Expository Thoughts
on Genesis

Expository Thoughts
on Genesis

James Dixon

 EVANGELICAL PRESS

EVANGELICAL PRESS
Faverdale North Industrial Estate, Darlington, DL3 OPH,
England

Evangelical Press USA
P. O. Box 825, Webster, New York 14580, USA

e-mail: sales@evangelicalpress.org

web: www.evangelicalpress.org

First published 2005

British Library Cataloguing in Pulication Data available

ISBN 0 85234 569 0

Scripture quotations in this publication are from the King James version of the Bible.

Printed in the United States of America

To Joan M. Dixon
whose hard work and self-sacrifice
allowed me to fulfil my dream of writing this book

Contents

Acknowledgements

One is always indebted to many people when completing a project such as this book. I would like to acknowledge some of the key people who made this work possible.

First, I need to say 'thank you' to the corporate body of the First Baptist Church of Sierra Vista, Arizona. During my ministry with them, during the 1990s, they constantly encouraged me and validated my preaching, teaching and writing ministry with them. Their encouragement gave me the confidence to pursue the writing of this book. It began as a daily devotional written to them, and gravitated into the expository thoughts written here. This work is greatly due to their encouragement.

Linda Sturm, the secretary for First Baptist Church, typed many of the pages of the first draft from my handwritten notes. Her patience in deciphering my handwriting is duly noted and appreciated.

I am most deeply indebted to my wife, Joan, who also was involved in the typing of many first draft pages from handwritten notes, but in addition worked with me through many tireless hours of revisions, and changes in the format. There were long nights she tirelessly laboured with me knowing she must get up early the next day to go to her own job. Without her, this project would not exist. It is to her that this book is dedicated.

Foreword

For far too many Christians, the Old Testament is foreign territory—and thus it is ignored, neglected, and frequently misunderstood. This is to the shame and embarrassment of evangelical Christianity.

The first problem is reduced to shear ignorance. With serious Bible study displaced in so many churches by other programs and activities, many Christians simply lack knowledge about the content and riches of the Old Testament. Furthermore, the decline of expository preaching in favor of more trendy approaches has robbed God's people of the biblical sustenance they so desperately need.

The second problem is the absence of a comprehensive biblical theology. A majority of Christians—including even churchgoers—demonstrates this absence by a failure to interpret the Old Testament accurately and Christologically. Thus, the Old Testament is often reduced to a set of books containing historical narratives, moving stories, ancient wisdom, and courageous prophesy, but without any unifying theme or interpretive scheme.

For these reasons and more, many evangelical preachers avoid Old Testament texts. Even many preachers committed to biblical exposition have never preached through an entire Old Testament book, mining its riches and instructing the people of God in the ways God revealed himself to ancient Israel—and to us.

Expository Thoughts on Genesis by James Dixon is a healthy corrective to these trends. Dr. Dixon is a skilled and faithful pastor, whose serious study and pastoral concern are combined in a remarkable book that brings the book of Genesis to life for God's people and serves as a model for the teaching and preaching of the Old Testament.

The book of Genesis is not only the first book of the Bible, it is also the great text that introduces the God of Abraham, Isaac and Jacob—the self-revealing God who is determined to redeem a people of his own choosing. God reveals himself as the Holy One of Israel, promising Abraham descendents more numerous than the stars in the sky. This book takes us all the way back to God's act of creation, when the worlds were brought into being and all things were ordered according to God's glory.

Of course, the book of Genesis also tells us about the origin and nature of humanity, establishing human beings as the pinnacle of God's creation—the only creatures bearing the divine image and able consciously to know and glorify the Creator. Importantly, the book of Genesis also serves as an essential corrective to the confusion of our day, making clear that God made human beings as male and female, establishing the covenant of marriage as the most basic institution of society.

Of course, Genesis also tells us of the Fall and its inevitable consequences. Human existence is literally inexplicable without the category of sin and Genesis explains sin's beginning and its impact on humanity. The many historical narratives in this book contain, among other truths, repeated demonstrations of human sinfulness lived out in the arena of human history.

The book of Genesis comes to life in Dr. Dixon's exposition. His theological and pastoral insights apply the truths of this great book to the realities of life in this postmodern age.

We can only hope that this book will serve as an encouragement to evangelical preachers, so that they will also take up the challenge of preaching the Old Testament and sharing the riches of God's Word with God's people. Those who read this book will be greatly blessed, greatly challenged, and spiritually nourished.

R. Albert Mohler, Jr.

Genesis 1:1-31

I. God Created (1:1)
1. The source of all things
2. God and evil
3. God in control
4. Obedience taught in creation

II. The Holy Spirit (1:2)
1. Presence
2. Hope

III. The Light (1:3-5)
1. Reason for light
2. Day and night

IV. Behold the Creation (1: 6-19)
1. Waters
2. God's spoken Word
3. Dry land
4. Dynamic vegetation
5. Heavenly bodies

V. The Creatures (1:20-25)
1. Ocean and sky
2. Animal purpose
3. Learning of greatness

VI. The Human Equation (1:26-28)
1. God's conversation

2. Human distinction
3. Image of God
4. The blessing
5. Dominion

VII. God's Evaluation of Creation (1:29-31)
1. Food source
2. 'Very good'

Genesis 1:1-5

1. In the beginning God created the heaven and the earth. 2. And the earth was without form, and void; and darkness was upon the face of the deep. And the Spirit of God moved upon the face of the waters. 3. And God said, Let there be light: and there was light. 4. And God saw the light, that it was good: and God divided the light from the darkness. And God called the light Day, and the darkness he called Night. And the evening and the morning were the first day.

The source of all things

As a human being trying to develop a love for God, the easiest, most direct route to love is to think in terms of relationship. Love is developed within the framework of intimacy and knowing. Therefore, the most attractive and most compelling features of God appear in the stories of people's lives. However, if we only concentrate on God's relationships with human beings, we miss an important part of knowing God. As our love for other human beings is expanded by appreciation for the parts of their existence which are not fixed explicitly on their direct relationship with us (such as the charitable things they do for others, or their hard work on significant projects), so we must come to appreciate God's work in areas not explicitly involving human beings.

The story of God's creation of the earth can provide such insight, and guide our meditation in a way that enriches our love for God. The word 'created' is a marvellous word that bears examining. Modern secular education has much trouble with any idea of creation, and prefers the idea of the accidental development of the order of things. The scientific methodology of creation is not part of biblical thought. The origin is clear. 'In the beginning God created the heaven and the earth' (1:1).

The reader is asked to accept a basic and wonderful premise. Everything that his senses can experience or his mind can imagine is available only because of God's activity. There is nothing possible without God. He is the 'Creator.' The phrase '...the heaven and the earth' is the biblical way of including every possibility. In trying to understand the application of this, we immediately note that all understanding must start with God. He is the source of all things. It would continue that he is the source of the knowledge of all things. If God created all things, he created the knowledge of all things.

In what many would describe as a tendency of secular education to make the creator-God a non-entity, the biblical stance requires reflection. With the increase of knowledge in our day, and at the same time the idea of a creator-God being viewed as unintelligible, how do we explain the biblical view? Consider this: Humans only have the knowledge that God allows them to have when he allows them to have it. God said to Daniel '...seal the book, even to the time of the end: many shall run to and fro, and knowledge shall be increased' (Daniel 12:4). God knew that knowledge would increase at the end. That was easy for him to know. That was when he, as Creator of all knowledge would allow human beings to have it.

The Christian will note that God's ultimate revelation of himself was through the incarnation, God becoming flesh. It was the Incarnate One who is the Creator in Genesis (John 1:1-3). One is reminded of the nature of the wonderful, progressive revelation of God found in the Bible.

God and evil

The creation of the universe is not directly related to God's personal dealings with human beings. The meditation of his creation activity will, however, reflect on much that is applied to God's activity with humans. When the biblical premise '...God created....' (1:1) is accepted, other conditions become axiomatic. As God is the source of all things, humans can only understand all things as God grants them knowledge. To leave God out of any equation is to lead humans down a pathway that can mean total misuse of knowledge. This means that whatever God grants to humans knowledge-wise will be utilized in a way that leads to self-destruction, not to self-edification.

One of the most frightening aspects of the fact of God's 'creation' lies in its total inclusion. Man's mind cannot know, sense, or imagine anything that is not part of God's created order. This becomes a real dilemma when evil is considered. Did God create evil? This is a philosophical question with which humans have wrestled throughout the ages. The answer lies in a meditation beyond the surface of things.

If 'God is good', meaning that he is the pure and total essence of good, and that no creation of God can ever be anything more than a created being, all of his creation will, of necessity, be less than himself, thus it cannot be the essence of good. When God creates, he must set the standard of what is acceptable or not acceptable for that part of his creation. Only as that part of his creation continues by his set standard can it continue to be good. If God allows his creation a choice of living by another standard than the one he sets, then evil is the result of the created one's choice. God is not the author of evil, but God made it possible.

Here is the frightening part. When one is guilty of evil, he often thinks he is acting totally independent of God. He prides himself in the mocking of his Creator. He mistakenly believes he has created a world in which God has no control. He fails to understand that God, through a loving act of creation, made possible everything the rebellious person does.

One may ask, 'What is the difference between God being the author of evil, and God making it possible?' Look at it from the other side. The difference is in the ability to know God through the intimacy of our choosing a relationship with him. Without the possibility of evil there is no capacity of choice. Without choice, our intimacy, knowledge, and understanding of God are radically short-changed, because without choice, the human is not personality in its fullest sense. Thus it is not the control of God the rebellious person escapes. It is the knowledge of God.

Paul suggests the most wonderful thing for humans is the opportunity to know Christ (Philippians 3:7). Even in creation, the importance of the knowledge of the Creator is emphasized.

God in control

There is much to contemplate in the reality that 'God-created....' The creation implies all things seen, and all things unseen. When this is contemplated fully, it leads to many fearful and many comforting insights. One of the first things is that all knowledge comes from God. Humans only have knowledge that God allows them to have when he allows them to have it. Second, every person falls within the framework of God's authority. The evil person, in rebellion against God, can act only because God gave him the mind and God made him in a manner that allows him the choice to rebel. This reality leads to many sublime understandings.

God, as Creator, necessarily means that every created being is less than God. When God creates, God sets the standard for what his creation should be. When God grants a choice to live by, or to not live by his standard, it means that anything short of his standard is wrong. Hence the definition of sin in Romans 3:23: 'For all have sinned, and come short of the glory of God.' In accordance with this reality, it is customary for humans to think along the following terms. To live by God's standard is to accept the control of

God in life. To rebel is to reject the control of God in life. That is correct. But the thinking gets a little weak when we take it to the next level. We will follow with, 'The more one rebels, the less he is under God's control, the more one obeys, the more he is under God's control.' Think about it further. The reality is the opposite. The rebellious person loves to think of himself as in complete control of his own life. The obedient person (in the rebellious person's mind) is weak and dependent. It is the rebellious one, however, who actually comes more and more under the control of God.

To understand, compare with the rearing of children. As children are raised, and prove themselves competent, dependent, and obedient, do we place tighter and more restrictive controls on them, or do we lessen control and tighten up on the rebellious? The same is true of our relationship with God. As he is loved, known, and understood by us, we willingly walk according to his commands, and covet knowledge of his direction. There is great freedom for the person walking in that kind of relationship. The rebel, however, is continually rushing into a greater and greater restrictive situation. As humans, we put criminals in restricted areas called prison. The ultimate restriction is hell, where one has capacity to do only one thing, 'suffer!' 'God created' translates into God's total control. After all, he created all things, and thus he controls all things.

Obedience as taught in creation

The 'creation' of God is a theological principle that explodes into many applications and understandings about life. It is impossible for man to explore its depths completely. A few meditative thoughts about it leave us with awe and wonder. It creates a great paradox. The more we know, the more mysterious God becomes. The mystery of God makes the unfolding of knowledge about him a great and wonderful adventure.

The mystery lies in certain realities. God as Creator demands an explanation of evil. God as the essence of good and as the Creator of all things is the one who makes evil possible. If personality and mind are part of God's creation it is inherent that the possibility be in place for one to choose to be the opposite of God. Good is only understood as good when there is something to measure good against. The more we know of God, and the more we understand the measuring sticks, the more glorious God becomes.

God as Creator demands a reckoning for all creation. No created being can ever be equal to God. Everything, outside of God himself, is a created entity. Created entities can only function within the framework God establishes. This reality is at the heart of the troubles of humanity. Humans, as beings with choice, get angry that there are limits on what they can be. God is an enemy because he established those limits. Frustration sets in, and a desire to rebel is prominent. Thus, the big test for any creation of God is, 'Will it function obediently in the standards set for it?'

As one comes to understand the big question, it is not difficult to explain why the theological principle of God's creation is under attack by the scientific community. Once the creation of God is denied, it is then logical that the supposed standard set by the fictional Creator is irrelevant. Humans deem themselves free to establish a standard more suitable to their own desires. When this happens, every human is free to set his own standard, thus there are no standards, except what is right for each individual, as he perceives it.

Clearly, the contemplation of God as Creator gets very complicated, philosophically deep, and mentally taxing. Yet, it should be clear that any compromise or short-changing of the concept of a God who 'created the heaven and the earth' has devastating consequences to individuals and to culture. A belief that '...God created the heaven and the earth', is foundational to any ordered society.

Humanity today seems to be absorbed with the notion of happiness and its pursuit. The Incarnate One said that happiness was the result of obedience (John 13:17).

Holy Spirit presence

Genesis 1:2 begins the story of God's preparation of the earth for
the habitation of man. There is a great deal of speculation about
the statement, '...the earth was without form and void....' Some
have implied that there was an earlier creation of beings inhabiting the earth who sinned and brought the earth under judgment.
Verse two would be the beginning of a new creation. It is more
commonly believed that verse two simply adds detail to verse one.
Whatever view one holds, it is clear that God is portrayed as one
who can take chaos and make something beautiful of it. He is
often seen doing it in the individual lives of human beings. The
concluding line of verse two is meant to be an extremely comforting word in a dismal situation: '...the Spirit of God moved upon
the face of the waters' (1:2).

There is much to understand in the simple words '...God created..,', and there is much to understand in the picture of the Spirit
of God that is placed before us. There was chaos, but the presence
of God's Spirit was enough for life to be present. This theme shall
be restated often in the Word of God. The Psalmist notes, 'Thou
sendest forth thy spirit, they are created: and thou renewest the
face of the earth' (Psalms 104:30). The prophet Isaiah adds, 'For
I will pour water upon him that is thirsty, and floods upon the dry
ground: I will pour my spirit upon thy seed, and my blessing upon
thine offspring: And they shall spring up as among the grass, as
willows by the water course' (Isaiah 44:3-4).

When Jesus left his disciples on the earth, he left an awesome
command. They were to be witnesses to the whole world about the
miraculous event of the resurrection they witnessed. They were to
do it without the visible, bodily presence of Jesus. The command
was followed by these words '...tarry ye in the city of Jerusalem,
until ye be endued with power from on high' (Luke 24:49). That
power was to be the same Spirit of God that moved on the waters
during the darkness and void of the earth. Jesus said, '...ye shall
receive power, after that the Holy Spirit is come upon you: and ye
shall be witnesses unto me....' (Acts 1:8).

The activity of God's Spirit is the greatest word of comfort that human beings can know. He moved upon the face of the waters indicating that the chaos is not the final story. He moved upon the apostles, and began the great missionary movement that would provide spiritual light to a world of darkness. Genesis 1:2 opens the door to the theology of the Spirit of God. In chaotic times, we should watch for his movement.

Hope wrought by the Holy Spirit

Among many Christians, the doctrine of the Holy Spirit may be the least known and understood of all theological doctrines. He is mentioned here by way of introduction, and it provides a big key for understanding the doctrine. '...And the Spirit of God moved upon the face of the waters' (1:2). The picture here is one of desolateness. Clearly, there is the presence of raw material. Science would call it 'matter'. However, there is no form, no purpose to it. Then comes the statement indicating the presence of the Spirit of God. The word which the KJV translates 'moved' is the same word the Scripture uses to describe an eagle that is fluttering her wings above the young in her nest. 'As an eagle stirreth up her nest, fluttereth over her young, spreadeth abroad her wings, taketh them, beareth them on her wings....' (Deuteronomy 32:11). Careful meditation helps us to reflect upon the Spirit of God hovering over the formless earth in careful examination, and with a clear plan in mind. The Spirit did not see formlessness, but the raw materials of a great creation.

The presence of the Spirit of God is a gigantic picture of hope. If thought about, there is the sense of great anticipation. The Spirit of God is hovering, what is he about to do? One can be sure that it shall be awesome. The picture of Acts 2 comes to mind where the same Spirit is said to have entered the upper room. 'And suddenly there came a sound from heaven as of a rushing mighty wind, and it filled all the house where they were sitting. And there appeared unto them cloven tongues like as of fire, and it sat upon (dare we say 'hovered above') each of them' (Acts 2:2-3).

The concept of the Holy Spirit has grandeur beyond imagination. There is unspeakable power. There is heart-pounding anticipation of his activity. There is holiness that overrides every other condition that is present. The Spirit of God hovered upon the face of the waters. His presence overrides the condition of the earth. Think of the divine majesty that is wrapped in the understanding the Spirit of God. Think about what we are asking when we ask for the presence of the Holy Spirit. We are asking that he override everything else around us. The hovering of the Spirit is prequel to the awesome. Are we ready for that when we pray?

> An awesome work of the Spirit of God is in his convicting power making men aware of their sins. Only in the mystery of a changed life do we begin understand the work of God's Spirit.

The reason for light

Trying to understand the ramifications of God's creation of the world from a material perspective is a study in futility. There is no eyewitness to the event except God, so how he did it will ever be speculation. The narrative that is before us is not meant to help us understand creation, but to help us understand the thinking of God. God had spoken all things into existence which were necessary for his unique activity upon the earth (1:1). The Spirit of God hovers above that part of the raw material that God shall use to make the earth. The material is without form and is covered in darkness. God continues by speaking light into existence.

Neither the reason for establishing the light, nor the nature of the light is explained. Certainly, it was not because God could not see. The Psalmist notes the reality. 'His going forth is from the end of the heaven, and his circuit unto the ends of it: and there is nothing hid from the heat thereof' (Psalms 19:6). One must keep in mind the long-term view. The light was not made that God might see, but for the larger purpose that his ultimate creation on earth (humankind) might be able to see his glory. This concept is later reflected in the writing of the Psalms. 'The heavens declare the glory of God; and the firmament sheweth his handiwork' (Psalms 19:1). The Psalms also express amazement that the God of created splendour would have a relationship with created beings. 'When I consider thy heavens, the work of thy fingers, the moon and the stars, which thou hast ordained; what is man that thou art mindful of him?' (Psalms 8:3-4).

The whole creation allows created human beings to behold his glory. The beholding of God's glory is an unspeakable joy that is his desire to provide for us. It continues to be the ultimate goal of God. This understanding gives light to the wondrous manifestation of God in human flesh, 'And the Word was made flesh, and dwelt among us, (and we beheld his glory, the glory as of the only begotten of the Father), full of grace and truth' (John 1:14).

There is some confusion for the reader in an arriving at a rational understanding of 'the light.' It appears prior to God's positioning of the sun, yet, there is an evening and a morning indicating the presence of the sun. Without any clarification, the reader is called upon to believe that God is the source of all light. In view of the many world religions that came to worship the sun as the source of light, the fact that light preceded the sun is compelling and important.

One cannot help but focus on the wonder of the Incarnate Christ, of whom John said, 'That was the true light...' (John 1:9).

The day and night

Wrapped in God's command, '...Let there be light...' (1:3), is a world of potential theological development. First, we are to see that light is the result of the spoken Word of God. He is the source of light, and controls the light. As human beings, we experience the light as the result of the sun. By our experience, it is hard to think of 'light' in any other fashion. Artificial light invented by man does not carry the same dynamic as the glorious advent of the rising sun. With light coming prior to God's positioning of the sun (1:16), biblical scholars are left to debate the meaning of verse 5. 'And God called the light Day, and the darkness He called Night. And the evening and the morning were the first day.'

Some would argue that the sun had to be in place for the events of verse 5 to occur. It would seem just as logical in the progression of things that God's intention at the start of creative activity was that the earth would rest in darkness for a while, and enjoy the light for a while. As this is exactly how the created order worked out, it is not difficult to allow God, as Creator and the true source of light, to create evening and morning without the sun. In a practical, religious way, the understanding of evening and morning without the sun condemns worship of the sun. Why should we force upon God a situation of necessity, simply because we cannot understand it by virtue of our experience?

In addition, the beginning of the Bible and the end of the Bible are vitally connected. Just as light precedes the positioning of the sun, so light continues after the sun is removed. '...the first heaven and the first earth were passed away...and I saw... the new Jerusalem, coming down...they need no candle, neither light of the sun; for the Lord God giveth them light...' (Revelation 21:1-2; 22:5).

The light is the first act of God in creation, and the assurance of the continuation of light brings the earth to culmination in the New Jerusalem. In the grand design of God, he is providing for his creation the words and illustrations (the light, the day, the night) to inspire belief in him.

The gospel of John adds further fuel to inspire belief. 'In the beginning was the Word...all things were made by him...That was the true light...And the Word was made flesh...' (John 1:1,3,9,14). The light that started it all and will be there when everything ends is the same one who revealed himself in the flesh. Genesis and Revelation are connected by the one who is '...Alpha and Omega, the first and the last...' (Revelation 1:11).

The glory of God's creation rests in the revelation of the source of light. A prayerful reflection on the light that reveals God's creation and the light that shines on the darkness of our sin brings to mind the wonder of God's redemption.

Genesis 1:6-19

6. And God said, Let there be a firmament in the midst of the waters, and let it divide the waters from the waters. 7. And God made the firmament, and divided the waters which were under the firmament from the waters which were above the firmament: and it was so. 8. And God called the firmament Heaven. And the evening and the morning were the second day. 9. And God said, Let the waters under the Heaven be gathered together unto one place, and let the dry land appear: and it was so. 10. And God called the dry land Earth; and the gathering together of the waters called he Seas: and God saw that it was good. 11. And God said, Let the earth bring forth grass, the herb yielding seed, and the fruit tree yielding fruit after his kind, whose seed is in itself, upon the earth: and it was so. 12. And the earth brought forth grass, and herb yielding seed after his kind, and the tree yielding fruit, whose seed was in itself, after his kind: and God saw that it was good. 13. And the evening and the morning were the third day. 14. And God said, Let there be lights in the firmament of the heaven to divide the day from the night; and let them be for signs, and for seasons, and for days, and years: 15. And let them be for lights in the firmament of the heaven to give light upon the earth: and it was so. And God made two great lights; the greater light to rule the day, and the lesser light to rule the night: he made the stars also. 17. And God set them in the firmament of the heaven to give light upon the earth, 18. And to rule over the day and over the night, and to divide the light from the darkness: and God saw that it was good. 19. And the evening and the morning were the fourth day.

Division of waters

The Scripture here recites the activity of God as he takes the raw materials which he spoke into being (1:1) and begins to shape them into the habitat for humanity. He begins by clearing the place for land. It is helpful to see the unfolding of this part of God's creative act through our imagination. The part of God's raw material here discussed is the water. The activity of God is to separate the water and create an expanse, 'firmament' (1:6-8) between. God's action produces waters in the heavens and waters upon the earth. At God's Word the water begins to move, and a vast atmosphere develops. The atmosphere created will provide space for the air which man will breathe.

'God called the firmament Heaven...' (1:8). 'Heaven' in this passage is not to be understood as the place of the God's abode, but as the expanse of the earth's atmosphere. In our mind's eye is the picture of waters in the heavens, and waters mixed with the other raw materials of the earth, with a vast atmosphere between them. Job provides a very colourful description of this part of God's creative act. 'Hast thou with him spread out the sky, which is strong, and as a molten looking glass' (Job 37:18)?

The picture in Job is of a master-craftsman. '...spread out....' and '...molten....' are vivid images contrasting one who stamps metal to smoothness and spreads it out to the point of reflection as in a mirror. God, in the separation of the waters, spreads them out over the vast horizon of the sky as one who presses metal into a looking glass and increases its dimensions.

As we try to visualize this event, it becomes apparent that there are no words to describe the splendour of the occurrence. Humanity's attempt to explain the heavens and the earth by such things as millions of years of evolution, or by some accidental gigantic explosion denies the majesty. If one observes the part of the finished product of creation which one set of eyes can manage, there is recognition of the grandeur. It goes beyond the empty attempts of the created being to explain the Creator's work. The glory of Genesis 1 is an absolute necessity, and the only truly natural way to understand what our eyes behold. Its description is too wonderful to be from the lips of man. It is God-inspired, and it is using the only adequate words to explain the wonder of the creation. 'The heavens declare the glory of God; and the firmament showeth his handiwork...There is no speech nor language, where their voice is not heard' (Psalms 19:1, 3).

The glory of the Creator recalls the words spoken of the Incarnate Christ in Hebrews. '...Thou, Lord hast, laid the foundation of the earth; and the heavens are the works of thy hands.' (1:10).

God's spoken Word

In Genesis 1:6 and Genesis 1:7, there is an interesting contrast which provides insight into the biblical understanding of God. The reader will note the duplication of action. It the same event in both verses, but there is this difference. Verse 6 begins with 'And God said....' Verse 7 begins with 'And God made...' The writer is expressing a theme that is consistent in biblical thought. It may be stated in this fashion. 'When God speaks, his word is supreme.' The author of Genesis is reinforcing this doctrine. The Word of God is immediate authority. God said the Word, '...Let there be a firmament....' (1:6). Thus, it is the natural conclusion, '...God made the firmament....' (1: 7).

As one traces the history of humanity it becomes clear why there is so much emphasis placed on this theme 'from the beginning'. (Note: 'God said...it was so....' (1:9), 'God said...it was so....' (1:11), 'God said...it was so....' (1:14, 15). One of the first things that comes to our mind is the first words of the serpent to the woman. '...Yea, hath God said...' (Genesis 3:1)? The attack on the Word of God is the beginning of troubles. To go against the Word of God is to cause one's destruction. Creation teaches us that God's Word is supreme. If his Word has the force to stamp out the heavens and to spread out the vastness of its great dimensions, what force must we be fighting against when we try to rebel against his Word!

When Moses spoke to the children of Israel before he died, he stated, '...take heed to thyself...Specially the day that thou stoodest before the Lord thy God in Horeb, when the Lord said unto me, Gather me the people together, and I will make them hear my words, that they may learn to fear me all the days that they shall live upon the earth....' (Deuteronomy 4:9-10). It is a strange thing to note the God of creation, who speaks the earth and the heavens into existence, talking to humans about the need to fear him. It denotes the extreme foolishness as well as the total depravity of man.

The majesty of God's creation can lead to our wonder and our worship. The power of his Word can create in our hearts a hunger to know it and thus to know him. The power of his word can also crush us when we reject it. When seen completely, it places an awesome slant to the statement of God, 'So shall my word be that goeth forth out of my mouth: it shall not return unto me void...' (Isaiah 55:11).

The opportunity to reflect on the majesty of the Incarnate Christ arises in every part of Scripture. The emphasis on God's Word reminds of another Scripture, 'In the beginning was the Word...' (John 1:1). A prayer to know the Word and to hear his words can be especially helpful to any day.

Appearance of dry land

On the third day of creation, God continues his development of the raw materials which he has spoken into existence (1:1). He is preparing the earth to be a place where his ultimate creation (humanity) will reside. Using imagination to envision the moment provides help to understand the action. 'And God said, Let the waters under the heaven be gathered unto one place, and let dry land appear:, and it was so' (1:9).

As we experience the earth in present form, the image of the land in one place and the water in one place is bothersome. The biblical accounting does not seem accurate. It becomes easier to understand when we see the sequence from verse one. God began his activity by separating waters to form an atmosphere for the earth (1:6). The raw materials of God's creation of earth were all in place. He begins the defining and shaping of those materials. The dry land emerges from the deep as a separate entity from the waters. The '...one place....' is not a problem when understood as defining distinction as opposed to position. The dry land appears and is now distinct from the water. Thus, on the third day, for the first time, there is the visual distinction between water and dry land.

One should not take this creative event lightly. It is critical to theological development in the establishment of the nation of Israel. The separation of waters to cause the dry land to appear is told in graphic display as part of God's creative act. When sin entered the human race, mankind was drawn to the worship of the created world through establishing gods of various elements (harvest, seas, sun, etc.). The ability to separate waters and reveal dry land would be a crucial element in identifying the true God. In light of this, consider this moment: 'And Moses stretched out his hand over the sea; and the Lord caused the sea to go back by a strong east wind all that night, and made the sea dry land, and the waters were divided. And the children of Israel went into the midst of the sea upon the dry ground: and the waters were a wall unto them on their right hand, and on their left' (Exodus 14:21-22).

God brought the earth into existence through the separation of waters. God established a nation as witness to himself through another separation of the waters. There could be no doubting on Israel's part about the author of their redemption from Egypt. As we see the biblical themes come together, our own admiration for God is expanded just as he expanded the heavens.

Dynamic of vegetation

When the dry land is separated (becomes visible) from the water, God speaks into existence all the vegetation that shall be born by the land. Two things are of note. First, all vegetation is the result of the spoken Word of God. Second, God provides the land a capacity to reproduce the vegetation. '...Let the earth bring forth grass, the herb yielding seed, and the fruit tree yielding fruit after his kind, whose seed is in itself, upon the earth: and it was so' (1:11). There are two creative acts in the spoken Word. God creates the vegetation, and he creates a way for the vegetation to continue without a new creative act necessitated.

Immediately, one can see the ramifications of such creative forethought. The earth becomes a dynamic entity. God did not intend for his creation to stand still as in a picture to be viewed. He intended the appearance of the earth to be ever changing and renewing itself. There is a kind of awesome reality that is present. Science fiction has often entertained us with the possibilities of that reality. A creation with power to renew and sustain itself, but without mind or reason, is a fascinating thought. The science fiction route will give this creation mind and reason, and in that arena, the vegetation that is dynamic has horrifying possibilities.

The marvellous thought of dynamic vegetation is wonderful when humanity gets placed in the mix. 'So God created man in his own image...and said unto them...fill the earth and subdue it....' (1:27-28). Mind and reason are added to the mix and the possibilities for God's dynamic creation become endless. The little touch of creating that which can recreate and sustain itself is mind boggling when meditated upon.

With every step of creation, the wisdom of God is more and more revealed. The caveat that is placed upon this creation of dynamic vegetation is also a revelation of wisdom. There is power to re-create and sustain, but not to create something new. Each re-creation must stay within its own kind. '...grass the herb yielding seed, and the fruit tree yielding fruit after his kind...the herb yielding seed after his kind...' (1:11-12). There would be no re-creation of a brand new species. That decision is, and always will be, God's decision. Every part of God's creation will always know that it is from the Word and the hand of God. '...all the trees of the field shall know that I the Lord...have done it' (Ezekiel 17:24).

The more one sees the marvellous hand of creation, the more one wonders at the nature of a God which would make himself personally known to human flesh (John 1:14).

Heavenly bodies

On the fourth day of God's creation activity, God acts to separate the light into various entities in the heavens. Light on the earth (day and night), will be governed by the skies. In this accounting, there is a new revelation of the meaning of light. There is also knowledge associated with light. The human beings that will be placed on the earth must have a way of denoting time. They will be creatures that live in the realm of time passing, rather than as God, whose realm is the eternal present (knowing the end from the beginning). Humans must have the means to denote occurrences, and to remember them and date them. The entities of light placed in the heavens (allowing the telling of time) are the beginning of the humans' storehouse of knowledge. '...Let there be lights in the firmament of the heaven to divide the day from the night; and let them be for signs, and for seasons, and for days, and years....' (1:14).

It is important to see the real reason for the lights in the heavens. Light is in place because of God's pronouncement (1:2). The light God created will now be diffused through the sun, moon, and stars. Their benefit to humanity will go far beyond the lighting of dark places, and will be guides for direction, (note: the wise men at Jesus' birth were guided by a star), resources for navigating the oceans, signs for tracking the seasons, and much more.

The creation of the entities of the heavens as dividers of light is a critical theological issue. Because of the great storehouse of knowledge that a study of the stars will provide for humans, it is important to know that the entities of the heavens are not the cause of light; they are simply the purveyors of light. The tendency for humans to worship the entities of the heavens will be strong. There is so much in the heavens that guide the affairs of humans. If there is not a clear understanding of their creation, the human will believe that the heavenly entities are the controlling elements of the knowledge they purvey. Creation teaches that God has that control.

As one examines the creation story completely, it emerges that each creation carries certain risks for humans. That which is very good when properly understood and properly used can turn very bad if humans misuse it. Therefore, the issue is its source. Is it directly from God, and accountable to God, or of itself? Unless the Creator is first, the creation is paramount, thus commanding worship.

The nature of man's worship is key to life. True worship comes only in the atmosphere of the all-consuming importance of God. All knowledge comes from God. Thus, without full acquiescence to his will, man is left destitute.

The phrase '...that hath life....' represents a totally different creation. 'Life' has two elements in combination that the other parts of God's creation did not have. The two elements are the ability to experience things and to know that you are experiencing things. Vegetation will experience the elements of nature, but there is no knowledge.

The phrase '...that hath life....' represents a totally different creation. 'Life' has two elements that the other parts of God's creation did not have. The two elements are the ability to experience things and to know that you are experiencing things. Vegetation will experience the elements of nature, but there is no knowledge within vegetation that the experience is occurring. The fifth day of creation brings forth life that will experience in unique ways the waters and firmament, and to know it is having the experience. The knowledge is extremely limited, and their experiencing is confined to the areas they are to populate. The experiencing of the fish of the sea and the birds of the air will provide action, and ever-changing beauty and renewal to two parts of God's creation.

Observing creation from the view of God's revelation to humans offers us many things upon which the soul of man might meditate. One might picture the grandeur of earth as a majestic place of beauty. It is awe-inspiring in its impact. Allow your mind's eye to gaze upon the newly created horizon; picture the sunrise coming over the trees at the edge of the lake. The serenity is wonderful to behold. Is there something missing? We think not! Then, over the trees there flies a flock of geese, an eagle swoops down and flies low across the lake, a fish leaps out of the water. From the trees comes the sound of the birds singing. We realize that as beautiful as was the sunrise, there was something missing. Life!

The reader is confronted with a phenomenal insight. This creation story has the clear sound of historical reality. There is logic to it that no other explanation of existence carries. This narrative makes sense. It could only be seen as revealed through the mind of the only one who was there when it happened, God!

Purpose of animal life

On the sixth day of creation, God's activity is focused on bringing life and vitality to the land. As he had added fish to the sea, and birds to the air, he creates the animal kingdom uniquely suited for life on the land. The animals of the land are divided into three groups: domesticated animals (cattle), crawling animals or creepers located close to the ground (creeping things), and wild animals or game (beast of the earth). The animals will be partners with humans in bringing of life to the land. The domesticated animals will have a much more defined partnership with humans than the other animals, but all will help to enrich the grandeur of the creation of God that shall be forever called 'the land.'

The air, the oceans, and now the land will have creatures that experience and know they are experiencing the elements of creation. The sounds of the animals, the movement and playful activities of the young, the stately elk surveying the landscape, the lion walking boldly and proudly to his den, are all part of a combination made to bring varieties of dynamic activity to earth.

It is clear that each animal was made to inhabit a specific part of the creation. The phrase 'after his kind' is repeated to emphasize the unique and individual nature of each created life. They are not developed one from another, for they are not meant to be the same. Though amazingly different, they are united by what the Bible calls 'life.'

As we imagine the dramatic change on the earth with the addition of animals, life seems a totally adequate word. We have all used slang terms that speak of a party with no 'life,' a sports team with no 'life,' a speaker with no 'life,' etc. Our meaning has reference to enthusiasm, excitement, and interest. The picture of earth without animals, though beautiful, is magnificently enhanced by life wrought in the animals. A child bored by the scenery becomes excited when an animal appears. There is interest, enthusiasm, and excitement.

As one considers the thinking of God at this point, the reality is that God would not make such a beautiful and wonderful place without providing creatures which can experience and enjoy it. In God's great wisdom, the two complement each other. The animals experience the land, and make the land an even more attractive creation. The forest is far more beautiful, and more memorable when you see a deer standing in its midst. They fit together perfectly. This is no accident.

Lesson about greatness

An examination of God's creation of the animal kingdom leads to some interesting questions. As man is the last of God's creation, he is surely the supreme creation of earth. It would appear that the order of creation is on an ascending scale. Each creation is of a higher order than the last. One moves from the inanimate to the animate, from creation of vegetation to creation of that which has life, from animals of the air and ocean to animals of the land. This leads to the creation of humans. One might legitimately ask at this point, 'What makes land animals superior to sea and air animals?' The answer is to be found in the arena of work and service. Certain of the land animals will be able to partner with humans in the work of the land, and are thus used as a servant to man. The service and work aspect alone makes the animals of the land superior.

There is a basic theology that is exposed. Jesus applied the theology to human beings when he said, '...whosoever will be great among you, let him be your minister; and whosoever will be chief among you, let him be your servant' (Matthew 20:26-27).

Many domesticated land animals became great servants to man in enabling him to fulfil God's command. The oxen and the horse were used in cultivating the land; the sheep provided wool for clothing, the donkey and horse for transportation. Many other examples may be added. The land animals (far above the creatures of the air and sea) were man's greatest servants.

One finds the great wisdom of God unfolding in the ascending order of creation. In the correct order of things, as God created them, it is the grandeur of servanthood that speaks of the greatest order. The sin factor distorted the human's ability to perceive this truth. The natural tendency is to believe the greatest are to be served by others. Humans tend to spend their lives looking for the day when they are boss and others serve them.

A part of this dynamic reaches the human psyche in terms of satisfaction. It is in the service we perform that our greatest satisfaction is derived. Being served satisfies for the moment, but carries no lasting memory or value. Service rendered can have lasting impact.

Humans are far more attached to the animals that serve them. The ones who work for us receive our greatest attention and affection. They serve us, and we love them! Should we carry that lesson over to humanity and its relation to God? Our greatness is in our servanthood.

It is left to the Creator, the Incarnate One, to teach the ultimate lesson of servanthood. He is the one who reminds
us of the greatest enjoyment of life, the ability to serve our
Heavenly Father. He did it through the act of redemption
(Isaiah 53:6).

God's conversation

On the day God creates the land animals, he also creates man.
The Scriptural record of this event is astounding on several fronts.
There is the appearance of a council which makes the decision to
proceed. God converses about this last creation. 'And God said,
Let us make man in our image, after our likeness: and let them
have dominion over the fish of the sea, and over the fowl of the air,
and over the cattle, and over all the earth, and over every creeping thing that creepeth upon the earth. So God created man in his
own image, in the image of God created he him; male and female
created he them' (Genesis 1:26-27).

God's comment begins with '...Let us....' It is quite unlike the
other creations where there is a direct moving forward with creative activity. First, the plural is used. Who are the ones considered
in the 'us?' Second, why is there no 'us' in the rest of God's creative activity?

As one reads the full story of Scripture, the answers appear.
There are hints at the presence of another person in Genesis 1:2.
'...And the Spirit of God moved....' There is God, and there is the
Spirit of God that is involved in this discussion. The creation upon
which God embarks is made in a way that shall allow disobedience
to God. As God is omniscient (knowing all things from beginning
to end), he knew that his creation would disobey. From this reality
there are several parts to the implied conversation. God's heart
may have heaviness attached as he proceeds. He knows what this
creation will become, and he knows what it will cost him. In that
pre-creation discussion is a third person. He is the one who shall
bear the brunt of the cost of this creation of God. The Bible says

that he was '...foreordained before the foundation of the world....' (1 Peter 1:20) to be a redeemer. That redemption would come by virtue of his own sacrifice (1 Peter 1:18-19). The 'us' in Genesis 1:26 is the Godhead looking upon this final creative act, and with full knowledge of what lies ahead, says, 'Let us make man....'

The 'us' is not mentioned in the narrative prior to this moment. It is because God is going to do the one thing that establishes and proves love. He is creating the creature to which he shall make himself vulnerable. Thus, we are let in on the fact of full ascent in the Godhead. 'For God so loved the word...' is brightly shining from the moment he says, 'Let us....'

> God created humans while knowing the cost to himself. It is an amazing love which humans can scarcely comprehend.

Human distinction

God's decision to make man, in spite of his knowledge about what this creation would cost him (1 Peter 1:18-20), is the foundation to the whole narrative of the Bible. There is further revelation given to help us understand the scene that shall unfold. Man is to be distinct from the rest of creation. The animals have provided life and vitality to the earth. They can experience the earth and know that they are experiencing the earth. Humans shall be given further ability. It shall be more than experience; it shall be to experience and to explain the experience. Humans shall provide a further dynamic to creation that the animals do not have. They shall not only experience the earth, but shall be charged with decision-making about the earth. That creativity will have good and bad possibility. 'And God said, Let us make man in our image, after our likeness...' (1:26). Much has been said about the meaning of 'God's image and likeness.' This is one of those statements best understood in its simplest and clearest expression. Humans are like God in that they are rational beings who make choices, with a moral nature inherent in them. Animals experience, they act and react according to their nature, but they do not sin. Humans (in God's image) are moral creatures. Thus, they act and react in a context of right and wrong, good and evil. They, unlike animals, can rebel against that for which they were created.

The ramifications for this in the way we think about the animal world, the human world, and the vegetable world are far-reaching. In those ramifications is to be found the underlying danger when humans are understood as having developed from the animal kingdom. When the 'image of God' is not part of the human equation, the moral aspect of humanity is distorted and diminished. Humans are encouraged to act and react according to their physical nature instead of as moral beings making choices in the framework of good and evil.

Animals cannot sin. If humans are nothing more than animals, it is obvious to conclude that they also do not sin. The modern culture's perplexity in trying to explain why humans can be so cruel is precisely the result of failing to understand the 'image of God' connection. Humans are not animals. They must connect with moral decisions in their lives. The writer of Genesis makes this very clear in the creation narrative. We act and react in a moral world. Why did God make us like this? He did it because he loves us, and desires fellowship with us!

> God's desire for fellowship with humans is more astounding in light of the fall. The Incarnate Christ demonstrated this desire in the most profound way imaginable (John 1:4).

Image of God

It requires in-depth theological reflection to grasp the concept of a person created in the 'image of God' (1:27). As believers, we have been taught the important reality of God's goodness. We know that, in God, there is no evil. This reality makes it difficult to explain the 'image of God' in humanity. This is because humans rebelled against God and became evil. Yet, to be fully in the image of God, we had to be placed in the context of beings who act and react, as moral beings within the possibility of evil. That is the essential thing that separates us from animals.

It is also the essential thing that provides us with the possibility of fellowship with God. If that is difficult to understand, consider it along these lines. How can humans have fellowship with animals? They are our pets. They humour us! They scare us! They work for us! They annoy us! We can study them and learn much about them. We can come to know and explain animals very well. They can come to know us in limited ways. They can respond to training, they can recognize our scent, our voice, etc. The missing ingredient is 'understanding'. We cannot communicate our inner selves to animals. We cannot have conversation with animals. They can never be in true fellowship with humans. True fellowship is based in the ability to make moral decisions. An animal can make certain kinds of decisions. They can choose to come to us when we call them. They can choose to run or to walk. They cannot, however, make moral judgments, and choose based on right or wrong. Without that ability, they can never fully appreciate what it means to be human, thus they can never fully appreciate us and be in fellowship with us.

When God created humans, he placed within us the one great and necessary ingredient for true fellowship with him. As creatures 'in his image', we can fully appreciate him. We cannot attain unto being God, but we can be like him through understanding him.

'Be ye therefore perfect, even as your Father which is in heaven is perfect' (Matthew 5:48). As this concept takes hold in one's conscience, it is a lightning bolt to the soul. Inherent is the reality that we were made for God. He created us to be a delight to himself, and that he might reveal his glory to us. This one concept alone can inspire a great love for God, and goes further to solve the modern 'self-esteem' problem that all the foolish social engineering that humanity can invent.

The importance of the life of Christ is magnified here. It is his life that can fully teach us what it is like to be in the image of God. In understanding him and emulating him we can best demonstrate the concept of the 'image of God'.

The blessing

The sixth day of creation saw the act of placing animals and humans on the earth. In Genesis 1:28, the biblical reader encounters the statement 'And God blessed them....' In the entire creation narrative, this statement is only mentioned twice. The first time is on the fifth day. God had created the creatures of the sea and the air. 'And God blessed them saying, Be fruitful, and multiply, and fill the waters in the seas, and let fowl multiply in the earth...' (1:22).

The only part of God's creation that is said to be blessed is that part which is given life, animals and humans. The blessing here has the idea of a 'salute' or 'well-wishing'. God is saying to the creatures with life, 'You have something special, use it well.' He goes on to inform how it can be used well. To animals, it is a simple statement, 'Be fruitful and multiply.' To humans is added another dimension. '...Be fruitful, and multiply, and replenish the earth, and subdue it: and have dominion over the fish of the sea, and over the fowl of the air, and over every living thing that moveth upon the earth' (1:28).

The blessing of propagation of the species is the meditation for this devotional. It has its own peculiar reality. In the animal kingdom, propagation will require an intimacy with other creatures of its kind. In its own way, this is reflective of God's great motivation in creating humanity. Sexual intimacy that results in propagation is the highest form of human intimacy. It is a notch below the kind of fellowship that God seeks, but mirrors the great vulnerability and surrender to another that must be in place for the fellowship that God wants to create.

Within the framework of propagation of the species, there comes another of those kinds of special positions reserved only for those blessed with 'life.' That is the nurture and care of the young. The blessing of re-creating yourself carries with it the awesome responsibility of caring for those you bring into the world. This is God's wisdom at work. The greatest thrill of humanity is wrapped in the fellowship and joy of those whom we were responsible for bringing into the world. God has truly blessed us with this reality. He is also teaching us. By our rejoicing over the young, we can consider the full meaning of God's rejoicing over his creation. Also, in this light, it helps us reflect on how God must react to those who sense no responsibility in the caring for the young.

Genesis 1:29-31

29. And God said, Behold, I have given you every herb bearing seed, which is upon the face of all the earth, and every tree, in the which is the fruit of a tree yielding seed; to you it shall be for meat. 30. And to every beast of the earth, and to every fowl of the air, and to every thing that creepeth upon the earth, wherein there is life, I have given every green herb for meat: and it was so. 31. And God saw every thing that he had made, and, behold, it was very good. And the evening and the morning were the sixth day.

Dominion

When God creates humans, he offers a blessing and issues a responsibility. The blessing is the joy of propagation of the species. The responsibility is the care of the earth. 'And God blessed them, and God said unto them, Be fruitful, and multiply, and replenish the earth, and subdue it: and have dominion over the fish of the sea, and over the fowl of the air, and over every living thing that moveth upon the earth' (1:28).

Humanity's dominion over the earth is a hotly debated topic in an environmentally sensitive generation. How are we to understand it? The two words used in this context (subdue and dominion) have rather harsh meanings in other biblical texts. The words are used in connection with domination and trampling under foot. In 1 Kings 9:23, the word that is translated 'dominion' in Genesis 1:28 becomes 'rule over.' The word 'subdue' is seen in Zechariah to describe a conquering army (Zechariah 9:14). From a simple reading of the text, one would assume that humans are to exploit the earth, and use it for their own advantage. The mistake that one makes when utilizing this interpretation is to ignore the greater context of creation. One must continue to read in chapter 2 where he will encounter a further word from God. 'And the Lord God took the man, and put him into the garden of Eden to dress it and to keep it. And the Lord God commanded the man, saying, Of every tree of the garden thou mayest freely eat: But of the tree of the knowledge of good and evil, thou shalt not eat of it...' (Genesis 2:15-17).

Humanity's dominion of the earth is established as safekeeping. He is free to 'subdue,' but must stay within the framework of being responsible for God's creation. The placing of the animals on the earth brought beauty and dynamic vitality to nature. Within God's parameters, there is much additional vitality that can be brought to God's creation when humans exercise their creative minds within it. In the twentieth century, we have seen human creativity used for both good and bad. Great dams have created beautiful lakes, and allowed cities to be given electrical power, and allowed deserts to blossom. We are to have dominion, but God laid down a law in forbidding man to eat the forbidden fruit, thus he is reminding us that humans are under the dominion of God. Dominion of the earth is the allowing of God's creation to be an ever-expanding dynamic entity contributing to the growth and versatility of nature, just as God seeks constant growth for humans.

Food service

The concluding verses of Genesis 1 involves an interesting assumption when one discerns that which is not stated. The text quotes God. '...I have given you every herb...and every tree, in the which is the fruit of a tree yielding seed; to you it shall be for meat. And to every beast...every fowl...every thing...wherein there is life, I have given every green herb for meat...' (1:29-30). The reader will note the absence of any sense of animals as food. The animal world, as well, seems to be herbivorous, not carnivorous.

There are a couple of things upon which one might ponder. First, God grants only that which is not seen as having life for use as food. The importance of life is subtly affirmed. As humans observe nature in the present organization of things, many animals are by nature carnivorous. Humans also slaughter many different animals for use as food. It is hard for us to imagine a world without the present order of nature. Scientists can only observe what is presently at work, and thus would scoff at any other reality. Yet, the Bible provides additional evidence that such order existed by predicting a future day when such respect for life will again be the order of things. 'And the cow and the bear shall feed; their young ones shall lie down together: and the lion shall eat straw like the ox' (Isaiah 11:7). The first time animals are slaughtered for human benefit (Genesis 3:21) is a sad commentary on the depths of human sin and reflects the loss of the intrinsic value of life that was once upon the earth. The use of animals for food may have begun at Genesis 3:21, or after the flood in Genesis 9:3. The sanctity of animal life will not be fully restored until the future age of God's reign on earth when sin is conquered by the dominion of Christ.

Second, the need requiring animal flesh as food is not fully explained. The permission for the eating of the flesh of animals comes after the flood which would indicate some kind of climatic change in the earth which would require the eating of flesh in order for there to be an adequate supply of food. The fact that carnivorous animals are also present is evidence of that which another biblical writer speaks. 'For we know that the whole creation groaneth and travaileth in pain together until now' (Romans 8:22). Taken together, these two things help us to understand the great value God placed in the 'life' that he gives. It also aids in our consideration of the depth of our sin. The very 'life' which was God's precious blessing upon his creation is diminished and totally devalued. One should consider further that the ultimate solution to the problem was the sacrifice of the most valuable life of all, the Son of God (John 3:16).

'Very good'

The work of God in creation is concluded at the end of the sixth day. God looked upon his creation and pronounced it '...very good' (1:31). Six times (1:4, 10, 12, 18, 21, 25) God pronounced his creation 'good.' In the end, it is 'very good.' In the light of what shall come, as man allows evil into his existence (Genesis 3:1-6), how do we explain God's pronouncement? The Hebrew word that is translated 'good' has a very broad interpretation. The meaning can range from desirable and beautiful to virtuous and right. Every aspect of the word fits in describing the creation of God. Taken as a whole, it is to be understood in terms of God's judgment on it, not just in its inherent quality. God said it was good. Thus, God is saying, 'It is what I intended it to be.' Everything created is capable of fulfilling its intended purpose. The creation is not 'good' in the sense that goodness is inherent in the creation. Inherent goodness can only belong to God. 'Goodness' in the creation is derived from fulfilling God's intended purpose for it. As God completes his creation, everything is in place for complete fulfilment of God's purpose.

The 'very good' statement of 1:31 shows completeness. Each entity of creation is good, but when seen in complement to the other parts of creation, it is very good. Each part has independence as a direct creation of God, but it needs the rest of creation to fulfil its own intended purpose.

The reader comes to the end of this sublime journey with the sense of a call to worship. After observing creation, worship is not a tedious affair; it is a joy and a need. One cannot be content with anything else. God has revealed his own splendour, and there is the overwhelming sense that there is nothing of repayment in kind that we can ever muster. The grand view to which the reader is treated demands appreciation and thanksgiving. Worship is the only resource.

Meditation on the creative act is essential to anyone wishing to understand a right relationship to God. It helps us to see the difference between worship as a duty, worship as a command, and worship as the natural, wonderful, and easy response to such glory. To be allowed into that kind of splendour is far more than even the most deserving human could expect or imagine. God has given us this literary glimpse. Let our meditation carry us beyond the literary to glimpse the glory.

Genesis 2:1-25

I. A Grand Revelation (2:1-7)
1. God's rest
2. The Sabbath
3. The garden
4. From the earth
5. Breath of life

II. The Human Test (2: 8-17)
1. Subdue the earth
2. Importance of freedom
3. Opportunity of freedom
4. Possibility of death
5. Understanding the choice
6. Nature of knowledge of good and evil

III. The Human Relationships (2:18-25)
1. Animals
2. Man and woman
3. Man and wife

Genesis 2:1-7

*1. Thus the heavens and the earth were finished, and all the host of them.
2. And on the seventh day God ended his work which he had made; and he rested on the seventh day from all his work which he had made. 3. And God blessed the seventh day, and sanctified it: because that in it he had rested from all his work which God created and made. 4. These are*

the generations of the heavens and of the earth when they were created, in the day that the Lord God made the earth and the heavens, 5. And every plant of the field before it was in the earth, and every herb of the field before it grew: for the Lord God had not caused it to rain upon the earth, and there was not a man to till the ground. 6. But there went up a mist from the earth, and watered the whole face of the ground. 7. And the Lord God formed man of the dust of the ground, and breathed into his nostrils the breath of life; and man became a living soul.

God's rest

The Scripture records six days of creation, and then brings us to a rather phenomenal and intriguing passage. 'And on the seventh day God ended his work which he had made; and he rested on the seventh day...' (Genesis 1:2). Human beings are conditioned to thinking of rest as a cessation of activity. That is not the meaning of God's rest. Jesus confirms that God has not ceased activity. 'But Jesus answered them, My Father worketh hitherto, and I work' (John 5:17). God's rest is the ceasing of one kind of activity to give attention to another. The sense of 'rest' as the ceasing of all activity is a fallacy that causes the child of God to misunderstand the purpose of the Sabbath.

The meditation required for the reader is to understand the beginning and the ending activity of the seventh day. It is fairly clear that it was God's creation activity that ceased. From Genesis 1:1, God is actively involved in putting together that which is very new. The first verse mentions God's creation of the heavens and the earth. God spoke into existence all the raw materials (matter) necessary for the forming of his creation. Day by day he placed all this raw material into the precise variety and form he desired. The kind of creation seen in 1:1 is that which theologians call 'ex-nihilo.' That is 'out of nothing'. God simply speaks into being what he needs for creative activity. It is unclear how much of the six days creation was ex-nihilo, and how much was developed out of the raw material already created. Genesis 2:7 offers additional detail not found in chapter one. 'And the Lord God formed man of the dust of the ground....' By the end of the sixth day, creation (the making of something out of nothing) is unnecessary.

In the next step a new activity begins and there is a startling reality. God begins to interact with his creation (2:6, 8-9, 15-22). God did not leave his creation but nurtures it. It is a magnificent picture of God's activity. His rest is in the personal involvement he now enjoys with his creation. It is somewhat beyond imagination to think of a God with such power and glory stopping to spend time with such lowly creatures. Surely, he would want to be rushing off to create some new universe, some grander world. No, he rests from that to enjoy us. That thought is too marvellous for words.

> God's desire for fellowship with humanity is demonstrated best when the Son of God '...dwelt among us...' (John 1:14). Human worship is designed in order that we may make the same kind of statement of desire for fellowship with God.

The Sabbath

God's creation activity has come to an end. The Scripture tells us that the work of God enters a new phase. 'And on the seventh day God ended his work which he had made; and he rested on the seventh day...' (2:2). His rest is not to be understood as the cessation of activity, but as the beginning of a new kind of activity, which shall be interaction and fellowship with his creation.

As humans attempt to grasp the meaning of the Sabbath, this understanding of God's rest is the proper foundation. God created us, and he will (in his rest) fellowship with us. Genesis 3:8 shows fellowship with his creation as part of his plan. 'And they heard the voice of the Lord God walking in the garden in the cool of the day....' Apparently, God made regular visits to be with the humans he created.

God's interaction and development of relationship with his creation is a wondrous concept. It shall be a work for God, but not creation work. Wrapped in the wonderful 'rest' (which means our fellowship with God) is the character of the Sabbath. It is to be a special day that is understood in the framework of rest. The 'rest' of the Sabbath is understood properly in activity changing, not in activity ceasing.

God gave man a work to do with his creation. '...replenish the earth, and subdue it: and have dominion over...every living thing that moveth upon the earth' (Genesis 1:28).

The command must be placed alongside another blessing of God that the writer records. 'And God blessed the seventh day, and sanctified it: because that in it he had rested from all his work which God created and made' (Genesis 2:3). The word 'sanctified' means 'to set apart.' The seventh day is set apart as a day of rest for humans.

It follows naturally that just as God's rest was not the cessation of activity, but the changing of activity, the same is true for humans. God's rest is to mean interaction and fellowship with his creation. Man's rest is to mean interaction and fellowship with his Creator. It is not that the Sabbath is the only day for fellowship, but that the Sabbath is to be understood as the day in which humans give undivided attention to that fellowship. The earth is the source of human work. Human work is made much easier when time is given to know the Creator of that earth. That is the essence of true rest.

Rest is part of the requirement for healthy bodies. Work is also a requirement for healthy bodies. Six days are given to work, the nights are for rest. On the Sabbath, another kind of work is required for health. It is the work of worship. The soul must be exercised in learning and fellowship with God.

The garden

One's journey through the book of Genesis will find regular encounters with a phrase introduced in our text. 'These are the generations of....' (2:4) will be seen ten times in the book of Genesis.
In each instance, its purpose is to begin a new section with a look
forward. The heaven and the earth were created. That which follows is the account of what happens after the creation. Thus, the
reader is able to prepare himself for a shift in the nature of the
written account. It is no longer a creation of a brand new thing. It
is a reflection of events that happen to the creation, or an adding
of details to the creation.

First, there is an account of God's personal action on behalf of
his created vegetation. 'These are the generations of the heavens
and of the earth...and every plant...and every herb...for the Lord
God had not caused it to rain...and there was not a man to till the
ground. But there went up a mist from the earth, and watered the
whole face of the ground' (2: 4-6).

There are two things requiring attention, and both reflect on
the blessing and the wisdom of God. Chapter two is the record of
the planting of the Garden of Eden. The plants and herbs have reference to the plants and herbs necessary for food. The most edible
parts of creation have always required the rain and have needed
the cultivation of man. There are edible plants that grow wild, but
the food that is the staple of human diets requires care. It is the vegetation that is most vulnerable to climate, and to being overtaken
and destroyed by other parts of vegetation. It is critical for the rain
to fall to grow those plants upon which mankind shall depend for
food. God provides for the necessary rain by a source of water
from the earth. The language seems to reflect that rain from the
skies was not necessary, though scholars debate that issue.

The role given to humans is to cultivate and carefully nurture
this land so that the edible plants will bear fruit. As Adam was
only one individual, it would be impossible for him to cultivate the
entire earth which God created. In God's wisdom, he sets aside a
particular part of that earth for a specific assignment, and provides

the detail that answers our concerns about Adam's ability to care for the entire earth. That particular part of creation is the Garden of Eden. The blessing that God provides is that humans shall not only enjoy God's creation, but will enjoy seeing the completed work of their own hands.

> Humans are prone to think of work as a curse. Genesis teaches that work was a gift of God nullifying the idea of a curse. Jesus Christ put the holy stamp on work, saying, '...I work' (John 5:17).

From the earth

It is sometimes taught that the account of Genesis two is a second account of the creation story of chapter one. It is even stated that they are two different accounts with differing origins and were at some point merged into the one story. Scholars have resorted to this methodology to explain the different emphases of the two chapters. In chapter one, the animals are mentioned before humans. In chapter two, the animals come after humans. It is not necessary, however, to take such radical steps to explain the differences in the two chapters. The phrase, 'These are the generations of....' always points to that which comes after. With that introduction in 2:4, one can instantly understand that the action is not on creation, but on the continuing story of creation.

The writer begins by adding some detail to the creation of humans. The human body is formed from raw materials found in the earth. 'And the Lord God formed man of the dust of the ground...' (2:7). One wonders why this information is provided. Most likely, it is there to reflect on the connection humans are to have with the earth. It is by cultivation of the earth that humans are to eat. It is from the earth that the vegetation will grow and provide the food to be eaten. 'And out of the ground made the Lord God to grow every tree that is pleasant to the sight, and good for food...' (2:9).

Further, the information that is provided looks past other religious systems of the world, and perhaps thousands of years into the future. In the act of man's creation, it is stated as fact that man comes directly from the earth. There was no intermediary (meaning the animal kingdom). It will require a direct argument with the clear statement of Scripture to postulate an evolutionary concept. Springing from the earth provides humans with the understanding of their creatureliness, but does not make them the descendants of the animal kingdom. Humanity is both humbled and given special position as unique from the rest of creation. He shall be the master of earth, as he will eat by the result of his own work, whereas, the rest of nature (including the animals) will be dependent on the earth without any power to affect its elements.

This understanding of creation is crucial to humans being able to form a proper theology of their personal responsibility to the earth, and to its Creator.

> It is important for humans to grasp the significance of their creatureliness. For, it is in this foundation that the wonder of the Incarnate Christ leads to another dimension. Consider: 'to them (us) gave he power to become the sons of God' (John 1:12).

Breath of life

In this text, there is a new name given to God. Throughout Genesis one, he is named (in Hebrew) by the general, ancient name for deity, *Elohim*. In verses 4, 5, 7 of chapter two, the English translation reads 'Lord God'. This places two names together. The Hebrew reads 'Yahweh Elohim'. Yahweh is known to many as Jehovah. Yahweh is the covenant name by which Israel is to know God. It is the name that God reveals to Moses when Moses asks for a name. Literally, Yahweh, in Hebrew, is the verb 'to be', hence, God responds to Moses with the name 'I am' (Exodus 3:14). It is by this name that Israel shall know its God in intimacy.

It is appropriate that the intimate name of God would be introduced in this passage of Scripture (2:4-7). It is here that God begins to act in very personal ways with his creation. In verse seven, it is revealed that God '...breathed into his nostrils the breath of life....' This is a sublime act of intimacy between the Creator and his creation. It is a special kind of activity with humans and is not given to animals. The beasts receive life by means of the spoken Word of God. Humans receive it in a way that clearly lifts them above the animals.

Often, this passage is read without understanding the biblical expression of God's special attention to humans. Humankind was created by a very unique touch from God. As the work of God among men is contemplated, it is well to return to this moment of creation. There is a tender loving care often expressed in God's work with humans. There is also judgment that is fierce and decisive (the flood, confusion of tongues, captivity of Israel). Yet, through all the judgments, God offers hope. In the flood, Noah and his family are spared. Abraham is called out after the confusion of tongues, and a remnant is spared from among the nation of Israel. Finally, God acts through sending his own Son into the world who offers himself as a sacrifice. The biblical reader is left to ponder such love and longsuffering patience. What is it that motivates God?

In the very beginning, God acted to show his intention for this creation. There is the picture of face-to-face intimacy. Metaphorically, one might say that the breath of life was bestowed with a kiss. This moment, contrasted with the betrayal of Jesus by means of the kiss of Judas Iscariot, becomes quite ironic.

No human can know the force of God's desire for intimacy with his creation. In the death of Christ when he prayed for the ones crucifying him to be forgiven, we see this passion for his creation demonstrated again.

Genesis 2:8-17

8. And the Lord God planted a garden eastward in Eden; and there he put the man whom he had formed. 9. And out of the ground made the Lord God to grow every tree that is pleasant to the sight, and good for food; the tree of life also in the midst of the garden, and the tree of knowledge of good and evil. 10. And a river went out of Eden to water the garden; and from thence it was parted, and became into four heads. 11. The name of the first is Pison: that is it which compasseth the whole land of Havilah, where there is gold; 12. And the gold of that land is good: there is bdellium and the onyx stone. 13. And the name of the second river is Gihon: the same is it that compasseth the whole land of Ethiopia. 14. And the name of the third river is Hiddekel: that is it which goeth toward the east of Assyria. And the fourth river is Euphrates. 15. And the Lord God took the man, and put him into the garden of Eden to dress it and to keep it. 16. And the Lord God commanded the man, saying, Of every tree of the garden thou mayest freely eat: 17. But of the tree of the knowledge of good and evil, thou shalt not eat of it: for in the day that thou eatest thereof thou shalt surely die.

Subdue the earth

God's intention for humans to be in a special relationship with him is revealed graphically by the biblical writer's phrasing of the giving to man the 'breath of life'. 'And the Lord God formed man of the dust of the ground, and breathed into his nostrils the breath of life…' (2:7). It is an awesome expression of the affection God has for this being called 'man'.

As the passage moves ahead, it is necessary to establish the situation which will satisfy the demands of a true relationship. Clearly, God has affection for his creation. Will the creation have the same affection for him? Thus, a test is presented.

The setting for man's test shall be a garden. He is to subdue the earth (far too great a task for one man). So, the first man is given one small part of the earth as his domain. There will be ample vegetation for food (2:9), ample water supply, by means of a river

(2:10-14), a supply of precious ore and metals by which he may utilize his creative craftsmanship (2:12), and a clear responsibility for cultivation (2:5). Finally, the first man is presented with the challenge of great opportunity. He has received life as a means of intimacy from God. That relationship with God can grow into a great storehouse of knowledge and glory if the man will do one thing. 'And the Lord God commanded the man, saying, Of every tree of the garden thou mayest freely eat: But of the tree of the knowledge of good and evil, thou shalt not eat of it: for in the day that thou eatest thereof thou shalt surely die' (2:16-17).

It is profitable to examine the nature of this test. It is forthright, without ambiguity, and very doable. It is not easy, however. God has told the humans to subdue the earth, yet he is ordered not to eat of a tree that is clearly good for food. This sets up the nature of the test. God said, 'subdue', but how can the man subdue the earth, if he cannot have mastery over one part of the earth? Let's take it one step further. The tree grows from the ground. Man himself, by the command of God, grew from the dust of the ground (2:7). The issue can thus be stated: Will the man attach himself more to his creatureliness, or to the creator who is giving him the opportunity for a special relationship? Will his mastery of the earth be more important than his servanthood to God? It is more than abstaining from the fruit of a tree. Man is being given the opportunity to define himself as one who relates to God or as one who relates to the earth.

> This trial, of the first man and woman, is stated by Jesus in command. '...seek ye first the kingdom of God, and his righteousness...' (Matthew 6:33).

Importance of freedom

As Christians have contemplated the story of the first humans' test of their obedience to God, the question, 'why', is often asked. Why did God allow this opportunity, knowing the devastating results that would happen to humans; not to mention the price he will personally pay by virtue of the sacrifice of Jesus Christ? There are many answers that manifest themselves as one meditates on the story.

First, humans are set apart from the animal kingdom to be in relationship to God. There must be a clear statement about that which makes them different. Animals shall be in absolute bondage to their environment without the ability to affect it. Humans will not have that enslavement, and will be empowered to affect the environment. One further step is required. There is freedom in the ability to move around on the earth, to affect the environment through the choices made, but is there full freedom to establish love for the Creator? That is only established with another level of choice.

The test placed upon these first humans is another biblical statement about the manifold wisdom of God. He gives to humans the second greatest gift that he could provide. Obviously, the greatest gift is life. The second greatest is freedom. Why is freedom such a great gift? It is only in freedom that the true potential for humanity can be reached. Without freedom, in the sense of being able to rebel against God, humans could never truly be more than animals. Though they have the ability to affect the earth, they are tied to the earth in terms of relationships. Humans are of the earth (2:7). Clearly, the highest potential for humans is to be discovered in the possibility for relationship with God. If that relationship is pre-set by the determination of God, where is the freedom? Where is the uniqueness of humans? Where is the clear differentiation from animals?

Freedom gives the human the opportunity to soar high. Of course, it also sets up the possibility for a crash. There are many who prefer the safety of never having to worry about the crash. They would choose never to soar high. A determination of that sort on God's part would have deprived every man the opportunity to be more than animals. Instead of accepting the lowest common denominator for humans, he appeals to the highest common denominator, and grants the freedom necessary to achieve it.

The profound love of God is clearly displayed. He knew what direction the humans would choose. He had already made provisions to redeem before he created them. '...with the precious blood of Christ...who verily was foreordained before the foundation of the world...' (1 Peter 1:19-20).

Opportunity of freedom

The test of Adam and Eve is not often thought of in the context of freedom. Because of the fallen nature of humans, we are prone to seeing the restriction, and being somewhat agitated by it. '...of every tree of the garden thou mayest freely eat: But of the tree of the knowledge of good and evil, thou shalt not eat of it...' (2:16-17). Immediately we rush to the notion of that which is forbidden.

This is the point where clear discernment becomes necessary. What has God truly offered to humanity? Physically, there is the fruit of every tree of the garden except the forbidden one. There is a principle involved that goes beyond the material. The chance is here for the humans to prove their mettle. The man and the woman are given the chance to set a clear direction for themselves, and to prove their ability to stick to it. At the end of the day, there would be a two-fold result. They establish themselves as worthy of the garden, and they receive the joy of enlightened knowledge of their Creator. At that point, they become more than the creation of God, they became the friends of God.

One should consider carefully the point. The decision was not about whether to enjoy the fruit of the tree of knowledge of good and evil. The decision was about whether to enjoy the knowledge of God. It was critical that the humans, being tested, refuse to fasten their eyes on the tree. There is a much greater, more wonderful fruit to be sought. If they begin to lust after the fruit of the physical tree, they will be lusting after that which is least rewarding. If the lust is for the greater fruit, they will have no problem with ignoring the tree of knowledge of good and evil.

In the light of modern day religious thirsting for happiness, which is very much related to earth-bound entities, we are again fastening our eyes on the tree that is least rewarding. Our focus is on the lowest element of our lives. Sometimes, our preaching and our teaching, is so grounded in our gardening chores of 'this-earth' related commandments, we lose sight of the greater opportunity. Our sense of the 'thou shalt not's' become great burdens because our eyes are looking hard at the one tree that entices us. Our focus is always on the lowest denominator of life. It would be wise to reflect on the great freedom God has offered by the test (the chance for a great relationship with him) and focus our eyes on learning of him, instead of eyeing that restriction. The more our focus is on what is restricted, the more we lose sight of the freedom offered by the test.

> The enticements of sin are always deceiving, and prevent our seeing the greater reward available to us. The restrictions are great opportunities to discover the greater reward. Thus, even in restriction, there is great freedom to seek what is greater.

Possibility of death

The test that God places on the first humans first impacts us as an easy assignment. The words, '...in the day that thou eatest thereof thou shalt surely die....' (2:17), would seem to provide a warning which will be all that is needed to effect a proper outcome. The man and the woman have the clear statement of God, and the rest of the Garden of Eden with which to be occupied.

This is the first place in the Bible that death is mentioned. It is quite a shock to the senses. The creation has been a fascinating study filled with splendour, and our mind's eye has been awestruck with the glory. God's gentle touch in bringing humans into the world (2:7) has thrilled us with the grandeur of the gentle and loving emotion from the great Creator. The wonder of the grand creation and the tender emotion for the Creator, which we sensed, as we observed the intimacy of his giving life to humans, is radically altered. The stark announcement takes us by surprise. God shall kill his creation if they disobey. That is a word that we did not expect.

The wonder of the possibility of humans enjoying their greatest fulfilment by knowing their God is met with the harsh reality of the alternative. One either starts the journey of knowing God or one dies. Since God is the source of all life, it should be easy to accept the reality that separation from the source of life is death. In the story, that aspect of things had not occurred to us until this pronouncement.

As one meditates on this word from God, the emotion and anxiety begin to stir. It is clear that a great drama is about to play out before us. The drama is of the highest stakes possible: life and death. The beautiful earth, the wonderful garden, the man and the woman, are all seen very differently with the sound of four words. '...thou shalt surely die...' (2:17).

In reality, it could be no other way. The greatest blessing is to know God intimately. There is no alternative but death. Why? God is the source of life. To choose other than God is to choose other than life. The feeling of dread comes over us in terms of the story, but we calm ourselves with the knowledge that it seems an easy test. They will not do what would cause them to die. It sounds easy, but the man and the woman must never become curious about that forbidden tree. God has given them a mind to think and the ability to affect the earth. Will they use their mind to think correctly? Proper thinking will determine the outcome of this drama.

Improper thinking is a deadly danger for all men. Jesus had this in mind when he noted '...He that abideth in me, and I in him, the same bringeth forth much fruit...' (John 15:5).

Understanding the choice

Could not God have come up with some other punishment? Death
will happen for eating the fruit of a tree. Sure, it is a fruit that is
forbidden, but how is that so bad? Many of us ask this question
as the situation of the first man and the first woman is pondered.
Why is disobedience to God such a deadly thing? Perhaps a little
meditation from a philosophical perspective can help.

God has created the man and the woman. He has given them
two great gifts. He has given them life, and he has given them
freedom. They can choose to accept themselves as coming directly
from the breath of God destined to be with him for eternity, or as
the simple creatures of earth destined to return to the earth. That
choice is made in the decision of refusing to eat the fruit of one
tree. The decision is not the simple eating of fruit. It is a decision
about how they will think. It is a decision that determines who and
what they will be. The perspective of the mind will be forever altered. God is telling the man and woman that eating the forbidden
tree will radically alter their nature, and they can never again be
what they were before. The mind will be so inextricably attached
to this earth that the creation will appear stronger and wiser than
the Creator. The Apostle Paul speaks of this situation in Romans
1:25: 'Who changed the truth of God into a lie, and worshipped
and served the creature more than the creator, who is blessed forever. Amen.'

There is a basic question to consider. Which is greater: the glory
of God, or the glory of God's creation? The quick response is that
God is greater, yet that is not the way that humans really think. The
glory of God is unfathomable. Without a Bible that tells us of God's
glory, and without the leap of faith to accept it, there is simply no
mechanism in our brain to grasp it.

The mind of the first man and the first woman had potential
beyond belief. When they made the choice to be attached to the
dust rather than to God, the mind's potential was forever altered.
God's glory would have to be taught to them, not inherently understood. That which is good will have to be explained and enforced

because the mind will turn to satisfying the urges of the flesh rather than to knowing God, who is the essence of good. At that point, death is as much a matter of grace as a matter of punishment. Without the mind to know God, humans can never achieve their intended potential. The task for the first man and the first woman is 'Think correctly now, for you will not be able to think correctly again if you fail this test.'

> Romans 12:2 speaks of the need to be 'transformed by the renewing of your mind.' This statement is clearer when we understand that our minds are presently conformed to the dust instead of God. It is only in the transformed mind through the redemption wrought in the Incarnate Christ that the needed transformation can occur.

Nature of knowledge of good and evil

The description of Genesis two tells us that there were two important trees planted in the Garden of Eden. They were called the tree of life and the tree of the knowledge of good and evil. The inference is clear. To eat of the tree of life shall impart an action of God leading to eternal life for the body. The eating of the second tree would cause death. It is assumed that the man and woman never got to the tree of life (Genesis 3:22-24).

One is left to ponder an interesting question. If the death tree is called the tree of knowledge of good and evil, why is it that good becomes so difficult for humans, and evil becomes so easy for humans after eating it? Should not good and evil be equally easy? The answer is found in the command of God. To discover knowledge of good and evil is to be found in obedience to God. Eating the fruit of the tree did produce knowledge, but in an unexpected form. The purpose of the fruit of the tree was in its testing. It is in not eating that knowledge of good and evil in terms of avoiding evil is to be gained. The only knowledge gained by the man and woman through eating the fruit of the tree is the knowledge of experiencing evil. The experience of it will alter the human mind in startling fashion.

If we meditate a little deeper, we will ask, 'If experiencing evil provides the knowledge of evil, why does the human return to evil a second time after being involved in it once?' In fact, the second time, it is easier, not more difficult. The mind does not develop a knowledge-controlling action of the body by experiencing evil, but often becomes addicted to the activity and rationalizes that it is an acceptable act. The lesson for us is the same as in the beginning. One gains control of evil in refraining from the commission of it.

In addition, one's knowledge of good begins with refraining from the commission of evil. The problem is, once man eats the forbidden fruit, his mind is not capable of arriving at correct conclusions of good and evil. Young people often complain about the seventh commandment and argue that in order to have a healthy sexual relationship after marriage, they must gain some pre-marital sexual experience. This is a clear example of foolish thinking and lack of knowledge. Healthy marriages come in 'not eating' the fruit before marriage. Eating the fruit before marriage is a strong detriment to the knowledge necessary to a happy marriage.

Genesis 2:18-25

18. And the Lord God said, It is not good that the man should be alone; I will make him an helpmeet for him. 19. And out of the ground the Lord God formed every beast of the field, and every fowl of the air; and brought them unto Adam to see what he would call them: and whatsoever Adam called every living creature, that was the name thereof. 20. And Adam gave names to all cattle, and to the fowl of the air, and to every beast of the field; but for Adam there was not found an helpmeet for him. 21. And the Lord God caused a deep sleep to fall upon Adam, and he slept: and he took one of his ribs, and closed up the flesh instead thereof; 22. And the rib, which the Lord God had taken from man, made he a woman, and brought her unto the man. 23. And Adam said, This is now bone of my bones, and flesh of my flesh: she shall be called Woman, because she was taken out of Man. 24. Therefore shall a man leave his father and his mother, and shall cleave unto his wife: and they shall be one flesh. 25. And they were both naked, the man and his wife, and were not ashamed.

Animals

The text reveals more of God's action with his creation and adds further insight to an earlier passage. 'So God created man in his own image, in the image of God created he him; male and female created he them' (Genesis 1:27). That which is revealed as a singular act in one event of creation is now explained as having a time-lapse involvement between the creation of the man and the forming of the woman from the man.

The need for the woman is explained. 'And the Lord God said, It is not good that the man should be alone; I will make him an helpmeet for him' (2:18). The narrative that follows is extremely curious. God leads Adam through an interesting exercise. He brings the animals before Adam in a mock search for a suitable helpmeet. Certainly God knew there would not be found a counterpart with Adam among the animals. Why the search? The text offers a clear reason, and another possibility can be gleaned from inference.

First, by bringing the animals before Adam, there is a bond established with the animal world. The giving of names to animals is to be seen as establishing an intimacy. Adam was to have dominion over the animals, and this exercise was to familiarize Adam with the animal world. It must have been a delightful and wonderful experience for Adam. God's exercise was a great moment of education and entertainment. Think of your trips to the zoo, or the times you have walked into a pet store to view the puppies, birds, fish, or other animals. Wouldn't you like to have been at God's zoo on this day with Adam? This exercise was to give Adam a love and appreciation of animals, and to prepare him for something more wonderful.

Second, there is a statement that seems to be aimed at an intellectual world that shall develop thousands of years later. 'And Adam gave names to...every beast of the field; but for Adam there was not found an helpmeet for him' (2:20). Throughout the biblical narrative of creation, there are those words that tell us of the distinctive difference in humans and the animals. To try to connect and preserve an evolutionary view with the biblical view is to give elasticity to Scripture that doesn't fit. There was no helpmeet, no animal that could serve in helping humans procreate. Human procreation required one like unto man. For evolution to function there has to be procreative possibility from one species to another. In the biblical view, it is not allowed. The animals are wonderful, but nothing compares to the male and female of the human race.

Let us thank God for his clear Word in creation which enables us to avoid the pitfalls of the worship of animals, and the truly comical, and senseless glorification of animals that seems to have control of so much of modern civilization.

Man and woman

The description of the creation of the woman from the man is noteworthy on several fronts. First, it adds further information to Genesis 1:27. The earlier passage reads as if male and female are created at precisely the same moment. The later description of Genesis 2:7 shows that the man was formed first (from the dust of the earth). The woman is formed from the man. God takes a portion of the man's bones and flesh to form the woman (2:23).

Second, the need for the woman is established by God in the words, 'It is not good that the man should be alone; I will make him an helpmeet for him' (2:18). This statement is not made about any of the animal kingdom though the animal kingdom is also male and female. One must dig deeper to see the significance.

Third, it is not stated of the animals that the female was formed from the flesh of the male, but that all animals came from the dust of the ground (2:19). The female of the human species was clearly on a different level. She shall be unique and special.

To discover the nature of her uniqueness, one must return to the first mention of human creation. 'And God said, Let us make man in our image, after our likeness...male and female created he them' (Genesis 1:26-27). It is in the phrase 'in our image' that the uniqueness of the human female is discovered. The biblical account reveals that the image of God is portrayed through the male-female relationship of humanity. How? It is in Adam's response to the woman (which God presents to him) that understanding is achieved. He notes, '...This is now bone of my bones, and flesh of my flesh: she shall be called Woman, because she was taken out of Man' (2:23). Adam looks upon the woman and sees one like unto himself, but unique unto herself. The two, though separate, had a natural affinity for each other that could mold two thoughts into one, two perspectives into one perspective, and the two could walk together as one. Their communication and intimacy would be far above the animal world, and would add the one ingredient the animal world could never achieve, love. The man shall love the woman as himself and the woman shall love the man as herself (Ephesians 5:28). How is this in the image of God? Jesus said, 'I and my Father are one' (John 10:30). Humans, in their fallen state as sinners, have much trouble with this, but it is the oneness uniting separate entities of husband and wife that is earth's closest parallel to the love manifest in the oneness of the Godhead.

From this story, it is clear that the male-female concept of humanity was not an afterthought, but was God's plan from the start. Real intimacy of two minds becoming one is always an unrealized picture for humanity. There can only be glimpses into it that can teach of God. The Incarnate One teaches us further of intimacy, and urges us to long for the greatest intimacy of all, oneness with God (Philippians 2:5).

Man and wife

God formed the woman to be a helpmeet for the man. There is much that theologians and sociologists try to make of this concept. The context seems to have one thing in mind. It is in the relationship that derives from oneness. The female is different from the male but corresponds to the male in such fashion as to cause the two to be drawn to each other. As separate entities they can forge a relationship that will unite their lives in one direction with complementing goals and aspirations. Though different, they shall be united. Though separate, they shall think as one. Though male and female, they shall call the other precious, and find a bond called 'love'. To lay the mantle of love on another, and call that which is outside one's self more precious than one's self is the pinnacle of oneness. A helpmeet is thus understood as one who can draw out the part of the human that creates love.

When one can love another as more precious than one's self, then a touch of the image of God is realized. It goes one step further in its appreciation and becomes real oneness when the mutual love two have for each other can be fused to create love for a third separate entity that is outside the two. When the two in love equally love a third as more precious than the love they share, the image of God is further clarified. In that light, consider God's love for the Son, and the Son's love for us. Add these words, 'For God so loved the world, that he gave his only begotten Son, that whosoever believeth in him should not perish, but have everlasting life' (John 3:16). In our children, we sense the great dynamic of God's love.

Humans, in a sinful state, often focus on certain elements of the great picture of male-female oneness and distort God's picture. The sexuality consumes us, and that which God provided to entice the male-female to each other is the picture upon which we dwell. The oneness God wishes to portray is far above the male-female sexuality. It is further distorted by human romanticism that speaks of our being made whole upon finding a wife or husband. Such language is the distortion of sin. The husband-wife imagery is to provide a picture of something greater. The oneness that comes in the male-female relationship is not the oneness of wholeness. That would mean that no single person could ever be whole. Jesus would not have been whole by that understanding. Nakedness without shame is a reflection of a clothing of righteousness emanating from God's creation. Marriage is a symbol that points to the wholeness that comes in our relationship with God and is pure and without shame. To make of it more than God intended is to lead us to great frustration. To understand its picture is to help us understand God.

Genesis 3:1-24

I. Elements of the Fall (3:1-6)
1. Identifying the serpent
2. Wisdom of the serpent
3. Invention of legalism
4. Human vulnerability
5. Elements of a confused mind
6. Understanding the work of confusion
7. Truth that is a lie
8. Wisdom of evil
9. Desire for evil

II. Paralysing Effects of Sin (3:7-14)
1. Horror of sin exposed
2. Clothing of righteousness lost
3. Voice of the Lord
4. Hiding from God
5. Naked
6. '...the woman...'
7. When God speaks

III. God's Response to Human Sin (3:15-19)
1. '...dust shalt thou eat...'
2. Judgement on the serpent
3. Seed of the woman
4. Judgement on the woman
5. Plight of the woman
6. Judgement on the man
7. Plight of the man

IV. A New Situation for Humanity (3:20-24)
1. Return to dust
2. A statement of faith
3. A new clothing
4. A new relationship with the creation
5. Out of the garden
6. '...as one of us.'
7. Cherubims

Genesis 3:1-6

1. Now the serpent was more subtil than any beast of the field which the Lord God had made. And he said unto the woman, Yea, hath God said, Ye shall not eat of every tree of the garden? 2. And the woman said unto the serpent, We may eat of the fruit of the trees of the garden: 3. But of the fruit of the tree which is in the midst of the garden, God hath said, Ye shall not eat of it, neither shall ye touch it, lest ye die. 4. And the serpent said unto the woman, Ye shall not surely die: 5. For God doth know that in the day ye eat thereof, then your eyes shall be opened, and ye shall be as gods, knowing good and evil. 6. And when the woman saw that the tree was good for food, and that it was pleasant to the eyes, and a tree to be desired to make one wise, she took of the fruit thereof, and did eat, and gave also unto her husband with her; and he did eat.

Identifying the serpent

At the beginning of chapter 3, the drama unfolds. The reader has been adequately prepared by the creation narrative. Adequate tension has been put in motion by virtue of the tree of knowledge of good and evil. In the reader's mind, there are some concerns. The nature of the warning about the tree is clear and horrifying. '... thou shalt not eat of it: for in the day that thou eatest thereof thou shalt surely die' (Genesis 2:17). This is enough, one would think, to prevent the eating of the tree by any purposeful choice. The concern is, can they be tricked? Will they eat of it by accident? The warning had no exception clauses.

The story that develops has an eerie presence. In its simple reading one imagines a snake talking, a woman listening, and being beguiled to eat of the forbidden fruit. The worst has happened. One of the animals that God created has tricked one of the humans into eating the forbidden fruit. To some extent, the story sounds like a child's fairy tale until you examine closely.

From where did this talking serpent come? The beasts of the field had not been able to talk in any of the creation narrative. The narrative provides us with a great mystery, and with an underlying clue. This was no ordinary serpent. The phrase, '...was more subtil than any beast of the field,' is better understood when read in a partitive sense. That is, this serpent is set apart from all beasts, meaning he is part of the animal kingdom, but is not necessarily from that kingdom. The text could be understood as '...subtil as no other of the beasts....' The eerie presence rocks us. The serpent has been there in the animal kingdom, but some other being is present of which the reader has not been informed. It has entered the serpent, and it is that other presence which speaks. This serpent is different from all the other serpents, as well as all the other beasts.

From this point, one thing shall be played out. Humans were established for the purpose of having relationship with, and knowledge of the Creator. There will be competition for that relationship, and an attempt by a presence, whose identity is not yet established, to undermine the human's capacity to have the knowledge for which he was intended. It will take many years and the unfolding revelation of God to reveal the nature and person of that other presence which inhabits the serpent.

The presence inhabiting the serpent is later revealed as one called Satan, the great enemy of humanity. Knowing his devices and tricks are a key to wise decision making.

Wisdom of serpent

The human (male and female) has been created by God, placed in charge of the earth, made different from the animals because of the ability to make choices of right and wrong. If the human chooses right, there is a great reward in store. It is eternal life and the opportunity for a growing relationship with his Creator. If he chooses wrong, there is punishment, '...thou shalt surely die' (Genesis 2:17).

A presence not yet revealed, enters one of the serpents. He is described as '...more subtil than any beast of the field...' (3:1). Separate from all other beasts by virtue of the cunning presence within him, the serpent speaks to the woman. The words reflect his genius. He does not begin with an argument, but a statement to redirect the woman's thinking. It is both amusing and enlightening to see the impact. The snake (a creature) engages in the parsing of words. Did God really say, '...Ye shall not eat of every tree of the garden' (3:1)?

In a brilliant stroke, the snake has recast God's words by two gimmicks. First, he added one thing. Second, he structures the statement in a way that could allow an unclear meaning on God's words. The snake wants the woman to feel good. He adds something to that which God said in order for her to correct him. The intimation is that God had instructed the male and female to abstain from eating the fruit of all trees in the garden. As the one who has dominion over the animals, she is now given the privilege of exercising dominion through correcting the statement of the serpent. Once the serpent is properly humbled, he will not be perceived as a threat. Upon acceptance of the humbling, he can make bolder statements because the woman would now feel properly empowered. She would feel somewhat invincible.

Also, the snake slyly asserts by the tone of the question that she may have misunderstood the meaning of God's statement. 'Thou shalt surely die' is hard to misunderstand. Nevertheless, the tone is effective in redirecting the mind to allow the possibility of misunderstanding. Modern lawyers have mastered this technique through the use of the term 'reasonable doubt'. The common use of 'reasonable doubt' has been restructured to mean the possibility of reasonable doubt, not the actuality of it. The possibility of misunderstanding is all that will be necessary for the snake to get to the next level. That level will be to totally change the meaning of God, and that changes the nature of discussion. The choice of right and wrong is thus confusing instead of simple. That is the difference between the wisdom of God and the wisdom of man.

> It is easy to have our thinking redirected in ways that will allow the distortion of God's Word. Jesus noted, '...if my words abide in you...' (John 15:7), calling attention to knowing his words that we might be protected from redirected thinking.

Invention of legalism

The snake has asked a question of the woman. The question is subtle and carries a strong insinuation. He (the presence occupying it) knows that God has not deprived the woman of eating from all the trees of the garden, yet he asks her if that is the case. The insinuation is that God is cruel. The woman is placed in the position of defending God and at the same time instructing the serpent. The possibility of God's cruelty has been placed in her mind. If God has forbidden one tree, maybe the next step is to forbid the eating from all the trees.

The woman's response indicates that the insinuation may have created concern about God's intention in her mind. She first gets the serpent's error corrected. 'And the woman said unto the serpent, We may eat of the fruit of the trees of the garden: But of the fruit of the tree which is in the midst of the garden, God hath said, Ye shall not eat of it...' (3:2-3). She quotes God accurately. However, she doesn't stop. She goes on to add her own understanding,

'...neither shall ye touch it, lest ye die' (3:3). Eve was engaging in application of God's command and adding that which would attribute some cruelty in God's requirements of her.

The response of the woman provides a typical human reaction to many of life's restrictions. It also illustrates how the Word of God gets distorted. Eve takes a restriction and magnifies it. She over-states what God had said. In her attempt to straighten out the error of the serpent, she adds a further restriction. It may sound like a good thing to her. The reasoning could be 'If I do not touch it, I will not eat it.' She can make things easier, she assumes, by adding a tougher restriction. In theological terms, we would call it 'legalism'.

The problem arises when the legalism she has established is applied. God has also told the humans to till the ground, to dress the garden and keep it (Genesis 2:15). The dressing and keeping also included the tree of knowledge of good and evil. To dress it and keep it would require touching it. The woman establishes a rule by her own addition that will safeguard one restriction, yet make it impossible to fulfil a clear work requirement. The woman has set up an impossible situation for herself.

Legalism always lays a trap for us. It magnifies restrictions, creates hardships that are impossible to fulfil, and leads us to situations that make it impossible to serve God. In effect we will only be serving the rules we created. It becomes sad because it leads us to believe that God is the one who so restricts, and thus weakens resistance to temptation.

In this passage, a fearsome thing is revealed that has been a horrifying aspect of Christianity, that is, the making of rules which add to the Word of God and end up only in cruelty. The Christian succeeds only in outsmarting himself when he adds his own rules to the Word of God.

Human vulnerability

As one meditates on the verses of this text, perplexity weighs upon the mind. It is one of the most confusing moments of all Scripture. The confusion is experienced in the way this episode defines humanity. No one wants to think of himself as being this vulnerable. It doesn't make sense. Yet, it is precisely what we all are.

After correcting the snake's misstatement about God's command, the woman does not discredit the serpent, but continues to listen. The snake offers another distortion. 'And the serpent said unto the woman, Ye shall not surely die' (3:4). Immediately, the woman should have cut off the conversation and walked away. Why would she continue to listen? The Scriptures often remind us of the importance of knowing God's Word because we are simply incapable of coming to right conclusions without God's revelation. The prophet Isaiah reminds us, 'For as the heavens are higher than the earth, so are my ways higher than your ways, and my thoughts than your thoughts' (Isaiah 55:9). The story of Eve demonstrates that even in a stage of innocence (without sin) humans were vulnerable to faulty thinking. A human listened to a snake instead of remembering the Word of God.

One may postulate several ways in which the woman's thinking was vulnerable. The woman may have reasoned that the serpent, being created before humans, thus older than humans, has some secret that God had shared with the animal world, and the humans were not yet told. The serpent was being kind enough to let them in on the secret. Humans are often deceived by charlatans and deceivers, who claim mystical secrets that can give great power or great reward to the properly initiated. The charlatans tell us that they are sent by God to let us in on the secret. The woman's vulnerability was that she allowed herself to meditate on the words of the serpent rather than the words of God.

The woman has already started the rebellion against God. She is accepting the fact that animals over which she has been given dominion may have knowledge that supersedes hers. She fails to keep the position of dominionship. She makes God's restriction tougher than it really is by adding the phrase '...neither shall ye touch it...' (3:3). Her addition means she will not be able to fulfil God's command to keep and dress the garden (Genesis 2:15). A simple command of God, 'don't eat', is now a maze of confusion. Clear thinking becomes impossible.

Elements of a confused mind

In the conversation with the serpent, the woman has allowed a discussion that ultimately twists her mind in knots. She sought to protect herself from the danger of eating the fruit of the tree of knowledge by adding a restriction, '...neither shall ye touch it' (3:3). Eve's legalistic approach to God's command serves only to confuse and bewilder. That which appears to be a protective device only serves to add another rule to remember. She is robbing herself of freedom, and creating a mystery in her mind (what does the fruit feel like) that will only serve as further temptation.

In addition, the woman has allowed a conversation with a snake. The serpent should have been under her control, not trying to be her teacher. The snake purports to have knowledge the woman does not have. '...Ye shall not surely die:...God doth know... your eyes shall be opened, and ye shall be as gods...' (3:4-5). There were several things to which the woman might turn in order to discern fact from fiction. First, she was given dominion over the animals. Why would a snake have more understanding? This is a clear refusal to accept her responsibility in having dominion over the animals. When one thinks about it, this same sin is committed in a similar fashion by modern day parents who seem to allow their own children to outsmart and intimidate them, and thus refuse to be responsible in their rulership of the home.

Second, what possible purpose could the knowledge of evil serve the woman? She had everything that was good. 'And God saw everything that he had made, and, behold, it was very good...'

(Genesis 1:31). Sound reasoning would have established that having evil is to deteriorate her life, not improve it. Why would she
want it?

Clearly, the woman became confused. The snake had led her to
think about the wrong things. He had induced her to make further
rules not established by God. She looked at the tree with a mindset
she had not previously considered. It is a tree, she thought, '...to
be desired to make one wise...' (3:6). She forgot that it was also a
tree to make one dead. So much of human thinking falls into this
kind of foolhardiness. 'There is a way that seemeth right unto a
man, but the end thereof are the ways of death' (Proverbs 16:25).
Every time humans try to reason in ways that carry us away from
the Word of God, whether in establishing legalistic rules to keep
ourselves in line, or in establishing brand new ways that we think
are wise, we are walking the path of destruction.

> A mistake of Christians is that we spend too much time
> looking for creative ways to enforce the Word of God and
> too little time trying to understand it.

Understanding the work of confusion

It is clear to the reader when meditating on the serpent's temptation to Eve that the woman has become confused, and has allowed
the words of the serpent to lead her mind in a faulty direction. It is
very telling to see how she reasons once she becomes confused.
'And when the woman saw that the tree was good for food, and
that it was pleasant to the eyes, and a tree to be desired to make
one wise, she took of the fruit thereof, and did eat...' (3:6).

Note the direction: she reverts to the only things she truly un-
derstands, her own passion. She knows the appetites of the flesh.
She knows what appeals to the eye, and she knows that she likes to
feel important. When confusion reigns, one always turns inward.
The truth no longer matters, one does what makes self feel good.
It just seems right. The problem is that humans refer to it as 'think-

ing'. In reality, it is only lusting. It is that which every human shares, and it is the lowest common denominator of human existence. Why does the woman turn to the lust of the flesh, the lust of the eye, and the pride of life? It's easy to know when one thinks about it. The serpent had gotten her mind so rattled, and her thinking so muddled that the only thing that made sense to her was her lusts.

This pattern can be seen consistently in the affairs of humankind. Whenever an issue becomes confused, we resort to the lowest common denominator. The marriage becomes complicated, an extramarital affair results. It feels right! The college life is tough, the studies are hard, relationships are complicated, so a drunken party, a wild night giving in to lusts is the answer. It feels right! The finances in life are bad, the times are tough, others are doing better financially, so taking what others have is the answer. People go to war, they fight, and seek to satisfy the lowest common denominator by taking from others. It feels right!

All of this kind of activity in humans results from the loss of proper thinking. It is confusion and bewilderment. It started when one simple command of God was thought about and a human and a snake engaged in conversation. One was trying to make the command easier to enforce, the other was trying to add a detail that would make things better than what God had provided. Ultimately, the only thing with which they are left is a body that struggles to use its mind, and consistently reverts back to the lowest element of itself to find satisfaction.

> The Incarnate One faced the same kind of problem. He encountered the same evil one, but did not waiver. How did he do it? Note: He answers the tempter with '…it is written…' (Matthew 4:4, 7, 10).

Truth that is a lie

In the temptation the first woman faces, she is called upon to believe this claim. '…ye shall be as gods, knowing good and evil'

(3:5). Consider what the woman hears, and compare to what the serpent actually means. For the woman, she hears that she can be the equal of God, at least in one capacity. The presence that is using the serpent in beguiling the woman has another thought in mind. The presence seeks to make the woman as he is.

When the woman understands good and evil as the snake suggests, it will be to know the full force of evil in experience of it. The inhabiting presence of the snake had already gone there. She had not thought in that framework. The awesome reality is that the snake was telling the truth. It is the most hideous kind of lying. It is the lie that states truth knowing that what is heard is not what is said.

The woman starts to act as if she already has such knowledge. She allows the promise of the snake to give her a vision of something better than the Garden of Eden. It is all there in the forbidden fruit. 'And…the woman saw that the tree was good for food, and that it was pleasant to the eyes, and a tree to be desired to make on wise…' (3:6). Her thoughts reveal much about the success of the snake.

She assumes that no other tree can properly satisfy her hunger as can this tree. The tree's attractive appearance is now irresistible. The feeling is that life is incomplete without the forbidden fruit. God cannot provide everything she needs. She must have the additional fruit. She will be wiser than before. She assumes that there is a wisdom that God cannot or will not give her.

The truly sad thing is that the woman's faulty thinking was started by the mind's interpretation of that which the serpent said. She did not realize that a god inhabited the serpent. The Bible refers to the presence that inhabited the serpent as the 'god of this world' (2 Corinthians 4:4). The mind when moved in the wrong direction easily leaps to false assumptions, and a true statement becomes a lie to us. Eve heard 'I'll be like God.' She should have heard 'I'll be like the snake.'

The tempter attempted to deceive Jesus with a similar technique of stating a truth which is a lie because of what gets heard. Quoting Scripture, he attempts to get Jesus to cast himself down from the temple (Matthew 4:6). Understanding that it was not the tempter's prerogative to make the suggestion, he quotes Scripture '...Thou shalt not tempt the Lord thy God (Matthew 4:7).

Wisdom of evil

The sinister nature that is before the woman is truly frightening. When one casually reads the story, there is the tendency to look beyond these words, and see them only as temptation. The tree, we argue, does not make one wise, so the woman is deceiving herself. What is there about this fruit that would cause her to believe it would provide wisdom? First, there is the name: tree of knowledge of good and evil. The Creator had given the tree its name (Genesis 2:17). Second, the serpent had led her to believe that he had a knowledge she did not possess.

Would the fruit of the tree of knowledge of good and evil make one wise? The answer is an unequivocal 'yes!' It is not just a faulty temptation to which the woman succumbs. The problem is the nature of the wisdom she pursues. Consider the snake. Was the approach to the woman wisely carried out? Was he successful in his goal? The snake used an evil logic to create doubt concerning the 'good' she already possessed. There is a greater 'good', he argues, to be found by eating the forbidden fruit. The wisdom the woman acquired upon eating the fruit was the wisdom of the snake. It was the wisdom of using the logic of evil to overcome good.

Unfortunately, the wisdom of the world is the wisdom of evil. It often outsmarts the wisdom of good. The Bible validates this through the words of Jesus '...for the children of this world are in their generation wiser than the children of light' (Luke 16:8). One of the most important biblical truths humans can ever learn is to be found here. It is to understand the nature of a truth that is a lie. To understand the concept, we might meditate along these lines. It is wonderful to be smart until one outsmarts oneself.

Eve saw correctly when she noted the tree was one that could make one wise. That much was true. She did not see that the wisdom noted would be the wisdom to use evil to overcome good. She would be like the snake that tempted her. Since the moment the male and female ate of the fruit of the forbidden tree, evil has come easy to humans, and good has come difficult. Humans find themselves capable of rejoicing in doing evil and getting away with it. They feel themselves extremely smart, extremely wise. They are indeed wise, but they are, as they shall discover in judgement, outsmarting themselves.

One of the most telling mistakes that Christians make is in trying to defend Christianity with the world's logic. We cannot fight evil with worldly wisdom, but only in the power of God, and his Word.

Desire for evil

The tragic story of the disobedience of humans unfolds in disaster. The woman, who had been created from the man, and is of the man eats first of the forbidden fruit. At the time she eats, she has been clearly deceived. She truly thinks she is doing a wise thing. All the ingredients of things most appealing to humans are present. The fruit is good food, it is pleasant to the eye, and there is wisdom to be had. What's wrong with that?

There is nothing wrong with it if those three things are the total equation. There is, however, an additional factor. God said '...thou shalt not eat of it...' (Genesis 2:17). God's Word always outweighs human reasoning.

The woman gives to the man. The intriguing thing is that he also eats. The man was not deceived, as was the woman. He knew that he was not doing a wise thing. The apostle Paul informs us of this reality. 'For Adam was first formed, then Eve. And Adam was not deceived, but the woman being deceived was in the transgression' (1 Timothy 2:13-14). The Scripture does not tell us why Adam ate when not deceived. There are many possibilities.

It is appropriate to examine why Adam ate of the fruit. It could be that his desire to please the woman outweighed his desire to please God. The Apostle Paul speaks of the result of sin in the distortion of worship. '...and worshipped and served the creature more than the Creator...' (Romans 1:25). The woman was beguiled by the serpent and was not necessarily engaging in an act that demonstrated her preference of the snake above God. Adam's sin could have been the beginning of placing the creature above the Creator as he received the 'good' from the woman's hand rather than cleaving to the good that God has given him in the other trees of the garden.

The most frightening prospect in Adam's choice is the prospect of a clear rebellion against God. His choice (if pure rebellion) would have registered in a specific way. He reasoned 'I have experienced good. I want to also experience evil.' As the reader understands it, that is extremely foolish, but humans still reason in just that way. The conscious choice to take the route of evil is often made, though there is clear knowledge that it is wrong. It is rationalized by talk of the 'rush of excitement' that one feels, or by the extreme pleasure it brings the flesh, or by the sense of taking control of one's own life. It is stated 'I'm doing my own thing!' There is no attempt at defence. It is acceptable simply because one wants to do it. The picture is one of rebellion at its most frightening. When Adam is understood as acting in this manner, it is easier to understand the phenomenal punishment he received for his sin.

The prophet Isaiah writes, 'All we like sheep have gone astray; we have turned everyone to his own way...' (Isaiah 53:6). The tragedy of every human is there is the desire to experience evil, and we often choose that road. Only in the power of God's redemption is there power to resist.

Genesis 3:7-14

7. And the eyes of them both were opened, and they knew that they were naked; and they sewed fig leaves together, and made themselves aprons. 8. And they heard the voice of the Lord God walking in the garden in the cool of the day: and Adam and his wife hid themselves from the presence of the Lord God amongst the trees of the garden. 9. And the Lord God called unto Adam, and said unto him, Where art thou? 10. And he said, I heard thy voice in the garden, and I was afraid, because I was naked; and I hid myself. 11. And he said, Who told thee that thou wast naked? Hast thou eaten of the tree, whereof I commanded thee that thou shouldest not eat? 12. And the man said, The woman whom thou gavest to be with me, she gave me of the tree, and I did eat. 13. And the Lord God said unto the woman, What is this that thou hast done? And the woman said, The serpent beguiled me, and I did eat. 14. And the Lord God said unto the serpent, Because thou hast done this, thou art cursed above all cattle, and above every beast of the field; upon thy belly shalt thou go, and dust shalt thou eat all the days of thy life:

Horror of sin exposed

There is an amazing, ironic twist that these verses provide for us. It goes to the heart of human vulnerability, if not human irrationality. Note the words uttered by the serpent to Eve. '...your eyes shall be opened, and ye shall be as gods...' (3:5). Compare the words of Genesis 3:7, 'And the eyes of them both were opened, and they knew that they were naked....'

To 'be as gods' has a wonderful sound. It carries all the promise that any human could desire. 'Eyes...opened' means you will see what you have not seen before. What happened? They were as gods. That is, they were like other creatures not of this earth which had rebelled against God. The other creatures would later be revealed as some of the angels in heaven, and defined in the New Testament. 'For we wrestle not against flesh and blood, but against principalities, against powers, against the rulers of the darkness of this world...' (Ephesians 6:12). These principalities and powers (gods) were angels who, like Adam and Eve, had followed the presence inhabiting the serpent. How are Adam and Eve now like them? They had experienced evil, and were exposed.

Their eyes were opened. The ironic twist is that they did not like what they saw. It sounds so wonderful. They will see what they had never seen before. They were not told about the horror they would experience. In a modern world, fascinated by pictures of nudity, and the emphasis on the beauty of the body, it is difficult to imagine the idea of horror at the human form. We are prone to the lust and cravings and curiosities of the human flesh. What did Adam and Eve see that horrified them and caused them to seek to cover their naked form?

It is extremely difficult for fallen man to understand. When first introduced, the two were exceptionally attracted to each other. There was an excitement, and a joy about the other's presence. They had a clothing of righteousness, now stripped from them. As attractive as they are to each other after their sin, it does not compare to the attractiveness they had before their sin. The woman knew that she could never be as beautiful in the man's eyes as she had been previously. The man knew that he would never be as admired and respected as previously. Yes, they saw, but they despised what they saw.

> The Christian knows, but needs regular reminding, that sin promises great enlightenment but produces only horror. One look at the Incarnate Christ's death is all that we need for proof (Isaiah 53:5).

Clothing of righteousness lost

The evil presence inhabiting the serpent has achieved his objective. Eve eats of the fruit of the forbidden tree, and Adam follows suit. The tree of the knowledge of good and evil, which was to make them as gods (Genesis 3:5), changes their lives dramatically. 'And the eyes of them both were opened, and they knew that they were naked...' (3:7). This raises an interesting question? Had they always been naked, and are only noticing it after eating of the forbidden fruit?

It has been stated by many that humans are the only species which are born naked on the earth. All other creatures are born with their clothes on. This statement has an interesting touch of reality. No one looks at animals, and thinks of them as naked. There is no shame in their being without clothing. In fact, the opposite is true. It is shameful, and somewhat laughable when humans try to manufacture clothes for animals. Why? The answer is in the shame? Nakedness, in them is not exposed.

Did Adam and Eve have clothing before they ate of the forbidden fruit? The answer has to be, 'yes'. The exact nature of the clothing is not as fallen beings would understand, but is in the sense of a clothing of righteousness, a clothing pure and undefiled. Clothing of purity is typified in the instructions which God gives to Moses when he initiates the priesthood for the nation of Israel. 'And thou shalt make holy garments for Aaron thy brother for glory and for beauty. And thou shalt speak unto all that are wise hearted, whom I have filled with the spirit of wisdom, that they make Aaron's garments to consecrate him, that he may minister unto me in the priest's office' (Exodus 28:2-3). Adam and Eve lost their clothing because they were no longer able to wear it, their purity and innocence were gone. They had not simply for the first time noticed their nakedness. They were, for the first time, naked. The holiness, naturalness, purity, and shamelessness with which they were created were gone. They looked upon each other and for the first time did not like what they saw, and desired to cover it.

God said, '...in the day that thou eatest thereof thou shalt surely die' (Genesis 2:17). One of the most important aspects of death is separation. Adam and Eve were separated from that which clothed them, their innocence and holiness.

The understanding of the loss of the innocence of Adam and Eve, and their clothing of righteousness, makes the words of the Apostle Paul more meaningful. 'But put ye

on the Lord Jesus Christ...' (Romans 13:14). We can reclaim clothing of righteousness only as we are clothed in
his righteousness.

Voice of the Lord

There is a phrase in this text that occurs often in the first five books
of the Bible. The man and his wife 'heard the voice of the Lord
God...' (3:8). The Hebrew word, voice, is often understood as the
'sound' of the Lord. There is plenty of room for the imagination
to wander when one considers the nature of the '...sound of the
Lord....'

It is particularly awesome in the light of the changed relationship. Adam and Eve are stripped of their clothing of righteousness.
They are naked, and God is coming. What is the sound? Throughout the Bible, the sound of the Lord is usually his voice. He created by speaking the elements of the earth into existence. Note the
phrase 'and God said...' in the first chapter of Genesis (vs. 3, 6, 9,
11, 14, 20, 24, 26, 28, and 29). In Deuteronomy 5:25, the same
Hebrew word is used. 'Now therefore why should we die? for this
great fire will consume us: if we hear the voice of the Lord our God
any more, then we shall die.' See also Exodus 20:18-19. 'And all
the people saw the thunderings, and the lightnings, and the noise
of the trumpet, and the mountain smoking: and when the people
saw it, they removed, and stood afar off. And they said unto Moses, Speak thou with us, and we will hear: but let not God speak
unto us, lest we die.'

As one pieces together the biblical accounts of the 'sound of
the Lord,' the theme that emerges is one of commandment and
obedience. The importance is on the hearing. One must hear the
Lord if one is to obey. The flip side to obedience is disobedience,
and the sound of the Lord is manifest in judgement. Revelation
portrays the God, who spoke all things into existence, exercising
his speaking power in a different way. 'After this I looked, and, behold, a door was opened...and the first voice which I heard was...

of a trumpet talking with me; which said, Come up hither...' (Revelation 4:1). This is a command given to John just prior to the demonstration of God's judgement.

Adam and Eve heard that voice of judgement. The sound of the Lord which before had given gifts, (Garden of Eden, the woman to the man, the earth to subdue), now sounds as a trumpet, as the thunder. Not only had their eyes been opened to see what they did not want to see, their ears now hear what they did not want to hear. One should hear the voice of the Lord in his command, and obey, and thus he will be spared the voice of the Lord in judgement.

> The understanding of the loss of the innocence of Adam and Eve, and their clothing of righteousness, makes the words of the Apostle Paul more meaningful. 'But put ye on the Lord Jesus Christ...' (Romans 13:14). We can reclaim clothing of righteousness only as we are clothed in his righteousness.

Hiding from God

From the reading of the creation narrative (Genesis 1-2), one has a glimpse of a Creator God who has benevolently acted to provide humans a wonderful place to live, and a great chance to grow in fellowship and knowledge of the Creator. When the Creator approaches them, there should be the gleeful excitement of a little child who is thrilled when he sees his daddy or mommy approaching at the end of the day. Instead, we read this sad refrain, '...and Adam and his wife hid themselves from the presence of the Lord God...' (3:8). It is helpful to consider this hiding from a level of meditative depth.

What caused them to hide? It is easy to say simply 'they sinned, and were feeling guilty.' That is true. However, the focus of the hiding is not the commission of the sin. It is not that they had committed a foul deed, it is the view they now have of themselves. They did not want God to see what they looked like. '...they knew they were naked; and they sewed fig leaves together, and made themselves aprons' (3:7). They despised themselves.

At this moment, Adam and his wife would have given anything to gain back what they had lost. She had lost the sense of being beautiful and adored by her husband. Adam had lost the respect and admiration of his wife. Their shame created the need for hiding. The only one who could give them back what they had lost was approaching, but he had said, '...thou shalt surely die' (Genesis 2:17). In the light of the horror they have just experienced, death would have been a better alternative than facing God.

It is shame, and its consequences, which provide the most notable marks of sin. The problem of self-esteem in the human condition is explained in this passage of Scripture as nowhere else. The despising of self came naturally to the man and woman after sin. They were horrified at what they had become. Every action of life will be dictated by the mental approach to overcoming shame. They first turned to wrapping themselves in fig leaves. A little meditation reveals to us the devastating results of shame. The frantic search for approval causes us to hide from God, become angry at others who do not appreciate us as we desire, flaunt whatever strength we may have as individuals, yet, it is never quite enough. It is the God from whom we have chosen to hide that has the answer. Of course, we do not want him to see us.

> Human shame is compounded in a look at the cross. '...the Lord hath laid on him the iniquity of us all' (Isaiah 53:6). A look at the cross reveals us as naked. As was the case with Adam and Eve, there is great shame in looking at the only one who can redeem us.

Naked

The man and the woman had viewed each other with awe and wonder. They were created as a perfect combination to complement each other in their responsibilities of earth, and to increase the enjoyment of the other in their mutual experience of Eden. They, in a word, were a delight to each other. Then came the sin. They ate of the forbidden fruit (3:6).

The result of eating was immediate shame. They looked upon themselves, and, for the first time, did not like what they saw. Stripped of the clothing of righteousness, their eyes looked at naked bodies with horror. Immediately, they sought to cover those bodies with fig leaves (3:7). They hear the voice of God, and they did not want God to see them without their clothing of righteousness, so they hid.

God discovers them, and Adam's reason for hiding is explained. '...I heard thy voice in the garden, and I was afraid, because I was naked; and I hid myself' (Genesis 3:10). It is important to note Adam's focus on his condition. 'I was naked.' He did not say, 'I ate of the forbidden fruit.' As is always the case with sin, the focus is on self, and the consequences of the sin. It is not on repentance and sorrow for the sin.

The question of God is revealing: '...who told thee that thou wast naked....' (Genesis 3:11)? The thrust of the question is simple. There were only two people present, the man and the woman. The only way that Adam could have known he was naked was to be told by the woman, or to have seen it himself. The reader has a strange revelation about the clothing of righteousness. The clothing is in one's view. This takes us back to the words of the snake '... your eyes shall be opened...' (3:5). If the woman saw nakedness in the man, she was now looking through eyes of evil. She had eaten of the fruit. Eyes opened to evil can no longer see righteousness. The clothing of righteousness is gone because they no longer had eyes to see. The snake had not said that the same act that opens your eyes to one thing closes them to another.

In effect, when God questions the man, the question is, 'which one of you saw the nakedness?' It is even a deeper question, 'why are you naked?' God's question is designed to force the man to look beyond the consequences of the act, to admit the act itself. '...Hast thou eaten of the tree...' (3:11)? It is the act which created the nakedness upon which Adam must focus, not the nakedness, itself.

'...the woman...'

God has pointed out the action of Adam that produced his nakedness. '...Hast thou eaten of the tree, whereof I commanded thee that thou shouldest not eat' (Genesis 3:11)? Shame, the first result of sin, reveals its ugly head in Adam's response. '...The woman whom thou gavest to be with me, she gave me of the tree, and I did eat' (3:12).

These are words to ponder from many directions. Adam looked upon his own nakedness and despised himself. In personal disgust he seeks to cover his form with fig leaves. He has lost his sense of manhood in two ways. First, he accepted the woman's offer of the fruit of the tree, noting his desire for that which came from the woman above that which came from God. In this he had abdicated his headship. He had known fully that the fruit the woman provided would have dissatisfying results, thus he had not been deceived as had the woman (1 Timothy 2:14). He had allowed his will to be conquered by the woman.

Second, the woman had been deceived by a snake, one of the beasts of the field, which he was to subdue. The humiliation and shame was fierce in his mind. As he thinks about it his shame explodes in anger. He will bring everything around him down to his level. In anger, he says, 'The woman...' (3:12). Perhaps he is foolishly trying to show his manhood with a juvenile display of anger after the damage is done. Adam cannot recover his manhood like this.

As Adam spoke, the words must have been a piercing arrow to the woman's heart. She is stung with the anger in Adam's voice. She has lost his love, and the resounding joy he had previously demonstrated in her presence is now resentfulness at her presence. For her, there is the deep sense of the loss of the man's love. Her response at this point is amazing. One would think that she would say to Adam 'you should have spoken up to the serpent, you should have stopped me.' Instead, she says, '...The serpent beguiled me, and I did eat' (3:13). The woman's shame is self-condemning; and self-excusing in the same moment. It is to say, 'I did it, but I wouldn't have done it if the serpent had not been there.' Her shame leads her to try to recapture the man's love, by accepting blame, and shifting responsibility. Thus, this exchange with God establishes the foundation of that which shall be the long-term dilemma of male-female relationships. The man shall be forever fighting to recapture his manhood and restore the admiration he lost. The woman shall be forever trying to recapture the man's wonder and joy at her presence.

> The male and female now have the knowledge of good and evil. Part of that knowledge is the consequences of evil. They had not considered the consequences as part of knowledge.

When God speaks

The sin has been exposed. Adam and Eve have eaten of the forbidden fruit. The consequence is total shame as they are exposed as naked, and lose respect for themselves and for each other. This is symbolized through haste in covering their nakedness with fig leaves. The concern most important to the man and woman is the consequences on their lives in terms of personal shame. God establishes the real problem by means of a question. '...Hast thou eaten of the tree, whereof I commanded thee that thou shouldest not eat' (3:11)? The man and woman must accept their shame, not try to cover it. They must accept that the problem is not their shame, it was the decision to disobey God's command.

At this point, the reader is remembering the words of God, '...in the day that thou eatest thereof thou shalt surely die' (Genesis 2:17). When will death be administered? As one thinks about the situation of Adam and Eve, it is clear that death has already occurred. The wonder and amazement they had one toward another, gone! The understanding of God as the benevolent Creator of whom they had no fear, gone! Eyes with which to see and appreciate the wonder and glory of righteousness, gone! A relationship between the two without rancour, division, and misunderstanding, gone! The ability to control their destiny, gone! The reader has never experienced the Garden of Eden and may not understand the dramatic turn of events for the first man and woman. They had experienced the holiness of their prior life, and the only way to adequately characterize the dramatic difference is in noting the difference in life and death.

The man and the woman will not experience the immediate death of the body, but they have lost the innocence and the righteousness of their lives. There is nothing they can do about that, and their bodies will ultimately return to the earth. That is the destination unwittingly chosen by eating the forbidden fruit. Without question, they have died. The one thing that can make for real life (righteousness) is now gone.

Is there any hope? Immediately, God begins to speak (3:14). The man and the woman will pay close attention. Their Creator must have an answer, or they are doomed. It is a comforting thought that God has an answer. He always does. The question is, 'Will the one needing an answer from God arrive at the place where he will hear when God speaks?'

God's voice is both a horror and a comfort at this point. More than ever, Adam and Eve, in a now sinful state must hear the voice of God. The Christian is reminded of the words of Christ, 'These things have I spoken unto you... that your joy might be full (John 14:11). It is hard to keep our attention focused on his words when our sin is in view, but it is more critical than ever.

Genesis 3:15-19

15. And I will put enmity between thee and the woman, and between thy seed and her seed; it shall bruise thy head, and thou shalt bruise his heel. 16. Unto the woman he said, I will greatly multiply thy sorrow and thy conception; in sorrow thou shalt bring forth children; and thy desire shall be to thy husband, and he shall rule over thee. 17. And unto Adam he said, Because thou hast hearkened unto the voice of thy wife, and hast eaten of the tree, of which I commanded thee, saying, Thou shalt not eat of it: cursed is the ground for thy sake; in sorrow shalt thou eat of it all the days of thy life; 18. Thorns also and thistles shall it bring forth to thee; and thou shalt eat the herb of the field; 19. In the sweat of thy face shalt thou eat bread, till thou return unto the ground; for out of it wast thou taken: for dust thou art, and unto dust shalt thou return.

'...dust shalt thou eat...'

The man and woman have rebelled against God. They had been involved in a relationship of growth and understanding of God. There had been no fear. The sound of God's voice was welcome. This time it is different. Adam says, '...I heard thy voice...and I was afraid...' (3:10). Joy, without fear, at the presence of God is forever lost. Adam and Eve must have been trembling mightily as God speaks. 'And the Lord God said unto the serpent..' (3:14). It was the serpent who had been used by an evil presence to deceive the woman. For allowing that use of his body, the serpent is judged. '...thou art cursed...' (3:14). The serpent is forever condemned to be a beast without legs, transporting itself in the dust, and upon its belly. The appearance of the serpent is not described before this moment.

It is noteworthy that part of the serpent's punishment was the eating of dust all the days of his life. One will also note that the man is told '...dust thou art, and unto dust shalt thou return' (3:19).

A very clear parallel is established with dust and death. Dust is part of the punishment of death. Death is the result of rebellion against God. Rebellion against God is to choose the things of earth as more precious than God. There is a famous quote that says, 'You become what you think about.' The love of the earth was so important to the serpent and the humans, God rewarded them by returning them to its essence (dust).

As Adam and Eve viewed the transformation of the snake from the subtle and captivating creature of Genesis 3:1 into the repulsive animal crawling on its belly, the horror of their sin must have been driven home dramatically. If that is what God pronounced on the serpent, how much more horrible will be the judgement on them?

The reader can now meditate on the mystery of his own guilt in rebellion against God. Why do we humans rush into acts that seem attractive, only to find them unfulfilling, and the aftermath so disgusting. The adulterer, the drunkard, the liar, the thief, can reap the rewards of passion, sense the excitement of valuing the flesh above God but will always wake up to the reality of a changed appearance. The serpent becomes the snake crawling on the ground. How repulsive! Humans with great potential are reduced to living only in dirtiness. Adam and Eve saw the transformation of the serpent. What kind of transformation had they seen in themselves that caused them to rush to cover their nakedness?

> Sin's ultimate result is the return to the dust. It is not just fable that sin makes one feel dirty. One is dirty. The great penitential prayer of David makes sense. 'Wash me...from mine iniquity...cleanse me from my sin' (Psalm 51:2).

Judgment on the Serpent

Genesis 3:15 provides one of Scriptures' most profound theological statements. To fully grasp its meaning, one should consider the following things. First, the serpent (a beast of the field who should be in subservience to humans) had tried to position himself as being superior to humans. He had questioned God, and instructed the woman (Genesis 3:1-3). Second, the presence inhabiting the serpent had tried to supplant God in the trust of the woman. It was his attempt to usurp and take over the creation of God by gaining control of the humans who were commanded to subdue the earth. Third, the serpent, and the presence that occupies it, face God with the sense of having won the first battle to seize control of God's creation. God speaks to all three issues in the curse.

The snake, which had lifted itself into a position of superiority to humans, is now doomed to crawl at humans' feet. The literal act of crawling on the belly is a symbolic statement that the snake will be seen as without majesty or dignity. Thus, the snake is clearly below humans, and more repulsive than the other parts of creation. The serpent will only be able to attack the human at his heels, whereas the human can apply the immediate and fatal blow of crushing the serpent's head.

Within the statement to the snake comes the condemnation of the presence occupying it (the seed). God's word to that presence could be paraphrased. 'You have tried to take over the creation of God by deceit of the woman. You have positioned yourself as superior and think you have brought down the human race. The reality is that the human race through the seed of the one you deceived will overcome you.' It is the height of humiliation for the 'presence' to know he shall be defeated by the woman's seed, not the man's. It was the woman, after all, he deceived.

The battle with God has just begun. It will play out over many years, and the presence that occupies the serpent will win other battles. The snake, crawling on its belly, will be a constant statement to the 'presence' behind the serpent of his impending defeat. He will win battles, but he will lose the war.

The Bible reveals the presence as Satan, or the devil, and speaks of his great anger, referring to him as a '...roaring lion... seeking whom he may devour' (1 Peter 5:8). Do you think his anger is fuelled when he observes the snake and ponders his own future?

Seed of the woman

The 'seed' of the serpent will be revealed in later biblical development as synonymous with the presence occupying it. As God pronounces his curse upon the serpent, he notes that the seed of the woman will bruise (crush) the serpent's head. To crush the head of a snake is to provide destruction. In the battle with one of the earth's creatures, the human race must engage the battle. The 'presence' that occupies the snake will not be so easy to crush. Additionally, the human personalities of Adam and Eve are now under the influence of that presence and are helpless against him.

God had established that the progeny of Adam and Eve would populate and subdue the earth. They will only be able to procreate creatures exactly as they are. They are now creatures in rebellion against God. Even if they could be spared punishment for their deed, their children will continue the rebellion. The issue of redeeming Adam and Eve becomes much more complicated. It is not just redeeming them, it is having a way to redeem them and their progeny.

In a microscopic way, God reveals his plan. It will be through the seed of the woman. Such a marvel will require a brand new kind of activity by the great Creator. Adam's seed is the way that all humanity will come to be born. Every human being will be just as Adam, in need of redemption. In some marvellous way, there must be born to the woman a child that is not of Adam's seed. In that child, a redemptive plan will be put in place that shall crush the head of the presence occupying the serpent. When that is accomplished, the woman's 'seed' must be able to act in the same capacity as Adam. That is, the woman's seed must have the ability to effect the whole human race. When Adam sinned, he cast the direction for humanity. When the woman's seed acts, there must be the same kind of ability. Otherwise, redemption is impossible.

It is by virtue of sitting where we sit in the realm of human history that we see this 'theology in microscope' fully revealed through the virgin birth of Jesus Christ, and the phenomenal redemptive plan of God enacted by Christ's atoning death. Looking beyond the horror of sin, and its great cost, one can almost see a sense of humour in God. The woman deceived by the serpent (devil) is also the vehicle that brings the redeemer into the world. It is a grand display of righteous 'in your face' redemption.

The whole of the book of Genesis, indeed the rest of the Bible, is the story of God's unfolding miracle of the seed of the woman solving the sin problem. When the Incarnate Christ is born, it is no wonder that it was announced by angels who sung 'Glory to God...and on earth, peace...toward men' (Luke 2:14). A little praise in our prayer is the only proper response.

Judgment on the woman

The curse that God pronounces on the woman is extremely profound and requires meditation and understanding. In many ways, it reverses the woman's position in the Garden of Eden, but is also a marvellous act of grace. In the Garden of Eden, the woman would bring forth children in the context of blessing and perfect harmony with her husband. God's great gift to Adam, aside from life, was Eve. The great blessing and thrill to his life shall now be viewed as a problem and a responsibility.

Pain and suffering shall be a part of the process of childbirth. In addition to the struggle that shall be the woman's at the moment of giving birth, children shall be both a blessing and a curse. They shall provide life's greatest joy, but also be the source for some of life's greatest heartache. Yet, it is through childbirth (the unique act of woman) that redemption shall come to the human race. The Apostle Paul writes, 'And Adam was not deceived, but the woman being deceived was in the transgression. Notwithstanding she shall be saved in childbearing...' (1 Timothy 2:14-15).

Why is there pain and suffering in childbearing? In a strange way, this is God's grace. It is a constant reminder of the consequences of sin. The Apostle Paul also comments on this. 'For we know that the whole creation groaneth and travaileth in pain (as in childbirth) together until now...waiting for the adoption, to wit, the redemption of our body (Romans 8:22-23). The woman's greatest blessing is now accompanied with the burden of pain.

The greater theological issue is wrapped in the 'seed of the woman.' As it is in her childbearing that redemption shall come, her pain and suffering symbolizes the pain and suffering that shall be the birthright of her 'seed'. The prophet Isaiah gives us a look at this theological truth. 'But he (the seed of the woman) was wounded for our transgressions, he was bruised for our iniquities: the chastisement of our peace was upon him; and with his stripes we are healed' (Isaiah 53:5).

The curse that is pronounced on the woman carries a strange irony. The suffering that is presupposed is ominous. The sound of God's judgement is frightening and creates the sense of trembling in one's bones. However, there is hope. God is establishing in his judgement that the sin of the man and the woman is not the final word. He will redeem. The only way back into relationship with God must be through the work of God. In the announcement of the curse, God is proclaiming, 'I have a plan.' Despite the ominous sound of judgement there is also a sigh of relief.

> The judgement on sin was harsh, but it was not the final word. The final word came when the seed of the woman uttered '...It is finished...' (John 19:30).

Plight of the woman

The woman (Eve) has seen her position of love and adoration in the eyes of the man (Adam) reduced to a position of burden and responsibility. He had accused her of eating of the forbidden fruit and providing it to him. The clear inference is that the woman used his love for her to tempt him. He had failed to exercise his role as the one to rule over the animals, and to subdue the earth. He had failed to insure the maintenance of purity by allowing the serpent to seduce the woman. His failure to exercise responsibility in that instance changes his view of the woman.

The position of Eve is now accurately described as a desire for restoration as being of great joy and blessing to Adam. In the light of this situation, God's words explain the nature of woman in the human race: '...in sorrow thou shalt bring forth children; and thy desire shall be to thy husband, and he shall rule over thee' (3:16). What is this desire the woman shall have to the husband? Simply, it is to replace that which she lost in the eating of the forbidden fruit. Her husband does not manifest the same love and adoration as before. The great longing of her heart is to be the source of his happiness. Her focus is on the relationship the two of them have. She will be forever in need of assurances of his love, that she has regained the favour in his eyes in which she had taken such delight. The thought that she is a burden and a responsibility to him stings her to the core of her being.

God also notes, '...he shall rule over thee' (3:16). The rulership of the husband is easy to understand in light of the curse. It is not so much a legalistic command as it is a description of the woman's plight. She shall always be striving for her husband's favour. She wants to be the great joy of his existence. This, in itself, places her in a somewhat precarious position. Her husband will always be somewhat distracted from the relationship (he, too, is cursed). In that frustration, her intense desire to please and win his love, in a way that forces him to acknowledge that love, creates the reality, 'he shall rule over thee.'

Consider the full theological dynamic. The focus of the woman is to win back what she lost in the relationship to the man. However, her fallen state causes her to lose focus on the greater loss, her relationship to God. She seeks to win that which she cannot have until there is redemption in relationship to God. The curse on the woman is there to motivate her to turn away from the earth's satisfaction and turn to God. After the fall, it is only in God's eyes that one can be fully adored.

In the woman's plight the words of Christ have an even greater dimension. 'For God so loved...that he gave his son.' (John 3:16). Here is the only place where love is fully satisfied and restored.

Judgment on the man

God's attention turns to the man following the announcement of the curse upon the woman. Certainly, Adam must be shaking with fear. He had seen the serpent reduced to crawling on his belly (3:14), and had heard the ominous statement of peril on the woman in her travail of childbirth (3:16). His own fate can be no better. It was not.

The earth was the gift of God to man. Man had been commissioned to subdue the earth. In the Garden of Eden, he was to eat freely of the fruit of the trees of the garden with the tree of the knowledge of good and evil as the only exception. He had been provided a woman who brought him great delight. He had enjoyed the fellowship of his God, and possessed opportunity for a vast experience of learning as God taught him about the wonders and mysteries of the earth and of relationship to its Creator. Adam chose to enjoy the fruit of the forbidden tree instead of the continued relationship to God. The judgement now placed on him reflects that choice.

The ground is cursed. He will struggle to gain authority over it, '...cursed is the ground for thy sake; in sorrow shalt thou eat of it all the days of thy life; Thorns also and thistles shall it bring forth to thee; and thou shalt eat the herb of the field' (3:17-18). The key is found in one simple utterance. God had given the man the command to subdue the earth (Genesis 1:28). In creation, a clear rule of order had been established for existence on the earth with the human in supremacy. His supremacy in the created order of earth has not changed, but his authority has changed. The thorns and thistles are the pronouncement of God that even the earth will struggle with the human, and will not accept his dominion. He will wrestle with the earth all the days of his life, only to discover the continued rebellion of the earth against him.

Symbolically, the man will learn, by virtue of his relationship with the ground, the nature of humankind in his rebellion to God. The curse will continue to manifest itself in spite of every victory the human gains. God will show his control of humans and manifest his glory on many occasions, yet most humans will never submit to God. The Earth, created for blessing to man, will continue to provide food, but only as the human struggles to subdue. Strangely, that which man was commanded, but refused, is now forced on him by judgement. The rewards, which would have been his in perpetual blessing, are now gained only in frustration and hardship.

> The first humans established themselves in rebellion seeking to be as gods, in control of their own existence. The result is that now they must learn their total lack of control as even the land they were to subdue is in rebellion against them.

Plight of the man

As one contemplates the curse upon the man, there are many ramifications that can be noticed. In the Garden of Eden, the man had control. He was the undisputed ruler of his surroundings. The woman, whom he adored, looked on him with admiration and respect. He had lost it all when the serpent (used by the devil) had been allowed to deceive the woman, and lead her to eat of the forbidden fruit. The man followed the woman's lead, and ate, though he was not deceived (1 Timothy 2:13-14). The admiration of the woman is gone, and he will be facing an earth that will constantly create thorns and thistles.

What can the man expect in the forthcoming conditions of his life? As the woman wanted to restore what she had lost in the Garden of Eden (the love and adoration of the man), so shall the man desire to restore that which he lost (respect and control). The man shall survey his world and say, 'Everything is against me.' His struggle is to regain respect and authority, and that is extremely difficult for even the ground is in rebellion against him. 'Thorns also and thistles shall it bring forth to thee...' (3:18).

Consider what this means in man's relationship to the woman. She is focused on gaining his love, and being the supreme joy of his life. He is focused on conquering those thorns and thistles so that he can return the Garden of Eden to her and recapture her respect and admiration. To the woman, the man is always somewhat distracted. She wants him to turn from those thorns and thistles and appreciate her value. He cannot, because the whole source of his manhood is at stake. He cannot understand why she doesn't see the necessity of conquering those elements of the earth that are so stacked against him. Tragically, her reaching out to him is often seen as a lack of respect, and a symbol of his failure. She is trying to give love, but it is manifest to him as sympathy and pity, which he despises.

Consider what it means in man's relationship to God. He is focused exclusively on restoring the Garden of Eden. He forgets that God created the garden and he, alone, can restore it. What should the man do? The sweat of man's face is there to remind him of his struggle, and of the lack of authority he has. His authority can never be regained except through the act of God. As the woman must turn to God to find the love and adoration she needs, the man must turn to God to recapture a sense of strength and control. Strangely, he must submit in order to be in control.

The only source of satisfaction for the man is in submission to God. It is stated by another scriptural author, 'I am crucified with Christ...and the life which I now live...I live by the faith of the Son of God, who loved me, and gave himself for me' (Galatians 2:20).

Genesis 3:20-24

20. And Adam called his wife's name Eve; because she was the mother of all living. 21. Unto Adam also and to his wife did the Lord God make coats of skins, and clothed them. 22. And the Lord God said, Behold, the man is become as one of us, to know good and evil: and now, lest he put forth his hand, and take also of the tree of life, and eat, and live for ever: 23. Therefore the Lord God sent him forth from the garden of Eden, to till the ground from whence he was taken. 24. So he drove out the man; and he placed at the east of the garden of Eden Cherubims, and a flaming sword which turned every way, to keep the way of the tree of life.

Return to dust

It is a strange and hard study to discern the words that God gives to Adam. Clearly, there is the sense of a curse. Life will be filled with struggle and frustration. He will seek to subdue the earth, but will never quite reach his goal. The ultimate winner is the earth itself. 'In the sweat of thy face shalt thou eat bread, till thou return unto the ground; for out of it wast thou taken: for dust thou art, and unto dust shalt thou return' (3:19). It is the ultimate frustration for the man. He shall die and become that which he sought to conquer.

People often speak of the emptiness in their lives. They become bitter about the fruitless search for something that truly lasts and has meaning. The great king of Israel, Solomon, noted this emptiness and vividly described it. 'I have seen all the works that are done under the sun; and, behold, all is vanity and vexation of spirit. That which is crooked cannot be made straight: and that which is wanting cannot be numbered' (Ecclesiastes 1:14-15). For every man who pauses to look, there is the awesome reality that everything returns to the dust.

The sin of eating the forbidden fruit has produced an incredible knowledge of evil that the man and woman would now prefer to give up. It is a knowledge that produces severe melancholy, despair, and anger. Emptiness is a good word to describe it.

Once one begins meditation on this reality, there is the desperate cry for hope. Can it be found in God's words to Adam? Note these words: '...cursed is the ground for thy sake...' (3:17). With all the frustration and emptiness that will be part of human existence, how can the phrase 'for thy sake' make sense?

Consider the alternative. If humans have lost their relationship with God, the greatest need of their life is to restore that relationship. However, their focus will be on trying to restore the Garden of Eden, and all of its amenities. What if the curse on the ground was not in place and humans could succeed? This would lead humans to totally ignore any need for God. The emptiness that man has in his soul is directly connected to the loss of relationship to his Creator. Only in learning of the foolishness of trying to restore Eden will he be able to accept the submission to his God that can fill that emptiness. The curse is there to drive humans to the only one capable of solving the problem their sin created.

A statement of faith

The mortality of all humans is firmly established, '...for dust thou art, and unto dust shalt thou return' (3:19). The curse under which humans will now labour leaves a powerful sense of inestimable burden. The man and woman must adjust to a brand new perspective, knowing that their bodies are now destined for death. The reader of this event is filled with anxiety, and labours under the sense of absolute gloom. There is a fatigue from the announced judgement, and a wish for a ray of sunshine in this clouded picture. From a literary standpoint, one longs for a happy ending. One might even wonder how the principals (Adam and his wife) are going to cope. They know they will die. They don't know when. How will they respond?

The ray of sunshine flashes. Hear Adam's voice. 'And Adam called his wife's name Eve; because she was the mother of all living' (3:20). This is the second time that Adam names his wife. Earlier, he had called her 'woman' reflecting his delight in the glorious creature that God had provided who was perfectly suited for him (Genesis 2:23). The name, Eve, is given in a sense of hope, and acknowledgement of God's plan. It is a much subdued naming because it is a statement of faith more than an exultation at a new reality. Adam had heard the words of God to the serpent. 'And I will put enmity between thee and the woman, and between thy seed and her seed; it shall bruise thy head, and thou shalt bruise his heel' (3:15). Adam's name for his wife reflects his confidence that the continuance of life for the human race will come through the seed of the woman. The words are a grand statement by Adam. In effect, he says, 'I will live by faith in the promise of God.'

Herein lies the basic ingredient that shall be the foundation of human responsibility in redemption. The prophet states it clearly, '...the just shall live by his faith' (Habakkuk 2:4). If the man and the woman will accept God's judgement, establish faith in God, and look to their relationship to him for the meaning of their life, as opposed to re-creating Eden to find meaning, there is hope through the woman's seed to restore Eden. It must be through faith in God, not through one's own effort. The curse will continue to manifest itself and produce emptiness for all seeking their own way. Faith in God offers the only ray of hope.

'By faith!' It is a most difficult way, yet, it is all that we have. The Garden of Eden was lost due to sin. God's plan is to restore all who come to him in faith through Christ. It is only through God's work that this can occur, and we must wait upon him to finish calling all his children to repentance.

A new clothing

The first visible change in the lives of Adam and Eve after their sin was the fact of their nakedness (3:7). This had caused them to hide from God, as well as to cover their nakedness from each other. With the judgement of God announced (3:15-19), their nakedness must be addressed. There are other problems. Instead of the unique relationship with God, when they easily heard and understood his Word, they are now in a position where they must exercise faith in his Word without full benefit of all his secrets. They no longer had minds to clearly understand God. Because their hearts and minds were now conditioned to evil, they will be fighting the condition of this earth for survival. This will be a perpetual battle that will help to keep them from mischief. It will keep their minds involved so that they will not as readily run to evil. Also, they must work at keeping faith in the Word of God, and live by that confidence. It is the only kind of relationship with God that is now available to them. The issue is, 'how do they do it?'

God acts to teach the man and woman how to relate to their new condition and to him. 'Unto Adam also and to his wife did the Lord God make coats of skins, and clothed them' (3:21). By this act, God was providing a covering for their nakedness. It was an important act for theological reasons. Adam and Eve witnessed the slaughter of animals. The slaughter provided for their clothing. The slaughter of animals had not been necessary in the Garden of Eden. The clothing of righteousness which they lost in their sin will be replaced only by the shedding of blood (Hebrews 9:22). The clothing from slain animals covers their physical nakedness symbolizing the greater spiritual truth. Additionally, from this moment on, the ritual offering of animals for sacrifice will be part of the humans' worship form that demonstrates faith in God.

This was a dramatic moment for Adam and Eve. One can sense the terror they felt as they watched what God did. They must now do the same thing. Certainly, this was a repulsive act to their sensibilities, but it reflects the vivid horror of the consequences of sin.

The nakedness of the man and woman is covered, but at an ugly price. The lesson here is subtle and difficult. The humans can have a relationship with God, but it will require a discipline on their part. The natural desire of their life will be to steer away from a relationship with God. It will be costly, but there can be no other route to redemption.

Adam and Eve learn that one of the disciplines of faith is obedience. God established the slaying of animals as necessary for providing human need. It is repulsive, but humans must learn that their redemption will be based in the most repulsive act of all, the slaying of God's Son.

A new relationship with the creation

In the slaughter of animals for clothing, God establishes a pattern of worship for humans. To properly cover their nakedness, blood must be shed. In this act, God was instructing the man and woman that the image of 'shedding blood' must be understood in order to know God's plan to redeem them from their sin. It would be instituted in their pattern of worship. It is not hard to understand this act of God in the light of the overwhelming teaching of Scripture. Jesus was referred to as '...the Lamb of God which taketh away the sin of the world' (John 1:29).

Meditation on the passage exposes other applications of God's slaughter of animals. The sovereignty of humans over animals is once again declared. This is a clear statement to the humans that they shall not give to the animal kingdom a position of equality. Eve's acceptance of the serpent as her equal led to her deception. When God clothed humans with the skins of animals, he was showing how the animals are to be used to benefit humans. The sacrifice of animal life in the framework of the preservation of human life will be a necessity. Once animals are treated with equality, neither human nor animal life is improved. It would, in fact, be the foundation for great deception. Animals will become the objects of worship, and not available for food. They can over populate the earth when not controlled and make certain parts of the earth un-inhabitable for man. Because animals are important to the survival of man, there is the responsibility of preservation of animal life within the framework of human sovereignty. When the animals are given equality to men, the result is the abandonment of human decision-making and proper responsibility to the animal kingdom.

It was important for God to teach this lesson to Adam and Eve. In their now fallen state, they may question their right to sover-eignty over the animals. They will find frustration in their attempt to subdue the earth because of its thorns and thistles. Likewise the animals, which had been on friendly terms with humans in the Garden (note the ease with which Eve listened to the serpent), will now be at enmity with the humans. They must wage the same battle with the animal world that they will be waging with the veg-etable world. Man will not get any respect at all. God's established order of creation remains, in spite of the human sin and its judge-ment. It is however, going to be a battle to maintain.

Out of the garden

The nakedness of the two humans has been solved by the act of God. He has provided clothes that he made from the skins of ani-mals. The act was a demonstration of the cost of sin, and demon-stration to the man and woman of the struggles facing them. The elements of nature are unleashed against them by virtue of thorns and thistles (3:18), and by the requirement to overcome the animal kingdom. The awful and gory sight of animal slaughter as taught to Adam and Eve will be a part of worship to God. They will need to sacrifice animals in order to maintain any relationship to God. The blood-shed was required to provide a covering for their nakedness. The same kind of symbolism is revealed in the New Testament as providing a covering for sin. '...Blessed are they whose sins are forgiven, and whose sins are covered' (Romans 4:7).

Following the clothing of Adam and Eve, there is another event of consequence. The Garden of Eden is closed to the man and woman. Their task of subduing the earth is greatly multiplied. That which had been relatively simple and confined becomes overwhelming as they must do battle with the earth's elements, and search for the best place to make their habitat. If their way to the garden had not been blocked, they would fail to do the work that was now necessary. Their nature, and the desire to restore their previous position in the garden, would have led them to stay there.

There are two things that need considering. First, the Garden of Eden was a place of life, not death. It was not a place designed for death. The man and the woman will die one day. Also, God has already demonstrated that proper living until their death will require the sacrifice of members of the animal kingdom (3:21). The Garden of Eden was not a place where death could be allowed. God said, '...and now, lest he put forth his hand, and take also of the tree of life, and eat, and live forever' (3:22). Clearly, the meaning is that man would live forever in his sinful state if he eats of the tree of life. The application is probably more expansive. As long as man stays in the garden, a place of life, he cannot die.

Second, man must slaughter animals in order to conduct the necessary affairs of his life, including worship. Without this activity, there can be no relationship to God, and the quality of man's life would steadily deteriorate, even though it would not end. Living in the Garden of Eden without the possibility of relationship to God would ultimately be the worst kind of hell.

The slaughter of animals for worship causes modern sensibilities to be very repulsed. This reaction is derived from a lack of appreciation for the awfulness of sin. Redemption ultimately comes from a greater sacrifice. '...we are sanctified through the offering of the body of Jesus Christ once for all' (Hebrews 10:10).

'...as one of us...'

In tossing the man and woman out of the Garden of Eden, God says something that is worth a little meditation. 'And the Lord God said, Behold, the man is become as one of us, to know good and evil...' (3:22). How have the man and woman become as God? Think about these factors. They have a propensity to evil! Their clothing of righteousness is gone, leaving them naked! They are going to die! God's words are awkward when these factors are considered. The image of being 'as God' is a complicated theology and an unflattering one when fully understood.

The prophet Isaiah tells us of the fall of the powerful angel, Lucifer, who became known in the Bible by many other names (Satan, Devil, etc.). It was the same Lucifer who entered the serpent and deceived Eve. The words of Lucifer, at his fall, provide a telling clue to God's statement about the man and woman. '...I will exalt my throne...I will ascend above the heights of the clouds; I will be like the most High (Isaiah 14:13-14). How would he be like God? The focal point of Lucifer's desire was the enthronement of self. He desired independence from God. Being like God is to be an entity that made his own decisions about the character and nature of his being. The only being who has the privilege of that decision is God. Any creature desiring to make the decision for himself is in rebellion against God. He is doing evil. The creature has not become God. He is merely acting as if he is God.

When God says, '...the man is become as one of us,' the meaning is condemnatory. The man is trying to be the one who makes the decision about the character and nature of his being. He is certainly aware of evil. He became evil the minute he sought to be the decision-maker about his own creation. The serpent said, '...ye shall be as gods... (3:5). The apostle Paul offers a variation on this same kind of attitude when he asks, '...O man, who art thou that repliest against God? Shall the thing formed say to him that formed it, Why hast thou made me thus' (Romans 9:20)?

The sadness of the matter rests in the tragedy of the thinking process. Humans, in committing their sin, looked to have a sense of authority. They desired to be as gods. The goal was to make life better. The woman was deceived into thinking life would be better if she had the sovereignty. The man desired sovereignty despite the consequences. The problem is found in the reality that grasping sovereignty of their life meant separation from the one that gave them life. He, alone, understands the purpose of their creation and the way to get them to their fullest glory and the knowledge to know if they succeed or fail.

> The issue of who has the sovereignty in our life must be settled once for all in redemption. There is 'one Lord' (Ephesians 4:5), the apostle Paul declares. It is Christ who is set '...above all principality, and power, and might, and dominion, and everyone that is named...' (Ephesians 1:21).

Cherubims

When the man and the woman are cast out of the Garden of Eden, God placed cherubims and a flaming sword to prevent any re-entry into the garden. The Bible does not tell us how long the Garden of Eden remained in place. It is reasonable to assume that it was destroyed at the time of the flood in Noah's day. The cherubims are one of the various orders of angelic beings (Ezekiel 1:5, 10:15), and are placed here as representative of the impossibility of re-entering the garden. The flaming sword is a statement that any human attempt at regaining the Garden of Eden is rebellion against God.

There is to be a way God shall provide for restoring fellowship with him. It is fellowship with God, not the Garden of Eden, which must be the focus of man's restorative interests. The furniture prepared for the Holy of Holies, the most sacred place in the temple of Israel, reinforces this truth. 'And he made the mercy seat of pure gold...And he made two cherubims of gold...And the cherubims spread out their wings on high, and covered with their wings over the mercy seat, with their faces one to another; even to the mercy seatward were the faces of the cherubims' (Exodus 37:6-9). As cherubims blocked entrance to the Garden of Eden, symbolically, cherubims stand over, and point the way to renewed fellowship with God at his mercy seat.

The mercy seat is the place where the blood of the sacrifice, offered on the Day of Atonement, shall be sprinkled. The way of the Garden of Eden is blocked, but the way of atonement is available by the shedding of blood. When one contrasts the pictures of the Garden of Eden with the bloody, stained mess that would be the condition of the mercy seat, it is little wonder that man would prefer to spend his energy to recapture the Garden of Eden rather than traverse the Holy of Holies.

The extreme difficulty of gaining atonement for sin is captured by the cherubims blocking of the garden, and by the forbidding of any except the high priest to enter the Holy of Holies. He (the high priest) entered, acting as representative of the people, and sprinkled blood upon the mercy seat. With the death of Christ, who was the only one who could truly act on behalf of all, entrance to the Holy of Holies is made available to all. 'But Christ being come an high priest...by his own blood he entered once into the holy place, having obtained eternal redemption for us' (Hebrews 9:11-12). The cherubims block the path to the garden, but also stand over the mercy-seat, where full entry is available to the fellowship of God.

Genesis 4:1-26

I. The Story of Cain and Abel (4:1-16)
1. Birth of two sons
2. Work and worship
3. Worship in pride
4. Worship in humility
5. Possibility for repentance
6. Difficulty of repentance
7. Attitude of the non-repentant
8. The blame game
9. A terrifying witness
10. An acute loss
11. A heritage of dissatisfaction
12. Judgement of Cain
13. '...land of Nod.'

II. The Generations of Cain (4:17-24)
1. '...he builded a city...'
2. Unholy genius
3. Reasoning of Lamech
4. Understanding human vengeance

III. Another Son is Given (4:25-26)
1. Birth of Seth
2. Establishment of hope
3. The attitude of Seth

Genesis 4:1-16

1. And Adam knew Eve his wife; and she conceived, and bare Cain, and said, I have gotten a man from the Lord. 2. And she again bare his brother Abel. And Abel was a keeper of sheep, but Cain was a tiller of the ground. 3. And in process of time it came to pass, that Cain brought of the fruit of the ground an offering unto the Lord. 4. And Abel, he also brought of the firstlings of his flock and of the fat thereof. And the Lord had respect unto Abel and to his offering: 5. But unto Cain and to his offering he had not respect. And Cain was very wroth, and his countenance fell. 6. And the Lord said unto Cain, Why art thou wroth? and why is thy countenance fallen? 7. If thou doest well, shalt thou not be accepted? and if thou doest not well, sin lieth at the door. And unto thee shall be his desire, and thou shalt rule over him.

8. And Cain talked with Abel his brother: and it came to pass, when they were in the field, that Cain rose up against Abel his brother, and slew him. 9. And the Lord said unto Cain, Where is Abel thy brother? And he said, I know not: am I my brother's keeper? 10. And he said, What hast thou done? the voice of thy brother's blood crieth unto me from the ground. 11. And now art thou cursed from the earth, which hath opened her mouth to receive thy brother's blood from thy hand; 12. When thou tillest the ground, it shall not henceforth yield unto thee her strength; a fugitive and a vagabond shalt thou be in the earth.

13. And Cain said unto the Lord, My punishment is greater than I can bear. 14. Behold, thou hast driven me out this day from the face of the earth; and from thy face shall I be hid; and I shall be a fugitive and a vaga-bond in the earth; and it shall come to pass, that every one that findeth me shall slay me. 15. And the Lord said unto him, Therefore whosoever slayeth Cain, vengeance shall be taken on him sevenfold. And the Lord set a mark upon Cain, lest any finding him should kill him. 16. And Cain went out from the presence of the Lord, and dwelt in the land of Nod, on the east of Eden.

Birth of two sons

Humans have sinned. Their bodies are destined to return to the dust of the earth, from which they came (Genesis 3:19). Throughout their lives, they will wrestle with their relationships (Genesis 3:16), and with the elements of the earth (Genesis 3:17-19). Their only hope shall be in the framework of God's promise (Genesis 3:15), and their faith in his provision for them (Genesis 3:20-21). The slaughter of animals was to be an act of worship which proclaimed trust that God would one day clothe them again in righteousness just as he had provided clothing for their physical nakedness. God had placed the whole destiny of the human race within the context of worship. They could never re-enter the garden (Genesis 3:24), but they could live by faith in the promise of God, and worship him.

It is interesting that the very first major story that occurs in the family of Adam centres on the issue of worship. Cain and Abel, the first two sons born to Eve engage in an act of worship that reflects human tendency and the weakness of human wisdom after the fall. Before the worship event, however, is the record of their birth. There are some thoughts that are worth a little meditation.

With the birth of Cain, Eve proclaims '...I have gotten a man from the Lord' (4:1). The NIV and the NASV translate the words of Eve differently, and render a better understanding of her expression. 'With the help of the Lord, I have brought forth a man....' (NIV). 'I have gotten a manchild with the help of the Lord...' (NASV). There is a two-fold meaning. First, there is the hope of redemption promised in Genesis 3:15 through the seed of woman. Eve is expressing hope that her labour and travail has produced that redemption. Second, Eve is expressing a profound ignorance. When she states, '...I have gotten a man...' she means, 'God and I have equally created a man.' This is a dramatic error. It is to claim a partial role in redemption. She failed to understand that her son is Adam's seed, and that the woman's seed will be the exclusive work of God.

By the time that Abel is born, Eve's optimism has diminished. In Hebrew, Abel means 'vanity' or 'mere breath'. Eve has recognized the uselessness of obtaining redemption by her own effort. Everything rests in God. Adam and Eve must be faithful. They must do battle with the earth's elements and worship God. To change that perspective will be a waste of time.

Two mistakes are made by humans in their working lives. One is to complain that work is necessary, the other is to be proud and look to it for redemption. Let us ask for wisdom to do neither.

Work and worship

The first two sons born to Adam and Eve grew up and accepted differing occupations. Both occupations reflect the requirements that God had established for human struggle. Cain chose the work of tilling the ground; Abel chose the work of caring for the sheep. Humans would always be in struggle with the vegetable world and the animal world. To the extent that the brothers are accepting the struggle and working hard, there is nothing to criticize. It is, in effect, a credit to Adam that he has taken the role given to him, and passed along a good work ethic to his sons.

Sheep are attached to humans very early. They are extremely important because they shall provide food, and their wool will be one of the most important means of clothing. In addition, sheep are very dependent on humans for survival, and make for an easy and early conquest for humans in their attempt at subduing the animal kingdom.

Sheep are attached to humans very early. They are extremely important because they shall provide food, and their wool will be one of the most important means of clothing. In addition, sheep are very dependent on humans for survival, and make for an easy and early conquest for humans in their attempt at subduing the animal kingdom.

Agriculture will produce the largest part of human food supply. Cultivation of the ground is extremely hard work, but very rewarding. It is one of those special kinds of tasks which allow one to see, rather quickly, the fruits of labour. There is no other occupation that so clearly gives humans the sense of subduing the earth. The land is utilized for human benefit. It has often been said that the life of the farmer provides a great deal of serenity, though the work is fierce and hard. Perhaps the serenity is derived from the clear examples of victory in his battle with earth's elements.

Though Cain and Abel have chosen differing occupations, they are not mutually exclusive. Abel must eat of the fruit of the ground. Cain will need to utilize the benefits that are obtained from the wool, and if eating meat is part of the fallen condition of humans prior to the flood, he will also need the meat provided from sheep. Bartering and trade between the two will be essential, and will become part of human affairs as they attempt to relate to each other as well as subjugate the animal and vegetable kingdom.

One issue remains. How will the two brothers approach their responsibility in worship? Eve had begun her life outside the garden by believing she could partner with God in producing the child for redemption. Will the brothers look on the fruits of their labours, note their success, and feel they are half the way back to the Garden of Eden? Will they, too, forget that they cannot re-create Eden, and try to partner with God in their redemption? Or, will they worship God as their only hope?

Worship in pride

The narrative on Cain and Abel centres on an act of worship. Cain brings an offering to the Lord from the fruit of the ground. Abel brings one of the sheep. The narrative records God's response. '... And the Lord had respect unto Abel and to his offering: But unto Cain and to his offering he had not respect...' (4:4-5). The implication is that Cain has failed in his worship. Why? Is it the nature of the offering? He brings an offering from the ground. The Scripture later records that the shedding of blood is required for redemption from sin (Hebrews 9:22). Yet, there are appropriate offerings prescribed in the law given to Israel that are not blood sacrifices. One of the sweet savour offerings required in Leviticus is an offering of fine flour with oil and frankincense poured upon it. Leviticus 2:2 records, 'And he shall bring it to Aaron's sons the priests: and he shall take thereout his handful of the flour thereof, and of the oil thereof, with all the frankincense thereof; and the priest shall burn the memorial of it upon the altar, to be an offering made by fire, of a sweet-savour unto the Lord.' From the Levitical offering we can affirm that there is more to Cain's worship failure than the absence of a blood sacrifice.

Is it the quality of the offering? The beginning of Genesis 4:4 notes 'And Abel, he also brought of the firstlings of his flock...' The 'also' would indicate that, as Cain, he brought the first-fruits, which would indicate that neither offering is inferior as a product of its own realm. There is a deeper problem at work.

The needed insight is found in 4:5. '...And Cain was very wroth, and his countenance fell.' Obviously, the issue for Cain was his pride. Having been successful in his subjugation of the earth, he comes to God showing off his own labour and success. He had failed to understand the basic nature of worship, which is full sub-mission to God. Cain was saying 'my work will get me part of the way back to the Garden of Eden.' It is a slap in God's face. Cain was telling God that it would not be all that hard to redeem him. 'Just look at what I accomplished on my own,' he says.

When rejected, Cain's pride was injured. Such reaction should have occurred before the offering. We cannot partner with God to earn our redemption. There is no room for pride. Redemption is all of God, or it is not at all. That is the foundation for true worship.

Cain fell prey to the trap of work success. He wanted to have part in his own redemption. Instead of accepting God's plan (the seed of the woman), and living by faith, he sought too carve another niche. The Incarnate one, born of woman, is the only route to redemption.

Worship in humility

The act of worship in which Cain and Abel engage is the act of bringing an offering to the Lord. It is interesting that the very first recorded act of worship involves an offering to God. It is also interesting that the first narrative about humans following the banishment from Eden is an act of worship. Two things are clearly laid out as primary.

First, worship is the single, most important activity of humankind. Worship must be regular and correct, or everything else in life becomes a shambles. Cain did not come to worship with the proper appreciation of the moment. When his offering was rejected, his pride was hurt. 'His countenance fell' reflects the nature of one who carries a downcast appearance. He came to worship to show off. He did not understand that worship is the moment when God is the centre of attention.

Second, worship is an act that declares God's ownership of his creation. A gift to God is not done to replenish God's kingdom but to acknowledge his sovereignty. Abel's act of worship was acceptable to God because his heart was in full submission to God. How do we know?

Abel's offering required an action on the part of the worshipper demonstrating great significance. He must stand before God and slay the lamb. In the act, the focus is not on Abel, but on the lamb. The lamb's life was taken. In that sense, the lamb gave more than did Abel. There was no sense of giving the greater offering in Abel's mind. Even the lamb was superior to him. In Abel's mind, worship was not a competition with his brother, it was an expression of the opposite. There was no competition here, only complete submissiveness fully typified in the submissiveness of the lamb.

Also, Abel's offering was based on complete faith in God. He was not attempting, by virtue of his offering, to partner with God in his redemption. Hebrews 11:4 validates this. 'By faith Abel offered unto God a more excellent sacrifice than Cain....' Because of Cain's desire to have some part in his own redemption, his offering would have been unacceptable even if he had traded his vegetables to Abel and sacrificed the lamb. Likely, he would have sheared the wool first, made a nice cloak, roasted the lamb, and served it as lamb chops, and put his handiwork on display for God to appreciate.

The lamb giving more than did Abel is a keynote concept that cannot be forgotten. John the Baptist said of the Incarnate One: '...Behold the lamb of God, which taketh away the sin of the world.' (John 1:29).

Possibility for repentance

Two great theological themes manifest themselves in this scriptural passage. Both come under the general doctrinal perspective of salvation. The themes are those of repentance and restoration. To understand them, we must see what is taught here about another doctrine, sin!

God states, 'If thou doest well, shalt thou not be accepted? and if thou doest not well, sin lieth at the door. And unto thee shall be his desire, and thou shalt rule over him' (4:7). The phrase, 'sin lieth at the door,' reflects the image of an enemy or a wild animal crouching at the door ready to leap upon us and to devour us. '... unto thee shall be his desire...' manifests a hunger for domination. Sin is never small, and never inconsequential. It may appear only as a small thing, but it is always ready to totally consume us. One cannot play with sin, and not be mastered by it. God's word to Cain is a warning, and an encouragement. He is suggesting that Cain, instead of being downcast about the rejection of his offering, be grateful for the warning that can, if heeded, prevent him from being mastered by sin. In fact, Cain can have the mastery over sin. '...and thou shalt rule over him.'

Repentance comes into play as God promises, 'If thou doest well, shalt thou not be accepted?' In light of the biblical narrative, this is an extremely encouraging word. When Adam and Eve committed sin, there was swift and overwhelming punishment: banishment from the garden, struggle in relationships and with the earth's elements, and death. The reader sees that God's dealing with the new condition of man has a provision for grace. God will restore and accept Cain's offering if he understands and turns from the sinful attitude in which he approached God.

Restoration is found in the word 'accepted'. This conveys a 'lifting up'. There is a subtle reference to both Cain's acceptance before God, and to his own sense of esteem which was lost in God's rejection of his offering. The Word of God is hereby marvellous. There is a methodology by which Cain can stop the sin that is stalking him and gain mastery over it.

In the light of man's struggle with the elements, and with the fierceness of the punishment for his original sin, this should come as a great relief, and be a moment for rejoicing. Repent of your sin before it devours you and you can gain mastery over it.

Difficulty of repentance

God had offered to Cain a methodology for dealing with sin in his life. 'If thou doest well...' The intention is not that Cain can control sin by doing well, but that Cain should change his attitude. In theological terminology, he should repent. The willingness to repent of his sinful attitude would reflect a condition his of heart, which, though battling sin, will not be mastered by it. It seems a simple principle, but the humans will be forever learning how difficult repentance is.

Verse eight is the first clear establishment of the difficulty of repentance. '...when they were in the field...Cain rose up against... his brother, and slew him' (4:8). One may ponder at length the nature of one who would become so filled with anger that he kills his brother. In the light of other Scripture, where the elder brother is seen as owning the majority rights of family headship, Cain may have seen his brother ascending to the position of elder in the household by virtue of God's rejection of his offering. With the rejection of God, he may now see himself as losing the favour of his father, Adam. He removes the competition.

God had said to Cain, '...sin lieth at the door. And unto thee shall be his desire...' (4:7). The meaning is that sin wants to control him. Cain becomes an illustration of the individual that sin totally masters. What began with an offering to God demonstrating his pride at overcoming the earth's thorns and thistles, leads to anger at God for not appreciating his fine work. The problem is how does one get back at God? One cannot! The only thing open to him is to strike at the one who God accepts. Sin has totally mastered man when he hates someone purely because God loves him. Herein, we learn the meaning of Jesus' profound statement. 'If ye were of the world, the world would love his own: but because ye are not of the world, but I have chosen you out of the world, therefore the world hateth you' (John 15:19).

Cain could have protected everything that was truly important in his life by submission to God. Unfortunately, as Adam and Eve learned, he had become as god, meaning, he wanted to be the final arbiter in the nature of his own being. He could only do that through equality with God. That is impossible, though he tries! He imitates God. God had pronounced death on humans. Cain pronounces death on Abel. It happens when man tries to be God instead of repenting and submitting.

Attitude of the non-repentant

The killing of Abel is a shocking statement about the consequences of sin. From the eating of the forbidden fruit where humans first disobeyed God, they evolve to the natural outcome that rebellion dictates. When humans tried to be the arbiter of their own being, they lost the ability to reason correctly. Desiring to be as gods led them to think independent of God's reasoning. In Cain's mind rested the typical human desire of having some power in the nature of his being.

Consider how he might have reasoned. By his pride in fulfilling the command to subdue the earth, he brings an offering of the vegetables he had cultivated. He had, for the moment, overcome the thorns and thistles that were part of the curse upon Adam (Genesis 3:18). As he brought his vegetables, he looked at their beauty, contemplated the joy that eating them could bring, and felt proud that he had laboured, overcome, and had such a fine offering to bring to God. His pride was his undoing. He had not connected the work he did with the curse that was placed upon humans for their sin. He thought the fruit of his labour had gained him merit with God, and gave him some bargaining power with God. He was rejected.

Think about the attitude of Cain as he observed the offering of Abel. The act of killing a lamb was a gory and ugly site. It certainly was repulsive to his senses. As he compared his beautiful vegetables to this freak show of Abel's, he could have been ridiculing it in his mind. It is not that it was new to him. His father, Adam, must have trained the two brothers in the activity, or Abel would not have known to do it. It's just that Cain had a better idea. He was certain that the beauty of his offering would be more acceptable than the ugliness portrayed in the slaughter of animals, and the smelly burning of flesh. Imagine how startled he was when the beauty of his offering was rejected and the ugliness of Abel's offering was accepted.

Cain began speaking to Abel, and led him into the field, perhaps into his vegetable garden. As he fumed, he looked at Abel, at his garden, and thought about the killing of the lamb. He thought, 'If its killing God wants, I'll give it to him.' '...Cain rose up against his brother and slew him' (4:8).

This little exercise of looking into Cain's mind explains how the human mentality, when not under the influence of God's word, destroys us. God had spoken to Cain, offering him the opportunity to be accepted, by acknowledging the reality of sin in his life, and bringing his offering under a different attitude. Instead, he listened to his own mind, ignored the Word of God, and did not reason correctly.

Humans continually think they have a better idea than God. The ugly picture of the cross repels. The better idea of humanity always fails to take into account the ugliness of the human heart.

The blame game

Following Cain's killing of his brother, the Lord speaks to him. From Cain's encounter, we can contrast him to Adam and Eve and ascertain certain developments in the human mindset. Adam and Eve became ashamed. '...they knew that they were naked... they sewed fig leaves together, and made themselves aprons... and... hid themselves from the presence of the Lord...' (Genesis 3:7-8). The brash answer of Cain shows no such shame. '...Am I my brother's keeper' (4:9)? Cain is angry at being exposed. Sin has progressed in the human spirit, spiralling downwards in one's appreciation of God.

'Where is Abel thy brother?' The question stung Cain. In an attempt to hide his act, he had successfully steered Abel into his field (4:8). Because he was a keeper of sheep, one would not look for Abel in Cain's field. The fact that God came searching for Abel in the field of Cain further exposes the shortcoming of Cain. He knew by the fact of the question that God was on to him. He had not successfully hidden his dastardly act. His answer reflects that knowledge. If he did not know where Abel was, he could, and would have answered, 'I don't know.'

The nature of Cain's answer reflects bitterness toward God. 'Am I my brother's keeper?' Likely, Cain still had God's rejection of his offering in mind. In effect he is saying to God, 'You liked him so well, why didn't you take care of him?' Cain is not so much denying what he has done, as he is blaming God. Adam and Eve had also attempted to shift blame. Adam had subtly tried to put partial blame on God when he said, '...The woman whom thou gavest to be with me, she gave me of the tree...' (Genesis 3:12). Cain's words take it a step further. God not only caused his sin to happen, God should have prevented it.

Cain places a new perspective on the blame game in explaining sin. In Cain's inner being there was no accepting of his state as a sinner. The desire to be 'as god' knowing good and evil has led him to the point of claiming authority for discernment of evil. His is a high-handed way of saying to God that Abel was his favourite, but when Abel needed him he wasn't there.

Blaming God for the mess we make of our own life is a nifty little trick that humans often try. Cain's question of God was a proclamation of innocence. He was innocent because God could have prevented it. It is weird reasoning, but perfectly normal for a mind that refuses to admit that it is depraved.

A terrifying witness

After Cain's insolent argument to God, 'Am I my brother's keeper,' the Lord speaks again. '...What hast thou done? The voice of thy brother's blood crieth unto me from the ground' (4:10). The statement of God is rich in biblical analogy. There is more than just the fact that God knows of Cain's killing of Abel. Other biblical passages refer to God hearing the voices of the dead. Jesus noted, 'And shall not God avenge his own elect, which cry day and night unto him, though he bear long with them' (Luke 18:7)? The book of Revelation carries further evidence. 'And when he had opened the fifth seal, I saw under the altar the souls of them that were slain for the Word of God, and for the testimony which they held: And they cried with a loud voice, saying, How long, O Lord, holy and true, dost thou not judge and avenge our blood on them that dwell on the earth' (Revelation 6:9-10)?

A sense of terror must have gripped Cain. He thought he had rid himself of Abel. Instead, Abel is a witness against him before the Lord. It is one thing for Cain to try to excuse himself by subtly hinting that it was God's responsibility to protect Abel. It is another thing to have Abel, himself, calling for justice. Here is stark, compelling evidence that one cannot hide sin from God. The apostle Paul says, 'Be not deceived; God is not mocked: for whatsoever a man soweth, that shall he also reap' (Galatians 6:7). The evidence that Cain believed to be hidden is clearly visible and speaking to God. Man may try to destroy the evidence against him, but it is always readily available to God. As humans contemplate sin, and think it will be secret, and no one will know, it would be wise to remember God's words to Cain, 'The voice of thy brother's blood crieth unto me from the ground' (4:10).

Human conversation sometimes refers to a crime and speaks of it crying out for vengeance. We are not surprised that victims cry out for God to avenge their blood. There is, however, one notable exception in the Bible. 'And to Jesus the mediator of the new covenant, and to the blood of sprinkling, that speaketh better things than that of Abel' (Hebrews 12:24). The blood of Jesus cries out, not for vengeance, but for grace. When we think of the evidence that is stacked against us in our sin, we understand the meaning of being under the blood. The evidence against us was placed at Jesus feet.

An acute loss

When God pronounced a curse upon Adam, it was effectively a curse upon the ground. Humankind would have to battle the elements of the earth while it brings forth thorns and thistles, and is in rebellion to the human's attempt to subdue it (Genesis 3:18-19). Cain had effectively fought the earth's elements, and was proud of his mastery over the ground, and brought an offering of the fruit of the ground. His offering was delivered in the sense of 'showing off' his prowess in subduing the earth, instead of in acknowledgement of submission to God, thus his offering was rejected. Cain's rage at being rejected led to his murder of Abel, whose offering was accepted. God speaks to reveal Cain's punishment. The irony is noticeable. 'And now art thou cursed from the earth, which hath opened her mouth to receive thy brother's blood from thy hand; When thou tillest the ground, it shall not yield unto thee her strength...' (Genesis 4:11-12).

The one thing of which Cain was most proud, which he believed demonstrated his own effectiveness, and his right of acceptance, is stripped from him. The ground, which he battled to produce the vegetables brought for an offering, was cursed in order to force humans into dependence on God. Cain had used it for the exact opposite, to show off his independence. The Lord's curse on Cain insures that the ground will never again produce for him.

The theological theme demanding the reader's consideration is the importance of God's control in the affairs of our life. Our work is blessed by God to the extent that we do not allow it to become a source of pride which leads us to ignore our dependence on God. Israel was to learn the same thing in countless situations. When God brought them out of Egypt, they were led to a land reported to be flowing with milk and honey (Numbers 13:27). It was a good land that would produce as they laboured in it. Notice, however, God's warning. 'Take heed...that your heart be not deceived, and ye turn aside, and serve other gods...And then the Lord's wrath be kindled against you, and he shut up the heaven, that there be no rain, and that the land yield not her fruit...' (Deuteronomy 11:16-17). Our work is a good thing! It is done because of the requirement that we do battle with the elements of earth. It is not our work that wins that victory, however, it is the will of God which allows it.

A heritage of dissatisfaction

The punishment that God places on Cain for his slaying of Abel is in two parts. First, he is made aware that the ground will no longer yield her fruit. He was most proud of the way that he had conquered the ground. He had seen it as the essence of meaning for himself, but that is now taken from him. The second part of the punishment is phrased '...a fugitive and a vagabond shalt thou be in the earth' (4:12).

It is no wonder that Cain bemoans '...My punishment is greater than I can bear' (Genesis 4:13). Place yourself into the thinking of Cain. He had loved his success with subduing the land. With all his being, he wanted this to be the source of his satisfaction. By his own decision making power, he had determined that his own work is sufficient to satisfy every demand of his being. Being sold out to the concept, he is left with no place to turn.

Cain's condition is a testimony to the total human experience. It is a constant problem that we sell out to all kinds of things. We crave that they bring us the definition of our being. We so want our work, our human relationships, and our possession of this earth's realities to fulfil and satisfy. The ultimate result is that we are left with only those things. As we should have learned from the original curse placed upon the man and the woman (Genesis 3:16-19), they only produce frustration. The conquering of the earth, which Cain thought was so valuable, is no longer available to him. This is clearly symbolic of death. Everything to which we might sell out is lost at death, unless, we are sold out to God.

The words 'a fugitive and a vagabond' speak to the concept of banished and homeless. To see the full tragedy of it, one should think in a spiritual sense. There is no place for the soul to find rest. Cain abandoned God, and sold out to a source he deemed a better idea. He is incapable of admitting that he does not have the right of being 'as god' in his life. Thus, he actually prefers to continue in his frustration and punishment than submit to God. It is an accurate description of the human experience.

The modern rock music mantra, 'I can't get no satisfaction,' plays well in this setting. Clearly, the way humanity tries to find satisfaction leads to the wail of the rock musician.

Judgement of Cain

It is a curious thing that Cain was allowed to live after committing murder. After the flood, God established that murder was to be punished by death. 'Whoso sheddeth man's blood, by man shall his blood be shed...' (Genesis 9:6). In Cain's case, however, God forbade capital punishment. '...Whosoever slayeth Cain, vengeance shall be taken on him sevenfold....' (4:15). God made Cain this promise following Cain's expression of fear about others seeking vengeance for his murder of Abel.

There are some things in God's statement that require meditation. Even at this early stage in the development of human rebellion against God, and without law for society, humans would have realized that proper vengeance is a life for a life. Cain expressed such understanding. '...And it shall come to pass, that everyone that findeth me shall slay me' (4:14). Thus, the question remains, why is Cain allowed to live?

Part of the answer will be revealed in this same chapter when human rebellion deteriorates further (4:23-24). In the present context, the lack of capital punishment for Cain is to be discerned in the nature of sin itself. When humans determined to be 'as gods' (Genesis 3:5), they lost the ability to reason correctly. They opted for their own kind of reasoning instead of the reasoning of God. At the early stage of rebellion against God, humans would not understand vengeance. The act of violence committed in exacting vengeance is likely to be worse than the original crime. The only purpose it will serve is inciting passion and creating further crime. Without clear law established by God, the humans in a fallen state cannot be trusted with vengeance. The protection of Cain was also a protection for others to prevent them from further violence.

Also, the inability of humans to reason properly kept them from understanding the total, debilitating nature of sin. It must be allowed to run its course, and be fully revealed. The mark on Cain (4:15) would be a constant reminder to the early humans populating the earth of the consequences of sin. Cain's mark was, in a strange way, a testimony to God. Despite the mark on Cain, humans would continue in growing rebellion against God. A testimony, such as Cain's, combined with growing human rebellion leaves no doubt as to where true wisdom lies, and whose reasoning is best.

> Human reasoning is so easily flawed. Every Christian should depend on the Word of God for protection of his thinking. Deuteronomy states it and Jesus quotes it in his fight with Satanic temptation. '...man doth not live by bread only, but by every word that proceedeth out of the mouth of the lord...' (Deuteronomy 8:3).

'...land of nod...'

The textual reading of Genesis 4:16-24 appears as a simple genealogical table with a few noteworthy comments. The author is interested in conveying more than genealogy.

A meditative moment on the text reveals the development of a vast and diversified culture. It is clear that human knowledge is rapidly expanding, and that the developing knowledge is leading them further and further from dependence on God.

It all starts with '...Cain went out from the presence of the Lord, and dwelt in the land of Nod, on the East of Eden' (4:16). 'The land of Nod' is a curious statement and not easily discerned. Nod means 'wandering'. The fact that Cain acted to build a city (4:17) indicates that he was not a constant wanderer moving from place to place. The best understanding is probably in a spiritual context. An unrepentant Cain who had rejected God moves to a part of the world where the gate of Eden would not be visible to him, and he could continue his quest to be in control of his own being. His wandering is likely a spiritual wandering to be out from under the control of God.

Cain's building of a city is further sign of his continued attitude of independence from God. He is determined to be successful on his own. It is quite interesting to note that the person who feared that '...everyone that findeth me shall slay me' (4:14) now wants to have many people around him. As one thinks about Cain's situation, the thought can be carried to the next logical step. God had put a mark on him to protect him from human vengeance (4:15). God had shown him mercy. He reacts to God's mercy by flagrantly tempting God's promise. It is human arrogance at its worst. The God, who he had tried to blame for not protecting Abel, now must protect him. Cain must have felt very proud and probably claimed for himself a victory over God. He was dependent on God's protection, but independent in every other way. This reflects the whole human condition in rather pointed fashion.

The lesson for the reader is discovered as one mediates on the intricate workings of his own mind. We long for the protection of God, but want full credit for ourselves when things go our way. We resent it if God's protection does not manifest itself exactly as we desire, but never feel guilty about failing to worship and give God praise for the blessings of our life.

It is a worthy meditation to consider the ways that we so often demand the care of God in our lives, yet flaunt that protection by our disobedience to him, and by our tempting him through careless living.

Genesis 4:17-24

17. And Cain knew his wife; and she conceived, and bare Enoch: and he builded a city, and called the name of the city, after the name of his son, Enoch. 18. And unto Enoch was born Irad: and Irad begat Mehujael: and Mehujael begat Methusael: and Methusael begat Lamech. 19. And Lamech took unto him two wives: the name of the one was Adah, and the name of the other Zillah. And Adah bare Jabal: he was the father of such as dwell in tents, and of such as have cattle. 21. And his brother's name was Jubal: he was the father of all such as handle the harp and organ. 22. And Zillah, she also bare Tubalcain, an instructer of every artificer in brass and iron: and the sister of Tubalcain was Naamah. 23. And Lamech said unto his wives, Adah and Zillah, Hear my voice; ye wives of Lamech, hearken unto my speech: for I have slain a man to my wounding, and a young man to my hurt. 24. If Cain shall be avenged sevenfold, truly Lamech seventy and sevenfold.

'...he builded a city...'

The generations spawned by Cain are traced in these verses. It begins with the birth of a son. People have often played games with this passage of Scripture by asking where Cain got his wife. The answer is found in chapter five. 'And the days of Adam after he had begotten Seth were eight hundred years: and he begat sons and daughters' (Genesis 5:4). Cain would likely have married one of his sisters. It is not as unthinkable as present mindsets find it. First, the genetic devolution in terms of disease, and risk of birth defects had not entered the human race. That occurs after many years and many generations of sinful activity and abuse of the body. Second, there are many ancient historical records, such as in Egypt, where rulers are recorded to have married sisters. Third, God had commanded the first man and woman to populate the earth. God would have known that the early generations of humans would be marrying within the family. This question is of no consequence when fully understood.

Cain's building of a city, and naming it after his first born son, Enoch, symbolizes his desire to build an earthly kingdom for himself. Disenfranchised from the family of God, he creates a family of the ungodly, or as it might be described theologically, a family that wanted to be 'as gods.' The city would carry other benefits for Cain. He could no longer grow vegetables from the ground because of his punishment for the murder of Abel (4:12). He will have to glean what he can from the wild fruits and berries, and the city will help establish some means of barter with others to acquire the food that he needs for himself and family. The more Cain succeeds in providing for himself despite the punishment placed on him, the more he will congratulate himself on overcoming God.

The name, Enoch, is believed to mean 'beginning' or 'commencement'. For Cain, it is the start of a new way for himself. It is likely another reflection of his independence. The child and the city by the same name are human statements reflecting an attitude of anger and hatred toward God. Cain's embitterment still stands. He says to God 'who needs you?'

The more one understands Cain, the more one understands the human struggle against God. It is the nature of humans to want, and demand, acceptance based on our own worth, and our own ability to be 'as gods' to ourselves. That struggle leads to greater and greater desire for independence from God, and ultimately to hatred of God because his acceptance doesn't come until we admit our unworthiness.

> Human acceptance before God is a matter of imputed righteousness (Romans 4:22-24), the righteousness of God's Son being applied to our account. It is our tendency to fight the idea that we have nothing with which to bargain before God.

Unholy genius

Cain has successfully created his own place in the world. A city has been established apart from the rest of the family of his father, Adam. It is a culture independent of God, but worldly-wise. The family will be inventive and proud of its accomplishments. Yet, with all its accomplishments, it creates a shambles of life, and brings steady moral deterioration.

The reader is taken through five generations and encounters Lamech. The moral deterioration shows in a lack of discipline in protecting the sanctity of family. 'And Lamech took unto him two wives : the name of the one was Adah, and the name of the other Zillah' (4:19). The purpose of God, clearly seen from the beginning, was that one man and one woman be united to each other and procreate children in an ethical and orderly society. Jesus affirmed this in his teaching on divorce (Matthew 19:4-8). Lamech's action is the first recorded case of polygamy, and reflects the attitude of the dwellers of Cain's city, built with an independence of God. Lamech says, 'I have a better idea.' When his idea is allowed to dominate, marriage is changed from the sense of producing order in a society, and allowing for what is best for the community. Instead, what is best for Lamech becomes the rule. It is the rearing of the ugly head of the serpent's temptation again. '...ye shall be as gods....' (Genesis 3:5). It is easy to project what such an attitude will do to the community.

The children produced by Lamech's marriages show an independent genius. Jabal domesticates the larger animals expanding human control beyond the sheep (4:20). Jubal is the inventor of musical instruments (4:21). Tubal-cain originated the use of metals expanding human understanding of earth's elements and creating expansive possibility for easing labour, and producing commerce (4:22). As one reads this narrative, one thinks positively. These are all wonderful things. Human life can be improved. Human minds are used to subdue the earth. It is a sobering thought however, that it is the ungodly line of Cain that is making these discoveries. Why is it the ungodly, and not the godly, who are the creative ones?

It is important to remember that God controls all knowledge. Humans do not have any knowledge until God allows them to have it. The arrogance, pride, and independence of the ungodly line is granted grace to make earthly life better, yet, a hard lesson is before them. With all their genius about earthly elements, they will not be able to control themselves. That is an interesting indictment for those who want to be 'as gods'.

The first generations of men outside the Garden of Eden had to learn that they could not re-create the Garden. It is a sad commentary on humans that every generation must re-learn this lesson. Genesis 3:15 offered the only hope, but humans continually rebel against it.

Reasoning of Lamech

The descendants of Cain have been allowed the knowledge to advance earthly civilization. How will humans who are independent of God use the knowledge? Humans love to believe the best about themselves. If given the right environment, they will always choose the best path, or so we think. It is clearly demonstrated here that human reasoning is wrong. In fact, reality is the exact opposite of human reasoning. The arrogance of wanting to be as god comes to full fruition.

Why was Cain allowed to live after killing Abel? In Lamech, one can see why God allowed it, and what he was trying to teach. 'And Lamech said unto his wives, Adah and Zillah, Hear my voice, ye wives of Lamech, hearken unto my speech: for I have slain a man to my wounding, and a young man to my hurt. If Cain shall be avenged sevenfold, truly Lamech seventy and sevenfold' (4:23-24).

There are several points of meditation for the reader. The context has reported wonderful events in the development of the arts (4:21), animal husbandry (4:20), and metallurgy (4:22). Humans have better living circumstances. Would this not result in better humans? The nature of Lamech hits us like cold steel against a warm body. Lamech brags about killing a young man (literally, a young boy) for a small hurt. The spirit of Cain is not lessened in his descendants, but is expanded.

Lamech brags, 'If Cain shall be avenged sevenfold, truly Lamech seventy and sevenfold' (4:24). The statement, which follows immediately on the advancement in metallurgy, indicates that Lamech saw this advancement as a means to establish his own superiority, not as a means of advancing civilization. The belief that he has, in his own power, the ability to inflict his will upon others indicates that the working in brass and iron has been used for the fashioning of weapons. Desiring to be as god has led Lamech to a better idea. God had refused capital punishment for Cain when he murdered Abel. Lamech inflicts capital punishment for the slightest of wounds. Human nature, independent of God, is dramatically revealed. That is precisely what God intended. The lesson for every individual is to see the reasoning presented, and compare it with our own minds, and thus learn that we are all prone to the reasoning of Lamech.

> Human reasoning, when one is personally hurt, does not act with proper retribution, but seeks to respond in anger, needing to doubly repay for the hurt.

Understanding human vengeance

Cain commits murder (Genesis 4:8). He is punished through the loss of that for which he was most proud, his subduing the earth to produce quality vegetables (4:3, 12). In addition, he is a fugitive, a vagabond in the earth. He will never carry a sense of peace or understanding of his own being. However, God does offer grace, and places a mark upon him that will not allow anyone to do him harm. The issue of vengeance is put before the reader and calls for meditative examination.

Lamech's story offers further resource for that meditation. A question that must be asked is, 'What kind of attitude would Cain and his descendants have if they are the ones who are harmed?' Would they show grace? Lamech reveals the answer.

In Lamech is found the intensely selfish nature that is inherent to all human beings. It is often spoken of as being in one who thinks the world revolves around self. This condition is the nature of a child. As one matures, he must be taught differently. It is a difficult transition to move from a selfish perspective to one who considers the rights of others. When there is no protective societal device such as law, or faithfulness to God, human selfishness will reign.

God gave full allowance for humans to show what they are when he showed grace and did not apply the law to Cain. Lamech is the natural result. Selfishness always believes that its hurt is the greatest hurt, its need is the greatest need, its thoughts are the most important thoughts, and that everyone else is its enemy. Others, the selfish one thinks, do not seem to notice how much he hurts, or how great his needs are, or how important his thoughts are. Consequently, any harm felt is extremely cruel (even if minor) and demands great and severe retribution on those supposed others. Listen to Lamech. '...Hear my voice...hearken unto my speech: for I have slain a man to my wounding, and a young man to my hurt. If Cain shall be avenged sevenfold, truly Lamech seventy and sevenfold' (4:23-24). Lamech says, 'If you hurt me a little bit, I will kill you.' Without proper training, proper discipline, and the enforcement of law, it is where the human mind naturally goes. God allowed humans the chance to prove differently. Cain's descendants, living 'as gods' to themselves, failed.

> Obsession with self is a dangerous thing to which we are all prone. Jesus gave us a way to handle this obsession within the parameters of the golden rule (Matthew 7:12)

Genesis 4:25-26

25. And Adam knew his wife again; and she bare a son, and called his name Seth: For God, said she, hath appointed me another seed instead of Abel, whom Cain slew. 26. And to Seth, to him also there was born a son; and he called his name Enos: then began men to call upon the name of the Lord.

Birth of Seth

The reader of Scripture has been astounded as he has seen the dramatic creation of God, gloriously displayed in the relationship between Adam and Eve, deteriorate into the boastful and evil arrogance of Lamech. The first two sons born to Adam and Eve bring them great heartache. In their grief, we have the first notable and awesome by-products of sin. It is easy to observe that sin leads to greater sin. But, sin also leads to great heartache and misery. Abel is dead, slain by Cain. Cain is a fugitive and a vagabond in the earth. Adam and Eve have lost both of their first two sons.

When another son is born to Eve, the reader can hear the sadness in her voice. '...and she bore a son, and called his name, Seth: For God, said she, hath appointed me another seed instead of Abel, whom Cain slew' (4:25). The statement of Eve has an important application. Her hope for immediate redemption expressed when she bore Cain, has been destroyed by Cain's sin. As she observed the rebellion of her first-born son, there has to be concern about the survival of the human race. Will God allow its survival until the promised seed of the woman (Genesis 3:15) can appear? The birth of Seth is God's action to calm the fears of Adam and Eve.

Seth means 'appointed.' It is clear that God is easing the fears of Adam and Eve. Through Seth, the human race will survive. His line is set aside for salvation. This is key when we come to the awesome words of Genesis 6:3. 'And the Lord said, My spirit shall not always strive with man, for that he also is flesh: yet his days shall be an hundred and twenty years.' That which had begun with eating the forbidden fruit escalated to Cain's murder, and moves to the spirit of Lamech, ultimately pervades the whole of the human race. Cain had been spared from death, but the nature of sin is clearly revealed after humans continue in their rebellion against God.

The ray of hope is in the children who are born from Seth. That is God's promise to Eve. The lesson for the reader is easily discerned. Adam and Eve know that their life is to be based in faith. Their experience with Cain and Abel could easily destroy that faith. But, to all refusing to turn from God, He will have a word of comfort and rebuilding of faith. For Adam and Eve, it is Seth. He can't take away their sadness, but he does insert hope.

One of life's most precious possessions is hope. We learn here that hope is the product of God. The hope is in the 'seed of the woman' (Genesis 3:15). In the New Testament that same hope is seen, but in a different light. '...the glorious appearing of...Our Saviour Jesus Christ' (Titus 2:13).

Establishment of hope

In the birth of Seth, and the promise that he brings, the reader is introduced to a principle that shall be carried throughout the Old Testament. The first-born son always carried great promise and hope, but is rarely the chosen one. It is not Cain who is righteous, but Abel. Abel is murdered, and the third son, Seth, becomes the one who shall be the guarantor of the human race. This guarantee carries both the promise of survival, and the continuing hope first mentioned in Genesis 3:15 as the seed of the woman. Japheth, the elder son of Noah (Genesis 10:21), was passed over for Shem, the younger son, who numbered Abraham among his descendants (Genesis 11:10, 29). Ishmael, the elder son of Abraham was passed over for Isaac, the younger (Genesis 17:20-21). Esau, the elder son of Isaac was passed over for Jacob, the younger (Genesis 25:23). In a more subtle form, the same reality is present when the first king of Israel (Saul) is rejected as the kingly line of Israel, and David, the second king is accepted (1 Samuel 15:26; 16:1). This is one of those marvellous theological issues that establish the unity of Scripture. How?

The New Testament book of Romans places the sense of rejection of the first and accepting of the second into the greater biblical context. 'For if by one man's offence (Adam, the first man) death reigned by one; much more they which receive abundance of grace and of the gift of righteousness shall reign in life by one, Jesus Christ' (Romans 5:17). Adam, who held the seed of the entire human race, sins, and guarantees that all who are born after him are sinners, just as he. Jesus, as the seed of woman, not of Adam, comes as a complete human being without the tarnish of Adam's sinful nature. As man, without sin, he is thus only the second human about whom that statement can be made. In Adam, we are all condemned, but when placed in the second man, Christ, we inherit his righteousness. Adam, the first man without sin, failed. Jesus, the second man, without sin, succeeded. In Christ, a brand new race of human beings can be established, the race of human beings who shall be saved by faith.

With each story in the Old Testament where the elder is rejected for the younger, the reader is called upon to remember the great promise that was there in Adam, as is always there, in the first born. He is also soberly reminded of the great fall, but in the acceptance and faithful service of the younger, there is hope and redemption. When it all comes together in Christ, the vibrancy and life of the Word of God, not to mention its unity, is clear.

> The Scripture's wonderful unity is seen easily when one's focus is on the promise of Genesis 3:15. The Incarnate One is the unity of Scripture. Wonderful words of life are the wonderful Word of life, Jesus Christ.

Attitude of Seth

The birth of Seth renews the hope of Adam and Eve. He replaces the righteous Abel (4:4), and sets the proper example of worship toward God. The narrative places Seth and his descendants in direct opposition to Cain and his descendants. Cain names his first son Enoch, signifying a new beginning apart from God. He builds a city and names it after his son (4:17) in perhaps an arrogant display of his intention to do things his own way. The person familiar with Scripture might want to consider comparing the attitude of Cain who '...builded a city....' with that of Abraham whom the writer of Hebrews tells us '...looked for a city which hath foundations, whose builder and maker is God' (Hebrews 11:10).

In contrast, Seth names his first son Enos (4:26). The name means 'man' with respect to all the frailty and weakness that the term reflects. This concept is reflected in the Psalms. 'As for man, his days are as grass: as a flower of the field, so he flourisheth'

(Psalms 103:15). The spirit of humility, an acceptance of human weakness, and need for God, are expressed in the naming of Seth's son. The descendants of Cain expand on their independence from God, and produce the type of individuals characterized by the evil Lamech (4:19, 23-24). Compare what is said of Enos. '...and he called his name Enos: then began men to call upon the name of the Lord' (4:26).

Public worship makes its appearance at this time. The population of humans has arrived at a place where men worship together. The son of Seth leads in this practice. '...the name of the Lord...' (4:26) is the first biblical use of the name by which God referred to himself in the days of Moses (Exodus 3:13-14). It is the name 'Yahweh,' better known by many as Jehovah. When translated into English, the name is 'I Am.'

The lesson for the reader is found in comparison. Whereas the line of Cain rejoiced in itself, in its own works, and in building up its own name, the son of Seth rejoices in the name of God. Enos placed his hope, his life, and his destiny in the hands of God. Worship in the name of God reflects the total nature of worship. It is humanity, understanding its weakness, and specifically its moral weakness, acknowledging the need of mercy from God. For the writer of Genesis, man's entire relationship with God rests in this fact. Enos is praised because he led his brethren to worship God.

Reverence for the name of God is at the root of worship. The reader of Scripture will recall that Jesus referred to himself by the same name used here (John 8:58).

Genesis 5:1-32

Genesis 5:1-5

1. This is the book of the generations of Adam. In the day that God creat-
ed man, in the likeness of God made he him; 2. Male and female created
he them; and blessed them, and called their name Adam, in the day when
they were created. 3. And Adam lived an hundred and thirty years, and
begat a son in his own likeness, after his image; and called his name Seth:
4. And the days of Adam after he had begotten Seth were eight hundred
years: and he begat sons and daughters: And all the days that Adam lived
were nine hundred and thirty years: and he died.

Giving a name

The writer of Genesis redirects the reader's attention back to
creation and provides a strong reminder of mankind's purpose in

having relationship with his God. In very subtle fashion, God is shown as the Father of man, and this illustrates the importance of the institution of fatherhood. The methodology for accomplishing this is in the naming of children. '...in the likeness of God made he him; Male and female created he them; and blessed them, and called their name Adam, in the day when they were created' (5:1-2). This is the first time the Scriptural account tells us that God named Adam. Previously, Adam had given names to the animals, and to Eve. The narrative of Chapter 5 continues: 'And Adam lived an hundred and thirty years, and begat a son in his own likeness, after his image; and called his name Seth' (5:3).

Two very clear applications are placed before the reader. First, God established himself as the Father of all humans. He created us and named us. By creating us in his image, he takes on a personal responsibility. There is potential for the kind of relationship with him that no other created being carries. God gives himself an obligation and responsibility to do what is necessary to develop that relationship. That is what is meant in the fatherhood of God. When this is fully understood, it is the source of wonderful comfort and sublime blessing for the believer. God gave to himself a responsibility to have relationship in a unique way with this creation called humans.

Second, God established 'fatherhood' as the premise of earthly civilization. The first man, Adam, clearly understood that he had ruptured the relationship for which he was created. With children now created in his likeness instead of in the likeness of God, it would become his responsibility to be the teacher of the purpose of creation, and to point children to their true father, God. He will name his sons, as God named him. One should not miss the powerful symbolism that lies in giving one his name. It is to say 'I am offering to you the possibility of a personal relationship with me such as no other being has. As God did not bypass his obligation to me, I will not bypass my obligation to lead you into a relationship with our mutual father.' Of course, we humans continue to fail miserably here. The requirement was made more forceful to the nation of Israel. 'Hear O Israel: The Lord our God is one Lord...

And these words which I command thee this day...thou shalt teach them diligently unto thy children....' (Deuteronomy 6:4-7).

For any parent, especially Christian parents, the nature of giving a child his name should be kept in mind in terms of the eternal, spiritual responsibility such as act intimates.

Understanding fatherhood

The reader of Genesis 5 is confronted with a series of statements that appear as mere reciting of genealogical tables. The line of Adam's son, Seth, is recited. 'And Seth lived...and begat Enos...and Seth lived after he begat Enos eight hundred and seven years, and begat sons and daughters: and all the days of Seth were nine hundred and twelve years: and he died' (5:6-8). The same format is repeated through ten generations with only two exceptions, Enoch and Noah. When reading a recitation like this, the tendency is to think it is unimportant, and to pass over the people mentioned as unimportant. There is an important lesson, however, that should be noted.

One should compare with the genealogy of Cain. 'And unto Enoch was born Irad: and Irad begat Mehujael: and Mehujael begat Methusael...' (Genesis 4:18). Note there is no mention of length of life, no mention of extended families ('...begat sons and daughters...'), and no mention of the time of their death. Clearly, each individual named in the Seth line is to be seen as important to his time. His importance rests in his family. It is the first born son who shall have the responsibility (unless overruled by God) to carry the religious history, and carry the teaching of God, and the understanding of God as Father, to the next generation. This theme will reappear often in the rest of Genesis.

The methodology that the Genesis narrative uses to enforce the importance of the father's continuing the teaching of God is the formula of the father blessing his son. It shall be seen most clearly in Noah (Genesis 9:24-27), Isaac (Genesis 27:27), and Jacob

(Genesis 49:1-28). The reader should carefully consider the writer's determination to present each of these individuals as centred in a family, and it is that family which carries the name of God in a teaching manner for the civilization of humans. This is the foundational understanding in Scripture of a loving father.

A loving father is concerned about the well-being of his children. He best insures the well-being of his children through teaching of their true origin (belonging to and emanating from the hand of God). The seemingly unimportant names of Chapter 5 had no great inventions such as Cain's descendants (Genesis 4:20-22), but they are to be seen as true heroes because they keep alive the name of God. When a father passes this along to his children, he has truly blessed them. This could call for a little meditation on the words of Paul. 'For ye have not received the spirit of bondage again to fear; but ye have received the spirit of adoption, whereby we cry, Abba Father' (Romans 8:15).

Long life

One of the most fascinating aspects of this part of Scripture is the accounting of the number of years which people lived. There are a number of explanations that biblical scholars have offered. Some have said these are lunar years, meaning that age is accounted for in the changes of the moon. This would have made for some very young fathers. Enoch would have been five years old (Genesis 5:21). Others have attributed it to mythical writing. Ancient stories of the Sumerian kings record them as living more than 30,000 years. What can we learn from this portion of Scripture?

First, the biblical story does not carry the fantasy-like portrayals of long life such as the Sumerian culture. The author clearly meant to place the people in his genealogy squarely into a particular historical framework. The sons were born at a specific age of the fathers and presented in a way that traces their births in specific years from Adam. When traced carefully, the entire period from Adam to Noah carries the lifespan of two individuals, Adam and Methuselah. In effect, the total devastation of human civilization occurs in the life spans of two generations, though covering two thousand years. The many kings who lived so many years in the Sumerian myths can easily be explained by fantasy portrayals of the corporate memory that came from the tales of the sons of Noah, and had reference to the long lives of the original inhabiters of earth. Imagine the status that Adam and his many sons (5:4) would have as the population grew.

Second, the biblical story of the long lives emphasizes the value of living godly lives. This genealogy has reference to the godly line of Seth. In Cain's ungodly line, we read of selfish living and murderous activity (Genesis 4:23). In the line of Seth, we discover a man like Enoch. 'And Enoch walked with God; and he was not; for God took him' (5:24). In the book of Hebrews we are told that Enoch was 'translated', and did not see death (Hebrews 11:5). The lesson here is to understand the connection between life, and the giver of life, who is God.

Jesus said, '...I am come that they might have life, and that they might have it more abundantly...' (John 10:10). The early writing of Genesis emphasizes that life comes from God, and the closer one keeps himself to God, the closer he is to life.

For the one who desires to stay close to the giver of life the words of Jesus are important. '...Learn of me...' (Matthew 11:29). The Incarnate one is the source of life, and only as we learn of Jesus can we remain close to life.

Genesis 5:6-32

6. And Seth lived an hundred and five years, and begat Enos: 7. And Seth lived after he begat Enos eight hundred and seven years, and begat sons and daughters: 8. And all the days of Seth were nine hundred and twelve years: and he died. 9. And Enos lived ninety years, and begat Cainan: 10. And Enos lived after he begat Cainan eight hundred and fifteen years, and begat sons and daughters: 11. And all the days of Enos were nine hundred and five years: and he died. 12. And Cainan lived seventy years and begat Mahalaleel: 13. And Cainan lived after he begat Mahalaleel eight hundred and forty years, and begat sons and daughters: 14. And all the days of Cainan were nine hundred and ten years: and he died. 15. And Mahalaleel lived sixty and five years, and begat Jared: 16. And Mahalaleel lived after he begat Jared eight hundred and thirty years, and begat sons and daughters: 17. And all the days of Mahalaleel were eight hundred ninety and five years: and he died. 18. And Jared lived an hundred sixty and two years, and he begat Enoch: 19. And Jared lived after he begat Enoch eight hundred years, and begat sons and daughters: 20. And all the days of Jared were nine hundred sixty and two years: and he died. 21. And Enoch lived sixty and five years, and begat Methuselah: 22. And Enoch walked with God after he begat Methuselah three hundred years, and begat sons and daughters: 23. And all the days of Enoch were three hundred sixty and five years: 24. And Enoch walked with God: and he was not; for God took him. 25. And Methuselah lived an hundred eighty and seven years, and begat Lamech. 26. And Methuselah lived after he begat Lamech seven hundred eighty and two years, and begat sons and daughters: 27. And all the days of Methuselah were nine hundred sixty and nine years: and he died. 28. And Lamech lived an hundred eighty and two years, and begat a son: 29. And he called his name Noah, saying, This same shall comfort us concerning our work and toil of our hands, because of the ground which the Lord hath cursed. 30. And Lamech lived after he begat Noah five hundred ninety and five years, and begat sons and daughters: 31. And all the days of Lamech were seven hundred seventy and seven years: and he died. 32. And Noah was five hundred years old: and Noah begat Shem, Ham, and Japheth.

Enoch is translated

One of the most puzzling pieces of Scripture lies in the account of Enoch's life. 'And Enoch walked with God: and he was not; for God took him' (5:24). From the time of Adam's sin, the great pall cast over humanity is the awesome statement of God. '…thou shalt surely die' (Genesis 2:17). From the murderous activity of

Cain and Lamech to the simple pronouncement '...and he died' (5:5, 8, 11, etc.), God's statement is seen as certain and unchangeable. Why is Enoch different?

The reader will want to consider the nature of Enoch's life. It is wrapped in the phrase '...walked with God....' Obviously, the writer of Genesis sets Enoch apart by this phrase. The nature of his communion with God makes him unlike any of his contemporaries. There may be a subtle connection to the Garden of Eden where God is mentioned as walking with Adam (Genesis 3:8). Enoch was a notch above all his generation in the yearning of his soul and the ability to gain intense enjoyment from his knowledge of God. It is that intense connection with God that led to the statement '...God took him.'

There are two applications which meditation on this passage provides. First, God will provide beacons of hope for those who attempt to follow him. The sixth chapter of Genesis will reveal the total corruption of the human race. In Enoch's day, the world was quickly racing toward the moment when God would judge the earth. Any who were remaining true to God must have seen the pattern reflected in the moral decay of persons living and the consistent refrain of those in the godly line '...and he died.' All hope can easily be lost in that scenario. The promise of redemption, and the reversal of the punishment of death first mentioned in the seed of the women (Genesis 3:15), comes into question. When God spares Enoch from the curse of death, he re-establishes himself as the giver of life, and brings hope for the godly line.

Second, the writer reaffirms that the true wonder of the Garden of Eden was not in the fruit of the earth, but in the glory of unfettered fellowship with God. Man's continuing attempt to remake the garden, and ignore the wonder of fellowship with God is the route of death. It is in fellowship with God that the true garden is re-created. '...Thou shalt love the Lord thy God....' (Matthew 22:37) is suddenly seen as a commandment with great promise when one is able to discern the message of Enoch's life.

The Apostle Paul wrote 'Set your affection on things above, not on things on the earth' (Colossians 3:2). These are difficult words to learn and apply. We can find it more easily done through the personal application of relationship with the Incarnate Christ, who walked on this earth.

A walk with God

'And Enoch walked with God....' For any person who desires a relationship with God, there is wonder and curiosity to be found in these words. Enoch is looked upon as an example, but how are we to emulate him? The phrase 'walked with God' does not carry any detail. One wishes it did. How did Enoch conduct his day? What did he say? What were the actions and activities that denote walking with God? What did he read? How did he formulate his thinking? When one says, 'walking with God,' there are many gaps that need to be filled, but the writer of Genesis leaves those gaps in place.

In this is to be found a great lesson. What if we found great detail about Enoch's life? We discovered that Enoch began each prayer with a particular phrase and we knew that he went for a walk in the field at a certain time every day? What if the writer had told us that he said a certain ritual prayer each day at mealtime, and fasted on the third day of each week. How would we respond? Would we not want to do the same thing? Each activity of Enoch would become a necessity. In fact, there would be rules laid out requiring a true walk with God to rigidly follow the same pattern that Enoch followed. Ultimately, God would be unimportant. The only thing that mattered would be 'keeping the rules.' It is a good thing that the writer tells us nothing about Enoch's pattern. However, by not giving details, he does state one thing very clearly: A walk with God is not about knowing the rules.

Every time human beings try to define God in terms of rules, we become silly and cruel. When Enoch walked with God, there was no law except that one could not harm Cain (Genesis 4:15). A set of laws would later be given to Israel to bring order to their society, and to govern human relationships, and guide the nature of worship. When the nation tried to equate the keeping of their set of laws as the earmark of having a walk with God, the result was seen in the scribes and Pharisees. Jesus said of them '...ye shut up the kingdom of heaven against men: for ye neither go in yourselves, neither suffer ye them that are entering to go in' (Matthew 23:13). The rules actually become a stumbling block to a walk with God.

Remembering that Enoch walked with God prior to the 'set of laws,' we can infer that Enoch sought to know God. His desire was to be God's friend in a loving relationship. The cultivation of friendship only requires one law, love. Everything else comes naturally.

> Jesus said the greatest commandment is '...Thou shalt love the Lord thy God...' (Matthew 22:37). This is a good place to begin learning what a walk with God is like. We should pray that God would teach us all the nuances of love and how to apply them when it comes to our love for him.

Carrying a spiritual burden

As the genealogical recitation of chapter five comes to an end, the reader encounters the name of the man who lived longest on the earth, Methuselah. One should not attach any special significance to the age as his life span is only seven years longer than his grandfather Jared (5:20). A careful check of the chronology has led to the belief that Methuselah died just prior to the coming of the flood recorded in chapter seven. It is believed in some quarters that the name, Methuselah, represents a prophecy given to Enoch of the coming destruction of the earth. It is that prophecy which prompted Enoch's walk with God. It is difficult to make an emphatic case as there is no certainty about the meaning of the name, Methuselah. However, in the words of Methuselah's son, Lamech, there is indication that this family carried a heavy spiritual burden. 'And Lamech lived an hundred eighty and two years, and begat a son: and he called his name Noah, saying, This same shall comfort us concerning our work and toil of our hands, because of the ground which the Lord hath cursed' (5:28-29).

If Enoch had been given a revelation of the impending judgement of God, he had certainly passed his understanding to his son, and thus to his grandson. Lamech's words could be a reflection of two things. The first is his belief in the coming judgement of God. The second is his yearning for the redemption promised in Genesis 3:15 via the seed of the woman. Through Noah, Lamech is making a statement of faith in God. Either he sees in Noah the hope for continuing the human race after the judgement of God, or he is keeping alive the promise of ending the curse that the seed of the woman offers. In the latter sense, Lamech is a preacher of the message of God. In the former, he is expressing confidence that God will not destroy humanity until his redemptive plan is enacted. In either sense, Lamech is rewarded with a faithful and righteous son in Noah. '...Noah was a just man and perfect in his generations, and Noah walked with God' (Genesis 6:9).

Noah was the same kind of individual as his great grandfather, Enoch. Only of these two is it said that he 'walked with God.' The meditative moment for the reader lies in understanding the conditions of the world in which Enoch, Methuselah, Lamech, and Noah lived. They were one small family trying to keep alive the worship and the name of the creator-God. Except for themselves, they were failures. Nevertheless, God comforted them and used them as spokesmen for his name.

Arthur W. Pink, *Gleanings in Genesis*, suggests that the name, Methuselah signifies 'when he is dead, it shall be sent...' (p. 78). This implies a revelation given to Enoch, that when Methuselah dies God will deal with the world in judgement.

Two Lamechs

Before one continues a look at the teaching of Genesis, an interesting parallel is presented that bears some meditation. Every line and word of the Bible is presented for edification, and the parallel that is seen here is proof of the value of thorough examination of the Bible. Two genealogical lists have been presented. The first was the genealogy of Cain, the ungodly son of Adam, and murderer of Abel. The second was the genealogy of Seth, second brother of Cain, and the third son of Adam. Seth's descendants are seen as preserving the teaching of God, and maintaining a purity of worship. Each genealogy ends with the sons of a person named Lamech. The Lamech of Cain's genealogy has two wives, and four sons. The Lamech of Seth's genealogy has several children but only one is named. The interesting parallel occurs in the fact that each Lamech is notable for the words he spoke.

The Lamech of Cain brags about a murder and emphasizes his own importance. '...I have slain a man to my wounding, and a young man to my hurt. If Cain shall be avenged sevenfold, truly Lamech seventy and sevenfold' (Genesis 4:23-24). Note that Lamech's words point to himself, express independence, and demand that others respect him because of the fierceness of his actions. When God is left out of one's life, self dominates. It is easy to see the destructiveness that comes to a culture when self dominates. When all are demanding respect above everyone else, no one gets respect, and chaos occurs.

The Lamech of Seth reflects a personal burden and emphasizes the importance of God. In naming his son, Noah, he said '...The same shall comfort us concerning our work and toil of our hands, because of the ground which the Lord hath cursed' (5:29). The second Lamech understood his lack of importance. He did not call for men to respect him, but spoke of the curse, which was the result of human sin. He was not independent, but looked for help from his God. He gave his son a name, and pronounced a hope in his birth, reflecting a father's intention to teach his son about God.

Of the first Lamech's sons, we read of their great inventions (Genesis 4:20-22). Of the second Lamech's son, we read, 'Noah walked with God' (Genesis 6:9). The inventors died in the flood. Noah lived. What is the writer of Genesis trying to convey?

Genesis 6:1-22

I. Evil Overcomes the World (6:1-7)
1. '…evil continually…'
2. '…sons of God…'
3. '…daughters of men…'
4. Giants
5. '…it repented the Lord…'

II. Noah Found Grace (6:8-13)
1. Noah walked with God
2. Corrupt
3. The end of all flesh
4. '…I will destroy them…'

III. The Making of an Ark (6:14-22)
1. Dimensions of the Ark
2. '…I will establish my covenant…'
3. '…two of every sort…'

Genesis 6:1-7

1. And it came to pass, when men began to multiply on the face of the earth, and daughters were born unto them, 2. That the sons of God saw the daughters of men that they were fair; and they took them wives of all which they chose. 3. And the Lord said, My spirit shall not always strive with man, for that he also is flesh: yet his days shall be an hundred and twenty years. 4. There were giants in the earth in those days; and also after that, when the sons of God came in unto the daughters of men, and

they bare children to them, the same became mighty men which were
of old, men of renown. 5. And God saw that the wickedness of man was
great in the earth, and that every imagination of the thoughts of his heart
was only evil continually. 6. And it repented the Lord that he had made
man on the earth, and it grieved him at his heart. 7. And the Lord said,
I will destroy man whom I have created from the face of the earth; both
man, and beast, and the creeping thing, and the fowls of the air; for it
repenteth me that I have made them.

'...evil continually...'

A student of Scripture will here encounter a description of terrible times. If one has been thoroughly involved in the story to this
point, the heart will beat more swiftly, and the tension will be felt
as God states: '...My spirit shall not always strive with man, for
that he also is flesh...' (6:3). Adam was told that he would die if
he ate the forbidden fruit. The sentence of death fell upon Adam
and upon all men because he sinned. God had given hope that
the sentence might be reversed by one he calls the 'seed of the
woman' (Genesis 3:15). However, the seed of the woman has not
appeared. Conditions on the earth are far worse than when Adam
sinned. After two thousand years, there are millions of people living on the earth, and they are all wicked as compared with only
two (Adam and Eve) when the first humans sinned. With all the
wickedness, will God abandon the promise?

It gets worse. 'And God saw that the wickedness of man was
great in the earth, and that every imagination of the thoughts of
his heart was only evil continually. And it repented the Lord that
he had made man on the earth...' (6:5-6). That which began with
a simple act of disobedience to God ends with this horrifying expression. God had promised redemption, but that was when one
might still hope that there is something in humans worth redeeming. God's words have ended that hope.

Before one can fully absorb the story of the flood, and its meaning, one must grasp the significance to be found in this description

of human wickedness. There is nothing in us worth redeeming. All mouths are stopped before God. As one looks deep into his own soul, he has a hard time with God's statement.

Nothing worth redeeming! Aren't there good deeds? Aren't there other people who think of me as worthwhile? God speaks. '…I will destroy man whom I have created…' (6:7). One doesn't see what God sees. The prophet says, 'The heart is deceitful above all things, and desperately wicked: who can know it' (Jeremiah 17:9)? We argue with that statement. 'Some hearts are that wicked.' we say, 'but not mine.'

Can we see the implications? Humans forget that it was only a sin of eating the forbidden fruit that created a heart capable of murder (see Cain, Genesis 4:8; Lamech, Genesis 4:23). Instead of understanding the potential of our heart, we argue with God about his statement. The subtlety of evil is far more frightening than anything we can understand, except by the revelation of God.

It is always difficult to understand human evil, especially when it must be applied personally. A glimpse at the sacrifice of The Incarnate One provides some help.

'…sons of God…'

The text presents a difficult picture. '…the sons of God saw the daughters of men that they were fair; and they took them wives of all which they chose' (6:2). The difficulty occurs in several ways. First, the term 'sons of God,' as used in this passage, is found elsewhere in Scripture, and clearly means 'angels' (Job 1:6, 2:1). In an interpretation that sees the understanding as angels, a very unique intermarriage of species is presented. However, this is problematic in the light of Jesus' words. '…they neither marry, nor are given in marriage, but are as the angels of God in heaven' (Matthew 22:30). Jesus implies that angels do not marry, thus would not be sexually oriented.

Second, the passage speaks only of sons of God marrying the daughters of men. There is no indication that there were women of God who married the sons of men. The perception one receives is that there is more than just the righteous (the line of Seth) marrying the unrighteous (the line of Cain). One would assume that intermarriage would involve male and female descendants of both lines. If angels are not meant, why would the passage be worded the way it is? However, if angels are meant, there is nothing in the context of Scripture (to this point) to give the reader any knowledge that there are beings called angels. They are not mentioned in the creation story.

Angels appear later in Genesis without any prior mention of their existence, but are clearly called 'angels' (Genesis 19:1). The appearance of the serpent in the temptation of Eve is an angelic being utilizing the serpent as an approach to humans. The being, however, is introduced through a creature whose origin is implied in the creation story. Thus, the immediate context gives us no reason for the assumption that the 'sons of God' are angels. In fact, the context strongly emphasizes the awfulness of human sin. Angelic beings choosing humans would make the sin a much stronger condemnation of angels than of humans. '...the Lord said, My spirit shall not always strive with man...' (6:3). Clearly, humans are the greater sinners in this context.

The story of the Bible is about the glory of God. It is impossible for humans to grasp the glory of God without full encounter with their own wickedness. To insert angels into this account of human depravity fails to recognize the depths to which humans can go in their own wickedness. Sin has its fruit in us. Angels cannot make us worse than we already are. That is the message upon which we must meditate.

In biblical interpretation we should be careful about any approach that may minimize human depravity. The only route to a regular lifestyle of dependence on God, and growing in faith to him is in full recognition of the total depravity of the human condition.

'...daughters of men...'

The 'sons of God' marry the 'daughters of men.' The clearest and most biblically consistent understanding of this passage is that the people mentioned in the genealogical lines of Seth and Cain have intermarried. Those of the line of Cain have no respect for God and have committed themselves to a carnal state, and to re-creating paradise according to their own understanding. Their understanding is recorded in the hideous words of Lamech. '...I have slain a man to my wounding, and a young man to my hurt' (Genesis 4:23). The attitude of total self-worship and self-absorption is to be contrasted with another Lamech who mourned the condition of this earth created by human sin. 'And Lamech...begat a son: And he called his name Noah, saying, This same shall comfort us concerning our work and toil of our hands, because of the ground which the Lord hath cursed' (Genesis 5:28-29). Intermarriage between the two lines meant that humans, which would be more attracted to the selfish and flesh-gratifying aspects of the first Lamech, would cease teaching children the ways of God.

Arguments have been made by some to present this intermarriage as between angels and men. There is an awkward phrase that would lead to that belief if not adequately explained. The reference to 'sons of God' and 'daughters of men' (6:2) leaves the appearance that only men from the line of Seth married women from the line of Cain, and that there was no sin in which the women of Seth married men of Cain. That would seem unlikely.

There are two answers one might posit. First, throughout the book of Genesis, it is the men who are the pursuers of wives, not the reverse. This is seen in the stories of Isaac and Jacob, and in other instances, such as the ill-fated attempt of the sons of Ham to attain wives of the daughters of Jacob (Genesis 34). Second, the total moral breakdown of humanity began with the compromise of the godly line. The fact that it was the sons of Seth who made the first approach to intermarriage is the probable meaning here. It is not an exclusive argument that the intermarriage was only between men of Seth and women of Cain, but that it started that way.

The second argument is consistent with the rest of Scripture. The people of God are constantly warned against taking wives from among those who are not followers of God (Ezra 9:1-3; 1 Corinthians 6:14). These marriages automatically create great difficulty in passing values on to children.

Giants

There are two references in verses three and four that are worth some reflection. God said, 'My spirit shall not always strive with man...' (6:3). 'There were giants in the earth in those days....' (6:4). The two statements are related.

First, the reader has been through a genealogical litany and told of the long lives of men (Chapter 5). The author evidently wanted the reader to note the lengthy life spans of these individuals. The writer now records a different perspective. God says of man '...his days shall be an hundred and twenty years' (6:3). The long life granted to the individuals of chapter five is because of the Spirit of God. Thus, as flesh, man's life span is totally in the purview of God's decision. It is the first clear statement that God will shorten the life span of humanity.

Second, the 'giants' of verse four provide a strange, new kind of insertion into the story. The mind is led to wonder and speculate at this point. The best approach with any difficult portion of Scripture is to meditate carefully on the context. In verse three, we have been told of a shortening life span providing a clear contrast with the long lives of chapter five. In verse four, the author gives another explanation that helps to identify these giants: '...the same became mighty men which were of old, men of renown' (6:4). It is likely that 'giants' and 'men of renown' are synonyms, representing the long-lived men of chapter five. The wording of verse four does not allow for the giants to have been the offspring of the intermarriage that is condemned in verse two. Note the giants (men of renown) were present before and after the sons of God married the daughters of men (6:4).

As one considers the issue carefully, there is more to giants than great size. Giants (in the meaning of the Hebrew) can also be people with greatness as in people of 'a great name.' This would be particularly enlightening in the context of those who were the obedient followers of God trying to keep the name of the Lord alive among the people of antiquity. The extra long lives given to the faithful children of Seth did not contribute to the repentance of humanity in spite of God's clear message. In verse three God specifies that humanity will not have the benefit of that kind of message from God anymore.

'...it repented the Lord...'

When one fully understands the extreme wickedness revealed in man, one cannot be shocked with the words of verse six. 'And it repented the Lord that he had made man on the earth, and it grieved him at his heart' (6:6). There is no way in which humanity has achieved or kept the standard that God had set for it in creation. Humans had been created in God's image, but now reflect the exact opposite of God's nature. The passion of God is stirred, which we can readily understand. Anger? Yes! Hurt? Yes! We can identify. Repentance! That is a different story.

Does one not need to sin or at least make an error in order to repent? Is the writer of Scripture implying that God made an error? Meditation on the context reveals clearly that it is not God who has changed, but man. It is human error that is the problem. God's repentance is a reflection of God's control. Humans had been living under the grace of God. One should again note that Cain was salvaged from the punishment of immediate death (Genesis 4:15) after murdering his brother. Long lives had been granted to the ancients in spite of their sin, but exceptionally long lives had been granted to the faithful of the godly line of Seth. By this, there was a constant reminder of the value of following God. The repentance of God reflects that God will take a different approach in dealing with his creation. Whereas Cain had been spared, God now states '...I will destroy man whom I have created...' (6:7).

The horror one feels at the sound of God's words is immediately calmed by the writer's words. 'But Noah found grace in the eyes of the Lord' (6:8). One should recall the words of Noah's father. 'And he called his name Noah, saying, This same shall comfort us concerning our work and toil of our hands, because of the ground which the Lord hath cursed' (Genesis 5:29). In a masterful stroke the writer provides an interesting literary twist. Noah has indeed brought comfort, both to man and to God. See the words in full context: '...for it repenteth me that I have made them. But Noah found grace in the eyes of the Lord' (6:7-8). Out of all the men of the earth, there is one who still prefers the paradise that only God can provide, to the fleshly kind of paradise that he might build for himself. Noah, though a sinner, longed for righteousness. This comforted the heart of God, and Noah was separated for salvation.

> Grace is one of those great theological truths that is beyond human comprehension. It is enlightening to consider the words spoken of the Incarnate Christ. '...we beheld his glory, the glory of the only begotten of the Father, full of grace and truth' (John 1:14).

Genesis 6:8-13

8. But Noah found grace in the eyes of the Lord. 9. These are the generations of Noah: Noah was a just man and perfect in his generations, and Noah walked with God. 10. And Noah begat three sons, Shem, Ham, and Japheth. 11. The earth also was corrupt before God, and the earth was filled with violence. 12. And God looked upon the earth, and, behold, it was corrupt; for all flesh had corrupted his way upon the earth. 13. And

God said unto Noah, The end of all flesh is come before me; for the earth is filled with violence through them; and, behold, I will destroy them with the earth.

'...Noah walked with God...'

The description of Noah gives another insight into the mystery first seen in the life of Enoch. We are told that Noah, as Enoch, 'walked with God' (6:9). As with Enoch there is no description of how Noah performed his walking with God. There is, however, a clue that helps the reader formulate some understanding of the nature of Noah's walk. 'And God looked upon the earth, and, behold, it was corrupt; for all flesh had corrupted his way upon the earth' (6:12). Noah, who 'found grace in the eyes of the Lord' (6:8), conducted his life in a way that did not corrupt the way of God. Thus, a 'walk with God' involves the absence of corrupting God's way.

Corruption is the act of perversion. It is to redefine virtue in a way that is pleasing to self. It is to make the decisions of life based on a narrow way. That is, to ask, 'what is best for me?' Corruption asks this question without thought for the consequences of decisions on a larger stage than self. It is to be without thought for consequences on others, or for consequences in terms of precedent set, or for the impact on culture and rule. The way of God is to be able to think beyond self, which can only happen in an attitude of submission to God.

One should look carefully at the conditions of the earth: '...the earth was filled with violence' (6:11). It should not require great intelligence to understand that a civilization of each person acting in terms of 'what is best for me' will create violence. When two people meet, acting out of a self-centred foundation, the only outcome possible is collision.

In such conditions, how are problems solved? Humans love to talk about compromise. Each person should learn to accept only part of that which he wants. The only problem is that an attitude which thinks of right and wrong in terms of 'what's best for me' feels wronged in any compromise. Until one comes to a position of surrender to God he is likely to face all of life in terms of being wronged. Of course, it is only in surrender to God, and laying claim to him that one will never feel wronged. Interestingly, in the possession of God, there is no need for compromising and accepting only a part of him. He is fully available to everyone.

Jesus expressed the concept of surrender to God in this way. '...Whosoever will come after me, let him deny himself, and take up his cross, and follow me' (Mark 8:34).

Corrupt

The ancient prophet, Isaiah, speaks profound words. As the voice of God to men, he states, 'For as the heavens are higher than the earth, so are my ways higher than your ways, and my thoughts than your thoughts' (Isaiah 55:9). Isaiah's statement is dramatically illustrated in the verses of our meditation. The notion of corruption is the notion of destruction. Humans were living long lives, were actively involved in pleasing themselves, and from their perspective, were advancing the quality of life on the earth (see the inventions and developments of Genesis 4:19-22). To say 'flesh is destroyed' would not be the human perception.

God's view was very different. The wonderful opportunity for which humans existed was to have intimacy with God. They are, instead, living independent of God and enjoying it. An observer of human motivation knows that humans evaluate quality of life in the concept of enjoyment. If one is enjoying self, life is fulfilled. Yet, God looks on man's enjoyment and says of him, 'life is destroyed.' In the light of verse eleven, one might wonder if there was enjoyment in the earth. The verse states '...the earth was filled with violence....' How can humans be enjoying life? One only needs to examine modern culture. The constant news of violence and man's inhumanity to man is met with angry outcries, but not sober repentance. Humans are determined to enjoy themselves despite the violence. In fact, any message that calls for sobriety and repentance is met with ferocity in the culture. 'Who are you to tell me what to do?' the general culture responds. Certainly, life is getting better. We are making great strides in technology, travel, entertainment, and communication. We are getting closer and closer to creating paradise on earth. Shall we say, 'we are re-creating the Garden of Eden?'

As God looks, the view is very different. Human thought is only for self. There is little or no hunger for God. We are swiftly rushing toward our own destruction. Jesus' words come to mind. 'But as the days of Noe were, so shall also the coming of the Son of man be' (Matthew 24:37). Humans say, 'life is in the enjoyment of life.' God says, 'life is in the enjoyment of God.' The humans that God was about to destroy had already destroyed life.

> Seeking enjoyment as the meaning of life is one of the mis-understandings about life that makes humans so prone to sin. A better approach is provided by the Apostle Paul. '...I count all things but loss for the excellency of the knowledge of Christ Jesus my Lord' (Philippians 3:8).

'...The end of all flesh...'

The phrase, 'These are the generations of' will be frequently used in Genesis, and usually signals a brand new start in God's dealings with humanity. As everything unfolds, it is clear that God's work is not by a reaction he exercises but is a thorough plan carried out in great wisdom. From the utterance of God's promise in Genesis 3:15 through his dealings with the generations of Abraham, God is never taken by surprise, but carefully orchestrates the affairs of humans. These humans act independently of him while he moves them toward his redemptive purpose. The skilled literary artist of Genesis has created great mystery and plot with the majestic aura of suspense as God's plan works in apposition to human rebellion. At every turn, redemption seems impossible, and humanity lost, but God brings a surprise.

The corruption of human flesh has come to completion, but one man continues to 'walk with God'. He desires to know God even if the rest of humanity is in total rebellion. The clear meaning for the reader is that God will restart the human engine through one family. There are three sons of Noah who will repopulate the earth (6:10). The significance in biblical history is that the line of humans descended from Cain, and from all other of Adam's sons, except for Seth, shall be forever eliminated from the earth. Only Seth's line (through Noah) will survive. Other changes will come which God shall define for Noah after his judgement is complete.

The reader is encouraged on at least two fronts. First, God is in control. One of the wonderful aspects of judgement, in spite of its frightening quotient, is the aspect of control. Clearly, the condition of humanity is at a hopeless state. There is no stopping the force of its sinfulness. More frightening than judgement is the sense that things are spinning out of control, with no one to stop it. God steps in. He can stop it! That is very encouraging.

Second, God can create a new beginning. One family will be spared God's judgement. That is all God needs to keep alive the hope of Genesis 3:15. The sad commentary that multitudes will die is tempered by looking through God's eyes. They have already died morally, and are vessels fit only for destruction. Turning to their own devices, they became totally immoral creatures unable to even think 'good' (6:5). With only one good man left, all others must die before he dies, lest the judgement happen without hope for the new beginning.

'...I will destroy them...'

God begins giving instruction to Noah with these words. '...The end of all flesh is come before me...' (6:13). 'End' carries a very sobering note for humans. It has the idea of extremity. Flesh has reached its natural extreme. It has arrived at the place to which all flesh ultimately comes when left to its own devices. There is only one cure. God says '...I will destroy them with the earth' (6:13). Humanity (except for Noah) is beyond redemption.

It is appropriate to reflect on a New Testament concept at this point. Jesus spoke to the Pharisees about an awesome situation. 'Wherefore I say unto you, All manner of sin and blasphemy shall be forgiven unto men: but the blasphemy against the Holy Ghost shall not be forgiven unto men' (Matthew 12:31). In the Old and in the New Testament, there is a point at which humans arrive where sin cannot be forgiven. It can only be judged. Jesus refers to that point as the blasphemy of the Holy Spirit. There is much speculation on the nature of the blasphemy of the Holy Spirit. The account of the flood and its judgement provides a clue.

As God looked upon men he noted, '...every imagination of the thoughts of his heart was only evil continually' (6:5). When Jesus spoke to the Pharisees, he spoke to people who looked at the good works of Jesus (casting out demons), and pronounced those good works as being from the devil. They saw that which was good, and called it evil. Sin, in the human heart, will ultimately reach a point that is incapable of discernment of good. It is the condition God describes in the humanity of Noah's day.

When the reader of Genesis looks at today's western world, the awesome spectre of the 'end of all flesh....' considered in the light of the unpardonable sin should give great concern: Could one be watching all discernment of morality disintegrate? Is moral relativism replacing clear rules of conduct? Is ethical behaviour becoming merely a scientific debate, and the product of political squabbling?

The question rises 'can a culture commit the unpardonable sin?' With that question, the words of God are sobering, '...The end of all flesh is come before me...' (6:13). Where are the people, like Noah, who will find grace in the eyes of God?

Genesis 6:14-22

14. Make thee an ark of gopher wood; rooms shalt thou make in the ark, and shalt pitch it within and without with pitch. 15. And this is the fashion which thou shalt make it of: The length of the ark shall be three hundred cubits, the breadth of it fifty cubits, and the height of it thirty cubits. 16. A window shalt thou make to the ark, and in a cubit shalt thou finish it above; and the door of the ark shalt thou set in the side thereof; with lower, second, and third stories shalt thou make it. 17. And, behold, I, even I, do bring a flood of waters upon the earth, to destroy all flesh, wherein is the breath of life, from under heaven; and every thing that is in the earth shall die. 18. But with thee will I establish my covenant; and thou shalt come into the ark, thou, and thy sons, and thy wife, and thy sons' wives with thee. 19. And of every living thing of all flesh, two of every sort shalt thou bring into the ark, to keep them alive with thee; they shall be male and female. 20. Of fowls after their kind, and of cattle after their kind, of every creeping thing of the earth after his kind, two of every sort shall come unto thee, to keep them alive. 21. And take thou unto thee of all food that is eaten, and thou shalt gather it to thee; and it shall be for food for thee, and for them. 22. Thus did Noah; according to all that God commanded him, so did he.

Dimensions of the ark

God's plan is to spare Noah and family from the destruction he is to unleash on the earth. 'Make thee an ark of gopher wood....' (6:14). God establishes the dimensions and notes the things necessary to assure the full safety and protection of the ark. Air and light shall be available through a window (hole) that shall go around the top of the ark. The window would be about 18 inches (l cubit) deep. The size of the ark is extremely unusual for wooden vessels. It is important to remember that its purpose was for housing, not for travelling. The ark would be the abode of Noah, his family, and the animals, which he places on it, for one full year.

The meditative moment for the reader lies in the command of God. The assignment placed before Noah is an awesome one. The writer does not tell us of Noah's expertise in construction. It is unknown if Noah knew how to do the thing that God commanded him in the moment of God's command. It is not unusual for God to lead one into extraordinary things for which he feels inadequate. Certainly, Moses was a clear example of a human protesting God's command. 'And Moses said unto the Lord, O my Lord, I am not eloquent, neither heretofore, nor since thou has spoken unto thy servant: but I am slow of speech, and of a slow tongue' (Exodus 4:10). Noah's predicament did not allow for much protest. If he did not know how to build an ark, he better learn how, or he will be destroyed with the rest of the earth's population.

For the next one hundred and twenty years, Noah will be involved in building a huge, floating house in which he shall live one year. It is a breath-taking concept. Did Noah recruit others to help him? Did he hire workers? The reader is not given such detail but one thing stands out in the narrative. 'Thus did Noah; according to all that God commanded him, so did he' (6:22). In effect, the only important issue is, 'would Noah take the Word of God seriously, and begin to implement the plan?'

The reader will note that God gave the blueprint (6:14-16). When God asks the extraordinary of an individual, He will give the blueprint. Christians are sometimes prone to dream extraordinary dreams, and wonder if it is of God. It can be, but if it is, remember, He will give the blueprint for accomplishment of the dream.

It is a common habit of Christians to talk of accomplishing great things for God. That may be a misnomer. We are not called upon too accomplish great things, only to be obedient. The greatness is determined only by the size of God's instruction to us. The great accomplishment is his. Remember, he holds, and provides, the blueprint.

'...I will establish my covenant...'

By ancient standards, the house (ark) which Noah built was huge. Even in the modern era, wooden vessels would still be much smaller. When measured against the modern steel constructed ships, it would not seem as large, but this does not diminish the massiveness of Noah's task. Several things could have contributed to a negative reaction by Noah, had he decided to disobey God. The enormity of the task set beside the fact that he had the only family on earth that still worshipped God would obviously create ridicule. He would have to endure the ridicule of others and continue with the task. He could simply be overwhelmed, and give up, noting the difficulty of proceeding. He, also, was taking a chance on God's word. Would God deliver once the house is built, or would Noah be a fool?

To show that God knew the difficulty, in which he was placing Noah, he offers a comforting word. 'But with thee will I establish my covenant; and thou shalt come into the ark, thou, and thy sons, and thy wife, and thy sons' wives with thee' (6:18). The word, 'covenant,' is introduced in this text. It is spoken in a way which directs attention to that which has already transpired. What is the covenant which God will establish (reaffirm) through Noah? The reader's attention is drawn back to Genesis 3:15 where God made a promise. 'And I will put enmity between thee and the woman, and between thy seed and her seed; it shall bruise thy head, and thou shalt bruise his heel.'

The comfort that Noah receives from God is the simple reminder that he has not forgotten, nor abandoned, his promise to Eve. It will be an awesome and nearly unbearable strain for Noah to observe God's judgement. Imagine the intensity of the moment when he steps out of the special house, built to sustain his family through the flood, to feel the impact that his family is the only family left upon the earth. The judgement he lived through was made necessary by human sin. Certainly, he wondered, 'Can the sin-nature of man be reversed? Will it happen again?' By the mention of the 'covenant,' God tells Noah, 'Yes, it can be reversed. I know how to reverse it. I have a plan, and I will fulfil it, through your family.' Except for being alive, the new start after the flood leaves much about which Noah could grieve. Thank God for his comforting Word.

'...two of every sort...'

Many Bible readers have great trouble with the animals in the flood story. How could Noah have found all the land animals in the whole earth much less have housed and fed them for a year? It is a foolish exercise to try and explain this phenomenon outside a super-natural mechanism. Yet, there are certain native elements of the natural world that would render the flood narrative as being possible. The reader is not told how much hibernation (winter sleep), and aestivation (escape from summer heat and draught) may have been involved in the animals' stay on the ark. Also, the narrative does not demand that animals of every species be taken onto the ark, but only those animals being representative, or 'after their kind' (6:20). Zoology has demonstrated the amazing diversification of animal species within the framework of the basic Genesis 'kinds.' Thus, it is reasonable to assume that the animal kingdom, as presently constituted, would not require the presence of millions of animals on the ark. Considering that very young animals would fulfil the requirement, the ark was of sufficient size to handle the few thousand 'after its kind' animals which would have been required.

Additionally, climatic conditions of the earth were radically different in its pre-flood era. It is likely that Noah had access to all the 'kinds' within the smaller geographic area of his own habitat in the world.

The meditative moment for the reader lies in the sovereign control of God, and his ability to bring final judgement and to start over in the same action. The beginning of the animal kingdom is reported in Genesis 1. 'And God said, Let the earth bring forth the living creature after his kind, cattle, and creeping thing, and beast of the earth after his kind: and it was so. And God made the beast of the earth after his kind, and cattle after their kind, and everything that creepeth upon the earth after his kind: and God saw that it was good' (Genesis 1:24-25). Doubtless, there were many species within the various kinds that had been developed in the two thousand years since creation. Many of these would be destroyed by the flood and become extinct. The 'kinds' taken onto the ark will face differing climatic conditions when the judgement of God is completed. Because of the new climatic conditions, humans will face a different relationship with the animal kingdom, perhaps being more vulnerable to them and more dependent on them for survival. The new species will accommodate the new situation (both human need and climatic survival). God's original creation remains intact, but a new beginning will be established. Could this explain the extinction of the dinosaurs?

> It is a common human mistake to look at phenomenal stories in the Bible and rule them as fable because the situation does not fit our understanding of reality. The story of Noah demonstrates how a little common sense and understanding of God's plan destroys that kind of human reasoning. When God created, he made possible any and all phenomena that he would require of men.

Genesis 7:1-24

I. The Command to Enter the Ark (7:1-9, 13-16)
1. Planning ahead
2. Two by two

II. The Flood arrives (7:10-12, 17-24)
1. Destruction
2. Fountains broken up
3. Eyes on the ark

Genesis 7:1-9, 13-16

1. And the Lord said unto Noah, Come thou and all thy house into the ark; for thee have I seen righteous before me in this generation. 2. Of every clean beast thou shalt take to thee by sevens, the male and his female: and of beasts that are not clean by two, the male and his female. 3. Of fowls also of the air by sevens, the male and the female; to keep seed alive upon the face of all the earth. 4. For yet seven days, and I will cause it to rain upon the earth forty days and forty nights; and every living substance that I have made will I destroy from off the face of the earth. And Noah did according unto all that the Lord commanded him. 6. And Noah was six hundred years old when the flood of waters was upon the earth. 7. And Noah went in, and his sons, and his wife, and his sons' wives with him, into the ark, because of the waters of the flood. 8. Of clean beasts, and of beasts that are not clean, and of fowls, and of every thing that creepeth upon the earth, 9. There went in two and two unto Noah into the ark, the male and the female, as God had commanded Noah. 13. In the selfsame day entered Noah, and Shem, and Ham, and Japheth, the sons of Noah, and Noah's wife, and the three wives of his sons with them, into the ark;

14. They, and every beast after his kind, and all the cattle after their kind, and every creeping thing that creepeth upon the earth after his kind, and every fowl after his kind, every bird of every sort. 15. And they went in unto Noah into the ark, two and two of all flesh, wherein is the breath of life. 16. And they that went in, went in male and female of all flesh, as God had commanded him: and the Lord shut him in.

Planning ahead

The day for entering the ark finally arrived. A new facet of the story appears in God's directive to Noah. 'Of every clean beast thou shalt take to thee by sevens, the male and his female: and of beasts that are not clean by two, the male and his female. Of fowls also of the air by sevens, the male and the female; to keep seed alive upon the face of all the earth' (7:2-3). The reader will note that clean animals were taken aboard by sevens rather than by twos.

A little meditation manifests the wonderful difference in the biblical narrative of the flood and mythological flood stories. Why are there seven clean animals? A clean animal is later revealed in Scripture as one suitable for eating, and for sacrifice (Leviticus 1:10, 14; Leviticus 11:2f). Clearly, God was planning ahead. When Noah's family abandons the ark a year later, they will encounter a vastly changed world. It will take time to plant, harvest, and to raise animals for eating purposes. With two of each animal, it will be necessary to leave them alive until mating and procreation occurs. What will the family eat until such time as adequate growing and procreating time has past? The extra animals of the clean variety will be a source of food when the year has ended. Also, the nature of worship to God has been by animal sacrifice.

The extra animal (number seven) which breaks the pattern of 'twos' shall be the animal of sacrificial worship (Genesis 8:20-22). It is in placing the two (eating and worship) together that we get a feel for God's planning. Human survival is dependent on maintaining the worship of God in the world. Through the 'sevens' of the clean animals, God manifests his loving care and concern for humans. He is thinking ahead! In the activity and the spectre of destruction under which Noah is operating, it would be extremely difficult to think beyond the moment. Noah must be careful to obey God fully. He must survive the flood, but he also must be able to survive after the flood. In God's command, He was making provision for the flesh, and for the spirit, after the flood is past. Thus, life can begin anew. When we obey God, we can have the confidence that God is thinking ahead.

> God turns the human mind toward the nature of sacrifice in worship. It is only in remission of sin through sacrifice that there is route to God. Each animal sacrifice in worship is connected to the promise of Genesis 3:15. The seed of the woman, the Incarnate Christ, shall solve the sin problem through the sacrifice of himself, and the shedding of his own blood. 'Neither by the blood of goats and calves, but by his own blood he entered in once into the holy place, having obtained eternal redemption for us (Hebrews 9:12).

Two by two

This passage is one to inspire meditation. It is phenomenally and clearly laid out. The notable concepts that strike the reader lie in the author's repetitiveness. Twice he recounts the activity of the processional into the ark (7:7-10, 13-16). Twice he mentions that Noah was six hundred years old when he enters the ark (7:6, 11). Twice he refers to a period of seven days that it took to complete the processional (7:4, 10). Three times the reader is told the rain lasted forty days (7:4, 12, 17). Within the framework of the author's repetitiveness, the reader will note the command of God was mentioned once, and the obedience of Noah was repeated twice.

The reader is invited to meticulously follow the processional into the ark. 'There went in two and two unto Noah into the ark, the male and the female, as God had commanded Noah...And they that went in, went in male and female of all flesh, as God had commanded him: and the Lord shut him in' (7:9, 16). The Bible does not waste words. There is great method to what appears as writer redundancy. For one hundred and twenty years Noah has been building this great house. He arrives at the dreadful moment. It is also the moment of his salvation. It is at the invitation of God that the processional begins. '...come thou and all thy house into the ark....' (7:1). It is as if the writer is taking the extra time to allow us to observe the salvation of the Lord.

There is great biblical stress on this very issue. It is generally believed that Moses penned the first five books of the Bible as we have them in present form. The same author records the following words when standing at the Red Sea with the Egyptian army closing behind him. 'And Moses said unto the people, Fear yet not, stand still, and see the salvation of the Lord, which he will shew to you today...' (Exodus 14:13). The people of Israel, as well as the reader, are called upon to gaze intently on the Lord's salvation.

As Noah, the animals, and Noah's family entered the ark, one can only be amazed at the spectacle. It is one long and glorious parade. The people of the world looked. They were probably amazed. Man stood watching and wondering, not knowing that they were seeing a divine work of salvation in progress. The biblical student's mind, as he places himself in the mind of the observer of Noah's day, remembers another Scripture. 'How shall we escape if we neglect so great salvation...' (Hebrews 2:3)?

> Peter contrasts the salvation afforded Noah and his family with the salvation afforded all who trust in Christ. 'Which sometimes were disobedient when once the longsuffering of God waited in the days of Noah, while the ark was a preparing, wherein few, that is, eight souls were saved by water. The like figure whereunto even baptism doth also now even save us (not the putting away of the filth of the flesh, but the answer of a good conscience toward God), by the resurrection of Jesus Christ' (Peter 3:20-21).

Genesis 7:10-12, 17-24

10. And it came to pass after seven days, that the waters of the flood were upon the earth. 11. In the six hundredth year of Noah's life, in the second month, the seventeenth day of the month, the same day were all the fountains of the great deep broken up, and the windows of heaven were opened. And the rain was upon the earth forty days and forty nights.

17. And the flood was forty days upon the earth; and the waters increased, and bare up the ark, and it was lift up above the earth. 18. And the waters prevailed, and were increased greatly upon the earth; and the ark went upon the face of the waters. 19. And the waters prevailed exceedingly upon the earth; and all the high hills, that were under the whole heaven, were covered. 20. Fifteen cubits upward did the waters prevail; and the mountains were covered. 21. And all flesh died that moved upon the earth, both of fowl, and of cattle, and of beast, and of every creeping thing that creepeth upon the earth, and every man: 22. All in whose nostrils was the breath of life, of all that was in the dry land, died. 23. And every living substance was destroyed which was upon the face of the ground, both man, and cattle, and the creeping things, and the fowl of the heaven; and they were destroyed from the earth: and Noah only remained alive, and they that were with him in the ark. 24. And the waters prevailed upon the earth an hundred and fifty days.

Destruction

Many commentators on the Bible love to speak of its mythological elements. Contrasts and comparisons are made with the phenomenal stories of other cultures. Biblical commentators often compare the biblical flood story to the Babylonian myth known as the Gilgamesh epic. A careful study reveals details in the biblical narrative not found in myth. In fact, it is those very details that set it apart. One of the most important parts of the biblical story lies in the reiteration of the age of Noah at the beginning of the flood. 'And Noah was six hundred years old when the flood of waters was upon the earth' (7:6). The inherent emphasis is, Noah was a real man who really lived. The writer continues the same theme.

He inserts details that are totally unnecessary unless the desire is to plant the flood squarely in human history. 'In the six hundredth year of Noah's life, in the second month, the seventeenth day of the month, the same day were all the foundations of the great deep broken up, and the windows of heaven were opened' (7:11).

The flood story is undoubtedly, a story of cosmic proportions. There is great difficulty in giving it a precise historical date. Outside the best attempts at explaining biblical chronology, there is no secular historical data to validate a specific historical moment. However, the way that precise timing of the years of Noah is woven into the story is consistent with biblical character. There is the careful note of specificity. The impact on the reader is the emphasis of a factual presentation. It is fact well known and clearly remembered.

It is here that the true meditative moment arrives. God commanded! Noah obeyed, and was saved. It happened! One must not be distracted by intense speculation on the many gory details. There is just enough detail to emphasize that it happened, and more than enough detail to know why it happened, and how the man and his family received salvation. Why would God do it? That is, why would he destroy the whole world?

In the last fifty years, humans have lived in what historians have dubbed the nuclear age. We are absorbed with our own inventions that might destroy the world. Make no mistake! If left alone by God, humans would destroy the world, if not literally, certainly morally, and there would be no means of survival. In Noah's day, God acted first, so that there was a means of survival for humans. A student of the Bible and of human nature will see the validity of the flood, and the necessity of it.

> Human reasoning often misses the grace that is pervasive in God's judgemental action. Humans were well on their way to destruction of themselves in Noah's day, but God acted first. It is of great comfort to note the ark was God's provision. It was built to God's specifications. The art foreshadows the salvation from sin found in Christ as the

only one to live in perfect conformity to God's specificity for humans. He could thus be the perfect sacrifice to remove God's judgement from all who trust in him. 'Forasmuch as ye know that ye were not redeemed with corruptible things...But with the previous blood of Christ, as of a lamb without blemish and with spot (1 Peter 1:18-19).

Fountains broken up

To fully understand the devastation of the flood, one must examine the geological implications recorded in the narrative. 'In the six hundredth year of Noah's life, in the second month, the seventeenth day of the month, the same day were all the fountains of the great deep broken up, and the windows of heaven were opened' (7:11). One should pay attention to the phrase 'fountains of the great deep'. Biblical scholars note that this has reference to underground waters. Rivers, oceans, and streams that are under ground are hurled violently upward. This process continues for 150 days or for five months (Genesis 8:2-3). As humans have told the flood story, the focus is generally on the forty days and nights of rain, but clearly it involves much more.

The 'windows of heaven' is the firmament of waters placed above the earth in the creation story (Genesis 1:6-8). The waters under the earth and the waters above the earth all come crashing together in one mighty crescendo. The change in the heavenly firmament will produce climate changes on the earth. The torrent of waters hurling upward from beneath the earth will produce dramatic changes in the earth's geological structure. Much of the water of the world's oceans and lakes is from the waters God originally placed in heaven? The new conditions demand a new understanding from humans. The rain that was so terrifying when it fell in a flood will now be regular and necessary for human survival. With the changes in geological structure, the dew that regularly watered the land (Genesis 2:6) will no longer occur. Human life span will decrease. God had already declared it (Genesis 6:3) and the changes in climatic conditions may be a factor in producing it. The rain, which likely had never occurred prior to the flood, will be depended upon in the future. The new process of recycling the waters of the earth through evaporation and condensation will replace the dew. Noah will have an entirely new set of earthly conditions with which he must wrestle. For meditative purposes, the reader may want to note the implications.

Obviously, there is a great deal of melancholy for all that was lost. The issue for the reader, however, becomes clear. When it is remembered that the human psyche is prone to be independent of God, and to attempt to rebuild Eden after his own human image, the new conditions are God's way of affixing greater dependence on him. Since he is the true source of life, the act, which causes humans to need a relationship with him, is a true act of grace.

> Can there be great hope, and a new sense of wonder, at the new kind of dependency the human family will face in the post flood earth? It is the most important lesson of life that dependency on God is the best and most secure place for the human.

Eyes on the ark

In rather striking fashion, the reader's attention is focused on: the house that Noah built, the long parade of animals as they are herded into the house, the statement and restatement of Noah's obedience, and the resulting salvation of his three sons and their wives. A vivid image of waters crashing down from the heavens, and hurling upward from subterranean levels is brought to the reader's attention. The mind's eye observes as Noah's ark rises with the waters. 'And the waters prevailed, and were increased greatly upon the earth; and the ark went upon the face of the waters' (7:18). The whole focus is on the salvation that God provides. For the moment, the reader has forgotten something. Suddenly, the narrative brings the reminder: 'And all flesh died that moved upon the earth...All in whose nostrils was the breath of life...died...And every living substance was destroyed...' (7:21- 23).

As the narrative scene is surveyed, several emotions are stirred. There is gratefulness that eyes were focused on the ark, and not on the awesome spectacle below. It would have been more awful than one's soul can absorb. One can only hope that the end of 'all flesh...upon the earth' came swiftly, and that their terror was short-lived. However, one wonders at the callousness of it all. It is stated as a matter of fact '...all flesh died....' One family lives and millions die, but all the attention is placed on the one family. Are the millions of lives so insignificant? What does this say about the God who inspired the writing of the narrative, and engineered the devastation? The answer is given in subtle form. '...and Noah only remained alive, and they that were with him in the ark.' (7:23).

The answer is simple. Focus on the one who was saved. The only way to truly understand God is to understand his salvation. It is not difficult to understand judgement, though one doesn't like it. Humans easily rush to judgement in our own affairs with others. To forgive, to provide salvation, is not so easy, and requires a great exercise of mind. It is in salvation, not in judgement, that one understands the significance of lives. What is there in Noah that helps us to understand? Reference must be made to the writer's tendency for redundancy. Note the repeated sentiment. Noah did 'all that God commanded him' (Genesis 6:22; 7:5, 9, 16). That says it all. The writer emphasizes, 'Do as God commands you, for only there is salvation found.' His salvation is as sure and certain as the ark in which Noah rode the flood.

> Just as the author wants all eyes focused on the life in the ark, not on the death in the flood, so the Scripture is a telling of God's redemption in Christ. There is death and destruction in the world. One cannot make sense of things with eyes focused there, but logic can rule again when eyes see the life to be found in the Incarnate One.

Genesis 8:1-22

I. A Summary of the Flood and its Aftermath (8:1-14)
1. God remembered Noah
2. Comfort of the wind
3. The decreasing waters
4. The birds
5. Mt Ararat

II. The Command to Leave the Ark (8:15-19)
1. Dry ground
2. Starting over

III. Facing the New Conditions (8:20-22)
1. A promise
2. Primacy of worship
3. Summer and winter

Genesis 8:1-14

1. And God remembered Noah, and every living thing, and all the cattle that was with him in the ark: and God made a wind to pass over the earth, and the waters asswaged; 2. The fountains also of the deep and the windows of heaven were stopped, and the rain from heaven was restrained; 3. And the waters returned from off the earth continually: and after the end of the hundred and fifty days the waters were abated. 4. And the ark rested in the seventh month, on the seventeenth day of the month, upon the mountains of Ararat. 5. And the waters decreased continually until the tenth month: in the tenth month, on the first day of the month, were the tops of the mountains seen. 6. And it came to pass at the end of forty days, that Noah opened the window of the ark which he had made: 7. And he sent forth a raven, which went forth to and fro, until the waters were dried up from off the earth. 8. Also he sent forth a dove from him, to see if the waters were abated from off the face of the ground; 9. But the dove found no rest for the sole of her foot, and she returned unto him into the ark, for the waters were on the face of the whole earth: then he put forth his hand, and took her, and pulled her in unto him into the ark. 10. And he stayed yet other seven days; and again he sent forth the dove out of the ark; 11. And the dove came in to him in the evening; and, lo, in her mouth was an olive leaf pluckt off: so Noah knew that the waters were abated from off the earth. 12. And he stayed yet other seven days; and sent forth the dove; which returned not again unto him any more. 13. And it came to pass in the six hundredth and first year, in the first month, the first day of the month, the waters were dried up from off the earth: and Noah removed the covering of the ark, and looked, and, behold, the face of the ground was dry. 14. And in the second month, on the seven and twentieth day of the month, was the earth dried.

'...God remembered Noah...'

Spend a moment thinking about the meditations of Noah upon the ark. His family is with him, but all else he had known on the earth is destroyed. Outside the ark, there is devastation. All human beings live with a private world known only to them. The private world is filled with thoughts, fantasies, and a personal understanding of reality. Reality for each person will include the people one knows, the buildings in the personal environment, and the conditions of nature in that environment. The person will build reality within the framework of familiar images. There will be some understanding of the proper people to seek when answers to questions are needed. For Noah, that private world is now gone. What will be the character of the new world? To whom can he go when he needs another creative mind to solve an agricultural or a construction problem? How will he calculate what to do with the new kind of earth he will face outside the ark? How long will he be on the ark? Most likely he is filled with a sense of stir-craziness on the ark, and anxiety to get off, and a dread of actually facing the new world.

When thoughts of that sort are added to the reality that the only word from God is the torrential rains, and the flood of waters upon the earth, Noah's anxiety must be phenomenal. Certainly, there was enough activity in caring for the animals to keep Noah busy and keep his mind off his concerns to some degree. Yet, the anxiety had to be there. God had destroyed the population of the world. Noah's family was unharmed but would that be the end of it? Would God abandon Noah and force him to fend for himself?

There are moments in the life of every believer (sometimes extremely long periods) in which these kinds of questions come to mind. Has God forgotten me? I have my tasks to do, but it is the same thing day after day, and all I seem to be doing is staying afloat. The writer must have had Noah's anxiety in mind when he says, 'And God remembered Noah...' (8:1). He is not indicating that God had temporarily forgotten. The Hebrew word 'remember' carries the context of God's continuing action. The word is a tender expression showing a movement on God's part toward a certain future. Noah need not worry for he had God's undivided attention. It wasn't much, but the writer says, 'God made a wind to pass over the earth...' (8:1). It is creative action all over again (see Genesis 1:2). Noah! Relax! The wind is blowing.

> Has God forgotten me? Every Christian knows what it is to struggle with that question. The reminder for Noah that God had not forgotten was small, but if he knew the story of creation, he would have seen God's reassurance in the wind.

Comfort of the wind

As one ponders the thought of a wind passing over the waters upon the earth, one should be reminded that the author of these words is Moses, author of Genesis through Deuteronomy. The 'wind' appears in other places. In the Hebrew, 'wind' and 'spirit' are the same word. In Genesis 1:2, the word is translated into English as 'spirit'. '...And the Spirit of God moved upon the face of the waters.' The context indicates whether spirit, or wind, is the best translation. The intent of Moses rests in the reality of God's action. 'Wind' can also refer to 'breath' as in exhaling. The wind is the result of God's exhalation.

In another passage in which Moses depicts the action of God, we see a similar kind of statement. 'And Moses stretched out his hand over the sea; and the Lord caused the sea to go back by a strong east wind all that night, and made the sea dry land...' (Exodus 14:21). In the flood narrative, the creation account, and the Red Sea story, waters depart for the appearance of dry land. The direction this image provides for meditation is a comforting and special moment. There are two notes of emphasis that one might ponder.

First, consider that waters are made dry. It has to be a warm wind blowing over the face of the waters. The action is powerful, but warm wind on the waters produces a refreshing and invigorating breeze. One is seeing something wonderful, but is also enjoying the refreshing feel of God's breath. It is a special comfort, and an awesome one. Such power has the image of the gentle summer breeze blowing off the ocean. It is the simple wind but something supernatural is occurring.

Second, the three stories are similar, but different. The 'wind' of the flood narrative takes five months to dry the earth. In the Genesis account, the dry land appears on the third day. The dry land at the Red Sea appears in the course of one night (Exodus 14:21). The result is always the same, but the timing is varied. Moses personally experienced the Red Sea, and writes of the other two events under the inspiration of God.

The striking thing is how the awful judgement of God is welded to the very comforting breath of God in the flood narrative and in the Red Sea event. The reader longs for the experience of the comforting breeze, but must remember that it is often accompanied by the surrounding judgement of God. We do not long for that. The reader must keep in mind that in God's timing, 'the wind will blow.'

> The most comforting word for the Christian is the promise of the return of The Incarnate One. Yet, the excitement and glorious anticipation of that event is that he returns in judgement. It is a hard lesson to learn, but the comforting breath of God in our lives is often felt in God's judgement of our sins.

The decreasing waters

The rains of the flood lasted forty days and forty nights. The upheaval of waters from the subterranean oceans appears from the scriptural language to have lasted for five months. 'And the waters prevailed upon the earth an hundred and fifty days' (Genesis 7:24). It is at the end of five months that God sends the wind to start settling the waters. The wind is a comforting factor for those on the ark signalling the activity of God. 'And God remembered Noah…and God made a wind to pass over the earth…' (8:1).

The drying breeze upon the waters would be welcome following the five months of torrential upheaval and storm. During the storm, those who rested in the ark had assurance of their own safety. The need following the storm is for assurance that God is still present, and will guide them in the future. The theme of being able to make it through the storms of our life is often used in literature. For the believer, the presence of God in the storm is usually symbolized in some fashion. It is that to which we cling. It may be the sympathetic voice of another person, or the strength of a church family, or to a simple personal faith in God.

It is a paradox that the most trying moments of our life can sometimes be the times after the storm. The fear of facing the normal struggles of the new situation, which the storm has wrought, is frightening. The faith, so real and powerful in the storm, does not carry the same kind of dynamic help after the storm. Where does one turn? For Noah, God provided the answer. He sent the wind.

One should remember that in the crashing waves, there was great comfort in seeing the lumber of the ark holding together. With no wave with which to be concerned, there is the fear that the ark which made them feel so safe could now be a tomb as they float forever (though gently) on top of the waters. Will there ever be dry land again? The wind begins to blow. It is drying up the waters.

Where might one look for the gentle breeze of God after the storms of life? For Noah, there was a continual procession of signs. The ark comes to rest on the mountain top (8:4), the waters continually decrease (8:5), the tops of mountains are seen (8:5), the raven finds no need to return to the ark, surviving outside (8:7). All of these signs are small tokens, but each give proof that the wind is at work. For the obedient believer, God will place the feel of his breath upon us. There will be the small signs (though not as dramatic as the ark that does not break) that the wind of God is at work. The believer must be alert to them.

> One should note that the reassuring things of God to Noah are not spectacular, but instead are within the realms of normality. Before we look for the spectacular for our reassurance, perhaps we should ask God to help us see his work in the normal things of our life.

The birds

When reading the flood story, many are stirred by the portrayal of the two birds, the raven and the dove. Much has been written about the typology represented, and the symbols to be found in the birds. There is little or no information in the rest of Scripture to inform about a symbolic significance to the birds. It is better to focus one's meditation on the story itself. There is a common feature within the account of the raven and the dove.

Clearly, the birds are sent out as a means of determining conditions outside the ark. It was a practice of ancient mariners to take birds on long sea voyages. When they were released, the direction of their flight would be a guide to the nearest place to find land. The raven and the dove were also meant for guidance for the ark's dwellers. Each had a specific nature suited for Noah's purposes. The raven (an unclean bird) can feed on the carcasses floating in the water, and will light on them and rest there while eating. '...he sent forth a raven, which went to and fro, until the waters were dried up from off the earth' (8:7). The narrative reports that the raven never re-enters the ark, but does land upon it when not feeding on the carcasses in the water. He will cease landing on the ark once there are other places of dry land or vegetation upon which he might perch. The raven thus provides a regular reading of conditions outside the ark.

The dove (a clean animal) will not light on anything that is not dry, and will return to the safety of the ark where he may be fed. 'But the dove found no rest for the sole of her foot, and she returned...unto the ark...' (8:9). The focus of the reader should be on the faithful acts of Noah, not upon the birds. The sending of the birds is a statement to Noah's family of his faith in God. The raven goes first because he will be a constant sign. His leaving and reappearing provide a regular encouragement to the nervous residents of the ark, and demonstrate the fact of Noah's faithful expectation. The dove represents finality. When she lights, there is dry land. The dove returns the second time with the olive branch indicating vegetation and growth in the new earth.

The writer's depiction of the time passing between each journey of the dove shows a patient Noah who calmly waits and believes God, but in the meantime, acts to encourage his family. The prophet states, '...they that wait upon the Lord shall renew their strength; they shall mount up with wings as eagles...' (Isaiah 40:31).

Certainly Noah must have had his own doubts and concerns as he waits on God to finish the work of the flood. Yet, he provides a great example to his family in his unwavering trust in God. His trust was not seen in bold acts or in great stirring speeches, but in simple acts of doing wise things in his circumstances.

Mt. Ararat

It is appropriate, as the flood ends, to reflect on the wisdom of God. The later narrative of Genesis will note the development and scattering of the generations of humans who shall descend from Noah. As the various people of the earth move from the place the ark rests and begin to populate the land, the geographic student will note that Mt Ararat is perfectly positioned for that purpose. It is at a central point of the ancient world sitting on a landline that extends from the southern tip of Africa to the Bering Straits of Siberia. This fact provides another moment providing a clear ring of truth to the Bible, and setting it apart from fable. As Noah's family gets off the ark, they will be ideally situated for their descendants to spread throughout the world.

One's meditation upon this fact will create great wonder at the magnificence of God's continual design. Imagine the devastating power of the flood, the seven months of the ark being moved about upon the floodwaters and coming to rest at the very centre of the landmass. The ring of truth is carried out in providing the name of the place, Mt. Ararat, without mention of its centrality. How could the ancient storyteller have known of its geographical centrality? God knew!

This understanding should provide a great deal of comfort to the believer in the struggle to make sense of life. As Noah leaves the ark, there are some things he will definitely know. He will know he is alive because God allowed him to be alive. He will remember the 120 years of labour to build the ark that protected him. He will know that he is in the centre of God's will when he leaves the ark. He will not know that he is perfectly centred on the earth's landmass for the re-population of the earth. He will not know that God will, with a future generation, bring a new kind of judgement (the confusion of human languages) which will force the geographical scattering of the population. God knew! The believer can look at the things of life that are known. There is the struggle to be obedient to God. There is the knowledge that obedience to God often leads through trial. There is knowledge that obedience to God carries the reward of being in God's will. There may not be any knowledge of a large plan of God, or the knowledge of being centrally located to guarantee the effectual work of God, or that a truly phenomenal thing has occurred, which may in life's struggle appear as simple coincidence. God knows!

> Simple coincidences in our life can often reveal a master planner. Such wonder should cause every believer to be vigilant in obedience to God's direction, so that the master plan may redound to our benefit instead of to our judgement.

Genesis 8:15-19

15. And God spake unto Noah, saying, 16. Go forth of the ark, thou, and thy wife, and thy sons, and thy sons' wives with thee. 17. Bring forth with thee every living thing that is with thee, of all flesh, both of fowl, and of cattle, and of every creeping thing that creepeth upon the earth; that they may breed abundantly in the earth, and be fruitful, and multiply upon the earth. 18. And Noah went forth, and his sons, and his wife, and his sons' wives with him: 19. Every beast, every creeping thing, and every fowl, and whatsoever creepeth upon the earth, after their kinds, went forth out of the ark.

Dry ground

After nearly eleven months on the ark, Noah and his family arrive at a fateful moment. The dove, being sent out a third time, does not return. The action of the dove is good.

After nearly eleven months on the ark, Noah and his family arrive at a fateful moment. The dove, being sent out a third time, does not return. The action of the dove is good news. The dove found a clean, dry place upon which to rest. The blowing wind has succeeded in bringing about the process of the waters receding. Noah makes a decision to remove part of the roof. 'And it came to pass in the six hundredth and first year, in the first month, the first day of the month, the waters were dried up from off the earth: and Noah removed the covering of the ark, and looked, and, behold, the face of the ground was dry' (8:13).

It is at this point in the narrative that a phenomenal thing happens. The reader should be careful that the phenomenon is not missed. After nearly one year, the family would be anxious to leave the ark. The ground is dry. One might think that Noah's reaction would be to immediately rush to the door and out onto the dry ground. Instead, the reader encounters this: 'And in the second month, on the seven and twentieth day of the month, was the earth dry. And God spake unto Noah, saying, Go forth of the ark, thou, and thy wife, and thy sons, and thy sons' wives with thee' (8:14-16).

One will note that it is fifty-seven days after Noah discovers the dry land before he attempts to leave the ark. Fifty-seven days! There are two possible scenarios that may apply to the human situation. First, there is the fear factor. It is a brand new world outside the ark. The familiarity of the ark does have its comfort. It is known. The new situation of a dry land that has been flooded for all this time is unknown. What will it mean to walk on land now? Will it be the same as before the Flood? The fear is helpful because it keeps them from acting hastily.

Second, the word from God had not yet come. The reader should recall a significant statement. 'And they that went in, went in male and female of all flesh, as God had commanded him: and the Lord shut him in' (Genesis 7:16). It was God who had closed the door to the ark. Noah must now be patient. If God closed it, it must be God who decides when it is to be opened. The open and closed door is an oft-used metaphor when the believer talks about discerning the Lord's will. It is very difficult to know how to discern the open or closed door. For Noah and his family, it may have been the simple fear of God that kept them from acting too soon.

Starting over

Starting over! Depending on the situation, these are words of great excitement and spirit, or they are words of despair and hopelessness. The start of a new football season presents the starting over for teams that did poorly the previous season. Spirit and enthusiasm are high, the past is forgotten. For the teams that did well, the new season is also filled with hope and spirit. The chance of adding to success of the past is a wonderful challenge. The past is easily forgotten, and the future is filled with opportunity. However, the family that looks at the ashes of a home that has burned thinks 'starting over,' and sees only the reliving of the hard times of the past. Starting over is not a fresh start. First, the ashes of the burned out home must be worked through. The resources to recoup what was lost may no longer be present. 'Starting over' are words that mean only loss, not new chances and opportunities. The past is not so easily forgotten.

As Noah and family disembark from the house in which they had lived for the past year, they face 'starting over'. What kind of 'starting over?' Will there be great energy and enthusiasm, or the reality that the world is not what it used to be? Their lives had been built around people. Though those people were not followers of God, there had to be many close acquaintances and friends lost in the flood, and for whom Noah's family grieves. The grief will only be intensified as Noah surveys the new post-flood earth, and considers how he is to survive.

The writer's depiction of the events carries an eerie similarity to the creation story. 'Bring forth with thee every living thing that is with thee, of all flesh, both of fowl, and of cattle, and of every creeping thing...that they may breed abundantly in the earth...' (8:17). The creation account reads, 'And God created...every living creature...and God blessed them, saying, Be fruitful, and multiply, and fill the waters in the seas, and let fowl multiply in the earth...And God made the beast of the earth after his kind, and cattle after their kind, and every thing that creepeth upon the earth after his kind: and God saw that it was good' (Genesis 1:21-25).

The big difference in the initial creation, and in Noah's situation is the earth's post-trauma condition. God had blessed the first people (Adam and Eve) with perfect conditions. Noah is 601 years old and starting over with less than perfect conditions. Can he look at it with enthusiasm as a new creation, or will he only mourn that which is lost?

A promise

Noah's offering to God is received by God as a smell of 'sweet savour' (8:21) Immediately, God reacts. '...I will not again curse the ground anymore for man's sake; for the imagination of man's heart is evil from his youth; neither will I again smite anymore every thing living, as I have done' (8:21). There are three parts of God's statement that provide ground for reflection. First, God promises that he will not 'curse the ground any more'. His reference is to the flood. Curse has the meaning of 'esteem lightly.' There will not be another situation in which God will devastate the land because of human sin. He will relate to men based on an acceptable sacrifice such as Noah brought. Individual sin will still be judged, but the earth will not be devastated, and the sacrifice provides a proper vehicle for depraved humans to approach God.

Second, God makes clear that it is human sin that caused the judgement of the flood. The fault was not in the creation of God. The flood did not occur because God had somehow messed things up when he initially hung the waters in the heavens. Humans should not be so foolish as to think that the sacrifice of Noah satisfies some insatiable appetite of God that was stirred because of the chaos of the flood. The Babylonian flood story has the gods feverishly eating the offerings as if starved for what the humans could provide them. The Genesis writer records a very different view of the sacrifice. It is a confession of human need, not a reflection of God's need.

Third, there will not be another 'starting over' for the human creation. The fresh start God gives to human creation through Noah will be carried to its ultimate conclusion. There will be no parts of the generations of Noah (as with the non-Seth generations of Adam), that shall be destroyed from earth. All of Noah's sons will have their part in the impending drama of human history. The hope of Genesis 3:15 is alive and well, and will not go through another test of worldwide devastation.

The thought for meditation lies in contrast and comparison. The world had just been devastated by flood. God now says a simple animal sacrifice shall be sufficient to hold back destruction. It sounds almost preposterous. That preposterous nature changes, however, when one understands that solution of the sin problem is even more devastating than the flood. 'So Christ was once offered to bear the sins of many...' (Hebrews 9:28). The value of the one life, 'Christ', is more than equal the value of all the lives in the world.

Primacy of worship

It is not unusual for humans when faced with trauma to turn to God. Generally, there is the sense of great need, and God is approached with the sense of a last hope, with nowhere else to turn. When Noah's family leaves the ark, a new kind of world confronts them. They have each other, but the way of life previously known will radically change. All will be facing a certain degree of the unknown. Consider their human instincts! In the light of normal human instincts, consider as well how they would understand their greatest need.

The family has survived within the safety of the ark for a full year. The floodwaters have receded, and they must now survive outside the ark. Human instinct would call 'survival' the greatest need. How would Noah approach his situation? The narrative states, 'And Noah builded an altar unto the Lord; and took of every clean beast, and of every clean fowl, and offered burnt offerings on the altar' (8:20). The first official act of Noah upon leaving the ark was an act of worship. This act is extremely significant. The reader should meditate beyond the simple picture of the animal sacrifice to the framework of human survival.

Clean animals were brought onto the ark in larger numbers than unclean animals (Genesis 7:2). The clean animals would be for sacrifice in worship and for food after leaving the ark. As Noah surveys his surroundings, he has family to feed (a wife, three sons and their wives), with knowledge that it will take time to plant and grow crops. Edible vegetation growing wild would be somewhat limited. The clean animals will be his major food supply. If survival is the greatest need, it would make sense to use the animals for food, and hold off the sacrifice until the other animals have procreated and the food supply is more abundant. Noah has a different perception. His greatest need is for God. Thus, it is better to give God his offering first, and allow God to take care of the survival issue.

In human trauma there is the cry for survival and the meeting of one's needs. God is normally approached out of that survival need rather than out of a need for God. Offerings to God are made as bribes to get God's focus on the survival. Noah's approach reminds us of why Noah first found grace in the eyes of God (Genesis 6:8). He worshipped God not because he needed to survive but because he needed God. How does the reader know? The writer reports God's response. 'And the Lord smelled a sweet savour...' (8:21).

The Incarnate One instructed men in the concept that Noah understood: '...If any man come after me, let him deny himself, and take up his cross and follow me' (Matthew 16:24).

Summer and winter

God, in response to Noah's offering, lays out the nature of the new earth Noah will be facing. He first promises that he will not destroy the earth because of human sin (8:21). Because '...man's heart is evil from his youth up...' (8:21), there must be a way to establish and keep a relationship with God. Noah's offering had reflected a desire on Noah's part for his relationship with God to continue. Noah's attitude is not typical of humans, who are more likely to flee from God and turn to evil. The new situation will require thorough teaching of and adherence to sacrificial worship to meet the demands of maintaining relationship with God.

Further, God calms the troubled minds of the ark's survivors. He prescribes a succession of times and seasons that shall never cease. It will be the responsibility of the humans to carefully plan and orchestrate the events of their lives around the times and seasons. The water that had been in the heavens prior to the flood, and had given the world a consistent climate is now in the seas. The world will see regular changes, 'cold and heat, and summer and winter' (8:22). The words of God explain the pattern so that the new situation will not cause the ark's survivors to panic. In addition, the struggle to survive in the changing climate will provide a needed challenge to humanity. The continuing evil imagination of his heart can be better put to use by the labour-intensive efforts of dealing with the earth's climatic conditions.

Interestingly, the seasons, when read correctly, are a story of God's grace and renewal. Mythological tales have projected this, and have seen in the springtime a rebirth of nature. Humans created fertility gods and goddesses and worshipped them as a part of the seasonal changes. Pagan worship has noticed a divine element to the changing seasons that the worshippers of the true God often miss. The dark and difficult days of winter are endured based on the promise of spring, and its renewal of life.

The new climatic changes told a story to Noah, and it is the same story for the reader. God acted in judgement on the earth, and devastated it because of human sin. Winter is the constant reminder that God is the owner of this earth, and holds judgement in his hand. The regular changes in the seasons remind us of God's commitment that the earth, as long as it remains populated with depraved humans, will never be destroyed again. Life on the earth will be difficult. Humans will have to use creative energy in survival, but can trust God that winter will never last forever. Spring and summer will come but must be fully used for seedtime and harvest. The seasons are a sure sign that God keeps his Word.

There are several things in nature that establish God's glory in the concept of the seasons. The animals are well aware of the need to store up for winter. There is a purpose for the seasons, specifically designed for man's work, and to keep him from sin.

Genesis 9:1-29

I The Shedding of Blood (9:1-6)
1. Subduing the animals
2. The sanctity of blood

II. The Noahic Covenant (9:7-17)
1. A life for a life
2. Rainbow

III. The Family Lineage (9:18-29)
1. The father of Canaan
2. Populating the earth
3. Noah's drunken state
4. The sin of Ham
5. The sons' defining
6. The curse of Canaan
7. Shem and Japheth
8. Noah dies

Genesis 9:1-6

1. And God blessed Noah and his sons, and said unto them, Be fruitful, and multiply, and replenish the earth. 2. And the fear of you and the dread of you shall be upon every beast of the earth, and upon every fowl of the air, upon all that moveth upon the earth, and upon all the fishes of the sea; into your hand are they delivered. 3. Every moving thing that liveth shall be meat for you; even as the green herb have I given you all things. 4. But flesh with the life thereof, which is the blood thereof, shall ye not eat. 5. And surely your blood of your lives will I require; at the hand of every beast will I require it, and at the hand of man; at the hand of every man's brother will I require the life of man. 6. Whoso sheddeth man's blood, by man shall his blood be shed: for in the image of God made he man.

Subduing the animals

God continues his message to Noah's family concerning the new post-flood conditions of the earth. There will be a new climate (Genesis 8:22). In addition, the relationship which humans have with animals shall take on a new dimension. 'And the fear of you and the dread of you shall be upon every beast of the earth, and upon every fowl of the air, upon all that moveth upon the earth, and upon all the fishes of the sea; into your hand are they delivered' (9:2).

The reader will note the addition of 'fear of you and dread of you' from the early relationship that humans had with animals. 'And out of the ground the Lord God formed every beast of the field, and every fowl of the air; and brought them unto Adam to see what he would call them: and whatsoever Adam called every living creature, that was the name thereof' (Genesis 2:19). There is no indication of any fear of Adam in the animal world. The prophet may have reference to this pristine relationship in his prophecy for the future. 'The wolf also shall dwell with the lamb, and the leopard shall lie down with the kid; and the calf and the young lion and the fatling together; and a little child shall lead them (Isaiah 11:6).

When sin entered the human race, the animal kingdom had to be sacrificed to provide clothing for humans, and to demonstrate the awfulness of sin, and provide the means of worship to God (Genesis 3:21). The relationship with animals took on an adversarial role. They must be sacrificed for the sake of humans. Subduing the animal kingdom took on a different perspective. The fear that shall be in the animal kingdom following the flood adds a whole new element to human relationship with animals. It will be more difficult then ever to subdue the animal kingdom. In fact, it is worth noting that God's command to Adam to 'subdue' the earth (Genesis 1:28) is absent from his statement to Noah. Does the new post-flood condition make the command impossible?

Is grace to be found? Consider the next statement of God. 'Every moving thing that liveth shall be meat for you...' (9:3). The words that aren't there are clearly implied: 'But you will have to hunt it and kill it.' In addition to the easily domesticated sheep and cattle, humans will have to search for food sources among the rest of the animal kingdom. The grace is to be found in the intensive labour situation. Just as the new climate will involve man's creativity and energy, so the new relationship with animals will require creativity and energy. It is all less time for humans to spend on the evil imagination of their heart.

The sanctity of blood

Noah has learned from God that the whole animal world shall be a basis of food for humans. Some scholars believe that animals had not been part of the food supply prior to the flood. Though there is a case to be made for that understanding, it is likely that the statement of God simply expands the food supply from the more domesticated sheep and cattle. The new situation will be necessary because of a much more difficult and unfriendly environment on the earth.

There are certain conditions that are outlined in the human use of animals for food. 'But flesh with the life thereof, which is the blood thereof, shall ye not eat' (9:4). Man shall not eat blood. This requirement has great theological significance. First, the blood is symbolic of life. When the sacrificial system of worship was declared through Moses, for Israel, the prophet stated 'For the life of the flesh is in the blood...' (Leviticus 17:11). The human was to understand the dynamic of taking life. It is true that animals must be part of the human food chain, but humans should never forget the reality of the taking of life. The sacrifice of the lesser creation (animal) for the greater creation (human) is there because of the greater creation's sin. To eat the blood would be a desecration, and would mean that humans were forgetting the reality of sin's consequences.

Second, the blood would play a major role in human worship. The blood is set apart as holy and will forever depict the reality of the innocent being sacrificed for the guilty. The rest of Leviticus 17:11 reads '...and I have given it (blood) to you upon the altar to make an atonement for your souls: for it is the blood that maketh an atonement for the soul.' Humans must not forget that innocent animals must be sacrificed for their survival, but an even greater principle is at work. The innocent will be sacrificed for the guilty as atonement for sin. It is in the shedding of blood, and the acknowledgement of the life-giving nature of the blood as set apart for God's use only, that humans will understand God's work. God is teaching that a greater than humans (an innocent one) will be sacrificed as atonement for sin. 'But Christ being come an high priest..., by a greater and more perfect tabernacle,...not...by the blood of goats and calves, but by his own blood he entered in once into the holy place, having obtained eternal redemption for us' (Hebrews 9:11-12). Humans were to see both the lesser innocent sacrificed for the greater guilty, and beyond, to the sacrifice of Christ, where the greater innocent shall be sacrificed for the lesser guilty.

> The blood atonement is the heart of the biblical story. It is an amazing truth at which the redeemed stand in awe, and the unredeemed stand in ridicule. It is impossible to grasp with an unredeemed mind. Even the redeemed need the entire revelation of the Bible to begin to plum the depth.

Genesis 9:7-17

7. And you, be ye fruitful, and multiply; bring forth abundantly in the earth, and multiply therein. 8. And God spake unto Noah, and to his sons with him, saying, 9. And I, behold, I establish my covenant with you, and with your seed after you; 10. And with every living creature that is with you, of the fowl, of the cattle, and of every beast of the earth with you; from all that go out of the ark, to every beast of the earth. 11. And I will establish my covenant with you, neither shall all flesh be cut off any more by the waters of a flood; neither shall there any more be a flood to destroy the earth. 12. And God said, This is the token of the covenant which I make between me and you and every living creature that is with you, for perpetual generations: 13. I do set my bow in the cloud, and it shall be for a token of a covenant between me and the earth. 14. And it shall come to pass, when I bring a cloud over the earth, that the bow shall be seen in the cloud: 15. And I will remember my covenant, which is between me and you and every living creature of all flesh; and the waters shall no more become a flood to destroy all flesh. 16. And the bow shall be in the cloud; and I will look upon it, that I may remember the everlasting covenant between God and every living creature of all flesh that is upon the earth. And God said unto Noah, This is the token of the covenant, which I have established between me and all flesh that is upon the earth. 17. And God said unto Noah, This is the token of the covenant, which I have established between me and all flesh that is upon the earth.

A life for a life

Prior to the flood God had not allowed humans to be involved in the judicial aspects of justice. The killer, Cain, had his life spared by God (Genesis 4:15). Further, there is no indication that any kind of judicial action was taken against the murdered Lamech (Genesis 4:23-24). In the conditions of human relationships on the post-flood earth, God establishes a new rule. 'Whoso sheddeth man's blood, by man shall his blood be shed: for in the image of God made he man' (9:6). It is appropriate to ask why the new rule is established.

The reader should give some meditative thought to the post-flood conditions of earth. Life will be more difficult and life spans will be shorter. Humans will need to give creative attention to survival and to worship. Without human government, the lawless will be a much graver threat to human survival. There is a time that must be utilized for planting and harvesting, not for constantly guarding against the lawbreaker (Genesis 8:22). With the shortened life spans, time must be dealt with imaginatively to insure that humans maximize quality of life. Humans cannot afford to have one who seeks to take life when life will be difficult enough.

Also, the pre-flood condition of earth had the constant reminder of the cherubim at the Garden of Eden. Their presence, though perhaps not visible to the ones who lived faraway would still be very frequently spoken of, and be a force in crime prevention. The reminder of God's presence through the cherubim will no longer be present. Humans will have to take on that role for themselves.

In addition, God is declaring a distinct difference in the killing of animals as a part of the food chain, and in the taking of human life. Even the beast that is caught killing humans must be slain. 'And surely your blood of your lives will I require; at the hand of every beast will I require it...' (9:5). The beast must not be allowed to develop the lust for human blood. It will be a desecration of God's created order. For humans, the problem is more complicated. The 'evil imagination' of man's heart (Genesis 6:5) could cause him to love the killing of animals, and lose the proper understanding of the value of life. The only way to protect from that kind of distorted thinking is for humans to establish and maintain clear laws that continuously, and without ambiguity, place a high premium on human life. In the world of humans, the only way the value of human life is clearly maintained is in the principle of a 'life for life' (Exodus 21:23). Human sin is truly amazing in the many distortions it creates in our life.

The new rules placed on humans after the flood reflect the depravity of the human heart. This knowledge only serves to make God's continuous movement toward redemption more amazing.

Rainbow

Having laid down the basic foundation of human government in the protection of, and the validation of human life (9:6), God proceeds with the renewal of blessing on Noah. For a second time, he states, '...be...fruitful...multiply; bring forth abundantly in the earth...' (9:7). See also 9:1. The repeat of the blessing has the note of comfort. God has established that conditions will be different. Humans will have to govern themselves, and be more creative in their task of survival, but God says, 'you can do it.' The blessing is a reaffirmation that God has given the survivors of the flood the mental power to properly deal with the new conditions of their life.

There is one comforting factor that is still needed. The new climatic conditions will see the watering of the earth occurring through evaporation of waters off the earth, the density forming in the clouds, and the precipitation that follows. It is going to rain!

The ark's survivors have only one experience with rain. It lasted forty days and nights, flooded the earth, and killed every bit of flesh on the earth except for those on the ark. Place yourself in their position. With the first cloud, and the first drop of rain, there will be terror. God understands and prepares their minds for the moment. 'And God said, This is the token of the covenant which I make between me and you...I do set my bow in the cloud, and it shall be for a token of a covenant...And it shall come to pass, when I bring a cloud over the earth, that the bow shall be seen in the cloud' (Genesis 9:12-14).

The rain can be accepted as a normal part of the new conditions on the earth. The rainbow, with its beauty accompanying the rain, will be a reminder of God's covenant. It is placed before the entire community of land-creatures as an unconditional promise.

The unconditional nature is critical because it will soon be clearly manifest that human nature will continue with its evil ways. There will be no comfort found in human action. To make a conditional bargain with humans is to guarantee failure.

The rainbow is more than a comfort. It is a reminder of God's control. It is not that God cannot destroy the earth, but that he will not. The rainbow is God's signature. It is a statement of his will. God's judgement will never again manifest itself in the form of the elimination of depraved humanity. Any judgement from this point on will be utilized in the inexorable movement of God toward his purpose of redemption. It sounds trite, but God is teaching Noah that sin will always be with humans until God's redemptive action removes it.

Genesis 9:18-29

18. And the sons of Noah, that went forth of the ark, were Shem, and Ham, and Japheth: and Ham is the father of Canaan. 19. These are the three sons of Noah: and of them was the whole earth overspread. 20. And Noah began to be an husbandman, and he planted a vineyard: 21. And he drank of the wine, and was drunken; and he was uncovered within his tent. 22. And Ham, the father of Canaan, saw the nakedness of his father, and told his two brethren without. 23. And Shem and Japheth took a garment, and laid it upon both their shoulders, and went backward, and covered the nakedness of their father; and their faces were backward, and they saw not their father's nakedness. 24. And Noah awoke from his wine, and knew what his younger son had done unto him. 25. And he said, Cursed be Canaan; a servant of servants shall he be unto his brethren. 26. And he said, Blessed be the Lord God of Shem; and Canaan shall be his servant. 27. God shall enlarge Japheth, and he shall dwell in the tents of Shem; and Canaan shall be his servant. 28. And Noah lived after the flood three hundred and fifty years. 29. And all the days of Noah were nine hundred and fifty years: and he died.

The father of Canaan

In very subtle fashion the writer connects the present (Noah and family) with the future. Throughout the writing of Genesis, there will be the recurrent theme of the father's blessing upon his sons. Noah's family will provide the start of this practice. The most compelling thing about Noah's words to his sons is not a blessing, but a cursing. The curse shall fall on a grandson. The writer teases his readers, and in great literary style sets up the drama. 'And the sons of Noah...were Shem, and Ham, and Japheth: and Ham is the father of Canaan' (9:18). Immediately, the reader is attracted to the last words. Who is this Canaan? Why is his name mentioned while the other grandchildren are ignored? We have a mystery. The writer shall tease us again in verse 22. 'And Ham, the father of Canaan, saw the nakedness of his father.'

It becomes clear to the reader that Canaan is going to play an important role, in some capacity, as the narrative continues. One who is familiar with the Old Testament will recognize that Canaan is the father of the inhabitants of the land of promise who will be dispossessed by Israel in the accounts of Joshua. It is fair to assume that the narrative will reveal something of the original Canaan that has direct relevance to the Canaanites of later years. Thus, the writer has connected the future with the present. The reader should be alert for this kind of scenario throughout Genesis.

The devotional moment comes in trying to understand what this teaches us about God. As one considers the moment, it becomes apparent that God is the great teacher. It is not so much what we learn of God, but what God teaches us about ourselves. It is unpleasant to think about, but it is a reality, that any one generation can take actions that shall affect his progeny for generations to come. Many families celebrate great wealth in America today because the generation of one hundred and fifty years ago endured great hardships, and a life of suffering, to transplant their family from Europe to America. By the same token, some people live in great hardship because some patron taught his children to be dependent, and gave them no sense of pride and ambition, and no one in the progeny has risen to break the cycle. The mention of Canaan is God's attention to detail in order to teach us. Pay attention to him, the father of Canaan, and much of the destiny of the Canaanites will be explained. We should pay attention to our own actions. We are setting precedents for our progeny.

> The subtle lessons of Scripture are not to be ignored. The story of Canaan is critical for parents. Your children will not answer to God for your sins, but you can steer them in a way that will lead them away from God, and their sins may become worse than yours.

Populating the earth

When meditating on the Scripture, one should take note of the subtleties that help to validate Scripture as truthful, accurate, and God-inspired. In this short passage, there is such subtlety.. The three sons of Noah are named. They are Shem, Ham, and Japheth. They had been mentioned previously when entering the ark with Noah (Genesis 7:13). The mention of their names does not seem notable. Further attention reveals otherwise. The reader's eyes fall on these words: 'These are the three sons of Noah: and of them was the whole earth overspread' (9:19).

Biblical scholars of the nineteenth and twentieth centuries have come to debate the truthfulness of a world-wide flood. It is quite common to speak of a localized flood covering only the ancient Middle East, because a flood that destroyed all flesh is seen as unlikely. World population derived from one family that survived the flood is incredulous. This opinion is adopted despite the fact that universal flood stories are part of cultures all over the world, giving evidence of having sprung from a common source. Verse 19 carries the weight of a forward-looking passage. It is written in anticipation of a day when the truth of one family being the foundation for the earthly population will come under ridicule. Consider this: In light of a story that has emphasized on several occasions that all flesh is destroyed (Genesis 6:7, 13, 17, 7:4, 21-23; 8:21; 9:11, 15), there is no need to utter a statement as in verse 19. Any person intelligent enough to read the story would know that the earth's re-population will evolve from the only family alive. The statement is emphatic '...of them was the whole earth overspread.' It leaves no doubt that the writer intends for everyone whoever reads the passage to know that wherever people are found on the earth, they are the descendants of Noah. Though the fact is clearly obvious, there is a need for an emphatic statement for those doubters and gainsayers who would come centuries later.

The truth carries a delightful devotional moment. It is a seemingly insignificant statement, but it is written with a matter of fact authority. It requires either a faith acceptance, or and accusation of pure falsehood. When God acts in history, he will not accept human efforts to rationalize away his work. From Noah came all the peoples of the earth. If you reject that premise, you must explain your rationale to God. In his Word, he lays it on the line so that there is a requirement for decision, not ambiguity.

Noah's drunken state

The illustration impacting the reader in this passage is rather startling. The mental image of Noah is one who built an ark, withstood the ridicule of friends, stood tall in difficult times, and rode the ark during the devastating flood. Here is a real man. The Scripture adds the descriptive statement. '...and Noah walked with God' (Genesis 6:9). Thus, our senses are shocked when we read '...he drank of the wine, and was drunken...' (9:21). What can be made of this?

There are some things that will connect the actions of Noah with the original family of earth. The wine that is made from the fresh fruit of the grape is not nearly as intoxicating as humans have in modern wines. It took a great deal of drinking to arrive at a state of drunkenness. Clearly, self-indulgence is implied. Proverbs declares, 'Who hath woe? Who hath sorrow?...They that tarry long at the wine...' (Proverbs 23:29-31). Noah could not resist the fruit of the vine. He became foolish in his action. The original family has a similar story. 'And when the woman saw that the tree was good for food, and that it was pleasant to the eyes...' (Genesis 3:6). The first parents, and Noah, in his new start, allowed the lust of the flesh and the lust of the eye to overcome the best of their senses.

Some have suggested that Noah accidentally became drunk, not knowing that the fruit of the vine would ferment over time and create intoxication. This may be possible in the light of the new climatic conditions. However, Jesus refers to 'eating and drinking' (Matthew 24:38) before the flood, which would lead to the belief that the fermentation process is a prediluvian as well as postdiluvian reality. The application is more the indictment of self-indulgence than of the actual drunkenness.

As Cain before him had been so proud of the fruit of the ground (Genesis 4:3), Noah had taken great pleasure in the product of his labour. This kind of self-indulgence always leads to a kind of drunkenness. We humans get so carried away with self-indulgent pleasures that we create those appetites that can never be satisfied. We simply thirst for more and more.

Jesus gave us the answer for such indulgence. '...Take no thought for your life, what ye shall eat, or what ye shall drink...Is not the life more than meat...But seek ye first the kingdom of God and his righteousness...' (Matthew 6:25, 33).

Self-indulgence is a sin with which most of humanity can identify. In fact, Christians often joke about this sin, such as in overeating. Jesus taught us that only in a hunger for righteousness can we defeat the other hungers in our life.

The sin of Ham

Biblical interpreters have observed this passage with great curiosity. It has been used as ammunition to condemn the sin of homosexuality, and to validate the slavery of people of African heritage in modern western history. Instead of reaching such conclusions, it is better to have a closer examination of the text.

Ham, whose progeny will populate the African continent, and much of the near East (as Chapter 11 will show), walks in on his father's nakedness. Ham's response shows no reverence for his father. He goes to his brothers and reports it. The attitude was totally inappropriate. 'You will not believe what I have just seen' is Ham's perspective. Noah's nakedness had clearly been the product of drunkenness. He lay down without awareness of his own condition. Ham reacted by thinking it was funny, or by concluding that there was something to gain from his father's condition. Ham's activity is thought by some to be homosexual in nature but that does not seem to be apparent in the immediate context.

A contextual understanding will take into account that nakedness has been mentioned before. When Adam and Eve first sinned, we read, 'And the eyes of them both were opened, and they knew that they were naked...' (Genesis 3:7). When this realization struck, the first parents acted in a futile attempt to cover their nakedness. '...they sewed fig leaves together, and made themselves aprons' (Genesis 3:7). The key is in their shame. Ham, upon discovering the nakedness of Noah sought not to cover it, but to exploit it. There was no sense of shame. A heart bereft of shame is a heart that is far from conversion, and far from listening to God.

In the modern world, nakedness is often applauded, and spoken of in such reverential terms as 'the beauty of the human body.' Those who would find shame in nakedness are ridiculed as uptight, or old fashioned, or out of touch. The ridicule comes from a shallowness of thinking. It fails to see the deeper problem. The naked form (in and of itself) is not where the problem lies. It is in the eye of the beholder who is a sinful being. When God clothed Adam and Eve (Genesis 3:21) it was because he knew that humans could not look on the naked form of another human and maintain concentration on righteousness. One may find a helpful way to understand this in the nakedness of a little baby, perhaps the only place where a degree of holiness can be found in the naked form. Why? It is in the innocence. The eye of the beholder will see the innocence and not be distracted. As the baby grows, the innocence is lost.

> One of the problems of dealing with sin lies in the inability of humans to think beyond what meets the eye. It is the heart attitude that is the major issue. This is hard to hear, much less to understand.

The sons' defining moment

The brothers of Ham, upon hearing of their father's nakedness, react with respect for their father. Unlike Ham, they did not see the event as something to exploit. Acting in reverence to their father, they took a blanket, and after backing into their father's tent covered his body. There was no desire for a visual image that might damage respect for their father, and thus limit his authority.

It is curious that this story is the only thing written about Noah's three sons (other than their place in genealogy). It is immediately followed by the announcement of Noah's blessing and cursing upon the sons. The writer clearly intends us to understand this moment as the defining moment in their lives. The reader may be reminded of the fifth commandment. As the nature of life for the progeny of Noah's sons turned on the attitude of Noah's sons toward their father, the future of Israel hinged on the same thing. 'Honour thy father and thy mother: that thy days may be long upon the land which the Lord thy God giveth thee' (Exodus 20:12).

In the defining moment of Shem, Ham, and Japheth's lives, there is a precursor to the law given to Israel, and a clear standard for orderliness in society. God took very seriously the irreverent attitude that Ham had toward his father. What kind of devotional thought might the reader glean from this incident?

There is much to be said for any individual who holds his father in reverence. He is, indeed, blessed. The sense of identity that one derives from the father, and the foundation that one has when the father is honoured is a key to sound mental health, and to the ability to make wise decisions. When Shem and Japheth did not look upon their father's nakedness, they were choosing a positive approach to their relationship with the father. They honoured him rather than mocking him as Ham had done.

Why would Ham's sin be manifest in a curse upon his progeny? Could it be possible that Ham was so blind that he did not understand the irreverence he had demonstrated toward his father? It is likely that he lived out his life and never understood that he had actually committed a foul act. How can one teach his sons that a deed is wrong and dishonourable when he personally sees no dishonour. It is likely that Ham reported the moment to his sons as well as to his brothers, and left in them a fascination for, and lack of regard about, nakedness. The curse is less a prophecy than a simple analysis about reality.

> It is a frightening thing to look at the nations which came from the generations of Ham and Canaan. It is a reminder that deeds of the moment may be an accurate prediction of the future. '…for whatsoever a man soweth, that shall he also reap' (Galatians 6:7).

The curse of Canaan

The book of Genesis is often called the 'book of beginnings.' As one reads and meditates on the book, one sees the truth of the statement. It is far more than a history of how the earth began. It explains both what and why. One not only learns of the handiwork of God's creation, but discovers why men and women are different, and why we react to each other way we do (Genesis 3:16-19). It explains the origins of history and establishes the nature in which the earth becomes populated (Genesis 10). Also, the book will define the nature of certain historical phenomena through the picture of prophecy known as blessing and cursing. The book of Genesis carries the sense of blessing and cursing of the family patriarch beyond the character of any other biblical writing. Each blessing and each cursing demonstrates the continuing sovereignty of God upon his creation, and demonstrates the always awesome and devastating results of sin. When the 'book of beginnings' ends, the need of such blessing and cursing will also end, except as they come directly from the mouth of God through the prophets. The patriarchal blessing is replaced by the prophet's pronouncements.

The first such blessing and cursing comes from the lips of Noah. It is caused by the actions of his three sons in reaction to Noah's nakedness. Ham saw it, and reported it. Shem and Japheth refused to look on Noah's nakedness covering him with a garment. Noah responds, 'Cursed be Canaan; a servant of servants shall he be unto his brethren' (Genesis 9:25). It is Ham who sinned. Why is the curse upon Canaan, the son of Ham (Genesis 9:18)?

There are two things to remember. First, God is in control of the curse. It is a reflection of a historical fact that shall fall upon the descendants of Canaan. It is the Canaanites Israel shall displace from the land of promise, and it is the Canaanites who carry the legacy of Ham. The Canaanite forms of worship were characterized by nakedness. It was in regard to Canaanite worship that God gave the command to Moses concerning the worship of Israel. 'And thou shalt make them linen breeches to cover their nakedness; from the loins even unto the thighs they shall reach' (Exodus 28:42). Canaan would have no sense of shame, even in worship.

Second, for Ham, there was cursing in the sense that there was no blessing. This should be understood in the religious sense. It is Ham's descendants that shall begin the defilement of religion in the world. It shall start at Babel. Ham shall father the progeny of all false religions. That is a truly awesome curse. He shall as Japheth, have no place in redemptive history, and he will have a more notorious history.

The human tendency is to read all sense of blessing and cursing purely from a materialistic perspective instead of a spiritual perspective. In the eyes of God (from whose eyes we need to view things), it was a fearsome and awful curse that fell upon Ham. The loss of spiritual insight is the worst fate humans can have.

Shem and Japheth

The respect Shem and Japheth demonstrated for their father, by refusing to look upon his nakedness (9:23), was rewarded, by blessing, from Noah. The blessing of Noah is the first of a series of patriarchal blessings that will be noticed in Genesis (Genesis 27:38-39). Noah's father, Lamech, had spoken of Noah in a similar fashion without the use of the term, blessing (Genesis 5:28-29). There are two things one notes in the first blessings that provide foundation for future blessings.

First, Shem receives the superior blessing. In Genesis 10:21, Japheth is reported to be the elder brother, but Shem shall receive the spiritual blessing. The purpose is to clearly establish God's sovereignty, and to draw attention to the nature of the superior blessing.

The blessing of Shem reads: '...Blessed be the Lord God of Shem; and Canaan shall be his servant' (9:26). The better understanding of the words is in translating the Hebrew with an extra article, hence, 'Blessed be the Lord, the God of Shem.' The Hebrew name for the covenant God of Israel is used in this verse. Yahweh, better known by some as Jehovah, is the name translated 'the Lord'.

The reality for the reader is that Shem's blessing shall come in a very special kind of relationship to his God. This theme shall be seen very clearly when Abraham, in the progeny of Shem, is specifically chosen by God to begin a new nation. The greater blessing is noted. To be in a special relationship with God is superior to everything else this earth can offer. 'Canaan shall be his servant' carries the prophetic hope of the land of promise. God shall give to the new nation the land that shall first be occupied by the descendants of Canaan. '...the Lord...said unto Abram, Get thee out... unto a land that I will shew thee' (Genesis 12:1).

Second, Japheth is also rewarded for his respect to his father. God, in his sovereignty chose Shem for the spiritual blessing. Japheth shall not have the same kind of special covenant with God in terms of the land, and of being a unique nation, but Japheth shall be enlarged. The descendants of Japheth shall come to political dominance in the world. This first occurred partially in the Medo-Persian ascendancy and came to full bloom in Greek rule. The land of promise, by the time of Messiah, was under the dominance of Japheth. The world's political dominance by the Indo-European descendants of Japheth is a historical reality. Japheth dwelling in the tents of Shem (9:27) is considered by Bible scholars to be seen in the promise to Abraham. '...in thee shall all families of the earth be blessed' (Genesis 12:3). It finds its ultimate fulfilment in Israel's Messiah, Jesus of Nazareth.

> Though Shem and his progeny are the recipients of the superior blessing, let it not be forgotten that the blessing is part of God's redemptive plan. Jesus Christ proved that God's love was not restricted to one family, but was only a part of the larger picture to bring redemption to humanity. 'For God so loved the world...' (John 3:16).

Noah dies

The story of Noah is a wonderful and captivating event. As the one who built and rode the ark to safety in the great deluge which destroyed the world, he easily holds place as one of the great heroes, if not the first of the great heroes, of the Bible. One is surprised by the rather perfunctory statement about Noah's life ending. 'And all the days of Noah were nine hundred and fifty years: and he died' (9:29). For such a great hero, one would expect a little more information, but it is not there. Is there a reason?

A possible answer may be found in the full narrative of Genesis. Noah is placed in lineage with the genealogical table of chapter five. He is the last of the ten great men in the pre-diluvian line of Seth. Of each one except Enoch, who was translated, it is said, '...and he died...' (Genesis 5:5, 8, 11, 14, 17, 20, 27, 31). Noah has the extensive narrative about himself, providing the link between the pre and post-diluvian worlds, and the reader is to see in the perfunctory end of his life the last of the world that used to be. He had a total life span that compared with the other great men of chapter five, but he would be the last to have that kind of life span. Chapter 11 shall record the steadily decreasing life span of humans from Shem's six hundred years (Genesis 11:10-11) down to Terah's two hundred and five years (Genesis 11:32). When Genesis ends, the human life span will have decreased another hundred years (Genesis 50:26).

During the remaining 350 years of Noah's life, he must have been a very influential figure. As his sons have children, and the population begins to spread into the distant places of the earth, his legend, and his story would be regularly told. As long as he is alive, he will grow in stature and in the development of legendary tales. None of those legendary tales remain except in the various flood stories in the world. It would be reasonable to assume that people might travel far to meet the man who lived on the other side of the flood, and had built the ark.

In the Bible, the story we have of the great man, after the flood, is that he offered sacrifice to God, got drunk, blessed two of his sons, pronounced a curse on his grandson, and died. The stark reminder is very evident. The Bible is the story about God, and human rebellion against him. Noah had a grand story, but mostly, it was God's story, and in the end, Noah proved himself a sinner. God acted in grace to spare humans. Even at their best, humans are just sinners in need of redemption. We do not need the legendary stories of great heroes. We need God's grace.

One would be wise to take a moment and reflect on the end of Noah's life. As profound and meaningful as it was, in the end, he died. The Bible is not the story of great men, but of a great redemption (Hebrews 2:3).

Genesis 10:1-32

I. Understanding the Heritage of Japheth (10:1-5)
1. Table of nations analyzed
2. Progeny of Japheth

II. Understanding the Heritage of Ham (10:6-20)
1. Sons of Ham
2. Nimrod

III.Understanding the Sons of Shem (10:21-32)
1. Progeny of Shem
2. '…was the earth subdued…'

Genesis 10:1-5

1. Now these are the generations of the sons of Noah, Shem, Ham, and Japheth: and unto them were sons born after the flood. 2. The sons of Japheth; Gomer, and Magog, and Madai, and Javan, and Tubal, and Meshech, and Tiras. 3. And the sons of Gomer; Ashkenaz, and Riphath, and Togarmah. 4. And the sons of Javan; Elishah, and Tarshish, Kittim, and Dodanim. 5. By these were the isles of the Gentiles divided in their lands; every one after his tongue, after their families, in their nations.

Table of nations analyzed

Chapter 10 provides a genealogical table explaining the division of nations in the world. The careful analysis of the table provides limited answers to other biblical questions. The descendants of Ham (10:6-20) were the nations with which Israel was in conflict throughout the Old Testament. The constant warfare between the sons of Ham and Israel reflect the lack of blessing upon Ham, and the scar of being at odds with the chosen people. God's grace enters at the call of Abraham when Ham's descendants are placed under the blessing found in the Word of God to Abraham. '...in thee shall all families of the earth be blessed' (Genesis 12:3).

The genealogical table of the chapter is somewhat confusing for the modern reader as individual names are sometimes replaced by the names of peoples (10:16, 18). The names of cities are also interspersed (10:12). These are in the narrative to give the sense of historical reality, and to isolate the political and religious nature of those cities and to clearly align them with their ancestral heritage. Additionally, the table of nations is unique to ancient literary style. The writer is clearly portraying the population of the world disseminating from the sons of Noah. It is a remarkable description and carries no peer in ancient literature.

The meditative moment is in comparing the genealogical table of this chapter with the tables of Genesis four and five. There is no table of nations, and no description of the way that people spread out upon the earth in the earlier tables. Two things are occurring. First, it is being made clear that all people of the earth have a common ancestry in Noah. Racial distinctive will result from the Tower of Babel incident, but humanity is one, and therefore, racial and national distinctive that would attempt to paint a superior nature to any race or cultural is irrelevant. The only relevance to all humans is that all are sinners. This is another distinctive that separates Genesis from genealogical lists of other ancient writings. In other writings, there is usually a clear attempt to establish the superiority of an individual or a race through direct lineage with the gods.

Second, the foundation is laid for a redemptive solution to the sin problem. As humanity is one, the promise of God to Abraham (Genesis 12:3) has believability and viability. When the redemptive history begins, Abraham will be chosen from among many nations, languages, and races of men. One should not be troubled by many nations. They all sprung from the family of one man, Noah. The drama is in how God will make them one again. See Galatians 3:28.

Progeny of Japheth

The table of nations begins with Japheth. He is the elder son of Noah (10:21). Ham is the youngest. The genealogical table of Japheth and Ham ware placed first to prevent disruption in the order of redemptive history through the progeny of Shem. The tables are somewhat cumbersome reading, and one would think it worth passing over. Yet, a little closer examination reveals teaching moments on the sovereign control of God.

The Japheth table consists of two groups of 'sevens.' There are seven sons, and seven grandsons. At least two of the grandsons (Kittim and Dodanim), have names with plural endings meaning that nations spawned by the grandsons may be in view. It is difficult to tie any specific significance to the combination of sevens in the table. The writer may be emphasizing the movement of Japheth's progeny on the earth. In that case, one might ask why there is mention of Gomer's and Javan's grandsons while the grandsons of the other Japhethite children are not mentioned.

If one pieces together the full context, there is a partial answer. First, there is the Japheth blessing. Noah said, 'God shall enlarge Japheth...' (Genesis 9:27). Second, most scholarly efforts at tracing the geographical setting of the two sets of grandsons place their progeny in the Mediterranean world, west of Israel. The Kittim and Dodanim are people who populated Cyprus, and the Aegean island of Rhodes. The other grandsons' progeny can also be, with some certainty, placed in the Mediterranean world, and they probably continued a movement westward. Third, when God directed the missionary movement of the Apostle to the Gentiles, He moved him westward in the direction of Japheth's grandsons. 'Now when they had gone throughout... Galatia, and were forbidden of the Holy Spirit to preach...in Asia...a vision appeared to Paul...a man of Macedonia...prayed him, saying...Come over into Macedonia, and help us' (Acts 16:6-9).

Noah said, 'God shall enlarge Japheth...' (Genesis 9:27). More than two thousand years before the time of Paul, God inspired the author of Genesis to specifically note the movement of the descendants spawned from two of Japheth's grandsons. He thereby demonstrates how he shall fulfil the blessing of Noah, and demonstrates anew that he is in control of history.

The genealogy of Japheth provides one of those interesting tidbits of information that can thrill the heart of the redeemed. This is truly a divine book inspired by God. It is only in his wisdom that there can be such accurate forecasting of world history, and redemptive history, wrapped in one simple statement.

Genesis 10:6-20

6. And the sons of Ham; Cush, and Mizraim, and Phut, and Canaan. 7. And the sons of Cush; Seba, and Havilah, and Sabtah, and Raamah, and Sabtecha: and the sons of Raamah, Sheba, and Dedan. 8. And Cush begat Nimrod: he began to be a mighty one in the earth. 9. He was a mighty hunter before the Lord: wherefore it is said, Even as Nimrod the mighty hunter before the Lord. 10. And the beginning of his kingdom was Babel, and Erech, and Accad, and Calneh, in the land of Shinar. 11. Out of that land went forth Asshur, and builded Nineveh, and the city Rehoboth, and Calah, 12. And Resen between Nineveh and Calah: the same is a great city. 13. And Mizraim begat Ludim, and Anamim, and Lehabim, and Naphtuhim, 14. And Pathrusim, and Casluhim, (out of whom came Philistim,) and Caphtorim. 15. And Canaan begat Sidon his firstborn, and Heth, 16. And the Jebusite, and the Amorite, and the Girgasite, 17. And the Hivite, and the Arkite, and the Sinite, 18. And the Arvadite, and the Zemarite, and the Hamathite: and afterward were the families of the Canaanites spread abroad. 19. And the border of the Canaanites was from Sidon, as thou comest to Gerar, unto gaza; as thou goest, unto Sodom, and Gomorrah, and Admah, and Zeboim, even unto Lasha. 20.

These are the sons of Ham, after their families, after their tongues, in their countries, and in their nations.

Sons of Ham

The son, who received no blessing from his father, has his progeny traced in these verses. As with Japheth, individual names in Ham's genealogy are sometimes to be understood as nations. There are four sons named, only three of which (Cush, Mizraim, and Canaan) have mention of their historical development. Nothing is said of Phut. The best answer for 'why?' is probably in the reality that the progeny of Phut played little or no role in the developing life of the nation of Israel. The other three sons had descendants that were very prominent in Israel's history.

From Mizraim came Egypt and the Philistines. From Canaan came the many nations Israel must dispossess to conquer the promised land. From Cush came the Ethiopians, and the great kingdoms who were predecessors of the eastern Mesopotamian empires that would beleaguer Israel.

The descendants of Ham would people the African continent, but the Africans are not the only descendants of Ham. Nimrod took many of the descendants of Cush into the land of Shinar, the great Tigris-Euphrates valley, and established himself as the first of the world's great rulers. Some have speculated that many of mythology's great tales, and images of gods were based on the exploits of Nimrod. The centaur, half horse and half man, may have been inspired from Nimrod's prowess in domesticating the horse. The writer makes plain that Nimrod's kingdom began at Babel (10:9-10). It is logical to assume that he was the instigator of the Tower of Babel crises that led to the 'tongues' judgement on the nations in Chapter 11. This would be consistent with the writer's tendency to state something in the genealogy which lays the foundation for a coming narrative (See Genesis 9:18, 22, 25).

As one visualizes the developing geographical situation, there is concern for Shem's progeny. Japheth's sons have moved north and west populating the Mediterranean. Ham's sons take the African continent, the land of Canaan, and build a powerhouse empire to the east in the Tigris-Euphrates valley. What is left for Shem? Remember the words of Noah '...Blessed be the Lord God of Shem; and Canaan shall be his servant' (Genesis 9:26). Shem is hemmed in on all sides. He has nothing as one reads the genealogical table. Yet, he does have one thing. He has God. One should not miss that this is all happening to demonstrate the wonder of God's creative power. From Genesis 1:1 on, he continues doing something new. His re-creation is as exciting as creation 'ex-nihilo'.

The jumbled mass of nations coupled with the blessing and cursing of Noah's sons make for a wonderful mystery for the first time reader of Genesis. It is clear that the orchestration of the nations will serve the clear purpose of demonstrating God's control of human history.

Nimrod

One cannot move past this passage without giving due consideration to the intriguing character, Nimrod. The name, itself, carries the idea of revolt, and suggests a rebellious spirit. It is noteworthy that the ascendancy of Nimrod came by virtue of his own distinct prowess and exploits. It is not the development of his progeny that is in view. The word 'mighty', used three times of Nimrod (10:8-9), reflects a warrior. The idea of military strength, and military leadership is the prime characteristic.

The phrase 'before the Lord' (10:9) should be understood as 'against the Lord'. This would provide an understanding of the rebellious nature in the man. This kind of attitude is rebuked in Psalms 66:7: 'He ruleth by his power forever...let not the rebellious exalt themselves.' Nimrod began his kingdom at Babel, and later built the great city of Nineveh. Thus, the two most notorious of Old Testament cities from Israel's standpoint, have their origin with

Nimrod. (Note: Most scholars see the statement 'Out of that land went forth Asshur...' (10:11) to mean Nimrod journeyed from Babel to Assyria).

The picture that the writer of Genesis is portraying is of a very deadly sin. The sin was on display in Ham's disrespect for his father (Genesis 9:22). That attitude is now carried to the next level in total disrespect for God. Nimrod is not just disobeying God, but is setting himself as equal with God. The reader also saw this disrespect for God when Lamech committed murder (Genesis 4:23). Nimrod's great power and heroism would allow him to bring much of the earth's population into alliance with him and his disrespect for God.

Meditation at this point can be very enlightening for the reader. Human beings are very prone to hero worship. There are very charismatic individuals, with great skill and power, who can mesmerize us, and cause us to have a great desire to follow them, to be like them, to be close to them. One should always be able to discern the religious quotient in hero worship. The heroic figure we seek to imitate, who is he, really? Is he one, like Nimrod, who is in total rebellion against God? When you seek to imitate his exploits, will you discover that you, instead of equaling his exploits, succeed only in imitating his rebellion? Do you become as he is religiously, but never arrive at his physical prowess? It is a wonderful thing to have heroes who establish great examples of humility before God. It is extremely dangerous to become involved in hero worship, only to have one in rebellion against God to capture our minds.

An epic such as the exploits of Nimrod, and the way he captured the imagination of the people of the world should lead us to a constant prayer for discernment in the nature of the people we choose as our heroes and who we wish to emulate.

Genesis 10:21-32

21. Unto Shem also, the father of all the children of Eber, the brother of Japheth the elder, even to him were children born. 22. The children of Shem; Elam, and Asshur, and Arphaxad, and Lud, and Aram. 23. And the children of Aram; Uz, and Hul, and Gether, and Mash. 24. And Arphaxad begat Salah; and Salah begat Eber. 25. And unto Eber were born two sons: the name of one was Peleg; for in his days was the earth divided; and his brother's name was Joktan. 26. And Joktan begat Almodad, and Sheleph, and Hazarmaveth, and Jerah, 27. And Hadoram, and Uzal, and Diklah, 28. And Obal, and Abimael, and Sheba, 29. And Ophir, and Havilah, and Jobab: all these were the sons of Joktan. 30. And their dwelling was from Mesha, as thou goest unto Sephar a mount of the east. 31. These are the sons of Shem, after their families, after their tongues, in their lands, after their nations. 32. These are the families of the sons of Noah, after their generations, in their nations: and by these were the nations divided in the earth after the flood.

Progeny of Shem

The reader of Genesis will now encounter the genealogy of Shem. It is through this son of Noah that redemption history shall occur. Attempting to trace the nations that are Shem's progeny is recognized immediately as more problematic than the Japheth and Ham lines. The descendants of Shem occupied parts of the Tigris-Euphrates Valley and Syria. Aram is one of Shem's children and probably gives his name to the Aramean kingdom located in the same area. The title, Aramean, seems to have stuck with the patriarchal family of Abram, though Aram was not directly related to Abram, but to Abram's brother, Arphaxad. Jacob is called a 'wandering Aramean' (Deuteronomy 26:5, NASV). One will also note that Abraham and Isaac were careful to choose their sons' wives from Shem instead of the descendants of Ham who occupied the land of Canaan (Genesis 24:1-3; 28:1-2).

However, as the biblical historian tries to follow the geographical development of the line of Shem, the picture is blurred. The clarity is that Shem's descendants seem to dwell in places in which they were not dominant. Shem's progeny simply does not rise to prominence. Though the Assyrian and Babylonian empires have traces of Semitic heritage, their beginnings are with Nimrod, and are thus more a heritage of Ham than of Shem.

The reader's information takes on a marvellous significance when the beginning of Genesis 12 is fully grasped. 'Now the Lord had said unto Abram, Get thee out of thy country, and from thy kindred, and from thy father's house, unto a land that I will shew thee: And I will make of thee a great nation...' That which the Shemites could not do on their own, God was going to do for them. God adds the promise of miracle. '...I will bless thee, and make thy name great...and in thee shall all families of the earth be blessed' (Genesis 12:2-3).

From modern perspective, there is no way to know if the descendants of Shem, in Abraham's day, felt somewhat trodden upon, and without respect in the world. We can certainly see the possibility of it from the overview of Genesis 11. In such likelihood the words of God to Abraham would have carried extra meaning, and would have excited the emotions. It would also have seemed preposterous and impossible. Further, God is going to give Abraham a land, the very land occupied by the descendants of Canaan. The drama unfolding here is truly mesmerizing!

This wonderful story could only be written by God. It traces a kind of wisdom no human can claim.

'...was the earth divided...'

The writer's methodology for tracing the line of Shem has an interesting dynamic. A great deal of attention is given to the generations of Arphaxad, son of Shem. In Arphaxad's progeny, each generation has one son mentioned, until the name, Eber, appears. Eber has two sons mentioned. Peleg's genealogy takes the reader to the birth of Abram (Genesis 11:26), which is the beginning of God's redemptive history through the new nation of Israel. When Peleg's name is mentioned, the writer adds this note: '…for in his days was the earth divided…' (10:25). Discovering the meaning to this note provides a moment of meditation.

There are two kinds of division that are in view. The first is the separation of the two generations of Eber. The second is the separation of the peoples of the world by confusion of languages after the Tower of Babel. Why is the mention of Peleg being alive at the time of the Tower of Babel incident important? The writer's emphasis on understanding the best part of this world as having a proper relationship with God provides the answer. As the line of Seth kept alive the worship of the true God in the pre-flood era, it is the line of Peleg that shall keep the worship of the true God alive in the post-Tower of Babel era. Thus, the earth is divided as part of Shem's progeny deserts the worship of God. Joktan's generations participate in following Nimrod. Peleg shall have sons who follow God. Once again, the author subtly shows that humanity is exceedingly sinful, but that God's plan of redemption cannot be halted.

The second division will come at the Tower of Babel incident where God's judgement confuses the language of humans. Peleg is alive, but will not succumb to the great temptation of the rest of the world. In this sense, Peleg stands out as one, like Noah, who refused to go along with the world's wisdom.

It is only a genealogy. It is a brief mention of a name. Yet, because he kept alive the worship of God, he is notable, thus the brief mention, '…in his days was the earth divided…' (10:25). God makes sure that Peleg's name will be noticed by any passing the way of this biblical passage.

The desire for a relationship with God carries no weight in this world. It will not mark you for greatness. Let us be grateful for every note in the Word of God that shows that it carries great weight with God.

Genesis 11:1-32

Genesis 11:1-9

1. And the whole earth was of one language, and of one speech. 2. And it came to pass, as they journeyed from the east, that they found a plain in the land of Shinar; and they dwelt there. 3. And they said one to another, Go to, let us make brick, and burn them throughly. And they had brick for stone, and slime had they for morter. 4. And they said, Go to, let us build us a city and a tower, whose top may reach unto heaven; and let us make us a name, lest we be scattered abroad upon the face of the whole earth. 5. And the Lord came down to see the city and the tower, which the children of men builded. 6. And the Lord said, Behold, the people is one, and they have all one language; and this they begin to do: and now nothing will be restrained from them, which they have imagined to do. 7. Go to, let us go down, and there confound their language, that they may not understand one another's speech. 8. So the Lord scattered them abroad from thence upon the face of all the earth: and they left off to build the city. 9. Therefore is the name of it called Babel; because the Lord did there confound the language of all the earth: and from thence did the Lord scatter them abroad upon the face of all the earth.

Making a name

Generally, the Tower of Babel story has been understood simply as the explanation for the many different human languages in the world. A closer look reveals that the author has some very clear lessons that go beyond the historical significance. Established themes continue to dominate the context, but with differing forms.

First, the people moved to the east. '…as they journeyed from the east…' (11:2). The phrase 'from the east' is more accurately understood as simply 'toward the east.' In the parlance of Genesis, journeying eastward is to journey away from God (Genesis 3:24; 4:16; 13:11). By noting their direction, the author provides an immediate clue that the intention of the travellers is evil. Under the leadership of Nimrod (Genesis 10:9-10), the people were seeking to build their own kind of glory. Once again, as with the generations of Cain, it is the human effort to rebuild Eden without redemption from sin, and without submission to God. It is the same kind of sin that had tempted man from the beginning. The people will build a tower from the crude materials of the earth for the purpose of showing off their own ability. They will be proud, they will have re-created Eden. Who needs God?

Second, the people sought their security in themselves rather than God. '…let us make us a name, lest we be scattered abroad upon the face of the whole earth' (11:4). There is a subtlety at work in this situation that should not be missed. In the human heart, evil can always be justified if others are involved. Humans cloak themselves in the hiddeness of 'other people do it.' The reality that (in Genesis) it is always the rebellious humans who are the builders of cities helps to establish this point (Genesis 4:17; 10:8-12). The safety in numbers instead of in God is a flawed concept, but plays out continually in human minds. Cain built a city, but Enoch and Noah walked with God, is a contrast that should not be missed.

The idea is not mentioned here, but the destruction of the earth via the flood must still be prominent in the people's minds. Despite God's covenant with Noah that he would not again destroy the world by flood (Genesis 9:11), the tower could possibly have been viewed as a place of safety if a flood reoccurs. Many such towers (called Ziggurats) have been unearthed by archaeologists, and were part of ancient religious culture.

The meditative moment arrives when the reader understands that safety in the world is in the correct worship of God. Trust, obedience, and gaining redemption from sin is God's' safety net.

The making of a name carries New Testament overtones, and this helps us to understand the great sin of Nimrod's followers. 'That at the name of Jesus every knee should bow…' (Philippians 2:10). The name of Jesus could not be desecrated even though it was still 2000 years from his appearance as The Incarnate seed of the woman..

Dawn of counterfeit religion

A consideration of the 'Tower of Babel' incident is necessary to an understanding of Scripture. It is here that a great spiritual warfare is established which shall be seen throughout human history. The worship of idols, which is the heart of the downfall of Israel, has its roots here. The evil enemy in this warfare is labelled in the last book of the Bible. 'And upon her forehead was a name written, Mystery, Babylon the Great, the mother of harlots and abominations of the earth' (Revelation 17:5). The enemy (mystery, Babylon) is counterfeit religion. It is the substitute established and created by humans as an alternative to the worship of God. The creator of this counterfeit religion is a son of Ham through Cush. That which makes the religion of Nimrod unique is that it is not just rebellion against God, it is the creation of an alternative god.

When this is understood, the statement about Nimrod in Chapter 10 has greater clarity. '…Even as Nimrod the mighty hunter before (against) the Lord' (10:9). Nimrod set out to gain the affection of men's hearts, which rightly belonged to God. It is the birth of counterfeit religion.

When God established the ten commandments with his chosen nation, the first three of those commandments spoke directly to mystery, Babylon, the awful dynamic begun by Nimrod.

'Thou shalt have no other gods before me' (Exodus 20:3).

'Thou shalt not make unto thee any graven image…' (Exodus 20:4).

'Thou shalt not take the name of the Lord thy God in vain…' (Exodus 20:7).

The devotional moment for the reader rests in considering how Nimrod came to the point of leading this revolt. From Genesis 10:9, it is clear that Nimrod was an exceptional man for his time. The 'mighty hunter' reflects one who was extremely successful in the human struggle to 'subdue the earth.' He was conqueror of the animal world. He was a leader among men as he built cities, and became a hero. While he is admired and adored by men, he leads them a step further. '…let us build us a city and a tower, whose top may reach unto heaven; and let us make us a name…' (11:4). The idea of 'reach unto heaven' is and in-your-face declaration against God. The tall tower may be Nimrod's way of saying to people, 'Follow me, and I will show you how to protect yourself against the judgement of God.' It sounds preposterous, but refusal to submit to God leads to such foolishness. Human success led to tragedy. It becomes easy to see why true wisdom begins with the fear of God (Psalms 111:10).

> In the story of Nimrod is illustrated the greatest reason for humility among men. It seems preposterous that one destined for death could be considered as a god, yet humans have never stopped making this mistake.

One speech

When the evil Nimrod fashioned the idea of building a tower, and bringing all the people of the world together for worship of an alternative god ('...let us make us a name...' 11:4), there was only one language spoken (11:1). The clear act of rebellion against God was for the express purpose of creating a worship, which could be so appealing, and so enticing, that humans would easily be drawn into it. It is clear that Nimrod's plan was working. The literary insertion of '...Go to, let us...' (11:3, 4) expresses great excitement among the people. In their minds, Nimrod has a wonderful idea. It is an interesting study of the human mindset to note how often rebellion against God manifests itself as a wonderful idea. The ability to unite the whole world of humanity around one counterfeit religion is dependent, however, on effective communication. The confusion of languages prevented the full success of Nimrod. Yet, he did give birth to the creation of alternative gods, which came to rule national identities.

Bible students see God's great control, and can also look forward to a future kind of irony. Nimrod, when the world spoke one language, sought to unite them into counterfeit worship. God acted to prevent it. There will come a day, however, when one language and speech will again be the rule, and men shall be united in worship. It will not be worship of a counterfeit. God shall once again prove his control. 'For then will I turn to the people a pure language, that they may all call upon the name of the Lord, to serve him with one consent' (Zephaniah 3:9). When common language and speech returns to the world, it will be for the express purpose of common worship of the one true God.

In terms of devotional thought, the reader should consider the great danger posed by the one great worship system proposed by Nimrod. If it is successful, where is the place that God shall find the individual upon whom to show grace? Because there was Noah, humanity was spared, and God's redemptive history continued. If Nimrod succeeds in turning every man's heart to a counterfeit religion, redemptive history is in jeopardy (11:6). The promise of

Genesis 3:15 is once again under attack. God's judgement insures that there will be no single world religion to disrupt his redemptive plan. His glory is revealed in the confusion of languages to prevent a unified counterfeit worship. It will ultimately be revealed in a greater way in restoration of pure speech which shall unify humanity in perfect worship. Humans always get excited about their ideas, but God's idea always carries the day.

> Humans always seems to have a better idea than God. Just as in the Garden of Eden when the first woman was deceived, it is easy to be deceived when the Word of God is not kept prominent in our hearts. 'Thy word have I hid in mine heart, that I might not sin against thee' (Psalms 119:11).

Many languages

As one reads carefully the story of the Tower of Babel, some important biblical themes arise. A portrait of human rebellion contrasted with God's control is brilliantly displayed. God's command to Noah was 'replenish the earth (Genesis 9:1). Nimrod, 'the mighty hunter,' had a better idea '…let us build us a city…lest we be scattered abroad…' (11:4). Under Nimrod's leadership, the people sought independence of God, and would feel safer if they made their own way. In disobedience to God, they thought, 'we are out from under God's control, and will be free of God.' We shall devise protection for ourselves.

The biblical writer's portrait draws out a humorous irony. The people were proud and free. 'We will not scatter abroad on the earth,' they said. Did it mean they were independent of God, that God had lost control? The 'in your face' attitude of the people was returned by God with a stroke of divine brilliance. '…the Lord said...let us go down...and confound their language, that they may not understand one another's speech' (11:6-7). Though seeking to be out of the control of God, they found themselves totally controlled by God.

The confounding of speech would do two things. First, they could not find adequate safety in numbers. They would now find themselves suspicious of, and angry at, each other as communication is rendered impossible. Nimrod's power could not be as effective because the people he sought to lead would not understand him. People of each language would require heroes who knew their language. They had sought a name under which all could unite in rebellion against God. That is now impossible.

Second, they will do as God commanded, not through obedience, but through necessity. 'So the Lord scattered them abroad... upon the face of all the earth...' (11:8). One should not miss the humour. The freedom, which they so grandly proclaimed, turned into a greater kind of slavery. It is true that they rebelled against God, but they are now under greater control than before. They did not want to be scattered, so what happened? They were scattered. The rebellion of the people did not mean that God was not in control. When the writer of Genesis states '...God created...' (Genesis 1:1), he left no doubt about who is in charge. Nimrod, and his followers, discovered God controls through judgement. Every human who rebels will ultimately discover the same thing. It is the tragic-comic at its most sublime.

It is the continuing saga of Scripture that the greatest freedom comes in complete obedience to God. It runs counter to human logic, but then, God's Word always runs counter to what humans prefer.

Significance of Babel

The Tower of Babel story ends with the judgement of God in the confusion of human language, the stoppage of the city building, and the scattering of the people. Once again humans have tried to re-create the Garden of Eden, and have succeeded only in creating a much more complicated situation on the earth. The reader is left to contemplate the new circumstances, and to wonder! As one looks back on the story of Genesis, and remembers the pristine beauty of the original creation, the grandeur and promise of Adam and Eve, and sees now this scattered and confused world, the reaction can only be amazement. How could that which began so marvellously and with such order now be so complicated?

The name of the place is Babel, taken from the Hebrew root 'bll' which means confusion. The reader should note a larger context than mere confusion of languages.

Nimrod, though stopped in his attempt at creating the one great counterfeit religion to rival God, has created the basic idea of counterfeit religion. Many gods will now arise as humans are scattered and languages are confused. The far greater confusion than languages is the religious confusion. Who is the true God? How shall he be worshipped? What is the truth? Will the true God ever reveal himself to man? As people with their new languages begin to make sense of the new situation, and learn to think in their new languages, the religion of Nimrod will manifest itself in a thousand different ways. Humans shall forever be confused. Wars will occur as the differing language groups attempt to establish superiority. The feeling of superiority will often be based in religion. It all happened because humans originally followed a 'mighty hunter' (Genesis 10:9), who sought to create an alternative to God.

Further, the reader looked at the original order of Genesis, and saw it collapse in the evil of humanity. '...every imagination of the thoughts of his heart was only evil continually' (Genesis 6:5). The result was that God destroyed the world and started over with one man and his family. We can see the possibility (though remote) for getting things in order when there is one man with which to begin and one language with which to communicate. How will God solve the mess of Genesis 11? Many languages! Many religions! Total confusion! Is there a way?

Think about it, and observe the glory of God. Humans keep confusing things, and God keeps acting, moving forward, and does not miss a beat. Contemplate this, '...the Lord had said unto Abram...I will... make thy name great' (Genesis 12:1-2). The great name will not be Nimrod who had sought it for self.

> Here is a wonderful place to pause and enjoy the magnificent drama that is presented in Genesis. The act of God in confusing the tongues appears to have created a literal mess. The way God goes to work to clear it up, and re-establish his name is glorious.

Two lines from Shem

The interjection of the Tower of Babel incident has provided a clear picture of the direction humanity goes when it abandons true worship of God. From Shem, two genealogical lines are traced. The two lines are through Eber, the third born from Shem. The first genealogical line was that of Joktan (Genesis 10:26-30), whose descendants brought us to the time of rebellion of Babel. It is a reminder of the ungodly generations of Cain (Genesis 4:16-24). The Joktan branch of Shem's progeny did not separate itself as a follower of God, but bought into the apostasy of Nimrod and the builders of Babel.

With the confusion of tongues established, the writer turns his attention to the second genealogical line from Shem through Eber. This is the line of Peleg. This genealogy culminates with the family of Terah who has three sons (11:27). There is similarity here to the tracing of the genealogy of Seth, the son of Adam (Genesis 5:6-32). In the line of Seth, the true worship of God was preserved. By the time of Noah, it was only alive in one man, and through that man's family, there was grace given by God. Through Noah, the human race was spared, a new beginning occurs, and the hope of Genesis 3:15 is kept alive. In the genealogy of Peleg, there is a similar situation. The worship of God is kept alive through the descendants of Shem, in the Peleg branch of Eber.

The awful consequences of Babel leave the world in a mass of confusion. The many different peoples go on their way establishing their cultures and creating their gods in the image of Nimrod. The reader of Genesis looks on in bewilderment. There was the blessed hope for redemption in the seed of the woman. Will there be a place of grace (like Noah) in this massive corruption? As if in a giant pictorial display, the reader is called upon to take a visual trip from the lofty perch of many nations and follow his vision to focus more and more narrowly on the one group of individuals that are born from Peleg. Keep your eyes focused! There is born Reu, and Serug, and Nahor, and Terah. It is important to notice because, somewhere in this family, the worship of God is being kept alive. The reader will remember the flood and the memory may create some anxiety. What will happen now? There are many languages, many nations. How can they all be united in worship of God? How will the seed of the woman be a redemptive agent? The Genesis writer is taking us to a sublime announcement of God. '…I will make of thee a great nation…' (Genesis 12:2). Out of the many tongues, God is going to make a nation. Wow! His creative activity continually takes on new dimensions.

Introduction of Abram

In a few short lines, the writer of Genesis prepares the reader for the narrative to follow. The family that is being traced (Shem to Peleg to Terah) is the family that God has ordained for his plan of action. When most of the world is scattered, and has turned to the worship of the gods of its own creation (the heritage of the Babel rebellion), there is one family through whom God's name survives. As the story of the family moves forward, one of Terah's sons (Haran) dies. In Chapter 12:1, another of the sons, Abram, receives instructions from God. '...Get thee out of thy country, (the place of thy birth) and from thy kindred, and from thy father's house, unto a land that I will shew thee.'

From the command of Chapter 12, the reader knows that Terah's decision to leave Ur of the Chaldees and travel northwest to Haran was actually the result of a call that was given to Abram. A third son of Terah (Nahor) is evidently left behind in Ur. Abram, in addition to his father, takes his dead brother's son (Lot) on the journey. God had commanded Abram to leave them behind. In Joshua 24:2, it is stated that Terah was one who worshipped idols. One does not know from which member of the family Abram had his knowledge of God. Perhaps it was through his grandfather, or through his brother Haran, who died. The Joshua text notes that Terah and Abram's brother, Nahor, served other gods, but does not mention Haran. It is possible that Abram's call to separate himself from his idolatrous father and brother came at Haran's death.

With the evidence mounting that it is more and more difficult to keep alive the name of God, the story takes on a new dimension. God will begin a dramatic work in the historical affairs of humanity to keep alive his name. There are many languages, and many nations resulting from God's judgement at the Tower of Babel. God begins by taking Abram, out of the shadow of Babel, in Ur of the Chaldees, and promises, 'From you, I will make a nation.' The nation that God will build will be a testimony, which shall identify the true God, to a world that has forsaken him.

The biblical student finds an incredible devotional moment in this realization. Nimrod's goal was, '...let us build us a city...' (11:4). The New Testament reflects on the life of the man in whom God would do his building of a nation. '...he looked for a city...whose builder and maker is God' (Hebrews 11:10). Nimrod sought a great name for himself by building his own city. Abraham received a great name by desiring the city of God.

Another beginning

The beginning of chapter 12 marks a stark contrast in the telling of God's action with his creation. In the first eleven chapters, there has been no historical development in the lives of individuals. They are noted for character, for one or two specific incidents in their life, or for their relationship with others. Noah's story is the longest, but it deals only with the flood, and the immediate aftermath. With the introduction of Abram (later called Abraham), the reader will be taken on a journey through the lives of four individuals who shall be known as the patriarchs of Israel. The journeys are not biographies in the twentieth century sense, but are historical narratives dealing with what might be called the 'God event' in their lives.

Each of the four lives carry great interest for the biblical student. Understanding the work of God in each life provides a framework to help every Christian to discern the specific work of God in his or her own life. The critical aspect for the reader is to note the nature of God's individual work with humans in a world that is aligned against God. The confusion of tongues (Genesis 11:7) leaves a massively confused religious system. God will begin his work to bring a redeemed portion out of the masses that shall give testimony to his power and glory.

As one reads the story of Abram and his descendents, careful meditation should be given to the wonderful ability of God to focus on the smallest detail of the individual's life while weaving it into his own world wide plan. Each event reported by the writer carries the divine imprint of inspiration as it reveals the way God thinks. In effect, God is speaking to every believer throughout the ages when he manages the times of obedience and disobedience of the patriarchs.

There is so much frustration in the lives of Christians who search for God's will that could be avoided through meditation on these lives. It is possible that many prayers seeking God's will would be unnecessary if there were adequate time spent looking at the lives where God has already spoken. The reader should ponder the possibility that the answer to many prayers might be, 'Open your Bible, and meditate on the lives of Abraham, Isaac, Jacob, and Joseph.'

Genesis 12:1-20

10. And there was a famine in the land: and Abram went down into Egypt to sojourn there; for the famine was grievous in the land. 11. And it came to pass, when he was come near to enter into Egypt, that he said unto Sarai his wife, Behold now, I know that thou art a fair woman to look upon: 12. Therefore it shall come to pass, when the Egyptians shall see thee, that they shall say, This is his wife: and they will kill me, but they will save thee alive. 13. Say, I pray thee, thou art my sister: that it may be well with me for thy sake; and my soul shall live because of thee. 14. And it came to pass, that, when Abram was come into Egypt, the Egyptians beheld the woman that she was very fair. 15. The princes also of Pharaoh saw her, and commended her before Pharaoh: and the woman was taken into Pharaoh's house. 16. And he entreated Abram well for her sake: and he had sheep, and oxen, and he asses, and menservants, and maidservants, and she asses, and camels. 17. And the Lord plagued Pharaoh and his house with great plagues because of Sarai Abram's wife. 18. And Pharaoh called Abram and said, What is this that thou hast done unto me? why didst thou not tell me that she was thy wife? 19. Why saidst thou, She is my sister? so I might have taken her to me to wife: now therefore behold thy wife, take her, and go thy way. 20. And Pharaoh commanded his men concerning him: and they sent him away, and his wife, and all that he had.

Hard choices

Trying to walk with God in a relationship of love has its ups and downs. There are those moments that require choices. The teenager gets his first night to be away from his parents, and to spend an evening with his friends. He is confident that he will do nothing wrong, his parents have taught him well, but two of the group want to take advantage of the freedom to try an experiment with drugs. Suddenly, the evening that was so eagerly anticipated is filled with trial. If he doesn't participate, he can be rejected and the evening, so anticipated, is cut short. If he does participate, he will break the trust of his parents. Which is the more important for him: the trust that his parents have or the inclusion into the group? This is a tough decision because there are no immediate rewards in a parent's trust. They will only know of this event if the teenager reports the event to his parents. The reward of acceptance into the group, however, has immediate benefits.

The choices that a Christian make fall into categories of this type. Abram had been obedient to God. He had pulled up stakes, left his homeland, to the country that God showed him. He had every reason to feel good about his spiritual willpower. Then it is tested. 'And there was a famine in the land...' (12:10b). Based on God's promise, Abram had every reason to expect that entrance into the land of promise would begin a time of great prosperity. Instead, there was famine. What will he do? The Bible says, '...and Abram went down into Egypt to sojourn there...' (12:10b). He leaves the land of promise.

There is a lesson that should be very clear. Love is a command that is never totally proved. It is constantly on the testing ground. Abram proved that he valued his relationship to God when he left his homeland. In the Promised Land, he must prove it again. It was in the land of promise that Abram's relationship with God would grow because that is where God had wanted him. For Abram, there was a new lesson. The victory was in his choice of a relationship with God. The reward is his opportunity to deepen that relationship through the trial of the famine. God can become even more wonderful to him. In this moment, Abram chose to be blessed by Egypt rather than God. It was to lead him to sin. Whose blessing will the teenager accept? Our value system is wrapped in those kinds of choices.

Discerning bad choices

Trying to solve a problem that we have by committing sin is like placing a baby in a pen with a rattlesnake hoping that the presence of the baby will awaken a sense of compassion in the snake. Abram had made a great step of faith in leaving home, obeying God by journeying into the Promised Land. A problem arises when the land is hit by famine. Humans are to use their heads in dealing with problems, but when the conclusion involves sin, they have not thought wisely. Abram follows a great step of faith with the exact opposite. He knows that God wants him in the land, but makes a decision that says God cannot provide for him in the land. It seems like a good decision. Abram can provide for his family in Egypt, so where is the sin? His sin was in not trusting God. Love for someone requires the aspect of trust. Love cannot be maintained where trust is lacking.

Decisions of this sort are very difficult for us. The sin of failing to trust God is often hard to discern. The famine obviously was overwhelming to Abram. He was responsible for his family and needed to do something. It is likely that he was feeling pressure from some of his family and servants, though the Scripture does not report it. Under the pressure that Abram faces, the need to do something (anything) is surely urgent.

Other aspects of discerning failure to trust God often arise. How much of my own creativity am I to use in solving problems? Christians sometimes worry that their creativity is sin. Should we pray for God to bless what appears to be a human idea? How can we discern when our actions may reflect a lack of trust? And, when can we be confident in the exercise of human ingenuity?

Abram's experience provides a very clear illustration which can give guidance. That which opposes right will manifest wrong if we are alert. Abram had a capital idea. Let's go to Egypt. He was putting the baby in the pen with the rattlesnake. How could he have known this in light of his good idea? In order to pull off his scheme, he realizes he must lie to the Pharaoh and tell him that Sarai (his wife) is his sister. Sarai must be willing to commit adultery to spare Abram's life. Abram's lack of trust led to a second sin that is more easily discerned. The snake bites. Loving God is to have an aversion to sin. The lack of trust is fully exposed when our schemes require us to compromise. We may not quickly discern the lack of trust factor, but there will be a sin that is clear if the lack of trust is present. Abram could have seen his lack of trust in his proposed compromise.

> It is easy for humans to try to force answers to the problems of their lives, and in that forcing of answers excuse a compromise to sin. We should always seek to know the Word of God, so that, in the midst of our difficulties, we may be alert to our error when we are compromising with sin.

'...the Lord plagued Pharaoh...'

One of the great tendencies of Christians is to notice possessions, and to reflect on the way God blesses some with many material things while others who may be better Christians have little. As one examines this story of Abram, the dilemma is even more complicated. It is made clear to us that Abram had sinned in two ways. First, he had failed to trust God (12:10). Second, he had lied to the Pharaoh, passing off his wife, Sarai, as his sister, exposing her to adultery (12:13-14). God intervenes, punishing Pharaoh, who then forces Abram to leave. Abram leaves! Abram sinned! The Pharaoh is punished! It doesn't seem right.

In the New Testament, the apostle Paul states, 'For the gifts and calling of God are without repentance' (Romans 11:29). This verse helps in reflecting on Abram's situation. The promise God made to Abram was, 'And I will make of thee a great nation...And I will bless them that bless thee, and curse him that curseth thee...' (12:2-3). Abram sinned, and Pharaoh, by taking Abram's wife to himself, was interfering with God's promise to Abram (12:2-3).

Though Pharaoh did not know it, God's Word was at risk. When God punished Pharaoh, he was not validating Abram; he was validating his own Word. God will be true to himself.

Abram returns to the land where he should have stayed in the first place instead of taking the journey into Egypt. He returns to an altar he had earlier built at Bethel. He 'called on the name of the Lord' (Genesis 13:4), are words which present the idea of offering a sacrifice of repentance. It is clear that Abram did not see his additional wealth as God saying to him, 'Well done!' In fact, that wealth is an ever-present reminder of his sin. The Pharaoh did not seek the return of that which he gave to Abram. It was now tarnished. It was a lesson to Abram that the material things of this world carry no value without a clean heart and mind before God, and that God's Word is more valuable than all material blessings. Learning the value in God's Word is part of a true love for God.

Genesis 13-14

I. Abram and Lot Separate (13:1-13)

II. Abram's Superiority in the Land (13:14-14:24)
1. '...toward Sodom...'
2. Lift up your eyes
3. An honour from Melchizedek

Genesis 13:1-13

1. And Abram went up out of Egypt, he, and his wife, and all that he had, and Lot with him, into the south. 2. And Abram was very rich in cattle, in silver, and in gold. 3. And he went on his journeys from the south even to Bethel, unto the place where his tent had been at the beginning, between Bethel and Hai; 4. Unto the place of the altar, which he had made there at the first: and there Abram called on the name of the Lord. 5. And Lot also, which went with Abram, had flocks, and herds, and tents. 6. And the land was not able to bear them, that they might dwell together: for their substance was great, so that they could not dwell together. 7. And there was a strife between the herdmen of Abram's cattle and the herdmen of Lot's cattle: and the Canaanite and the Perizzite dwelled then in the land. 8. And Abram said unto Lot, Let there be no strife, I pray thee, between me and thee, and between my herdmen and thy herdmen; for we be brethren. 9. Is not the whole land before thee? separate thyself, I pray thee, from me: if thou wilt take the left hand, then I will go to the right; or if thou depart to the right hand, then I will go to the left. 10. And Lot lifted up his eyes, and beheld all the plain of Jordan, that it was well watered every where, before the Lord destroyed Sodom and Gomorrah, even as the garden of the Lord, like the land of Egypt, as thou comest unto Zoar.

Then Lot chose him all the plain of Jordan; and Lot journeyed east: and they separated themselves the one from the other. 12. Abram dwelled in the land of Canaan, and Lot dwelled in the cities of the plain, and pitched his tent toward Sodom. 13. But the men of Sodom were wicked and sinners before the Lord exceedingly.

Abram and Lot separate

Choices are the stuff of life. Everyone's life is the consummate result of the choices made. Every choice is a test, but every choice is not a determinative one in the course of our life. There are those choices from which there is no turning back. They will have permanent and enduring effects. Learning the ability to discern when I am making that kind of choice, and knowing how to choose wisely is critical to the development of maturity.

Abram and Lot faced a choice. They could no longer stay together. Both had great wealth and the servants of the two families were quarrelling about which family had priority in grazing lands, water, etc. Abram offered to Lot the choice of which part of the country he would take. At this point Abram had learned his lesson about the danger of trusting in the physical circumstances of life as opposed to trusting God. Lot chose the part more pleasing to the eyes, and believed he had made a capital choice. 'And Lot lifted up his eyes, and beheld all the plain of Jordan, that it was well-watered everywhere, ...Then Lot chose him all the plain of Jordan; and Lot journeyed east...' (Genesis 13:10-11).

The Scripture gives us an indication of a severe miscalculation on Lot's part. It is the ongoing dilemma of all Christians to this day. He did not fully examine that which attracted him. Note verses 12-13 '...and Lot dwelled in the cities of the plain, and pitched his tent toward Sodom. But the men of Sodom were wicked and sinners before the Lord exceedingly.'

Lot, without question, told himself that his decision was based totally in the need to care for his family and servants, but he was also curious about the enticements of Sodom, clearly inferred by

'... pitched his tent toward Sodom' (Genesis 12:12). Lot's choice gives us a clue about discerning when we are about to make one of those life-altering choices from which there is no return. The clue is wrapped in this question: How does this choice reflect on my love of God? Is it demonstrating a greater curiosity and concern about the things of this world than I have about God's word and my relationship with him?

> It is common to fool ourselves into thinking that we are making right decisions because they materially prosper us, or our family. We should seek wisdom to discern those moments we are making choices that say our love for the world is greater than our love for God.

Genesis 13:14-14:24

14. And the Lord said unto Abram, after that Lot was separated from him, Lift up now thine eyes, and look from the place where thou art northward, and southward, and eastward, and westward: 15. For all the land which thou seest, to thee will I give it, and to thy seed for ever. 16. And I will make thy seed as the dust of the earth: so that if a man can number the dust of the earth, then shall thy seed also be numbered. 17. Arise, walk through the land in the length of it and in the breadth of it; for I will give it unto thee. 18. Then Abram removed his tent, and came and dwelt in the plain of Mamre, which is in Hebron, and built there an altar unto the Lord. 1. And it came to pass in the days of Amraphel king of Shinar, Arioch king of Ellasar, Chedorlaomer king of Elam, and Tidal king of nations; 2. That these made war with Bera king of Sodom, and with Birsha king of Gomorrah, Shinab king of Admah, and Shemeber king of Zeboiim, and the king of Bela, which is Zoar. 3. All these were joined together in the vale of Siddim, which is the salt sea. 4. Twelve years they served Chedorlaomer, and in the thirteenth year they rebelled. 5. And in the fourteenth year came Chedorlaomer, and the kings that were with him, and smote the Rephaims in Ashteroth Karnaim, and the Zuzims in Ham, and the Emims in Shaveh Kiriathaim, 6. And the Horites in their mount Seir, unto Elparan, which is by the wilderness. 7. And they returned, and came to

Enmishpat, which is Kadesh, and smote all the country of the Amalekites, and also the Amorites, that dwelt in Hazezontamar. 8. And there went out the king of Sodom, and the king of Gomorrah, and the king of Admah, and the king of Zeboiim, and the king of Bela (the same is Zoar;) and they joined battle with them in the vale of Siddim; 9. With Chedorlaomer the king of Elam, and with Tidal king of nations, and Amraphel king of Shinar, and Arioch king of Ellasar; four kings with five. 10. And the vale of Siddim was full of slimepits; and the kings of Sodom and Gomorrah fled, and fell there; and they that remained fled to the mountain. 11. And they took all the goods of Sodom and Gomorrah, and all their victuals, and went their way.

12. And they took Lot, Abram's brother's son, who dwelt in Sodom, and his goods, and departed. 13. And there came one that had escaped, and told Abram the Hebrew; for he dwelt in the plain of Mamre the Amorite, brother of Eshcol, and brother of Aner: and these were confederate with Abram. 14. And when Abram heard that his brother was taken captive, he armed his trained servants, born in his own house, three hundred and eighteen, and pursued them unto Dan. 15. And he divided himself against them, he and his servants, by night, and smote them, and pursued them unto Hobah, which is on the left hand of Damascus. 16. And he brought back all the goods, and also brought again his brother Lot, and his goods, and the women also, and the people. 17. And the king of Sodom went out to meet him after his return from the slaughter of Chedorlaomer, and of the kings that were with him, at the valley of Shaveh, which is the king's dale. 18. And Melchizedek king of Salem brought forth bread and wine: and he was the priest of the most high God. 19. And he blessed him, and said, Blessed be Abram of the most high God, possessor of heaven and earth: 20. And blessed be the most high God, which hath delivered thine enemies into thy hand. And he gave him tithes of all. 21. And the king of Sodom said unto Abram, Give me the persons, and take the goods to thyself. 22. And Abram said to the king of Sodom, I have lift up mine hand unto the Lord, the most high God, the possessor of heaven and earth, 23. That I will not take from a thread even to a shoelatchet, and that I will not take any thing that is thine, lest thou shouldest say, I have made Abram rich: 24. Save only that which the young men have eaten, and the portion of the men which went with me, Aner, Eshcol, and Mamre; let them take their portion.

'...toward Sodom...'

Being able to anticipate the unforeseen thing is a gift that many of us would like to have. Predicting the future is seen as a phenomenal way to attain wealth, or gain, for self. Of course, no one but God can do that. Yet, it is incumbent on Christians that we have a certain degree of discernment about the future. By knowing how to think, there are certain kinds of predictions that we can accurately make.

Lot, when he had the choice of dwelling places after his breakup with Abram, 'pitched his tent toward Sodom' (Genesis 13:12). In the very next chapter we discover the natural result. When certain kings of the area made war with Sodom, we read, 'And they took all the goods of Sodom and Gomorrah, and all their victuals, and went their way. And they took Lot, Abram's brother's son, who dwelt in Sodom, and his goods and departed' (Genesis 14:11-12). Lot now dwells in the city of wickedness. His compromise with evil continues. In chapter 19, he offers his daughters as sexual partners to certain men in the city to prevent them from attempting a homosexual encounter with the two guests in his house (Genesis 19:7-8). Lot found himself in this predicament for one reason. He refused to adequately read the future.

It takes spiritual discernment to know that curiosity about evil leads to defining down the defilement of evil, and that leads to compromise with evil. Though it takes spiritual discernment, it does not take genius. Lot should have known when he chose to pitch his tent toward Sodom that it would lead to his living in Sodom. Though he may not have predicted that he would commit such foul acts as offering his daughters to be sexually abused, it is the kind of filthiness that described the city in which Lot was so anxious to dwell. A love for God would have prevented the attraction to Sodom. Because Lot exercised no spiritual or moral authority in his family, we see the ultimate tragedy. 'But his wife looked back from behind him, and she became a pillar of salt' (Genesis 19:26).

A little spiritual discernment would have allowed Lot to adequately predict the future, and the great downfall of his life would have been prevented.

Lift up your eyes

Consider the emotional impact on Abram. He had been very kind to Lot, the son of his dead brother, Haran. Lot had travelled with Abram to Canaan, and had prospered by virtue of Abram's kindness (13:5). The day arrives when the two must separate because of friction between the two families. Abram again shows his kindness, offering Lot the choice of the highlands or the plains. With all of the kindness Abram had demonstrated, one might assume that Lot, in his gratitude would offer to his uncle the more beautiful plains, and would accept the highlands. In a clear display of a lack of appreciation, Lot chose the plains for himself. It is not that the highlands were so bad, it is just that the contrast with the well-watered plain made them far less appealing. Abram would have to feel disappointed both in Lot's lack of gratitude and in the result of settling for the less attractive highlands.

God sees the need for encouragement. He states, '...look from the place where thou art...For all the land which thou seest, to thee will I give it, and to thy seed...I will make thy seed as the dust of the earth...Arise, walk through the land...' (13:14-17). There is great irony in God's words. They are clearly meant to comfort Abram in a moment of disappointment, but what is the comfort? He reminds Abram of a promise of things he will never possess in his lifetime. 'Arise, walk through the land...' (17)! Your descendants will possess it, but you will never own it, Abram. So, rejoice and be glad! Would such a promise be that comforting to you and me?

In Abram's response, we have a moment which reveals that which so clearly endeared Abram to his Lord. 'And Abram...came and dwelt in the plain of Mamre...and built there an altar unto the Lord' (13:18). He worshipped God! It is a notable contrast to Lot's unappreciative attitude. Lot could not be grateful for that which he clearly possessed. Abram had a great appreciation for, and took delight in, that which he could possess only in faith. Abram's possession of God's promise was no more than the possession of a promise, yet, it made his heart glad. It is a revealing glimpse into why God chose him.

As one looks ahead to the coming of the Incarnate One, there is the same reality that the man, Christ Jesus, must face. He shall have a bride for himself, a church, (Ephesians 5:31-32), but he must die first! It is a lesson in faith that every Christian must learn God's greatest blessing awaits the return of Christ.

An honour from Melchizedek

When Abram's nephew, Lot, was taken captive by a group of city-state kings (14:12), Abram pursued after them. He overcame them, rescued Lot, and rescued the others who were part of the cities of the plain and had been taken captive. The kings of the cities of the plain came to Abram to express their gratitude. Two of those kings came bearing gifts. Melchizedek, a king of Salem (later to be called Jerusalem) is also a priest of God. Abram pays tithes to the priest, who provides bread and wine for Abram. The king of Sodom offered Abram the goods robbed from Sodom, which Abram retrieved in victory. Abram accepted the gifts of the priest of God and rejected the gifts of the king of Sodom. It is a curious event, but illustrates much about loving God, and about the choices that we make.

First glance will tell us that Abram gave more to Melchizedek then he received in return. The tithe represents one tenth of Abram's possessions, while the bread and wine Abram received were mere symbols. In the Old Testament, bread is the symbol of life, and wine is the symbol of the provisions of life (Note Jesus said 'I am the bread of life' John 6:35). Abram had been asked to trust God for all the provisions of life, and his acceptance of the priest's gifts, and his payment of the tithe was Abram's expression of gratitude and reaffirmation of his full trust in God. His love for God is expressed in the value he placed on the offering that came from the priest.

The gift of the king of Sodom, at first glance, would seem much greater. Abram's discernment allows him to see into the future, which dramatically devalues the gift of the king. 'And Abram said to the king of Sodom, I have lift up mine hand unto the Lord, the most high God, the possessor of heaven and earth, that I will not take from a thread even to a shoe latchet, and that I will not take anything that is thine, lest thou shouldest say I have made Abram rich' (14:22-23). The gift of the king of Sodom would place Abram in the king's debt, and remove Abram's ability to make his own decisions. He was wise enough to understand that there are many kinds of debts that we can incur. Decisions, which give anyone but God control of our life, are very insidious.

Why would the same thing not apply with the gifts accepted from Pharaoh. Those gifts from Pharaoh came not from a ruler in the land which was now promised to Abram. The Pharaoh's gifts were a reminder of a sin committed, not a prerequisite to further sin. Abram could not allow himself to be perceived in debt, in anyway, to rulers of the land. It could affect the future of his descendants.

The observant reader of Scripture can discover many gems of wisdom in the story of Abraham. Here lies one of the greatest pieces of wisdom: the importance of rejecting any thing that relinquishes control of our life to anyone or anything but God.

Genesis 15-16

I. A Vision of Comfort and Horror
1. Faith for things not seen
2. A prophecy of affliction
3. Iniquity of the Amorites

II. A Solution from Sarai (16:6-16)
1. Sarai's offer
2. Sarai's motivation
3. The God who sees

Genesis 15:1-21

1. After these things the word of the Lord came unto Abram in a vision, saying, Fear not, Abram: I am thy shield, and thy exceeding great reward. 2. And Abram said, Lord God, what wilt thou give me, seeing I go child-less, and the steward of my house is this Eliezer of Damascus? 3. And Abram said, Behold, to me thou hast given no seed: and, lo, one born in my house is mine heir. 4. And, behold, the word of the Lord came unto him, saying, This shall not be thine heir; but he that shall come forth out of thine own bowels shall be thine heir. 5. And he brought him forth abroad, and said, Look now toward heaven, and tell the stars, if thou be able to number them: and he said unto him, So shall thy seed be. 6. And he be-lieved in the Lord; and he counted it to him for righteousness. 7. And he said unto him, I am the Lord that brought thee out of Ur of the Chaldees, to give thee this land to inherit it. 8. And he said, Lord God, whereby shall I know that I shall inherit it? 9. And he said unto him, Take me an heifer of three years old, and a she goat of three years old, and a ram of three years old, and a turtledove, and a young pigeon. 9. And he took unto him all these, and divided them in the midst, and laid each piece one against another: but the birds divided he not. 11. And when the fowls came down upon the carcases, Abram drove them away. 12. And when the sun was going down, a deep sleep fell upon Abram; and, lo, an horror of great darkness fell upon him. 13. And he said unto Abram, Know of a surety that thy seed shall be a stranger in a land that is not theirs, and shall serve them; and they shall afflict them four hundred years; 14. And also that nation, whom they shall serve, will I judge: and afterward shall they come out with great substance. 15. And thou shalt go to thy fathers in peace; thou shalt be buried in a good old age. 16. But in the fourth generation they shall come hither again: for the iniquity of the Amorites is not yet full. 17. And it came to pass, that, when the sun went down, and it was dark, behold a smoking furnace, and a burning lamp that passed between those pieces. 18. In the same day the Lord made a covenant with Abram, saying, Unto thy seed have I given this land, from the river of Egypt unto the great river, the river Euphrates: 19. The Kenites, and the Kenizzites, and the Kadmonites, 20. And the Hittites, and the Perizzites, and the Rephaims, 21. And the Amorites, and the Canaanites, and the Girgashites, and the Jebusites.

Faith for things not seen

Trying to make sense of our world, and to understand God, leads us into very unexpected places. This event in the life of Abram is fascinating, and extremely challenging to our imagination. It immediately follows Abram's wise choice to refuse the spoil of this earth, reflected in the gifts of the king of Sodom, in favour of trust in God, reflected in the gifts of the king of Salem. God comes to him and assures him that he has chosen wisely, '…Fear not, Abram: I am thy shield, and thy exceeding great reward' (15:1). Abram uses the moment to remind God of his original promise that still goes unfulfilled. '…Behold, to me thou has given no seed…' (15:3). God responds with '…Look now toward heaven, and tell the stars, if thou be able to number them…So shall thy seed be' (15:5). God reiterates his promise that Abram would inherit the land upon which he had travelled. Abram asked for assurance, and God gives this incredible word '...Know of a surety that thy seed shall be a stranger in a land that is not theirs, and shall serve them; and they shall afflict them four hundred years' (15:13).

Abram was concerned that there was no son, and no land, and God's word of comfort was about that which will not happen for four hundred years. What would you think if you went to your preacher with a concern, and he said, 'Relax, four hundred years from now, your concern will be solved!' We read Scripture in the light of four thousand years of history. Abram did not have that luxury. He was called upon to rejoice in his God for what God was doing which would directly impact his family, but four hundred years later. In our world of instant gratification, this is mind-boggling. Yet, it is a great motivator for love of God. The teaching of Scripture is to lead us to be spiritually perceptive enough to be able to know what kinds of predicaments that our choices create. It is to learn to discern the future in order that we do not make foolish moral mistakes. This little event in Abram's life shows that God works to grant us a little of his wisdom if we demonstrate willingness to use it. It also tells us that God thinks a long way ahead, and that what he is doing in us is much greater than we could possibly fathom. He is worthy of our love and our trust.

The validity of present sacrifice for spiritual reward in another life is the heart of the Christian experience. The Apostle Paul uses Abram as example to explain the faith condition of the believer. Though still in a body prone to sin, the believer accepts a future hope as a present reality. He is justified, made fit for God's presence, in satisfaction of God's holiness by virtue of sin's punishment in Christ. God has redeemed without compromising his holy demand for justice. The Christian's claim to justification is his faith in the Word of God. As Paul said of Abraham, 'For what saith the Scriptures? Abraham believed God and it was accounted unto him for righteousness' (Romans 4:3). In the present state, the believer does battle with sin, but carries the promise (by faith) of total victory over sin. ' Likewise, reckon ye also yourselves to be dead indeed unto sin, but always alive unto God, through Jesus Christ, our Lord' (Romans 6:11).

A prophecy of affliction

The picture in Genesis 15 is very strange to our modern mind. It was, however, a relatively common custom in the ancient Near East. There is a fascinating touch of realism provided by the writer. The carcasses of three animals are halved and laid upon the ground along with the unsevered carcasses of two birds, a turtledove and a pigeon. Note the action in verse 11. 'And when the fowls came down upon the carcasses, Abram drove them away.' This charming touch of realism lightens up a very sombre event.

Abram is placed in a trance, '...horror of great darkness' (15:12). In the trance, Abram views a torch ('burning lamp' and a 'smoking furnace') passing between the carcasses. Clearly, the torch represents God. In the ancient world, humans would often make covenants with each other with this kind of ritual (see Jeremiah 34:18-20). The strange part of the vision of Abram is that God is the only one who passes between the carcasses. God allows Abram to view the covenant that God makes with himself.

The devotional moment for the reader is in the impact on Abram. He has confronted God with the reality that the promised son has not been given him (15:3). In effect, he is asking, 'why?' In this strange ritual and pronouncement, God answers the question. Both Abram and the reader must understand that God must be true to himself.

Consider the following: There are nations in the land of promise with which God must demonstrate his authority. The commitment he makes to Abram does not exclude God's responsibility to himself to act with patience toward the nations he will dispossess (15:16). He is telling Abram, 'Do not be so possessed with what I am doing in you that you lose sight of the reality that I am also at work everywhere else.' It is a wonderful, personal moment Abram receives as God reveals this aspect of himself.

Also, God communicates to Abram a harsh reality. His descendants will go through a horror that he will not have to experience. Abram had a wonderful promise, but wrapped in the promise is a horror. Be grateful, Abram, for what you will get, but be grateful as well, for what you do not get.

> The history of the redemptive plan of God offers another view into the human inability to see fully God's design. Israel longed for the coming of Messiah. When he came, they did not like what they got. They had failed to see the horror in addition to the glory. The messiah was also the promised seed of the woman (Genesis 3:15). He must first suffer in order to deal with the sin problem of humanity before he could deal with the frustrations of Israel.

Iniquity of Amorites

God's words to Abram present a problem in interpretation. It can only be understood in the full context of biblical revelation. 'But in the fourth generation they shall come hither again; for the iniquity of the Amorites is not yet full' (15:16). What is meant by '...not yet full.' There is connectedness with other biblical events. Of the people of Noah's day, it was stated, '...the thoughts of his heart was only evil continually' (Genesis 6:5). Sodom and Gomorrah were destroyed because their sin was very grievous (Genesis 18:20). The children of Israel were told to kill all the inhabitants of Jericho (except for Rahab and her family, Joshua 6:17). In all those instances, the population had passed the point of repentance. Evil had come to its climax in their lives, and no repentance is possible. It is the same sin of which Jesus spoke '...but the blasphemy against the Holy Spirit shall not be forgiven unto men' (Matthew 12:31).

When God spoke of the iniquity of the Amorites (an alternative name for Canaanites) as being full, he is referring to a mindset beyond the possibility of redemption. This is a horrifying picture, and one that most people do not want to consider. It was clearly seen in the people of Noah's day that they were incapable of recognizing good (Genesis 6:5). That is the point at which the Amorites (Canaanites) must arrive.

All vestiges of the worship of the true God will disappear from Canaan with the removal of Abram's grandson (Jacob) and his family to Egypt. During the four hundred years the nation is developing in Egypt, the Amorites will be in the process of confirming their wickedness, so that God's judgement on them will clearly manifest his wisdom and righteousness, just as had the judgement on the earth in Noah's day.

The reader can be comforted in the knowledge of God's long-suffering. He does not judge on mere whim, or anger. He allows every opportunity for repentance. Individuals and nations must remember that with every moment of opportunity one has to repent, it is also an opportunity to become hardened. Thus, when one arrives at the place of inability to distinguish good from evil, his iniquity is full.

> The opportunity for the heart to harden beyond the point of repentance is a concept difficult to imagine. Yet, the Scripture is replete with such imagery. God is patient! But patience has two sides. It provides both opportunity for repentance, and opportunity for hardening.

Genesis 16:1-16

1. Now Sarai Abram's wife bare him no children: and she had an handmaid, an Egyptian, whose name was Hagar. 2. And Sarai said unto Abram, Behold now, the Lord hath restrained me from bearing: I pray thee, go in unto my maid; it may be that I may obtain children by her. And Abram hearkened to the voice of Sarai. 3. And Sarai Abram's wife took

Hagar her maid the Egyptian, after Abram had dwelt ten years in the land of Canaan, and gave her to her husband Abram to be his wife. 4. And he went in unto Hagar, and she conceived: and when she saw that she had conceived, her mistress was despised in her eyes. 5. And Sarai said unto Abram, My wrong be upon thee: I have given my maid into thy bosom; and when she saw that she had conceived, I was despised in her eyes: the Lord judge between me and thee. 6. But Abram said unto Sarai, Behold, thy maid is in thy hand; do to her as it pleaseth thee. And when Sarai dealt hardly with her, she fled from her face. 7. And the angel of the Lord found her by a fountain of water in the wilderness, by the fountain in the way to Shur. 8. And he said, Hagar, Sarai's maid, whence camest thou? and whither wilt thou go? And she said, I flee from the face of my mistress Sarai. 9. And the angel of the Lord said unto her, Return to thy mistress, and submit thyself under her hands. 10. And the angel of the Lord said unto her, I will multiply thy seed exceedingly, that it shall not be numbered for multitude. 11. And the angel of the Lord said unto her, Behold, thou art with child and shalt bear a son, and shalt call his name Ishmael; because the Lord hath heard thy affliction. 12. And he will be a wild man; his hand will be against every man, and every man's hand against him; and he shall dwell in the presence of all his brethren. 13. And she called the name of the Lord that spake unto her, Thou God seest me: for she said, Have I also here looked after him that seeth me? 14. Wherefore the well was called Beerlahairoi; behold, it is between Kadesh and Bered. 15. And Hagar bare Abram a son: and Abram called his son's name, which Hagar bare, Ishmael. 16. And Abram was fourscore and six years old, when Hagar bare Ishmael to Abram.

Sarai's offer

God restates his promise to Abraham (15:18), and provides a list of nations whose countries shall establish the clear boundaries of God's promised land (15:19-20). As an insignificant descendant of Shem, Abram is to become a great nation. His nation will supersede all the nations around him. And it is even more phenomenal, they shall first be slaves for four hundred years. God gave to

Abram with this proclamation his legacy. It was quite a legacy for one whose greatest accomplishment can be written in three words: he trusted God.

The reader then is faced with a human tragedy. Human failure complicates the promise of God. Sarai's suggestion to Abraham is a perplexing dilemma to the mindset of Christianity with a long tradition of placing great stress on monogamy and faithfulness. Despite her barrenness, one struggles to understand Sarai's action. There is a powerful theological connection in Genesis that helps in analysing the story. It takes the reader back to the moment of the first childbirth. Eve rejoiced in the birth of her son, Cain, as hope of the fulfilment of God's promise in Genesis 3:15. The seed of the woman would bring redemption to humanity. It was not to be found in Cain, as he was the seed of man. Yet, it is in childbirth that the woman shall produce her 'seed.' The promise of the woman's seed was certainly taught to the followers of God in the coming generations. When Noah was born, his father's words about his son, Noah, reflect his hope in the promise. '...This same shall comfort us concerning our work and toil of our hands, because of the ground which the Lord hath cursed' (Genesis 5:29). Noah was a redeemer, in that humanity was delivered from total destruction through Noah's faithfulness. Nevertheless, he was not the hoped for seed of the woman.

When God chose Abram and gave him the great promise that he would make of him a great nation, the greater hope, that is rooted in that promise, is the hope of Genesis 3:15. The hope of bearing children, for Sarai, was wrapped in the child-bearing instinct of the woman, but it was also a theological necessity when considered in the light of God's promise of redemption, and God's promise to Abram. As both promises come from the mouth of God, both, are vitally connected, and become part of the same promise. If Sarai did not completely understand it in this manner, it is certain that the writer of Genesis intends the reader to make the connection.

When Sarai sends her husband to her handmaiden, it was an act acceptable to the culture, but more is in view. For Sarai, as the two promises are one, a son must be born to Abram or the first promise dies. She is to be chastised for her lack of faith, but on the other hand, her act has a certain kind of nobility. She wants to make sure that God's word does not fail. Many times we Christians act in the attitude of guaranteeing that God's word is done, forgetting that our actions are a demonstration of a lack of faith in God.

It is sometimes a difficult thing for the Christian to discern the difference between trying to guarantee the success of God's work, and simply doing God's work.

Sarai's motivation

In a conversation, a young man expressed a rather common human complaint. He was in a quandary about a perplexing problem, and said, 'There are so many people giving me advice, I don't know who to believe.' There are many voices that are always available to tell us what we should do. We all know the experience of having listened to the wrong voice.

In the story of God's promise to Abram to multiply his seed and to make of him a great nation, we seldom focus on another who is central to this promise. It is Abram's wife, Sarai. The curse of barrenness was a great burden for women of that generation. As Sarai had waited for God's promise to be fulfilled, she felt responsible. Trying to reason things out in her mind she evidently concluded that God would not grant Abram a son because of her. 'And Sarai said unto Abram, Behold now, the Lord hath restrained me from bearing: I pray thee, go in unto my maid; it may be that I may obtain children by her…' (16:2). Note the dynamic: Sarai reasoned very personally, and applied her personal distress to Abram. She becomes a voice seeking to counsel Abram.

The voice of Sarai was powerful. First, Abram cared for her and did not like seeing her hurting. Second, she had a solution. Third, Abram probably liked the solution. Here was Sarai giving him permission to do something that was already a temptation. The result, '...And Abram hearkened to the voice of Sarai' (16:2).

The text lays out for us the truth that Sarai added to her burden when the handmaiden conceived. The solution only brought heartache. The failure of Abram here was in the choice of the voice to which he listened. We might ask, 'Why should he not listen to the one who loved him, for she would have his best interest at heart?' Discernment for Abram could have come on two fronts. First, Sarai had stated that God had kept her from bearing a child meaning that she was at fault. The promise, however, had been made to Abram. It was his prerogative to make that determination, not Sarai's. Sarai was in need of consolation from Abram, not acquiescence. Second, the solution was a distortion of God's word. This is sin. Even if Sarai's sin had created the problem, God would not fulfil his promise by allowing the sinner to dictate the methodology. Those voices that talk to us can be well meaning, and sincere, so we must determine if they are speaking out of the baggage of their own hurts, needing spiritual comfort themselves, and we must be able to discern if another sin is involved.

Humans must always realize how easily they are attracted to sin. Sincere voices can sometimes be the leading instrument in directing us to sin. We should always seek wisdom to know when those sincere voices may be leading us to sin.

The God who sees

Once Hagar becomes pregnant, her disposition towards Sarai changes. Upon seeking Abram's help and not getting it, Sarai acted in a way that created great fear for Hagar. She flees into the Wilderness of Shur on the way back to Egypt. Here, she is confronted by 'the angel of the Lord' (16:7). The angel of the Lord is an appearance of God, for only God could make the kind of promise that is here made (16:10). The words are very comforting for Hagar and assure her that her son, though rejected by the house of Abram would be well able to survive. Note the term 'wild man (16:12). He shall be particularly skilled at surviving in the desert.

Hagar's response to the message of the 'angel of the Lord' is an expression of faith and of submission. She recognizes that it is the God of Abram who speaks to her. She notes '...Thou God seest me...' (16:13). Her immediate recognition of the God of Abram likely comes from the nature of God's promise. '...I will multiply thy seed exceedingly...' (16:10). She must have heard Abram and Sarai use these words regularly as they discussed God's promise to them. For Hagar, the ability to accept these comforting words from God is significant.

She is afraid of the reaction of Sarai and Abram. She has already run from them because of Sarai's harsh treatment. She must return and face their anger about her attempt to leave. Her faith must be bold enough to accept the promise she hears from a God who had promised a son to Abram and Sarai, a son that has never been born, much less conceived. She acknowledges trust in the God of Abram, though she is yet to see him deliver on his promise to Abram. What was the motivation behind such trust?

Hagar gives this God a name. '...Thou God seest me: for she said, Have I also here looked after him that seeth me?' (16:13). In the Hebrew, it is simply, El Roi, or 'the God who sees'. There are two aspects to understanding the God who sees which is relevant to Hagar.

First, She had felt left out of the promise, thus could have no part in the God of Abram. In her mind, having fled the house of Abram would have meant the God of Abram is also left behind. Instead, He follows her into this wilderness, and finds her. The fact that he saw her need is an overwhelming revelation. She may not have a share in the specific promise of Abram, but she can have Abram's God. She will accept.

Second, 'the God who sees', can also be understood as the God of sight, or appearance. He can make himself known as he did by appearing as the Angel of the Lord. Hagar's choice is clear. Abram's God blessed her with the manifestation of his presence. He spoke a clear word. She can return to the house of Abram and place her destiny in the promise of this God who has seen her, or she can proceed to Egypt, and abandon this God. She names the place where God met her, Beerlahairoi, a fitting title.

The thought that God has abandoned us, or that God has lost sight of us is ridiculed in sermons demanding faith, yet it is not uncommon for one to fee this way in times of trouble. The story of Hagar offers a ray of hope that God will let us know that we are in his sight. But, we must be alert to teaching moments along the way if we are to discern the vice of God. Because Hagar had been alert to the teaching of God through the voice of Abram and Sara, she recognized the voice of God when it came to her.

The thought that God has abandoned us, or that God has lost sight of us, is ridiculed in sermons about faith. Yet, it is not uncommon for one to feel this way in times of trouble. The story of Hagar offers a ray of hope that God will let us know that we are in his sight. But, we must be alert to teaching moments, along the way of our life, if we are to discern the voice of God when he offers the ray of hope. Because Hagar had been alert to the teaching of God through the conversation of Abram and Sarai, she recognized the voice of God when it comes to her.

Genesis 17:1-27

Genesis 17:1-14

1. And when Abram was ninety years old and nine, the Lord appeared to Abram, and said unto him, I am the Almighty God; walk before me, and be thou perfect. 2. And I will make my covenant between me and thee, and will multiply thee exceedingly. 3. And Abram fell on his face: and God talked with him, saying, 4. As for me, behold, my covenant is with thee, and thou shalt be a father of many nations. 5. Neither shall thy name any more be called Abram, but thy name shall be Abraham; for a father of many nations have I made thee. 6. And I will make thee exceeding fruitful, and I will make nations of thee, and kings shall come out of thee. 7. And I will establish my covenant between me and thee and thy seed after thee in their generations for an everlasting covenant, to be a God unto thee, and to thy seed after thee. 8. And I will give unto thee, and to thy seed after thee, the land wherein thou art a stranger, all the land of Canaan, for an everlasting possession; and I will be their God. 9. And God said unto Abraham, Thou shalt keep my covenant therefore, thou, and thy seed after thee in their generations. 10. This is my covenant, which ye shall keep, between me and you and thy seed after thee; Every man child among you shall be circumcised. 11. And ye shall circumcise the flesh of your foreskin; and it shall be a token of the covenant betwixt me and you. 12. And he that is eight days old shall be circumcised among you, every man child in your generations, he that is born in the house, or bought with money of any stranger, which is not of thy seed. 13. He that is born in thy house, and he that is bought with thy money, must needs be circumcised: and my covenant shall be in your flesh for an everlasting covenant. 14. And the uncircumcised man child whose flesh of his foreskin is not circumcised, that soul shall be cut off from his people; he hath broken my covenant.

A name change

By the time the command to 'love the Lord thy God' was given to Israel (Deuteronomy 6:5), they had a vast array of historical narrative behind them to guide them in understanding the command. The requirement of love should never be considered lightly, or considered only in the sense of giddy excitement and good feelings. In Abram the nation could look and see that love for God exacts a toll on us. Love, in human terms, is never really proven. Because of our sin nature, it is a discipline to which we must constantly be recommitting ourselves. Abram's life establishes this point. As we come to understand this, it gives us reflection on Abram's faith (the concept for which he is best known). How do we define a life of faith? From Abram, we can postulate that a life of faith is one that accepts the reality of constantly reproving our love for God.

In this Scripture reading, God gives to Abram the name by which we know him, Abraham. He is ninety-nine years old when God gives him the name. Note the irony. Abraham has one son born of his wife's handmaiden, and God commands him to start telling people your name is Abraham. The name means, 'Father of many nations.' This will carry some degree of embarrassment for Abraham. The only motivation to accept this embarrassment would be his relationship with God.

Further, Abraham is given a sign that shall be an everlasting covenant with the nation which shall be established as seed of Abraham. It is circumcision. At ninety-nine years old he is called upon to circumcise himself, and all males in his house, as token of God's promise. Do you love God, Abraham? In many ways, Abraham was called upon to look foolish in order that God's greatness might be manifest. Are Christians still called on to do that? Certainly!

We may be enduring great personal suffering, but we are asked to praise God, and test him. The world often appears to be in the hands of mad men, and Christians are called upon to say, 'God is in control!' If you feel somewhat frustrated, so did Abraham. He begged God to stop toying with him. 'And Abraham said unto God, O, that Ishmael might live before thee!' (Genesis 17:18). By loving and trusting God, Abraham was ultimately validated, and God was glorified. That promise is no less certain for us.

> The sincere Christian desires for his life to glorify God. This desire often exposes us to trial. Even our Lord understood this as he prayed for 'the cup' to pass from him (Matthew 26:39). The human can grow weary. We must accept the reality that our validation may not come soon, or even in this life, and that we can fully understand that his promise is all that we need here.

A task to perform

The Genesis writer has reported the unfortunate action of Abram and Sarai's attempt to usurp the decision making of God and to produce a son by virtue of Abram's liaison with Hagar, the handmaid of Sarai. After the action proves to be an unsatisfactory answer, and complicates Abram and Sarai's life, God speaks. His words bear the force of a stinging rebuke, but also resound with the note of reassurance. The act of Abram and Sarai was the result of a lapse in their faith. God's word to Abram is '...I am the Almighty God; walk before me, and be thou perfect' (17:1). It is to tell Abram that he should have known better. The God he serves is El Shaddai, 'the Almighty God.' He is totally sufficient and does not need the help of Abram. In addition, Abram's name is changed to Abraham, 'father of many nations' (17:5). The name Abram will carry gives testament to his faith in God every time he introduces himself. 'Perfect' (17:1), has the idea being upright and confident in God.

At ninety-nine years old, and with only one son in the household (born to his wife's handmaid), Abraham's name is foundation for ridicule. Yet, it is a name he is required to carry.

It is at this point in Abraham's life that God introduces something else. In effect, instead of God doing something, he gives Abraham something to do. '...Every man child among you shall be circumcised. And ye shall circumcise the flesh of your foreskin; and it shall be a token of the covenant betwixt me and you' (17:10-11). Circumcision was a rather common practice in a number of cultures, but it was to be a requirement for the descendants of Abraham who shall inherit the promise of Genesis 12:2, 'And I will make of thee a great Nation...'

The significance of circumcision is a matter of much discussion, but the context lends itself to some clear themes. First, though there is evidence that circumcision was common with several nations, the practice was not found among the Canaanites, the dwellers of the land. The practice was to be another of God's mandates for separating the nation he would build from the present occupants of the land God has destined for the 'great nation.' They are to engage in this very painful action as a demonstration of their extreme sensitivity to the leadership of God. As the foreskin is separated from their flesh, so they shall be a separate people unto God.

Second, God is providing something for Abraham to do which will ease his aching mind. Often, the struggles of life are eased when one can provide an assignment to the life. Worry and consternation are great destroyers of the spirit. One must be doing something. 'Abraham, you shall be the father of many nations, but you shall be a 'great nation.' Start separating yourself and your family from the family of nations among which you dwell. Stop your frustration and get busy with my assignment.

Sometimes making sense of life is very hard. The explanation will often not help even if we had it. At those moments, it is often best to have an assignment to carry out. We should seek to be so in tune to God's leading that we will not mistake his assignment even though we might not be able to make sense of our life.

Genesis 17:15-27

15. And God said unto Abraham, As for Sarai thy wife, thou shalt not call her name Sarai, but Sarah shall her name be. 16. And I will bless her, and give thee a son also of her: yea, I will bless her, and she shall be a mother of nations; kings of people shall be of her. 17. Then Abraham fell upon his face, and laughed, and said in his heart, Shall a child be born unto him that is an hundred years old? and shall Sarah, that is ninety years old, bear? 18. And Abraham said unto God, O that Ishmael might live before thee! 19. And God said, Sarah thy wife shall bear thee a son indeed; and thou shalt call his name Isaac: and I will establish my covenant with him for an everlasting covenant, and with his seed after him. 20. And as for Ishmael, I have heard thee: behold, I have blessed him, and will make him fruitful, and will multiply him exceedingly; twelve princes shall he beget, and I will make him a great nation. 21. But my covenant will I establish with Isaac, which Sarah shall bear unto thee at this set time in the next year. 22. And he left off talking with him, and God went up from Abraham. 23. And Abraham took Ishmael his son, and all that were born in his house, and all that were bought with his money, every male among the men of Abraham's house; and circumcised the flesh of their foreskin in the selfsame day, as God had said unto him. 24. And Abraham was ninety years old and nine, when he was circumcised in the flesh of his foreskin. 25. And Ishmael his son was thirteen years old, when he was circumcised in the flesh of his foreskin. 26. In the selfsame day was Abraham circumcised, and Ishmael his son. 27. And all the men of his house, born in the house, and bought with money of the stranger, were circumcised with him.

Comfort for Sarai

God's renaming of Sarai has an extremely gentle and understanding touch that may be missed unless one spends a little meditative time. When one considers the positioning of this narrative within the Genesis story, the realization of God's comforting for Sarai stands out. The fact that she had offered her handmaid to Abraham to provide him a son indicates that she had come to believe herself left out of the Abrahamic promise. Certainly, this thought was a painful one for her. She clearly loved Abraham, and was willing to sacrifice herself for him. It would be depressing to think of being left out of a joy which the two of them had mutually owned by virtue of the shared promise.

The change from 'Sarai' to 'Sarah' (17:15) seems minor, and has no defining distinction. Its practical import is to say to Sarai, 'You are a part of the promise!' God understood Sarai's motivation in her decision about the handmaid. She had sinned but God does not want her fretting for a long period about the sin. He is providing a word of forgiveness, and a word of reaffirmation. '...she shall be a mother of nations...' (17:16). Yes, 'she,' that is Sarai, not another, shall bear the promised son. The new name by which she shall call herself will be the daily reminder of the covenant God makes with her. For Abraham, the change in name (17:5) was a witness to the nations. For Sarai, now Sarah, the witness is strictly personal, just for her. It reveals to us God's tender and loving forgiveness.

At this moment, Abraham's humanness took hold. 'Then Abraham fell upon his face and laughed...And Abraham said unto God, O that Ishmael might live before thee!' (17:17-18). Abraham was ninety-nine years old. Sarai was well past child-bearing years. When Abraham laughed, it was not in derision, but out of personal struggle. In effect, he was saying to God, 'Why are you making this hard? Ishmael is here, why not let things be as they are?' God was asking Abraham to have faith for a miracle. Abraham was saying, 'It is hard to have faith for a miracle, why cannot I have faith in that which I can see and understand.' Abraham had become somewhat weary of tough faith, a condition not uncommon to the Christian pilgrimage.

A blessing for Ishmael

Abraham makes a plea to God that Ishamel (the son born to Hagar) might be accepted as the child of promise (17:18). God rejects Abraham's plea, and instead reaffirms the promise that Sarah shall have a son who shall be the child of promise. In fact, God proceeds to name the child, '...and thou shalt call his name Isaac...' (17:19). The name carried the meaning, 'laughter.' Abraham had laughed (17:17) when God had reaffirmed his promise to Sarah. It was a laughter that came out of Abraham's anxiety, not out of the humour in God's promise. It is, as though God ignored the true nature of Abraham and gave it a new slant. Abraham laughed! God says, 'Good, that is what you shall name your son.'

Further, God proceeds to encourage Abraham's heart concerning Ishmael. Though, he shall have no part in the 'great nation' (Genesis 12:2), he shall not be separated from blessing. '...I have heard thee: Behold, I have blessed him, and will make him fruitful, and will multiply him exceedingly...' (17:20). Abraham follows this promise by circumcising his household, including Ishmael (17:26). The significance should not be lost on the reader.

Circumcision, seen as a symbol of exclusiveness, separating the nation which shall develop from Abraham through Isaac, now takes on a special kind of inclusion. Ishmael shall father a nation, himself. It will not be the nation of promise, but it shall be blessed by the promise. Ishmael's inclusion in the circumcision symbolizes the greater part of the covenant which God made to Abraham which reads, '...in thee shall all families of the earth be blessed.' (Genesis 12:3). Ishmael was excluded, but also included. This is another of those great ironies often found in the Genesis narratives.

One can imagine that Ishmael may have questioned the value of that inclusion at the time of the circumcision, but is that not the nature of the promise of God? Suffering is a key part of inclusion into God's promise in this world. The Apostle Paul writes of the great desire of the Christian. 'That I may know him (Christ), and the power of his resurrection, and the fellowship of his sufferings...' (Philippians 3:10). Jesus said '...If any man will come after me, let him deny himself, and take up his cross...' (Matthew 16:24).

Inclusion into God's promise is a wonderful and glorious thing to which all Christians rejoice. It is not quite so easy to rejoice when the reality sets in that the promise carries suffering as well.

Genesis 18:1-33

I. Entertaining Strangers (18:1-16)
1. '…they did eat…'
2. Emotional hardness
3. Confronting weakness of faith

II. A Story of Intercession (18:17-33)
1. Friend of God
2. Plea for Sodom

Genesis 18:1-16

1. And the Lord appeared unto him in the plains of Mamre: and he sat in the tent door in the heat of the day; 2. And he lift up his eyes and looked, and, lo, three men stood by him: and when he saw them, he ran to meet them from the tent door, and bowed himself toward the ground, 3. And said, My Lord, if now I have found favour in thy sight, pass not away, I pray thee, from thy servant: 4. Let a little water, I pray you, be fetched, and wash your feet, and rest yourselves under the tree: 5. And I will fetch a morsel of bread, and comfort ye your hearts; after that ye shall pass on: for therefore are ye come to your servant. And they said, So do, as thou hast said. 6. And Abraham hastened into the tent unto Sarah, and said, Make ready quickly three measures of fine meal, knead it, and make cakes upon the hearth. 7. And Abraham ran unto the herd, and fetcht a calf tender and good, and gave it unto a young man; and he hasted to dress it. 8. And he took butter, and milk, and the calf which he had dressed, and set it before them; and he stood by them under the tree, and they did eat. 9. And they said unto him, Where is Sarah thy wife? And he said, Behold, in the tent. 10. And he said, I will certainly return unto thee according to the time of life; and, lo, Sarah thy wife shall have a son. And Sarah heard it in the tent door, which was behind him. 11. Now Abraham and Sarah were old and well stricken in age; and it ceased to be with Sarah after the manner of women. 12. Therefore Sarah laughed within herself, saying, After I am waxed old shall I have pleasure, my lord being old also? 13. And the Lord said unto Abraham, Wherefore did Sarah laugh, saying, Shall I of a surety bear a child, which am old? 14. Is any thing too hard for the Lord? At the time appointed I will return unto thee, according to the time of life, and Sarah shall have a son. 15. Then Sarah denied, saying, I laughed not; for she was afraid. And he said, Nay; but thou didst laugh. 16. And the men rose up from thence, and looked toward Sodom: and Abraham went with them to bring them on the way.

'...they did eat...'

This is a delicate and beautiful passage of Scripture. Angels pay a visit to Abraham. In the New Testament, human beings are cautioned about such a possibility. 'Be not forgetful to entertain strangers: for thereby some have entertained angels unawares' (Hebrews 13:2). Scripture records many instances in which angels have appeared to men just prior to God's specific activity on the earth. In Abraham's case, there are two events the visit of the angels portend. First, they are there to confirm the Word of God (which Abraham heard in Genesis 17:15-16) and later heard by Sarah (18:10). Second, God is going to judge the sin of Sodom and Gomorrah (18:20-22).

The meditative moment for the reader comes in considering the reality of this visitation of the angels. Abraham acted in a manner consistent with the Eastern laws of hospitality. In the nomadic society of the culture, there is a dependence factor making such reception of strangers a survival necessity. Thus, such reception, was to be a sign of great virtue in the one showing hospitality. However, Abraham recognized the majesty of these visitors as seen in verses two and three '...he...bowed himself toward the ground, And said, My Lord, if now I have found favour in thy sight, pass not away, I pray thee from thy servant.' For Abraham it is more than showing hospitality, it is worship. He recognizes one of these as the Lord who had previously spoken to him (17:11).

He prepares water to wash their feet (18:4), offers to feed them (18:5), and instructs Sarah to prepare the bread (18:6), while he proceeds to kill and prepare the calf (18:8). The reader may be surprised, and somewhat repelled by the thought of angels eating food prepared by humans which is designed for our physical bodies. What can this mean?

New Testament images are relevant, as is the recalling of the very beginning of God's relationship with humans in the Garden of Eden. This kind of fellowship with God had been available daily to Adam (Genesis 3:8). Also, the resurrected Christ, ate a meal with his disciples before the ascension (Luke 24:30, John 21:10-12). The intimacy displayed between Abraham and the Lord manifests a desire the creator still has with his creation despite their sin. Intimacy with his creation is the goal of God and the great theme of Scripture often symbolized in eating. It is the hope of the restoration of the Garden of Eden. After sharing the last supper, Jesus said, '...I will not drink henceforth of this fruit of the vine, until that day when I drink it new with you in my Father's kingdom.' (Matthew 26:29).

> The story here is a beautiful picture of a future time when the Bride and the Lamb shall dine together at the great marriage feast (Revelation 19:7-10). The wonder of intimacy with God no matter where it is founded in the Scripture should not be lost on the reader.

Emotional hardness

The paths of life lead us to many things. Disappointments, shattered dreams, plus our successes all leave their mark on us. We are both hardened and softened by them. The hardness that occurs is not always bad. There is protection in it. After all, a wall of concrete is not nearly so harmed by a flying rock as is the pasteboard dry wall. Hardness can be a sign of strength.

Abraham and Sarai (now called Sarah) have waited years for God to fulfil his promise of providing a son. Sarah has been well past her time of child bearing, and she and Abraham hear once again the promise of God. '…I will certainly return unto thee according to the time of life; and, lo, Sarah, thy wife shall have a son… (18:10). Sarah's response was exactly what we might expect. 'Therefore Sarah laughed within herself, saying, After I am waxed old shall I have pleasure, my Lord being old also?' (Genesis 18:12). The laughter of Sarah was not the laughter of caustic unbelief, but the laughter of hardness that the years of disappointment had produced. She was not being sarcastic, she was just accepting reality. You can sense the melancholy.

God rebuked Abraham for Sarah's laughter, and Abraham, in turn comforted Sarah. The Bible says that she denied the laughter, being fearful (18:15). Nothing more is said. Sarah has no punishment except for the gentle rebuke of the Lord. This is a clear statement about God's knowledge of the difficulty humans have in loving him. We often fall prey to hard times and find ourselves growing hard for self-protection. We anticipate that God will be very angry with us and expect his punishing sword to fall. We are fearful, as Sarah was that our hardness may cost us any relationship with God that we have left. The rebuke without punishment becomes a word of comfort. It is God saying to Sarah, 'I know how you feel.' The fact that we build up emotional shields to protect ourselves does not mean loss of relationship to God. Sarah was okay. God was going to do his work. Sarah still had her misgivings about the promised son becoming reality. God was telling her 'I understand. It's hard to love me in this world!' Understanding a God like that does make him somewhat easier to love, however.

The world's disappointments can feel like having rocks thrown at us. At times we can find ourselves growing emotionally hard in order to keep the rocks from doing their damage. It is nice to know that this will not cause us to lose our relationship with God.

Confronting weakness of faith

The angels who visited Abraham and Sarah are there to reaffirm the promise to Sarah. The angel to whom Abraham had referred as 'Lord' (18:3) speaks. '...I will certainly return unto thee according to the time of life; and lo, Sarah thy wife shall have a son. And Sarah heard it in the tent door...' (18:10). This is a repeat of the same thing God had spoken in chapter 17:16. Evidently, Sarah is not comforted by Abraham, and it is evident that he was unable to convince her. It is conjectured that Sarah may have stopped any sexual activity with her husband because of her distress. Her painful expression of verse 12 may indicate such action. '...After I am waxed old shall I have pleasure...?' This may or may not be true, but Sarah's harsh look at reality has caused her faith to go weak.

Recent actions of Abraham may not have helped her faith. Prior to the visit of the angels, Abraham had acted to circumcise himself, and all the men of his house including Ishmael, his son by Hagar, handmaid of Sarah. As a woman of sensitivity, Sarah must certainly have looked on this action as brutal, and may have been very put off by it. It could have profoundly affected her attitude about sexual activity. In addition, she was probably very confused as she sought to understand her life. This brutal action was commanded by the same God who had promised to provide a son, and had not delivered. Why would Abraham engage in such brutality when she could no longer deliver a child to him?

If Sarah had indeed cut off sexual activity with her husband, the visit of the angels is a word of authority, which should help her acceptance of God's promise and encourage her return to the marriage bed. For the reader, the action of God in gently working with these two human vessels (Abraham and Sarah) is a picture of divine grace and infinite wisdom. One can be somewhat caught up in the emotional charm. As fellow human beings, we cannot be too hard on Abraham and Sarah. Our heart goes out to them. It is comforting to note that God's grace acted to comfort them. He understands Sarah's reluctance to believe Abraham, so he came to say it again when she can hear.

> Humans often sin! Humans are often simply weak! It is not a given, however, that weakness is a sin. God sees every sin, but he also sees and has understanding for our weakness. Was it not said of the Incarnate One that he was '...tempted like as we are, and yet without sin' (Hebrews 4:15).

Genesis 18:17-33

17. And the Lord said, Shall I hide from Abraham that thing which I do;
18. Seeing that Abraham shall surely become a great and mighty nation, and all the nations of the earth shall be blessed in him? 19. For I know him, that he will command his children and his household after him, and they shall keep the way of the Lord, to do justice and judgement; that the Lord may bring upon Abraham that which he hath spoken of him. 20. And the Lord said, Because the cry of Sodom and Gomorrah is great, and because their sin is very grievous; 21. I will go down now, and see whether they have done altogether according to the cry of it, which is come unto me; and if not, I will know. 22. And the men turned their faces from thence, and went toward Sodom: but Abraham stood yet before the Lord. 23. And Abraham drew near, and said, Wilt thou also destroy the righteous with the wicked? 24. Peradventure there be fifty righteous within the city: wilt thou also destroy and not spare the place for the fifty righteous that are therein? 25. That be far from thee to do after this manner, to slay the righteous with the wicked: and that the righteous should be as the wicked, that be far from thee: shall not the Judge of all the earth do right? 26. And the Lord said, If I find in Sodom fifty righteous within the city, then I will spare all the place for their sakes. 27. And Abraham answered and said, Behold now, I have taken upon me to speak unto the Lord, which am but dust and ashes: 28. Peradventure there shall lack five of the fifty righteous: wilt thou destroy all the city for lack of five? And he

said, If I find there forty and five, I will not destroy it. 29. And he spake unto him yet again, and said, Peradventure there shall be forty found there. And he said, I will not do it for forty's sake. 30. And he said unto him, Oh let not the Lord be angry, and I will speak: Peradventure there shall thirty be found there. And he said, I will not do it, if I find thirty there. 31. And he said, Behold now, I have taken upon me to speak unto the Lord: Peradventure there shall be twenty found there. And he said, I will not destroy it for twenty's sake. 32. And he said, Oh let not the Lord be angry, and I will speak yet but this once: Peradventure ten shall be found there. And he said, I will not destroy it for ten's sake. 33. And the Lord went his way, as soon as he had left communing with Abraham: and Abraham returned unto his place.

Friend of God

Chapter 18, verses 13-19 provide some opportunity for consideration of a great Genesis theme. For many of us, it is a theme hard to imagine, much less to understand. It is the concept of 'friend of God.' The idea has been noted before when Enoch and Noah were described as men who walked with God (Genesis 5:22, 6:9). The additional information provided in this text is found in the revelation of God's reassuring. 'Shall I hide from Abraham that thing which I do...For I know him, that he will command his children, and his household after him, and they shall keep the way of the Lord...' (18:17, 19). God considers the need to share his thoughts with Abraham.

It is interesting to note that which God said was the thing he most valued in Abraham. There was a clear confidence that Abraham would not abandon his teaching responsibility to his household. As one tries to examine what it means to have a walk with God, and specifically to wonder if he or she may be walking with God, the example of Abraham provides one of the Scripture's best measuring sticks. Is the responsibility of teaching the way of God to One's family taken seriously?

God delighted in the fact that Abraham was one who would 'command his children' in 'the way of the Lord.' The word, 'command' carries the idea of 'to set up,' or to 'establish.' It is the idea of foundational thinking. Major decisions in our lives are based in certain believed realities. The Genesis narrative enforces the importance of the foundational reality of remembering the way of God in all of life. It is a reality that must be taught from generation to generation, or it will be lost. Humans cannot come to the way of God without the continual preaching and teaching of successive generations. The Apostle Paul reiterates the importance of God's command in the form of a series of questions. 'How then shall they call on him in whom they have not believed? And how shall they believe in him of whom they have not heard? And how shall they hear without a preacher?' (Romans 10:13-14). The words of Paul are generally understood with only an evangelistic application. It's true meaning is to be found in the development of a solid foundation in the knowledge of God's way, which shall direct every facet of life. The willingness to teach, especially to teach our own household, is a sure measuring stick to the closeness of one's walk with God. Abraham had God's confidence that he would teach. If God is confident that you and I will teach, we might be called a 'friend of God.'

> Teaching one's own household the way of God is a small thing, and does not win great rewards or praise for us on this earth, but it is extremely important in the mind of God. It is part of being the friend of God.

Plea for Sodom

We have here an interesting story of intercession on the part of Abraham. God has told him that Sodom, where Abraham's nephew, Lot, is living, will be destroyed. Abraham begins a peculiar prayer in which he barters for the people of Sodom. He secures a promise from God that Sodom will not be destroyed if ten righteous souls are found. Two things catch our attention. First, God reveals to Abraham his plan. 'And the Lord said, Shall I hide from Abraham that thing which I do?' (Genesis 18:17). From God's standpoint, this is a wonderful expression of intimacy with Abraham. The fact that God would choose to have this kind of intimacy with any human should come as a great surprise to us. Yet, the Bible teaches that all who are in Christ have such intimacy and more. 'Beloved, now are we the sons of God...' (1 John 3:2).

A second curious thing is that Abraham bartered with God to spare Sodom if ten righteous souls could be found. Note what happens next. 'And the Lord went his way, as soon as he had left communing with Abraham: And Abraham returned unto his place' (Genesis 18:33). There is no effort made by Abraham to find those ten souls. Even with his nephew, Lot, in the city, he fully trusts the men to do the finding. It is often stated that Abraham's faith came up short in that he stopped at ten and did not continue the bartering until he got it to one soul. The fact, however, that Abraham did not attempt to find those ten leads to another conclusion. Abraham, through his intercession, realized the grace and long-suffering of God and came to acknowledge God's wisdom in the destruction of Sodom. Abraham's ceasing of the prayer was his acceptance of God's will. We have here another major step in understanding the meaning of the love of God. The next chapter reveals God's rescue of Abraham's nephew, and the destruction of the wicked city. God honoured Abraham's trust in yielding to his will to destroy the city.

Sometimes in the affairs of our life it is hard to see that God is gracious, and long-suffering to us. This makes it difficult to give in to his will. There was no promise made to Abraham that Lot would be spared. His acceptance of God's will is made doubly tough. It is hard to pray 'thy will be done,' but love for God often demands it.

Genesis 19-20

I. The Destruction of Lot's Family (19:1-38)
1. An unholy barter
2. A family tragedy

II. Abraham and Abimelech (20:1-18)
1. Making the same mistake again
2. Selfish love

Genesis 19:1-38

1. And there came two angels to Sodom at even; and Lot sat in the gate of Sodom: and Lot seeing them rose up to meet them; and he bowed himself with his face toward the ground; 2. And he said, Behold now, my lords, turn in, I pray you, into your servant's house, and tarry all night, and wash your feet, and ye shall rise up early, and go on your ways. And they said, Nay; but we will abide in the street all night. 3. And he pressed upon them greatly; and they turned in unto him and entered into his house; and he made them a feast, and did bake unleavened bread, and they did eat. 4. But before they lay down, the men of the city, even the men of Sodom, compassed the house round, both old and young, all the people from every quarter: 5. And they called unto Lot, and said unto him, Where are the men which came in to thee this night? bring them out unto us, that we may know them. 6. And Lot went out at the door unto them, and shut the door after him, 7. And said, I pray you, brethren, do not so wickedly. 8. Behold now, I have two daughters which have not known man; let me, I pray you, bring them out unto you, and do ye to them as is good in your eyes: only unto these men do nothing; for therefore came they under the shadow of my roof. 9. And they said, Stand back. And they said again,

*This one fellow came in to sojourn, and he will needs be a judge: now will
we deal worse with thee, than with them. And they pressed sore upon the
man, even Lot, and came near to break the door. 10. But the men put
forth their hand, and pulled Lot into the house to them, and shut to the
door. 11. And they smote the men that were at the door of the house with
blindness, both small and great: so that they wearied themselves to find
the door. 12. And the men said unto Lot, Hast thou here any besides?
son in law, and thy sons, and thy daughters, and whatsoever thou hast in
the city, bring them out of this place: 13. For we will destroy this place,
because the cry of them is waxen great before the face of the Lord; and
the Lord hath sent us to destroy it. 14. And Lot went out, and spake unto
his sons in law, which married his daughters, and said, Up, get you out
of this place; for the Lord will destroy this city. But he seemed as one that
mocked unto his sons in law. 15. And when the morning arose, then the
angels hastened Lot, saying, Arise, take thy wife, and thy two daughters,
which are here; lest thou be consumed in the iniquity of the city. 16.
And while he lingered, the men laid hold upon his hand, and upon the
hand of his wife, and upon the hand of his two daughters; the Lord being
merciful unto him: and they brought him forth, and set him without the
city. 17. And it came to pass, when they had brought them forth abroad,
that he said, Escape for thy life; look not behind thee, neither stay thou
in all the plain; escape to the mountain, lest thou be consumed. 18. And
Lot said unto them, Oh, not so, my Lord: 19. Behold now, thy servant
hath found grace in thy sight, and thou hast magnified thy mercy, which
thou hast shewed unto me in saving my life; and I cannot escape to the
mountain, lest some evil take me, and I die: 20. Behold now, this city
is near to flee unto, and it is a little one: Oh, let me escape thither, (is it
not a little one?) and my soul shall live. 21. And he said unto him, See,
I have accepted thee concerning this thing also, that I will not overthrow
this city, for the which thou hast spoken. 22. Haste thee, escape thither;
for I cannot do any thing till thou be come thither. Therefore the name
of the city was called Zoar. 23. The sun was risen upon the earth when
Lot entered into Zoar. 24. Then the Lord rained upon Sodom and upon
Gomorrah brimstone and fire from the Lord out of heaven; 25. And he
overthrew those cities, and all the plain, and all the inhabitants of the cities, and that which grew upon the ground. 26. But his wife looked back
from behind him, and she became a pillar of salt. 27. And Abraham gat*

up early in the morning to the place where he stood before the Lord: 28. And he looked toward Sodom and Gomorrah, and toward all the land of the plain, and beheld, and, lo, the smoke of the country went up as the smoke of a furnace. 29. And it came to pass, when God destroyed the cities of the plain, that God remembered Abraham, and sent Lot out of the midst of the overthrow, when he overthrew the cities in the which Lot dwelt. 30. And Lot went up out of Zoar, and dwelt in the mountain, and his two daughters with him; for he feared to dwell in Zoar: and he dwelt in a cave, he and his two daughters. 31. And the firstborn said unto the younger, Our father is old, and there is not a man in the earth to come in unto us after the manner of all the earth: 32. Come, let us make our father drink wine, and we will lie with him, that we may preserve seed of our father. 33. And they made their father drink wine that night: and the firstborn went in, and lay with her father; and he perceived not when she lay down, nor when she arose. 34. And it came to pass on the morrow, that the firstborn said unto the younger, Behold, I lay yesternight with my father: let us make him drink wine this night also; and go thou in, and lie with him, that we may preserve seed of our father. 35. And they made their father drink wine that night also: and the younger arose, and lay with him; and he perceived not when she lay down, nor when she arose. 36. Thus were both the daughters of Lot with child by their father. 37. And the firstborn bare a son, and called his name Moab: the same is the father of the Moabites unto this day. 38. And the younger, she also bare a son, and called his name Benammi: the same is the father of the children of Ammon unto this day.

An unholy barter

The Bible is filled with stories about the sin of good men. Here, the sin of Lot is shocking, even to twentieth century sensibilities. Even in our extremely promiscuous society, it is hard to imagine a father making the offer that Lot made. Two men, identified as angels (19:1), had come to Lot's house. Evidently, these were the same two men who had accompanied the Lord in visiting Abraham in Genesis 18. The men had attracted the attention of the Sodomites, who desired them for homosexual activity. Lot makes this incredible offer '...I pray you, brethren, do not so wickedly. Behold now, I have two daughters which have not known man; let me I pray you bring them out unto you, and do unto them as is good in your eyes: only unto these men do nothing...' (19:8).

This extremely wicked offer of Lot is from one who is nephew of Abraham, the great patriarch and father of the nation of Israel. The New Testament speaks of Lot as a 'just' man. 'And delivered just Lot, vexed with the filthy conversation of the wicked: (For that righteous man dwelling among them, in seeing and hearing, vexed his righteous soul from day to day with their unlawful deeds)' (I1 Peter 2:7-8). How does the image of a just and righteous Lot, nephew of Abraham, compute with the offer that Lot made?

For any, who have a desire in their heart to love God, and have a sense of troubling in the soul about sin, this is a frightening prospect. Lot had earlier made the choice to live in Sodom based on a curious fascination with the city (Genesis 13:12). It was not so much that he loved the sin as that he saw the potential for material gain. Thus, the wickedness of the city was made more palatable. When this happens, another result logically follows. When one lives with evil, he finds his choices are no longer between good and evil, but between the lesser of two evils. This is where Lot found himself. Choosing the lesser of two evils will never bring honor or good to our lives. Though Lot had a vexation in his soul about the sin around him, he could not escape without sacrificing the material gain he had so cherished. In his barter with the men, he opted for the lesser of two evils. His daughters shall be defiled instead of the angels who are his guests. If one can learn to make every decision based in love for God, he can avoid this kind of dilemma.

A family tragedy

The destruction of a city, or a nation, is seen in several places in the Old Testament. Sodom's downfall is one of the most famous. The devastation to Sodom, however, appears secondary in this

Genesis account. The focus is on one family. Lot, a just man, living in Sodom is the only individual who is given information which will allow escape. He and his family are allowed to leave. Lot had built his entire identity on the material gain he had accrued in Sodom. He 'pitched his tent toward Sodom' (Genesis 13:12) identified the nature of the choices in his life. Contrast that with what is said of Abraham in the New Testament. 'For he looked for a city which hath foundations, whose builder and maker is God' (Hebrews 11:10).

Though the New Testament gives Lot credit for being 'vexed' by the sin around him (2 Peter 2:7-8), his story ends in tragedy. His wife dies, because she looks back at the city (19:26), his daughters engage in incestuous activity with him (Genesis 19:31-36), and he is seen as losing his credibility with the world, dwelling in caves. (19:30). He loved the world more than God, and it led to his ruin. Perhaps the attitude of his family provides the greatest tragedy. His wife (probably learning from Lot) loved her material gains so much she could not bear to leave the possessions behind. Looking back toward Sodom, she was destroyed with the city. His daughters, once offered as harlots to the evil men of Sodom (19:8), see nothing wrong with an incestuous relationship with their father. If harlotry is right (which Lot demonstrated), then the incest must be right. Two nations are born of the incestuous relationship, Moab and Ammon (19:37-38), which will prove to be great enemies to Israel. There is no further record of Lot's life.

Clearly, Lot is to be contrasted with Abraham for our learning. One can choose to love the world and prosper from it in material ways. It will, however, take its toll. Most people want to be successful, hard-working, and leave something for their family. Lot's story teaches us that leaving only material gain for our family is extremely nebulous and shallow. It can be taken away instantly. When our attitude demonstrates that material gain is what we love most, our families will come to interpret right and wrong based in what obtains or loses those possessions. They will not be 'vexed' with sin as we were.

The critical lesson here should not be missed. Though we may not succumb fully to sin, our slight compromises can teach harmful lessons to others. Lot's righteous soul was vexed, yet he raised daughters who saw no problems with their incestuous relationship.

Genesis 20:1-18

1. And Abraham journeyed from thence toward the south country, and dwelled between Kadesh and Shur, and sojourned in Gerar. 2. And Abraham said of Sarah his wife, She is my sister: and Abimelech king of Gerar sent, and took Sarah. 3. But God came to Abimelech in a dream by night, and said to him, Behold, thou art but a dead man, for the woman which thou hast taken; for she is a man's wife. 4. But Abimelech had not come near her: and he said, Lord, wilt thou slay also a righteous nation? 5. Said he not unto me, She is my sister? and she, even she herself said, He is my brother: in the integrity of my heart and innocency of my hands have I done this. 6. And God said unto him in a dream, Yea, I know that thou didst this in the integrity of thy heart; for I also withheld thee from sinning against me: therefore suffered I thee not to touch her. 7. Now therefore restore the man his wife; for he is a prophet, and he shall pray for thee, and thou shalt live: and if thou restore her not, know thou that thou shalt surely die, thou, and all that are thine. 8. Therefore Abimelech rose early in the morning, and called all his servants, and told all these things in their ears: and the men were sore afraid. 9. Then Abimelech called Abraham, and said unto him, What hast thou done unto us? and what have I offended thee, that thou hast brought on me and on my kingdom a great sin? thou hast done deeds unto me that ought not to be done. 10. And Abimelech said unto Abraham, What sawest thou, that thou hast done this thing? 11. And Abraham said, Because I thought, Surely the fear of God is not in this place; and they will slay me for my wife's sake. 12. And yet indeed she is my sister; she is the daughter of my father, but not the daughter of my mother; and she became my wife. 13. And it came to pass, when God caused me to wander from my father's house, that I said unto her, This is thy kindness which thou shalt shew unto me; at every place whither we shall come, say of me, He is my brother. 14. And Abimelech took sheep, and oxen, and menservants, and women servants, and gave them unto Abraham, and restored him Sarah his wife. 15. And Abimelech said, Behold, my land is before thee: dwell where it pleaseth thee. 16. And unto Sarah he said, Behold, I have given thy brother a thousand pieces of silver: behold, he is to thee a covering of the eyes, unto all that are with thee, and with all other: thus she servants, and told all these things in their ears: and the men were sore afraid. 9. was reproved. 17. So Abraham prayed unto God: and God healed Abimelech, and his wife, and his maidservants; and they bare children. 18. For the Lord had fast closed up all the wombs of the house of Abimelech, because of Sarah Abraham's wife.

Making the same mistake again

The story of Abraham continues to demonstrate the struggles of a human being attempting to live a life characterized by faith and a love of God. One of the most sublime lessons is what Abraham's story teaches us of God's reaction and faithfulness to us. Abraham is very old at this point, but he commits a sin that is identical to the sin he committed many years earlier when he passed Sarah off as his sister to the King of Egypt. At Sarah's advanced age, her physical attraction would have been less a factor than her great wealth as part of Abraham's family, though the longer life span of that time meant that one kept youthful vitality and appearance at advanced ages. Abraham's deception, this time, is to a ruler among the people who occupy the land. The ruler's name is Abimelech.

As in the earlier narrative, God intervenes. He appears in a dream to Abimelech, and rescues Abraham. Our judgement on Abraham would be that he makes the same mistake twice. How would he not have learned? The human condition is such that it takes only dispassionate observation to see humans regularly make the same mistake again. For some, it is a clear pattern of life that the same mistake occurs repeatedly. Yet, in Abraham, we have one who supposedly lives by faith and is one who loves God, thus, not vulnerable to this error.

For all whose life takes the journey of living by faith, there is a dilemma. The love for God calls us to do the right thing, but the pressure of life, the concern of the moment distracts us. The reason Abraham gave for his action is, 'Because I thought, Surely the fear of God is not in this place; and they will slay me for my wife's sake' (20:11). As in the earlier instance, Abraham was putting the promise of God at risk. Having a son by Sarah does not seem a possibility at this point, so Abraham's action has a small excuse. However, God's constant restatement of his promise to Abraham should have made Abraham aware that he was placing Abimelech in danger. God's word to Abimelech was 'Now, ...restore the man his wife...and if thou restore her not, know that thou shalt surely die...' (Genesis 20:7). Abraham failed to ask the question, 'What will my actions create for others?' This reflects on how the one attempting to love God may rationalize the committing of sin. When the relationship with God is so intensely personal that one only thinks in terms of how an action impacts self, without thought for others who are part of our influence, the tendency can be to make a wrong decision, even to making the same mistake a second time in our life.

> It is a popular idea in the modern world that people can live their lives in a vacuum, that is, what one does affects no one else. Extremely personal decisions that do not take ramifications to others into consideration can create great ham to ourselves and to others.

Selfish love

We all know that love is a characteristic of life that makes one unselfish. Or is it? There is an aspect of love that can turn it into a very selfish thing. This aspect manifests itself in immature love, and in the context of loving the idea of love as opposed to accepting the realities of love. Sometimes, it is hard to discern. The aspect becomes manifest through the extremely personal nature of love. When one loves, there is an internal part that has only to do with self and self's relationship to the object of love. When the mind thinks only in terms of the love one feels, and the personal benefit one shall receive from that love, it leads to total selfishness. Love used in this way is not unselfish at all. Meditation on this passage is a reflection of such an event.

Abraham, afraid for his own life, asks Sarah to help save him by passing herself off as his sister. He deceives Abimelech, and gets Abimelech in trouble with God. The intervention of God spares Abimelech. Note first, Abraham thought in terms of his wife's responsibility to him. It never entered his mind that he was endangering Abimelech. Our text offers another thing about which Abraham did not think. 'And Abimelech said, Behold, my land is before thee: dwell where it pleaseth thee. And unto Sarah he said, Behold, I have given thy brother a thousand pieces of silver: behold, he is to thee a covering of the eyes, unto all that are with thee, and with all other: thus she was reproved' (Genesis 20:15-16). This rather strange statement is obscure to us. It means that Abimelech did something for Abraham that protected Sarah and himself. '...a covering of the eyes...' is better rendered, 'it is your vindication.' Abraham's sin included the setting up of a possibility he did not discern. What if Sarah had entered Abimelech's bed? She would have returned to Abraham ultimately, but he could never have looked at her the same. Though he loved her, his very selfish application of their relationship set up the possibility of his despising her. Abimelech's gift established that Sarah had not been defiled.

Our love of God can be applied in such intensely personal fashion that we think only of how we feel, how we are benefiting, how we need to be cared for. That often leads us to make demands that can put others at risk. Our prayers to God can be so intensely personal and selfish that it does not dawn on us that there are consequences of our requests. Thankfully, we have a God that will refuse to answer that kind of prayer, and will even rescue us from our selfishness if we, like Abraham, have demonstrated a pattern of desire to love God.

Genesis 21:1-34

I. The Promised Son is Born (21:1-8)
1. The promise kept
2. '...God hath made me to laugh...'
3. A nation's greatness

II. The Son of a Bad Decision (21:9-21)
1. Joy, but a sobering reality
2. Ishmael sent away

III. An Interesting Learning Experience (21:22-34)
1. A redemptive lesson
2. '...the everlasting God...'

Genesis 21:1-8

1. And the Lord visited Sarah as he had said, and the Lord did unto Sarah as he had spoken. 2. For Sarah conceived, and bare Abraham a son in his old age, at the set time of which God had spoken to him. 3. And Abraham called the name of his son that was born unto him, whom Sarah bare to him, Isaac. 4. And Abraham circumcised his son Isaac being eight days old, as God had commanded him. 5. And Abraham was an hundred years old, when his son Isaac was born unto him. 6. And Sarah said, God hath made me to laugh, so that all that hear will laugh with me. 7. And she said, Who would have said unto Abraham, that Sarah should have given children suck? for I have born him a son in his old age. 8. And the child grew, and was weaned: and Abraham made a great feast the same day that Isaac was weaned.

The promise kept

A promise is delivered! A promise is kept! There are many years that roll by in the interim. By human rationalization, we may question whether the promise was really kept. Do you think Abraham and Sarah reasoned at the time of the promise that Sarah must wait until her old age before a child is given to her? Her youth is spent, and the time that people are normally enjoying their children passed her by. There are always two parts to any promise: The promise spoken! The promise heard! What was the promise spoken? We go back to Genesis 12:2-3. '...I will make of thee a great nation, and I will bless thee, and make thy name great; and thou shalt be a blessing: And I will bless them that bless thee, and curse him that curseth thee: and in thee shall all families of the earth be blessed.' Note that the promise is totally about what God would do. At the time of promise, it did not seem so remarkable that Abraham might have many sons. The great nation would only occur after Abraham's death, so it is easy to trust God for that. He had no choice. At least he could enjoy the blessing of the family God would give him.

There is subtlety in the promise that Abraham did not hear. God is saying, 'I promise to show you the working out of my power in your life, so that there will be no mistake that I did it!' This is the painful part of loving God. I want my love to present me with pleasant moments, with good feelings and a sense of security. I do not want my love to present me with questions, with testing, with insecurity. Why does God's love inflict us with such pain?

Herein lies another of those wonderful teaching moments. The human condition is such that insecurity is a natural part of our being. Sin has created that beast. The ability to know and love God is very unnatural because of that sin. God's desire is to reveal himself to us, so that our insecurity will leave. God knows our tendency, however, to find other explanations for the events of our lives besides the working of God. Thus, it is by God's grace that we must be taken to the absolute limits before we will fully accept God's work in us. That old tendency in us is to always question. Be sure that God's work is to leave no questions.

'It is common for Christians to desire to see the work of God in their life. It is just as common to ignore it and become lifted up in pride when it happens. We seldom consider that a request to see God work in our lives may be a request for testing and trial.

'...God hath made me to laugh...'

We have before us a very enlightening passage of Scripture. There is a moment of merriment, and spontaneous joy that will draw almost everyone into the emotion. 'And Sarah said, God hath made me to laugh, so that all that hear will laugh with me' (Genesis 21:6). Sarah, you are so right. After 4000 years, your story still resounds with wonder, and creates that feeling of joy as we appreciate the special moment of the birth of your son.

There was another moment when Sarah laughed. It was several years before when God had reiterated his promise of the son to be born to Abraham and Sarah. 'Therefore Sarah laughed within herself, saying, after I am waxed old shall I have pleasure...' (Genesis 18:12). Sarah reflected on life's reality at that point, and soothed her troubled mind with laughter. It was not as much laughter of derision as a means of finding comfort. When heartache abounds in our life, we find laughter in the ironic. Having a baby for Sarah would indeed be an ironic twist at her age. The improbability of it all prompted a laughter that you and I have perhaps experienced. I would call it the laughter of 'nervous hope.' It may happen, but it is not likely.

When God finally delivers on his promise, Sarah laughs again. Note the way the Scripture phrases it, 'God hath made me to laugh...' (21:6). The laughter is clearly on two levels for her. Of course, there is the purely human delight with her infant son, but there is also the teaching aspect of the God-relationship. As Sarah looked upon her newborn, the reality strikes, God, alone, made it happen. God was at work in me. There is no earthly joy that can quite compare with those moments of life that clearly bring the knowledge that God is at work in us.

The journey for Abraham and Sarah has been long. The wait has been agonizing. Sarah's words reveal that she has learned the importance of being able to know when God is at work, to be able to give God all the glory, and to see that God often has a purpose in mind she could not fathom. '…all that hear will laugh with me,' even 4000 years later. When God brings us to the point that we know it is God, and nothing else, at work, our love for him reaches another plateau. To know God is at work in me is indeed special. God made the moment with Sarah even more special by leaving no doubt about who did it.

One may not have knowledge of any unique promises God has made to you such as the ones made to Abraham. Yet one can know the work of God in the life if properly attuned to his mind through the Word of God.

A nation's greatness

A child is born to Abraham and Sarah that is the child of promise. He will be the son out of whom a great nation will arise. As one looks back over four thousand years of history, one might legitimately ponder the concept of 'greatness' for that nation. As humans account for greatness, we look for empires and kingdoms that dominate the earth. During the reigns of David and Solomon, the nation of Israel enjoyed great wealth and occupied much territory, but there was no world empire. Israel has spent most of the years of its history as a scattered people, often hated in the countries in which they live. Their re-emergence as a recognized nation was precipitated by one of the most notorious slaughters in human history during World War II. Israel occupies none of the greatness which history would apply to Babylon, Greece, Rome, the British Empire, modern America, the great civilizations of China, or even to Ancient Egypt. Where is the greatness? What kind of descendants did Abraham perceive as he observed the growth of his son?

In Genesis 15, God revealed to Abraham that the nation, which his son would beget, would be in slavery for four hundred years. Abraham, through the eyes of faith, must have known a bit more. He knew that the great nation would not have greatness as the world measures it. Hebrews tells us as much. 'By faith Abraham... went out...For he looked for a city which hath foundations, whose builder and maker is God (Hebrews 11:8, 10). The greatness of the nation of Israel is that it shall point the world to that city.

Abraham lived in a world where there was worship of many gods. Nature, and human aspirations, had come to be moulded into worship forms as gods. The worship of the true God and creator was mostly lost. Out of this son, born to Abraham, would come the nation that would reunite the world with its creator. That great city, and the greatness of the nation, would be in a unique position as directly from the hand of God. The promised son, born to Abraham, is a precursor of a similar promise made to the nation and to the world. '...unto us a child is born, unto us a son is given...' (Isaiah 9:6). All Christians know that this points to Jesus Christ. Abraham may not have had full understanding of God's plan, but the knowledge that his family would be God's vehicle for reuniting the world with himself must have been a source of heart-pounding excitement. The lesson for us is clear. There must be a different understanding of greatness for those who speak of 'loving God.'

There is no greater contrast between human thinking and God's thinking than the concept of greatness. Humans must accept true greatness in a theological context and interpret it in the light of a relationship with God. God's idea for Israel as he established his law with them was never to be fulfilled except in the 'seed of the woman!' True to every facet of the law, perfect in the eyes of the Father, that which God would desire to say of Israel, he said of Christ, '...Thou art my beloved Son; in thee I am well pleased' (Luke 3:22). The prophet Isaiah further highlighted this distinction in his look ahead to the day of Messiah. Israel is seen as the chastened servant of the Lord in Isaiah 42:19. 'Who is blind, but my servant or deaf as my messenger that I sent? Who is blind as he that is perfect, and blind as the Lord's servant.' In a beautiful prophetic look into the future, Isaiah saw Messiah fulfilling that which the original servant could not. Here was the ideal servant acknowledging his faithfulness. 'The Lord God hath given me the tongue of the learned, that I may know how to speak a word in season to him that is weary: he wakeneth morning by morning, he wakeneth mine ear as the learned. The Lord God hath opened mine ear, and I was not rebellious, neither turned away back' (Isaiah 59:4-5). Because it was said of Christ who fulfilled the ideal, in his perfections and through his imputed righteousness, it can be said of all who believe 'Beloved, now are we the sons of God, and it doth not yet appear what we shall be: but we know that, when he shall appear, we shall be like him, for we shall see him as he is' (1 John 3:2).

Genesis 21:9-21

9. And Sarah saw the son of Hagar the Egyptian, which she had born unto Abraham, mocking. 10. Wherefore she said unto Abraham, Cast out this bondwoman and her son: for the son of this bondwoman shall not be heir with my son, even with Isaac. 11. And the thing was very grievous in Abraham's sight because of his son. 12. And God said unto Abraham, Let it not be grievous in thy sight because of the lad, and because of thy bondwoman; in all that Sarah hath said unto thee, hearken unto her voice; for in Isaac shall thy seed be called. 13. And also of the son of the bondwoman will I make a nation, because he is thy seed. 14. And Abraham rose up early in the morning, and took bread, and a bottle of water, and gave it unto Hagar, putting it on her shoulder, and the child, and sent her away: and she departed, and wandered in the wilderness of Beersheba. 15 And the water was spent in the bottle, and she cast the child under one of the shrubs. 16. And she went, and sat her down over against him a good way off, as it were a bowshot: for she said, Let me not

see the death of the child. And she sat over against him, and lift up her
voice, and wept. 17. And God heard the voice of the lad; and the angel of
God called to Hagar out of heaven, and said unto her, What aileth thee,
Hagar? fear not; for God hath heard the voice of the lad where he is. 18.
Arise, lift up the lad, and hold him in thine hand; for I will make him a
great nation. 19. And God opened her eyes, and she saw a well of water;
and she went, and filled the bottle with water, and gave the lad drink. 20.
And God was with the lad; and he grew, and dwelt in the wilderness, and
became an archer. 21. And he dwelt in the wilderness of Paran: and his
mother took him a wife out of the land of Egypt.

Joy, but a sobering reality

The New International Version's translation shows when God reveals the set time. 'Then the Lord said, I will surely return to you
about this time next year, and Sarah your wife will have a son'
(Genesis 18:10). Sarah had laughed at the time nervously hoping
that it was true. Perhaps wanting us to recall the nervousness of
Sarah the author drives home the trustworthiness of God's word.
Three times it is stated: '…visited Sarah as he had said…did unto
Sarah as he had spoken…at the set time of which God had spoken
unto him' (21:1-2). The writer wants us to see the great joy of God
as he watches Abraham and Sarah celebrate. It is sobering to realize that this event is the foundation for Abraham to be able to face
even greater testing in his life.

Several years earlier, he and Sarah had tried to help God fulfil
his promise. Sarah offered her handmaiden to Abraham in order
to conceive and bear the son she had not been able to conceive
(Genesis 16:1-4). The relationship produced a son, Ishmael. He
is the elder son of Abraham, and now that Sarah has given birth
to Isaac, the natural problem of inheritance and family authority
arises. Ishmael's 'mocking' of Isaac (21:9) could reflect many
things. It may be cruelty of an intense form, or a manifestation
of arrogance by Ishmael, or childlike jesting that shows a lack of
respect. In any event, Sarah perceived wisely that Ishmael lacked
understanding about Isaac's position in the household, and to

allow him to remain would mean much difficulty later on. '...cast out this bondwoman and her son: for the son of this bondwoman shall not be heir with my son, even with Isaac' (21:10).

This request brought a great deal of grief to Abraham. Ishmael was also his son, and he clearly loved Ishmael. In many ways, this decision is the most difficult he has faced to this point, even greater than the first one to leave his father's homeland and follow God. It is a clear reminder of that which moral mistakes will produce in our life. It is not unusual for us to desire to make ourselves feel better, and to engage in sin because it seems good at the moment. The problem is that moral mistakes will lead us to the need to make painful decisions. Abraham finds himself with this dilemma. He must cast his older son out of his house in order to protect the future harmony of his family. If he keeps him, he spares one kind of pain, but inflicts a greater one later.

In our quest to love God, we may find ourselves facing serious and heart-wrenching decisions created by moral mistakes of the past. From Abraham's story, we learn that some sins will leave a price to pay which cannot be avoided. God does not always let us off the hook.

Ishmael sent away

The very painful moment of disowning his elder son presents Abraham with the kind of decision everyone dreads. It is a decision of doing the right thing, though it hurts supremely. God promised Abraham that he would care for Ishmael (Genesis 17:20), but this will have to be entirely entrusted to God. Abraham could no longer treat him as an heir. The fate of Ishmael and Hagar, his mother, is given in this brief record. '...and God was with the lad; and he grew, and dwelt in the wilderness, and became an archer. And he dwelt in the wilderness of Paran: and his mother took him a wife out of the land of Egypt' (21:20-21).

As we reflect on the whole of Scripture, there are certain ironies before us. First, Ishmael should never have been born. He was the product of an immoral decision made by Abraham and Sarah. Human conflict and tragedy result from the event. Abraham must deal with his own bitter sorrow, and Ishmael must deal with being an outcast. Here is the irony. God builds a larger picture and makes his perfect plan a reality in spite of the sin of Abraham and Sarah. In fact, the apostle Paul will use the story two thousand years later to show that the event is an exact portrait of God's salvation (Galatians 4:21-31). God was able to take that which should never have happened, and turn it into a picture of his redemption. Instead of a tangled web of destruction, God made a beautiful picture.

Second, there is bitterness, grief, and tragedy all over this story. Sarah loses her long time handmaiden, Hagar. Abraham disowns his son. Ishmael and Hagar are out of the household and must struggle in the wilderness alone. The irony is, God pronounced this the right thing to do. 'And God said unto Abraham, Let it not be grievous in thy sight because of the lad, and because of thy bondwoman; in all that Sarah hath said unto thee, hearken unto her voice...' (21:12). It is extremely hard for human beings to understand the difficult things that must happen, and the hard choices we must make to straighten out the problems created by our sinful choices. Full obedience to God can seem wrong because it may involve pain, but it is only in that full obedience that God can make right what we made wrong. The ultimate blessing of Ishmael stands as an eternal testimony to what God can do when we love him more than our attachments to this world.

Genesis 21:22-34

22. And it came to pass at that time, that Abimelech and Phichol the chief captain of his host spake unto Abraham, saying, God is with thee in all that thou doest: 23. Now therefore swear unto me here by God that thou wilt not deal falsely with me, nor with my son, nor with my son's son: but according to the kindness that I have done unto thee, thou shalt do unto me, and to the land wherein thou hast sojourned. 24. And Abraham said, I will swear. 25. And Abraham reproved Abimelech because of a well of water, which Abimelech's servants had violently taken away. 26. And Abimelech said, I wot not who hath done this thing; neither didst thou tell me, neither yet heard I of it, but to day. 27. And Abraham took sheep and oxen, and gave them unto Abimelech; and both of them made a covenant. 28. And Abraham set seven ewe lambs of the flock by themselves. 29. And Abimelech said unto Abraham, What mean these seven ewe lambs which thou hast set by themselves? 30. And he said, For these seven ewe lambs shalt thou take of my hand, that they may be a witness unto me, that I have digged this well. 31. Wherefore he called that place Beersheba; because there they sware both of them. 32. Thus they made a covenant at Beersheba: then Abimelech rose up, and Phichol the chief captain of his host, and they returned into the land of the Philistines. And Abraham planted a grove in Beersheba, and called there on the name of the Lord, the everlasting God. 34. And Abraham sojourned in the Philistines' land many days.

A redemptive lesson

In this text, Abraham is approached by Abimelech, king of a city named Gerar. This is part of the land that was, in Abraham's day, controlled by the Philistines. We are told in verse 34, '...Abraham sojourned in the Philistines' land many days' (21:34). Here, we are hit by a stark realism. The New Testament explains, '...By faith he sojourned in the land of promise, as in a strange country, dwelling in tabernacles with Isaac and Jacob, the heirs with him of the same promise' (Hebrews 11:9). God's promise to Abraham had been without ambiguity. He would possess the land upon which he walked (Genesis 13:17). Yet, he lived out his life as an exile among other people. The promised son, Isaac, was born while Abraham lived among the Philistines.

Just before Abraham faces the biggest test of his life, he receives another stark reminder of his alien status. Abimelech remembers an earlier encounter when Abraham had allowed Abimelech to believe that Sarah was his sister. Only God's intervention prevented

Abimelech from a serious mistake (Genesis 20). Abimelech's appeal is for Abraham to deal honestly with him from that moment on. In fact, at that moment, Abimelech had dealt dishonestly with Abraham. His men had seized possession of a well that Abraham had dug. Both had something for which to atone. Abimelech denied having any knowledge about the theft of the well. Abraham gave seven lambs to Abimelech as proof of ownership. The cost of being an alien is that Abraham must pay to get his own well returned.

Abraham must establish his own name to prove his ownership and get possession of what already belonged to him. In the story of Abraham's life, God had to do the same thing. He must establish his own name to have full possession of Abraham. Abraham's worship of 'the everlasting God' (21:33) is Abraham's recognition that his true possession is in God. The land may never be his in this earthly life, but the faith he had in God has a quality that does not end with this life. He had God, and now God truly had him. God's ability to give the land to the nation that Abraham's offspring will produce is no more significant than the victory God had just won.

> The lesson here has redemptive theology overtones. God was our Creator. He owns us! Yet, he will pay a supreme price to get us back via the sacrifice of the Incarnate one, the seed of the woman, his own Son.

'...the everlasting God...'

Among the most interesting learning experiences the reader of Genesis encounters are those moments when the narrative reveals the human to have a new understanding of God, and worships God under a new name corresponding to that new understanding. Abraham learns a new relationship with God through the struggle with Abimelech. Abraham wanted his well returned (21:25).

Abimelech also had a request, he wanted to know that Abraham could be trusted (21:23). This was the result of Abraham's earlier deceit of Abimelech (Genesis 20:1-2).

Abraham gave a gift to Abimelech to establish his trustworthiness. The gift was seven ewe lambs. Abimelech accepted the lambs and the two established a covenant, naming the place Beersheba which means 'well of the seven.' It is in the light of Abraham's worship that the real significance of the moment strikes the reader. 'And Abraham…called there on the name of the Lord, the everlasting God' (21:33). The transaction between the two men carried an everlasting consequence for Abraham. What was it?

Two things give us the clue. First, the number 'seven' is significant to the Hebrews. It signifies completion. Though Abraham had only solidified ownership of a well, he saw the event through the window of God's promise, '…Unto thy seed will I give this land…' (Genesis 12:7). For Abimelech, Abraham had required a well, but for Abraham, he had just taken possession of the land. The hand of God was at work in this seemingly insignificant event.

Second, the later testimony of Scripture and the history of Israel validates the significance that Abraham attached to the moment. This very spot, Beersheba, will come to be known as the Southernmost boundary of the land. '…I…set up the throne of David over Israel…from Dan even to Beersheba' (II Samuel 3:9-10). Through trust in the everlasting God, Abraham is able to transcend time and space and own the promised possession.

A true devotional moment arrives when one understands that Abraham's method of ownership was worship. This cannot be lost upon anyone who seeks a better relationship with God. As Abraham owned the land, though a sojourner, the present Christian pilgrimage is no different. I must lay claim to many of God's promises through worship. In the activity of calling on the name of the Lord, I can appropriate the hope of the future kingdom of God into my present existence.

The Christian is a creature of time. Yet, through faith, claim is laid to an everlasting existence. '…whosoever believeth in him should not perish…' (John 3:16). As Abraham could boldly lay claim to a land he did not possess, so we can boldly lay claim to eternal life based on the promise of Christ, the Incarnate redeemer.

Genesis 22:1-24

I. The Call to Sacrifice Isaac (22:1-10)
1. '…God did tempt Abraham…'
2. '…God will provide…'
3. Developing mental tenacity
4. A hope that comes in faith
5. '…offer him…'

II. An Interesting Confirmation for Abraham 22:11-24)
1. '…lay not think hand…'
2. Jehovah-Jireh
3. '…God did tempt Abraham…'
4. '…children unto thy brother…'

Genesis 22:1-10

1. And it came to pass after these things, that God did tempt Abraham, and said unto him, Abraham: and he said, Behold, here I am. 2. And he said, Take now thy son, thine only son Isaac, whom thou lovest, and get thee into the land of Moriah; and offer him there for a burnt offering upon one of the mountains which I will tell thee of. 3. And Abraham rose up early in the morning, and saddled his ass, and took two of his young men with him, and Isaac his son, and clave the wood for the burnt offering, and rose up, and went unto the place of which God had told him. 4. Then on the third day Abraham lifted up his eyes, and saw the place afar off. 5. And Abraham said unto his young men, Abide ye here with

*the ass; and I and the lad will go yonder and worship, and come
again to you. 6. And Abraham took the wood of the burnt offering, and laid it upon Isaac his son; and he took the fire in his hand,
and a knife; and they went both of them together. 7. And Isaac
spake unto Abraham his father, and said, My father: and he said,
Here am I, my son. And he said, Behold the fire and the wood: but
where is the lamb for a burnt offering? 8. And Abraham said, My
son, God will provide himself a lamb for a burnt offering: so they
went both of them together. 9. And they came to the place which
God had told him of; and Abraham built an altar there, and laid the
wood in order, and bound Isaac his son, and laid him on the altar
upon the wood. 10. And Abraham stretched forth his hand, and
took the knife to slay his son.*

'...God did tempt Abraham...'

When Abraham willingly offered to Abimelech seven ewe lambs as
proof of his ownership of a well, Abraham was acknowledging that
though he had dug the well, he must now sacrifice to obtain and
keep possession (Genesis 21:22-33). It wasn't fair, but it was a reality. The Philistines, among whom he lived, did not have the kind of
knowledge of Abraham to allow any other means to establish his
ownership. This was a very enlightening moment for Abraham. In
it, he learned something of God's love in reclaiming ownership of
his creation. That which he learned is now to be expanded upon
by the strangest request in the Bible.

God asks Abraham to offer Isaac as a sacrifice. This is the beloved son of promise. Ishmael (the elder son by Sarah's handmaiden) has been disowned at God's command (Genesis 21:10-
12). Abraham has one son. The son had been given by miracle of
God, born in Abraham and Sarah's old age. Why does God want
him slain? The Bible student immediately recognizes the powerful
imagery pointing to Jesus Christ, and God's own sacrifice of his

Son, '...that he gave his only begotten Son (John 3:16). The lesson for Abraham is of a wonderful redemption.

Consider Abraham's previous lesson (Genesis 21:30). In order for God to establish his ownership of us, he will provide an offering that proves it. As humans and sinners we do not have the kind of knowledge that can accept God's claims on us. Abraham did for Abimelech what God must do for us by validating his own testimony through an offering. Abraham showed a great understanding of God, and acknowledged that his possession of God was his greatest treasure in worshipping 'the everlasting God' (Genesis 21:33). It was more, however. It was the confession that God possessed him.

Abraham has confessed it! Will he demonstrate it? Basically the test is this: God is giving Abraham a marvellous opportunity to validate his confession. 'Take now thy son...whom thou lovest...and offer him...for a burnt offering...' (22:2). Though he has shown a great understanding of God, Abraham must take another step. The greatest test of his life comes precisely at the moment he has demonstrated the greatest confession of his life. The reader may look back on the event knowing how it turned out. What did Abraham know? He knew that God had given him a land he had not yet received, had promised that he would be a great nation which he would never see in this life, and that the only means of having that nation was Isaac whom he must now slay. He also knew that his greatest treasure was God. Disobedience might cost him that relationship. He dared not disobey. His love for God leads him to value God above all else, even his son, Isaac.

This is one of the more sobering stories in the Bible. It is an indescribably fearful moment when contemplated. If God would ask this of the faithful servant, Abraham, what might he ask of us? It is more sobering when looked at through the mirror of Jesus Christ What did God ask of himself?

'...God will provide...'

The story of Abraham's life teaches a radically important lesson. That lesson is circular, consisting of two parts. First, the route to a growing love of God is in learning of God. Second, loving God will provide great results in learning of God. Abraham had made great strides in his knowledge of God. This knowledge enabled him to discern correctly how to deal with the Phillistine ruler, Abimelech (Genesis 21:22-33). His love of God was manifest in his worship of God, and he noted his increased knowledge of God through his use of the name, 'the everlasting God' (Genesis 21:33).

Abraham understands by this point that he is being taught what God is like. Every step is an exciting learning experience into eternal truth. God is ready to teach more, but it is through a phenomenal request. '...Take now thy son, thine only son Isaac...and offer...him...for a burnt offering....' (22:2). You and I wonder, 'How could Abraham follow through on this?' There is only one explanation. Abraham had just worshipped 'the everlasting God' (Genesis 21:33). He had experienced God's test many times and had seen the way that God used the tests to teach of himself. Abraham was hungry for what God would teach him, and that could only come through obedience. God always has more to teach us. He can never exhaust himself. The question is, 'Do we want to learn?' Jesus said, 'Take my yoke upon you, and learn of me...' (Matthew 11:29). We cannot learn something new about God until we have been obedient in what we already know.

When Abraham started his journey to the mountain where he must offer Isaac, it is certain that the journey was not one of eager anticipation. He had a heaviness of heart about the request. He certainly must have been confused. Why is God asking him to do this? How will God grant me the son to fulfil his promise? No doubt, he wondered how he would explain the event to his wife, Sarah. He also knew that God would not let him down. He would come down from that mountain with answers, but he must obey first.

On the journey, Abraham gives us a clue to his thinking. Isaac asked, '...where is the lamb for a burnt offering' (22:7)? Abraham replied, '...God will provide himself a lamb for a burnt offering...' (22:8). This moment strikes like a lighting bolt. John the Baptist introducing Christ said, '...Behold the lamb of God, which taketh away the sin of the world' (John 1:29). Indeed God does provide himself a sacrifice. Abraham had a belief that he would come away from that mountain knowing the kind of offering that the Lord really required.

Developing mental tenacity

We must deal with a passage of Scripture that is blessed and frightful. Abraham is asked by God to do that which is unthinkable '...Take now thy son...whom thou lovest...and offer him...for a burnt offering...' (22:2). It is easy for us from our vantage point to look back and cheer Abraham's great faith, and God's ultimate response in stopping Abraham, and make comparison to the offering of Jesus Christ as sacrifice for sin. To that extent the story is blessed, and that is why we never tire of hearing it. The frightening part comes when we ask, 'Would God ask me to make the same, or similar, commitment?'

The kind of obedience Abraham exhibited is incredible. He was willing to offer his son as a burnt offering. Clearly, God did not intend to have Abraham actually slay Isaac. It was to teach Abraham of the kind of sacrifice that God, himself, would make to redeem man from his sin. 'For God so loved the world that he gave his only begotten Son... (John 3:16). The question Abraham had to answer was the question of value. Does he truly understand what his treasure is? His treasure was not in Isaac for he is merely the gift of God. Abraham's treasure is God, and God alone. His is the journey from placing value on earthly treasure to placing value on heavenly treasure.

As Abraham makes the trek up the mountain to sacrifice Isaac, he must have been in an emotional quandary. This great test, and we might call it the final crossroads of Abraham's life, involved a mental tenacity. Abraham could not afford to go by feelings. He must make up his mind before the moment comes that he will obey God, no matter the feelings of his heart. The battle Jesus had in the Garden of Gethsamane reflects a similar struggle. '...Nevertheless not my will, but thine, be done... (Luke 22:42). Abraham is seeking to gain strength with each step up the mountain.

'And Abraham took the wood on the burnt offering, and laid it upon Isaac his son...' (22:6). Abraham knows he is going to sacrifice Isaac, and yet forces Isaac to carry the wood. Obviously, there is a clear picture of the cross being carried by Christ, but what are we to make of Abraham's attitude? Is he a sick human being, filled with cruelty?

With all the emotion of the moment, Abraham steeled himself for the task that was ahead. His commitment to obey God was already in place. Even before the final moment of testing, he demonstrates that God is his treasure. His will comes first. The lesson for us is the importance of prior commitment to God. Our love for him must be in place before the testing, so that the issue of obedience is not a question at the time of testing. Jesus made sure of this point as he wrestled in prayer during the fitful night in Gethsemane.

> There is an important factor at work here. It is very helpful to have a prior commitment to God in place before any time of testing. To understand that God is the greatest treasure of life and to have a fear of losing that treasure can be the greatest advantage we have in the time of our testing.

'A hope that comes in faith'

When one commits himself to a loving relationship, he commits himself to pain. Love requires sacrifice and hanging in there when people hurt you. Love for God is also a relationship of pain.

Because a relationship with God often requires a lifestyle that is not accepting of that which the world loves, the world will turn on you. Obedience to God means accepting the enmity of the world. Abraham, however, is called upon to endure pain that he would never have expected that God would require. '...Take now thy son, thine only son Isaac, whom thou lovest...and offer him...for a burnt offering...' (22:2).

The fact that Abraham proceeded in obedience to God's command is indication that Abraham had grown in understanding of God. He has a desire to know all that God would teach him. It is a strange request that God has made. Why does he make it? Abraham can only discover the answer in obedience. Many things may run through his mind. He saw what God did to Sodom. Has Isaac sinned in such a way that he should be punished by death? That would not fit the nature of sacrifice in which the innocent lambs have been the burnt offerings, so if Isaac is a burnt offering to God, he must be innocent.

Abraham could question his own actions. Has he sinned in such a way that requires the death of Isaac? If that be true why would God have protected him in those moments when he had said Sarah was his sister and allowed her to be taken as wife to someone else (Genesis 12:10-20; 20:1-18). The questions for Abraham had no answer, so he continues.

There is indication that Abraham hoped that God would change his mind, or that there would be another command to replace the one he received. He said to those journeying with him '...Abide ye here...I and the lad will go yonder, and worship, and come again to you' (22:5). He expected, or hoped, that both he and Isaac would return from the mountain.

Ultimately, the issue for Abraham is 'What does the Lord require of me? What kind of offering must I make to have God satisfied?' Abraham knew that when he had sinned, God had protected him and even prospered him. This test is different. Can God be trusted to prosper him when he is fully obedient? This is real pain! Jesus faced the same kind of test in fully trusting the Father in his submission unto death.

Did Abraham expect that he would have to slay Isaac, but trusted that God would then raise him from the dead? Hebrews 11:19 intimates this possibility. 'By faith, Abraham, when he was tried, offered up Isaac...accounting that God was able to raise him up, even from the dead...In this sense, Isaac prefigured Christ as the beloved son who is slain, but who also provides a picture of Christ in resurrection.

'...offer him...'

The aspect of the request that God makes of Abraham that is the most provocative for us is the concept of knowing and doing the will of God. Abraham heard the will of God named. 'Take now thy son...and offer him...for a burnt offering...' (22:2). That kind of command is not exactly what one expects when he seeks to know the will of God. The experience of Abraham teaches a lot about what this 'will of God' thing truly means.

When I seek to know the will of God in my life, for what am I asking? Is it to grow in relationship to God, or is it to have God make something great of me? Abraham had begun his walk with God with the promise that God would make something great of him. 'And I will make of thee a great nation, and I will bless thee, and make thy name great...' (Genesis 12:2). Most of the promise could only occur after Abraham was dead, yet Abraham followed God, and pursued the promise. The only visible testimony that Abraham had of his future greatness is his son, Isaac. The test here takes on another dimension. God is not only asking Abraham to slay the son he loves, but to slay the dream he has of greatness.

Jesus said, '...If any man will come after me, let him deny himself, and take up his cross, and follow me' (Matthew 16:24). Nowhere in Scripture is the idea of 'denying oneself' better illustrated than in this great test of Abraham's life. Abraham must understand that the greatness that God promised was about God's greatness, not Abraham's. The people of God will come to marvel at Abraham's willingness to obey. In that moment, however, there was no evidence, no great applause, and no one to speak of him as the great example of faith. It was just he, Isaac, and God. He must look his son in the eye, perhaps with tears, and say 'My God takes precedence over you' (Genesis 22:10). Mostly, it was to say, 'My God takes precedence over me.' Abraham was willing to give up the greatness that God had promised him in order to keep his relationship with God. When we ask to know the will of God, we must always remember that when the knowledge comes, it is apt to be by means of a test. Is our relationship with God more important than our greatness?

The will of God can invade our lives in many forms. We should not seek to discern it in validation and exoneration of ourselves. The command of God upon Abraham is to show sacrifice in order to have a relationship with God. After all, he had to sacrifice for a relationship with us. In the end, that is the lesson that dominates this episode in Abraham's life. The awesome reality is what God is doing for Abraham. He is opening up his heart and showing to this man, Abraham, exactly what he is going to do to provide answer to the sin problem. The sacrifice is not a one way street. In fact, it is God who shall sacrifice most.

Genesis 22:11-24

11. And the angel of the Lord called unto him out of heaven, and said, Abraham, Abraham: and he said, Here am I. 12. And he said, Lay not thine hand upon the lad, neither do thou any thing unto him: for now I know that thou fearest God, seeing thou hast not withheld thy son, thine only son from me. 13. And Abraham lifted up his eyes, and looked, and behold behind him a ram caught in a thicket by his horns: and Abraham went and took the ram, and offered him up for a burnt offering in the stead of his son. 14. And Abraham called the name of that place Jehovah-jireh: as it is said to this day, In the mount of the Lord it shall be seen. 15. And

Genesis

the angel of the Lord called unto Abraham out of heaven the second time, 16. And said, By myself have I sworn, saith the Lord, for because thou hast done this thing, and hast not withheld thy son, thine only son: 17. That in blessing I will bless thee, and in multiplying I will multiply thy seed as the stars of the heaven, and as the sand which is upon the sea shore; and thy seed shall possess the gate of his enemies; 18. And in thy seed shall all the nations of the earth be blessed; because thou hast obeyed my voice. 19. So Abraham returned unto his young men, and they rose up and went together to Beersheba; and Abraham dwelt at Beersheba. 20. And it came to pass after these things, that it was told Abraham, saying, Behold, Milcah, she hath also born children unto thy brother Nahor; 21. Huz his firstborn, and Buz his brother, and Kemuel the father of Aram, 22. And Chesed, and Hazo, and Pildash, and Jidlaph, and Bethuel. 23. And Bethuel begat Rebekah: these eight Milcah did bear to Nahor, Abraham's brother. 24. And his concubine, whose name was Reumah, she bare also Tebah, and Gaham, and Thahash, and Maachah.

'...lay not thine hand...'

Knowing the will of God is often approached as open-ended. That is, we don't see it as a matter of fact entity. By this, God's will is not seen as directing me to go to the store and buy a jar of mayonnaise. That is an act that takes only a few minutes to perform and it is over. God's will is usually perceived in dynamic terms and is continually in motion. When Abraham was told to slay his son Isaac by making of him a burnt offering (22:2), it was very matter of fact. It would be done, and it would be over. There is no sense of 'what next?' When Isaac is dead, he is dead, unless God chooses to resurrect him. The possibility of God raising him from the dead could have been Abraham's hope. He had seen God resurrect the womb of Sarah so that Isaac could be born in Sarah's old age. Yet, the matter of fact of offering him as a burnt offering didn't give hope that any such miracle would be forthcoming.

Fortunately, that for which Abraham certainly hoped did come to pass. He had told Isaac, '...God will provide himself a lamb for a burnt offering...' (22:8). As Abraham was poised to plunge the knife into Isaac's body, God stopped him, and provided a ram to replace Isaac. The 'angel of the Lord' (22:11), an Old Testament reference to the second person of the Trinity, spoke to Abraham and said, '...Lay not thine hand upon the lad ...for now I know that thou fearest God, seeing thou hast not withheld thy son, thine only son from me' (22:12).

The moment was magical. Abraham had come to this moment eager to learn about God's requirements of him, and that which he learned was beyond anything he could have imagined. He gave a name to the place, 'Jehovah-jireh,' which means, 'The Lord will provide' (22:14). These words are directly related to God's deliverance. Abraham understood that God had let him in on a divine master plan. God was going to do exactly what he had just requested that Abraham be willing to do. Jesus tells us, '...Abraham rejoiced to see my day: and he saw it and was glad' (John 8:56). Before the words were ever written, and the history was finished, Abraham heard God saying 'For God so loved the world that he gave his only begotten Son....' (John 3:16). What seemed a very matter of fact request without continuing motion has become the most dynamic act of history. Abraham saw it 2,000 years ahead of time because he obeyed God.

Jehovah-Jireh

Abraham had just been through the darkest valley of his life. He had been tested by God as to his willingness to obey God despite the personal losses that might accrue, specifically, the loss of his son and possibly the loss of the rest of God's promise relating to the land. Abraham would have God, and God, alone, but would that be sufficient for Abraham? Abraham passed the test. Thus he has a new and precious understanding of God, which is defined by a new name for God, 'Jehovah-jireh' (22:14). It means 'The Lord will provide.' It is a moment in time that added great wisdom to Abraham. God took Abraham through the dark valley because it was only through the valley that this wisdom could be obtained.

As we examine the issue of loving God, it should be clear that as much as Abraham did not like the valley, he rejoiced about the learning he gained. His relationship with God was strengthened. His ability to trust in God was increased, and his faith was given very solid foundation. 'The Lord will provide' is a defining moment of peace for every believer. It is a walk of love that feeds on the certainty of God's care. The place at which Abraham now stood is the place of everlasting covenant. 'God will provide' is a knowledge that extends beyond the vale of this life.

It is sin that creates the difficulties that this life presents. It is relationship to God that overcomes sin. It is God's sacrifice of his own son that accomplishes that feat. When that is accomplished, the care of God is guaranteed through the giving of eternal life. It is a truly wonderful event when we can learn to think in terms of provision that is for eternity. When Jesus said '…Abraham rejoiced to see my day, and was glad…' (John 8:56), he was speaking of the value of an eternal vision.

For Abraham, it was the great joy of possessing the promise even though much of it still awaited fulfilment when he died. He had learned the great lesson of faith. It is the possession of that which is not yet obtained. Hebrews says, '…faith is…the evidence of things not seen' (Hebrews 11:1). How wonderful to latch on to that which is not subject to the ups and downs of this earth's system. 'The Lord will provide' is the language of loving God.

It is difficult to understand that the Christian must possess that which he cannot see, and claim that which he has no power to produce. It is only through faith that this is accomplished.

'…Children unto thy brother…'

After the extreme trial that Abraham has just been through, he may have been wondering what comes next? The Lord must have sensed this anxiety, and offered this word of reassurance. '…because thou hast done this thing, and has not withheld thy son...I will bless thee...I will multiply thy seed as the stars of the heaven...and in thy seed shall all the nations of the earth be blessed...' (22:16-18). Because of his obedience Abraham knew that somewhere among his seed would be born the Son of God who would be the sacrifice that God required. A further word of encouragement is to follow.

It has been many years since Abraham made his initial journey into the land of promise. He had left other family behind when he went out from Haran. The land in which Abraham lived was to be the possession of Abraham's descendants, but Abraham would know it only in the promise of God. Trusting God, and being obedient to God, based on a promise, which shall only come after his lifetime, had brought Abraham into a special relationship with God that no one of his generation could equal. The promise of God has just been repeated to Abraham (22:16-18).

By this time, Isaac is in his mid-teen years, and it will be his children that shall receive the continuation of God's promise. Who will Isaac marry? There is some tension in the story as Abraham lives as a stranger in the land of Canaanites. It appears that God is providing a comforting word for Abraham via the news that Abraham's extended family which he had left behind has grown. This word comes at a crucial time for Abraham. Having tested him by his willingness to sacrifice Isaac, God does not allow Abraham distress about who Isaac will marry. God has been taking care of that issue himself. This news further solidifies for Abraham that there will be no further test when it comes to Isaac.

God knew that Abraham needed an encouraging word, and he gave it. It is important to know that the encouragement comes in the light of obedience. Abraham knows that his descendants will possess the land. The great nation will be great because it is the vehicle that will be used to present the Son of God, who will be the sacrifice to God, which Isaac typified. Without Abraham's knowledge of God, which he learned through obedience, he might still be wrestling with the issues of his present life and would have no basis of encouragement.

Genesis 23-24

Genesis 23:1-20

1. And Sarah was an hundred and seven and twenty years old: these were the years of the life of Sarah. 2. And Sarah died in Kirjatharba; the same is Hebron in the land of Canaan: and Abraham came to mourn for Sarah, and to weep for her. 3. And Abraham stood up from before his dead, and spake unto the sons of Heth, saying, 4. I am a stranger and a sojourner with you: give me a possession of a buryingplace with you, that I may bury my dead out of my sight. 5. And the children of Heth answered Abraham, saying unto him, 6. Hear us, my lord: thou art a mighty prince among us: in the choice of our sepulchres bury thy dead; none of us shall withhold from thee his sepulchre, but that thou mayest bury thy dead. 7. And Abraham stood up, and bowed himself to the people of the land, even to the children of Heth. 8. And he communed with them, saying, If it be your mind that I should bury my dead out of my sight; hear me, and intreat for me to Ephron the son of Zohar, 9. That he may give me the cave of Machpelah, which he hath, which is in the end of his field; for as much money as it is worth he shall give it me for a possession of a buryingplace amongst you. 10. And Ephron dwelt among the children of

Heth: and Ephron the Hittite answered Abraham in the audience of the children of Heth, even of all that went in at the gate of his city, saying, 11. Nay, my lord, hear me: the field give I thee, and the cave that is therein, I give it thee; in the presence of the sons of my people give I it thee: bury thy dead. 12. And Abraham bowed down himself before the people of the land. 13. And he spake unto Ephron in the audience of the people of the land, saying, But if thou wilt give it, I pray thee, hear me: I will give thee money for the field; take it of me, and I will bury my dead there. 14. And Ephron answered Abraham, saying unto him, 15. My lord, hearken unto me: the land is worth four hundred shekels of silver; what is that betwixt me and thee? bury therefore thy dead. 16. And Abraham hearkened unto Ephron; and Abraham weighed to Ephron the silver, which he had named in the audience of the sons of Heth, four hundred shekels of silver, current money with the merchant. 17. And the field of Ephron which was in Machpelah, which was before Mamre, the field, and the cave which was therein, and all the trees that were in the field, that were in all the borders round about, were made sure. 18. Unto Abraham for a possession in the presence of the children of Heth, before all that went in at the gate of his city. 19. And after this, Abraham buried Sarah his wife in the cave of the field of Machpelah before Mamre: the same is Hebron in the land of Canaan. 20. And the field, and the cave that is therein, were made sure unto Abraham for a possession of a burying place by the sons of Heth.

A burial place for Sarah

The event presents such irony that its meaning can easily escape us. There is a strong correlation to what it means to love God when walking through this life. On its surface, it is only Abraham purchasing a burying place for Sarah. The irony comes in the reality of God's promise. 'For all the land which thou seest, to thee will I give it, and to thy seed forever' (13:15). God promised to give it. Abraham is now purchasing it. That which he purchases will be the place of burial in the land. It is the first and the last mention of Abraham's ownership of any parcel of the promised land, and it is only a gravesite.

Ephron offered to give the gravesite to Abraham, but just as Abraham had refused the gifts of the king of Sodom, he refused the gift of the land. There is a note of absolute contentment with Abraham. He wanted only what God could provide, not that which men could provide. He would pay for the burial place knowing that God would provide the rest of the land to his descendants. The writer of Hebrews expresses the attitude of Abraham and Sarah. 'These all died in faith, not having received the promises, but having seen them afar off, and were persuaded of them, and embraced them...' (Hebrews 11:13).

The knowledge of God is indeed a wonderful thing. By claiming God and his promises as his possession, Abraham is able to accept a burying place as full possession of the land. In many ways, this sounds like a great mystery to the modern reader. It even sounds foolish and deluded. Yet, which is more secure, God's promise or a tangible possession? Abraham has seen how tangible possessions come and go (Note Lot's fortune and misfortune, and the loss of Ishmael). He has also seen how God resurrected Sarah's dead womb in order to provide the promised son. Clearly, God's promise is the more secure.

Abraham had now obtained such great love of God that he claimed possession of everything God promised on the pure wonder of that love relationship. The gravesite among strangers was his title of possession. The Christian will always be among strangers in the world. The promise is one day to rule with Christ. Can we be content with the promise, as was Abraham?

> Jesus said, '...My kingdom is not of this world...' (John 18:36). It is also true that our treasure is not here. '...Lay not up for yourselves treasures upon earth...' (Matthew 6:19). Our treasure is in God, and his promise is secure, eternal, and beyond the vale of this life.

Genesis 24:1-67

1. And Abraham was old, and well stricken in age: and the Lord had blessed Abraham in all things. 2. And Abraham said unto his eldest servant of his house, that ruled over all that he had, Put, I pray thee, thy hand under my thigh: 3. And I will make thee swear by the Lord, the God of heaven, and the God of the earth, that thou shalt not take a wife unto my son of the daughters of the Canaanites, among whom I dwell: 4. But thou shalt go unto my country, and to my kindred, and take a wife unto my son Isaac. 5. And the servant said unto him, Peradventure the woman will not be willing to follow me unto this land: must I needs bring thy son again unto the land from whence thou camest? 6. And Abraham said unto him, Beware thou that thou bring not my son thither again. 7. The Lord God of heaven, which took me from my father's house, and from the land of my kindred, and which spake Unto me, and that sware unto me, saying, Unto thy seed will I give this land; he shall send his angel before thee, and thou shalt take a wife unto my son from thence. 8. And if the woman will not be willing to follow thee, then thou shalt be clear from this my oath: only bring not my son thither again. 9. And the servant put his hand under the thigh of Abraham his master, and sware to him concerning that matter. 10. And the servant took ten camels of the camels of his master, and departed; for all the goods of his master were in his hand: and he arose, and went to Mesopotamia, unto the city of Nahor. 11. And he made his camels to kneel down without the city by a well of water at the time of the evening, even the time that women go out to draw water.

12. And he said O Lord God of my master Abraham, I pray thee, send me good speed this day, and shew kindness unto my master Abraham. 13. Behold, I stand here by the well of water; and the daughters of the men of the city come out to draw water: 14. And let it come to pass, that the damsel to whom I shall say, Let down thy pitcher, I pray thee, that I may drink; and she shall say, Drink, and I will give thy camels drink also: let the same be she that thou hast appointed for thy servant Isaac; and thereby shall I know that thou hast shewed kindness unto my master. 15. And it came to pass, before he had done speaking, that, behold, Rebekah came out, who was born to Bethuel, son of Milcah, the wife of Nahor, Abraham's brother, with her pitcher upon her shoulder. 16. And the damsel was very fair to look upon, a virgin, neither had any man known her: and she went down to the well, and filled her pitcher, and came up. 17.And the servant ran to meet her, and said, Let me, I pray thee, drink a little water of thy pitcher. 18. And she said, Drink, my lord: and she hasted, and let down her pitcher upon her hand, and gave him drink. 19. And when she had done giving him drink, she said, I will draw water for thy camels also, until they have done drinking. 20. And she hasted, and emptied her

pitcher into the trough, and ran again unto the well to draw water, and drew for all his camels. 21. And the man wondering at her held his peace, to wit whether the Lord had made his journey prosperous or not. 22. And it came to pass, as the camels had done drinking, that the man took a golden earring of half a shekel weight, and two Bracelets for her hands of ten shekels weight of gold; 23. And said, Whose daughter art thou? tell me, I pray thee: is there room in thy father's house for us to lodge in?

24. And she said unto him, I am the daughter of Bethuel the son of Milcah, which she bare unto Nahor. 25. She said moreover unto him, We have both straw and provender enough, and room to lodge in. 26. And the man bowed down his head, and worshipped the Lord. 27. And he said, Blessed be the Lord God of my master Abraham, who hath not left destitute my master of his mercy and his truth: I being in the way, the Lord led me to the house of my master's brethren. 28. And the damsel ran, and told them of her mother's house these things. 29. And Rebekah had a brother, and his name was Laban: and Laban ran out unto the man, unto the well. 30. And it came to pass, when he saw the earring and Bracelets upon his sister's hands, and when he heard the words of Rebekah his sister, saying, Thus spake the man unto me; that he came unto the man; and, behold, he stood by the camels at the well. 31. And he said, Come in, thou blessed of the Lord; wherefore standest thou without? for I have prepared the house, and room for the camels.

32. And the man came into the house: and he ungirded his camels, and gave straw and provender for the camels, and water to wash his feet, and the men's feet that were with him. 33. And there was set meat before him to eat: but he said, I will not eat, until I have told mine errand. And he said, Speak on. 34. And he said, I am Abraham's servant. 35. And the Lord hath blessed my master greatly; and he is become great: and he hath given him flocks, and herds, and silver, and gold, and menservants, and maidservants, and camels, and asses. 36. And Sarah my master's wife bare a son to my master when she was old: and unto him hath he given all that he hath. 37. And my master made me swear, saying, Thou shalt not take a wife to my son of the daughters of the Canaanites, in whose land I dwell: 38. But thou shalt go unto my father's house, and to my kindred, and take a wife unto my son. 39. And I said unto my master, Peradventure the woman will not follow me. 40. And he said unto me, The Lord, before whom I walk, will send his angel with thee, and prosper thy way; and thou shalt take a wife for my son of my kindred, and of my father's house: 41. Then shalt thou be clear from this my oath, when thou comest

to my kindred; and if they give not thee one, thou shalt be clear from my oath. 42. And I came this day unto the well, and said, O Lord God of my master Abraham, if now thou do prosper my way which I go: 43. Behold, I stand by the well of water; and it shall come to pass, that when the virgin cometh forth to draw water, and I say to her, Give me, I pray thee, a little water of thy pitcher to drink; 44. And she say to me, Both drink thou, and I will also draw for thy camels: let the same be the woman whom the Lord hath appointed out for my master's son.

45. And before I had done speaking in mine heart, behold, Rebekah came forth with her pitcher on her shoulder; and she went down unto the well, and drew water: and I said unto her, Let me drink, I pray thee. 46. And she made haste, and let down her pitcher from her shoulder, and said, Drink, and I will give thy camels drink also: so I drank, and she made the camels drink also. 47. And I asked her, and said, Whose daughter art thou? And she said, The daughter of Bethuel, Nahor's son, whom Milcah bare unto him: and I put the earring upon her face, and the bracelets upon her hands. 48. And I bowed down my head, and worshipped the Lord, and blessed the Lord God of my master Abraham, which had led me in the right way to take my master's brother's daughter unto his son. 49. And now if ye will deal kindly and truly with my master, tell me: and if not, tell me; that I may turn to the right hand, or to the left. 50. Then Laban and Bethuel answered and said, The thing proceedeth from the Lord: we cannot speak unto thee bad or good. 51. Behold, Rebekah is before thee, take her, and go, and let her be thy master's son's wife, as the Lord hath spoken. 52. And it came to pass, that, when Abraham's servant heard their words, he worshipped the Lord, bowing himself to the earth.

53. And the servant brought forth jewels of silver, and jewels of gold, and raiment, and gave them to Rebekah: he gave also to her brother and to her mother precious things. 54. And they did eat and drink, he and the men that were with him, and tarried all night; and they rose up in the morning, and he said, Send me away unto my master. 55. And her brother and her mother said, Let the damsel abide with us a few days, at the least ten; after that she shall go. 56. And he said unto them, Hinder me not, seeing the Lord hath prospered my way; send me away that I may go to my master. 57. And they said, We will call the damsel, and inquire at her mouth. 58. And they called Rebekah, and said unto her, Wilt thou go with this man? And she said, I will go. 59. And they sent away Rebekah their sister, and her nurse, and Abraham's servant, and his men. 60. And they blessed Rebekah, and said unto her, Thou art our

sister, be thou the mother of thousands of millions, and let thy seed pos-
sess the gate of those which hate them. 61. And Rebekah arose, and her
damsels, and they rode upon the camels, and followed the man: and the
servant took Rebekah, and went his way. 62. And Isaac came from the
way of the well Lahairoi; for he dwelt in the south country. 63. And Isaac
went out to meditate in the field at the eventide: and he lifted up his eyes,
and saw, and, behold, the camels were coming. 64. And Rebekah lifted
up her eyes, and when she saw Isaac, she lighted off the camel. 65. For
she had said unto the servant, What man is this that walketh in the field
to meet us? And the servant had said, It is my master: therefore she took
a vail, and covered herself. 66. And the servant told Isaac all things that
he had done. 67. And Isaac brought her into his mother Sarah's tent, and
took Rebekah, and she became his wife; and he loved her: and Isaac was
comforted after his mother's death.

A wife for Isaac

Abraham is determined that his own commitment to God be carried on through his son. He will not allow the people of the land
(Canaanites), who are to be dispossessed, to have claim to the
land, even through marriage. In this way, he is faithful to live by
God's promise. He tells his servant '...go unto my country, and to
my kindred, and take a wife unto my son Isaac' (24:4).

This story provides a compelling insight into a most interesting
person that is a minor character in the Bible. He is referred to as
the 'eldest servant' of Abraham (24:2). He is asked to do the most
delicate of tasks. He must travel to a far country and find a wife for
Abraham's son, Isaac. How would you like that assignment? There
are many obvious risks, not to mention the most obvious – what
if he makes a bad choice, and Abraham and Isaac are displeased?
There are some noteworthy things about the servant.

First, he is mentioned in Genesis 15:2 as the likely heir of Abraham's fortune because, at that time, Isaac was not born. This
verse also tells us his name, Eliezer. The person who once stood to
inherit Abraham's wealth is now called upon to find a bride for the
true heir. The strength of character displayed by Eliezer is some-

what remarkable in light of the personal loss he accrued by virtue of Isaac's presence.

Second, his relationship with Abraham had given him an appreciation for God. As he came near the city where Abraham had sent him, he prayed, '...O Lord God of my master Abraham...shew kindness unto my master Abraham' (Genesis 24:12). He came to trust in God just as he had seen Abraham do. The amazing thing is his concern that God would continue to bless Abraham. There is a certain kind of beauty here. Just as Abraham had come to accept that his greatest blessing was in his knowledge of God and in that relationship, Eliezer understood that his relationship with Abraham was a greater blessing than the material wealth that he might have inherited from Abraham. Thus, his service to Abraham demonstrates a loyalty beyond any material payment. It is done in gratitude, and in full acceptance of that which is the will of God.

Third, the sign that he asks of God in revealing the chosen woman is not some weird or magical manifestation, but something that will identify the character of the woman (24:14). Eliezer has learned from Abraham the importance of humility. He had seen it in Abraham's consistent submission to the will of God. He seeks the same attitude for the bride of Isaac.

> Eliezer becomes a great study in what it means to love God. He is a servant who places great value in being a servant.

Rebekah

In the framework of a master storyteller comes this delightful recitation of the servant's meeting the woman who will be wife to Isaac. We saw her name earlier. It was almost like an after-thought that the writer tells us of the word that came to Abraham. '...it was told Abraham, saying, Behold, Milcah, she hath also born children unto thy brother Nahor... and Jidlaph, and Bethuel. And Bethuel begat Rebekah...' (Genesis 22:20-23). Immediately after this inserted statement, our minds are refocused on Abraham as we are told of Sarah's death, and of Abraham's purchase of a burying place (Genesis 23). Afterward, Eliezer is sent to Abraham's extended family to find a wife for Isaac. On his journey the servant faithfully prayed that God would show him the right person for Isaac. He asked for a specific kind of sign that, if seen, would provide insight into the woman's character (24:14). Into the scene walks none other than Rebekah.

Immediately, we are charmed. She is very pretty (24:16), She is extremely likable (24:17-19), and she is of the right family (24:24). It is immediately clear to the servant that God is at work (24:26). The reader of Scripture is stricken by how quickly this occurs. We have agonized with Abraham over the length of time he had to wait before the birth of the promised son.

There was the famine in the land to which God had brought Abraham. There is his constant sojourning in the land without any ownership. Even now, he owns only a gravesite. We are conditioned to waiting. Why is this incident so different? Abraham's words tell us. 'The Lord God of heaven, which took me from my father's house, and from the land of my kindred...and that sware unto me...Unto thy seed will I give this land; he shall send his angel before thee, and thou shalt take a wife unto my son from thence' (24:7). Abraham knew that the timing was right. How? Sarah is dead. Abraham had been challenged to sacrifice Isaac, and was halted. There is no longer any chance that God will revive the womb of Sarah to produce the promised son. Put it all together and Abraham simply knew. It was the right time and God had set the stage. The beauty and attraction of this story provides great encouragement to all believers struggling with the will of God. When God writes the story, it always has a beautiful ending.

We may wonder if God is writing a story for us, and if there can be a beautiful ending. Many times we cannot see how it is possible. It is really not important to know how. It is only important to know that the beautiful ending is always based in submission to him.

'...I being in the way...'

Have you ever been astonished at an event or happening? I'm talking about the sense of fate. It is the knowledge that something greater than yourself has been at work, and though you were very much part of it, you did not realize it. The hero of this story in Genesis 24 is the servant of Abraham, and he experiences this kind of astonishment.

He has been commissioned by Abraham to find a bride for Isaac, Abraham's son. There must be some degree of anxiety as he approaches the city to which he has been sent. He has prayed, asked a specific sign of God, and the prayer has been answered. It has been a long journey, but in the context of the story, there is a lightning-like quickness to the events. All the angst of the servant is quickly ended and the pieces of the puzzle that is in his mind fall into place at once. The reaction of the servant reveals more of his exemplary character. He places the ornaments of gold upon her (24:22). These ornaments are the symbols of honor. It is more than thanks for the service she had performed (24:17-20). The one served gives the honor to the servant, and says in effect 'I am now your servant.' This is to be a reality if Rebekah accepts the forthcoming offer.

The story proceeds and the servant learns that Rebekah is of the family of Abraham (24:24), and she invites him to lodge in her father's house for the evening (24:25). The servant, whose name is Eliezer (15:2), is astonished. He had traveled all those miles, stopped at this particular well, encountered this particular woman, who is of the particular house of Abraham's brother, and he is going to lodge there for the evening. His actual words reflect the wonder he felt. 'And the man bowed down his head, and worshipped the Lord...Blessed be...God...who hath not left destitute my master...I being in the way, the Lord led me to the house of my master's brethren' (24:26-27). Note the subtlety! Eliezer establishes a claim in Abraham's blessing. We have a little insight into Eliezer's learning. He knew God blessed him. All the glory goes to the God of Abraham. The wonder of Abraham's story is that God reveals himself to all through Abraham. Remember the promise '..in thee shall all families of the earth be blessed' (12:3). Eliezer understood that having Abraham's God meant having a share in Abraham's blessing.

> Eliezer's spirit is one of great example. He was in the place of blessing because he was where God led him. He was not worried about his lack of possessions but took great pride in the knowledge that God was at work in him.

'...the Lord hath prospered my way...'

The servant of Genesis 24 (whose name is Eliezer) has been on a remarkable journey. He has been astonished at the way God has worked. His footsteps were directed by God, to the very well, where he would encounter Rebekah, the woman that God has chosen for the wife of Isaac. He spends the evening at Rebekah's home, does the proper bartering with the family, and they immediately agree that Rebekah should be Isaac's bride. '...Rebekah is before thee, take her, and go, and let her be thy master's son's wife...' (24:51). Immediately, the servant worships God (24:52).

Twice in the story, we see the servant in an act of worship that is inspired by the development of events. The attitude of the servant, and his expressiveness is captivating. If this were a movie, he would steal the scene. It is with sheer joy and exuberance that he falls on the ground to worship God. His exuberance continues to manifest itself in the morning. He is ready to leave, but Rebekah's family urges him to stay a while before they leave. He replies '... Hinder me not, seeing the Lord hath prospered my way; send me away that I may go to my master' (24:56).

The servant's attitude manifests two wonderful learning experiences. The first is in the knowledge of a task completed well. He was given a job, by his master, and now it is finished. It is clear from his worship that he understood how the task had been accomplished. He had been faithful to obey his master, and God did the rest. In the New Testament, the Apostle Paul states, 'I have fought a good fight, I have finished my course, I have kept the faith' (I1 Timothy 4:7). The satisfaction comes from staying with the task in spite of fear. Loving God is manifest in faithfulness while experiencing anxiety.

The second is the anticipation of seeing his master. Clearly, the servant was now anxious to present to Isaac his bride. The delight would be Eliezer's when Isaac and Rebekah are face to face. He can't wait for the moment. Eliezer, the servant, is giving the master a gift, and what a gift it is! Eliezer did not create Rebekah, he did not choose her, but he has the privilege of presenting her. Note the attitude of Paul 'For I am jealous over you…that I may present you as a chaste virgin to Christ' (2 Corinthians 11:2).

> As a servant, the greatest joy is in a task done well. Eliezer felt that sensation. It is possible to lose that kind of thrill in the hope for material gain as the best reward. Let us not lose sight of the thrill of obedience and thus presenting to God the rewards of his work through us. If we are traveling his way, there will be gifts in our hands to present to him.

'…when she saw Isaac…'

Wouldn't you have liked to be there! The author magically brings our attention to the moment that Isaac and his bride meet for the first time. Isaac is in the fields meditating (24:63). No doubt, he was thinking about the return of his father's servant and the lady he would be bringing with him. The place name 'La-hai-roi' (verse 62) is relevant. It is the same place God had met Hagar and promised that she would give birth to a son who would father a nation (16:11-14). Isaac's mind is centered on his own situation as heir to the promise of Abraham that he would father a nation through whom the world would be blessed (12:3).

As the servant of Abraham (Eliezer) and Rebekah are traveling, their conversation must certainly have been about Isaac. I would imagine that Eliezer had described Isaac in much detail. Rebekah would know what he looked like as far as words could describe. She would know about his demeanor, his character, his likes and dislikes. The questions surely kept coming. The assumption is that Eliezer would never tire of telling her of Isaac.

The magical moment arrives. She sees Isaac approaching them, and in anticipation (maybe recognizing him from Eliezer's description) asks who he is? Upon knowing that it is Isaac, she jumps down from the camel upon which she rides and pulls the veil over her face. We have a visual picture of Rebekah's grace and humility, and a sense of the anticipation of Isaac. We are drawn into the magic of the moment. Isaac is very pleased. It is love at first sight. 'And Isaac...took Rebekah...she became his wife; and he loved her...' (24:67).

The knowledgeable reader of Scripture will note a beautiful spiritual picture. Isaac, by his willingness to be a sacrifice (Genesis 22) is a picture of Jesus Christ. Here, we have him in another portrayal of Christ. Eliezer, his servant, has painstakingly described him to his bride, Rebekah. Jesus said, 'But when the Comforter is come, whom I will send...from the Father, even the Spirit of truth...he shall testify of me...' (John 15:26). Just as Eliezer was sent to seek Rebekah and tell her of Isaac, so the Holy Spirit is sent to seek us, the bride of Christ (Ephesians 5:22-32), and tell us of him.

> The Holy Spirit stands always ready to teach us of Christ, and to impart to us his mind (1 Corinthians 2:16). It is logical to assume that we might have a great anticipation of seeing our Lord, and that we would flee to the Word of God with many questions of the Holy Spirit about him.

Genesis 25:1-34

I. The Generations of Abraham (25:1-21)
1. '…all tht he had to Isaac…'
2. '…she was barren…'

II. Two Sons (25:22-34)
1. '…the children struggled…'
2. '…elder shall serve the younger…'
3. '…what profit this birthright…'

Genesis 25:1-21

1. Then again Abraham took a wife, and her name was Keturah. 2. And she bare him Zimran, and Jokshan, and Medan, and Midian, and Ishbak, and Shuah. 3. And Jokshan begat Sheba, and Dedan. And the sons of Dedan were Asshurim, and Letushim, and Leummim. 4. And the sons of Midian; Ephah, and Epher, and Hanoch, and Abida, and Eldaah. All these were the children of Keturah. 5. And Abraham gave all that he had unto Isaac. 6. But unto the sons of the concubines, which Abraham had, Abraham gave gifts, and sent them away from Isaac his son, while he yet lived, eastward, unto the east country. 7. And these are the days of the years of Abraham's life which he lived, an hundred threescore and fifteen years. 8. Then Abraham gave up the Ghost, and died in a good old age, an old man, and full of years; and was gathered to his people. 9. And his sons Isaac and Ishmael buried him in the cave of Machpelah, in the field of Ephron the son of Zohar the Hittite, which is before Mamre; 10. The field which Abraham purchased of the sons of Heth: there was Abraham buried, and Sarah his wife. 11. And it came to pass after the death of Abraham, that God blessed his son Isaac; and Isaac dwelt by the well

Lahairoi. 12. Now these are the generations of Ishmael, Abraham's son, whom Hagar the Egyptian, Sarah's handmaid, bare unto Abraham: 13. And these are the names of the sons of Ishmael, by their names, according to their generations: the firstborn of Ishmael, Nebajoth; and Kedar, and Adbeel, and Mibsam, 14. And Mishma, and Dumah, and Massa, 15. Hadar, and Tema, Jetur, Naphish, and Kedemah: 16. These are the sons of Ishmael, and these are their names, by their towns, and by their castles; twelve princes according to their nations. 17. And these are the years of the life of Ishmael, an hundred and thirty and seven years: and he gave up the Ghost and died; and was gathered unto his people. 18. And they dwelt from Havilah unto Shur, that is before Egypt, as thou goest toward Assyria: and he died in the presence of all his brethren. 19. And these are the generations of Isaac, Abraham's son: Abraham begat Isaac: 20. And Isaac was forty years old when he took Rebekah to wife, the daughter of Bethuel the Syrian of Padanaram, the sister to Laban the Syrian. 21. And Isaac intreated the Lord for his wife, because she was barren: and the Lord was intreated of him, and Rebekah his wife conceived.

'...all that he had to Isaac...'

The life of Abraham comes to an end. The writer of Genesis tells us of further sons born to Abraham by Keturah. This woman was probably part of Abraham's household, perhaps one of Sarah's handmaidens, hence the reason she is referred to as a concubine in verse 6. These verses are a transition from focus on Abraham to a focus on Isaac. There are a couple of things that should be noted which speak of God's plan and should strengthen our faith.

The promise made to Abraham of possessing the land and being a blessing to all nations is to be fulfilled only in Isaac. Thus, at the appropriate time Abraham takes action. '...Abraham gave all that he had unto Isaac. But unto the sons of the concubine... Abraham gave gifts...and sent them away from Isaac his son...unto the east country (25:5-6). Such action seems terribly cruel to the casual reader. One must remember, however, that we are looking at the unique blessing that will be applied to all nations. Isaac was a picture of the one that would provide that blessing – the Son of

God, Jesus Christ. Isaac's willingness to be a sacrifice (Genesis 22) foreshadowed the great sacrifice for sin made by Jesus. He would enter the world via the nation that should come through Isaac. Without the nation spawned from Isaac, there would be no savior. The separation of Isaac's half-brothers validated Isaac's position, and made certain the reality of God's work in salvation history.

In verses 18:8-9 there is an interesting picture that lays out the true end of this tale. 'Then Abraham...died...And his sons Isaac and Ishmael buried him...' Ishmael is united with Isaac in the burial of his father, which foreshadows the coming together of nations by the atoning death of Christ. Ishmael lived out his life in the southern wilderness. He and the sons of Keturah were sent away in order that there may be a place of salvation to which they could come. The promise of God in its greater sense is the promise of salvation. Without Isaac's preeminence, man will not discern that salvation is a clear work of God alone, and that all nations must come to one source for salvation. Abraham's appearance of cruelty is based in the eternal love and grace of God.

'...she was barren...'

Isaac is one of the most intriguing persons of Scripture. His actual story is very short, and there are not the many events, which help us to understand his journey with God, as there was with Abraham. His story is almost anti-climatic after reading of Abraham and Sarah's long wait before he was born. The sense of rejoicing at his birth created the great sense of expectation of what he would become. However, the focus will quickly turn to Isaac's offspring.

There was a wait of many years before Abraham and Sarah will rejoice in the blessing of childbirth. With Isaac, the blessed event of having a son is immediately reported. It does have its adventure, however. As with Sarah, Rebekah is reported barren. We are not told how long this barren condition had existed before Isaac began praying that God would bless Rebekah with child. The condition of barrenness on the part of these women whom God has chosen as the ones to be the mothers of the blessed nation strike us with wonder. Is there a meaning to this? Does God enjoy playing games with his chosen vessels?

For an answer, we look at the consistent theme of Genesis. It starts with the very first verse. 'In the beginning God created the heaven and the earth' (1:1). We are brought ultimately to the creation of man, and man's ruination of God's creation by virtue of sin (Genesis 3). From that point on, God has been about the task of repairing that which man has ruined. With Abraham, God began to lay out his history of salvation that will climax in the blessed son, Jesus Christ. The problem for humans is that we have this unique capacity for crediting ourselves, for worshipping nature, and for not seeing the work of God. It is critical that the whole of salvation history be clearly pointing to God as the only source of redemption. The women's barrenness is not a practical joke that God is playing. It is the great wisdom of God who discerns our tendency to fail to understand the need for his work in our lives. Salvation is to be known as totally the work of God, and nothing of mankind. Even at the very beginning of the history of salvation, God must open the wombs of mothers for the children to be born which begin the history climaxing in the incarnation, the greatest miracle birth of all.

> Humans are constantly prone to forgetting how much we need God, and his work in our life.

Genesis 25:22-34

22. And the children struggled together within her; and she said, If it be so, why am I thus? And she went to inquire of the Lord. 23. And the Lord said unto her, Two nations are in thy womb, and two manner of people shall be separated from thy bowels; and the one people shall be stronger than the other people; and the elder shall serve the younger. 24. And when her days to be delivered were fulfilled, behold, there were twins in her womb. 25. And the first came out red, all over like an hairy garment;

and they called his name Esau. 26. And after that came his brother out, and his hand took hold on Esau's heel; and his name was called Jacob: and Isaac was threescore years old when she bare them. 27. And the boys grew: and Esau was a cunning hunter, a man of the field; and Jacob was a plain man, dwelling in tents. 28. And Isaac loved Esau, because he did eat of his venison: but Rebekah loved Jacob. 29. And Jacob sod pottage: and Esau came from the field, and he was faint: 30. And Esau said to Jacob, Feed me, I pray thee, with that same red pottage; for I am faint: therefore was his name called Edom. 31. And Jacob said, Sell me this day thy birthright. 32. And Esau said, Behold, I am at the point to die: and what profit shall this birthright do to me? 33. And Jacob said, Swear to me this day; and he sware unto him: and he sold his birthright unto Jacob. 34. Then Jacob gave Esau bread and pottage of lentiles; and he did eat and drink, and rose up, and went his way: thus Esau despised his birthright.

'...the children struggled...'

Isaac was the long awaited son for Abraham and Sarah. He is known to all the ages as the promised son. As such, he foreshadows the greater promised son (Isaiah 9:6). Yet, Isaac's birth produced controversy. His elder half-brother, Ishmael, was disowned (21:9-10). His other half-brothers were also disowned (Genesis 25:6). This also foreshadows the greater son, who said of himself, 'For I am come to set a man at variance against his father...And a man's foes shall be they of his own household' (Matthew 10:35-36).

Throughout the book of Genesis, controversy in the family has been a recurring theme: Cain and Abel (4:8-14), sons of Noah (9:20-27), Abraham and Lot (13:7-12). The controversy will continue with Isaac's children. In fact, it begins in the womb (25:21-22). Isaac's story is interrupted as we leap immediately to the grown-up twins, which had struggled in Rebekah's womb. The story documents the further controversy between the two.

The controversy makes for exciting and interesting reading, but its purpose is not to make a great story. It documents two things for us. First, humanity (wittingly and unwittingly) will do everything it can to disrupt the plan of God. Second, humanity's efforts always fail. God's plans will be accomplished in spite of man's efforts. The struggling twins in the womb gave foundation for God to reveal to Rebekah that he is never taken by surprise. '...Two nations are in thy womb, and two manner of people shall be separated...the elder shall serve the younger' (25:23).

We know that we can grow in our love of God by increasing our knowledge of him and here is one of those great moments where knowledge of God can develop. All around us there is controversy, trouble, and strife. Our own families cause us heartache and misery. God, however, is never taken by surprise. It is the nature of sinful humanity. The strife and controversy in the beginning could not alter or change the plan God put in place for salvation. It cannot alter God's plan today. He is, indeed, a God in whom we can put our trust.

> Though we cannot see beyond the controversy of our lives, it is comforting to know that God does. Human controversy cannot alter or change God's plan. He is never taken by surprise. There is great comfort this brings us when we are in need of forgiveness. God knew we would commit the sin, yet still reached out to us and stands ready to forgive.

'...elder shall serve the younger...'

The Genesis narratives of Abraham, Isaac, Jacob, and Joseph portray for us the very early stages of God's salvation history. This salvation history is the calling out of a nation through whom God will send a redeemer into the world to pay for human sin, and reunite mankind in fellowship with God. The stories reveal much about God, and reveal much about humans. Careful analysis provides answers about some of life's most perplexing problems, and creates wonder at such an awesome God who could execute his divine plan even through all of man's attempts to thwart him.

This verse (25:23) is a prophecy that says much to ancient minds, but not as much to the mindset of the modern Western

world. Of the twins in Rebekah's womb, God says they will produce separate nations, and the younger child will prevail. That is,
the younger shall have the rights to the blessing that God gave to
Abraham and ultimately passed to Isaac. '...the elder shall serve
the younger' (25:23). For the ancient mind this is clearly out of
the norm. The elder son has the right of inheritance. Part of the
privilege of the elder son included the birthright, which represented
a two-thirds share of the material possessions of the father. To reverse the process would create havoc in the culture. What is God
doing?

Just as controversy in the family is a constant theme in Genesis, so is the theme of the elder serving the younger. The younger
Abel had his offering accepted while the elder Cain was rejected.
The younger Isaac was accepted while the elder Ishmael was rejected. Later, among the sons of Judah, the elder Reuben does
not receive the blessing of the first-born son. Jacob's sons will be
one nation, not two (as was the case with Jacob and Esau), but
a younger brother, Judah, will receive the blessing of being the
greater among his brothers (49:8-13), for out of his descendants
will come the one who blesses all nations.

The learning event here is two-fold: God's blessings are not a
matter of privilege, but a matter of God's grace. Israel would later
try to claim salvation for themselves just by virtue of being sons
of Abraham (John 8:39). Yet, even the earliest in the birth lines
of salvation history did not have this kind of birth privilege as the
younger took precedence. This is not unlike those claiming privilege by denominational identity, the faith of a mother or a father,
or the simple status of prestige in church leadership, other than
understanding that all relationship with God are based in the simple statement of faith in Jeuus Christ. It is not privilege, but grace
that matters. Also, the principle of the elder serving the younger
reaffirms that the work occurring in putting the nation together is
totally God's work. We must never forget it.

The blessing of God is always based on grace, not merit.
This is a truth that all of Christianity needs to hear time

and again. It is so easy to forget because it is not the human way. The failure to understand leads to foolish activity on our part, even trying to one-up each other in service to God. Instead, we need simply to be thankful that his grace extends to the lowly place that we sit. The blessing of God is always based on grace, not merit. This is a truth that all of Christianity needs to hear time and again. It is so easy to forget because it is not the human way. The failure to understand leads to foolish activity on our part, even trying to achieve more than another in service to God. Instead, we need simply to be thankful that his grace extends to the lowly place that we sit. The possibility of grace is established through God'sjudgement on sin. All grace has its foundation in Jesus Charist. '...Even when we were dead in sins, hath quickened us together with Christ, (by grace are ye saved);...that in the ages to come he might show the exceeding riches of his grace in his kindness toward us in Christ Jesus. For by grace are ye saved through faith; and that not of yourselves: It is the gift of God...For we are his workmanship, created in Christ Jesus unto good works...' (Ephesians 2:5-10).

'...what profit this birthright...'

The controversy that will be the defining characteristic of Esau and Jacob is clearly outlined in their birth. They are very different, and will father two different nations. Esau shall develop into a rugged outdoorsman, while Jacob shall be the quiet tent-dweller. It is not hard to understand why Esau would be more pleasing to his father, and Jacob more closely attached to his mother.

After one of his hunting trips, Esau reveals the more important part of who he is. Hungry from his time in the field, he asked Jacob for part of the stew that Jacob was cooking. Jacob is already revealed as a trickster by virtue of grabbing Esau's heel at birth and receiving the name, Jacob, which means 'dogging another at his heels', the 'deceiver' or 'supplanter'. Jacob asks Esau for his birth-right in exchange for the meal. Esau agrees.

At first glance, our thoughts are that Esau gave up the inheritance of two-thirds of his father's property for a quick meal. We think of his material loss and are somewhat amazed that he would sell it for one meal. However, we must keep in mind that Isaac (Esau's father) was like Abraham, a tent dweller. He owned no land and was a sojourner in a foreign land. The riches of Isaac were of two types. The material wealth was primarily livestock. Esau would have ample time to build his own herds long before his father died. Isaac was also the owner of God's promise, which came to him through Abraham. The promise of God was future and had no visible manifestation.

There are two things that we see in Esau that teach us much about our relationship with God. First, Esau sacrificed the long term for the moment. Sin often ensnares us this way. The needs of the moment seem so great that we compromise the more important things of our life to meet the immediate need. Even more seriously, Esau devalued the promise God made to Abraham. 'I will make of thee a great nation...and in thee shall all families of the earth be blessed' (12:2-3). Esau's concern was only for the moment. If God's promise was not primarily material blessing, he was not interested. Unlike his grandfather, Abraham, and his father, Isaac, he was unwilling to look beyond the flesh for his rewards. Historically and spiritually, he is the lesser, and Jacob the greater, just as God predicted (25:23).

All humans must learn that the greatest problem we face is sin, not the lack of earthly possessions. The wonder of the angels singing when the seed of the woman finally entered the world reflected the view of God (Luke 2:13-14). The sin problem of humanity is being attacked and solved, providing the greatest reason humans could have for rejoicing.

Genesis 26:1-35

I. Testing for Isaac (26:1-11)
1. Facing the Famine
2. Balancing Faith and Fear
3. '…what hast thou done…'

II. Paradox of Blessing and Trial (26:12-35)
1. Trust and be Tested
2. '…Go from us…'
3. '…a grief of mind…'

Genesis 26:1-11

And there was a famine in the land, beside the first famine that was in the days of Abraham. And Isaac went unto Abimelech king of the Philistines unto Gerar. 2. And the Lord appeared unto him, and said, Go not down into Egypt; dwell in the land which I shall tell thee of: 3. Sojourn in this land, and I will be with thee, and will bless thee; for unto thee, and unto thy seed, I will give all these countries, and I will perform the oath which I sware unto Abraham thy father; 4. And I will make thy seed to multiply as the stars of heaven, and will give unto thy seed all these countries; and in thy seed shall all the nations of the earth be blessed; 5. Because that Abraham obeyed my voice, and kept my charge, my commandments, my statutes, and my laws. 6. And Isaac dwelt in Gerar: 7. And the men of the place asked him of his wife; and he said, She is my sister: for he feared to say, She is my wife; lest, said he, the men of the place should kill me for Rebekah; because she was fair to look upon. 8. And it came to pass, when he had been there a long time, that Abimelech king of the Philistines looked out at a window, and saw, and, behold, Isaac was sporting with Rebekah his wife. 9. And Abimelech called Isaac, and said, Behold, of a surety she is thy wife; and how saidst thou, She is my sister? And Isaac said unto him, Because I said, Lest I die for her. 10. And Abimelech said, What is this thou hast done unto us? one of the people might lightly have lien with thy wife, and thou shouldest have brought guiltiness upon us. 11. And Abimelech charged all his people, saying, He that toucheth this man or his wife shall surely be put to death.

Facing the famine

These verses begin a very short account of Isaac's walk with God. He serves the narrative of Genesis as a link between Abraham and Jacob. The promise of God to Rebekah has some very ominous reality for Isaac. There are two nations that Rebekah carries in her womb (25:23). This means that the true beginning of a blessed nation, which was God's promise to Abraham, must wait another generation. It will begin in the family of the younger child, as he shall spawn only one nation. For Isaac, this means exactly what it meant to Abraham. The hope of actually possessing the Promised Land in his lifetime is gone. That will belong to another generation.

With this reality in place, God appears to Isaac. He reassures Isaac of the Abraham promise (26:4-5). He then puts Isaac to the test. The test is the same as his father faced (12:10). 'And there was a famine in the land…' (26:1). When Abraham faced famine, he travelled into Egypt. God acts to insure Isaac will not do the same. '…Go not down into Egypt; dwell in the land…' (26:2). God gave a test and a promise. The mature Christian is aware that with every promise of God, there comes the test.

The instructive reality here is the similarity of Isaac's test with Abraham's. It tells us that our fathers before us may instruct us, but we will have to endure the test for ourselves. Neither Abraham's successes, nor his failures can qualify as growth for Isaac. All parents should know they cannot prevent their children from facing the test. The test and the promise are part of the same package.

In Isaac's life, he, like his father, must decide if he will claim God as his possession, and accept the hope of the promise as good enough. Will he see that God is the greatest prize? The meaning of love for God becomes more and more clear as we see how God has to teach each new generation that the greatest gift he can give is himself. Is that not the truth that is so beautifully stated in John 3:16? 'For God so loved the world, that he gave his only begotten Son....'

> The Word of God is all about teaching to humans another kind of glory than this earth can provide. The glory of the creator is much greater than the glory of the creation, though our sin hides it from us.

Balancing faith and fear

Isaac is faced with a situation the reader will recall from the life of Abraham. As with Abraham, it occurs immediately following an act of great faith (12:10). Famine has struck the land, and Isaac is instructed by God to remain in the land regardless of famine. Abraham had also faced famine when he first entered the land. He had been obedient to God's command to leave his homeland to come to a new country. The famine, however, led him to sin by going to Egypt. Abraham's act of faith was leaving his home to come into a new land (12:1). Isaac's act of faith was to obey God and stay in the land. However, because of fear, both Isaac and his father commit a similar sin in lying about having a wife. Both claim their wives as sisters, because they feared for their lives, believing the rulers of the land desired to take their wives. Abraham committed this sin twice. The second time, it was with a ruler named Abimelech. With Isaac, the same name reappears, indicating that Abimelech is probably a common name given to rulers of the Philistines.

The fact that Isaac and Abraham show such fear immediately following a great act of faith forces a meditation on a common frailty of many believers. We attempt to balance faith and fear. Why could Isaac trust God to see him through the famine, but could not trust God to protect him from Abimelech? That is the proverbial $64,000.00 question. It may be wrapped in Isaac's confidence that God would deal with natural crises and disaster, but didn't have confidence in God's ability to overcome human evil minds. Clearly, he figured that God needed his help, and he made a bad decision. Whatever Isaac's motivation, he must deal with two parts of his person-hood: his faith and his fear. Trying to act with both elements competing against each other led him to believe that God needed his help, and his decision-making is faulty. Love for God should prevail at this point. The Bible says, '...perfect love casteth out fear...' (1 John 4:18). How? If Isaac's concern had been, 'How do I please God,' instead of 'How do I protect myself,' he would have made a different decision. There would have been no room for fear to operate.

'...what...hast thou done...'

As one meditates on this story, there are several things that might puzzle us. It is made clear that Isaac sinned. His sin is discovered, and he is severely chastised by the Philistine ruler (26:10). The moment is markedly humiliating for Isaac. As possessor of God's promise, through Abraham, he carries the name of God. Because of sin, he is chastised by a pagan. It is always unfortunate when the people of God are instructed in proper behaviour by the world. Also, it is Abimelech, not Isaac, which acts to see the proper action is guaranteed (26:11).

The puzzling part is in the rest of the story. Isaac sinned, but God blessed him (26:12-13). This is a reversal of the age-old question, 'Why do bad things happen to good people?' Here, the question should be, 'Why do good things happen to bad people?' It is difficult for us to think of our biblical heroes as bad people, and one may be offended by using this terminology for Isaac. Yet, what would you think of a twentieth century Christian who exposed his wife to potential sexual abuse, or adultery, to protect his own skin? Why would God bless him?

To answer the question, look at the larger context. God was not rewarding Isaac's sin, he was keeping his Word of promise. he had instructed Isaac to remain in the land in spite of famine, and had promised to bless him. Isaac's sin did not invalidate the specific promise of God. We must remember that God, not Isaac, is the hero of our story. Isaac's decision to remain in the land was similar to his father's decision to leave his homeland and journey to a new country. It was the kind of decision that is foundational to one's existence. He staked his life on God. He would be a sojourner in a land that his descendants will possess, but he will not personally experience that possession in this life. God's blessing to Isaac is to remind him that his foundational decision to trust God is the correct one, and is the only safe guidepost to use in his life. The blessings of God are a test. He trusted God in the famine. Will he trust him in prosperity?

> It is a comforting thing to know that God will keep his promises regardless of the activity of humans. Isaac learned an important thing about God. The key question is, 'Will this lead him to a greater relationship with God, and to a greater trust in him?' That is a question that the believer often faces.

Genesis 26:12-35

12. Then Isaac sowed in that land, and received in the same year an hundredfold: and the Lord blessed him. 13. And the man waxed great, and went forward, and grew until he became very great: 14. For he had possession of flocks, and possession of herds, and great store of servants: and the Philistines envied him. 15. For all the wells which his father's servants had digged in the days of Abraham his father, the Philistines had stopped

them, and filled them with earth. 16. And Abimelech said unto Isaac,
Go from us; for thou art much mightier than we. 17. And Isaac departed
thence, and pitched his tent in the valley of Gerar, and dwelt there. 18.
And Isaac digged again the wells of water, which they had digged in the
days of Abraham his father; for the Philistines had stopped them after the
death of Abraham: and he called their names after the names by which
his father had called them. 19. And Isaac's servants digged in the valley,
and found there a well of springing water. 20. And the herdmen of Gerar
did strive with Isaac's herdmen, saying, The water is ours: and he called
the name of the well Esek; because they strove with him. 21. And they
digged another well, and strove for that also: and he called the name of it
Sitnah. 22. And he removed from thence, and digged another well; and
for that they strove not: and he called the name of it Rehoboth; and he
said, For now the Lord hath made room for us, and we shall be fruitful
in the land.

23. And he went up from thence to Beersheba. 24. And the Lord
appeared unto him the same night, and said, I am the God of Abraham
thy father: fear not, for I am with thee, and will bless thee, and multiply
thy seed for my servant Abraham's sake. 25. And he builded an altar
there, and called upon the name of the Lord, and pitched his tent there:
and there Isaac's servants digged a well. 26. Then Abimelech went to
him from Gerar, and Ahuzzath one of his friends, and Phichol the chief
captain of his army. 27. And Isaac said unto them, Wherefore come ye to
me, seeing ye hate me, and have sent me away from you? 28. And they
said, We saw certainly that the Lord was with thee: and we said, Let there
be now an oath betwixt us, even betwixt us and thee, and let us make a
covenant with thee;

29. That thou wilt do us no hurt, as we have not touched thee, and
as we have done unto thee nothing but good, and have sent thee away
in peace: thou art now the blessed of the Lord. 30. And he made them
a feast, and they did eat and drink. 31. And they rose up betimes in the
morning, and sware one to another: and Isaac sent them away, and they
departed from him in peace. 32. And it came to pass the same day, that
Isaac's servants came, and told him concerning the well which they had
digged, and said unto him, We have found water. 33. And he called it
Shebah: therefore the name of the city is Beersheba unto this day. 34.
And Esau was forty years old when he took to wife Judith the daughter
of Beeri the Hittite, and Bashemath the daughter of Elon the Hittite: 35.
Which were a grief of mind unto Isaac and to Rebekah.

Trust, and be tested

We humans must always examine and analyse our relationship with God through the clear teaching of the Word of God and the experiences of our lives. Sometimes, our experience and the message of the word seem contradictory. Putting all the pieces together in a way that makes sense seems impossible. Consider Isaac's situation. He had obeyed God's command and avoided the attraction of Egypt when famine occurred (26:2-3). He followed his act of trust with an act of distrust when he lied about his relationship with Rebekah (26:7). He is caught in his sin, and God still prospers him (26:12-14).

For most of us, the intense questions about our relationship with God usually come in the context of our difficult times. We question ourselves! What sin have I committed that has caused God to punish me? We don't normally think of prosperity as punishment. As we examine Isaac's story, there is a sobering reality and it should give us pause for reflection. Note that Isaac's wealth was in flocks, herds, and many servants (26:14). His responsibility was great. All the flocks and herds, as well as the people for whom he is responsible will need water, but the Philistines had stopped up all his wells, and now drive him from their land (26:15-16). God's blessing was a test. Will he now turn his back on his earlier commitment to stay in the land? Going to Egypt is the easy way out. Is he willing to refrain from the sin of distrust, and return to a life of trust?

The human tendency is to look at our prosperity and think of it as proof that God's approval is on us. It may be only a second chance to prove that we love God more than we love this world. We think of our prosperity as proof that God sees nothing in us to punish, when it is only a reflection of God extending the time for us to prove our relationship to him.

Isaac's trial did not end quickly. He made a right choice by staying in the land. He went out and dug wells. The new wells were also taken from him (26:19-21). Note that God blessed him and then severely tested him. It is true that we must understand God through our experience, but our experience is only understood by obedience to his Word.

'...go from us...'

The human experience is lived in isolation. Most of us have many people around us through the context of work, family, school, and other relationships. Yet, our experiences are understood in the context of our own mind. No one hears our thoughts, or understands how words said, and experiences had, are applied in our private thoughts. We place analysis and definition on those experiences in the solitude of our minds, and know nothing of how others may be defining those same experiences. For us, life may be tough, and the world is against us. For others, it may be that no one is against us except ourselves and we are our own worst enemy. Sometimes, even if things are going well and we are achieving victory, the isolation of our minds see only the struggles and the battles that we fight daily. Others see the good things in our life, see only our victories, and wish to emulate what they see in us. The isolation of our mind laughs at that prospect. Yet, this is precisely the nature of the life that God intends for his people.

After Isaac had been told to leave the area of the Philistines, his life had been difficult. He had struggled to keep his flocks watered, and had been in constant arguments about ownership of the wells which he and his servants had dug. Isaac, in his own mind, would have sensed only the constant frustration of struggle in the light of great responsibility. God appeared to him and reassured him that the blessed promise made to Abraham was still alive (26:24). For Isaac's faithfulness, God promised to be with him.

Something wonderful and instructive happens. Isaac's old nemesis, Abimelech appears. Isaac assumes that more trouble is on the horizon. '...Wherefore come ye to me, seeing ye hate me...' (26:27). Abimelech replies '...We saw certainly that the Lord was with thee...' (26:28). That which Isaac needed a clear word from God to perceive, Abimelech and the Philistines had already seen in Isaac's life. Abimelech desires peace with Isaac. That is his way of being at peace with Isaac's God.

In the lonely isolation of our mind, we might know only the struggle, but if that struggle is in the context of obedience to God, there is victory that others perceive. Maybe you will hear about it, maybe you won't, but in due course, God will tell you.

'...a grief of mind...'

In our lives, there are things that are struggles, and there are things that are hurts. The struggles of life are seen in competition with others, the achievement of goals, the irritations of other people's mistakes that victimize us, and the disappointments we must overcome. Hurts are those moments when the people we love are harmed, or when they act in ways that break our heart. Most people will admit that life's most bitter moments fall in the latter category.

Isaac had struggled with his enemies to sustain his life, and meet his responsibilities. He had proven that God was the supreme possession of his life, and that he wanted his life characterized by obedience to God. There had been validation of his spiritual journey though God's personal word (26:24), and the testimony of his enemy (26:28). He had just celebrated a feast noting that one of the struggles of his life was over (26:30-31). Then comes this sobering word. The victory seems unimportant. 'And Esau...took to wife Judith...the Hittite, and Bashemath...the Hittite: Which were a grief of mind unto Isaac and to Rebekah' (26:34-35).

The nature of the parents' grief is in Esau's foolish decision. Esau's decision demonstrates an attitude of complacency about spiritual things. The promise of God was that he would father a nation (25:23). When he claims wives of the people of the land that will be possessed by the descendants of his brother Jacob, he establishes a potential for long-term enmity between the two nations. He had sold his birthright to possession of the land for his descendants. Yet, he maintains ties to the land through marriage.

He has no respect for God, nor Abraham, who did not want his sons marrying among the dwellers of Canaan (24:3). Esau's disdain for both Abraham, and God's promise, will be manifested by his descendants. Instead of seeking God's blessing on the nation he would father, he demonstrated no interest for God's promises, neither the one contained in the birthright, nor the secondary blessing of his own nation. Isaac had not been able to instill his own passion for God into his eldest son.

The hurts that attack our life can have major impact on our relationship with God. These hurts, if complicated by guilt, can cause us to try to tear apart and fix that which cannot be changed. Esau's actions verify the wisdom of God in choosing the younger Jacob over the elder Esau. How will Isaac and Rebekah respond? The important issue for them at this point is to recognize that some hurts must be accepted. Total trust in God is the only option. The Word of God at Jacob and Esau's birth should provide comfort. his Word, when remembered, always will.

> The greatest frustration of a parent's life is to watch their children make critical mistakes and know they are powerless to stop it. This produces some of life's most powerful hurts. To watch anyone we love be in difficult situations and be without power to affect it is difficult. Clearly, the ability to place full trust in God is critical in those moments.

Genesis 27:1-46

I. Rebekah and Jacob's Deception (27:1-33)
1. A particular disobedience
2. '...have blessed him...'

II. Isaac and Esau's Reaction (27:34-46)
1. A plea too late
2. Esau's threat

Genesis 27:1-33

1. And it came to pass, that when Isaac was old, and his eyes were dim, so that he could not see, he called Esau his eldest son, and said unto him, My son: and he said unto him, Behold, here am I. 2. And he said, Behold now, I am old, I know not the day of my death: 3. Now therefore take, I pray thee, thy weapons, thy quiver and thy bow, and go out to the field, and take me some venison; 4. And make me savoury meat, such as I love, and bring it to me, that I may eat; that my soul may bless thee before I die. 5. And Rebekah heard when Isaac spake to Esau his son. And Esau went to the field to hunt for venison, and to bring it. 6. And Rebekah spake unto Jacob her son, saying, Behold, I heard thy father speak unto Esau thy brother, saying, 7. Bring me venison, and make me savoury meat, that I may eat, and bless thee before the Lord before my death. 8. Now therefore, my son, obey my voice according to that which I command thee. 9. Go now to the flock, and fetch me from thence two good kids of the goats; and I will make them savoury meat for thy father, such as he loveth: 10. And thou shalt bring it to thy father, that he may eat, and that he may bless thee before his death. 11. And Jacob said to Rebekah his mother, Behold, Esau my brother is a hairy man, and I am a smooth man: 12. *My father peradventure will feel me, and I shall seem to him as a deceiver; and I shall bring a curse upon me, and not a blessing. 13. And his mother said unto him, Upon me be thy curse, my son: only obey my voice, and go fetch me them. 14. And he went, and fetched, and brought them to his mother: and his mother made savoury meat, such as his father loved. 15. And Rebekah took goodly raiment of her eldest son Esau, which were with her in the house, and put them upon Jacob her younger son: 16. And she put the skins of the kids of the goats upon his hands, and upon the smooth of his neck: 17. And she gave the savoury meat and the bread, which she had prepared, into the hand of her son Jacob. 18. And he came unto his father, and said, My father: and he said, Here am I; who art thou, my son? 19. And Jacob said unto his father, I am Esau thy firstborn; I have done according as thou badest me: arise, I pray thee, sit and eat of my venison, that thy soul may bless me. 20. And Isaac said unto his son, How is it that thou hast found it so quickly, my son? And he said, Because the Lord thy God brought it to me. 21. And Isaac said unto Jacob, Come near, I pray thee, that I may feel thee, my son, whether thou be my very son Esau or not.*

22. And Jacob went near unto Isaac his father; and he felt him, and said, The voice is Jacob's voice, but the hands are the hands of Esau. 23. And he discerned him not, because his hands were hairy, as his brother Esau's hands: so he blessed him. 24. And he said, Art thou my very son Esau? And he said, I am. 25. And he said, Bring it near to me, and I will eat of my son's venison, that my soul may bless thee. And he brought it near to him, and he did eat: and he brought him wine and he drank. 26. And his father Isaac said unto him, Come near now, and kiss me, my son. 27. And he came near, and kissed him: and he smelled the smell of his raiment, and blessed him, and said, See, the smell of my son is as the smell of a field which the Lord hath blessed: 28. Therefore God give thee of the dew of heaven, and the fatness of the earth, and plenty of corn and wine: 29. Let people serve thee, and nations bow down to thee: be lord over thy brethren, and let thy mother's sons bow down to thee: cursed be every one that curseth thee, and blessed be he that blesseth thee. 30. And it came to pass, as soon as Isaac had made an end of blessing Jacob, and Jacob was yet scarce gone out from the presence of Isaac his father, that Esau his brother came in from his hunting. 31. And he also had made savoury meat, and brought it unto his father, and said unto his father, Let my father arise, and eat of his son's venison, that thy soul may bless me. 32. And Isaac his father said unto him, Who art thou? And he said, I am

*thy son, thy firstborn Esau. 33. And Isaac trembled very exceedingly, and
said, Who? where is he that hath taken venison, and brought it me, and I
have eaten of all before thou camest, and have blessed him? yea, and he
shall be blessed.*

A particular disobedience

The story of Isaac's attempt to bless Esau presents Isaac in an unfa-
vourable light. Previously, Isaac had demonstrated respect of God,
and a willingness to obey (26:1-3). He now acts in a way that is in
opposition to the will of God. The blessing Isaac is to give Esau has
already been reserved for Jacob according to God's pronouncement (25:23).

The love Isaac had for Esau prompted him to act unwisely.
Before Isaac was born, his father, Abraham, also had an elder
son whom he loved. He had asked God to make that elder son,
Ishmael, the son of promise (17:18). God refused Abraham's request, noting that a son would be born to Abraham and Sarah.
Abraham had accepted the wisdom of God, and later, Isaac was
born. Isaac did not display the insight of his father. What made the
difference?

Isaac's sin was a direct attempt to thwart the will of God. It
is human tendency to sin through disobedience. Abraham often
disobeyed. His sins were, however, in the category of trying to do
God's will his own way rather than changing God's will, as Isaac
did. It is hard to discern why one will sin in the way that Isaac
sinned.

The history of the two men provides a small clue about their
approach to God that may help us to understand. In Chapter 26
we see Isaac in an act of worship following a revelation of God. We
are told that he '… called upon the name of the Lord…' (26:25).
Compare that with the worship events of Abraham '…and took
the ram, and offered him up for a burnt offering…And Abraham
called the name of the place Jehovah- jireh…' (22:13-14). 'And
Abraham planted a grove in Beersheba, and called there on the

name of the Lord, the everlasting God' (21:33). '...and Abraham said...I have lift up mine hand unto...the most high God, the possessor of heaven and earth...' (14:22). Note how Abraham at each act of worship spoke of the new aspect of God's nature that he had learned. 'Jehovah-jireh' means 'The Lord will provide' coming out of the provision of a ram for sacrifice. 'The everlasting God,' or 'the God of eternity,' came out of his conflict with Abimelech. 'The most high God' came out of submission to the priest, Melchizedek. Could it be that Isaac was faithful to worship his God but had been lax in learning about God?

> It is important that humans never short circuit worship as a mere praise event or feel-good event. Jesus said, '...learn of me...' (Matthew 11:29). True worship places great value in the learning experience. It is there that one gains the valuable knowledge that guides the decision- making events of life in positive ways.

'...have blessed him...'

Isaac establishes a plan that would have given to Esau the blessing reserved for Jacob (25:23). Rebekah, who had favoured Jacob over Esau (25:28) overhears Isaac's instruction. This sets off a rapidly developing chain of events. God's rule is to be broken, and Rebekah feels that God must have her help to prevent it. She schemes to deceive her husband into giving Jacob the blessing. Though fearful, Jacob goes along with the scheme. The results are predictable. Esau hates his brother and wants to kill him (27:41). Isaac is remorseful because he had sinned in attempting to give the blessing to Esau (27:33). Jacob must run for his life (27:42-45). These are all tragedies that are created out of one sin. It is a deadly chain reaction.

The great commandment of both the Old and New Testament is to '...love the Lord thy God with all thine (thy) heart, with all thy soul and with all thy might (mind)' (Deuteronomy 6:5; Matthew

22:37). In attempting to understand how this commandment affects our lives, it is worthwhile to examine this incident. Love for God would have stopped this sin somewhere along the chain. Isaac would have valued the directed will of God more than his desire to bless his elder son. Rebekah would have valued God too much to resort to trickery and deceit to effectuate God's will. Jacob would have refused to be involved based on his knowledge of the consequences (27:11-12), and the reality that God does not act in this manner.

The primary lesson for all Christians to understand is that one must not commit sin believing that one sin can make right that which another sin makes wrong. Rebekah may have told herself that she was acting to make sure that God's will was accomplished. A better understanding of God would have taught her that man cannot prevent or change the plan of God. The earlier encounter which Isaac had with Abimelech (26:1-16) should have taught the lesson, but she was not aware enough to discern and apply it. Esau had no interest in his birthright or the blessing (25:34), until Jacob deceives him and steals it. An enemy was created where none had previously existed.

Genesis 27:34-46

34. And when Esau heard the words of his father, he cried with a great and exceeding bitter cry, and said unto his father, Bless me, even me also, O my father. 35. And he said, Thy brother came with subtlety, and hath taken away thy blessing. 36. And he said, Is not he rightly named Jacob? for he hath supplanted me these two times: he took away my birthright; and, behold, now he hath taken away my blessing. And he said, Hast thou not reserved a blessing for me? 37. And Isaac answered and said unto Esau, Behold, I have made him thy lord, and all his brethren have I given to him for servants; and with corn and wine have I sustained him: and what shall I do now unto thee, my son? 38. And Esau said unto his father, Hast thou but one blessing, my father? bless me, even me also, O my father. And Esau lifted up his voice, and wept. 39. And Isaac his father answered and said unto him, Behold, thy dwelling shall be the fatness of the earth, and of the dew of heaven from above; 40. And by thy sword shalt thou live, and shalt serve thy brother; and it shall come to pass when thou shalt have the dominion, that thou shalt break his yoke from off thy neck. 41. And Esau hated Jacob because of the blessing wherewith his father blessed him: and Esau said in his heart, The days of mourning for my father are at hand; then will I slay my brother Jacob. 42. And these words of Esau her elder son were told to Rebekah: and she sent and called Jacob her younger son, and said unto him, Behold, thy brother Esau, as touching thee, doth comfort himself, purposing to kill thee. 43. Now therefore, my son, obey my voice; and arise, flee thou to Laban my brother to Haran; 44. And tarry with him a few days, until thy brother's fury turn away; 45. Until thy brother's anger turn away from thee, and he forget that which thou hast done to him: then I will send, and fetch thee from thence: why should I be deprived also of you both in one day? 46. And Rebekah said to Isaac, I am weary of my life because of the daughters of Heth: if Jacob take a wife of the daughters of Heth, such as these which are of the daughters of the land, what good shall my life do me?

A plea too late

There is an axiom among the wise that tells us people do not appreciate a good thing until they lose it. Esau was the older of Isaac's two sons. As such, the rights to the ownership of blessing, which came through the father's name, belonged to him. Materially, this represents two-thirds of the father's estate. In this case, it also represented the title to the promise of God that began with Abraham. The blessing was about that which was very much future. It involved the land which would be the possession of the descendants, the great 'name' that would be a historical reality, plus the great nation his seed would become, and the coming heir that would fulfil the promise by which all nations of the earth would be blessed. The promised heir would be the Son of God, Jesus Christ (12:2-3; 15:5; 17:4-8; Isaiah 9:6).

At the birth of Esau and his twin brother, Jacob, God offered this statement. '...the elder shall serve the younger' (25:23). The proceeding story of Esau explains why Jacob was chosen over

Esau. The blessing of his father and all of its accompanying benefits were treated as being worth no more than a small meal (25:27-34). Also, he had acted against the wishes of his father, mother, and against the clear direction of his grandfather, Abraham, in marrying women of the land (26:33-34). This was a repudiation of the promise of the land going to Abraham's descendants via the blessing belonging to Jacob.

Considering the attitude of Esau about the inheritance of the blessing, his reaction to its theft is somewhat contradictory. '...he cried with...a... bitter cry...and said...Bless me...also...my father...And Esau lifted up his voice, and wept (27:34, 38). After the blessing is gone, Esau finds it valuable. The words of Isaac confirm that the blessing is now Jacob's and that God's will has prevailed in spite of the attempts made to change it. '...I have eaten of all before thou camest, and have blessed him? ... and he shall be blessed (27:33).

The lesson for us falls clearly in the framework of the first commandment. '...Thou shalt love the Lord thy God with all thy heart...soul...mind...' (Matthew 22:37). At the end of our days, the only treasure that is worthwhile is the treasure that has eternity attached to it. By placing our greatest value in our love for God, we will be able to see clearly that which has potential for blessing and that which is no more valuable than a small meal, quickly eaten and gone forever.

The value of spiritual blessings always takes a supernatural touch for humans to grasp. It is easy to get attachments to this world and proclaim the less valuable as more valuable.

Analysing the aftermath

I believe that it was Sir Walter Scott who gave us the quote: 'Oh, what a tangled web we weave when first we endeavour to deceive.' We see this admonition played out in this text. Isaac sought to bless Esau without Rebekah's involvement, and then Rebekah acts to deceive Isaac and the blessing is given instead to Jacob. It is true that God intended the blessing for Jacob (25:23). Yet, it was not God's intention for the blessing to be given through fraud.

The biblical narrative has revealed that Rebekah had shown favouritism to Jacob while Isaac had showed favouritism to Esau (25:28). A differing perspective had set the two against each other, and resulted in aggravating the conflict between the sons (27:41). It is a tragedy of errors that ends with Rebekah sending Jacob away in order to protect his life (27:42-43). The Bible does not mention that Rebekah ever saw her younger son again. The one she loved most is permanently put out of her life. That which she hoped would be a short time (27:44) turned into twenty years away from home.

The learning events of this story in the life of the patriarchs are as follows. First, our heroes tried to do that which pleased themselves, but it was God's plan that triumphed. Whenever we try to do things our own way, we merely bring harm to ourselves. It is far better to submit to God.

Second, unlike this father, Abraham, Isaac could not keep his son at home in a place where he could be taught the ways of God. Jacob must flee. He will be choosing a bride without input from his father. Esau had already made this mistake. Jacob would ultimately return home with two wives. Unlike the comfort that Isaac found in Rebekah (24:67), Jacob will find that his wives are a constant source of stress in his life. The father's wisdom was not there for Jacob as it had been for Isaac. We never do our children any favours when we try to improve their lives by acting in ways that are displeasing to God.

Third, there is some degree of comfort to be found in the story. Isaac, Rebekah, Esau, and Jacob all sinned. Their lives are in chaos because of it. Yet, the will of God, announced to Abraham, is alive and well. When we truly love God, that is the primary wish of our life. It is difficult to work through all of our own fleshly desires and come to full trust and obedience, but it is comforting to know that God can accomplish His will even when we are disobedient.

Genesis 28:1-22

I. A Comparison of Spiritual Perception (28:1-16)
1. A demonstration of spiritual ignorance
2. '...I am with thee...'

II. Jacob's Spiritual Awakening (28:17-22)
1. '...How dreadful...this place...'
2. Marking the spot
3. The tenth

Genesis 28:1-16

1. And Isaac called Jacob, and blessed him, and charged him, and said unto him, Thou shalt not take a wife of the daughters of Canaan. 2. Arise, go to Padanaram, to the house of Bethuel thy mother's father; and take thee a wife from thence of the daughters of Laban thy mother's brother. 3. And God Almighty bless thee, and make thee fruitful, and multiply thee, that thou mayest be a multitude of people; 4. And give thee the blessing of Abraham, to thee, and to thy seed with thee; that thou mayest inherit the land wherein thou art a stranger, which God gave unto Abraham. 5. And Isaac sent away Jacob: and he went to Padanaram unto Laban, son of Bethuel the Syrian, the brother of Rebekah, Jacob's and Esau's mother. 6. When Esau saw that Isaac had blessed Jacob, and sent him away to Padanaram, to take him a wife from thence; and that as he blessed him he gave him a charge, saying, Thou shalt not take a wife of the daughters of Canaan; 7. And that Jacob obeyed his father and his mother, and was gone to Padanaram; 8. And Esau seeing that the daughters of Canaan pleased not Isaac his father; 9. Then went Esau unto Ishmael, and took unto the wives which he had Mahalath the daughter of Ishmael Abraham's son, the sister of Nebajoth, to be his wife. 10. And Jacob went out from Beersheba, and went toward Haran. 11. And he lighted upon a certain place, and tarried there all night, because the sun was set; and he took of the stones of that place, and put them for his pillows, and lay down in that place to sleep. 12. And he dreamed, and behold a ladder set up on the earth, and the top of it reached to heaven: and behold the angels of God ascending and descending on it. 13. And, behold, the Lord stood above it, and said, I am the Lord God of Abraham thy father, and the God of Isaac: the land whereon thou liest, to thee will I give it, and to thy seed; 14. And thy seed shall be as the dust of the earth, and thou shalt spread abroad to the west, and to the east, and to the north, and to the south: and in thee and in thy seed shall all the families of the earth be blessed. 15. And, behold, I am with thee, and will keep thee in all places whither thou goest, and will bring thee again into this land; for I will not leave thee, until I have done that which I have spoken to thee of. 16. And Jacob awaked out of his sleep, and he said, Surely the Lord is in this place; and I knew it not.

A demonstration of spiritual ignorance

Esau's character is clearly revealed. He was forty years old when he took the Canaanite wives, but totally missed the grief of his parents at the time. He comes to understand their grief after it is too late. He evidently had a spirit incapable of reading anything outside his own desires. A discerning son could not help but pick up on the desires of his parents.

Isaac's blessing on Jacob reiterates God's promise to Abraham showing that Isaac had come back to a position of acceptance of God's will. Esau demonstrates that a heart, which places no value in God, will be victimized by a lack of discernment.

One of the saddest features in the life of an individual is the refusal to understand. Humans are to be different from animals in that we do not react to stimulus-response as the only method to determine our actions. We are to learn how to look beyond the stimulus to discern what created it, and act on the true reality, not simply the appearance at the surface. A person whose life is not conditioned by a love for God often makes choices that are based merely in stimulus-response. It appears right, but the results are devastating. Note how Esau made such a choice. When he learned (too late) that his parents were displeased that he had taken wives of the Canaanites, he responded in stimulus-response fashion. He reasoned, 'I will make them happy! I will take a wife from among my kinfolk.' He chooses a third wife from the family of Ishmael, Esau's uncle by virtue of kinship with Abraham (28:9). This was the family that Abraham had disowned. Esau continued to reason incorrectly.

Esau's choice of placing no value in the birthright (25:30-33), demonstrates no understanding of the meaning of the birthright. God's promise of giving the land to Abraham's descendants held no fascination for Esau. The fact that he was intermarrying with those presently in the land, who would ultimately be dispossessed, was out of Esau's comprehension. He saw Isaac and Rebekah's displeasure as only a racially based dislike of his wives. He made no connection to the larger picture of God's plan. Isaac and Rebekah had no dislike for Esau's wives. They held only grief for the children who will be born to them. Esau's lack of discernment led to adding a third wife. His choice again proved him decisively ignorant of spiritual matters. Abraham had disowned Ishmael. Had Esau never asked why? He now comes to marry one of Ishmael's family, believing he will please Isaac and Rebekah. When they are unhappy with that choice, he is sure to continue reasoning that his mother and father are just being cruel.

It is hard for human beings to understand that the decision-making moments of their lives should be more than a stimulus-response to fleshly desires. We should ask God to help us prevent the series of mis-actions that a stimulus-response will always produce.

'...I am with thee...'

The life of one who loves God will be filled with many days of trial and anxiety. There are times when he or she feels alone. One will even question if God's presence is still there. Yet, in every life of a child of God, there are those rare moments in which God acts, and there is certainty of God's presence. Those are life's defining moments. It may come through a word from a friend used by the Holy Spirit to drive home a point we have been unable to see. It may be a moment in church when the pastor's sermon forced the decision that changed our life. It could be the new relationship God gives us at a critical moment in our lives. It happened, and because our mind is stayed on God, there is no doubt it occurred because God made it occur. In those kinds of moments, decisions are made which become foundational for us. It may be the giving up of a bad habit, or the start of a good one. It may be a vocational choice. It may be a sudden understanding of reality that gives us new perspective to our life.

For Jacob, this is his first encounter with the God of his father and grandfather. To this point the reader of Scripture has known him only as the deceiver. He is the one who stole his brother's blessing and took advantage of his brother's fatigue to lay claim to the birthright. He is running from his brother, and is journeying to the home of his mother's brethren many miles to the north. God sends him a dream, and makes a promise. '...the land whereon thou liest, to thee will I give it...thy seed shall be as the dust of the earth...in thy seed shall all the families of the earth be blessed. And...I am with thee...' (28:13-15). The promise may strike us as strange compared to what we know about Jacob. Should God not have chastised him before giving this promise? For the reader, we would feel better to see Jacob get some punishment here. Careful analysis would show, however, that punishment would be easier than what Jacob must bare. He was encountered by God. That is a moment of crisis, which brings a new awareness to his life.

Jacob had shown appreciation for the promises of God contained in the birthright. He had been keen to listen when the spiritual nature of the 'blessing' of the father was discussed. Would he, like his father, and grandfather, be willing to accept a unique relationship with God as full reality of the promise? How much does he really want God? Facing a decision like that can often be much tougher than punishment.

Most people struggle and don't particularly like it when tough decisions are forced upon them. Yet, it is difficult decisions that often bring us into a more clearly defined relationship with God.

Genesis 28:17-22

17. And he was afraid, and said, How dreadful is this place! this is none other but the house of God, and this is the gate of heaven. 18. And Jacob rose up early in the morning, and took the stone that he had put for his pillows, and set it up for a pillar, and poured oil upon the top of it. 19. And he called the name of that place Bethel: but the name of that city was called Luz at the first. 20. And Jacob vowed a vow, saying, If God will be with me, and will keep me in this way that I go, and will give me bread to eat, and raiment to put on, 21. So that I come again to my father's house in peace; then shall the Lord be my God: 22. And this stone, which I have set for a pillar, shall be God's house: and of all that thou shalt give me I will surely give the tenth unto thee.

'...How dreadful this place...'

Jacob, the deceiver, the one who had so enraged his brother that thoughts of murder were present (27:41), was encountered by God. He has a dream of angels walking up and down a ladder (literally a staircase). At the head of the ladder, the Lord appears and Jacob hears his voice repeating the promise originally made to Abraham (28:13-15). There are a couple of things here that require some meditation.

First, the significance of the angels is obscure. A way to understand may be found in the fact that the vision occurred while Jacob was asleep. In Abraham's experience, God put him into a deep sleep to reveal the horror that was to come upon the nation he would father (15:12-15). Jacob is at a very precarious position in his life. His sin is forcing him to leave the land of promise (27:42-45). The children that will come from him will also leave the land and go into Egypt as God had told Abraham. For Jacob, he must be made to realize that his destiny is the land, and he must keep in mind the importance of returning to the land. The years that lay ahead are going to be hard. The angels portray for Jacob the nearness of God. They are constantly and easily ascending into heaven and descending so that Jacob may have confidence. The message is 'Though you are out of the land, you are not out of the sight and governance of God.'

During the next twenty years, this vision would serve as a constant reminder to Jacob of his ultimate destiny. The person who loves God must always live in the reality of destiny. A look beyond the affairs of this world and a belief that God will accomplish his purpose even when we try to disrupt it must always guide us (28:15).

Second, Jacob's sudden reaction to learning that God was in the place where he slept opens a new chapter in his life (28:16). This is remindful of Psalms 111:10. 'The fear of the Lord is the beginning of wisdom...' Note the strange dynamic that confronts us. The vision of angels, meant to comfort, brings the reality of God's presence, which produces fear. A love for God has both elements. Jacob will confront very rough and trying times. God will not prevent that, but God will be with him and lead him to the fulfilment of his destiny. That is indeed comforting.

There is a Christological point to be made here. The ladder which Jacob saw was the bridge leading from himself to God. Angels ascending and descending gave Jacob the sense of God's presence with him. Jesus spoke of this same image when extending his call to Nathaniel. '...Verily, verily, I say unto you, Hereafter ye shall see heaven open and the angels of God ascending and descending upon the son of man' (John 1:51). The bridge that Jacob saw in the ladder becomes personalized. Christ is that ladder.

Marking the spot

The fear of the Lord is a theological subject that can absorb us for hours. Jacob, perhaps for the first time, encounters a sense of the fear of God (28:16-17). The reality of God's presence has him awestruck. Further, the reality that God was present and he did not know it has him quaking (28:16-17). For modern Christianity, the idea of a healthy fear of God is unpopular. It seems unnatural to speak of a love of God and a fear of God in the same context. Our focus is on the gentle aspects of God, and the easily approachable God. It is hard to understand the role of fear.

Note its impact on Jacob. First, he becomes accountable to God. The place where he lay his head he names Bethel (28:19). This means 'house of God.' It is recognition of God's ownership. God is in control. The recognition of God's control is critical because that leads to submission. For Jacob, there is a further irony. He knows that he is guilty of sin, yet that does not restrain the ability or the control of God. It is Jacob's introduction to submission, the first basic in spiritual understanding.

Second, Jacob marked the spot, '...Jacob...took the stone that he had put for his pillow, and set it up for a pillar, and poured oil upon the top of it.' (28:18). This represents Jacob's discernment that a defining moment has occurred. He knew that God would be at work in every decision of his life. If he sinned, God would counter to affect the proper outcome, though it would mean great pain for Jacob. If he obeyed, God would be at work to teach him. God would bring him smoothly, or roughly, to his destiny. There could be no turning around. Jacob knew that God had the reigns of his life and he marked the spot to give it emphasis.

Every child of God could learn from Jacob. There are times in the life when we must symbolically mark the spot. Just as Jacob will later be brought back to this place where his submission to God began (35:1), so must we identify the place of submission, the defining moments in our life, for God will regularly call us back to that place. Only in a healthy fear of God can the 'sinner which we mortals be' truly understand the need for submission.

> The Christian can know of a certainty that God is at work in his life. '...he which hath begun a good work in you will perform it until the day of Jesus Christ' (Philippians 1:6).

The tenth

Have you ever had a mountaintop spiritual experience? Every Christian knows about this either by personal experience or by listening to others. A great worship event, a summer camp, a retreat, are occasions which produce that moment when we feel especially close to God. We would like for life to always be the same. Peter, James, and John, the apostles closest to Christ wanted to maintain the transfiguration experience by building tabernacles on the mountaintop in which Moses, Elijah, and Jesus could dwell. They could stay on the mountaintop. The problem lies in the fact that the mountaintop is not the norm. It is designed for the retreat, not for everyday living. The question is how to bring the lessons of the mountain into the valleys of our life. Our answer might be in the new commitments that we make.

Jacob had a dynamic spiritual experience in the vision of the staircase. He does not seek to have the vision again, but rather to take a lesson from the vision that will enlarge his spiritual life. That lesson is in these words, '...and of all that thou shalt give me I will surely give the tenth unto thee' (28:22). Where did Jacob get that idea? He obviously had paid attention to lessons taught by his father and grandfather. Abraham had paid tithes (14:18-20) and had surely taught the lesson to his son Isaac, who passed it along to his children. Jacob's commitment is a grand statement that vitally connects him with God and with God's will.

The value of such commitments is in the motivation they produce. Until now, Jacob had not thought about tithing. There is no guilt, no stress, and no desire to implement it. Because there is no commitment, there is no thought about doing it. With the commitment comes the requirement. That commitment will create guilt and a sense of loss when not performed. The commitments that we make on the mountaintop will make us more effective Christians in the rest of our lives. For Jacob, in this instance, it was a commitment of finances. For us, it may be a commitment to clean up a foul language, a commitment to be more loving and sympathetic to family, or a commitment to be more loving and firm in discipline in our family. By making the commitment we create an automatic reminder that makes us think about our relationship to God, and our spiritual responsibilities.

The human being should be careful of his commitments making them according to the clear leading of God. Those commitments can be a guiding light for our life, but, we must remember that God will call us back to them. Le us never underestimate the value of our commitments.

Genesis 29:1-35

Genesis 29:1-22

1. Then Jacob went on his journey, and came into the land of the people of the east. 2. And he looked, and behold a well in the field, and, lo, there were three flocks of sheep lying by it; for out of that well they watered the flocks: and a great stone was upon the well's mouth. 3. And thither were all the flocks gathered: and they rolled the stone from the well's mouth, and watered the sheep, and put the stone again upon the well's mouth in his place. 4. And Jacob said unto them, My brethren, whence be ye? And they said, Of Haran are we. 5. And he said unto them, Know ye Laban the son of Nahor? And they said, We know him. 6. And he said unto them, Is he well? And they said, He is well: and, behold, Rachel his daughter cometh with the sheep. 7. And he said, Lo, it is yet high day, neither is it time that the cattle should be gathered together: water ye the sheep, and go and feed them. 8. And they said, We cannot, until all the flocks be gathered together, and till they roll the stone from the well's mouth; then we water the sheep. 9. And while he yet spake with them, Rachel came with her father's sheep; for she kept them. 10. And it came to pass, when Jacob saw Rachel the daughter of Laban his mother's brother, and the sheep of Laban his mother's brother, that Jacob went near, and rolled the stone from the well's mouth, and watered the flock of Laban his mother's brother.

11. And Jacob kissed Rachel, and lifted up his voice, and wept. 12. And Jacob told Rachel that he was her father's brother, and that he was Rebekah's son: and she ran and told her father. 13. And it came to pass, when Laban heard the tidings of Jacob his sister's son, that he ran to meet him, and embraced him, and kissed him, and brought him to his house. And he told Laban all these things.

14. And Laban said to him, Surely thou art my bone and my flesh. And he abode with him the space of a month. 15. And Laban said unto Jacob, Because thou art my brother, shouldest thou therefore serve me for nought? tell me, what shall thy wages be? 16. And Laban had two daughters: the name of the elder was Leah, and the name of the younger was Rachel. 17. Leah was tender eyed; but Rachel was beautiful and well favoured. 18. And Jacob loved Rachel; and said, I will serve thee seven years for Rachel thy younger daughter. 19. And Laban said, It is better that I give her to thee, than that I should give her to another man: abide with me.

20. And Jacob served seven years for Rachel; and they seemed unto him but a few days, for the love he had to her. 21. And Jacob said unto Laban, Give me my wife, for my days are fulfilled, that I may go in unto her. 22. And Laban gathered together all the men of the place, and made a feast.

Jacob seizes the moment

Jacob's story carries a kind of amazement. Earlier in the book of Genesis, we read of Abraham's servant, Eliezer, who came to this same country in the northeast to seek a bride for Isaac. That story is filled with the allusion of God's providential guidance. He arrives at the exact well where God's choice of a bride for Isaac will appear. There are similarities in Jacob's story. Were it not for the ring of truth that these stories carry, one might think them mere legendary tales. The attitude of the shepherds in the carrying out of their duties (29:7-8), the impulsive action of Jacob on seeing the attractive young woman, Rachel (29:10), the emotion that Jacob showed when he so quickly found the family he sought (29:11), all carry the flavour of actual history. The writer of Scripture is very concerned that we see something else. God is at work. Jacob is away from the land of promise but not out of the providence of God.

The activity of Jacob at this moment presents another of those marvellous learning events the scriptural narratives bring us. How does one react in unfamiliar territory? For many, there is the tendency to moan, to wait for something to happen and hope that it will be good. One prays for God to make something happen, and never perceives the opportunity God provides for one to act.

Jacob had come to the country of his mother's family to seek a wife (28:1-2). When he sees the beautiful Rachel, and realizes she is of the right family, he is alert to the moment. Jacob read the scenario. First, there were shepherds who were not doing their job (29:7). He realizes that Rachel is the daughter of Laban, the one he must ask for help (29:6). He immediately seizes an opportunity to serve (29:10). The rock, which the shepherds would not remove until there was help, Jacob removed. He proceeds to water the flocks of Rachel. He did not ask for payment, he simply saw something he could do. In this moment, Jacob saw an opportunity to give of himself, and he did. When you and I are in unfamiliar territory, the opportunity to give of ourselves may be the place we discover God's providential care. Jacob had promised to give the tenth (Genesis 28:22). Before he can give the tenth of his possessions, he must learn to give of himself.

Sometimes we Christians are very sincere in our desire to give of our possessions. We fail to understand that giving begins with the giving of self. The Incarnate One set the pattern. 'But made himself of no reputation, and took upon him the form of a servant...' (Philippians 2:7).

A desire for Rachel

The story in this Scripture carries much subtlety. Jacob, the deceiver, is deceived. Jacob, who promised to give to God a tenth of
all he earned, spends fourteen years gaining nothing out of which
he could tithe. The positive aspect of these years is the aggressive
mentality of Jacob. He seized the opportunity to introduce himself
to Rachel. He removed the stone that covered the well so that
the flocks could be watered (29:8-10). Note his aggressiveness as
compared to the lazy attitude of the other shepherds (29:7-8). This
willingness for hard work would serve Jacob well for many years.

There is a very operative spiritual lesson at work here. The story comes on the heels of Jacob's vow '...and of all that thou shalt
give me I will surely give the tenth unto thee' (Genesis 28:22). It is
normal human tendency to believe that when one makes a commitment of that sort, God will eagerly recompense and give the
opportunity to fulfil the vow. Yet, after fourteen years, Jacob possessed nothing of his own to tithe. According to ancient custom,
even Jacob's wives were still (as daughters) the property of Laban.
Everything belonged to his deceiving uncle, Laban.

Have you ever made a promise to God, and then had no opportunity to fulfil it? I have heard of Christians who volunteer to
teach a Sunday school class in church, and there are no vacancies.
Others want to preach, but there are no churches, which invite
them to preach. Some, like Jacob, commit to increase their giving
and find themselves in great financial stress. What is the lesson
here?

For Jacob, it seems clear. Note the subtlety in his promise '...of
all that thou shalt give me I will surely give the tenth unto thee'
(28:22). Jacob had a chronological order in mind. God gives to
Jacob and then Jacob gives to God. The receiving comes before
the giving in Jacob's vow. Jacob is to learn the reverse order. He
will give first, receive later. God was not concerned about Jacob's
tenth. God was interested in Jacob's character. This is a lesson that
every servant of God must learn.

Jacob wanted Rachel. He was willing to work seven years for her (29:18). He discovered that he must work fourteen years for her (Genesis 29:30). How serious was Jacob about giving? That very issue was being put to the test. Whatever we have that we want to give to God, whether it be talent or money, is given to God only when giving, not receiving, is the dominating factor. Seven years is not enough, give seven more.

It is not an easy thing to learn the spiritual lesson of giving. The Bible does not teach us to give in order to receive. Instead, it teaches to learn the blessing of giving, as blessed in and of itself.

The deceiver is deceived

To this point in Scripture, there have been three incidents in Jacob's life that have given us an understanding of the man. His birth revealed him grasping the heel of his twin brother, Esau. His name is Jacob, the deceiver. His deceitful nature is then reported in two other events. He persuaded Esau to bargain away his birthright, and he conspired with his mother to steal the blessing that Isaac tried to give to Esau. A person with the character of Jacob is often blind to his own deceitfulness. He will think of it as shrewd, being smart. He may even think it is wise. In our world, it might be called good business or politically astute. The only way the true nature of one's character is revealed is to be victimized by one who is more politically astute. As a victim, one defines shrewdness as deceitfulness.

When the need for God enters one's life, and God is considered in our affairs, the opportunity for true learning about our own character begins. Jacob, by virtue of a vow, has invited God into a ruling role in his life '...and of all that thou shalt give me I will surely give the tenth unto thee' (28:22). Jacob is now ready to learn, and he will indeed learn. He will meet his match.

Jacob strikes a bargain with his uncle to have the girl he loves (Rachel) for his bride. He will work without wages for seven years (29:18). Rachel had a sister who was unattractive, and unlikely to find a suitor (29:17). Laban was concerned about getting the elder daughter married. The story tells us that Jacob's love for Rachel made the seven years go by swiftly, but when the wedding night came, it was the unattractive sister who Laban (under the cover of darkness) slipped into the tent. Jacob spent the night with her and the deceiver had a taste of his own medicine. Clearly, Jacob was not happy. He must strike another bargain (29:25-30). The plan that Jacob had is set aside by the deceit of another. He can still get what he wants, but the deceit has severely complicated things. Jacob must learn that deceit does not make things easier. It does not provide a short-cut to blessing. It only complicates things. That is true on both ends of deception – for the deceiver and the deceived. If God is taken seriously in our lives, be certain that he will teach us that lesson.

> The one who tempts us, and who is also called the deceiver will often offer short-cuts that include deception. He showed to Christ a short-cut to glory. '…cast thyself down…' from the temple, he urged (Matthew 4:6). The seed of the woman would not succumb. He would not be derailed from fulfilling his mission. Instead, he turned to the Word of God for guidance. 'It is written…' (Matthew 4:7). It is fitting to ask for guidance to live our lives openly without turning to deceit, or preferring the short-cut way to blessing.

Genesis 29:23-35

23. And it came to pass in the evening, that he took Leah his daughter, and brought her to him; and he went in unto her. 24. And Laban gave unto his daughter Leah Zilpah his maid for an handmaid. 25. And it came to pass, that in the morning, behold, it was Leah: and he said to Laban, What is this thou hast done unto me? did not I serve with thee for Rachel?

wherefore then hast thou beguiled me? 26. And Laban said, It must not be so done in our country, to give the younger before the firstborn. 27. Fulfil her week, and we will give thee this also for the service which thou shalt serve with me yet seven other years. 28. And Jacob did so, and fulfilled her week: and he gave him Rachel his daughter to wife also. 29. And Laban gave to Rachel his daughter Bilhah his handmaid to be her maid. 30. And he went in also unto Rachel, and he loved also Rachel more than Leah, and served with him yet seven other years. 31. And when the Lord saw that Leah was hated, he opened her womb: but Rachel was barren. 32. And Leah conceived, and bare a son, and she called his name Reuben: for she said, Surely the Lord hath looked upon my affliction; now therefore my husband will love me. 33. And she conceived again, and bare a son; and said, Because the Lord hath heard that I was hated, he hath therefore given me this son also: and she called his name Simeon. 34. And she conceived again, and bare a son; and said, Now this time will my husband be joined unto me, because I have born him three sons: therefore was his name called Levi. 35. And she conceived again, and bare a son: and she said, Now will I praise the Lord: therefore she called his name Judah; and left bearing.

'...he opened her womb...'

As one looks at this rather unsavoury set of events from the vantage-point of 3800 years of history, it is easy to be indifferent about individuals so long removed from the earth. Careful attention, however, offers a very sympathetic character to us. It is still difficult to feel much sympathy for Jacob based on his background. Laban is clearly a scoundrel who used Jacob to solve what he perceived a family crisis (29:25-26). Rachel, the beautiful daughter, catches our attention because of Jacob's fascination with her, but as an attractive woman, there is no real sympathy for her plight. Leah, however, is another story (29:16-17). An elder sister who has a much more attractive younger sister is one for whom we can feel much sympathy. It is even worse when her father gets her married off by deceit (29:22-25). Even the most callous of us would look at this situation and have our hearts go out to Leah.

When Jacob sinned by conspiring to steal the blessing from Esau, there was plenty of sin on the whole family. Here, poor Leah is an innocent victim. Humans who take no thought for the plan of God, but move forward with selfish motivation, will often create a tragic position for an innocent person. This kind of deceit is not what God would condone.

It is the will of God that Jacob choose a wife from the family of Laban. Jacob had done so, and been deceived. He has a wife he does not love. He proceeds to work seven more years in order to have both the wife he did not desire, and Rachel, the one he loves. Poor Leah! She will live out her life knowing that her husband carries no love for her. The spiritual dilemma is this. God's plan is to make of Jacob a great nation. It is not to inflict this kind of misery upon Leah. Humans, as usual, have complicated things as they usually do. God, however, acts in marvellous grace. '...And Leah conceived, and bare... Reuben...Simeon...Levi...Judah...' (29:31-35). We shall later discover that Judah (Leah's son) will be the favoured tribe of Israel out of which the promise is fulfilled that all the nations of the earth will be blessed (12:3). We shall also discover that Levi (Leah's son) will be the favoured tribe which will carry the responsibility of the priesthood of the nation (Numbers 18:21). Leah was victimized by men, but given triumph by God.

> Leah's struggles may provide some degree of comfort to us, if we have learned the valuable lesson of prioritizing the spiritual above the temporal. It may not always be the comfort we seek, but it does have eternal ramifications. We might thank God for the knowledge that we can still triumph even if men victimize us.

'...my husband will love me...'

The birth of four sons to Leah is the result of God's looking with sympathy on her plight as the unloved wife (29:31). It is instructive for the reader of Scripture to note the grace of God to Leah. He did not leave her without blessing, yet, the tragic application that Leah gives to the blessings of God provide a sad note. Instead of focus on the blessing, her cry was still for that which she would not have. '...now therefore my husband will love me...will my husband be joined unto me, because I have born him three sons...' (29:32-34).

The story presents a common tragedy of humankind. Leah was a victim. There is no disputing it. Born as 'tender-eyed' and unattractive (29:17), given to Jacob as wife in a fraudulent manner (29:23-25), and captive in a marriage to a man who did not love her (29:30-31), she is one of life's unlucky ones. God changes her luck with the birth of sons. She hopes that the son will change her previous victim status. This kind of attitude will continue to keep her a victim. It is a sad commentary on humans that we can be just like Leah. The acts of others may have put us into a situation that is unhappy, so our mindset is determined to reverse the victim status. Leah wanted the love of Jacob, and could not appreciate the blessings of God. She attached a false meaning to the birth of her two sons, clinging to a hope that could never be a reality.

When we have been victimized, it is counterproductive to hope that a previous victim status can be reversed. The better route is to look to God for his work to be accomplished in us. A love for God will allow us to make the correct applications to the events of our lives. Bearing sons to Jacob did not win Jacob's love. Leah was risking the possibility of coming to despise her sons because they failed to give her what she desired. It should cause us to wonder if we have sometimes despised blessing because we attached the wrong application. The story indicates that Leah came to accept her victim status, and stopped making the wrong application. 'And she conceived...bare a son: and she said, 'Now will I praise the Lord: therefore she called his name Judah; and left bearing' (Genesis 29:35).

The Apostle Paul wrote '...forgetting those things which are behind...I press toward the mark for the prize of the high calling of God in Christ Jesus' (Philippians 3:13-14).

It would help all of us in forgetting any sense of victim status and to concentrate on present opportunities for obedience.

Genesis 30:1-43

I. The Bearing Children Competition (30:1-24)
1. '...Give me children...'
2. No control
3. Rachel's attitude

II. Another Bargain between Deceivers (30:25-43)
1. '...the Lord hath blessed thee...'
2. '...ringstraked, speckled, and spotted...'

Genesis 30:1-24

1. And when Rachel saw that she bare Jacob no children, Rachel envied her sister; and said unto Jacob, Give me children, or else I die. 2. And Jacob's anger was kindled against Rachel: and he said, Am I in God's stead, who hath withheld from thee the fruit of the womb? 3. And she said, Behold my maid Bilhah, go in unto her; and she shall bear upon my knees, that I may also have children by her. 4. And she gave him Bilhah her handmaid to wife: and Jacob went in unto her. 5. And Bilhah conceived, and bare Jacob a son. 6. And Rachel said, God hath judged me, and hath also heard my voice, and hath given me a son: therefore called she his name Dan. 7. And Bilhah Rachel's maid conceived again, and bare Jacob a second son. 8. And Rachel said, With great wrestlings have I wrestled with my sister, and I have prevailed: and she called his name Naphtali. 9. When Leah saw that she had left bearing, she took Zilpah her maid, and gave her Jacob to wife. 10. And Zilpah Leah's maid bare Jacob a son. 11. And Leah said, A troop cometh: and she called his name Gad. 12. And Zilpah Leah's maid bare Jacob a second son. 13. And Leah said, Happy am I, for the daughters will call me blessed: and

*she called his name Asher. 14. And Reuben went in the days of wheat
harvest, and found mandrakes in the field, and brought them unto his
mother Leah. Then Rachel said to Leah, Give me, I pray thee, of thy son's
mandrakes. 15. And she said unto her, Is it a small matter that thou hast
taken my husband? and wouldest thou take away my son's mandrakes
also? And Rachel said, Therefore he shall lie with thee to night for thy
son's mandrakes. 16. And Jacob came out of the field in the evening, and
Leah went out to meet him, and said, Thou must come in unto me; for
surely I have hired thee with my son's mandrakes. And he lay with her
that night. 17. And God hearkened unto Leah, and she conceived, and
bare Jacob the fifth son. 18. And Leah said, God hath given me my hire,
because I have given my maiden to my husband: and she called his name
Issachar. 19. And Leah conceived again, and bare Jacob the sixth son.
20. And Leah said, God hath endued me with a good dowry; now will my
husband dwell with me, because I have born him six sons: and she called
his name Zebulun. 21. And afterwards she bare a daughter, and called
her name Dinah. 22. And God remembered Rachel, and God hearkened
to her, and opened her womb. 23. And she conceived, and bare a son;
and said, God hath taken away my reproach: 24. And she called his name
Joseph; and said, The Lord shall add to me another son.*

'...Give me children...'

Genesis 30:1 offers a very colourful portrayal of human nature,
and the problems created by humans when they seek to act against
the will of God. Many themes come together: comedy and tragedy,
deep theology and human folly, plus the kind of sibling rivalry that
makes for some of history's liveliest moments. Here, the rivalry is
almost on an adolescent level. Rachel, who is the more attractive
and beloved sister, is childless. Leah, the sister who is unloved
has given Jacob four sons. There is a brand new understanding
of which sister is the more blessed. Rachel is now jealous of Leah
(30:1). From the information we have of the two, this is probably a
new emotion for Rachel. She shares her concern with Jacob who
is less than understanding '...Am I in God's stead, who hath withheld from thee the fruit of the womb' (30:2)?

From Jacob's point of view, Rachel had the position of most loved, why would she be upset at Leah's childbearing. From Rachel's point of view, she was not being a satisfactory wife. In her love for Jacob, she does what Sarah had done for Abraham. She offers her handmaiden. Jacob (playing the role of a good husband) accepts the offer. Two sons are born to which Rachel lays claim (30:6, 8). Leah, upon observing this phenomenon gets in on the act, and offers Jacob her handmaid, and Jacob (doing his duty) obliges. Two sons are born to Leah by the handmaid (30:9, 13).

As a story, these events have us laughing at the shenanigans created by two sisters fighting it out for the affection of Jacob. Except for his little irritation with Rachel, we are not told that Jacob paid much attention, and appears to be greatly benefiting. There is something of a much deeper activity at work. Humans are playing their silly games making life miserable for themselves, but God is still in control enacting his divine plan and purpose. Amusement, amazement, and awe interact. Two women think this is about pleasing a man. The man thinks this is about harmony in the family. In reality, it is about the demonstration of God's power to control the uncontrollable affairs of men and still bring his purpose to pass (18:12-15).

> Poor Leah! Poor Rachel! Poor Jacob! They perceived life only in a self-contained box. Their view was distorted and they were unhappy. We all know the feeling. God can give us the vision to think of life outside of our self-contained dimensions and within the framework of his plan and will.

No control

There are several fascinating questions that come to mind in the narrative of children being born to Jacob by his two wives and their handmaids. In rapid succession, we are told of Jacob's developing family. Though Rachel is barren for a time, the story develops quickly. When we ponder the situation of Jacob's grandmother,

Sarah, and his mother, Rebekah, who were each burdened with long term barrenness, we might question the sudden turn in the way God dealt with the patriarchs. The one great theme that keeps returning in the telling of their stories is the absolute control of God. But, why is Jacob blessed quickly with sons while Abraham and Isaac had to wait?

The answer is likely to be found in the many realities that come to play in a love for God. True love for God requires acknowledgement of his control. Abraham, as father of the nation of Israel had the severest test of submission. He must sacrifice everything for God. He must leave his homeland, wait many years for the promised son, and be willing to sacrifice him when God commanded it. As such, Abraham's name shines brightest among the three patriarchs. Isaac submitted to God's wisdom by remaining in the land during famine, and ultimately accepting the reality of Jacob's priority over Esau. Jacob's need for learning submission was in a different area. His submission was a surrender of pride. His favoured wife, Rachel, is barren. God has given no revelation about the ruling child in the family. There is no promise of children to Rachel, as Sarah had. Jacob's favoured wife may not be the favoured of God. Jacob had been a take charge person. He is now helpless, while his wives are in conflict.

Submission to God is a phenomenon with many variables. Abraham had been given a phenomenal promise. He and his son, Isaac, must submit to God's ability to fulfil the promise, thus the long wait through the barrenness of Sarah and Rebekah. Jacob must submit to the authority of God's promise. He must bring an end to his scheming and deceitfulness. Jacob, who was a person in complete control, must learn he has no control. The one who had seized the moment (bargaining for the birthright, stealing the blessing, moving the stone from the well to impress Rachel) has the moment seized from him by Laban, and then by God, who opened Leah's womb and shut Rachel's.

The stories of the patriarchs teach that there are many different themes in submission. We are to be continually learning of the nature of the submission required of us. The total submission of the Incarnate One, '...even the death of the cross...' (Philippians 2:8), provides the supreme example.

Rachel's attitude

Leah and Rachel's rivalry is one of the more intriguing narratives in Scripture. The reader is naturally drawn to Rachel by the writer's notes of her beauty (29:17). One is sympathetic to Leah, and somewhat relieved that God has blessed her with children. Yet, there is a question. Why did God so disfavour Rachel? Is it out of sympathy for Leah, or does God have a bias against the more attractive sister? Ultimately, Rachel's life will be short-lived, and carry a note of tragedy. The events in these verses help to clarify things.

Just as Esau's life and attitude helped to explain God's choice of Jacob, so in Rachel's decisions, we discover something about her. Though she was Jacob's beloved, she had not given attention to Jacob's God. There are two places that Rachel's attitude about God is revealed. The other is in Genesis 31:19, 30-35.

Rachel's competition with her sister in terms of bearing children to Jacob leads her to a strange bargain. She asks Leah's son, Reuben, to give her the mandrakes he had discovered while gathering wheat. Mandrakes are plants that have a divided fleshy root, and plum-like berries. The plant is reported to induce human fertility. For the sake of superstition, she toyed with the affections of Jacob and gave him to Leah for the night. Just as Esau had traded the birthright for a small meal, Rachel trades that which is greater for that which is lesser. The sad, human story is that Rachel who had Jacob's love did not supremely value it. Leah, who supremely valued Jacob's love (30:15), did not have it. The greater tragedy is in Rachel's valuing of silly superstition above trust in, and submission to, God.

As is so often the case in scriptural narrative, we see a touch of irony. Rachel, who went with the superstition remains barren, and Leah bears three more children to Jacob (30:16-20).

God will ultimately give Rachel a son, whom she names Joseph. Instead of appreciation for the blessing, she tempts God '...The Lord shall add to me another son' (30:24). Rachel seems to manifest the worst part of the character of Jacob, the attempt to be in control. She did this first with the bargain of the mandrakes, and does it again by trying to force a bargain on God. When will she fully acknowledge the authority of God?

The attempt to somehow strike a bargain with God and to have control of our life in that way is common to all. We can sympathize with Rachel. Can we learn from her?

Genesis 30:25-43

25. And it came to pass, when Rachel had born Joseph, that Jacob said unto Laban, Send me away, that I may go unto mine own place, and to my country. 26. Give me my wives and my children, for whom I have served thee, and let me go: for thou knowest my service which I have done thee. 27. And Laban said unto him, I pray thee, if I have found favour in thine eyes, tarry: for I have learned by experience that the Lord hath blessed me for thy sake. 28. And he said, Appoint me thy wages, and I will give it. 29. And he said unto him, Thou knowest how I have served thee, and how thy cattle was with me. 30. For it was little which thou hadst before I came, and it is now increased unto a multitude; and the Lord hath blessed thee since my coming: and now when shall I provide for mine own house also? 31. And he said, What shall I give thee? And Jacob said, Thou shalt not give me any thing: if thou wilt do this thing for me, I will again feed and keep thy flock. 32. I will pass through all thy flock to day, removing from thence all the speckled and spotted cattle, and all the brown cattle among the sheep, and the spotted and speckled among the goats: and of such shall be my hire. 33. So shall my righteousness answer for me in time to come, when it shall come for my hire before thy face: every one that is not speckled and spotted among the goats, and

brown among the sheep, that shall be counted stolen with me. 34. And
Laban said, Behold, I would it might be according to thy word. 35. And
he removed that day the he goats that were ringstraked and spotted, and
all the she goats that were speckled and spotted, and every one that had
some white in it, and all the brown among the sheep, and gave them into
the hand of his sons. 36. And he set three days' journey betwixt himself
and Jacob: and Jacob fed the rest of Laban's flocks. 37. And Jacob took
him rods of green poplar, and of the hazel and chesnut tree; and pilled
white strakes in them, and made the white appear which was in the rods.
38. And he set the rods which he had pilled before the flocks in the gutters
in the watering troughs when the flocks came to drink, that they should
conceive when they came to drink. 39. And the flocks conceived before
the rods, and brought forth cattle ringstraked, speckled, and spotted. 40.
And Jacob did separate the lambs, and set the faces of the flocks toward
the ringstraked, and all the brown in the flock of Laban; and he put his
own flocks by themselves, and put them not unto Laban's cattle. 41. And
it came to pass, whensoever the stronger cattle did conceive, that Jacob
laid the rods before the eyes of the cattle in the gutters, that they might
conceive among the rods. 42. But when the cattle were feeble, he put
them not in: so the feebler were Laban's, and the stronger Jacob's. 43.
And the man increased exceedingly, and had much cattle, and maidservants, and menservants, and camels, and asses.

'...the Lord hath blessed thee...'

One of the great banes of human existence is the way we can
struggle and waste much creative energy to achieve that which
we already have. Siblings in a household can be in competition
with each other for years to win the love and approval of parents
when they were in possession of it from the beginning. I have often
thought the human struggle for happiness falls into this category.
We search for it when we only need to possess it. The wives of
Jacob were both blessed: one with children, one with beauty and
the affection of her husband. Yet, each preferred that which the
other had (30:1-14). We are often victims to believing that happiness is based, not in what we have, but in what the other person

has. The approach of the actions of our life is thus guided by unnecessary struggle.

Jacob is at a point in his life of observing that which Laban possesses. '...and the Lord hath blessed thee since my coming: and now when shall I provide for mine own house also' (30:30)? Note the subtlety of Jacob's statement. He is saying, 'God has not blessed me.' Has Jacob forgotten that he had to leave home because his brother wanted to kill him, but God has provided for him (27:41)? Has Jacob forgotten the promise of God (28:13-15))? Has Jacob forgotten the blessing of his family, and the birth of many sons? Even though he is in a country far from home, Jacob has a blessing in his sons that Abraham and Isaac had greatly desired and did not possess for many years. At the moment, his eyes were only on that which belonged to someone else. Another subtlety, which Jacob and the reader of Scripture may have forgotten, is that Jacob owned the birthright to his father's possessions. Back in the country from which he came is an inheritance that is waiting. In the cloud of circumstances, he can't see it.

The struggle will continue for Jacob. He and Laban will continue their deceit with each other. Jacob, the deceiver, will still be trying to seize control as he had done in stealing the blessing from Esau. The whole scenario, played out for the next few years, is a labour in futility. God's control was no consolation for Jacob. He did not make a bad decision in staying with Laban, he just created for himself a lot of labour, worry, and frustration that were unnecessary. He could simply have done his job and trusted God. He could have enjoyed life instead of making life a burden.

'...ringstraked, speckled, and spotted...'

Jacob completed fourteen years of service to Laban. The years had been payment to Laban for the privilege of marrying Rachel. Through Laban's trickery, Jacob had also received Rachel's older sister, Leah, as his wife. The scriptural account of the fourteen years is a small capsule of the rivalry of the two sisters and the birth of Jacob's children. Leah has given birth to six sons. Rachel, at the end of the fourteen years also has a son. The handmaidens of the two women also bore two sons apiece to Jacob. At this point there are eleven sons. One daughter is mentioned (30:21), though there may have been more.

The activity of Jacob during this time (besides being passed around among the women) is to tend the flocks of Laban. He decides he wants to leave and return home to his father, Isaac (30:26). The fact that he owns nothing, except for his family, gives Laban opportunity to persuade him to stay. Since the debt for his wives is now properly paid, Laban offers Jacob the chance to obtain additional wages.

Jacob suggests that he work for ownership of the speckled and spotted portion of future livestock births. This was a modest request as most Palestinian sheep were white, and most goats were black. Laban and Jacob are involved in a battle of wits. Laban quickly moves to get the speckled and spotted portion of the herds out of Jacob's control. Under this situation, there would be little mixing of the herds and only the occasional exception would be of the kind Jacob could claim. Jacob retaliates.

The history of Jacob, the deceiver, shows him always ingenious and seeking control. His plan is in three parts: 1) He erects streaked rods in front of the ewes (30:37). 2) He separates newly born spotted lambs from the rest of the flock and arranges them to increase chances of their bearing spotted young (30:40). 3) He schemed to secure the young among the strongest animals (30:41). The result is that Jacob's herds increase and his wealth becomes substantial (30:43). It was not, however, the result of Jacob's scheming (31:11-13). The schemer still cannot give up scheming. God had promised to be with Jacob (28:13-15). He had demonstrated his power to Jacob by swiftly giving him a large family, the exact opposite of that which had been true for Isaac and Abraham. If God had provided the family, could Jacob not have trusted God to provide the cattle? Jacob wasted a lot of effort that could have been spent more wisely.

Another great lesson is portrayed for those willing to see it. It is the futile efforts of humans on things that are already in the purview and promise of God. Jacob schemed when he could have been without stress, and simply doing his job, while God took care of the rest. He lost an opportunity to better know his God.

Genesis 31-32

Genesis 31:1-52

1. And he heard the words of Laban's sons, saying, Jacob hath taken away all that was our father's; and of that which was our father's hath he gotten all this glory. 2. And Jacob beheld the countenance of Laban, and, behold, it was not toward him as before. 3. And the Lord said unto Jacob, Return unto the land of thy fathers, and to thy kindred; and I will be with thee. 4. And Jacob sent and called Rachel and Leah to the field unto his flock, 5. And said unto them, I see your father's countenance, that it is not toward me as before; but the God of my father hath been with me. 6. And ye know that with all my power I have served your father. 7. And your father hath deceived me, and changed my wages ten times; but God suffered him not to hurt me. 8. If he said thus, The speckled shall be thy wages; then all the cattle bare speckled: and if he said thus, The ring-straked shall be thy hire; then bare all the cattle ringstraked. 9. Thus God hath taken away the cattle of your father, and given them to me. 10. And it came to pass at the time that the cattle conceived, that I lifted up mine eyes, and saw in a dream, and, behold, the rams which leaped upon the cattle were ringstraked, speckled, and grisled. 11. And the angel of God spake unto me in a dream, saying, Jacob: And I said, Here am I. 12. And he said, Lift up now thine eyes, and see, all the rams which leap upon the cattle are ringstraked, speckled, and grisled: for I have seen all that Laban doeth unto thee. 13. I am the God of Bethel, where thou anointedst the pillar, and where thou vowedst a vow unto me: now arise, get thee out from this land, and return unto the land of thy kindred. 14. And Rachel and Leah answered and said unto him, Is there yet any portion or inheritance for us in our father's house? 15. Are we not counted of him strangers? for he hath sold us, and hath quite devoured also our money. 16. For all the riches which God hath taken from our father, that is ours, and our children's: now then, whatsoever God hath said unto thee, do. 17. Then Jacob rose up, and set his sons and his wives upon camels; 18. And he carried away all his cattle, and all his goods which he had gotten, the cattle of his getting, which he had gotten in Padanaram, for to go to Isaac his father in the land of Canaan.

19. And Laban went to shear his sheep: and Rachel had stolen the images that were her father's. 20. And Jacob stole away unawares to Laban the Syrian, in that he told him not that he fled. 21. So he fled with all that he had; and he rose up, and passed over the river, and set his face toward the mount Gilead. 22. And it was told Laban on the third day that Jacob was fled. 23. And he took his brethren with him, and pursued after him seven days' journey; and they overtook him in the mount Gilead. 24. And God came to Laban the Syrian in a dream by night, and said unto him, Take heed that thou speak not to Jacob either good or bad. 25. Then Laban overtook Jacob. Now Jacob had pitched his tent in the mount: and Laban with his brethren pitched in the mount of Gilead. 26. And Laban said to Jacob, What hast thou done, that thou hast stolen away unawares to me, and carried away my daughters, as captives taken with the sword? 27. Wherefore didst thou flee away secretly, and steal away from me; and didst not tell me, that I might have sent thee away with mirth, and with songs, with tabret, and with harp? 28. And hast not suffered me to kiss my sons and my daughters? thou hast now done foolishly in so doing. 29. It is in the power of my hand to do you hurt: but the God of your father spake unto me yesternight, saying, Take thou heed that thou speak not to Jacob either good or bad. 30. And now, though thou wouldest needs be gone, because thou sore longedst after thy father's house, yet wherefore hast thou stolen my gods? 31. And Jacob answered and said to Laban, Because I was afraid: for I said, Peradventure thou wouldest take by force thy daughters from me. 32. With whomsoever thou findest thy gods, let him not live: before our brethren discern thou what is thine with me, and take it to thee. For Jacob knew not that Rachel had stolen them. 33. And Laban went into Jacob's tent, and into Leah's tent, and into the two maid-servants' tents; but he found them not. Then went he out of Leah's tent, and entered into Rachel's tent. 34. Now Rachel had taken the images, and put them in the camel's furniture, and sat upon them. And Laban searched all the tent, but found them not. 35. And she said to her father, Let it not displease my lord that I cannot rise up before thee; for the custom of women is upon me. And he searched but found not the images. 36. And Jacob was wroth, and chode with Laban: and Jacob answered and said to Laban, What is my trespass? what is my sin, that thou hast so hotly pursued after me? 37. Whereas thou hast searched all my stuff, what hast thou found of all thy household stuff? set it here before my brethren and thy brethren, that they may judge betwixt us both. 38. This twenty years have I been with thee; thy ewes and thy she goats have not cast their young, and the rams of thy flock have I not eaten. 39. That which was torn of beasts I brought not unto thee; I bare the loss of it; of my hand didst thou require it, whether stolen by day, or stolen by night. 40. Thus I was; in the day the drought consumed me, and the frost by night; and my sleep departed from mine eyes. 41. Thus have I been twenty years in thy house; I served thee fourteen years for thy two daughters, and six years for thy cattle: and thou hast changed my wages ten times.

42. Except the God of my father, the God of Abraham, and the fear of Isaac, had been with me, surely thou hadst sent me away now empty. God hath seen mine affliction and the labour of my hands, and rebuked thee yesternight. 43. And Laban answered and said unto Jacob, These daughters are my daughters, and these children are my children, and these cattle are my cattle, and all that thou seest is mine: and what can I do this day unto these my daughters, or unto their children which they

have born? 44. Now therefore come thou, let us make a covenant, I and
thou; and let it be for a witness between me and thee. 45. And Jacob took
a stone, and set it up for a pillar. 46. And Jacob said unto his brethren,
Gather stones; and they took stones, and made an heap: and they did eat
there upon the heap. 47. And Laban called it Jegarsahadutha: but Jacob
called it Galeed. 48. And Laban said, This heap is a witness between me
and thee this day. Therefore was the name of it called Galeed; 49. And
Mizpah; for he said, The Lord watch between me and thee, when we are
absent one from another. 50. If thou shalt afflict my daughters, or if thou
shalt take other wives beside my daughters, no man is with us; see, God
is witness betwixt me and thee. 51. And Laban said to Jacob, Behold this
heap, and behold this pillar, which I have cast betwixt me and thee: 52.
This heap be witness, and this pillar be witness, that I will not pass over
this heap to thee, and that thou shalt not pass over this heap and this pillar
unto me, for harm.

'...return unto the land...'

In a sublime moment, Jacob, the deceiver makes a confession.
'...but the God of my father hath been with me' (31:5). This is a
critical statement for Jacob. The deceiver, the one who must be in
control and the one who always seizes the moment admits, 'God
did it.' He was in control all the time.

Jacob has been away from his father's house for twenty years
(31:38). He is now compelled to return through two kinds of revelation. First, Laban's attitude toward Jacob has radically changed
(31:2). Second, God appears to him in a dream and commands it
(31:13). The attitude of Laban is based on the reality that his herds
have depleted while Jacob's herds have grown. God has blessed
Jacob despite attempts by Laban to defraud him (31:7-8). When
Jacob first came into Laban's household, there were no sons. By
virtue of marriage to Laban's daughters, Jacob stood as heir to
Laban. Sons had since been born to Laban, and Jacob's prosperity would be endangering the inheritance of those sons. Laban was
not happy with Jacob on those two fronts.

When God appeared to Jacob and commanded him to return to Canaan, there were important spiritual overtones. First, Jacob is called back to the promise God made to Abraham. He must count as worthless the possessions of Laban and claim instead the yet unrealized Abrahamic promise '...Unto thy seed will I give this land...' (12:7). Jacob is called upon to place his treasure in the Word of God instead of whatever claim he might have elsewhere. Love for God always requires our desire for total possession of him as compared to partial possession of earth (Colossians 3:2). Additionally, Jacob's wives are called upon to do the same thing.

Second, God had been with Jacob to prosper him even in the face of the obstacle of Laban. Jacob and his wives could fight for more. They could argue for a share of the inheritance. Instead, Jacob is called upon to accept what God has provided as enough. He is owner of the birthright that entitles him to two-thirds of the possessions of his father, Isaac. He knows that he will have to deal with his brother, Esau, in order to claim it, so he is right where he was twenty years before. Will he trust God to deal with it, or is he going to be the old self, the deceiver? God has a way of bringing us back to the same old spiritual lesson until we learn it.

Third, there is Jacob's vow which must have closure '...and of all that thou shalt give me I will surely give the tenth unto thee' (28:22). The vow was made at Bethel. God is calling him back to the source of that vow (31:13). It was easy to make when he had nothing. Can he keep it when he has much? Is God the authority in his life?

> It is a sad, but true, commentary that we humans are stubborn learners. Often God works in us to keep drawing us back to the same lessons over and over. For Jacob, it is to go back to where he made his vow. Wouldn't it be wonderful if we had wisdom to clearly discern the lessons of our life so that we do not have the same test over and over. Perhaps a little paying attention to the instruction of his Word can help us here.

Stolen images

Life is a beautiful and wonderful thing. It is at its most beautiful, however, when viewed from the standpoint of potential. Everyone loves 'possibility.' The bright young student, the gifted athlete, the person with great looks and personality, excite our imagination and our envy with their potential. Life, for them, we assume, will be wonderful. Life, as it moves along, often changes that perspective. There is nothing so sad as wasted potential.

Every Christian can look at his or her life and find many areas of unmet potential. The question before us is, 'why?' The young person with much to offer the world can often squander every chance by laziness and lack of motivation. Spiritual potential is squandered through bad decisions based in misplaced priorities.

The first time that we saw Rachel, we were fascinated. She was beautiful, and Jacob immediately acted to impress her (29:8-10). The whole romantic notion of boy meets girl is before us. Jacob's selfish ambition, and the tendency towards deceit could (we hope) be wonderfully changed by his love for a good woman. He clearly demonstrates a willingness to do unselfish-like things to win her (29:18-20).

When it became clear that Rachel was not favoured by God, and that the elder sister, Leah, given to Jacob by deceit, was the one God blessed with children, we have a clue that the glorious potential of Rachel will not be achieved. In this text, we have the clearest explanation of her shortcomings. When it comes time for Jacob to leave Laban's household, and return to his own land, Rachel does not fully invest in her husband's life. She steals her father's gods (31:19, 30). The images, when possessed, were proof of being the proper heir of the family. Rachel's theft was her attempt to cling to the possessions of her father. It is also a statement of the way she devalued what she had in Jacob.

On a more subtle level, it is devaluation of the God of Jacob. Rachel, after twenty years of marriage to Jacob, has surely heard of the Abrahamic promise, part of Jacob's birthright, and of the covenant relationship with God to which Jacob was heir. Rachel's inability to establish the proper priorities led to bad decisions, and the sadness of lost potential. The beautiful young woman that so fascinated us in the beginning is no less a schemer than the one we hoped she could positively influence.

> It is rarely perceived that the normal processes of life are often leading us to set priorities. The priorities we set can lead to wise or to very unwise decisions.

'...I will not pass over...'

It is one of life's most common stories. When humans speak forth-rightly about their lives, they often focus on a particular agenda or thing, and can live in constant frustration because they never achieve or gain that thing. Much effort is expended, and life carries the sense of failure because of that singular pursuit that goes unfulfilled. There may be many things in our life for which we can rejoice, yet the rejoicing never occurs. We only bemoan the singular failure.

Rachel had sought to hang on to a claim of her father's possessions (31:19). The ownership of the images she stole signifies the proper heir to the father's estate. Rachel's error is that she could not sacrifice the one heritage (her father's) for the new heritage (her husband's). The spiritual application for human beings is seen by virtue of the same kind of inability. The New Testament speaks of the Christian as taking on a husband. Ephesians makes the analogy, '...a man... shall be joined unto his wife...This is a great mystery: but I speak concerning Christ and the church' (Ephesians 5:31-32). Christ is portrayed as husband of the church. From the moment that Christ enters our life as husband we are called upon to accept a brand new heritage. That heritage is acknowledgment of the Lordship of Christ.

The history of the patriarchs began when Abraham was called to leave behind his family, and sacrifice any claims to his father's estate, and lay claim to that which God would give him. Rachel is called upon to do the same thing, and fights it. When her father pursues after Jacob and his entourage, she hides the stolen images in her camel's saddlebag, sits upon it, tells her father she is in the monthly condition of women, and cannot get off the camel (31:35). The lie is a continued effort to have and to keep the inheritance of her father.

The conclusion of this story paints a solemn picture for Rachel, and leaves us with a principle that could help to rid us of the sense of failure about the unfulfilled agenda in our lives. Laban and Jacob establish a covenant. A pillar of stones is built, and the two pledge that they will never pass the stones with any attempt to lay claim to the possession of the other (31:51-52). Rachel's possession of the images is made null and void by the covenant. In spite of her scheming, God's plan prevails. It is time for Rachel to rejoice in what she has in her husband. She can do that and find great satisfaction, or she can fret over that which she did not achieve and have only failure and frustration. Acquiescence to God's will always opens the door to rejoicing and ends frustration and failure.

'...the God of my father...'

The Scriptures have taken us on a journey in the lives of three men known by readers of Scripture as the patriarchs, Abraham, Isaac, and Jacob. Their story is the historical development of the unique nation of Israel. The uniqueness of the nation is wrapped in the promise of God to the first patriarch, Abraham '...in thee shall all families of the earth be blessed' (Genesis 12:3). That promise became a reality when the sin problem that affects every human was affirmatively dealt with in the death of Jesus Christ, the greater son of Abraham. In Christ's death, we may know forgiveness of sin, and establish peace with our God by a trust in Jesus Christ as Lord.

Having been forgiven of sin that separates us from God, we must seek to live our lives in victory over sin. To gain that victory will produce difficulty and conflict. The Apostle Paul describes: '... in my flesh, dwelleth no good thing: for to will is present with me; but how to perform that which is good I find not...the good that I would I do not: but the evil which I would not, that I do' (Romans 7:18-19). Paul goes on to say that victory in this conflict is found by those '...who walk not after the flesh, but after the Spirit' (Romans 8:1). Walking after the Spirit is accomplished only by obedience to the greatest commandment, '...Thou shalt love the Lord thy God with all thy heart...soul...mind...' (Matthew 22:37). For Christians, this is the place where most spiritual battles are fought. In the patriarchs, this battle is portrayed vividly and poignantly.

Jacob's story has been one of progression. He knew about the promise of God (to Abraham) and gave it value. He displayed an attitude that saw great worth in the promise. He encouraged Esau to bargain away the birthright (25:29-34). With all the attention that Jacob gave to spiritual things and with his knowledge that God watched over him (31:5), there was still an initial step Jacob had not taken in his relationship with God. That step is clearly noted in Jacob's words. 'Except the God of my father, the God of Abraham, and the fear of Isaac (meaning Issac's fear of God), had been with me, surely thou hadst sent me away...empty...' (31:42). Jacob's understanding of God was still as the 'God of Abraham and Isaac.' He had not made the connection that God was Jacob's God. Many of us may be living daily with this dilemma. We have asked Jesus to be our Saviour, but we are not allowing him to be our God. Spiritually, we are short-changed.

Genesis 32:1-23

1. And Jacob went on his way, and the angels of God met him. 2. And when Jacob saw them, he said, This is God's host: and he called the name of that place Mahanaim. 3. And Jacob sent messengers before him to Esau his brother unto the land of Seir, the country of Edom. 4. And he commanded them, saying, Thus shall ye speak unto my lord Esau; Thy servant Jacob saith thus, I have sojourned with Laban, and stayed there until now: 5. And I have oxen, and asses, flocks, and menservants, and women servants: and I have sent to tell my lord, that I may find grace in thy sight. 6. And the messengers returned to Jacob, saying, We came to thy brother Esau, and also he cometh to meet thee, and four hundred men with him.

7. Then Jacob was greatly afraid and distressed: and he divided the people that was with him, and the flocks, and herds, and the camels, into two bands; 8. And said, If Esau come to the one company, and smite it, then the other company which is left shall escape. 9. And Jacob said, O God of my father Abraham, and God of my father Isaac, the Lord which saidst unto me, Return unto thy country, and to thy kindred, and I will deal well with thee: 10. I am not worthy of the least of all the mercies, and of all the truth, which thou hast shewed unto thy servant; for with my staff I passed over this Jordan; and now I am become two bands. 11. Deliver me, I pray thee, from the hand of my brother, from the hand of Esau: for I fear him, lest he will come and smite me, and the mother with the children. 12. And thou saidst, I will surely do thee good, and make thy seed as the sand of the sea, which cannot be numbered for multitude. 13. And he lodged there that same night; and took of that which came to his hand a present for Esau his brother; 14. Two hundred she goats, and twenty he goats, two hundred ewes, and twenty rams, 15. Thirty milch camels with their colts, forty kine, and ten bulls, twenty she asses, and ten foals. 16. And he delivered them into the hand of his servants, every drove by themselves; and said unto his servants, Pass over before me, and put a space betwixt drove and drove.

17. And he commanded the foremost, saying, When Esau my brother meeteth thee, and asketh thee, saying, Whose art thou? and whither goest thou? and whose are these before thee? 18. Then thou shalt say, They be thy servant Jacob's; it is a present sent unto my lord Esau: and, behold, also he is behind us. 19. And so commanded he the second, and the third, and all that followed the droves, saying, On this manner shall ye speak unto Esau, when ye find him. 20. And say ye moreover, Behold, thy servant Jacob is behind us. For he said, I will appease him with the present that goeth before me, and afterward I will see his face; peradventure he will accept of me. 21. So went the present over before him: and himself lodged that night in the company. 22. And he rose up that night, and took his two wives, and his two women servants, and his eleven sons, and passed over the ford Jabbok. 23. And he took them, and sent them over the brook, and sent over that he had.

'...God's host...'

One of the most intriguing scenarios in biblical narrative was the times that the saints of God saw angels (32:1). Some of us may even think that we would love to see angels. The visit of angels in the Bible, however, is often the forerunner to biblical heroes being called upon to do something extremely difficult. The visit of angels has a powerful burden attached. Jesus was visited by angels before his crucifixion. Abraham was visited by angels prior to the destruction of Sodom and Gomorrah. Isaiah saw angels in a vision before setting out on the prophetic ministry that would take him through extremely difficult times.

The ministry of angels was also to comfort in extremely stressful moments as Jacob experienced when first leaving home on his way to Haran (28:11-17). The comforting ministry of angels in the Old Testament is assumed by the Holy Spirit in the New Testament (John 14:16-18). The appearance of the angels to Jacob in Genesis 32:1 is to comfort him before a difficult encounter with Esau. This must be done in order to assume the ultimate working out of God's plan calling for Jacob to receive the benefits of the birthright and blessing. Jacob was in this predicament because he had stolen the blessing from Esau instead of relying on God. He must now reconcile with Esau and do things God's way.

In an extremely frightening moment for Jacob (Genesis 32:2), the presence of the angels assured him that he was doing the right thing. He says, '...This is God's host....' It is a further confirmation of God's earlier promise. '...I am with thee...I will not leave thee...' (Genesis 28:15). Every Christian will face the moment when he or she knows what must be done but is sorely afraid. We would love to have the vision that Jacob had. We must remember that the comfort of the angels is available to us through the Holy Spirit. The presence of the angels did not mean they were going to keep Jacob from his encounter with Esau. They only meant that God would be with him.

The greatest comfort you and I can have in our life is the knowledge that we are doing the right thing. The comfort that we seek is often there in that assurance. It does not mean we can avoid doing the difficult thing. It only means that God will be with us. When we have the sweet assurance of doing right, it is just as good as seeing angels.

The knowledge of doing the right thing is one of the most comforting elements of our life. However it is not often thought of in that way. But it is only in doing the right thing that we can have the assurance that God is with us.

The struggle for courage

As one looks at the lives of the great heroes of Scripture, the reality of Jesus' words, 'This is the...great commandment' (Matthew 27:38), takes on meaning. It is the great commandment because the impact of our obedience or disobedience to it radiates out to many other parts of our lives. This is the difficult and hard journey of every person who desires to be a person of God.

In Jacob's story, the beginning of chapter 32 provides a crossroads. The specifics of his problem speak of a much larger spiritual lesson every follower of God will face. It is the moment in which we must do the extremely difficult thing. It is the full knowledge of what we must do, and yet the thing we least want to do.

Twenty years before, Jacob had heard the voice of the Lord say, '...I am with thee...and will bring thee again into this land...' (28:15). Jacob had responded to the promise of God and made a vow of his own. '...and of all that thou shalt give me, I will surely give the tenth unto thee' (28:22). To keep the vow, Jacob must return to the place where he made it, Bethel. As we read the narrative, he does not go directly to Bethel, but travels a circular route that will take him past the land of his brother, Esau. The last time he had seen Esau, it was under the threat of death. Esau hated Jacob for stealing the father's blessing. Jacob's return to the land meant laying claim to the benefits of the birthright and blessing. Jacob's dilemma is simple. If he is to have the land which God had given him (25:22-23) he must deal with Esau in an honorable, God-fearing way. But Jacob was also very afraid of Esau, who had wanted to kill him.

Loving God will require Jacob to fear God more than he fears Esau. That is a monumental dilemma. Jacob is very sincere in wanting to return to Bethel. Geographically he can get there without ever encountering Esau. Spiritually, the road to Bethel goes through Esau. Doing the thing we most fear is sometimes the only way to get to peace with God. We must show that we fear him most, thus we love him most.

> To love God often requires great courage. It is the kind of courage that can only be found in a love for God. Thus the problem is a circuitous one. Before courage there must be love, but love is only established in courage. It is an uncomfortable position.

'...he cometh to meet thee...'

Facing the things we don't want to face is a major issue that can move a life forward in productive ways, or leave it stalled and in a kind of limbo. Many people can find themselves in life's great chasm called 'going nowhere' because they refuse to deal with that which holds them back. This is especially true in our spiritual walk with God.

Many times, the issue holding us back is our own anger. The requirement to overcome it is forgiveness. Another issue may be a desire to hang on to something of this world that God is calling on us to give up. The issue could be a debt needing to be repaid, in order to restore our integrity, so that our relationship with God may move forward. In Jacob's case, he must seek to rebuild a relationship that he had been responsible for destroying. It was the relationship with his brother, Esau.

Jacob had fled from Esau twenty years earlier. He had deceived Esau, stolen the blessing of his father, and left home before

Esau could take his life (27:41-43). Jacob had presumed the role of God. It was a blessing that God intended Jacob to have, but he had trusted his own scheming instead of God's work to provide it. His mistake was in believing that his own sin is justified because it would result in God's will being done. His scheme backfired and has brought him to this serious moment in his life. God's will shall be the end result, but Jacob must learn to do things God's way. He now faces the requirement of walking through the dark valley of this fearful encounter with Esau.

Two things are notable. First Jacob must consider the nature of his life. Its whole meaning is wrapped in that birthright and possession of the land of promise. The only way to be in the land without fear is by going past Esau. He must face the one person in the world he does not want to face. Until he does, his life is 'going nowhere.' God was telling Jacob, 'You could not trust me to provide the blessing. Now you will learn to trust me the hard way.' That seems to be the way we humans always learn.

Second, regardless of Jacob's decision at this point, God would keep his word. If Jacob did not act now, he would only create a much more difficult situation later on. He had already spent twenty years out of the land. How much longer did he want this predicament to continue? Humans often think we can make things better by acting against God. In reality, we always succeed in making things worse, and facing a more difficult decision later.

> It is a difficult thing to face life's issues realistically. Most people prefer a God who is a great big candy man, rather than a God who forces us to grow into mature people. God requires us to do the right thing even when we are afraid.

The schemer still

Esau, the brother of Jacob, is coming to meet Jacob, and he has four hundred men with him. When Jacob and Esau were last seen together, Esau's desire was to murder Jacob (27:41). Twenty years have passed, and Jacob has no reason to believe that things have changed. The ominous sound of 'four hundred men with him' (32:6), doesn't calm the nerves.

For Jacob, there are many thoughts. He obviously regrets the way that he had deceived his brother. He knows he must make peace with Esau, but has no idea whether that is possible. He is faced with trying to bargain with his brother for his own life, but knows he cannot use the birthright and blessing as bargaining chips. God had said they belonged to Jacob so God would not permit Jacob to try to dodge the issue. Besides, Isaac (Jacob & Esau's father), had said the blessing is irrevocable. Jacob has nothing Esau wants, but must strike a bargain.

Jacob had schemed to obtain the birthright and the blessing. At this moment, they were a curse. Think of the paradox. The birthright and blessing were both symbols of God's preference of Jacob over Esau (25:23-26; Romans 9:13), but at the moment they were the very things that might get Jacob killed. God's preference is not always glorious, especially when we are caught in disobedience.

The schemer in Jacob is still alive. He divided up the people that were with him into two groups. This would give one group the chance to escape if Esau attacked. Obviously, Jacob would be hoping to be in the group that escaped. He gave himself a 50-50 chance (32:7-8). Jacob then begins to pray.

There are a couple of points for meditation here. Jacob had the assurance that God was with him. Why not prepare for battle? That is the manly way to do things. Would he not believe that God would give him victory? A guilty conscience has a difficult time preparing for battle because there is always the sense of punishment. One guilty of deceitfulness, as Jacob was, always wonders where his punishment will be manifest. To do battle is inviting punishment.

Also, Jacob was in a quandry. He had always had the answers in his life. They just weren't God's answers. He is at this crossroads. Will he seek to know God's answer before he acts? If he had been praying throughout his life, he might already have the answer.

The ministry of our Lord Jesus, the Incarnate One, set
the standard for prayer. In fact, his disciples were enam-
oured of his prayer life, and asked him to teach them to
pray (Luke 11:1). Why pray? It is not always to be done
just for the immediate needs seen. In reality, it is a major
step toward preparation for tests not yet seen. The answer
for the needs of today can come in the form of revelation
given yesterday. Adequate praying, done in the past, often
spares us from trauma in the present because we already
have knowledge from God.

Keys to effective praying

With his brother Esau coming with four hundred men to meet him,
Jacob is afraid he will die (32: 6, 11). The harsh reality of the moment is there despite the fact Jacob has the assurance God is with
him (32:9, 12). Jacob's prayer is significant. He begins by saying to
God 'You told me to come back.' His words are, '...O God...which
saidst unto me, Return unto thy country...and I will deal well with
thee' (Genesis 32:9). In Jacob's mind, things weren't going well
at the moment. Yet, there is a note of great comfort. He is able to
begin his request to God by saying, 'I have been obedient.' There
is nothing any more important to a life of effective prayer than the
sense of obedience. Every Christian should learn that the basis of
confidence in God is to come to him with a pure heart. Jacob had
much guilt about his life. It is a sign of growth that he now recognizes the importance of his recent obedience.

The prayer is closed by reminding God of the promise God
made 'And thou saidst, I will surely do thee good, and make thy
seed as the sand of the sea, which cannot be numbered for multitude' (32:12). The critical thing to note here is the spiritual growth
of Jacob. His request is not based in his own schemes, but in the
revealed plan of God. When Jacob noted his fear, he said, '...I fear
him (Esau), lest he will come and smite me, and the mother with
the children' (32:11). His concern for the death of his children, and

their mothers, coupled with the promise of God '…make thy seed as the sand of the sea…' (32:12) reveals that Jacob's thoughts are on the long-term plan of God, not just the present dilemma. Whenever Christians can pray with the long-term plan of God as our primary motive, we are more likely to discern the right thing to do in the pressure of the moment.

Thus, we have two important learning events about prayer. The first is, successful and effective praying begins with our obedience. God will not show us what to do without obedience to what is already known. The second is, we must be primarily motivated by the desire to achieve God's plan. Abraham and Isaac learned it through the need to grasp their relationship with God as the primary possession of their life. Jacob is now beginning to grasp the same thing.

> It is somewhat significant and somewhat redundant that the lessons of the lives of the patriarchs keep returning to the same issue. The importance of learning that God is the most important possession of their life. It is a constantly repeating issue in our lives as well.

Pricing the priceless

The time has come for Jacob to fulfil the vow he made years earlier (28:22). He has prospered greatly in the last six years of service to his uncle Laban. There is an obstacle in the way. It is Esau. A spiritual principle, provided by Jesus, aids our understanding. 'Therefore if thou bring thy gift to the altar, and there rememberest that thy brother hath ought against thee; Leave there thy gift before the altar, and go thy way; first be reconciled to thy brother, and then come and offer thy gift' (Matthew 5:23-24). Anger against a brother, whether a brother in Christ, or a member of our earthly family, will block our relationship with God. The path always goes through that family member that we despise. The story gives us Jacob's attempt to reconcile with Esau.

Jacob's plan is both elaborate and desperate. It reflects one who is truly repentant for what he had done to Esau years before (25:27-34; 27:34-41), and one who is earnestly seeking to make amends.

Though Jacob's heart is in the right place, it does express the pitiable nature of his plight. He offers Esau a total of 580 beasts as amends. This, in material terms, would seem a grand gesture. The problem is, it places a price on that which is priceless. Jacob took from Esau that which couldn't be returned (27:34-37). One cannot question Jacob's sincerity, but his methodology is an insult. It is like a man raping a woman, and then writing her a check thinking that makes it all even. Proverbs 18:16 speaks of this kind of logic in the affairs of men. ' A man's gift maketh room for him....' It is to say that one can make anything right with the material gifts of the world. This is great foolishness and is believed when one is without knowledge. Jacob certainly senses the uselessness of this barter as he sends everyone ahead of him (32:20-23), as a further buffer between himself and Esau.

Jacob's attempt to barter with Esau can be a powerful spiritual lesson. With Esau, he is trying to put a price on the priceless. That is a foolish waste of time. Later, when he sacrifices to God, he must also know that the sacrifices are not a barter to win the favour of God. With Esau, he must reconcile by receiving a gift from Esau: the gift of forgiveness. When he fulfils his vow to God to give the tenth (28:22), it is an acknowledgement of God's grace in giving to Jacob; it is not a means of placating God. Man can give nothing to God unless God gives to him first. Here, Jacob must also receive from Esau before he can go to Bethel. The whole experience of giving to God is turned into an experience of humiliation. Just as favour with Esau will be through Esau's grace, which Jacob must accept, favour with God comes only through his grace, which we must accept.

Humans never cease in their endless belief that somehow they can earn the favour of God. The peace of God can never be understood until one comes fully to grip with a wonderful truth. The gifts of God are by grace and grace alone.

Genesis 32:24-32

24. And Jacob was left alone; and there wrestled a man with him until the breaking of the day. 25. And when he saw that he prevailed not against him, he touched the hollow of his thigh; and the hollow of Jacob's thigh was out of joint, as he wrestled with him. 26. And he said, Let me go, for the day breaketh. And he said, I will not let thee go, except thou bless me. 27. And he said unto him, What is thy name? And he said, Jacob. 28. And he said, Thy name shall be called no more Jacob, but Israel: for as a prince hast thou power with God and with men, and hast prevailed. 29. And Jacob asked him, and said, Tell me, I pray thee, thy name. And he said, Wherefore is it that thou dost ask after my name? And he blessed him there. 30. And Jacob called the name of the place Peniel: for I have seen God face to face, and my life is preserved. 31. And as he passed over Penuel the sun rose upon him, and he halted upon his thigh. 32. Therefore the children of Israel eat not of the sinew which shrank, which is upon the hollow of the thigh, unto this day: because he touched the hollow of Jacob's thigh in the sinew that shrank.

Wrestling with God

An oft-used phrase in contemporary preaching is the phrase 'wrestling with God.' The meaning of the phrase is in a person's struggle to yield himself to the revealed will of God, and do that which we do not desire to do. Another kind of wrestling with God comes in resisting the temptation to do what we want to do. Jacob's wrestling was the former.

We are told that he '...wrestled a man...until the breaking of the day' (32:24). Jacob later reveals who the man is '...for I have seen God face to face...' (32:30). This encounter with God has the following elements. Jacob has made a spiritual journey that taught him God is sovereign. Everything he has is because of God

(31:4-10). He must come to terms with the sin of his life by seeking to reconcile with his brother Esau whom he defrauded years before. This effort to reconcile places his life at risk (32:11). Jacob does not want to risk this encounter (32:11). His choices at this point are based in two questions. Has he come to the point where he honours God as the greatest treasure of his life? Is he willing to lose his own life rather than lose the promise of God? The literal wrestling match Jacob had with God was over the issue of control of his life (32:25-26).

It became clear that God had control of the situation symbolized by the crippling of Jacob (32:25). Jacob's plea was then for God's blessing (32:26). It is here that Jacob submits. He wants absolute assurance of never losing the presence of God. It is always a sweet moment for God when his children long for him as Jacob does in this situation. God gave him two signs to honour that plea. The first is a change of name from Jacob (the deceiver) to Israel (prince with God). It is interesting that the one who now has power with God and men (32:28) has it precisely because he has yielded himself to God. Jacob will still have many trying and hard days ahead of him, but instead of the proud deceiver, there will be the man, humbled before God. That humility will always be reflected in the limp he will carry for the rest of his life (the second sign). His look is not so arrogant, and his strength is now based in faith in God, not trust in self.

> The curse of the thorns and thistles (3:18) lead the male into many battles to show off external prowess. He longs for respect, and admiration for the deeds he has done. It is a different thing to long for blessing. Jacob's prayer was for blessing. He needs grace. It is a reflection of humility.

A plea for blessing

There are several biblical pictures that are found in Jacob's wrestling with God. These pictures provide insight to the Old Testament understanding of God, and upon meditation, create a learning experience. First, it was night when Jacob and God wrestled (32:24). It is very noteworthy that the periods of life when one struggles with the will of God seem as night. Those times are as darkness precisely because the resistance to God's will leaves one without direction. It is very much like walking in darkness. Submission to God is like experiencing the breaking of the dawn. The Psalmist writes 'Thy word is a lamp unto my feet, and a light unto my path' (Psalms 119:105).

Second, it is also interesting that one of the most important blessings of God is the promise of his presence. Jacob recognized the value of that in his first encounter with God at Bethel (28:15-16). This is significant in the context of Jacob's wrestling with God. At no time in his life was God nearer than at that very moment, but Jacob was wrestling with him. For the Christian, the same dynamic applies. God is closer to us in those moments of wrestling than at any other time in our life, but because we are not in submission, those are times of great struggle instead of times of blessing.

Third, note God's words to Jacob, '...Let me go for the day breaketh...' (32:26). These are critical words. In the Old Testament, to see the face of God means death (Exodus 33:18-20). Jacob later noted, 'I have seen God face to face...' (32:30). This is a reflection of being face to face with God in the cover of darkness without the full impact of God's glory. For Jacob's sake, God withdrew from him before the daybreak (32:26). Jacob does not walk away from the encounter without scar. He is given a limp that shall forever remind him of a face to face meeting with God. The limp is a reminder to him of weakness, but also of a brand new kind of power he has found (32:28). This is remindful of the same thing Paul discovered in the New Testament after he prayed for removal of a thorn in the flesh. God said to Paul '...my strength is made perfect in weakness...' (2 Corinthians 12:9).

Daily submission to the will of God is accomplished in prayerful meditation upon the Word of God. It is only in submission that the light is manifest to us. In that meditation we learn of his strength, also to accept and be thankful for our weakness. Let us pray for the wisdom of Paul's confession in 2 Corinthians 12:9.

Genesis 33:1-20

I. The Meeting Occurs (33:1-11)
1. '…Esau embraced him…'
2. Settling the account

II. Jacob Settles Down (33:12-20)
1. To Succoth, not Bethel
2. '…erected an altar..'

Genesis 33:1-11

1. And Jacob lifted up his eyes, and looked, and, behold, Esau came, and with him four hundred men. And he divided the children unto Leah, and unto Rachel, and unto the two handmaids. 2. And he put the handmaids and their children foremost, and Leah and her children after, and Rachel and Joseph hindermost. 3. And he passed over before them, and bowed himself to the ground seven times, until he came near to his brother. 4. And Esau ran to meet him, and embraced him, and fell on his neck, and kissed him: and they wept. 5. And he lifted up his eyes, and saw the women and the children; and said, Who are those with thee? And he said, The children which God hath graciously given thy servant. 6. Then the handmaidens came near, they and their children, and they bowed themselves. 7. And Leah also with her children came near, and bowed themselves: and after came Joseph near and Rachel, and they bowed themselves. 8. And he said, What meanest thou by all this drove which I met? And he said, These are to find grace in the sight of my lord. 9. And Esau said, I have enough, my brother; keep that thou hast unto thyself. 10. And Jacob said, Nay, I pray thee, if now I have found grace in thy sight, then receive my present at my hand: for therefore I have seen thy face, as though I had seen the face of God, and thou wast pleased with me. 11. Take, I pray thee, my blessing that is brought to thee; because God hath dealt graciously with me, and because I have enough. And he urged him, and he took it.

'...Esau embraced him...'

Throughout Jacob's life, he had acted hastily and used his cunning to advance his own schemes. The schemes always created a later problem for him. He has just finished a time of 'wrestling with God' from which he emerged with a changed character. He will no longer be known as the deceiver, but as one whose power comes from God (32:28). The first step in his new dependency is a meeting with Esau who had years earlier stated a desire to kill him (27:41).

For this meeting, Jacob positions his family, aligning the ones least revered as first in line to meet Esau, the most revered (Rachel and sons) last in line to meet Esau. If there is a battle, the most cherished would have a better chance for escape. Following this we see ample evidence of the new Jacob. He places himself in harm's way. He goes to the front of the line, and in typical oriental fashion bows seven times to Esau. There is no one to protect him except God.

The reader of the story is prepared for anything. We know that God will protect Jacob, but what kind of trial must he go through? Jacob, and the reader, learn that the trial has always been with God, not Esau. 'And Esau ran to meet him, and embraced him, and fell on his neck, and kissed him: and they wept' (33:4). Every time Jacob did things his own way, he created more problems. When he finally did it God's way, the problems are solved.

Certainly, this does not mean that serving God never takes us through difficult valleys. What it teaches is that God works things out for good, while our way only creates more problems to solve

(Romans 8:28). The wonderful conclusion to the Jacob-Esau controversy should create quite a bit of devotional thought. Esau's hatred of Jacob was stilled, but the nation (Edom) that he spawns will be a long-time enemy to the nation (Israel) that Jacob spawns. God finally brought Jacob to submission to God and proved that his way is best, but Jacob's deceitfulness and treachery left its stain, with problems that will span generations. Every time we submit our will to God's, we save ourselves many problems. Only God knows how many problems we may save for others.

> There is a profound lesson meditation can show us. Humans tend to think of consequences to their disobedience in terms of how they hurt themselves. There is another consideration. We do not live on islands where our actions only affect ourselves, but we live in a world where our rebellion or submission can have wonderful, or devastating, consequences on others.

Settling the account

The pangs of a guilty conscience lead men to do many things. For Jacob, he was trying to reconcile with his brother after many years of separation. This separation had been created by Jacob's treachery in stealing the blessing of Esau. Jacob had feared for his life as Esau had once threatened to kill him (27:41). When Esau and Jacob met again, the hatred had left, and they embraced (33:4). Jacob may have been greatly surprised. He most certainly was relieved. The incident that follows is somewhat curious.

Jacob has a sizeable gift to present to Esau totalling 580 of his sheep and goats (32:13-16). The gift has two aspects that require our thought. The first is that Jacob's guilty conscience cannot be relieved by the simple forgiveness of Esau. The offer is Jacob's attempt to repay Esau for the damage that he caused. He is trying to place a price on the priceless. The attempt to repay is admirable, but is somewhat of an insult. It is impossible to restore the value of that which he had stolen. Esau understood this and at first refused the offer. At Jacob's insistence, he accepted (33:11).

The second aspect is that of redemption. By refusing Jacob's gift, Esau would indirectly be saying to Jacob 'You still owe me, the account is not settled.' The minute Esau accepts, he says, 'The account is settled,' thus Jacob's guilty conscience is salved. He has received notice of full reconciliation. The gift allowed Jacob's guilt to be eased.

This provides a great picture of our relationship with God. Our sin has created separation from God and an awesome sense of guilt. It is that sense of guilt that makes facing God a fearsome thing. God created us! He has rights to us! Our sin has fouled his creation. We have stolen from him his holy creation. It takes the settling of accounts, not just forgiveness to ease a guilty conscience. We must repay that which is priceless. In Jesus Christ, God provided a way. '…Christ died for our sins…' (1 Corinthians 15:3).

As Jacob could never have enough to repay Esau, we can never have enough to repay God. In the sacrifice of the blood of Jesus Christ, God establishes a means of restoration. As Esau's acceptance of Jacob's gift acknowledged 'the account is settled,' God's acceptance of the blood of Jesus Christ, and our coming to God with that as our possession allows God to say 'the account is settled,' and our guilt is quieted.

> The easing of the guilty mind is one of the most wonderful, but least understood aspects of redemption. The blood of the Incarnate One, the promised seed of the woman, provides for us the gift we can bring to God and settle our account. A little meditation and thanksgiving for such salvation is appropriate here.

Genesis 33:12-20

12. And he said, Let us take our journey, and let us go, and I will go before thee. 13. And he said unto him, My lord knoweth that the children are tender, and the flocks and herds with young are with me: and if men should overdrive them one day, all the flock will die. 14. Let my lord, I pray thee, pass over before his servant: and I will lead on softly, according as the cattle that goeth before me and the children be able to endure, until I come unto my lord unto Seir. 15. And Esau said, Let me now leave with thee some of the folk that are with me. And he said, What needeth it? let me find grace in the sight of my lord. 16. So Esau returned that day on his way unto Seir. 17. And Jacob journeyed to Succoth, and built him an house, and made booths for his cattle: therefore the name of the place is called Succoth. 18. And Jacob came to Shalem, a city of Shechem, which is in the land of Canaan, when he came from Padanaram; and pitched his tent before the city. 19. And he bought a parcel of a field, where he had spread his tent, at the hand of the children of Hamor, Shechem's father, for an hundred pieces of money. 20. And he erected there an altar, and called it Elelohelsrael.

To Succoth, not Bethel

A term that has often been used to identify a Christian who is engaging in sinful activity is 'backslider.' It is a harsh sounding term, and is used to refer mostly to those who have dropped out of church and are involved in unacceptable lifestyles. There is a kind of respectable backsliding about which we rarely speak. This lifestyle may not be noticed, and would certainly not be called by such a harsh term. Every Christian, however, should be aware of its dangers.

This kind of backsliding is illustrated in Jacob's life. We note that Jacob had come through a momentous crisis. His fear of Esau had been unfounded, the two brothers are reconciled. Jacob is back in the land of promise. He is the first in the line of promise to purchase land that is more than a burial plot (33:18-19). He proceeds to do something admirable. He erects an altar and acknowledges

God (33:20) 'El-e-lohe–Israel' is Jacob's way of saying, 'My God is distinct from all other gods. I have separated myself for service to him.' Note the great relief of Jacob! See his confidence reflected in his purchase of property. His life is now good, and he obviously is happy about it. Jacob has, however, left something out.

Esau had invited him to journey southward with him. Jacob had declined, saying that he would only slow Esau down because of his young children (33:13). Jacob then turned north. Jacob either forgets or ignores God's direction to him. He must return to the place where he made a vow to God (31:13). Bethel was south. Jacob went north to Succoth.

One of the most vulnerable times for a Christian to backslide is right after God has provided blessing. Maybe a great financial crisis ends by getting a new job, and the promise made to him is forgotten. A period of great trial is past. An ordeal has ended, and the feeling about life is now good. We praise God, but we forget to follow through on our commitment to him. Jacob had just taken a great step in his life. He follows with a backward step. He does not continue his journey to Bethel to fulfil his vow. No one would know he is a backslider. He builds an altar to God.

Jacob could be congratulated for his building of an altar to God, and engaging in worship. It was a good thing, but at this point it was not the best thing. It is easy for us to construct substitutes to obedience in our lives. In fact, others may congratulate, even be impressed with, our spiritual commitment.

'...erected an altar...'

How does one discern when he or she may be backslidden? This story of Jacob gives a clue. Life was now good for Jacob. He evidently was content and confident. The fear of his brother was no longer part of his life. He was in the land of promise, and out from under the burdensome situation of employment to his uncle

Laban, who had often cheated him. He has his family, and he purchases a piece of land, and erects an altar to God (33:18-20). Life is good, and Jacob is grateful to God for it.

To what does Jacob now give his attention? 'And Jacob journeyed to Succoth, and built him an house, and made booths for his cattle...' (33:17). It is the very predictable tendency of humans to be at a place where life is good, and have our attention turned even more to self. God has blessed us by making life easier, and we basically say, 'Thanks, God, I can take it from here.' Before the altar was built, Jacob built himself a house. He built booths for his cattle.

The attention that he gave to God was in thanksgiving. That's admirable. Most Christians are pretty good at 'thanks.' He also let it be known that his God was the only God he would serve (33:20). That's also admirable. Christians are good at verbal confessional statements. The only thing missing was that he wasn't serving God, he served himself. And, he thought himself justified in doing it. That is demonstrated in the building of the altar.

As followers of God, we are often prone to giving all of our creative energy to serving ourselves. In fact, we pride ourselves in it. God can stop worrying about us now, and go to helping someone else. We're taking care of ourselves. This attitude can easily overtake a Christian's life, and before we know it, it is the modus operandi of a church and its membership.

Jesus noted such a church in his Revelation to saint John. 'I know thy works, that thou art neither cold nor hot...Because thou sayest, I am rich, and increased with goods, and have need of nothing...' (Revelation 3:15-17). It is a very deceiving thing for us to look at the moment when we are materially in great shape and believe it proves we are spiritually in great shape. Jacob had a problem. He had made a vow (28:22). He must return to Bethel and fulfil it. Bethel must come before Succoth. By placing Succoth first, he is backslidden. We must note when we are doing the same thing.

Discernment of a backslidden condition is critical for maintenance of the productive Christian life. It would be good to ask God to reveal where the commitments are that we failed to keep, or the commitments that we have failed to make that may have us backslidden.

Genesis 34:1-31

I. The Defilement of Dinah (34:1-18)
1. '...before the city...'
2. One people

II. The Revenge of Simeon and Levi (34:19-31)
1. Failure in asking the next question
2. '...ye have troubled me...'

Genesis 34:1-18

1. And Dinah the daughter of Leah, which she bare unto Jacob, went out to see the daughters of the land. 2. And when Shechem the son of Hamor the Hivite, prince of the country, saw her, he took her, and lay with her, and defiled her. 3. And his soul clave unto Dinah the daughter of Jacob, and he loved the damsel, and spake kindly unto the damsel. 4. And Shechem spake unto his father Hamor, saying, Get me this damsel to wife. 5. And Jacob heard that he had defiled Dinah his daughter: now his sons were with his cattle in the field: and Jacob held his peace until they were come. 6. And Hamor the father of Shechem went out unto Jacob to commune with him. 7. And the sons of Jacob came out of the field when they heard it: and the men were grieved, and they were very wroth, because he had wrought folly in Israel in lying with Jacob's daughter: which thing ought not to be done. 8. And Hamor communed with them, saying, The soul of my son Shechem longeth for your daughter: I pray you give her him to wife. 9. And make ye marriages with us, and give your daughters unto us, and take our daughters unto you. 10. And ye shall dwell with us: and the land shall be before you; dwell and trade ye therein, and get you possessions therein. 11. And Shechem said unto her father and unto her breth-

*ren, Let me find grace in your eyes, and what ye shall say unto me I will
give. 12. Ask me never so much dowry and gift, and I will give according
as ye shall say unto me: but give me the damsel to wife. 13. And the sons
of Jacob answered Shechem and Hamor his father deceitfully, and said,
because he had defiled Dinah their sister: 14. And they said unto them,
We cannot do this thing, to give our sister to one that is uncircumcised; for
that were a reproach unto us: 15. But in this will we consent unto you: If
ye will be as we be, that every male of you be circumcised; 16. Then will
we give our daughters unto you, and we will take your daughters to us,
and we will dwell with you, and we will become one people. But if ye will
not hearken unto us, to be circumcised; then will we take our daughter,
and we will be gone. 17. But if ye will not hearken unto us, to be circumcised; then will we take our daughter, and we will be gone. 18. And their
words pleased Hamor, and Shechem Hamor's son.*

'...before the city...'

The horrible story of Genesis 34 must be understood in the context of Jacob's delay in returning to Bethel to fulfil the vow made
to God (28:22). God had spoken to Jacob and called him back to
Bethel (31:13). Jacob's fear about reconciliation with his brother,
and his great relief when that ordeal ended had turned Jacob's
attention away from his commitment and toward making his life
even more pleasant (33:17).

There is a very telling statement in Genesis 33:18. '...and
pitched his tent before the city.' The attentive reader of Scripture
recalls another such statement. '..and Lot dwelled in the cities of
the plain, and pitched his tent toward Sodom (13:12). Jacob built
stables for his sheep and goatherds, and looked to the city for commerce. This was the same thing that Lot had done.

The results of such activity are immediately manifest in Jacob's
family. 'And Dinah the daughter of Leah, which she bare unto
Jacob, went out to see the daughters of the land...' (34:1). Jacob's
family became curious about the people of the land. Dinah was
drawn to the women, perhaps a fascination with their dress, their
ornamentation, or something else in their lifestyle that attracted

her. She is taken by one of the men of the city who is part of a ruling family. He forced his sexual attention on her, and then desires that she be his wife. The defining words for this story are, 'Then will we give our daughters unto you, and we will take your daughters to us, and we will dwell with you, and we will become one people' (34:16). That is the exact opposite of God's intention for the family of Jacob.

The nations of Canaan are to be disinherited by God and the land given to the new nation, which will be derived from Jacob's family (28:13). Jacob's family is clearly in danger of the same kind of compromise with the people of the land that had afflicted Lot and his family. This tragedy could have been averted had Jacob been at Bethel instead of dwelling with his tent pitched toward Shechem. Jacob had claimed loyalty to God when he built the altar (33:20). He must learn that loyalty to God means one hundred percent obedience. Jacob, you should have been at Bethel. Trying to have God in the life without obedience to God will always create only those things that bring us heartache.

> Attraction to the world's fascinations can come into our lives in very subtle ways. When they begin to consume our minds, we easily become distracted from God's way of productive living. We should hope that God guards us from the allurements of the world, and keeps our minds focused on the truth of his Word.

One People

The sordid tale leaves us gasping for air. In brilliantly told fashion, one unspeakable act after another is presented. The triumph of Jacob's surrender to God, (32:24-32), and the beauty of the reconciliation between Esau and Jacob (33:4), seem to crumble in this ugly affair. Dinah, the daughter of Leah and Jacob, became too friendly with the people of the land leading to a sexual encounter with one of the men (34:1-2). The man has a desire to make her his wife, and the people see an opportunity to make Jacob and his family one of them (34:16). '...one people' means that the family of Jacob will be absorbed into their community. Jacob, because of his newfound dependence on God, and the reality that his disobedience in not returning to Bethel was the facilitator to the incident, plus his desire to protect his family from hostility with the people of the land, finds himself unable to act (34:5).

Dinah's brothers have not the hesitancy of Jacob. They set out to deceive the people of the land, by accepting the union of the two peoples, provided the men of the land agree to circumcision. This act, which was a covenant identification for Abraham's generations (17:9-11) was sometimes done in the other cultures as initiation into marriage. It was, however, extremely painful during the healing process, particularly after two or three days. On the third day, Simeon and Levi went into the city and killed all the men while they were in a weakened condition. The reader is left stunned. How could this happen after Jacob is given a new name, Israel, signifying power with God?

There are many lessons here for the devout person. One of the most important is to learn how a values system wrongly applied can be destructive. The sons of Jacob began with their values in the right place. They saw the compromise. '...folly in Israel...' (34:7) reflects a mindset that has gone beyond what has been done to their sister. It reflects on the greater danger of compromise in the family of God. Jacob must have done some prior teaching with his sons, but it had not included applying their knowledge. Their scruples led them into a greater folly. Sometimes, a righteous indignation turns into an unholy anger, and a person assumes the role of avenging angel. The Bible clearly teaches '...Vengeance is mine; I will repay, saith the Lord' (Romans 12:19). Jacob, by virtue of his own actions already understood the trouble one creates by jumping ahead of God. It is a pity that he could not have taught that lesson to his sons.

It is important that evil be punished, but it must be within the parameters of God's methodology. All too often humans

want to rush ahead of God. Punishment in this manner is
never fair and equitable.

Genesis 34:19-31

*19. And the young man deferred not to do the thing, because he had de-
light in Jacob's daughter: and he was more honourable than all the house
of his father. 20. And Hamor and Shechem his son came unto the gate
of their city, and communed with the men of their city, saying, 21. These
men are peaceable with us; therefore let them dwell in the land, and trade
therein; for the land, behold, it is large enough for them; let us take their
daughters to us for wives, and let us give them our daughters. 22. Only
herein will the men consent unto us for to dwell with us, to be one people,
if every male among us be circumcised, as they are circumcised. Shall not
their cattle and their substance and every beast of theirs be ours? only let
us consent unto them, and they will dwell with us. 24. And unto Hamor
and unto Shechem his son hearkened all that went out of the gate of his
city; and every male was circumcised, all that went out of the gate of his
city. 25. And it came to pass on the third day, when they were sore, that
two of the sons of Jacob, Simeon and Levi, Dinah's brethren, took each
man his sword, and came upon the city boldly, and slew all the males. 26.
And they slew Hamor and Shechem his son with the edge of the sword,
and took Dinah out of Shechem's house, and went out. 27. The sons of
Jacob came upon the slain, and spoiled the city, because they had defiled
their sister. 28. They took their sheep, and their oxen, and their asses,
and that which was in the city, and that which was in the field, 29. And
all their wealth, and all their little ones, and their wives took they captive,
and spoiled even all that was in the house. 30. And Jacob said to Simeon
and Levi, Ye have troubled me to make me to stink among the inhabitants
of the land, among the Canaanites and the Perizzites: and I being few in
number, they shall gather themselves together against me, and slay me;
and I shall be destroyed, I and my house. 31. And they said, Should he
deal with our sister as with an harlot?*

Failure in asking the next question

Throughout the narratives of the patriarchal families, one can see the dangers in human thinking. The need to think beyond the obvious, to ask the next question, is always required for one to be in tune with the mind of God. Humans can easily be fooled by the first thought, the comment that makes us feel good. We never ask what the long-term effects will be if we follow through on the feel-good thought.

This event with all of its morbid tragedy teaches the importance of 'asking the next question' in several instances. First, the men of Shechem failed to ask the meaning of circumcision to the sons of Jacob. For them, it was an initiation into marriage, but for Jacob's sons, it was a covenant relationship that identified them with the hope of the promise of Abraham. That promise did not include the Canaanites. Abraham, Isaac, and now Jacob had carefully avoided intermarriage with the Canaanites who were to be dispossessed of the land. The Canaanites were looking to seal their own control of the patriarchal families (34:22-23). A little further investigation on their part would have helped them to know that Jacob's sons would not allow this marriage to occur.

Second, Jacob's sons perceived their sister as having been defiled. As part of the Abrahamic promise, they also viewed the land as theirs already, though not in their possession. With this attitude the brothers rightly perceived that the people of the land had nothing to offer them. Thus, the friendly gesture on the part of Hamor (34:8-10) would not have been perceived as so friendly by Jacob's sons. Jacob's sons asked the next question. What does this alliance mean to the hope of the promise? '...and the men were grieved, and they were very wroth, because he had wrought folly in Israel in lying with Jacob's daughter; which thing ought not to be done' (34:7).

As the story progresses, we see Jacob's sons devising the scheme for punishment. Their problem, in this situation was that they failed to ask the next question about their scheme. What will be the long-term effect of their solution? It obviously made them feel avenged (34:31), but did it accomplish the purpose of spot-lighting the sin against their sister, or only make them appear as the real sinners in the story?

> The need to think! It is a hard discipline. Most people would rather just feel. Thinking requires going beyond feelings, and asks difficult questions, and seek answers. We should seek wisdom in the next question to ask, so that we may be attuned to his answer in our life, and not simply respond to a feeling, whether it be good or bad.

'...Ye have troubled me...'

The life of Jacob was characterized by deceit. In this story (chapter 34), his sons show themselves to be chips off the old block. It is apparent that Jacob had taken the time to do some instruction about the hope of the promise of Abraham, now incorporated into his family. Jacob's new name, Israel, given to him by God (32:28), is already established as the covenant name for the community (34:7). Jacob had not taught his sons about the trouble one creates when trying to enforce God's will on humans by unholy ways. Jacob had evidently learned that the will of God cannot be changed, and God does not need human help to enforce it. This led to his own hesitancy to take action after the defilement of his daughter (34:5). Clearly, some action on the part of Jacob and his sons is required, but it must be action that does not dishonour God.

Simeon and Levi, full brothers to Dinah, slaughter all the men of Shechem after they had encouraged them to be circumcised, taking advantage of their weakened condition. Their only thought was for the honour of their sister. In their minds, they may have been establishing themselves as power brokers in the land. Jacob's words of chastisement tell a different story, '...Ye have troubled me to make me to stink among the inhabitants of the land, among the Canaanites and the Perizzites: and I being few in number, they shall gather themselves together against me, and ...I shall be destroyed, I and my house' (34:30).

The words of Jacob reveal that which a mature child of God should know. Punishment for sin is designed to clearly unmask and show the horror of sin. It must, therefore, be inflicted within the full framework of God's plan and action for it. When one assumes the role of God in inflicting punishment, he only opens the possibility of himself being punished.

Jacob's concern reflects his forgetting that the first requirement of his return to the Promised Land was the fulfilling of his vow at Bethel (28:19-22). At Bethel, in giving his tenth, he would have had great opportunity for teaching his family. At Shechem, he had been preoccupied with building stalls for his herds, and a house for himself (33:17-18).

Preoccupations! If we are not preoccupied with the things of God, we will forget to do the proper teaching to our children and forget the lessons we learned ourselves. Clearly Jacob had become preoccupied with the wrong things, and it led to his children's sins. God had this in mind when he gave the law to the nation of Israel. 'And these words...they shall be as frontlets between thine eyes' (Deuteronomy 6:6-8).

Genesis 35:1-29

Genesis 35:1-15

1. And God said unto Jacob, Arise, go up to Bethel, and dwell there: and make there an altar unto God, that appeared unto thee when thou fleddest from the face of Esau thy brother. 2. Then Jacob said unto his household, and to all that were with him, Put away the strange gods that are among you, and be clean, and change your garments: 3. And let us arise, and go up to Bethel; and I will make there an altar unto God, who answered me in the day of my distress, and was with me in the way which I went. 4. And they gave unto Jacob all the strange gods which were in their hand, and all their earrings which were in their ears; and Jacob hid them under the oak which was by Shechem. 5. And they journeyed: and the terror of God was upon the cities that were round about them, and they did not pursue after the sons of Jacob. 6. So Jacob came to Luz, which is in the land of Canaan, that is, Bethel, he and all the people that were with him. 7. And he built there an altar, and called the place Elbethel: because there God appeared unto him, when he fled from the face of his brother. 8. But Deborah Rebekah's nurse died, and she was buried beneath Bethel under an oak: and the name of it was called Allonbachuth. 9. And God appeared unto Jacob again, when he came out of Padanaram, and blessed him. 10. And God said unto him, Thy name is Jacob: thy name shall not be called any more Jacob, but Israel shall be thy name: and he called his name Israel. 11. And God said unto him, I am God Almighty: be fruitful and multiply; a nation and a company of nations shall be of thee, and kings shall come out of thy loins; 12. And the land which I gave Abraham and Isaac, to thee I will give it, and to thy seed after thee will I give the land. 13. And God went up from him in the place where he talked with him. 14. And Jacob set up a pillar in the place where he talked with him, even a pillar of stone: and he poured a drink offering thereon, and he poured oil thereon. 15. And Jacob called the name of the place where God spake with him, Bethel.

El-Bethel

The many ways that God works in the affairs of men leave us awestruck with each encounter. Jacob, at the beginning of Chapter 35 has just been through a very disappointing time. His daughter, Dinah, is defiled by a Canaanite (34:1-2). His sons had committed a foul act of deception and revenge for the deed done to their sister (34:25-27). Jacob is now terrified that the Canaanites will seek some sort of reprisal (34:30). During this series of events, Jacob lived near the city of Shechem, taking care of his private business interests (33:17-18). This was in clear disobedience to the command of God that had called for Jacob to return to Bethel, and fulfil his vow concerning the tithe (31:13).

The sadness of Dinah's defilement, and the treachery of Jacob's sons, were not God's plan. Bethel was! God uses this event to force Jacob back to Bethel. Jacob's fear of the Canaanites moved him to action. He had become comfortable, and life was pleasant for him, thus obedience to God was unimportant. With his fear established, his desire to obey God is re-established.

In a quickly paced series of events, Jacob seizes the spiritual headship of his family. He orders that all idols, and jewelry associated with idols, be given to him. Evidently, his servants had brought idols into the land upon leaving Padanaram. The demand, no doubt includes the idols Rachel had stolen from her father, Laban. All the trinkets are buried in the ground, and left behind (35:1-4). He then takes his family to Bethel, and builds an altar for the purpose of sacrifice (Genesis 35:7). He gives an additional name to the place. The original name, Bethel (house of God) is now called El-bethel. El is an ancient name for God. Jacob calls the place 'the God of the house of God.' Note the spiritual growth of Jacob. His first encounter with God was in this place. He stated at that time '...Surely the Lord is in this place...' (28:16). He takes a further step in the confession of Genesis 35:7. God is not limited to Bethel. He is the God of every place. By putting away all the idols, and by this confession at the altar, Jacob is being the teacher to his family that he should be. God is the God of every place. That confession requires full obedience and allegiance. God used the tragedy of the sins of Jacob's family to get him to keep his vow. Considering what it sometimes requires to move one to obedience to God should be sobering for all believers.

> It is always wonderful to see the work of God. His will is not changed, and cannot be stopped. His ways are indeed wonderful. He will take the foolishness of humans and use it to accomplish His purpose in us. This can sometimes mean great trouble for the Christian.

The greatest danger

The first few verses of chapter 35 reveal a man of action. The character of Jacob that we had come to know was one of a decisive person. There is a lapse in that decisive nature when he is faced with dealing with the defilement of his daughter (34:5), but the decisive Jacob has returned. There is a notable difference, however. In this instance, he is acting decisively to obey God instead of jumping ahead of God. The writer of the Scripture provides a marvellous explanatory note. It is one of those wonderful concepts that the believer can only know in hindsight. It must be accepted by faith in the context of the moment.

The explanatory note is in verse 5. 'And they journeyed: and the terror of God was upon the cities that were round about them, and they did not pursue after the sons of Jacob.' The words here are critical in light of Jacob's earlier statement '...they shall gather themselves together against me, and slay me; and I shall be destroyed, I and my house' (34:30). Jacob's terror was due to the actions of his sons (34:25-27).

Where might we find the learning event? Jacob had been putting off (evidently for years) the requirement of returning to Bethel and fulfilling his vow (31:13). In the midst of what he thought was perfect safety, and ideal living, he built up a reputation with the people of the land and expanded his personal business (33:17-19). The succeeding story about his daughter's fascination with the Canaanites, her defilement, and the violent reprisal of her brothers reveals the great danger in Jacob's life, which he had not perceived. Disobedience to God is the single greatest danger for any child of God. The irony here is that Jacob was in greatest danger when he thought he was safe, and was safest when he thought he was in the greatest danger. Thanks to the writer of Scripture, we know what Jacob could not know. He could only trust God. By returning to Bethel, he was in God's will and finally being obedient. There, he was safe.

Life has many kinds of dangers. We must learn that the greatest harm that can befall us is the defilement of the world. To avoid that defilement, we must love God more, and be vigilant to being in his will for our life.

One day, Jesus was asked the question, '...What good thing shall I do, that I may have eternal life (Matthew 19:16)? The reply, '...go and sell that thou hast, and give to the poor,...and come and follow me' (Matthew 19:21). The lesson is that humans must look beyond the material things of this world for their safety nets.

Drink offering

The text presents Jacob in a final defining moment. For most of his life, to this point, he has been on the run. He had hastened to take advantage of his brother, Esau, competed with his uncle Laban to see who could out-duel the other in deceitfulness and treachery, and hesitatingly returned to face his brother, Esau, whom he had deceived. In the middle of this, he had an encounter with God, and had made a vow (28:22). We finally see him fulfilling the vow (35:7-8). There is much heartache to come in Jacob's life, but he is now prepared to handle it, and knows the true source of his strength.

We are not told in this text that Jacob gave the tenth of his possessions in the sacrifice on the altar. Indirectly, however, it is made clear. Verse 14 states 'And Jacob set up...a pillar of stone: and he poured a drink offering thereon, and he poured oil thereon.' This is the first mention of a drink offering in Scripture. In Numbers 15, the drink offering is associated with the sacrifices of Israel once they possess the land. It is a sacrifice made in connection with a vow. '...When ye be come into the land...And will make...a sacrifice in performing a vow...and the fourth part of a hin of wine for a drink offering shalt thou prepare with the burnt offering...' (Numbers 15:2-5). Jacob's offering was the forerunner to the offerings that were connected with a vow.

At this point of commitment to the rulership of God, Jacob hears again the words of blessing from God, and for a second time, the change of his name is stated. '...thy name shall not be called any more Jacob, but Israel shall be thy name...' (35:10). The restatement of the new name is emblematic of God's grace and God's sovereignty. For too long, Jacob had delayed his return to Bethel. God has clearly forgiven him, and at the same time is making the statement that Jacob is at Bethel because God brought him there. Jacob will face some great disappointments, and he must be confident in the reality of God's control if he is to endure. Every believer is called upon to take the name of Christ (as Christian) acknowledging God's control. Jacob must take the name God has given him. It will be the reminder of his source of strength in the future.

Genesis 35:16-22

16. And they journeyed from Bethel; and there was but a little way to come to Ephrath: and Rachel travailed, and she had hard labour. 17. And it came to pass, when she was in hard labour, that the midwife said unto her, Fear not; thou shalt have this son also. 18. And it came to pass, as her soul was in departing, (for she died) that she called his name Benoni: but his father called him Benjamin. 19. And Rachel died, and was buried in the way to Ephrath, which is Bethlehem. 20. And Jacob set a pillar upon her grave: that is the pillar of Rachel's grave unto this day. 21. And Israel journeyed, and spread his tent beyond the tower of Edar. 22. And it came to pass, when Israel dwelt in that land, that Reuben went and lay with Bilhah his father's concubine: and Israel heard it. Now the sons of Jacob were twelve.

Rachel's death

The awful moments that enter our life at the death of someone we love are deep valleys. Those valleys are more often and more terrible for some but thankfully, rare, for most of us. The death of a spouse or child is bitter, and changes our lives forever. No one can ever be the same after walking through that valley. In this text, Jacob must deal with the death of his beloved Rachel. The writer shows the perspective of one who is submitted to the Lord.

Rachel dies in giving birth to her second son. It was at the birth of her first son, Joseph, that she called for God to give her another son (30:24). There is a sense in which one must be careful what he or she asks of God. One can only wonder, when examining the tragedy of Rachel, if God's grace had not been an active part of Rachel's many years of barrenness. Is it possible that barrenness prolonged her life, and that she unwittingly prayed for her own demise? Could that be why Jesus taught us to pray '...thy will be done...' (Matthew 6:10)?

Rachel names her second son 'Benoni' which means 'son of my sorrow.' The obvious application is about Rachel's dying moments, but there seems to be a greater spiritual reflection here. Perhaps she has reference to both a physical suffering and to her own disposition toward God. The name of her son could be a statement of repentance for her spiritual shortcomings. Rachel's name comes to be associated with the sorrow that is part of the nation punished for its sin and carried into exile (Jeremiah 31:15).

The new person, Israel, changes the name of his son, calling him Benjamin, 'son of my right hand' (35:18). The name signifies a place of honour in the family. Israel (Jacob) has lost the true love of his life. It could be one of those awful valleys that inspire bitterness. Benjamin's birth had cost him his beloved. It is not unusual for one to have many years of tragic resentment towards the child in this kind of situation. Because Israel had now submitted to God, he found triumph, and drew Benjamin to himself. The clear lesson is the difference that full submission to God can make in our lives when we are struggling with the hurts and the dark valleys of life.

> It is a very tough hill to climb, that hill in the midst of great loss, which requires us to believe God and trust him. Yet, that is the only place life can be rebuilt. A prior commitment to the concept aids us when the trial comes.

Jacob, or Israel

The rest of the Genesis narrative presents the reader with a perplexing problem. God has changed Jacob's name to Israel (35:10).

One would expect that the narrative would, from this point, be referring to the man, Israel. When Abraham's name was changed from Abram, he is never again called Abram. Why does the name go back and forth when the name of Abraham's grandson is changed? There does not seem to be a direct answer in Scripture, but there are some analogies.

The use of Jacob and Israel reflect two names but mostly two characters that dwell in the same person. Jacob is submitted to God, after several defining moments in his life (Genesis 25:33, 28:22, 32:28, 35:7). However, he is never fully comfortable, and his submission will be regularly tested. Abraham comes to the ultimate moment in his willingness to sacrifice Isaac.

This pattern seems to picture the life of most believers in Christ. We have those moments of commitment, and then we become weak and backslide. We question if obedience to the way of God will be best for us. We become attracted to the pleasures of this world and think God may be cheating us. We think God is working too slowly, and we must help, and speed things up in our life. Our inability to fully submit to God causes us to act like Christians sometimes, and like non-Christians sometimes. Sometimes we are Jacob, sometimes we are Israel.

The sad feature of the life of a follower of God is that spiritual life too often emulates Jacob, not Abraham. Would it not be wonderful if we could arrive at the point where we are in total and peaceful submission to the will of God? We can reach that position only when we fully immerse ourselves in the first commandment. '…Thou shall love the Lord thy God with all thy heart, and with all thy soul, and with all thy mind' (Matthew 22:37).

Genesis 35:23-29

23. The sons of Leah; Reuben, Jacob's firstborn, and Simeon, and Levi, and Judah, and Issachar, and Zebulun: 24. The sons of Rachel; Joseph, and Benjamin: 25. And the sons of Bilhah, Rachel's handmaid; Dan, and Naphtali: 26. And the sons of Zilpah, Leah's handmaid: Gad, and Asher:

these are the sons of Jacob, which were born to him in Padanaram. 27. And Jacob came unto Isaac his father unto Mamre, unto the city of Arbah, which is Hebron, where Abraham and Isaac sojourned. 28. And the days of Isaac were an hundred and fourscore years. 29. And Isaac gave up the Ghost, and died, and was gathered unto his people, being old and full of days: and his sons Esau and Jacob buried him.

'...Reuben...lay with Bilhah...'

This incident is briefly inserted into the Scriptures. There is no story development. We only know that Israel (Jacob) was aware of it expressing the reality of his grief about it. Nothing more is said. It is a shock to our senses coming on the heels of Jacob's spiritual triumph at Bethel. The eldest son takes his father's concubine to himself. For the twentieth century reader, the whole idea of a concubine is repugnant. We might wonder why this is even mentioned at all. If concubines are allowed by the culture, should Reuben be singled out as a great sinner?

There are several reasons that Reuben's act is singled out. First, he devalued his father, showing no respect for his authority. Second, he showed despite for his half-brothers, Dan and Napthali, by having sex with their mother. He is creating grounds for them to despise their mother. If Reuben, as first-born son, is not punished, and receives the privileges that come with that position, the two brothers have grounds for despising their father. Third, Rueben's act presented the possibility of adding a child to the house of Jacob that was not born of the loins of Jacob. The risk Reuben took was a total disregard for that which God was doing through the house of Jacob. In every way, Reuben's act was despicable.

There is a further feature of Reuben's sin. That is the sin of presumption. As the older son, he had the right to the father's possessions upon his death. The ancient cultures allowed possession of the father's wives as a statement of the right of succession. Reuben acted to make his case early. Again, Reuben showed a clear lack of discernment. His father was the second son born, but he,

not the firstborn, had received the blessing and the birthright from
Isaac. Was Reuben fearful of the loss of the birthright as the oldest
son? He also recognized Jacob's love for the two sons of Rachel,
and may have worried that they would supersede him. What did
Reuben not understand?

Throughout the story of the patriarchs, we see that the blessing
and the birthright are primarily fastened in the promise of God.
God always decided who got the birthright. There is an earthly
meaning, but the real attachment is not to the promise, but to the
God of the promise. Reuben's mistake was to fail to see the spiritual nature of the blessing and then to attach himself to God. Instead, he attached himself to the earthly promise that led him to
his despicable sin. Our lesson is to examine our hearts. How much
do we attach to this earth, and thus devalue our relationship with
God?

> With a little meditation, one can see a connection and ap-
> plication to the words of Christ in Reuben's sin. 'But seek
> ye first the kingdom of God, and his righteousness...' (Mat-
> thew 6:33). The need for the attitude Christ commanded
> is that failure to do his will causes us to devalue our re-
> lationship with God. Reuben became so enamoured with
> the promise of God that he failed to value the God of the
> promise. He could have saved himself a great deal of dis-
> appointment with a little different set of priorities.

Completion of a journey

This text doesn't seem to say much that would reflect upon one's relationship with God. It appears as a mere recitation of the names of
Jacob's sons, and of the death of his father. The recitation of these
names, however, is critical for understanding God's plan. Jacob's
new name is Israel. He shall be called by both names (Jacob and
Israel) as the narrative proceeds. The reader shall learn that God

was revealing his game plan by giving Jacob a new name. Abraham had many sons. One was by his handmaiden, Hagar. One was by his wife, Sarah, and there were many sons by Keturah, the wife he chose after the passing of Sarah. Only Isaac, Sarah's son, was chosen as part of the promise. Isaac had two sons who were Esau and Jacob. Only Jacob was chosen to be heir to the Abrahamic promise. Jacob had twelve sons. He is named Israel. For the first time in the patriarchal history, all sons are a part of the promised nation. The recitation of these names is a statement that God is in control of history. A new nation is created and it is totally at God's discretion and power that it happens. The God of Abraham, Isaac, and Jacob is not only in control of the patriarchs, he is in control of the nations. He creates them, and he can bring them to an end.

The death of Isaac brings us full circle in the life of Jacob. God has completed his promise to Jacob. 'And, behold, I am with thee, and will keep thee in all places whither thou goest, and will bring thee again into this land; for I will not leave thee, until I have done that which I have spoken to thee of' (28:15). Several events now come together. In the completion of his geographical journey, Jacob has also completed a spiritual journey. The spiritual journey is the most important. In his battles to be on top of circumstances, he has learned that being on top begins with submission to God's authority. The way to the top is at the bottom. He had fled from Esau who swore to kill him at his father's death. He now stands beside Esau at his father's funeral without fear. He has learned that the fear of God which he first encountered at Bethel (28:16-17), is the key to living without fear of all other things. The Psalmist expressed it, 'The fear of the Lord is the beginning of wisdom...' (Psalms 111:10). The story of Jacob is the story for many believers. We think the struggles of our life are about our need to get on top of our circumstances, when, in fact, they are actually our struggle to submit to God.

It is a wonderful thing, and a defining moment in a person's life, when he can truly understand the nature of the battle he has in life. Almost all of the major battles of life can be named in one's struggle to submit to the will of God. Our problem is that we think we are fighting some other battle.

Genesis 36-37

I. Esau's Genealogy (36:1-43)

II. Lessons from the Patriarchs (37:1)

III. Joseph's Conflict with His Brothers (37:2-28)
1. Coat of many colours
2. Joseph's dreams

IV. Lessons from Joseph's Family at His Loss (37:29-36)
1. Sad state of Reuben
2. Simplistic rationalization
3. '…he refused to be comforted…'

Genesis 36:1-43

1. Now these are the generations of Esau, who is Edom. 2. Esau took his wives of the daughters of Canaan; Adah the daughter of Elon the Hittite, and Aholibamah the daughter of Anah the daughter of Zibeon the Hivite; 3. And Bashemath Ishmael's daughter, sister of Nebajoth. 4. And Adah bare to Esau Eliphaz; and Bashemath bare Reuel; 5. And Aholibamah bare Jeush, and Jaalam, and Korah: these are the sons of Esau, which were born unto him in the land of Canaan. 6. And Esau took his wives, and his sons, and his daughters, and all the persons of his house, and his cattle, and all his beasts, and all his substance, which he had got in the land of Canaan; and went into the country from the face of his brother Jacob. 7. For their riches were more than that they might dwell together; and the land wherein they were strangers could not bear them because of their cattle. 8. Thus dwelt Esau in mount Seir: Esau is Edom. 9. And these are the generations of Esau the father of the Edomites in mount Seir: 10. These are the names of Esau's sons; Eliphaz the son of Adah the wife of Esau, Reuel the son of Bashemath the wife of Esau. 11. And the sons of Eliphaz were Teman, Omar, Zepho, and Gatam, and Kenaz. 12. And Timna was concubine to Eliphaz Esau's son; and she bare to Eliphaz Amalek: these were the sons of Adah Esau's wife. 13. And these are the sons of Reuel; Nahath, and Zerah, Shammah, and Mizzah: these were the sons of Bashemath Esau's wife. 14. And these were the sons of Aholibamah, the daughter of Anah the daughter of Zibeon, Esau's wife: and she bare to Esau Jeush, and Jaalam, and Korah. 15. These were dukes of the sons of Esau: the sons of Eliphaz the firstborn son of Esau; duke Teman, duke Omar, duke Zepho, duke Kenaz,

16. Duke Korah, duke Gatam, and duke Amalek: these are the dukes that came of Eliphaz in the land of Edom; these were the sons of Adah. 17. And these are the sons of Reuel Esau's son; duke Nahath, duke Zerah, duke Shammah, duke Mizzah: these are the dukes that came of Reuel in the land of Edom; these are the sons of Bashemath Esau's wife. 18. And these are the sons of Aholibamah Esau's wife; duke Jeush, duke Jaalam, duke Korah: these were the dukes that came of Aholibamah the daughter of Anah, Esau's wife. 19. These are the sons of Esau, who is Edom, and these are their dukes. 20. These are the sons of Seir the Horite, who inhabited the land; Lotan, and Shobal, and Zibeon, and Anah, 21. And Dishon, and Ezer, and Dishan: these are the dukes of the Horites, the children of Seir in the land of Edom. 22. And the children of Lotan were Hori and Hemam; and Lotan's sister was Timna. 23. And the children of Shobal were these; Alvan, and Manahath, and Ebal, Shepho, and Onam. 24. And these are the children of Zibeon; both Ajah, and Anah: this was that Anah that found the mules in the wilderness, as he fed the asses of Zibeon his father. 25. And the children of Anah were these; Dishon, and Aholibamah the daughter of Anah. 26. And these are the children of Dishon; Hemdan, and Eshban, and Ithran, and Cheran. 27. The children of Ezer are these; Bilhan, and Zaavan, and Akan. 28. The children of Dishan are these; Uz, and Aran. 29. These are the dukes that came of the Horites; duke Lotan, duke Shobal, duke Zibeon, duke Anah, 30. Duke Dishon, duke Ezer, duke Dishan: these are the dukes that came of Hori, among their dukes in the land of Seir. 31. And these are the kings that reigned in the land of Edom, before there reigned any king over the children of Israel. 32. And Bela the son of Beor reigned in Edom: and the name of his city was Dinhabah. 33. And Bela died, and Jobab the son of Zerah of Bozrah reigned in his stead. 34. And Jobab died, and Husham of the land of Temani reigned in his stead. 35. And Husham died, and Hadad the son of Bedad, who smote Midian in the field of Moab, reigned in his stead: and the name of his city was Avith. 36. And Hadad died, and Samlah of Masrekah reigned in his stead. 37. And Samlah died, and Saul of Rehoboth by the river reigned in his stead. 38. And Saul died, and Baalhanan the son of Achbor reigned in his stead.

39. And Baalhanan the son of Achbor died, and Hadar reigned in his stead: and the name of his city was Pau; and his wife's name was Meheta-bel, the daughter of Matred, the daughter of Mezahab. 40. And these are the names of the dukes that came of Esau, according to their families, af-ter their places, by their names; duke Timnah, duke Alvah, duke Jetheth, 41. Duke Aholibamah, duke Elah, duke Pinon, 42. Duke Kenaz, duke Teman, duke Mibzar, 43. Duke Magdiel, duke Iram: these be the dukes of Edom, according to their habitations in the land of their possession: he is Esau the father of the Edomites.

Esau's genealogy

At first glance, Chapter 36 presents a dull recitation of Esau's de-scendants. Most are ancient names that are strange to us and have an uncertain pronunciation. The recitation details the development of the nation of Edom, which shall be the subject of much hostility with Israel. The descendants of one named Seir, a Horite, are also named (36:20). Finally, there is a listing of the Kings of Edom, the nation descending from Esau. Evidently, there was a blending of the Horites and the children of Esau, and Esau's family became dominant. This is the fulfilment of God's promise to Rebekah '... Two nations are in thy womb, and two manner of people shall be separated from thy bowels...' (25:23).

This genealogical listing is critical to our developing under-standing of God. The reader is allowed closure on the tragic figure of Esau. His fate was settled at birth in God's choice. In many ways he was a sympathetic character. Esau is seen here as one who has personally triumphed. He leaves the land of Canaan and dwells in

Mount Seir. He has accepted that he has no place in the possession of the land, but he is personally prosperous. Esau appears wealthy and content. Clearly, God's grace has prevailed. There is no reason to feel sympathy for Esau. Though Jacob is the greater name and has the place of prominence as far as salvation and biblical history is concerned, Esau is rewarded according to that which he most valued. How can we question the judgement of God in that scenario?

Except for the deceit of his brother, Esau's life was much the easier. Jacob suffered greatly for his sins and deceitfulness. He is yet to pay an even heavier price as his own sons deceive him about his beloved son, Joseph. He will die outside the land of promise. He will live out the rest of his life as a cripple. Early on, Jacob had placed value on the promise of Abraham. He wanted the long-term blessing more than momentary satisfaction. It took a long time for him to learn how to relate to the God of the blessing. In the end, he does have the greater eternal reward because he valued the greater treasure.

It is not as easy as one might think to evaluate where one truly has his treasure. Often, it takes a trial to help us understand the misplaced priorities of our life. It is an effective prayer to ask God's revelation of that which we truly deem as the greater values in our life, and to make sure it agrees with God's standard of measurement.

Genesis 37:1

1. And Jacob dwelt in the land wherein his father was a stranger, in the land of Canaan.

Lessons from the patriarchs

The story of the patriarchs has taken us through three lives. Through their lives God will manifest his glorious action in the making of a nation. The stories of Abraham, Isaac, and Jacob are monuments to two great facts: First, the sovereignty of God in human affairs. Second, the struggle of humans to properly relate to a sovereign God.

Key lessons that we learn are: 1) Believers in God often rebel against God. This is caused by several things: circumstances that create a lapse in faith, a desire to run ahead of God and do things by one's own design instead of by faith, a lack of appreciation for the value of relationship to God, and a lack of sufficient knowledge about God. Most people are in a natural state of rebellion against God. Our three patriarchs (Abraham, Isaac, and Jacob) had a basic appreciation for God, and did not desire rebellion, but often fell into its trap because of the aforementioned things.

2) God's knowledge of humans is greater than our knowledge of self. God's choice of Abraham, and his choice of Isaac over Ishmael, Jacob over Esau was based on omniscience about the nature of these men. Filled with the natural human flaws, and weaknesses, they were each drawn to the importance of relationship to God. Who is to say why one person responds to the value of spiritual things and another will never be impressed? God knows every human heart, and that is why we must learn to trust his wisdom and choices above our own. Isaac desired to give the blessing to Esau, but God intended it for Jacob. Clearly, God knew best.

3) God never loses control. Humans may rebel, but they cannot thwart God's plan. The patriarchs teach us that our rebellion against God will make things tougher on us, and may lead us

through difficult valleys that we might have avoided by paying attention to our relationship to him. In the long run, he will prevail. God will make the nation through which all nations will be blessed. God will make the seed of Abraham, Isaac, and Jacob to multiply. God will straighten out whatever mess the patriarchs create. If we live by the great commandment, '...Thou shalt love the Lord thy God with all thy heart...soul...mind...' (Matthew 22:37), our lives will more easily achieve its purpose.

Genesis 37:2-28

2. These are the generations of Jacob. Joseph, being seventeen years old, was feeding the flock with his brethren; and the lad was with the sons of Bilhah, and with the sons of Zilpah, his father's wives: and Joseph brought unto his father their evil report. 3. Now Israel loved Joseph more than all his children, because he was the son of his old age: and he made him a coat of many colours. 4. And when his brethren saw that their father loved him more than all his brethren, they hated him, and could not speak peaceably unto him. 5. And Joseph dreamed a dream, and he told it his brethren: and they hated him yet the more. 6. And he said unto them, Hear, I pray you, this dream which I have dreamed: 7. For, Behold, we were binding sheaves in the field, and, lo, my sheaf arose, and also stood upright; and, behold, your sheaves stood round about, and made obeisance to my sheaf. 8. And his brethren said to him, Shalt thou indeed reign over us? or shalt thou indeed have dominion over us? And they hated him yet the more for his dreams, and for his words. 9. And he dreamed yet another dream, and told it his brethren, and said, Behold, I have dreamed a dream more; and, behold, the sun and the moon and the eleven stars made obeisance to me. 10. And he told it to his father, and to his brethren: and his father rebuked him, and said unto him, What is this dream that thou hast dreamed? Shall I and thy mother and thy brethren indeed come to bow down ourselves to thee to the earth? 11. And his brethren envied him; but his father observed the saying. 12. And his brethren went to feed their father's flock in Shechem. 13. And Israel said unto Joseph, Do not thy brethren feed the flock in Shechem? come, and I will send thee unto them. And he said to him, Here am I. 14. And he said to him, Go, I pray thee, see whether it be well with thy brethren, and well with the flocks; and bring me word again. So he sent him out of the vale of Hebron, and he came to Shechem. 15. And a certain man found him, and, behold, he was wandering in the field: and the man asked him, saying, What seekest thou? 16. And he said, I seek my brethren: tell me, I pray thee, where they feed their flocks. 17. And the man said, They are departed hence; for I heard them say, Let us go to Dothan. And Joseph went after his brethren, and found them in Dothan. 18. And when they saw him afar off, even before he came near unto them, they conspired against him to slay him. 19. And they said one to another, Behold, this dreamer cometh. 20. Come now therefore, and let us slay him, and cast him into some pit, and we will say, Some evil beast hath devoured him: and we shall see what will become of his dreams. 21. And Reuben heard it, and he delivered him out of their hands; and said, Let us not kill him. 22. And Reuben said unto them, Shed no blood, but cast him into this pit that is in the wilderness, and lay no hand upon him; that he might rid him out of their hands, to deliver him to his father again. 23. And it came to pass, when Joseph was come unto his brethren, that they stript Joseph out of his coat, his coat of many colours that was on him; 24. And they took him, and cast him into a pit: and the pit was empty, there was no water in it. 25. And they sat down to eat bread: and they lifted up their eyes and looked, and, behold, a company of Ishmeelites came from Gilead with their camels bearing spicery and balm and myrrh, going to carry it down to Egypt. 26. And Judah said unto his brethren, What profit is it if we slay our brother, and conceal his blood? 27. Come, and let us sell him to the Ishmeelites, and let not our hand be upon him; for he is our brother and our flesh. And his brethren were content. 28. Then there passed by Midianites merchantmen; and they drew and lifted up Joseph out of the pit, and sold Joseph to the Ishmeelites for twenty pieces of silver: and they brought Joseph into Egypt.

Coat of many colours

In Genesis 15:12-13, there is given to Abraham a prophecy. '… Know of a surety that thy seed shall be a stranger in a land that is not theirs, and shall serve them; and they shall afflict them four hundred years…' Chapter 37 begins the process of getting the seed of Abraham to that foreign land.

In the sons of Jacob, human passions are at their worst. Extreme cruelty is the result. In God's omniscience, he knew how the sons of Jacob would act. He uses their natural inclinations to work out his plan. The human tendencies to lie, to show bias, and envy all manifest themselves.

Joseph's story is introduced, and the writer makes clear that Jacob has not hidden his favouritism. '...he made him a coat of many colours' (37:3). This coat was typical of that worn by tribal leaders, and marked Joseph as chosen by Jacob to be the chief of the family, hence, ruler of the tribes of Israel. Jacob is committing a similar sin to Isaac, who sought to bestow the blessing on his favourite son. God has not yet declared who will be ruler in the household.

Close examination of this sibling rivalry provides scrutiny of one's own life, in addition to revealing how God works in human lives. Joseph, next to youngest of Jacob's twelve sons, is given a place of leadership in the family. After being in the field with his half-brothers, he '...he brought unto his father their evil report' (37:2). There is no mention of the nature of the evil, leading the reader to reason for himself. The 'coat of many colours' (37:3) denotes leadership. By connecting the coat and the evil report, it becomes clear that Joseph, the much younger brother, was put in charge of the older brothers.

Mistakes are everywhere. Jacob (perhaps the most culpable) should never have entrusted this kind of responsibility to one so young. He places Joseph in a position where he could not be successful. Joseph, instead of having a little humility, and looking to learn from his brothers, assumed knowledge he did not have. The brothers who could have shown kindness by tutoring Joseph only responded with envy, and grew to hate their brother (37:4).

Ultimately, Joseph will be placed in the position of being a ruler in the most powerful nation on earth (41:37-41). The early mistakes of leadership that he learns here will be lessons that will pay off in the future. Clearly, there were mistakes made by Jacob,

Joseph, and his brothers. God, however, was not taken by surprise, and used it as training ground. Joseph later understood this (Genesis 50:19-20).

There is a way to benefit from the mistakes of our life. The best way to keep a mistake from being a tragedy is to make sure we learn the right lessons from it. Joseph is a great example of one who always learned his lessons well, and did not repeat his mistakes.

Joseph's dreams

Joseph's youthful exuberance and naiveté are principle characteristics of this narrative. Yet, it is clear that the events are very much orchestrated by God. The enmity of Joseph's brothers is already apparent (37:4), and God allows their anger to be used in getting his divine plan in place.

Joseph has two dreams that he relates to his brothers. There is no mistaking the dreams' meaning. The brothers of Joseph immediately recognize the implications. 'And his brethren said to him, 'Shalt thou indeed reign over us? Or shalt thou indeed have dominion over us? And they hated him yet the more for his dreams…' (37:8). God ultimately uses the dreams to stir the brothers to action (37:18).

In the scriptural setting, there are other purposes. The writer is once again establishing the clear control of God. Just as Abraham, Isaac, and Jacob had learned to submit to God's will, it is now the sons who must learn the lesson. By the prophecy expressed in the dreams, the brothers (though years later) will understand who is in control of things. Ultimately, they will bow to Joseph, but it is to God that their submission is to be turned. Unfortunately, for most humans, we must be humbled before man before we will be humbled before God. Joseph will learn his humility, through many years of servant-hood, after his brothers commit their foul deed. By virtue of the hearing of Joseph's dream, the brothers will not fail to recognize the author of events when they encounter Joseph years later. As cruel as it seems for Joseph to be rubbing it in (so to speak), it was necessary because, through it, they would learn of God.

In addition, Jacob's reaction to the dreams is interesting. 'And his brethren envied him; but his father observed the saying' (37:11). The idea is that Jacob saw the dream as God's statement. Perhaps he was influenced by his own vision at Bethel. His earlier rebuke to Joseph (37:10) seems to be overruled by an acceptance of the dream as the plan of God. Jacob, too, is still learning submission to God. Isn't it interesting how the idea of submission to God keeps recurring over and over in Scripture? Perhaps it is because submission is the single most difficult step in learning to 'love the Lord thy God' (Matthew 22:37).

> Though not always readily apparent, there are many striking parallels that one may draw between the life of Jesus and Joseph. It is a touch of irony and of supernatural origin. The last hero in the book of Genesis reminds of he who is the beginning and the end (Revelation 1:11). In this story one is reminded of the jealousy of the religious elite of Israel towards Christ.

Genesis 37:29-36

29. And Reuben returned unto the pit; and, behold, Joseph was not in the pit; and he rent his clothes. 30. And he returned unto his brethren, and said, The child is not; and I, whither shall I go? 31. And they took Joseph's coat, and killed a kid of the goats, and dipped the coat in the blood; 32. And they sent the coat of many colours, and they brought it to their father; and said, This have we found: know now whether it be thy son's coat or no. 33. And he knew it, and said, It is my son's coat; an evil beast hath devoured

him; Joseph is without doubt rent in pieces. 34. And Jacob rent his clothes, and put sackcloth upon his loins, and mourned for his son many days. 35. And all his sons and all his daughters rose up to comfort him; but he refused to be comforted; and he said, For I will go down into the grave unto my son mourning. Thus his father wept for him. 36. And the Midianites sold him into Egypt unto Potiphar, an officer of Pharaoh's, and captain of the guard.

Sad state of Reuben

The words are extremely shocking. Joseph's brothers plan to kill him. They agreed to do so in an extremely cruel way. He would be placed in an abandoned cistern from which he could not escape without help, and left to die of exposure, starvation, and thirst (37:21-24). Reuben, the older brother intended to return and set him free, but before he could do so, the others seized the opportunity to sell Joseph to a merchant caravan on its way to Egypt.

The tragedy can fuel much speculation. The older brother, Reuben, obviously tries to rescue Joseph. His situation is quite revealing. Already in trouble in the family for his adultery with his father's concubine (35:22), Reuben knew, that as the eldest brother, he would receive the greatest blame for Joseph's demise. He did not desire to risk further harm in his relationship with his father. He may have wanted to return Joseph, secretly hoping, to regain lost favour by virtue of the private rescue.

Reuben's failure was his secrecy. Why would he hide his intention from his brothers? As the eldest, he was perfectly in his rights to step forward and call a halt to their scheme. Why did he not exercise it? He acted only to change the methodology, which gave him a chance to hide his intentions. Herein lies another of life's tragic traps. When Reuben acted to take possession of Jacob's concubine, he was staking his claim to the headship of the family. He wanted the leadership. In the situation he faces with Joseph, he refuses to lead by moral mandate. He will not take a stand that may make him unpopular with his brothers. Discretion is the better part of valour, but not when it means condoning evil. Many people want to lead, but will reject the most important part of leadership, moral authority. Reuben will condone evil to stay popular with his brothers.

Could it also be true that because of his action with Jacob's concubine, Reuben felt already estranged from his brothers, thus preventing him from taking a moral stand? Perhaps he did not desire to listen to his brothers speak of his immorality as he tried to stop their immoral act. His action with the concubine would forever make a farce out of any other attempts to lead. He was reduced to trying to lead by deceit, covering up his own intentions, and trying to maintain favour with his brothers.

> Actions in our lives are often taken for the purpose of pro-
> ducing momentary gratification. The permanent conse-
> quences to others, and to self, are not well thought out.
> The brothers thought only of satisfying their own jealousy,
> and did not see that this action would only serve to isolate
> them further from their father.

Simplistic rationalization

The selling of Joseph into slavery is a story that teaches much about the human mind and its reasoning. Reuben could have pre-vented the act by taking a moral stand and showing the leadership of the eldest brother. Instead, he opts for a secret plan that will ele-vate himself in his father's eyes and avoid the need to challenge his brothers. Judah, another of Joseph's brothers, is also mentioned by name. After Joseph is placed in the abandoned cistern, his brothers (Reuben absent) sat down to eat, and while eating, spot a caravan of Ishmaelites. These are descendants of the first son of Abraham (Ishmael). His descendancy has clearly grown very large by this time, and his family has become dominant in Midian. One should note that Ishmaelite and Midianite are used interchangeably (37:25-28). Judah takes centre stage with this suggestion, '...What profit is it if we slay our brother, and conceal his blood? Come, and let us sell him to the Ishmaelites, and let not our hand be upon him; for he is our brother and our flesh...' (37:26-27).

Judah's reasoning sounds familiar. Human rationalization often borders on the ridiculous with enough of a creative touch to makes it sound right and palatable. It is seen in two areas. First, why not make a profit out of Joseph's situation? They would sell him and increase their wealth. They might actually use the extra money to gain favour with their father, by claiming some special business action with the responsibility of the flocks. Have you ever heard someone justify a wrong action on the basis of a profit?

Second, if it is the Ishmaelites who harm Joseph, his brothers can claim innocence. '...and let not our hand be upon him; for he is our brother...' (37:27). This reasoning would be laughable were we not all guilty of it. Here is how: We talk ourselves down from a greater sin to a lesser sin, and then congratulate ourselves on overcoming temptation. We believe we have not sinned because we did not commit the greater sin. You and I may look at the statement of Judah and laugh at its simplicity and simple-mindedness. The benefit of distance from the moment gives us that perspective. Yet, in our own weak moments, we use the same logic without realizing its simple-mindedness.

The story here provides another allusion to the seed of the woman. As Joseph was betrayed for a few pieces of silver, so shall Jesus be betrayed for a few pieces of silver (Matthew 26:15-16). Both of these acts of betrayal work to great redemption as God's hand fashions the final results. Joseph was used in Egypt for his family's ultimate survival, the seed of the woman for providing redemption from sin. The tragedy in both instances was in the nature of the results on the perpetrators of betrayal. They each had their rationalisations. Let us pray that God will help us step back from our decisions and understand when our rationalisations may be foolish and simple-minded.

'...he refused to be comforted...'

Jacob's lamentation about the news of his son Joseph (37:32-35), leaves us feeling numb. One has no desire to make a life application, only to mourn with Jacob. He is truly to be pitied, and our hearts go out to him. Yet, there are points of learning that must be noted.

It was Jacob's partiality toward Joseph that had created this moment. The brothers of Joseph hated him. With the kind of venom in place that would lead to murder, it must have manifested itself in front of Jacob on many occasions. Why would Jacob send Joseph to his brothers where Joseph would be alone and helpless? Could it be that Jacob was so wrapped in his obsessive love for Rachel's son that he could not see what was going on around him? No doubt, Jacob prided himself on loving his son, but he lost sight of the larger picture. It is very common among us to be so involved in our own obsessions that we cannot imagine that the relationships around us are seeing things very differently. It is likely that Jacob didn't even know of the hatred of his sons. He may have assumed that they all thought as he did.

Also, when news of Joseph reached Jacob, he responded with total disdain for the family. 'And all his sons and all his daughters rose up to comfort him; but he refused to be comforted...' (37:35). Though Jacob could have no means of knowing or understanding, his refusal to be comforted did two things. First, he validated the evil that his sons had perpetrated on his beloved son, Joseph. If there had been any remorse that might lead them to confession and repentance, his shutting them out of his grief locked that possibility away. He guaranteed what they already believed. His love for Joseph was the sign of hatred for them. There are many times that our obsession with our own hurts and concerns lead to evil in others, and leads to helping them validate the rightness of their evil actions.

Second, Jacob failed to recognize the volatility of his grieving situation. Extreme tears and powerful grief leave visual images that others, especially those closest to us, never forget. If they are shut out of that grief process without explanation, and without the ability to provide aid, they will likely be shut off from ever knowing how to relate to us in a mutually beneficial fashion. We could grieve with Jacob, but the problem is, he won't let us.

> Emotions are the dessert of life. They give to life its most precious and memorable moments. And, emotions manifest themselves in very difficult moments. But dessert when eaten without other food that nourishes can create great harm to the body. A life based in emotions expended, without the nourishment of clear thinking can destroy us and those around us. Jacob was experiencing an extremely difficult moment. However, he used the emotion to shut others out of his life. His family perceived that Jacob's emotion was the only thing important to him.

Genesis 38-39

I. Judah's Moral Failure (38:1-30)
1. Judah takes a Canaanite wife
2. Judah goes in to Tamar
3. Judah's sons by Tamar

II. Joseph's Moral Test (39:1-19)
1. Joseph, a servant
2. A moment of temptation
3. '…how then can I…sin against God…'
4. '…and got him out…'
5. Importance of overcoming temptation

III. Joseph's Worsening Condition (39:20-23)
1. '…he was there in the prison…'
2. '…the Lord was with Joseph…'
3. The strength of Joseph

Genesis 38:1-30

1. And it came to pass at that time, that Judah went down from his brethren, and turned in to a certain Adullamite, whose name was Hirah. 2. And Judah saw there a daughter of a certain Canaanite, whose name was Shuah; and he took her, and went in unto her. 3. And she conceived, and bare a son; and he called his name Er. 4. And she conceived again, and bare a son; and she called his name Onan. 5. And she yet again conceived, and bare a son; and called his name Shelah: and he was at Chezib, when she bare him. 6. And Judah took a wife for Er his firstborn, whose name was Tamar. 7. And Er, Judah's firstborn, was wicked in the sight of the Lord; and the Lord slew him. 8. And Judah said unto Onan, Go in unto thy brother's wife, and marry her, and raise up seed to thy brother. 9. And Onan knew that the seed should not be his; and it came to pass, when he went in unto his brother's wife, that he spilled it on the ground, lest that he should give seed to his brother. 10. And the thing which he did displeased the Lord: wherefore he slew him also. 11. Then said Judah to Tamar his daughter in law, Remain a widow at thy father's house, till Shelah my son be grown: for he said, Lest peradventure he die also, as his brethren did. And Tamar went and dwelt in her father's house.

12. And in process of time the daughter of Shuah Judah's wife died; and Judah was comforted, and went up unto his sheepshearers to Timnath, he and his friend Hirah the Adullamite. 13. And it was told Tamar, saying, Behold thy father in law goeth up to Timnath to shear his sheep. 14. And she put her widow's garments off from her, and covered her with a vail, and wrapped herself, and sat in an open place, which is by the way to Timnath; for she saw that Shelah was grown, and she was not given unto him to wife. 15. When Judah saw her, he thought her to be an harlot; because she had covered her face. 16. And he turned unto her by the way, and said, Go to, I pray thee, let me come in unto thee; (for he knew not that she was his daughter in law.) And she said, What wilt thou give me, that thou mayest come in unto me? 17. And he said, I will send thee a kid from the Flock. And she said, Wilt thou give me a pledge, till thou send it? 18. And he said, What pledge shall I give thee? And she said, Thy signet, and thy Bracelets, and thy staff that is in thine hand. And he gave it her, and came in unto her, and she conceived by him. 19. And she arose, and went away, and laid by her vail from her, and put on the garments of her widowhood. 20. And Judah sent the kid by the hand of his friend the Adullamite, to receive his pledge from the woman's hand: but he found her not.

21. Then he asked the men of that place, saying, Where is the harlot, that was openly by the way side? And they said, There was no harlot in this place. 22. And he returned to Judah, and said, I cannot find her; and also the men of the place said, that there was no harlot in this place. 23. And Judah said, Let her take it to her, lest we be shamed: behold, I sent this kid, and thou hast not found her. 24. And it came to pass about three months after, that it was told Judah, saying, Tamar thy daughter in law hath played the harlot; and also, behold, she is with child by whoredom. And Judah said, Bring her forth, and let her be burnt. 25. When she was

*brought forth, she sent to her father in law, saying, By the man, whose
these are, am I with child: and she said, Discern, I pray thee, whose are
these, the signet, and bracelets, and staff. 26. And Judah acknowledged
them, and said, She hath been more righteous than I; because that I gave
her not to Shelah my son. And he knew her again no more. 27. And it
came to pass in the time of her travail, that, behold, twins were in her
womb. 28. And it came to pass, when she travailed, that the one put
out his hand: and the midwife took and bound upon his hand a scarlet
thread, saying, This came out first. 29. And it came to pass, as he drew
back his hand, that, behold, his brother came out: and she said, How
hast thou broken forth? this breach be upon thee: therefore his name was
called Pharez. 30. And afterward came out his brother, that had the scarlet thread upon his hand: and his name was called Zarah.*

Judah takes a Canaanite wife

Chapter 38 presents a strange story. It comes as an interlude between Joseph being sold into slavery and the discovery of what
happened to him in Egypt. Several things jolt us. Judah, who engineered the sale of Joseph into slavery, though sparing his life, had
already shown a propensity for cruelty. He continues his revolting
conduct. First, he marries a Canaanite woman who is not named.
She is referred to as the daughter of Shuah (38:2, 12). The act of
marrying a Canaanite woman is clearly a violation of the tradition
of the Abrahamic family that frowned on marriage to a woman
of the land. Abraham, Isaac, and Jacob had all taken their wives
from the family of Abraham in distant Haran. It is in this fact that
we discover why this story is presented.

We shall come to see that the chosen son which will receive
title to the promise given to Abraham, '...in thee shall all families
of the earth be blessed' (Genesis 12:3), is Judah. We will naturally
ask the question, 'How can Judah be the chosen son having taken
a Canaanite wife?' The answer is here. Note the pattern. 1) Judah
sins (38:2), forgetting the anger at the Canaanites for their action
with his sister, Dinah. 2) The first two sons born of this marriage are
evil (38:7, 9-10). When the natural heir, Er, dies, the second son

(Onan) is required to raise up children by him through accepting his brother's wife as his own. The children will be considered sons of the first-born. Onan refused to do this. He dies also. 3) The third son of Judah is too young, so Judah promised Tamar, whom Onan refused to honour, that she will be given to the third son when he reaches age (38:11). Judah evidently had no intention of doing this, perhaps feeling that Tamar was a bad omen having signalled the death of his first two sons. 4) Tamar deceives Judah, disguises herself as a harlot, and conceives children by him. Judah is later made aware of the deception. He can be commended for acting honourably in that revelation (38:26). 5) Ultimately, Tamar gives birth to twins (38:27-29). The significance of this story is that it is Judah's sons, by Tamar, not the Canaanite woman that is in the line of promise (Numbers 26:19-20). The genealogy of I Chronicles 2:3-5 indicates that no sons were born to Shelah. Israel, the nation, still in its birth stage, does not have its birth lines contaminated. The sins of Judah were an abomination, but God's plan still dominates, and Judah paid a heavy price in the death of his sons, and the revelation of his own character.

> The Bible teaches us that we shall reap what we sow. Judah's sin cost him the loss of two sons by death, estrangement from another, and the ultimate embarrassment of deception by his daughter-in-law.

Judah goes in to Tamar

Sometimes things in life are just unfair. Others get things we feel rightfully belong to us. We are victimized, and suddenly find ourselves in seemingly hopeless situations created by circumstances we could not have prevented. What do we do? Tamar had been chosen for the wife of Judah's son, Er. She was not the reason for the wickedness that caused his death (38:7). In her world, a woman's standing and security as a widow could only be maintained by having a child (preferably a son). She was given to Er's younger brother, Onan, to fulfil the role of near-kinsman and provide children in his brother's name. Onan's conduct causes his own death as he refuses to honour the responsibility of near kinsman (38:9). Tamar is promised that she will be given to Judah's third son when he reaches the proper age, but Judah does not act in accordance with the promise. Tamar is a victim who does not receive what is due her.

She acts to gain her rights by tricking Judah into being the near kinsman. Judah's wife dies (38:12), and Tamar plays the part of a Canaanite cultic harlot. The understanding of this cultic religious practice is in the family because Judah's wife was a Canaanite. Tamar, as wife, to the eldest son of Judah had become well schooled in its understanding, and knew exactly how to entice Judah. She had probably seen Judah doing this before.

The tragedy is an old story that keeps resurfacing in the narratives of Genesis, and in our lives. Tamar looked at her life and saw only the difficulty, and ignores trust in God, seeking to get what she deserves by actions displeasing to God. Our sympathy goes out to her. Judah's fascination with the practices of Canaanite worship leads us to believe that worship of the God of Abraham, Isaac, and Jacob has been ignored by Judah. He is enticed through his Canaanite wife. This background helps to understand many of the other stories of the Old Testament. The book of Judges is filled with narratives of the nation falling away from the faith of God, and turning to the worship of the people of Canaan. In the book of Ezra, the people are called upon to put away their foreign wives, because of the same problem revealed in the failure of Judah. Without a proper understanding of God, Tamar turned to the only thing she knew. Amazingly, it is where Judah was most vulnerable. A continued worship of the God of his father, and an abhorrence of Canaanite gods would have prevented this whole sordid mess.

Judah's sons by Tamar

The sordid story of Genesis 38 comes to conclusion in these verses. It describes a very difficult birth of twin sons. There was a struggle in the womb. The struggle of the sons at birth is typical of the struggle of their mother to conceive. Treated unjustly by the family of Judah (38:8-11, 26), she had tricked Judah into becoming the father of these sons.

Also, the struggle portrayed in this birth is remindful of the total narrative of the Genesis patriarchal families. Symbolically, it portrays the human struggle for submission to God. It is no accident that the author of Genesis gives us the very vivid scene of one of the twins putting out his arm, having a scarlet thread tied to it, but being overcome by the other twin in the birth sequence (38:28-30). The scarlet thread symbolized possession of the birthright, and heir to the Abrahamic promise '...in thee shall all families of the earth be blessed' (Genesis 12:3).

The Genesis narrative continually surprises us with these kinds of incidents. God keeps Sarah barren for many years, but allowed a situation for a child to be born of the handmaiden, Hagar, yet refused him as the child of promise. Jacob, the younger child of Isaac and Rebekah shall rule over the elder Esau. Rachel is the beloved wife of Jacob, but it is Leah that bears the sons that shall spawn the dominant tribes of the nation. In this text, human hands tie a scarlet thread around the one who will be heir, but he loses the struggle in the womb. What is the lesson?

A few moments of meditation are meaningful at this point. It should be clear that the sovereignty of God is being manifest at every turn. He is in absolute control. He chose Abraham. He is providing a family that shall become a nation. He has acted to maintain the purity of that family until it is fully established as a nation. This, he has accomplished, even though the family has consistently acted in ways that might destroy that purity. He has turned every action of humans who sought to control their own destiny into proof of his sovereignty. The decision about who receives the birthright, and the blessing, is his, not the family's. The scarlet thread on the loser signifies human defeat, and God's sovereign choice. Things must ultimately be God's way. The revelation of the Genesis narrative is overwhelming in its impact for the nation that shall come, and for us. It would do us well to return to them often as a reminder of who is truly in charge in the affairs of our life. It is indeed an awesome God that can allow us full freedom of choice, and still move the events of our lives to his own ultimate purpose.

It is a somewhat precarious analogy, but one can see a bit of redemptive overtones here. The favouring of the second over the first is a Genesis theme which may reflect the superiority of the second man to come directly from the creative hand of God (the seed of the woman) over the first (Adam). The scarlet thread has been seen by some as symbolic of the need for cleansing by the blood of the preferred man, the Christ. In any event, the struggle that humans have with the will of God is clearly in view.

Genesis 39:1-19

1. And Joseph was brought down to Egypt; and Potiphar, an officer of Pharaoh, captain of the guard, an Egyptian, bought him of the hands of the Ishmeelites, which had brought him down thither. 2. And the Lord was with Joseph, and he was a prosperous man; and he was in the house of his master the Egyptian. 3. And his master saw that the Lord was with him, and that the Lord made all that he did to prosper in his hand. 4. And Joseph found grace in his sight, and he served him: and he made him overseer over his house, and all that he had he put into his hand. 5. And it came to pass from the time that he had made him overseer in his house, and over all that he had, that the Lord blessed the Egyptian's house for Joseph's sake; and the blessing of the Lord was upon all that he had in the house, and in the field. 6. And he left all that he had in Joseph's hand; and he knew not ought he had, save the bread which he did eat. And Joseph was a goodly person, and well favoured. 7. And it came to pass after these things, that his master's wife cast her eyes upon Joseph; and she said, Lie with me. 8. But he refused, and said unto his master's wife, Behold, my master wotteth not what is with me in the house, and he hath committed all that he hath to my hand; 9. There is none greater in this house than I; neither hath he kept back any thing from me but thee, because thou art his wife: how then can I do this great wickedness, and sin against God? 10. And it came to pass, as she spake to Joseph day by day, that he hearkened not unto her, to lie by her, or to be with her. 11. And it came to pass about this time, that Joseph went into the house to do his business; and there was none of the men of the house there within. 12. And she caught him by his garment, saying, Lie with me: and he left his garment in her hand, and fled, and got him out. 13. And it came to pass, when she saw that he had left his garment in her hand, and was fled forth, 14. That she called unto the men of her house, and spake unto them, saying, See, he hath brought in an Hebrew unto us to mock us; he came in unto me to lie with me, and I cried with a loud voice: 15. And it came to pass, when he heard that I lifted up my voice and cried, that he left his garment with me, and fled, and got him out. 16. And she laid up his garment by her, until his lord came home. 17. And she spake unto him according to these words, saying, The Hebrew servant, which thou hast brought unto us, came in unto me to mock me: 18. And it came to pass, as I lifted up my voice and cried, that he left his garment with me, and fled out. 19. And it came to pass, when his master heard the words of his wife, which she spake unto him, saying, After this manner did thy servant to me; that his wrath was kindled.

Joseph, a servant

From this point, the Genesis narrative focuses on Joseph. The story is phenomenal in its portrayal. Joseph holds not the position of Abraham and Moses in the tradition of Israel, but he is no less remarkable as a person. Except for the Lord Jesus, no one in Scripture comes across with a more consistent character, and a poise that seems to react correctly to every situation. He is the man that every Christian male longs to be.

Chapter 39 begins where Chapter 37 left off. The Ishmaelites, who bought Joseph from his brothers, bring him to Egypt and sell him to an officer of Pharaoh. He is referred to as Potiphar (39:1). Immediately, a very bad situation is shown as being good. Our sympathy for Joseph is given relief. There is strength of character that Joseph manifests. He works hard, impresses his owner and is elevated to a position of authority. The slave becomes a boss. Joseph's actions were designed to be pleasing to Potiphar. It was a sign of character that he submitted himself. The narrative of Genesis regularly shows the ability to submit as a positive trait.

One is led to contrast this attitude with those of Joseph's brothers. When hearing of his prophetic dream, they became furious and agitated (37:8). Whereas they looked at the mere suggestion of submission as a negative, Joseph, when called upon to be a slave, willingly submitted himself. The brothers' attitude led them to sin. Joseph's attitude led him to success (39:2-3).

The attitude Joseph displays is seen in full bloom in the one whom he foreshadows. The apostle Paul writes this about Jesus Christ. 'But made himself of no reputation, and took upon him the form of a servant...' (Philippians 2:7). The common language of the Christian is the language of servant-hood. We turn to Jesus as an example, but seldom do we truly understand it. We look at the cross and wonder how we can achieve that kind of servant-hood. For an example that doesn't seem as impossible, we might try Joseph.

Joseph, as a victim, in a situation he could not change, acted in a way that would please God. The Genesis writer wants us to note how God honoured this attitude (39:3).

A moment of temptation

The text recounts one of the most intriguing episodes in Scripture. There are several truths about Christian living that Joseph's experience teaches. First, precisely when Joseph totally overcome the tragedy of being sold into slavery, he is burdened with a huge temptation. Potiphar's wife attempts to seduce him sexually. There is no point at which men are more vulnerable, and history (not to mention everyday occurrences), are replete with tragic stories of a man's fall in this arena. Joseph could have given many rationalisations. He had worked hard after being victimized. He was far from home. God had abandoned him. He deserved to have what he is being offered. Potiphar was gone, who would ever know? He could have argued that things were going well for him because of his recent promotion (39:5), and this is just another good thing. Christians should always remember that at the moment things are going well, we are at our most vulnerable moments to temptation.

Second, though tempted, Joseph used a correct methodology for his decision making. '...my master wotteth not what is with me in the house, and he hath committed all that he hath to my hand; There is none greater in this house than I; neither hath he kept back any thing from me but thee, because thou art his wife: how then can I do this great wickedness, and sin against God' (39:8-9)? Joseph looked at what he had, and rejoiced in it. This is unlike human nature. Most of us will look at what we don't have and fret over our lack, instead of being grateful for what we have. This tendency creates extreme unhappiness and causes us to covet and desire that which does not belong to us. Satan tempted Eve with the fruit of the one forbidden tree when there were many other trees from which she could have eaten. Whereas Eve, and all humanity after her, have been frustrated by the forbidden thing; Joseph believed himself blessed through that which is not forbidden. In a western culture that is so wildly in search of material happiness, we could take a strong clue from Joseph.

Third, he understood correctly the true nature of the offer from Potiphar's wife. He called it 'wickedness' (39:9). If we could learn to call our temptations by their proper name, we might avoid the fall into sin that so often takes hold of us.

Joseph's reaction to temptation foreshadows the perfection in the Incarnate One, who saw the logical suggestions of Satan as temptation to sin. '...Thou shalt not tempt the Lord thy God' (Matthew 4:7).

'...how then can I...sin against God'

One of the great difficulties in obedience to the great commandment, '...Thou shalt love the Lord thy God with all thy heart...
soul...mind' (Matthew 22:37), is in doing battle with temptation.
Human need and human desire are so intertwined that it is often hard to distinguish between what is really needed and what is
based only in desire. Desire is often translated in our mind as need,
and temptation is understood as mere friendly persuasion. Satanic
trickery is to get us to perceive desire as need.

The first step in overcoming temptation is in its recognition.
If we are deceived, we will pursue the desires of our lust, and feel
justified. How does one know if his pursuit is for desire or for true
need? This is discernable by asking the next question, 'What is
the long-term effect of giving in to the temptation?' This must be
examined internally on the effect of my own conscience. Can I
maintain authority with others to teach what is right when I have
knowledge of my own evil action? Externally, what effect will my
actions produce in others? Would others look at what I do, perceive it exactly as I do (a need), and use it to justify an even greater
wrong action on their part?

Joseph is faced with a powerful temptation. Potiphar's wife offers herself to him. This would have been very flattering to Joseph,
having come into the household as a slave, and finding the mistress of the house coming-on to him. The human in Joseph could
easily have rationalized that his needs as a slave had been ignored.
Now is a chance to think about self. This is a very common methodology of reasoning in our present culture. What did he do?

The answer of Joseph provides the clue for helping us analyse what is truly happening in the moments of temptation in our
lives. He said, '...how then can I do this great wickedness, and
sin against God' (39:9)? When we do not have the wisdom to
examine what the long-term effects will be, one can ask simply 'Is
my action pleasing to God?' The discernment ability that one has
when examining things in the light of the desire to please God is
amazing. 'Thou shalt love the Lord thy God...' (Matthew 22:37) is

difficult to fulfil because of temptation, but is also the single greatest aid we have in discerning whether our desire is a real need or
is the effect of temptation. Joseph was able to fight off the advance
of Potiphar's wife because he wanted to please God more than he
wanted to please himself.

'...and got him out'

There is an aspect of temptation that is seldom discussed. Usually one thinks of temptation in terms of a singular event. There is
that extra piece of pie that we refused, or the offer to go have fun,
instead of preparing for tomorrow's classes, or tomorrow's meeting, which we turned down. These are acts of self-discipline that
are to be applauded. The moment was there and we overcame.
The same kind of moment may arrive again, but it isn't a constant
imposing problem for us. Sometimes, there are temptations that
are as much a part of the daily routine as getting out of bed in the
morning. This kind of temptation may come from mental obsession or from an external source. Satan knows our weaknesses, and
will use the relationships of our life to constantly pressure us to do
things against our conscience. This can be very difficult to bear as
well as impossible to avoid.

Joseph found himself facing external pressure to do wrong.
This was coming from a superior, his master's wife. The Scripture
says the pressure was non-ending, 'And it came to pass, as she
spake to Joseph day by day...' (39:10). Joseph was trapped. He
was a slave. If he gives in to her and is not caught, he has gone
against his conscience and displeased God. If he gives in and gets
caught, he could be punished by death, depending on the decision of Potiphar. The wife, on the other hand, could make things
continually miserable for him and cause him to lose his favoured
position in the house if he does not succumb to her advances.

Many find themselves in similar circumstances. The mind will
give to us plenty of arguments about the thing to do. The arguments are often based in fear. What will we lose? And we make

decisions based in that which we perceive as the most immediate loss. Had Joseph acted on that fear, he would have given in, not wanting to lose the prestige he had obtained in the household. The moment came to a brutal confrontation when she physically assaulted him, and he ran from her, leaving his garment in her hand. The constant pressure and temptation from which Joseph had no escape comes to this kind of moment. He responded with the only alternative choice he had. He ran! The lesson is rather simple. He acted decisively to remove himself from the source of the temptation. The subtlety of temptation will often keep us hanging around until it has control of us. Knowing when to run is critical in this kind of temptation.

> Sometimes, our faith in God requires that we run. We are instructed to flee many things in Scripture (1 Corinthians 6:18; 10:14; 2 Timothy 2:22, etc.)

Importance of overcoming temptation

Joseph faced a situation that in modern terminology would be labelled sexual harassment. There are so many conflicting emotions that affect a person in a time like this. His loyalty to Potiphar, who had been kind to him, his fear of alienating Potiphar's wife, and having her create problems for him, the desire to please his God, are all conflicting elements. We are not told specifically if there was a sexual attraction to the woman on Joseph's part, but the inference is clearly there. The placing of this story is on the heels of Joseph's older brother's indiscretion (38:15-18). The author wants us to compare the strength of Joseph's character with that of Judah.

When one finds he in this kind of situation, there is a clear trap. The message provides one of the great lessons of life. That is, we cannot always control life in a way that will keep us from decisions that don't cost us. When one is facing this kind of trap, the issue is rather basic. A price will be paid for whatever decision one makes. There is no solution that does not have serious consequences. We would love to think that doing the right thing always produces results that are fair, and we will be properly rewarded. Often, as Joseph will learn, doing the right thing can produce great hardship.

Overcoming temptation will lead to his being thrown into jail. Joseph could not know it, but being in jail would lead to a rulership position in the whole nation of Egypt. Could he handle such a role? That would be proven by his ability to handle the temptation presented by Potiphar's wife. Had he not overcome temptation, he would not have landed in jail. Had he not landed in jail, he would not have become ruler in Egypt. God's intention for us probably does not have such grand design. The test, however, is still crucial. The design of God for us, whatever it may be, requires overcoming the temptation that may destroy our life. The overcoming of any one temptation may be God's defining moment.

There are different kinds of temptations. Some present themselves as relatively harmless, such as ordering the extra piece of pie. Others can be defined by the potential disaster they represent, such as the moral indiscretion that leads to the unwanted pregnancy. The problem is, lack of discipline in lesser temptations leads to giving in to greater temptations.

Genesis 39:20-23

20. And Joseph's master took him, and put him into the prison, a place where the king's prisoners were bound: and he was there in the prison. 21. But the Lord was with Joseph, and shewed him mercy, and gave him favour in the sight of the keeper of the prison. 22. And the keeper of the prison committed to Joseph's hand all the prisoners that were in the prison; and whatsoever they did there, he was the doer of it. 23. The keeper of the prison looked not to any thing that was under his hand; because the Lord was with him, and that which he did, the Lord made it to prosper.

'...he was there in the prison'

It is a frequently used ploy of literature to show the results of 'a woman scorned.' Obviously, men and women have created many cruel acts as a result of being scorned. The 'woman scorned' makes a much more interesting story, because it is a bit more shocking to see it coming out of the more gentle of the two sexes. Potiphar's wife is the subject of the 'woman scorned' here. This is a bit of a reversal of that which is seen in the earlier parts of Genesis. Both Abraham and Isaac worried about their wives being desired by a foreign ruler. Here the wife of the foreign ruler is desirous of Joseph's affections.

When she tries to seize him physically, and force him to respond to her, she creates a moment that brings an end to the situation once and for all. She will have him or lose him. Joseph flees from her and seals his fate. She grabs his garment, and reports attempted rape '...he came in unto me to lie with me, and I cried with a loud voice' (39:14). Joseph's fate is settled. When Potiphar hears the report of his wife, he must take action. He places Joseph in prison. The fact that Joseph is placed in prison probably reflects that Potiphar had some doubt as to the report of his wife. Such acts were usually punished by execution. This would serve to make the event more traumatic for Joseph. He goes to prison knowing that Potiphar may actually believe him innocent. The 'woman scorned' gets her way.

The focus turns to Joseph's reaction. He was faithful to God, but what did it get him? It gets him thrown into jail (39:20). This was a place of hopelessness. Consider these factors. Joseph was in a foreign land as a slave. The only people who knew him were responsible for putting him in jail. His family (in Canaan) thought he was dead. The last words of verse 20 have a solemn ring '...and he was there in the prison (39:20).' There was no one to which he could turn that might help get him out. Any hope of a real life was, by all human standards, over. There was one thing. '...the Lord was with Joseph...' (39:21). That is always the bottom line for those who love God. What was the last word of Jesus to his disciples? '...lo, I am with you alway, even to the end of the world' (Matthew 28:20).

It is a difficult situation to try and overcome the circumstances of life over which we have no control. Joseph's story teaches us at least one lesson in how we might do that. We must come to appreciate the presence of God, and trust that he has not abandoned us.

'...the Lord was with Joseph...'

As one reads Scripture, there is the consistent discovery of a grand message from God; his message often comes in a fascinating little touch of irony. Events in the lives of real people woven together by God create continual surprises. It is more than the work of a master storyteller. It is the work of God.

Joseph is the subject of this touch of irony. He was sold into slavery, but became the head of his master's house. The Bible says, '...the Lord was with Joseph...' (39:2). Our hearts are lifted by Joseph's success. Though not free, and not with family, at least, life isn't bad. Then, he is falsely accused of attempted rape (39:13-14). He is thrown into prison. This is a life sentence. The Bible reports '...the Lord was with Joseph...and the keeper of the prison committed to Joseph's hand all the prisoners that were in the prison...' (39:21-22). Joseph had truly risen in the world. He had gone from being the favoured son, to being the favoured slave, to being the favoured jailbird. He always rises to the top, but each top is lower than the bottom of his previous state. The reader may begin to question the wisdom of the author's excitement about the Lord's presence being with Joseph. The success that God has given Joseph to this point has a hollow, dare we say, 'ironic' ring to it.

Looking backwards from history, we know where this story is leading. What if we learned no more, and the story ends with Joseph in prison, and the final words of Chapter 39 are the conclusion of Joseph's life? '...the Lord was with him, and that which he did, the Lord made it to prosper' (39:23). Is there a lesson for us? The lesson goes back to that which Abraham, Isaac, and Jacob had to learn. Joseph is learning it through a totally different set of circumstances. It is, the greatest treasure of life is God. When one has him, he needs nothing else. The characters of Genesis learn this lesson over and over through differing situations. You and I must learn it as well in the trials of our life. What is the value of 'the Lord was with Joseph...?' It is more than the words. It is the ultimate value of life.

> God's presence! It is an oddity that every Christian con-
> fesses, yet struggles with in his own life. How can it be said
> that God was with Joseph when so many bad things were
> happening? How can it be said of us? It must be accepted
> by faith! As one considers the great struggle when he feels
> abandoned by God, the words of the Incarnate One have
> an awesome ring. '...why hast thou forsaken me' (Mark
> 15:34)? The fact that God loved us enough to forsake his
> Son to fashion our redemption should forever remove the
> doubt that he would then forsake us. It would be a betrayal
> of his Son's sacrifice. Let us give praise for life's most pre-
> cious words, '...thou art with me...' (Psalms 23:4).

The strength of Joseph

As we meditate on Joseph's life as a prisoner, there is one thing that demands attention. It is a characteristic of a child of God that all should seek. When Joseph was a slave, he worked hard and impressed his master. As a prisoner, he again works hard and impresses the keeper of the prison. Joseph's attitude was the same, no matter his circumstances. This is a phenomenal ability that is only accomplished by the power of God. It is no accident that of all the notable characters of Genesis, only Joseph is named as one '...in whom the Spirit of God is' (Genesis 41:38).

When Jesus Christ was nearing his ascension, he called his disciples together and said '...tarry ye...in ...Jerusalem until ye be endued with power from on high' (Luke 24:49).

Jesus knew that the disciples were to face many trials. Many would be thrown into prison, many would die, most would suffer for their faith. They would be required to carry the same attitude as Joseph no matter the conditions of life. The apostle Paul stated this principle 'Not that I speak in respect of want: for I have learned, in whatsoever state I am, therewith to be content. I know both how to be abased, and I know how to abound: every where and in all things I am instructed both to be full and to be hungry, both to abound and to suffer need. I can do all things through Christ which strengtheneth me' (Philippians 4:11-13).

The 'power from on high' for which the disciples of Jesus were to wait is the Holy Spirit (Acts 1:8). The same Spirit, which enabled Joseph to be the same person in all circumstances of his life, is a present reality in all Christians. You and I can have the attitude of Joseph because, as a believer in Christ, we possess the same Spirit.

All of us admire the person who demonstrates strength of character and consistency of attitude in good times or bad. It is a noteworthy goal. If we begin with the understanding that God is the greatest treasure of our life, and seek diligently to 'love him with all our heart...soul...mind' (Matthew 22:37), we might find that the power of the Holy Spirit is unleashed in us. We can manifest the consistency we see in Joseph.

Genesis 40-41

I. The Dreams of Prisoners (40:1-23)
1. The jailbird is demoted
2. '…tell me then…'
3. Interpreter of dreams
4. Forgotten

II. A Ray of Hope (41:1-14)
1. '…I'd remember my faults'
2. '...pharaoh called Joseph…'

III. The Challenge for Joseph (41:15-36)
1. God-confidence
2. Years of Plenty, years of famine
3. '…shortly bring it to pass…'
4. Pharaoh's humility

IV. Joseph's Appointment (41:37-44)
1. No hesitation
2. '…Joseph gathered corn…'

V. The Blessing of God (41:45-57)
1. Joseph's family
2. Joseph and Jesus
3. '…what he saidth, do…'
4. '…in all lands…'

Genesis 40:1-23

1. And it came to pass after these things, that the butler of the king of Egypt and his baker had offended their lord the king of Egypt. 2. And Pharaoh was wroth against two of his officers, against the chief of the butlers, and against the chief of the bakers. 3. And he put them in ward in the house of the captain of the guard, into the prison, the place where Joseph was bound. 4. And the captain of the guard charged Joseph with them, and he served them: and they continued a season in ward. 5. And they dreamed a dream both of them, each man his dream in one night, each man according to the interpretation of his dream, the butler and the baker of the king of Egypt, which were bound in the prison. 6. And Joseph came in unto them in the morning, and looked upon them, and, behold, they were sad. 7. And he asked Pharaoh's officers that were with him in the ward of his lord's house, saying, Wherefore look ye so sadly to day? 8. And they said unto him, We have dreamed a dream, and there is no interpreter of it. And Joseph said unto them, Do not interpretations belong to God? tell me them, I pray you. 9. And the chief butler told his dream to Joseph, and said to him, In my dream, behold, a vine was before me; 10. And in the vine were three branches: and it was as though it budded, and her blossoms shot forth; and the clusters thereof brought forth ripe grapes:

11. And Pharaoh's cup was in my hand: and I took the grapes, and pressed them into Pharaoh's cup, and I gave the cup into Pharaoh's hand. 12. And Joseph said unto him, This is the interpretation of it: The three branches are three days: 13. Yet within three days shall Pharaoh lift up thine head, and restore thee unto thy place: and thou shalt deliver Pharaoh's cup into his hand, after the former manner when thou wast his butler. 14. But think on me when it shall be well with thee, and shew kindness, I pray thee, unto me, and make mention of me unto Pharaoh, and bring me out of this house: 15. For indeed I was stolen away out of the land of the Hebrews: and here also have I done nothing that they should put me into the dungeon. 16. When the chief baker saw that the interpretation was good, he said unto Joseph, I also was in my dream, and, behold, I had three white baskets on my head: 17. And in the uppermost basket there was of all manner of bakemeats for Pharaoh; and the birds did eat them out of the basket upon my head. 18. And Joseph answered and said, This is the interpretation thereof: The three baskets are three days: 19. Yet within three days shall Pharaoh lift up thy head from off thee, and shall hang thee on a tree; and the birds shall eat thy flesh from off thee. 20. And it came to pass the third day, which was Pharaoh's birthday, that he made a feast unto all his servants: and he lifted up the head of the chief butler and of the chief baker among his servants. 21. And he restored the chief butler unto his butlership again; and he gave the cup into Pharaoh's hand: 22. But he hanged the chief baker: as Joseph had interpreted to them. 23. Yet did not the chief butler remember Joseph, but forgat him.

The jailbird is demoted

The story of Joseph continues its interesting twist. In chapter 40, he receives another setback. Having risen to the position of being in charge of all prisoners, he is now reduced in authority because two officials of Pharaoh are placed in prison. The 'captain of the guard' (presumably still Potiphar) makes the decision (Genesis 40:4). This condition will last only three days as we will discover, but it serves to reinforce the character of Joseph. He is not perplexed by the turn of events, and goes to the new prisoners in the morning to attend to their needs (40:6). The reader wonders if Joseph's story will ever work out positively for Joseph.

We are not told why the two men were placed in prison, but as we are engrossed in the story, we become excited about the possibility. Joseph's only hope to get out of prison is through the help of one more powerful than the captain of the guard. Will these two prisoners be a contact with the most powerful man in Egypt? Clearly, that will be the case. The mystery is, how?

Before the answer can unfold, there is a learning event that must be noted. Joseph has once again found himself facing a setback. His attitude toward these two is very crucial. Joseph could have resented this intrusion of the new prisoners. We would have forgiven him for that. Normal human thinking would have left Joseph with the sense that all is lost anyway, and the best he can hope for is to maintain the authority he had achieved in the prison.

Most of us would have said, 'Just my luck to have new prisoners placed here who have worked for Pharaoh.'

Instead of bitterness, Joseph showed compassion. He noticed that they were sad, and asked them about it (40:6). Would we have simply been glad they were sad and ignored them? If Joseph had responded in that way, the events that ultimately get him out of prison would not have occurred. Joseph continually amazes us. First, a slave, now a jailbird, and he shows compassion to those who made his life more difficult.

> Showing compassion when the soul longs to be angry and bitter is the position in which Christians are called upon to stand. Joseph demonstrates it, and is again a foreshadowing of the Incarnate One. Jesus said, '...Love your enemies...' (Matthew 5:44), and then demonstrated it on the cross. '...Father, forgive them...' (Luke 23:34).

'...tell me then...'

The scene comes as somewhat of a surprise, but it offers the reader a chance to do some reflection that may reveal a lot about Joseph. The time spent in prison has given Joseph much time for reflection. No doubt, he has thought about his father and his brothers in Canaan. He has contemplated what brought him to the situation he is in. He has carefully analysed every facet of his past. As a believer in God, he has tried to put together the pieces of that which God is doing in his life.

He encounters, in prison, two men troubled by dreams from the previous nights' sleep. The surprise comes when Joseph quickly interprets those dreams. From where did this ability suddenly derive? Though it appears as a sudden feature, the reader and Joseph were prepared for this event. 'And Joseph dreamed a dream, and he told it his brethren...' (Genesis 37:5-6). That dream of Joseph many years earlier, which predicted Joseph's rulership over his brothers, was a critical part of what ultimately led to Joseph being in Egypt, and in prison. In his meditation with the Lord, made possible by the imprisonment, Joseph had been able to put certain pieces of his life together. He had been introduced to dreams that were of a prophetic nature, and was confident he could discern the nature of the dreams of these two prisoners. If the dreams were significant, God could interpret them. Joseph's physical body had been in prison, but his mind was free.

By this time, Joseph also had a sense of destiny about his life. You may ask, 'how can that be possible for one who is languishing in prison?' The key is found in Joseph's words. '...Do not interpretations belong to God...' (40:8)? Joseph had utilized his time in prison to learn of God. As he examined the affairs of his life, it was never with a 'woe is me' attitude, but a 'what is God doing in my life attitude?' Joseph was human and must have often been in despair, but he used the despair to learn of God. In the critical moment when he needed a specific kind of knowledge, he had prepared himself to receive it. In the burdens of our life, we are called upon to think about them, but to really think, not to simply moan 'woe is me.' Only in that way can we be prepared. Joseph's great moment in prison was not a sudden happening, it was a life time of preparation. Jesus said, 'Take my yoke upon you, and learn of me...' (Matthew 11:29).

> God always delights in his children who take the time to ponder on his Word, and think in ways that induce learning. Humans don't like it, but reality is that some of the greatest opportunity for learning of God is in the difficult moments of life. It is there that we can be prepared for the tests of our life.

Interpreter of dreams

Joseph encounters the chief butcher and the chief baker of Pharaoh's court. Each had been placed in prison for unspecified reasons. Each has had a troubling dream. Joseph discerns that the dreams may be a message from God and asks to hear them (40:8). When the dreams are recited, Joseph makes a bold prediction in interpreting the dreams. The chief butler would be out of prison in three days and restored to his official position in the house of Pharaoh. The chief baker would also be out of prison in three days, but would be beheaded, and his body hanged on a tree for the birds to eat. For an Egyptian who believed immortality is gained only though preservation of the body, this is a particularly morbid thought.

Joseph's interpretation of the dreams proved correct. This offers hope for Joseph, and for the reader. The chief butler will speak to the Pharaoh for Joseph, and soon win his release from prison (40:14). Such was not to be (40:23). Another setback manifests itself for Joseph; nonetheless we have a new picture of Joseph. He is not only a man of great character, a man '...in whom the Spirit of God is' (Genesis 41:38), he is a man of great wisdom. He is a discerner of, and interpreter of dreams.

When one considers what Joseph has been through, this is a classic and great moment. Joseph must have often questioned the perplexing setbacks of his life. He would wonder why God hadn't just let him die. Why is he languishing in prison? His mind was sharp, he had continued to learn of God, and he had been faithful to God, but all of that faithfulness and knowledge was simply going to waste. The interpretation of these dreams is an oasis in the desert for Joseph. Yes, it was only one event! Yes, Joseph was still in prison, but Joseph had done something very special. God revealed to Joseph that a plan was still very much alive for his life. Joseph is still required to meditate on God, to consider all the pieces of his life and be prepared for the next event.

When we are going through the difficult valleys of our life, there are often these little oasis in the desert to provide a sense that God is still working. In order to discern the oasis, we must be one who loves God and is continually learning of him. Sometimes, the moment will be small and seem very insignificant, but it will be enough to carry us.

Forgotten

As our lives develop and time passes, we learn many things. One of those things is the importance of timing. This issue confronts us in many ways. When do we buy? When do we sell? When do we change careers? When is the right time to ask her for a date? Do I go to college or spend a term in the military first?

In addition, we are impacted by the timing of other people's lives. We receive a job offer because the right person came into our life at just the right time. We lost out on the big opportunity because we were a moment too late, and someone else got there first. The boss insists that we be at a suddenly called meeting, which causes us to miss our daughter's school play.

It takes hindsight to be able to examine life and see the hand of providential timing. There are events, which seem at the time to have significance, but nothing of significance results. Joseph had such an event. He had made contact with one close to the Pharaoh. He had interpreted a dream and it came to pass. Maybe his new friend would speak to the Pharaoh and get him out of prison. The reader also has hope for Joseph. Then comes the disappointing words, 'Yet did not the chief butler remember Joseph, but forgat him' (40:23).

The beauty of the scriptural account is that we are let in on the providence of God in this event in Joseph's life. We know that it is a matter of timing. God is controlling the affair so that the butler will remember Joseph at the time it will do him some good. In all likelihood, the chief butler could have said a kind word about Joseph that Pharaoh would have ignored. Later, that will not be the case. The interpretation of the dream will be very significant, only Joseph does not know it. The significance is to be found in God's timing, not Joseph's.

What appears to be good timing, bad timing, or no timing to us, may be in the perfect timing of God's plan if we are busy loving God and learning of him. Paul puts it like this. 'And we know that all things work together for good to them that love God, to them who are the called according to his purpose' (Romans 8:28).

Genesis 41:1-14

1. And it came to pass at the end of two full years, that Pharaoh dreamed: and, behold, he stood by the river. 2. And, behold, there came up out of the river seven well favoured kine and fatfleshed; and they fed in a meadow. 3. And, behold, seven other kine came up after them out of the river, ill favoured and leanfleshed; and stood by the other kine upon the brink of the river. 4. And the ill favoured and leanfleshed kine did eat up the seven well favoured and fat kine. So Pharaoh awoke. 5. And he slept and dreamed the second time: and, behold, seven ears of corn came up upon one stalk, rank and good. 6. And, behold, seven thin ears and blasted with the east wind sprung up after them. 7. And the seven thin ears devoured the seven rank and full ears. And Pharaoh awoke, and, behold, it was a dream. 8. And it came to pass in the morning that his spirit was troubled; and he sent and called for all the magicians of Egypt, and all the wise men thereof: and Pharaoh told them his dream; but there was none that could interpret them unto Pharaoh. 9. Then spake the chief butler unto Pharaoh, saying, I do remember my faults this day: 10. Pharaoh was wroth with his servants, and put me in ward in the captain of the guard's house, both me and the chief baker: 11. And we dreamed a dream in one night, I and he; we dreamed each man according to the interpretation of his dream. 12. And there was there with us a young man, an Hebrew, servant to the captain of the guard; and we told him, and he interpreted to us our dreams; to each man according to his dream he did interpret. 13. And it came to pass, as he interpreted to us, so it was; me he restored unto mine office, and him he hanged. 14. Then Pharaoh sent and called Joseph, and they brought him hastily out of the dungeon: and he shaved himself, and changed his raiment, and came in unto Pharaoh.

'...I do remember my faults...'

There are many different ways that people can reveal the true nature of their character as humans, we tend to look mostly on the external things. What has one done to help or hurt others? What kind of words do we speak? Are they words of kindness and sympathy, or words that seem harsh and unfeeling? Do we remember to return a kindness done to us? These things often reflect a person of character or a person with a lack of character. Fortunately, God looks at things in greater depth.

The chief butler of Pharaoh has not appeared to us in favourable terms. He received ministry from Joseph when imprisoned. Joseph requested the butler speak on his behalf to Pharaoh. 'Yet did not the chief butler remember Joseph, but forgat him' (Genesis 40:23). Our first thoughts are to call the butler an ungrateful slob. He could have shown some appreciation. He, in our mind, is one of low character.

Yet, the forces of life have produced the same kind of mistake in all of us. How many have written a letter to a teacher that helped us so much. How often have we had a kindness done that we did not seek to repay, and may have long since forgotten. We would not want to have our character judged on that alone.

The story of the butler does not come to an end with his forgetfulness. It is two years later, and after Pharaoh's dream, the butler remembers the one who had interpreted a dream for him. The revelation of the butler's character is more clearly revealed here than in his forgetfulness. He said, '...I do remember my faults this day' (41:9). Note the confessional nature of the chief butler's statement. There was no need for him to repent before Pharaoh. He could have told him about Joseph without admitting wrongdoing on his part. The willingness to bare himself (even his faults) is a reflection of a man of character. Jesus teaches this in the prayer of the publican. '...God be merciful to me, a sinner' (Luke 18:13). Isn't it nice to know that our character is often revealed as much in our repentance as it is in our great deeds.

It is another of the strange oddities of life. A man's character is sometimes better revealed in his repentance than in his deeds. Good things can be done with bad motives. Bad things can be done with good motives. Both things are sin. It is inescapable that all men are sinners. The key to character is who will admit it and be willing to confess it. Owning who we are and owning our sins is a way to build resistance to sin in the future.

'...pharaoh...called Joseph...'

Joseph had been used by God to interpret the dreams of the butler and the baker of the Pharaoh (Genesis 40). He had hoped that his prophecy to the chief butler might be useful in getting him out of prison (Genesis 40:14). Two years passed, and the chief butler had not thought of Joseph.

Pharaoh has a dream that greatly disturbs him, and none of the wise men of Egypt could provide the interpretation. It is at this time that the chief butler remembers Joseph (41:9). The observant reader of Scripture will be excited at the anticipation of an amazing twist in the story. It was the reciting of his own dreams that got Joseph in such great trouble with his brothers, and led to his being sold into slavery in Egypt (Genesis 37:8). Now, the dreams of someone else will get him out of prison. In hindsight, one can see the sovereignty of God at work. As a young man, Joseph was exposed to understanding a dream that was of prophetic nature (something God used to reveal his will in biblical times, but is no longer necessary after the Bible is completed). As a young man, Joseph had a gift and used it foolishly, but God would use Joseph's foolishness to develop his own plan. He had gifted young Joseph in a way that would lead to this moment.

Joseph will be called before the most powerful man in the world to exercise the gift that God had bestowed upon him. There is a very clear lesson here for the Christian in the struggle of life. The understanding of God's work is often in hindsight, not in foresight. As a young man, Joseph was somewhat proud of his dream, and used it in exaltation of self. He now stands before Pharaoh. The situation is far more serious, and involves a world, not just a family. As a young man, he simply had no conception of the purpose that God had in mind. It would take years of maturing and humbling for him to use the gift properly. Joseph is on the verge of the greatest lesson of his life. All those very bad things that had been happening to him for the last few years (sold into slavery, accused of rape, cast into prison) are in reality good things. They are good because God used them for his own purpose. In hindsight, he will know what he could never have known in foresight. God will do this for all who will do as Joseph did, submit daily to the sovereignty, and will of God in our life.

Victory in the struggles of life always begins with losing one battle, the battle for sovereignty in our life. God owns that role. He will, if submitted to, guide our life and will ultimately give us insight to the work that he is doing in us.

Genesis 41:15-36

15. And Pharaoh said unto Joseph, I have dreamed a dream, and there is none that can interpret it: and I have heard say of thee, that thou canst understand a dream to interpret it. 16. And Joseph answered Pharaoh, saying, It is not in me: God shall give Pharaoh an answer of peace. 17. And Pharaoh said unto Joseph, In my dream, behold, I stood upon the bank of the river: 18. And, behold, there came up out of the river seven kine, fatfleshed and well favoured; and they fed in a meadow: 19. And, behold, seven other kine came up after them, poor and very ill favoured and leanfleshed, such as I never saw in all the land of Egypt for badness: 20. And the lean and the ill favoured kine did eat up the first seven fat kine: 21. And when they had eaten them up, it could not be known that they had eaten them; but they were still ill favoured, as at the beginning. So I awoke. 22. And I saw in my dream, and, behold, seven ears came up in one stalk, full and good: 23. And, behold, seven ears, withered, thin, and blasted with the east wind, sprung up after them: 24. And the thin ears devoured the seven good ears: and I told this unto the magicians; but there was none that could declare it to me. 25. And Joseph said unto Pharaoh, The dream of Pharaoh is one: God hath shewed Pharaoh what he is about to do. 26. The seven good kine are seven years; and the seven good ears are seven years: the dream is one. 27. And the seven thin and ill favoured kine that came up after them are seven years; and the seven empty ears blasted with the east wind shall be seven years of famine. 28. This is the thing which I have spoken unto Pharaoh: what God is about to do he sheweth unto Pharaoh. 29. Behold, there come seven years of great plenty throughout all the land of Egypt: 30. And there shall arise after them seven years of famine; and all the plenty shall be forgotten in the land of Egypt; and the famine shall consume the land; 31. And the plenty shall not be known in the land by reason of that famine following; for it shall be very grievous. 32. And for that the dream was doubled unto Pharaoh twice; it is because the thing is established by God, and God will shortly bring it to pass. 33. Now therefore let Pharaoh look out a man discreet and wise, and set him over the land of Egypt. 34. Let Pharaoh do this, and let him appoint officers over the land, and take up the fifth part of the land of Egypt in the seven plenteous years. 35. And let them gather all the food of those good years that come, and lay up corn under the hand of Pharaoh, and let them keep food in the cities. 36. And that food shall be for store to the land against the seven years of famine, which shall be in the land of Egypt; that the land perish not through the famine.

God confidence

Joseph, the Hebrew slave, imprisoned for many years, stands before the most powerful man in the world to interpret a dream. Joseph is well aware of the skill that God has given him to discern the dreams of a prophetic nature. He has a degree of confidence that he can function in this task, yet, he knows well the true source of this skill. He states, '...It is not in me: God shall give Pharaoh an answer of peace' (41:16).

There are some interesting implications within this scenario. We are not told that Joseph was afraid. He stood before the King of Egypt with confidence. He has surely been told the purpose for which he has been summoned. Joseph has the following things going for him. First, he has faced the situation before. He interpreted the dreams of the chief butler and the chief baker accurately. Second, God has been with him and brought him through many trials. He may have the sense that God has prepared him for such a moment as this.

Within the development of the Christian life, many would be amazed if they compared the times of being afraid and insecure, with the fearful moments in which they were calm and confident.

It is often that Christian confidence is ridiculed as inappropriate and out of place. We are called upon to be humble. Confidence, we sometimes interpret as arrogance. However, for the person who walks with God, is daily seeking to do his will, and is learning through the trials of his life, a godly confidence will manifest itself at crucial times. The Psalmist has in mind the confidence of one who delights in the law of the Lord. 'And he shall be like a tree planted by the rivers of water, that bringeth forth his fruit in his season; his leaf also shall not wither; and whatsoever he doeth shall prosper' (Psalms 1:3).

The confidence that God provides is often seen in Scriptures: Elijah before the prophets of Baal, Stephen before the Sanhedrin, Paul and Silas in the Philippian jail. What is this confidence? Joseph tells us, '…God shall give Pharaoh an answer…' (Genesis 41:16). It is to have the kind of walk with God whereby we know what God will do. It is not self-confidence but God-confidence.

> When the apostle Paul petitioned God for healing from his thorn in the flesh, he heard these words from God. '…My grace is sufficient for thee: for my strength is made perfect in weakness…' (2 Corinthians 12:9). This is the foundation of God confidence, and the secret of living without fear. God will demonstrate his grace to us. The question is, 'Will we be in the kind of relationship with God where we can see it?'

Years of plenty, years of famine

Joseph was called into Pharaoh's presence in order to interpret the dreams of the Pharaoh. The dreams are repeated twice (41:1-7; 41:17-24). A detail is added in the second recounting. '…I never saw in all the land of Egypt for badness' (Genesis 41:19). In the dreams there is the clear announcement of good and bad, and as

Joseph interprets, the analogy is clear, yet the very simplicity of it may have baffled the wise men of Egypt.

Humans often make that mistake in understanding God. We overlook the simple, plain parts, hoping for something more mysterious and bizarre.

The good thing in the dream is that Egypt was going to enjoy seven great years of prosperity (41:29). The rains at the source of the Nile would be regular, and Egypt would enjoy the full benefits of the flood season for watering and for growing of crops. The bad thing is that the seven years of prosperity would be followed by seven years of famine (41:30). God has acted to reveal these coming events to Pharaoh.

There is much to be understood here about the bad times that people as individuals and people as nations have. Our tendency is to always look at bad times as the judgement of God. In this instance, the bad times were not judgement, they were part of a plan that God was implementing. It will be a while before we understand that God would use this situation to bring into Egypt the family, which shall become the nation spawned from Abraham. Egypt would be a source (during the bad years) for the survival of other nations experiencing the famine. The world was experiencing bad times, but God was in complete control of the situation.

Try to soak in the richness of this. One little Hebrew slave is to be brought out of prison in Egypt, is to be given high office in Egypt, and will be responsible for helping to feed a world while God manoeuvres the family of that Hebrew slave into Egypt. Bad times are often the prequel to seeing the magnificent unfolding of the majesty of God. The role that you and I must play whether in the years of plenty or the years of famine is to always pay attention to God. Our obedience will bless us by causing us to be able to behold that majesty when it is manifest. Our disobedience will cause us to be looking elsewhere when God does his work.

We should pray that God would help us to keep our eyes on him so that we will not be looking elsewhere as he does his work. Our tendency is to think that God is not working

in bad times, yet biblical study teaches that bad times may
be precisely the time that God is doing his most profound
work. When Herod was executing all male babies trying to
destroy the Christ child, God brought him (as he did Jacob's
family) to Egypt for safekeeping (Matthew 2:13). The Word
of God continues to give us these wonderful allusions to
the work of God in the 'seed of the woman.'

'...shortly bring it to pass'

The dreams of Pharaoh, which Joseph interpreted, provide an interesting couplet. There are two dreams, but one interpretation.
The writer of Genesis presents the dreams in their entirety twice
(41:1-7; 41:17-24). It is interesting to ask why there were two pres-
entations of the dreams. Would one presentation not have suf-
ficed? It is also interesting to ask why there were two dreams when
both had the same meaning.

Part of the answer is derived from the subtleties of speech.
Have you heard a speaker say 'Let me repeat that?' One of the
things that readers of Scripture often miss is the reality that this
would not be first time that Pharaoh had dreamed. As with any
human, he must have had other dreams. Why is there the urgency
to have this dream interpreted? Clearly, Pharaoh had received a
message. Through the retelling of the dream, the writer gets our
attention. God is about to do something. The writer wants us to
be alert.

Joseph, himself, provides an additional part of the answer. 'And
for that the dream is doubled unto Pharaoh twice; it is because the
thing is established by God, and God will shortly bring it to pass'
(41:32). This is a revelation of God that requires immediate action
on the part of Pharaoh. The couplet is for emphasis. This is not
presented for Pharaoh to think about, it is presented for Pharaoh
to act upon.

As the reader reflects on Joseph's life, it is somewhat of a relief
that immediate action is necessary, seeing that he has languished

in prison for two extra years due to the inaction of the chief butler (Genesis 40:23). Will Pharaoh manifest the same inaction? One of the most difficult things for the Christian is to discern when a situation requires action, not just meditation. Knowing how to discern such things is part of the spiritual maturing process. The mind that is truly tuned to God will have such wisdom. One will note that God makes it easy for Pharaoh. The dreams and their interpretation have a natural fit. It is two dreams with one interpretation. And it is easy to see the analogy. Also, Joseph has a record of success to which the butler testifies (41:9-13). Third, even if Joseph turns out to be wrong, there will still be benefit from the action. God gives the right clues to those willing to act.

> Christians often love their inactivity, using the excuse of waiting on the Lord. Sometimes the Lord may be waiting on us. Differentiation between knowing when to wait and when to act is not always easy to discern. The one who is tuned to God in the difficult times of life is more likely to have the discerning power to make that decision.

Pharaoh's humility

Joseph has recommended that the nation of Egypt embark on an extremely difficult workload for seven years (41:34-36). When there is plenty, such a workload presents problems. The building of storage houses, taking in the harvest, saving a large part of each harvest, are all required when there seems no reason to do it, except for one man's dream, and the interpretation of a former slave. The view that we can have from this perspective has to bring a smile. God's action amazes.

Consider the situation of Joseph. The prisoner is cleaned up, given new clothes, brought before the Pharaoh, and asked to interpret a dream. It is almost absurd. One might hear the Pharaoh questioning himself. 'Bringing one out of jail to interpret a dream,

this has to be stupid!' The only reason Pharaoh did it was desperation. He must find an answer to his dreams.

Joseph, however, does not disappoint Pharaoh. Instead,
Joseph's interpretation makes Pharaoh look very wise. Pharaoh
had done well. For the reader of Scripture, we are again amazed
at the sovereignty of God. We are reminded of one of the great
statements of Jesus Christ. 'For whosoever exalteth himself shall
be abased; and he that humbleth himself shall be exalted' (Luke
14:11). Pharaoh humbled himself before the lowly Joseph, God's
servant. He was made to look good by his humbling. One must
note that he could have refused, and continued searching for other
wise men, but he would never have the answer to his dreams, and
Egypt would not have been prepared for the coming famine.

The theme of humility is one of those themes that is often
discussed in the Bible, and requires many different illustrations to
understand. The fact of Pharaoh, a heathen, being rewarded for
his humility demonstrates the statement of Jesus to be a universal
principle, not just a spiritual word applied only to Christians. During the famine, the holdings and wealth of Pharaoh will be greatly
expanded. It all started with his humility before God's servant.

The most beautiful thing presented is that the confidence of
Joseph in his God (Genesis 41:16) and the humility of Pharaoh
before God's servant, are combined to teach us two differing parts
of the same unity that is humility. The right kind of confidence
mixed with the right kind of submission produces humility.

Genesis 41:38-44

*37. And the thing was good in the eyes of Pharaoh, and in the eyes of all
his servants. 38. And Pharaoh said unto his servants, Can we find such a
one as this is, a man in whom the Spirit of God is? 39. And Pharaoh said
unto Joseph, Forasmuch as God hath shewed thee all this, there is none
so discreet and wise as thou art: 40. Thou shalt be over my house, and according unto thy word shall all my people be ruled: only in the throne will*

I be greater than thou. 41. And Pharaoh said unto Joseph, See, I have set thee over all the land of Egypt. 42. And Pharaoh took off his ring from his hand, and put it upon Joseph's hand, and arrayed him in vestures of fine linen, and put a gold chain about his neck; 43. And he made him to ride in the second chariot which he had; and they cried before him, Bow the knee: and he made him ruler over all the land of Egypt. 44. And Pharaoh said unto Joseph, I am Pharaoh, and without thee shall no man lift up his hand or foot in all the land of Egypt.

No hesitation

The reader of Scripture is given much to ponder in this text. Within hours, Joseph has gone from being in prison to being the Prime Minister of Egypt. As we read the story, we delight in Joseph's fortune. Certainly, he deserves some good luck. Yet, we have seen him have good fortune before, only to have a bad time afterward. We wonder if something bad is about to befall him again after this good event. Would Joseph be wondering the same thing?

Also, we are somewhat stunned at Pharaoh's analysis. 'Can we find such a one as this is, a man in whom the Spirit of God is' (Genesis 41:38). Joseph had been in jail!

The Pharaoh's statement is stunning, even with Joseph's ability to interpret the dreams. Would Pharaoh not have asked how a man 'with the Spirit of God' happens to be in jail?

In addition, if we are skeptical about this new situation for Joseph, would he (Pharaoh) not be somewhat skeptical? Some would look at this situation of Joseph and say 'Enjoy the ride while it lasts.' It is also normal to look at a situation like this with bitterness. The circumstances of Joseph's life had been so disappointing, he could have said 'This won't last either, and set about to make the worst of it, guaranteeing that it wouldn't last.

Pharaoh and Joseph made the best of their situation. Neither hesitated. '...And Joseph went out from the presence of Pharaoh, and went throughout all the land of Egypt. ...And he gathered up all the food of the seven years...' (41:46-48). Why did neither

Joseph nor Pharaoh fall into the possible pitfalls that could have
caused them to hesitate, and miss the work that must be done?
Perhaps the answer lies in Genesis 41:16. '...It is not in me...'
In Hebrew, Joseph's words are much stronger. It has an explo-
sive quality. 'It is not in me' is a single word. It has the strength
of 'No!' with authority. '...God shall give Pharaoh an answer of
peace' (41:16). 'God will do it,' is the next statement. In spite of all
his pitfalls, Joseph had come to interpret life in the framework of
God's providence. He has willingly submitted to it. Even in front
of the Pharaoh, he would do no less than submit to God. Pharaoh
observed this amazing attachment to God and rewarded it. What
is the attachment in us that others can readily see!

> It is an amazing thing and a wonderful moment of Christian
> growth when one can accept life in terms of God's provi-
> dence, and be submitted to it. It is also amazing that others
> will see it in us and respond to it. Joseph had shown his
> commitment to God before, and it had been responded to
> before, only then, it got him thrown into prison. This time,
> he becomes the second most powerful man in Egypt. One
> might want to read Philippians 4:11-13. Let us ask God for
> understanding.

'...Joseph gathered corn...'

This part of Joseph's life is a climactic moment for Joseph. Certainly there are many, as yet, unanswered questions. What will
happen to Joseph's family back in Canaan? Will his brothers be
punished? Will Jacob ever learn that his son is alive? However,
even if those questions never get answered, the ultimate triumph of
Joseph leaves the reader with a certain kind of satisfaction. Joseph,
our hero, has triumphed. Good guys can finish first.

The whole story of Joseph has been an emotional roller coaster.
We have been very attracted to him from the beginning. He may
have made some misjudgments with his brothers, but he never

deserved what he got. We admired his tenacity, and faithfulness to God, in spite of terrible circumstances. He is the person we wish to be. Unlike Jacob whom we loved, and hated, Joseph has garnered only our love.

What are we to make of his life and his ultimate triumph? It would be nice to say that it proves that all our lives will turn out with that kind of triumph if we are as faithful as Joseph. We know, however, that Christians get martyred, most Christians never become rulers, and many will suffer much and receive little or no earthly reward. Yet, Joseph's remarkable life does teach us about ourselves.

It teaches us that it is possible to be faithful in trying times. Joseph did not know what would happen. He simply grasped God as his possession and refused to turn loose. One recalls that it took Jacob a long time to learn to do that. He only understood it after an all night wrestling match with God (Genesis 32:24-26).

Also, the life of Joseph provides a lesson to a church as a whole. What might God be able to do through us if we refused to turn loose of God and, refused to run in our own directions every time things get tough? Christians who have followed God for years can testify to their personal growth, and even point out certain triumphs that can only be attributed to God. They may not have the grandeur of being Prime Minister of Egypt, but they do have the grandeur of quieting the soul and providing the on-going assurance that God is with them. And, in the end, that in itself, is the greatest reward the Christian can have.

> Again, it is important to return to the lesson that God, himself, not the triumphs associated with this world, is the greatest possession of the Christian. Joseph ended up with a great and wonderful position of worldly status, but the greater thing, he had all along, a relationship with God. That relationship is still paying dividends for Joseph thousands of years after his rulership in Egypt is buried in the pages of history. Let us give thanks to God for our relationship with him.

Genesis 41:45-57

45. And Pharaoh called Joseph's name Zaphnathpaaneah; and he gave him to wife Asenath the daughter of Potipherah priest of On. And Joseph went out over all the land of Egypt. 46. And Joseph was thirty years old when he stood before Pharaoh king of Egypt. And Joseph went out from the presence of Pharaoh, and went throughout all the land of Egypt. 47. And in the seven plenteous years the earth brought forth by handfuls. 48. And he gathered up all the food of the seven years, which were in the land of Egypt, and laid up the food in the cities: the food of the field, which was round about every city, laid he up in the same. 49. And Joseph gathered corn as the sand of the sea, very much, until he left numbering; for it was without number. 50. And unto Joseph were born two sons before the years of famine came, which Asenath the daughter of Potipherah priest of On bare unto him. 51. And Joseph called the name of the firstborn Manasseh: For God, said he, hath made me forget all my toil, and all my father's house. 52. And the name of the second called he Ephraim: For God hath caused me to be fruitful in the land of my affliction. 53. And the seven years of plenteousness, that was in the land of Egypt, were ended. 54. And the seven years of dearth began to come, according as Joseph had said: and the dearth was in all lands; but in all the land of Egypt there was bread. 55. And when all the land of Egypt was famished, the people cried to Pharaoh for bread: and Pharaoh said unto all the Egyptians, Go unto Joseph; what he saith to you, do. 56. And the famine was over all the face of the earth: and Joseph opened all the storehouses, and sold unto the Egyptians; and the famine waxed sore in the land of Egypt. 57. And all countries came into Egypt to Joseph for to buy corn; because that the famine was so sore in all lands.

Joseph's family

The teller of Joseph's story provides some very interesting detail in these passages. The information provides insight into the thinking of Joseph, and reveals more of his character. Upon meditation, there is much the reader is taught. Released from prison, Joseph has a great amount of energy to burn. The statement, '...And Joseph went out from the presence of Pharaoh, and went throughout all the land of Egypt' (Genesis 41:46), reveals an excitement and vitality to Joseph's newly found situation. As we read, we are excited for him.

Joseph receives an Egyptian bride, and is given an Egyptian name (41:45). The intent is clearly for Joseph to be accepted by the people of Egypt. His name is generally thought to mean 'the god speaks and he lives.' Pharaoh is noting that Joseph spoke with words from a god. He gave to Joseph the daughter of a priest for a wife. The religious implications are not to be missed. Pharaoh had seen a divine power in Joseph, and this is the best that he can do in acknowledging it. We, the readers, may be somewhat uncomfortable with the Egyptian bride in the light of God's judgement on the patriarchal families for taking wives of the Canaanites. The Egyptian bride, however, is not of the land, has no connection with it, and does not fall under the same kind of condemnation. God granted the two sons of this union a place in the nation of Israel. God is providing reward to Joseph for faithfulness in his actions with Potiphar's wife.

The two sons are given names that are very revealing. The first born, Manasseh, means 'making to forget.' Joseph is saying that God has made it possible for the trials of his earlier days to be forgotten. He does not walk in anger or bitterness. It would be nice if all Christians could learn that lesson from Joseph. The second born, Ephraim, means 'fruitful.' Joseph is looking at the situation of his life and rejoicing in what God has done. We have a man taking charge of his family. Married to the daughter of a priest of an Egyptian god, Joseph leaves no doubt as to the God that he and his family will worship (41:51-52). There could still be much sadness in Joseph's heart as he remembers his father, but he will not allow his mind to let the sadness define him.

All Christians have an option. They could allow the heartbreak and disappointments of life to define them, or rejoice in their opportunities.

Joseph and Jesus

One must be careful that one does not give to much glory to the great people of the Bible. Yet, there are certain things about Joseph's experience that should be celebrated. His life draws certain contrasts and comparisons to Jesus Christ that cannot be ignored.

First, he was betrayed by his brothers, and sold him into slavery. It shall turn out that the very evil act they committed became the means of their redemption. The Scripture teaches that Jesus '...came unto his own and his own received him not' (John 1:11). Like Joseph, Jesus was betrayed for a few pieces of silver (37:28; Matthew 26:15).

Second, Joseph was thirty years old when he began the work of his ministry that would result in saving the family that had betrayed him. It is no mere coincidence that Luke records 'And Jesus himself, began to be about thirty years of age...' (Luke 3:23). The statement about Jesus comes immediately after receiving his commission from the heavenly Father '...Thou art my beloved son; in thee I am well pleased' (Luke 3:22). For Joseph, it comes upon receiving commission from the Pharaoh. 'And Pharaoh said unto Joseph, See, I have set thee over all the land of Egypt' (41:41). In both instances, there is the clear intimation of God's establishment of those who are faithful. The biblical connection in the lives of Joseph and Jesus give evidence to the unity of Scripture.

Also, Joseph went from being the beloved son of his father, Jacob, part heir to the Abrahamic promise, to a stranger in a foreign land, to a ruler in the pagan nation. His brothers who betrayed him will ultimately bow to him acknowledging his authority. Jesus gave up the position at the right hand of his father. He came to a people who betrayed him. He also will ultimately find his own people bowing to him as Lord (Zechariah 12:10; 13:9; Philippians 2:10). For the Christian, these are all wonderful accounts that magnify the wonder of one God who used all events of Joseph's life to foreshadow the life of his own son, Jesus. As Pharaoh told the people, '...what he saith to you, do' (41:55), Jesus said, 'Ye are my friends, if ye do whatsoever I command you' (John 15:14).

> It takes some study and meditation, but one is amazed at the glimpses of eternal purpose in the events of our Biblical heroes. They are there for our learning, and should teach us that God is never bound by our limitations.

'...what he saith to you, do'

Joseph's story takes the turn for which we have been warned. '...the seven years of plenteousness...ended. And the seven years of dearth began to come...' (Genesis 41:53-54). The reader has known this is to happen but the words hit us like a thud. What will this mean for Joseph? Will the Pharaoh now turn on Joseph? As we have followed his life, that would not be unexpected. The tension rises as we read, '...the people cried to Pharaoh for bread...' (41:55).

The life of Joseph now swings back to hard times. The roller coaster of his life good times to hard times to good times and back to hard times again leaves us somewhat emotionally exhausted. This is something that mirrors life for many of us. A few will experience life as a constant bed of roses, many will see life as nothing but a bed of thorns, but the roller coaster is more common. The final line of children's fairy tales, 'and they lived happily ever after,' does not accurately reflect life. We have seen the character of Joseph hold him in good stead before. Will it continue to do so?

The author removes some of our concern. '...and Pharaoh said unto all the Egyptians, Go unto Joseph; what he saith to you, do' (41:55). Joseph will not be removed from his charge. He is, however, faced with a massive responsibility. How will he deal with the masses, who are clamouring for food?

For seven years, all of Joseph's energy had been for the purpose of gathering and storing food. His success was phenomenal. 'And Joseph gathered corn as the sand of the sea, very much, until he left numbering; for it was without number...' (41:49). He must now turn his creative energy to a different kind of task, the dispensing of food. He knows the problem will last seven years. He must be careful to maintain the supply.

It is not something that we think about very much, but maintaining the supply is a constant human dilemma. In times of plenty, we worry about recession and loss. Even in our problem solving, we worry if we will have an adequate supply of knowledge or wisdom. It is in this area as much as any area, that we learn one of the great aspects of loving God, 'trust.' Jesus was faced with a problem of adequate supply when the wine ran out at a wedding feast. The problem was brought to Jesus. His mother said of him 'Whatsoever he saith unto you, do it' (John 2:5). We've heard these words before (41:55).

> The constant pursuit of humanity, and guaranteed as a human right in the American Declaration of Independence, is for happiness. The Bible provides a better way. The better way is mirrored in the instructions of Pharaoh (41:55), and said by Mary concerning her son, the promised seed of the woman (John 2:5). In John 13:17 Jesus says, 'If ye know these things (my words), happy are ye if ye do them.' Let us pray that God will help us to be more concerned for his words than for the adequate supply.

'...in all lands...'

If one were reading the story of Joseph, noticing all the ups and downs, and wondering how it is going to conclude, he gets his first hint in this passage. 'And all the countries came into Egypt to

Joseph for to buy corn; because that the famine was so sore in all lands' (41:57). One can almost feel the tingle of expectancy. So this is what has been going on. Those brothers who betrayed him are going to eventually show up in Egypt. The suspenseful wait for that encounter is established in the reader's mind.

Once more the grandeur and the sovereignty of God is on display. As we read biblical history, our minds are swept away in wonder at this amazing God. When one thinks of the greatest commandment, 'Thou shalt love the Lord thy God with all thy heart... soul...mind' (Matthew 22:37), it becomes an easier command as the wonder of his works among men is observed. In this Scripture, we are told a marvellous detail. It is that God affected the conditions of a whole world in order to get one little family into Egypt that he may work out his divine purpose.

The methodology of God that is displayed in the story of Joseph will be seen again when God does another work in the affairs of men. 'And it came to pass in those days, that there went out a decree from Caesar Augustus, that all the world should be taxed' (Luke 2:1). These words reflect the work of God in moving the whole world to get one couple (Joseph and Mary) to Bethlehem in order for Jesus to be born there in fulfilment of the prophecy of Micah 5:2.

In loving God, there is the desire to know God. The action of God, in moving a whole world to impact one family, helps us read the thinking of God. His plan is nearing completion. In Joseph's case, the promise of Abraham fathering a great nation (12:2) will come to fruition in Egypt (Exodus 1:7). In the case of Jesus' birth, the promise made to Abraham that '...in thee shall all families of the earth be blessed' (12:3) is coming to fulfilment. God's plan comes to fruition in the quietness of the actions of one family, but the stamp of God is on it as the whole world is involved. What a mighty God we serve!

Genesis 42:1-38

I. The Decision to Seek Food in Egypt (42:1-9)
1. '...get you down...'
2. '...bowed down themselves...'
3. Joseph remembers the dream

II. Joseph's Brothers Face Deja-vu (42:10-24)
1. Family must come to Egypt
2. Joseph establishes a test
3. '...this do and live...'
4. '...his blood is required'

III. Guilty Reactions (42:25-38)
1. Money restore
2. Lost leadership

Genesis 42:1-9

1. Now when Jacob saw that there was corn in Egypt, Jacob said unto his sons, Why do ye look one upon another? 2. And he said, Behold, I have heard that there is corn in Egypt: get you down thither, and buy for us from thence; that we may live, and not die. 3. And Joseph's ten brethren went down to buy corn in Egypt. 4. But Benjamin, Joseph's brother, Jacob sent not with his brethren; for he said, Lest peradventure mischief befall him. 5. And the sons of Israel came to buy corn among those that came: for the famine was in the land of Canaan. 6. And Joseph was the governor over

the land, and he it was that sold to all the people of the land: and Joseph's brethren came, and bowed down themselves before him with their faces to the earth. 7. And Joseph saw his brethren, and he knew them, but made himself strange unto them, and spake roughly unto them; and he said unto them, Whence come ye? And they said, From the land of Canaan to buy food. 8. And Joseph knew his brethren, but they knew not him. 9. And Joseph remembered the dreams which he dreamed of them, and said unto them, Ye are spies; to see the nakedness of the land ye are come.

'...get you down...'

The long-sought reuniting of Joseph with his brothers is now in sight in Joseph's story. As it begins to develop, the scene changes from Egypt to Canaan. The famine has begun to have disastrous effect on the family of Jacob. He calls for his sons and instructs them. '...I have heard there is corn in Egypt: get you down thither, and buy for us from thence; that we may live, and not die' (42:2). With that statement by Jacob, the irony of Joseph's story increases. The brothers, who had sought to kill Joseph (37:18) will now turn to him to save their lives.

There are two other things of note to be seen in Jacob's words. He is rather caustic to his sons. 'Why do ye look one upon another' (42:1)? Here, one is reminded of Jacob's attitude when he first encountered the shepherds of Haran. '...Neither is it time that the cattle should be gathered together: water ye the sheep, and go and feed them' (29:7). The impatience of Jacob with those who do not take action in a serious situation is reflected in both instances. There is a certain lack of trust in his sons Jacob displays. In his mind, they should have already acted to go to Egypt. This lack of trust may be part of his reason for sending Joseph years earlier to discover how his sons were doing (37:14).

Also, Jacob's thoughts reflect that he had come to suspicion that Joseph's demise was due to the actions of the brothers. 'But Benjamin, Joseph's brother, Jacob sent not with his brethren; for he said, 'Lest peradventure mischief befall him' (42:4). This little passage tells us that the twenty years of trials for Joseph in Egypt were paralleled by twenty years of stress and suspicion, and conflict with the family in Canaan.

In a few cryptic words, the author has covered twenty years of history. In fact, our imaginations can fill in the blanks about the last twenty years for Jacob and his sons. The great tragedy for the brothers' of Joseph is that they sought to gain the love of their father by removing from him his greatest love in this earth, the favoured son Joseph; and had succeeded only in further condemning themselves. The biblical narratives amaze us with the incomprehensible thoughts of God, but they also anger us with the constant and utterly foolish thinking of we humans.

'...bowed down themselves...'

Joseph's brothers, who had sold him into slavery twenty years earlier, make their journey to Egypt to buy corn. In a master story-teller's stroke, we have this picture. '...and Joseph's brethren came, and bowed down themselves before him with their faces to the earth' (42:6). Instantly, the reader of the story is reminded of the dreams Joseph told his brothers '...the sun and the moon and the eleven stars made obeisance to me' (Genesis 37:9). God was writing this story. Only he could have scripted man's life like this.

Joseph immediately understood. 'And Joseph remembered the dreams which he dreamed...' (42:9). This is another of life's defining moments. For years, Joseph had been loyal to God. In spite of years of hurt, bad luck, wrongful treatment, he continued to trust God. There is every reason for him to despise his brothers, and to want revenge. Joseph remembered the dream, and in that moment, it all came together for him. God had done something wonderful, even though his brothers meant him harm. For Joseph, remembering the dream meant instantaneous forgiveness.

One might look at Joseph's treatment of his brothers and question whether forgiveness is present. Joseph's actions, however, are not meant for punishment, but for discovery. He must know of their present attitudes, if they had also turned on his brother, Benjamin, as they had turned on him. Also, any sudden revelation of himself before that discovery might create an angry reaction in the brothers, which would force disciplinary action by the Egyptians, and cause the brothers to fail in getting corn back to their father, Jacob. Joseph wants to get help to his father and to reconcile with his brothers. He must not do anything to damage those desires.

Joseph's long journey of trial, tribulation, and blessing had taught him much in the way of discerning situations. '...Tribulation worketh patience...' (Romans 5:3).

> Tribulation can do many wonderful things in the development of maturity. It can work patience. It can also help develop discernment. Joseph was now wise enough to refrain from a hasty reaction. His haste in telling the dreams as a young man had gotten him into trouble. He will not make the same mistake again.

Joseph remembers the dream

The process of learning involves the ability to properly interpret the events of our lives. Every human being makes judgements. Others impact our lives and we make judgements about whether the impact is good or bad. We make judgements on the motivation of the person who impacted us. We look at circumstances and events and try to interpret what they mean. Sometimes, we are wrong, and a wrong interpretation creates an attitude, which leads to incredibly foolish action.

Joseph's brothers had listened to Joseph's telling of his dream. Their interpretation was that Joseph believes he will someday be their master, and he will rule over them. 'And his brethren said to him, Shalt thou indeed reign over us? Or shalt thou indeed have dominion over us...' (37:8)? Their interpretation of the events created anger, which had led to their selling him into slavery.

The brothers' missed badly on their understanding. They erred on two fronts. First, there was no discernment that the dream was prophetic in its nature. They saw it only as arrogance on Joseph's part. It was only an attempt (as they saw it) for Joseph to rub it in their faces that he was their father's favourite son. The prophetic nature of the dream meant that the dream was from God, not from Joseph.

Second, had they understood that God was providing the message, there would have been a tendency to understand it in the light of spiritual implications. Their obedience in that light would be to God, not to Joseph. Instead of fastening attention on Joseph, they could have turned attention to God, thus preventing the great wrong that they inflicted on Joseph.

The irony of it all is that they heard the idea of bowing to Joseph as being slaves to Joseph. The facts are made clear when they bow before Joseph here that the obeisance is for the preservation of life, not for the lessening of life's advantages. Bowing down isn't so bad when you are on the verge of starving to death. The reality is a totally different take than their original foolish interpretation. It is important to learn from the moment in which a foolish analysis is made about a situation in our life? When our eyes are on our self and not on God, foolish analysing is the norm.

> When trouble strikes in our lives, there is usually instant analysis. Blame is placed everywhere, often, most stringently on self. It may be wise to learn from Joseph's brothers, and refrain from too hasty an analysis of the trials of our life. There are times when we just don't know the reasons. Perhaps there is a larger plan of God at work.

Genesis 42:10-24

10. And they said unto him, Nay, my lord, but to buy food are thy servants come. 11. We are all one man's sons; we are true men, thy servants are no spies. 12. And he said unto them, Nay, but to see the nakedness of the land ye are come. 13. And they said, Thy servants are twelve brethren, the sons of one man in the land of Canaan; and, behold, the youngest is this day with our father, and one is not. 14. And Joseph said unto them, That is it that I spake unto you, saying, Ye are spies: 15. Hereby ye shall be proved: By the life of Pharaoh ye shall not go forth hence, except your youngest brother come hither. 16. Send one of you, and let him fetch your brother, and ye shall be kept in prison, that your words may be proved, whether there be any truth in you: or else by the life of Pharaoh surely ye are spies. 17. And he put them all together into ward three days. 18. And Joseph said unto them the third day, This do, and live; for I fear God: 19. If ye be true men, let one of your brethren be bound in the house of your prison: go ye, carry corn for the famine of your houses: 20. But bring your youngest brother unto me; so shall your words be verified, and ye shall not die. And they did so. 21. And they said one to another, We are verily guilty concerning our brother, in that we saw the anguish of his soul, when he besought us, and we would not hear; therefore is this distress come upon us. 22. And Reuben answered them, saying, Spake I not unto you, saying, Do not sin against the child; and ye would not hear? therefore, behold, also his blood is required. 23. And they knew not that Joseph understood them; for he spake unto them by an interpreter. 24. And he turned himself about from them, and wept; and returned to them again, and communed with them, and took from them Simeon, and bound him before their eyes.

Family must come to Egypt

The actions of Joseph are clearly designed to bring his father's family to Egypt. The narrative of the patriarchal families has always been to keep the family in the land. Abraham sinned because of fleeing the land when famine struck (Genesis 12:10-12). Why would Joseph's actions to get the family out of the land be blessed by God. There are a couple of clues in the Scriptures.

First, Joseph remembered his dreams (42:9). He had seen the dream partially fulfilled when his brother bowed to him. All the parts of the dream were not yet in place. 'Behold, I have dreamed a dream more; and, behold, the sun and the moon and the eleven stars made obeisance to me. And he told it to his father…and his father rebuked him…shall I and thy mother and thy brethren indeed come to bow down ourselves to thee to the earth' (37:9-10)? Joseph knew that the prophetic nature of the dream required the presence of the entire family. It was not that Joseph was prideful, but that he knew this was part of God's plan.

Second, God had earlier given a vision to Abraham. '…Know of a surety that thy seed shall be a stranger in a land that is not their's, and shall serve them: and they shall afflict them four hundred years…' (15:13). In Joseph's move to fulfil the requirements of the prophetic dream, he is putting in motion that which shall bring to pass the prophecy received by Abraham. The 'land that is not theirs' (15:13) shall be Egypt.

The question remains as to why it is being done at this time. And why go to a foreign land? The answer lies in the reality that Jacob's family is Israel. Unlike Abraham's children, and Isaac's children, there is no special son for becoming a nation. They shall all be part of the nation. In a foreign land, the nation shall develop without the threat of taking Canaanite wives, and without taking on the 'gods' of the Canaanites as their own. In Egypt, (as we shall see), they shall be placed in a specific part of the land isolating them from the affairs of Egypt. Ultimately, their plight will deteriorate, and they will need to understand their position as uniquely separated unto the one God when he delivers them from bondage. The point for us is to daily pay attention to the learning of God's process, so that we may act in his will, as did Joseph.

Joseph was made aware of the plan of God because he paid attention to the activity of God in his life. At the proper moment, things were brought to his remembrance. The thing for us to remember is that things that were never in our mind cannot be brought to our remembrance. Let us be aware of God daily, and pray that he will make our learning complete so that we will never be lacking in what we need to remember.

Joseph establishes a test

Joseph immediately recognizes his brothers, but they did not recognize him. He was without beard (customary for Egypt), plus they would not have expected him to be such a powerful person. Joseph accuses his brothers of being spies. In their fear, they recite the family history. In a stroke of genius, Joseph says they must bring their youngest brother to Egypt to prove they are not spies. The youngest brother is Benjamin, Joseph's full brother by Rachel. He is testing the brothers' relationship with their father. Will they now be honest with their father or use the same kind of deceitfulness that they had used before? He comes to the conclusion that one should stay as hostage, while the others return. The brothers cannot make that decision, so Joseph makes it for them. The irony is, the decision about who to sacrifice was once easy, but now hard. Simeon is the one chosen.

Joseph's plan carries an extremely interesting twist. In effect, Joseph is saying, 'sacrifice one for the benefit of everybody else.' That is exactly what they thought they had done with Joseph. The actual result was that everybody suffered. They are now placed in the situation of again returning to the father with one brother missing. The memories are now clearly stirred. 'And they said one to another, We are verily guilty concerning our brother, in that we saw the anguish of his soul...' (42:21).

How did they so easily make the connection? Each one faced the reality that he could be the one remaining behind, and dealing with all the uncertainty of such an event. The cries of Joseph came easily to their minds.

Further, Joseph's words, '...This do, and live...' (42:18), removed any possibility that they could lessen their guilt, by rationalizing their sparing of Joseph's life, through selling him into slavery instead of killing him. It is an Egyptian prince who had just accused them of being spies who said this. A promise from this person would carry no real guarantee in their mind. Very skilfully, Joseph had placed the brothers in the same position in which they had placed him years earlier. The words of verse 24 'And he turned himself...from them and wept...' reveal that his motive was not vengeance. The point is to lead them to the place of desiring forgiveness, which is already in place.

> The thought that people must be brought to the point of desiring forgiveness is a strange thought, yet this is the nature of human beings. We prefer to think of ourselves as the ones wronged and that others need our forgiveness. Certainly, when Joseph's brothers sold him into slavery, they looked at themselves as the wronged ones.

'...this do and live...'

Joseph's plan to bring his family to Egypt, and to bring his brothers to the place of repentance, and accepting of forgiveness, is a powerful story told with many underlying themes. Each theme should be examined one at a time. His brothers have come to Egypt to buy grain. Recognizing them when they did not know who he was, he accused them of being spies, and works out a plan to spare their lives. One must be left behind while the rest take the grain home, and then return to Egypt with their youngest brother, which will secure the release of the brother kept behind.

When Joseph offers the plan he states, '...This do, and live; for I fear God' (42:18). In his statement, there are two realities. First, he is requiring them to trust a stranger with the life of their brother. With no guarantee, except the word of the stranger, they must bring their youngest brother back to Egypt. By placing their brother's life in the hands of strangers, they are repeating what they had done with Joseph years earlier.

Second, Joseph states, '...I fear God' (42:18). Joseph is speaking through an interpreter, but the name for God that is used is the name, Elohim, used by the children of Abraham. This must have struck a nerve as the words of Reuben testify '...Spake I not unto you, saying, Do not sin against the child; and ye would not hear? therefore...also his blood is required' (42:22). His brothers were not aware that he understood their language.

What is the significance? As Joseph heard the discussion, it is clear that the brothers were in anguish and had accepted that they had done evil against Joseph years earlier. Joseph's tears reflect a desire to reveal himself immediately, and begin the restoration process. However, it is one thing to repent, it is another to accept forgiveness. The family could not be reconciled until the brothers were willing to accept forgiveness. Otherwise they would continue to squabble as they are doing here.

In a very subtle and wise move, Joseph is allowing his brothers the opportunity to make retribution for the wrong they did to him. Through the retributions, they have paid for their sin, and forgiveness is more readily acceptable. Sometimes it is much easier to forgive than to accept forgiveness.

> Sometimes one can be so overwhelmed with the sense of one's sin, forgiveness seems impossible. The ability to make retribution in some way aids the acceptance of forgiveness. In a marvellous way, this is what God did through the sacrifice of Christ. Retribution is made to a Holy God, and sin can be forgiven.

'...his blood is required'

When Joseph presented his plan to his brothers to prove they were not spies, the brothers react in debate with each other. Reuben's comment brings up an old theme in Genesis and calls for some meditation. He states '...Spake I not unto you saying, Do not sin against the child, and ye would not hear? Therefore, behold, also his blood is required' (42:22). The statement reflects the obligation of restitution for wrong done to others. One of the brothers must be sacrificed to pay for the loss of Joseph.

The theme first appears in Genesis 4:8-10. '...Cain rose up against Abel his brother, and slew him. And the Lord said unto Cain...the voice of thy brother's blood crieth unto me from the ground' (4:8-10). Early on, the Bible makes plain the responsibility that man has for his brother. God would not allow anyone to slay Cain because there was no human government established. However, God punished Cain by banishment from the family and placing on him a mark that would forever show others his character. He would be marked as one who owed a debt that he did not pay (4:15).

The theme also appears later in Genesis when God establishes the pattern of human government. 'Whoso sheddeth man's blood, by man shall his blood be shed...' (Genesis 9:6). Reuben's statement reflects on the concept of human government God gave to Noah. The brothers knew well the punishment for their offence. The most obvious choice to accept the punishment would be the eldest brother, Reuben. However, Reuben was the one who made an effort to save Joseph. His statement, at this point, might be an attempt to salvage himself from being the one left behind.

Joseph listened to the debate of his brothers, and selects the next older brother, Simeon, to stay behind. It may be that Joseph was influenced by Reuben's statement. For our purposes, this even plays out the importance of restitution in God's redemptive plan. Joseph's life could not be restored by his brothers. They presumed him dead. The blood that is required for his life is not so much punishment, but acknowledgement of the value of his life. By taking his life into their hands, they said it was of no value. By losing their own life, they acknowledge that value. Reuben said, '...his blood is required' (42:22). It means, 'We owe a debt.' This acknowledgement was critical for the brothers' redemption. Debts are usually not paid until we own them.

It would be appropriate here to spend a moment in meditation of our sins, and spend time claiming ownership of
them, and accepting the payment of the blood of Christ as
full payment.

Genesis 42:25-38

*25. Then Joseph commanded to fill their sacks with corn, and to restore
every man's money into his sack, and to give them provision for the way:
and thus did he unto them. 26. And they laded their asses with the corn,
and departed thence. 27. And as one of them opened his sack to give his
ass provender in the inn, he espied his money; for, behold, it was in his
sack's mouth. 28. And he said unto his brethren, My money is restored;
and, lo, it is even in my sack: and their heart failed them, and they were
afraid, saying one to another, What is this that God hath done unto us?
29. And they came unto Jacob their father unto the land of Canaan, and
told him all that befell unto them; saying, 30. The man, who is the lord
of the land, spake roughly to us, and took us for spies of the country.
31. And we said unto him, We are true men; we are no spies: 32. We be
twelve brethren, sons of our father; one is not, and the youngest is this
day with our father in the land of Canaan. 33. And the man, the lord of
the country, said unto us, Hereby shall I know that ye are true men; leave
one of your brethren here with me, and take food for the famine of your
households, and be gone: 34. And bring your youngest brother unto me:
then shall I know that ye are no spies, but that ye are true men: so will I
deliver you your brother, and ye shall traffick in the land. 35. And it came
to pass as they emptied their sacks, that, behold, every man's bundle
of money was in his sack: and when both they and their father saw the
bundles of money, they were afraid. 36. And Jacob their father said unto
them, Me have ye bereaved of my children: Joseph is not, and Simeon is
not, and ye will take Benjamin away: all these things are against me. 37.
And Reuben spake unto his father, saying, Slay my two sons, if I bring him
not to thee: deliver him into my hand, and I will bring him to thee again.
38. And he said, My son shall not go down with you; for his brother is
dead, and he is left alone: if mischief befall him by the way in the which ye
go, then shall ye bring down my gray hairs with sorrow to the grave.*

Money restored

The subtle impact of this story is remarkable. It reveals the soul's reaction when it is filled with guilt. Guilt makes it impossible to read the circumstances of our life correctly. The motives of others are misconstrued, and good things in our life can appear as bad things. Note the events of this story.

Joseph, after deciding to keep Simeon captive, sends his brothers home to their father, Jacob. In order to secure Simeon's release they must return to Egypt with their youngest brother, Benjamin. Before the brothers leave, Joseph places their money in the sacks of grain. Along the way, one of them sought to feed his donkey a little of the grain and discovered the money had been returned. Their reaction provides an insightful look at human nature. '...their heart failed them, and they were afraid, saying one to another, What is this that God hath done unto us' (42:28)? The reader will note that a very good thing has been interpreted as a bad thing. The stirrings of a guilty soul will often create such a reaction.

The Bible narrative tells us nothing of Joseph's motivation in giving the money back to his brothers. It is thus assumed that Joseph returned it as a matter of grace. He had no need for their money, and was sending it back to his father. This was a positive thing. Joseph's brothers could only see it in the light of their guilt. In fact, the return of the money is viewed as the punishment of God upon them.

It is also noteworthy to see how Jacob reacted to the news. '...Me have ye bereaved of my children: Joseph is not, and Simeon is not, and ye will take Benjamin away: all these things are against me' (42:36). Jacob turned responsibility back on his sons. He is saying, 'this is what you have done.' He is accusing his sons of stealing the money. Twenty years of guilt on the part of these brothers had created actions that led their father to mistrust their words to him.

An act of grace on the part of Joseph created an awful lot of anguish in the family. This is instructive of how God's grace can often affect us. Joseph's brothers did not deserve his grace and could only see it as a precursor to judgement when that was not the intent. God may manifest his grace to us, and we only see it as bad, because our guilty soul expects judgement.

This story presents another of the learning events about grace. God's grace is seen in its ultimate expression in the death of Jesus Christ. Grace is that two-edged sword that can be seen as precursor to great punishment, or it can be seen as the vehicle to total freedom from guilt.

Lost leadership

The oldest son in the house of Jacob makes for an interesting and tragic study. He is seen here in a bold gesture trying to show leadership before his father and brothers. Reuben seems to go back and forth between taking a stand and doing the right thing, to waffling and showing weakness. The attempts at leadership are always pathetic and ill- timed.

At the moment of standing before his father, offering to sacrifice his own sons if he is not successful in saving Simeon (held captive in Egypt), and restoring Benjamin to his father, he is coming off a cowardly display before the Egyptian prince. As the oldest brother, he was the logical choice to remain in Egypt, but had, instead, chastised his brothers for their actions against Joseph years earlier (42:22). It was the Egyptian prince (Joseph, whom they did not recognize), who made the decision to hold Simeon, the next oldest brother (42:24). On the journey home, it is likely that Reuben received somewhat of a cold shoulder from his brothers. In typical Reuben-like fashion, he wants to make up for it by bold talk after the time for bold action has passed. The fact that Jacob refused Reuben indicated that Jacob understood Reuben's penchant for not showing up when bold action is required.

The story of Reuben can make many of us uncomfortable. Most of us can identify with being 'missing in action' when difficult moments arise. Guilt from those times along with the attitude of others around us will cause us to try to make amends. We will make promises, or push for bold action, while in safe environments. The problem is 'our actions speak louder than our words'.

Many people would love to be leaders, and try to do it in safe moments, or in self-benefiting situations, such as Reuben taking his father's concubine (35:22). Their desire is to have other people think of them as leaders. However, when the situation calls for leadership to manifest itself, they never can discern the moment, and simply run for cover. They cry for others to name them as leader, but when the opportunity to simply lead, without validation from others arrives, they don't recognize it. For them, leadership is only self-serving, never self-sacrificing.

Genesis 43:1-34

I. Debate About Taking Benjamin to Egypt (43:1-14)
1. Judah shows some class
2. '...live and not die...'
3. Moment of inevitably
4. The last hope

II. A Second Meeting with the Egyptian Prince (43:15-34)
1. Again in Egypt
2. '...he brought Simeon out...'
3. Theology for the moment
4. '...five times as much...'

Genesis 43:1-14

1. And the famine was sore in the land. 2. And it came to pass, when they had eaten up the corn which they had brought out of Egypt, their father said unto them, Go again, buy us a little food. 3. And Judah spake unto him, saying, The man did solemnly protest unto us, saying, Ye shall not see my face, except your brother be with you. 4. If thou wilt send our brother with us, we will go down and buy thee food: 5. But if thou wilt not send him, we will not go down: for the man said unto us, Ye shall not see my face, except your brother be with you. 6. And Israel said, Wherefore dealt ye so ill with me, as to tell the man whether ye had yet a brother? 7. And they said, The man asked us straitly of our state, and of our kindred, saying, Is your father yet alive? have ye another brother? and we told him according to the Tenor of these words: could we certainly know that he would say,

Bring your brother down? 8. And Judah said unto Israel his father, Send the lad with me, and we will arise and go; that we may live, and not die, both we, and thou, and also our little ones. 9. I will be surety for him; of my hand shalt thou require him: if I bring him not unto thee, and set him before thee, then let me bear the blame for ever: 10. For except we had lingered, surely now we had returned this second time. 11. And their father Israel said unto them, If it must be so now, do this; take of the best fruits in the land in your vessels, and carry down the man a present, a little balm, and a little honey, spices, and myrrh, nuts, and almonds: 12. And take double money in your hand; and the money that was brought again in the mouth of your sacks, carry it again in your hand; peradventure it was an oversight: 13. Take also your brother, and arise, go again unto the man: 14. And God Almighty give you mercy before the man, that he may send away your other brother, and Benjamin. If I be bereaved of my children, I am bereaved.

Judah shows some class

The famine that first sent the sons of Jacob to Egypt has not eased. Inevitably, they would run out of grain. The fateful day has arrived, and Jacob calls for his sons to make a second trip to Egypt. Judah protests! '...The man did solemnly protest unto us, saying, Ye shall not see my face, except your brother be with you. If thou wilt send our brother with us, we will go down...But if thou wilt not send him, we will not go down...' (43:3-5).

An interesting pairing, seen earlier, is once more before the reader. Earlier, Reuben had pled to Jacob for the allowing of Benjamin to go to Egypt. He had been rebuffed (Genesis 42:37-38). Here, Judah makes the same request. It was these same two brothers who were involved in keeping Joseph from being slain. Judah had taken the initiative in his being sold into slavery. At that time, the brothers had a plan against Joseph. It is Joseph's plan against the brothers to which they are now reacting.

Judah will succeed where Reuben failed. Though there are very practical reasons for this, such as the imminent threat of starvation, God has a much larger historical view in mind. Judah's supremacy, as the tribe from which God shall fulfil his promise, is already in view. Later, the tribe of Judah shall endure while the other tribes shall disappear following the invasion of Assyria. The reader of Genesis is provided the rationale for a true historical reality.

As we examine the argument of Judah against the statement of Reuben, there is an interesting lesson to be learned. Judah argues forcefully without wild claims. Reuben attempts a grand gesture, '...Slay my two sons, if I bring him not to thee...' (42:37). Judah makes no such wild promises, but spoke with realism. '...if I bring him not unto thee, and set him before thee, then let me bear the blame forever' (43:9).

An effective leader must always face realistically the possibility of failure. There is no grand gesture from Judah, no misplaced arrogance, simply, a promise to be responsible. He knew this was a risk, and he would not attempt to arbitrarily parcel out the responsibility to others as Reuben had done in his outlandish statement. Judah's kind of direct honesty and realism was much more comforting than Reuben's foolish confidence. All of us could learn a lesson here in the light of modern Christianity's penchant for loving the outlandish and the arrogant.

> Realistic honesty is lost on a culture that is enamoured of promises based in grandiose claims and charismatic personalities. We should pray that God would give us a new appreciation of simple and direct honesty.

'...live and not die...'

Jacob has instructed his sons to return the second time to Egypt to buy grain. Knowing they must take Benjamin, their youngest brother, with them, Judah pleads with his father to entrust Benjamin to his care. During the plea, Judah utters words that we have seen before and the words require some theological reflection. The author is recounting the story of the lives of the patriarchs, but more than that, he is recounting the details of God's working with men. He has presented a theme in Judah's words that drive home the point that this is God's story more than the story of Jacob and his family. Judah's important words are, '...send the lad with me, and we will arise and go; that we may live, and not die...' (43:8). Jacob had earlier said the same thing (Genesis 42:2). Joseph intimated the same idea (42:18).

The narrative of Genesis began with God's creation of man and the story of man's losing of life. 'And the lord God commanded the man, saying, Of every tree of the garden thou mayest freely eat: But of the tree of the knowledge of good and evil, thou shalt not eat of it: for in the day that thou eatest thereof thou shalt surely die' (2:16-17). The failure of the man to obey God brought death upon him. Thus, the theme of the book of Genesis (indeed of the entire Bible) is the theme of restoration of life.

'We shall live and not die' are powerful words in the context of Joseph's story. The writer leaves no doubt that God has masterfully engineered Joseph into being a preserver of life for the family of Jacob. This has critical ramifications for the whole story of the nation of Israel. It is Jacob's family that shall become the nation. Joseph becomes the protector of God's promise to bless all nations of the earth through the seed of Abraham. Jacob's family shall 'live and not die.' That shall be true in the earthly circumstances of the moment, but true in a larger historical and theological context.

A nation shall rise out of this family. It shall be Israel. The great son of Judah, who shall be the Saviour, Jesus Christ shall come. It is he who will say, 'I am come that they might have life...' (John 10:10). Jacob's family would say, 'Ye shall live and not die.'

The Word of God comes alive as the reader is confronted with the many moments, which are stories of people's lives, yet foreshadow much larger issues, even historical events, that shall not occur for centuries.

Moment of inevitability

Jacob's travail over allowing his youngest son, Benjamin, to go on the journey to Egypt comes to the point of his dread. The famine has not eased, and his intransigence about Benjamin has placed everyone in danger. The irony is that Benjamin's life is at risk if he stays or if he goes.

Knowing what he must do, Jacob reacts in typical human fashion. He complains! 'And Israel (Jacob) said, wherefore dealt ye so ill with me, as to tell the man whether ye had a brother' (43:6)? We can forgive Jacob for complaining because it is intrinsic to human nature. Complaining develops in the circumstance we can't change forcing the decision we don't want to make, so we bemoan all who might be implicated in our woes. Judah's reply is a repeat of the obvious. '...could we....know that he would say, Bring your brother down' (43:7)?

Jacob, aware that he has no alternative, gives in. He sends a few gifts of nuts, almonds, and spices to the Egyptian Prince. These were certain delicacies of the land, and for which the land was famous. With the famine in place, even these delicacies were probably rare, so Jacob was clearly hoping that sending what little he had to spare would appease the Egyptian Prince. Such a gift was an important custom when coming before one as high in position as Joseph. However, one must also see the sense of desperation in Jacob. It is a plea for life. He is searching for a way to bargain when he has nothing with which to bargain. Such is the plight of all men when it comes to our relationship with God.

When the sons leave, the sense of Jacob's despair is verbalized. '...If I be bereaved of my children, I am bereaved' (43:14). His statement represents two things. First, he has no hope except for what may be the decision of the Egyptian Prince. Second, a negative decision by the Egyptian Prince only hastens the inevitable death of his family. There is a strange kind of rest that comes in this. Jacob has accepted reality. The important lesson is expressed in Judah's words. 'For except we had lingered, surely now we had returned this second time' (43:10). The inevitability of Jacob's situation had been there when Reuben wanted to return to Egypt immediately after coming home (Genesis 42:37-38). By postponing the decision, Jacob had prolonged his agony. Instead of seeking to discover the answer to the mystery of the Egyptian Prince, he concentrated on his misery, thus guaranteeing his misery remains.

The last hope

Have you ever said, 'I have come to the end of my rope?' It is that statement that acknowledges limitations. You have used up every ounce of energy and creativity to solve a problem, and the problem remains. Sometimes the 'end of the rope' means doing what you did not want to do. Parents can face it as their children enter young adulthood carrying a rebellious attitude. Difficult decisions about whether they can remain in the home must be faced, sometimes with unpleasant, but necessary, requirements. We can face it in financial circumstances that have us in despair. It may be just depression about relationships that don't work out. Jacob faced it when the famine that may create starvation for his family required that he send his sons back to Egypt, risking the life of Benjamin in order to buy grain so that they may 'live and not die' (43:8).

This time, Benjamin must be sent, or the sons all risk execution. Simeon, the next to oldest brother was held prisoner there now. Jacob presumed he was dead (42:36), because on the previous trip the brothers had been accused of being spies (42:14). The only way to prove they were not spies was to return to Egypt with Benjamin. When Jacob finally realizes there is no way to avoid the inevitable, he sends his sons (Benjamin included) to Egypt.

The fact that Jacob is at the end of his rope is expressed. 'And God Almighty give you mercy before the man, that he may send away your other brother, and Benjamin...' (43:14). The words provide a great theology, and a lesson for life, which is worth grasping. The only hope that Jacob had was in the benefaction of the Egyptian Prince. That benefaction would be decided by a power higher than the prince, God.

From this moment, the story begins to turn. The writer of Genesis has skilfully led the reader to understand that when one is fully at the mercy of God, it is a good place to be. Being at the end of the rope is indeed a very good place to be if we find God there. Jacob could not know the wonderful thing his sons would discover in Egypt. He probably did not understand the depth and wonder in his total dependence on the mercy of God.

Stubbornness in the lives of Christians causes us to miss the value and blessing of our life that are to be found in relying on God's mercy. It is available many times, and we fail to see it. It was already at work for Jacob. A fact he would discover. God must occasionally bring us 'stubborn ones' to the end of our rope in order to see his mercy.

Pride can keep many people from seeing the value of mercy. No one ever receives the redemption from sin wrought in the seed of the woman without recognizing the need of mercy. Needing God's mercy! It is a good place to be positioned.

Genesis 43:15-34

15. And the men took that present, and they took double money in their hand and Benjamin; and rose up, and went down to Egypt, and stood before Joseph. 16. And when Joseph saw Benjamin with them, he said to the ruler of his house, Bring these men home, and slay, and make ready; for these men shall dine with me at noon. 17. And the man did as Joseph bade; and the man brought the men into Joseph's house. 18. And the men were afraid, because they were brought into Joseph's house; and they said, Because of the money that was returned in our sacks at the first time are we brought in; that he may seek occasion against us, and fall upon us, and take us for bondmen, and our asses. 19. And they came near to the steward of Joseph's house, and they communed with him at the door of the house, 20. And said, O sir, we came indeed down at the first time to buy food: 21. And it came to pass, when we came to the inn, that we opened our sacks, and, behold, every man's money was in the mouth of his sack, our money in full weight: and we have brought it again in our hand. 22. And other money have we brought down in our hands to buy food: we cannot tell who put our money in our sacks. 23. And he said, Peace be to you, fear not: your God, and the God of your father, hath given you treasure in your sacks: I had your money. And he brought Simeon out unto them. 24. And the man brought the men into Joseph's house, and gave them water, and they washed their feet; and he gave their asses provender. 25. And they made ready the present against Joseph came at noon: for they heard that they should eat bread there. 26. And when Joseph came home, they brought him the present which was in their hand into the house, and bowed themselves to him to the earth.

27. And he asked them of their welfare, and said, Is your father well, the old man of whom ye spake? Is he yet alive? 28. And they answered, Thy servant our father is in good health, he is yet alive. And they bowed down their heads, and made obeisance. 29. And he lifted up his eyes, and saw his brother Benjamin, his mother's son, and said, Is this your younger brother, of whom ye spake unto me? And he said, God be gracious unto thee, my son. 30. And Joseph made haste; for his bowels did yearn upon his brother: and he sought where to weep; and he entered into his chamber, and wept there. 31. And he washed his face, and went out, and refrained himself, and said, Set on bread. 32. And they set on for him by himself, and for them by themselves, and for the Egyptians, which did eat with him, by themselves: because the Egyptians might not eat bread with the Hebrews; for that is an abomination unto the Egyptians. 33. And they sat before him, the firstborn according to his birthright, and the youngest according to his youth: and the men marvelled one at another. 34. And he took and sent messes unto them from before him: but Benjamin's mess was five times so much as any of theirs. And they drank, and were merry with him.

Again in Egypt

Jacob's sons return to Egypt bringing Benjamin with them. One wonders what the journey was like. What did they talk about? How much conjecture was there about the mystery of events that would befall them in Egypt? Is Simeon still alive? The Scriptures tell us nothing of the events of the trip. We have only the abrupt '...and went down to Egypt, and stood before Joseph' (43:15).

They are invited to Joseph's house, attended to by Joseph's steward, and prepared to meet with Joseph. The brothers take an early moment to tell their story to Joseph's steward. They were hoping for some pronouncement about their own fate. The steward casually brushes off their story. Joseph appears and asks about their father, and asks if the new person with them is Benjamin. When this is acknowledged, Joseph is overcome with emotion and leaves the room. The meal is laid out when he returns. The brothers are seated according to their age, and wonder how the steward could have known this particular order (43:33).

Throughout the events of the day, Jacob's sons are put through an emotional trauma. At first they worried that they would be taken as slaves for Joseph (43:18), thus they hurried to make ready the present they had brought to him (43:25). Then, they are confused at the steward's knowledge of the order in which to seat them, but engage themselves in the festive atmosphere (43:34). Uneasiness has to be prevalent. The steward would not let them give back the money that had been placed in their sacks from the previous trip. The Egyptian Prince was more concerned with their father's health, and with the introduction to Benjamin, than with business (43:27-29).

Even more curious is that the steward of Joseph (an Egyptian) had made a theological statement about the God of their father, Jacob (43:23). Why would this Egyptian care about the God of Jacob? This statement had been totally missed, and no curiosity is shown. It was the God of their father who had given them treasure in their sacks. Why did they not focus on the steward's statement? When they first discovered the money, their response was, '...What is this that God hath done...' (42:28)? Their focus was God's punishment, not God's mercy. That's what our sin does, it has us focused on punishment so that we miss the grace.

It is a rather charming, and a major learning moment, to note that Joseph's brothers could not see the work of grace and mercy that is before them. They focused on their punishment because of their sin. We should ask God to help us understand the many ways we get so focused on the punishment we deserve that we do not see the offers of grace.

'...he brought Simeon out...'

The scene of the banquet in which Joseph feted his brothers reveals many subtle lessons. One of the most interesting is the brothers' attempt to explain one of their worrisome situations to the steward of Joseph. On the previous trip to Egypt, they had been accused of being spies. When arriving home, and opening the sacks of grain they purchased, they discovered that the money for purchase was placed in their sacks. With their brother, Simeon, already held hostage awaiting their return to Egypt to disprove the charge, they become terrified that they would be called thieves as well as spies (42:35).

On the second trip, they have brought the money back. Joseph does not talk to them, but through his steward invites them to his house for a feast. The brothers want the money issue settled, so they hastily tell their story to the steward (43:19-22). The motive was to get somebody to take the money back, so that another could testify that they were not thieves. The response of the steward was to say that God returned their money, and that he (the steward) had received the money they originally paid. It was evidently this same steward who had followed Joseph's orders to put the money in the sacks.

The steward's words could not be very comforting to the brothers. They needed to give the money back, but there was no one to accept it. Having the money in their possession was making them more and more uncomfortable. The steward's refusal to accept the money would have left them thinking 'what are they plotting against us? Are they purposely going to search us, take our money, and accuse us of thievery?' They make no further mention of the money. It is curious that they also make no mention of their brother, Simeon. The brothers are paralysed by fear, unable to ask questions that they need to be asking.

Abruptly, Simeon is delivered to them. If there was curiosity about their brother, Joseph acted immediately to remedy that concern. Joseph gave his brothers a lesson in setting priorities. They had come to purchase grain, and to eliminate the possibility that they would be charged as thieves. That was uppermost in their mind. When Simeon is put before them, they have something better if they acknowledge it. Sometimes, in our lives, fear has us paralysed. We are focused on some kind of immediate need trying to get something in our life fixed. God answers by giving us something else, something greater, in order to straighten our priorities, but we have no joy in it, because of our fear.

Theology for the moment

At the second encounter of Joseph's brothers with the one whom they had sold into slavery years earlier, we have another reminder of Joseph's dreams as a lad (37:5-11). The dreams noted that Joseph's brothers would bow before him. 'And when Joseph came home, they brought him the present which was in their hand into the house, and bowed themselves to him to the earth' (43:26). The scene projected in the dream literally comes to pass a second time (see 42:6). The same scene is repeated in Genesis 43:28. It is clear for the writer of Genesis that God is the orchestrator of these events and he emphasizes it for his readers. The same purpose is in mind in the words of the steward to Joseph's brothers. '...Peace be to you, fear not: your God, and the God of your father, hath given you treasure in your sacks' (43:23). Again, Joseph states to his brother, Benjamin, '...God be gracious unto thee, my son' (43:29).

The strong emphasis on the sovereignty of God throughout the stories of the patriarchal families should give pause to the reader of Scriptures. It is one of the great doctrinal truths of the Bible. The apostle Paul declares it, 'Nay but, O man, who art thou that repliest against God? Shall the thing formed say to him that formed it, Why has thou made me thus? Hath not the potter power over the clay...' (Romans 9:20-21)?

The sovereignty of God is a doctrine that will bring either great comfort or great horror to the soul of man. Consider: If one is attempting to know God, and please him, he has the great assurance that in whatever circumstances he finds himself, God is in control, and that he will be the master of events. 'And we know that all things work together for good to them that love God...' (Romans 8:28). What if one is in rebellion against God? One can, in the vanity of his life, think he is master of his own fate. He rebels in pride. Consider his horror when he understands that God has been in control of his life as well, orchestrating all the events toward his destruction. 'What if God, willing to show his wrath, and to make his power known, endured with much long-suffering the vessels of wrath fitted to destruction' (Romans 9:22)? God's sovereignty has two sides, horror and comfort. The writer of Genesis clearly wants us to perceive the comfort zone of God's sovereignty.

'...five times as much...'

The story of the banquet that Joseph provides for his brothers concludes with a very curious statement. 'And he took and set messes unto them from before him: but Benjamin's mess was five times so much as any of theirs...' (43:34). Joseph had not seen his only full brother since Benjamin was an infant. The statement that he favoured Benjamin would not be surprising to the reader. Is there, however, a larger meaning? The way the story reads would indicate such. The very next words describe the actions of the other brothers. '...And they drank, and were merry with him' (43:34).

One will note that there is no indication of jealousy or disturbance about Joseph (as Egyptian Prince) favouring Benjamin over the rest of them. In fact, this is probably a great relief to them. It is proof that the Egyptian Prince found favour with Benjamin, and will drop his charge that they are spies.

There is a very subtle message that the brothers will absorb later, and that the reader can pause and meditate upon at this point. The subtlety lies in this: the fact that one is favoured above the rest is not necessarily a bad thing. The favouritism shown to Benjamin worked to their salvation. The brothers seem to understand this at the moment Benjamin was favoured for they were merry. This demonstrates that the favouritism shown Benjamin produced great relief for them. Not only were they without resentment, they were ecstatic about it.

One of the most difficult lessons for humans to learn is acquiescence to the will of God even if others are favoured above us. God's actions are always to the benefit of all. The brothers' attitude with Benjamin was present because they perceived the reality of benefit to all. In this, they provide a contrast to later sinners of Israel, the scribes and Pharisees, who resented heavily the favouritism of the Father to the son, Jesus Christ. Matthew records that they sent Jesus to the cross for '...envy...' (Matthew 27:18). They could not recognize that in the favouritism of Christ, there is benefit for all.

The brothers of Joseph will not fully learn this until Joseph (whom they sold into slavery) is fully revealed to them. We should know it immediately in our acknowledgment of Jesus Christ as Lord.

The way of life can be made so much better if it can be lived without envy. Fortunate is the man who has the kind of relationship with God, which can produce such a life. A look at the cross, giving us an eternal view of life, and recognizing that all stand before God equal, with only the sacrifice of Christ to offer as redemption from sin, can help create the attitude that carries no envy.

Genesis 44:1-34

I. Charged with a Serious Crime (44:1-13)
1. '…evil for good…'
2. Theft of the divining cup

II. Facing the Charges (44:14-34)
1. A moment of confession
2. '…let thy servant abide…'
3. '…how shall I go up to my father…'
4. Learning the sacrifice of self

Genesis 44:1-13

1. And he commanded the steward of his house, saying, Fill the men's sacks with food, as much as they can carry, and put every man's money in his sack's mouth. 2. And put my cup, the silver cup, in the sack's mouth of the youngest, and his corn money. And he did according to the word that Joseph had spoken. 3. As soon as the morning was light, the men were sent away, they and their asses. 4. And when they were gone out of the city, and not yet far off, Joseph said unto his steward, Up, follow after the men; and when thou dost overtake them, say unto them, Wherefore have ye rewarded evil for good? 5. Is not this it in which my lord drinketh, and whereby indeed he divineth? ye have done evil in so doing. 6. And he overtook them, and he spake unto them these same words. 7. And they said unto him, Wherefore saith my lord these words? God forbid that thy servants should do according to this thing: 8. Behold, the money, which we found in our sacks' mouths, we brought again unto thee out of the land of Canaan: how then should we steal out of thy lord's house silver or

gold? 9. With whomsoever of thy servants it be found, both let him die, and we also will be my lord's bondmen. 10. And he said, Now also let it be according unto your words: he with whom it is found shall be my servant; and ye shall be blameless. 11. Then they speedily took down every man his sack to the ground, and opened every man his sack. 12. And he searched, and began at the eldest, and left at the youngest: and the cup was found in Benjamin's sack. 13. Then they rent their clothes, and laded every man his ass, and returned to the city.

'...evil for good...'

The brothers go on their way, clearly feeling good. Both Simeon and Benjamin are alive and returning home. One does have to wonder, in the light of the previous trip, why did they not check their sacks of grain before leaving. Perhaps they were too anxious to leave. Their fear produced the overlooking of a detail that should have been obvious. The missing of an important detail was to lead to greater trauma for them.

Before they could get very far Joseph sends his steward after them. He had secretly given back the money his brothers paid. As before, he put the money back in their sacks. This time there was a new wrinkle. He placed his silver cup, a very valuable cup (due to its religious significance as a divining cup), into Benjamin's sack. He instructs his steward '...follow after the men; and when thou dost overtake them, say unto them, Wherefore have ye rewarded evil for good (44:4)?

The question requires some reflection. When had the brothers been guilty of this? The most notorious moment was in the treatment of their father, Jacob. It was true that Jacob had favoured Joseph over the elder brothers, yet they had never lacked for provision. Jacob may have done more good for Joseph than for his brothers, but Jacob had certainly done them good. They interpreted the good for Joseph as evil for them. They rewarded Jacob by selling his beloved son into slavery, and reporting that he was dead. When the brothers heard the question from the steward, their consciences must have been pricked.

Listen to the brothers' protestations. '…how then should we steal out of thy Lord's house silver or gold? With whomsoever of thy servants it be found, both let him die, and we also will be my Lord's bondmen' (44:8-9).

It is pertinent that they were not accused of stealing gold, only the divining cup (44:8). Their guilty minds led them to attach additional complaints that were not there. Also, their guilty conscience led them to make an irrational judgement '…let him die …' (44:9). It is not unusual for a guilty party to act like a judge. That was exactly what the brothers had been, when they judged Jacob's treatment of them, but they had judged that which was good, not that which was evil. What if Joseph reveals himself as their brother, and expresses that God has done this for their good? Will they react in jealousy and continue to return evil for good? When one is in rebellion against God, he usually does just that. Joseph had to be sure of his brothers' attitude.

Theft of the divining cup

A most interesting aspect of this story is in the implications of the goblet Joseph placed in Benjamin's sack. The divining cup was a religious relic. It was used in the prophesying of future events. Water would be placed in the cup, and certain precious stones would be dropped in the water. Those with divining power would read the designs in the water for understanding of the future. Joseph, as we know from his interpretation of Pharaoh's dream, relied on God, not this kind of magic, to understand things to come (41:16). The fact that he had such a cup should not be surprising in the light of his power and position in Egypt, which had come from his prediction of the future in the dream interpretation.

When the steward came, accusing the brothers of the theft of the cup, he was making an extremely serious charge. It goes back to Joseph's original accusation against the brothers. They were accused of being spies (42:9). The theft of the divining cup would be construed as trying to learn the secrets of Egypt through having their magic goblet. The Egyptian Prince would have his proof that they were spies. When the cup appears in Benjamin's sack the brothers were distraught. 'Then they rent their clothes...and returned to the city' (44:13). We saw this same grief when Jacob was told of Joseph (37:34).

Joseph's plan was coming together. The steward had stated that the only brother in trouble would be the one who had stolen the cup. This left the brothers in the precarious position of having to return to their father, Jacob, without Benjamin. Their argument was that taking Benjamin to Egypt is the only way that we can prove we are not spies. They are now in the situation of saying, 'we cleared ourselves, but incriminated Benjamin.' How would Jacob receive this news? The brothers would then be responsible for the loss of both sons of Jacob's beloved Rachel.

As the brothers rode their donkeys into the city, the weight they were carrying was enormous. They knew they were guilty of Joseph's loss, and innocent of Benjamin's plight. They had seen the anguish of their father and Joseph. They could not be angry. They deserved this, but their father, and their brother, Benjamin, didn't! How can minds, who know they are guilty, protest their innocence? Before God, every human being is in that dilemma.

> One of the reasons that humans are so angry with God is that they know God has the evidence against them. When one has no argument, the only recourse is emotion, usually expressed in anger. At some point the anger must be replaced with humility which can accept grace.

Genesis 44:14-34

14. And Judah and his brethren came to Joseph's house; for he was yet there: and they fell before him on the ground. 15. And Joseph said unto them, What deed is this that ye have done? wot ye not that such a man as I can certainly divine? 16. And Judah said, What shall we say unto my lord? what shall we speak? or how shall we clear ourselves? God hath found out the iniquity of thy servants: behold, we are my lord's servants, both we, and he also with whom the cup is found. 17. And he said, God forbid that I should do so: but the man in whose hand the cup is found, he shall be my servant; and as for you, get you up in peace unto your father. 18. Then Judah came near unto him, and said, Oh my lord, let thy servant, I pray thee, speak a word in my lord's ears, and let not thine anger burn against thy servant: for thou art even as Pharaoh. 19. My lord asked his servants, saying, Have ye a father, or a brother? 20. And we said unto my lord, We have a father, an old man, and a child of his old age, a little one; and his brother is dead, and he alone is left of his mother, and his father loveth him. 21. And thou saidst unto thy servants, Bring him down unto me, that I may set mine eyes upon him. 22. And we said unto my lord, The lad cannot leave his father: for if he should leave his father, his father would die. 23. And thou saidst unto thy servants, Except your youngest brother come down with you, ye shall see my face no more. 24. And it came to pass when we came up unto thy servant my father, we told him the words of my lord. 25. And our father said, Go again, and buy us a little food. 26. And we said, We cannot go down: if our youngest brother be with us, then will we go down: for we may not see the man's face, except our youngest brother be with us. 27. And thy servant my father said unto us, Ye know that my wife bare me two sons: 28. And the one went out from me, and I said, Surely he is torn in pieces; and I saw him not since: 29. And if ye take this also from me, and mischief befall him, ye shall bring down my gray hairs with sorrow to the grave. 30. Now therefore when I come to thy servant my father, and the lad be not with us; seeing that his life is bound up in the lad's life; 31. It shall come to pass, when he seeth that the lad is not with us, that he will die: and thy servants shall bring down the gray hairs of thy servant our father with sorrow to the grave. 32. For thy servant became surety for the lad unto my father, saying, If I bring him not unto thee, then I shall bear the blame to my father for ever. 33. Now therefore, I pray thee, let thy servant abide instead of the lad a bondman to my lord; and let the lad go up with his brethren. 34. For how shall I go up to my father, and the lad be not with me? lest peradventure I see the evil that shall come on my father.

A moment of confession

The whole scope of Joseph's dealings with his brothers is now in view. As we read of all the little schemes (accusing them of being spies, holding Simeon hostage, insisting that Benjamin be brought to Egypt, etc.), we have confusion about what he is doing. It is now very clear that Joseph was manoeuvring the brothers into the position where they will clearly see what they had done. Once, they had sold their brother, Joseph, into slavery. They had covered up their culpability by claiming that he had been slain by wild animals (37:31-33). Now, Benjamin will go into slavery, and they are innocent, but will be blamed by their father because of the stolen cup. The guilt, they escaped with Joseph, is inescapable with Benjamin.

Judah becomes the spokesman for his brothers. We might ask, 'Where is Reuben, the eldest brother?' As is always the case with Reuben, he abdicates when the moment for leadership arrives. Judah clearly expresses the trap in which the brothers find themselves. '...God hath found out the iniquity of thy servants...' (44:16). The statement of Judah is sublime. Only a guilty mind coupled with a repentant heart could have expressed it.

The brothers were innocent of the immediate charge of stealing the cup of the Egyptian Prince. The evidence of guilt, however, is there. The cup was in Benjamin's sack. As Judah spoke, he understood that the present moment was the work of God. The Egyptian Prince had them charged with the theft of the cup. God had them charged with what they had done to Joseph. He speaks with an attitude that no longer tries to escape responsibility, but willingly accepts the role of slave to the prince '...we are my Lord's servants...' (44:16).

In a scenario of amazing twists and turns, we come to a moment of truth that almost takes our breath. More than twenty years have passed. Twenty years of emotional suffering for Jacob, twenty years of guilt for Jacob's sons, twenty years of tribulation and ultimate triumph for Joseph, and it culminates in this sublime picture. Finally, a public confession of sin by Joseph's brothers! The brothers were about to go into slavery (or so they thought), but you can almost feel the release of the burden of their guilt as it is stated '...God hath found out the iniquity of they servants...' (44:16).

> The lesson here is in the value of confession and repentance of sin. Ultimately, it is worth more than the release of the burden of hidden guilt. It is the route to rediscovery of our own well-being, and to proper discernment of our circumstances.

'...let thy servant abide...'

Judah's great confession and submission to the Egyptian Prince is highly laudable in the sense of its acknowledgement of sin and repentance. Judah, however, had not reached his peak in a spiritual sense. He had addressed himself on behalf of his brothers recognizing that though innocent of the immediate charge, he and his brothers are guilty before God for the crime done to Joseph years earlier. '...God hath found out the iniquity of thy servants...' (44:16). Judah's opportunity to take another step spiritually comes with the announcement from the Prince. '...the man in whose hand the cup is found, he shall be my servant; and as for you, get you up in peace unto your father' (44:17).

To the brothers who had recognized their crime, and finally, through Judah's eloquence had publicly admitted it, this is a devastating word. They vividly recall the grief of their father at Joseph's loss. They had lived with the guilt for twenty plus years. It is better to be a slave than to once again face their father with their sin before them. Judah acts! He recounts to the Egyptian Prince the suffering of their father, the fact that Benjamin is the only child left of the beloved Rachel (44:20), and the devastation that would fall upon Jacob if Benjamin does not return.

Benjamin is the one in whose sack the important divining cup has been found. As such, it is Benjamin who is guilty. Judah makes an offer to the ruler that must be reflected on in the light of salvation history. It is an offer of vicarious suffering. Another must be substituted for the one charged. Though this does not attain the level of the innocent suffering for the guilty, it still fits in the biblical picture. The sacrificial lamb, in the religious offerings of Israel, is the symbolic principle of this great truth. The vicarious suffering of Jesus Christ for the sin of the world is minutely in view here. Judah offered himself as Benjamin's substitute. It is no wonder that it is Judah's tribe that shall be blessed as the one through whom the Saviour comes. Judah's words carry the ring of nobility '...let thy servant abide instead of the lad a bondman to my Lord; and let the lad go up with his brethren' (Genesis 44:33). My, what a powerful change comes in the heart when one repents of sin.

> Christians often struggle with the desire to be more consistent in their walk with Christ. The inability to reflect a life of grater spirituality may be connected to sin not confessed.

'...how shall I go up to my father...'

The picture that has been seen by the reader of Genesis in the character of Jacob's sons has left little to impress. One has been consistently shocked by their fierceness (Chapters 34, 37) by their immorality (35:22), by their religious compromise, and failure to keep their word (38:2-26), and ultimately by their jealousy and intense cruelty to Joseph, their brother (37:20-34). There is not much to like in these characters.

Joseph, on the other hand, has been a superb character. He has won our hearts at every turn except for the immature way that he, in youthful foolishness, shared his dream with his brothers.

One wonders how they could have all been sons of Jacob. Certainly, part of the answer lies in timing. Joseph was much younger and would have known his father in greater clarity. Joseph must have been impacted, in his rearing, by Jacob's experience of wrestling with God, when Jacob was given a new name, Israel. A more concentrated effort at spiritual training would have been provided for the younger Joseph.

If we have any sympathy at all for Joseph's elder brothers, it is in the knowledge that they had been cheated emotionally by Jacob. Having the misfortune of being born of the unfavoured wife, Leah, or of the concubines, Bilhah and Zilpah, these brothers did not merit Jacob's greatest affection. One can identify with the emotional disconnect they had with Jacob. Perhaps, for this reason, we have longed to see something in them that we could cheer. Finally, Judah provides it.

The great speech he makes, the offer to be a substitute for Benjamin, is a gesture we would not have expected. There is something further to please us. It is noted in the last sentence of Judah's plea. 'For how shall I go up to my father, and the lad be not with me? lest peradventure I see the evil that shall come on my father' (44:34). Couched in these words is the memory of Judah's promise to his father. 'I will be surety for him; of my hand shalt thou require him; if I bring him not unto thee, and set him before thee, then let me bear the blame forever' (43:9). This is a great journey in Judah's life, and should be an example for us of the progress we can make. He journeys from the one who would not keep his word to his daughter-in-law, Tamar (38:26), to one who stands on his word to the extent of offering himself as sacrifice for Benjamin. If Judah can make that kind of progress, maybe there is hope for us.

Learning the sacrifice of self

Judah has stood before Joseph, the Egyptian Prince, and has made a grand and eloquent speech. Brought to the place of repentance and acknowledgment of old sin, Judah had received a new take on life. He had offered himself as a vicarious replacement for Benjamin. Instead of returning home to his father, Jacob, without Benjamin, he would stay and become the Prince's slave. He would rather never see his father again than to see his father grieve himself to death (44:31).

It is a side of Judah the reader of Genesis would never expect to see. Such change can only be created by the repentance of sin. The amazing thing is that this kind of change is the norm when one truly acknowledges and repents of sin.

The brothers of Joseph had been jealous of Joseph. They had sought the love of their father. They had competed for leadership in the family. They had gone after all sorts of worldly pleasures and lusts. They had thought that those kinds of pursuits were really living. Judah did not understand what real life was all about until he said, 'Now therefore, I pray thee, let thy servant abide instead of the lad a bondman to my lord; and let the lad go up with his brethren' (44:33). When Judah gave up all those other pursuits, and was willing to sacrifice himself for the benefit of someone else, he truly understood real living.

Jesus said, 'I am come that they might have life...' (John 10:10). To put that into perspective, he also said, 'He that findeth his life shall lose it: and he that loseth his life for my sake shall find it' (Matthew 10:39). The principle of losing life in order to find life is explicitly illustrated in Judah.

A deeper examination shows that Judah came to full submission to God. '...God hath found out the iniquity of thy servants...' (44:16). When the moment arrived that he was willing to submit to God, he found strength that he, and we, didn't know he had. The strength he found was the boldness to sacrifice self. It sounds strange, but it is the route to real living.

Sacrificing worldly gain for a better relationship with God is the battle of all Christians. It can only be accomplished through supernatural aid.

Genesis 45:1-28

I. The Revelation We've Been Waiting for (45:1-8)
1. Repentance opens options
2. '...they were troubled...'
3. '...I am Joseph'
4. '...not you...but God...'

II. The Reconciliation Is Made (45:9-15)
1. '...Thou shalt dwell in Goshen...'
2. '...your eyes see...'
3. The value of forgiveness

III. Plans for a Reunion (45:16-28)
1. A glimpse of God
2. '...fall not out by the way...'
3. '...the words of Joseph...'
4. '...he saw the wagons...'
5. '...I will see him...'

Genesis 45:1-8

1. Then Joseph could not refrain himself before all them that stood by him; and he cried, Cause every man to go out from me. And there stood no man with him, while Joseph made himself known unto his brethren. 2. And he wept aloud: and the Egyptians and the house of Pharaoh heard. 3. And Joseph said unto his brethren, I am Joseph; doth my father yet live? And his brethren could not answer him; for they were troubled at his presence. 4. And Joseph said unto his brethren, Come near to me, I pray you. And they came near. And he said, I am Joseph your brother, whom ye sold into Egypt. 5. Now therefore be not grieved, nor angry with yourselves, that ye sold me hither: for God did send me before you to preserve life. 6. For these two years hath the famine been in the land: and yet there are five years, in the which there shall neither be earing nor harvest. 7. And God sent me before you to preserve you a posterity in the earth, and to save your lives by a great deliverance. 8. So now it was not you that sent me hither, but God: and he hath made me a father to Pharaoh, and lord of all his house, and a ruler throughout all the land of Egypt.

Repentance opens options

The long story of Joseph's toying with his brothers is coming to an end. Joseph decides to reveal who he is. As one reads the narrative, one is led to the conclusion that Judah's impassioned plea on behalf of Benjamin settled it all. Joseph had seen what he needed to see. The repentance of Judah (44:16), led to the magnificent offer of Judah (44:33). Because the brothers (through Judah) dealt eloquently with the question, '...Wherefore have ye rewarded evil for good?' (44:4), there is a new option that is now available.

The brothers had been guilty of rewarding evil for good when they had taken the goodness of their father, Jacob, and sold his beloved son Joseph, into slavery. Here, through the majesty of Judah's offer, they return good for evil. The theft of the silver cup for which Benjamin (though innocent) was accused, is the issue. Joseph had placed the cup there (44:2). Judah, in his speech does not proclaim innocence, but offers himself and his brothers as slaves to Joseph (44:16). It is an about-face for Judah and his brothers, and is expanded on by Judah's offer to be a vicarious sacrifice.

Joseph had heard enough and with great emotion reveals himself to his brothers. 'And he wept aloud: and...said unto his brethren...I am Joseph your brother, whom ye sold into Egypt' (45:2-4). There is one overriding spiritual lesson that is in this event. When the brothers were facing a hostile prince, who had just accused their brother of theft, there were few options before them. Their fate was in the hands of the prince. They could be angry and vindictive, and loudly protest their innocence. This approach would have profited little because of the knowledge the prince had about the earlier sin in their lives. Repentance allowed the magnificent offer of Judah to occur. When that occurs, there is an option that opens which they could not have anticipated. Repentance has a trust factor. It is the sense of throwing oneself on the mercy of the court. Within repentance is always the plea and the hope for mercy. Judah's eloquent words placed the brothers in a 'faith' situation. Only by trust in the benefaction of the Prince is there hope. Maybe the Prince will be merciful to them. Their brother, Joseph, had been sold into slavery. The possibility that he could rise to the power of second in Egypt to Pharaoh would be an absurd dream. They could not have perceived this to be true. And if it is true, they would certainly not presume that he would be filled with grace toward them. The great spiritual truth is that options, which we could never perceive, are often opened to us when we open ourselves to God through our repentance of sin.

> It is a deep and perplexing theological truth, but wonderful and majestic in its application. Situations, which our sins produce, often leave us in circumstances with very few options. Repentance can open options, which we have not, and could not, have seen without the confession becoming a reality. In essence, that is a faith statement about a repentant heart. There is no emotion but remorse, but there is an expression that God may be able to change the remorse into a glad heart. Psalms 51:10 states the faith element of repentance, 'Create in me a clean heart, O God; and renew a right sprit in me.'

'...they were troubled...'

Joseph finally reveals himself to his brothers. It is an extremely emotional moment for Joseph reflected in the words, 'And he wept

aloud…' (45:2). At the moment of the announcement, his brothers were stunned. '…And his brethren could not answer him; for
they were troubled at his presence' (45:3). It is a classic picture.
The writer is very intelligent in not elaborating on the moment. We
can feel the tension and imagine the picture. This stern, Egyptian
Prince has turned into a mass of weeping humanity, and cries out,
'I am Joseph…' (45:3). What would you say if you were one of
the brothers?

There are too many emotions and questions to imagine. Shock!
Disbelief! Fear! That ironic sense of sickness in the pit of the stom-
ach! Is this guy an imposter? Did he know Joseph and is making
a pretence? Maybe Joseph was his slave. The reaction of Joseph's
brothers was certainly not the tone of a happy reunion.

As one ponders the emotions and considers the kinds of
thoughts running through their minds, it must be wondered if the
thought that they had earlier expressed is uppermost. '…What is
this that God hath done unto us' (42:38)? There is an interesting
kind of twist that is a real part of the spiritual life of human beings,
and it is manifest in this incident. The sense of judgement that was
before them prior to Joseph's revelation was that they would be
slaves to an Egyptian Prince. If this is truly Joseph, they will be
slaves to their younger brother whom they had sold into slavery.
There was one thing worse. They had already bowed down to him
on several occasions (a fulfilment of Joseph's dream in Genesis
37:5-11), and did not know it was Joseph. In every case, Joseph
knew them. It is one thing to bow before a stranger who does not
know you, but to bow before someone who knows you intimately,
gives them a control over you that is eerie, and is a double and
triple humiliation. As the brothers stand there, they are shocked,
and if this is Joseph, they are already deeply humiliated.

Joseph's great desire is to reconcile, and restore a familial
relationship with his brothers. That is not an easy trick with all
the heavy emotion that is filling this room. In that light, consider
what God is facing in attempting to reconcile us to himself. We
have no secrets from him. With his perfection and holiness, we are
clearly already humiliated. Our tendency is not toward rushing to

him being grateful for the reunion, because we are 'troubled at his presence'. God made a way to bring us to himself, but we must accept our humiliation and be comfortable with God's answer.

It is always God who makes the first move toward us. It is his desire to reconcile with us that makes salvation possible. We can be thankful for a God who understood that his work must enable us to come to him even out of the awfulness of our humiliation.

'...I am Joseph...'

With all the emotion that fills the room following Joseph's announcement to his brothers 'I am Joseph...' (45:3), the next step is extremely awkward. The brothers of Joseph are shocked senseless. '...And his brethren could not answer him; for they were troubled at his presence' (45:3). In this moment, Joseph, who is extremely emotional, himself, must take control, end the emotion, and explain the moment, so that everyone can leave the room in a proper frame of mind. How shall he do it?

Joseph wisely understands the humiliating position in which his brothers find themselves. Not only had they sold him into slavery more than twenty years ago, they had just found themselves bowing before him and pleading for his mercy. They had hated him twenty plus years earlier because he told them of a dream where this would happen. Now that it happened in reality, how will they react?

Joseph's words to his brothers are ingenious. There are three great theological themes that come together in one place. First, there is the punishment for sin. Joseph's brothers have paid a price of great humiliation and suffering. Second, there is the wisdom of God. He used the crime the brothers had (years before) committed against Joseph to be the means by which he is now saving their lives, '...for God did send me before you to preserve life' (45:5). Third, there is the release of guilt that comes through forgiveness of sin. 'Now therefore be not grieved, nor angry with yourselves, that ye sold me hither...' (45:5).

The restoration of family is made possible by means of theological thinking. That which could not be accomplished by all the earthly reasoning in the world is accomplished by a different focus. Interestingly, the question of the brothers many months earlier, '...What is this that God hath done unto us?' (42:28) is answered in a way they did not expect. God has restored them as a family. In all of this scenario, God revealed the true nature of these sons of Jacob, forced them to humiliation and repentance, and gave them far more than the grain for which they had come to Egypt to buy. He gave them family and a future. 'And God sent me before you to preserve you a posterity in the earth, and to save your lives by a great deliverance' (47:7). It is one of the great teachings of the Bible that in God we have an eternal future.

'...not you...but God...'

Many years earlier, a teenage boy had told a dream to his older brothers. It was a dream that indicated a time when his older brothers would bow down before him. Their reaction was bitterness and anger. 'And his brethren said to him, Shalt thou indeed reign over us? Or shalt thou indeed have dominion over us? And they hated him...' (37:8). The dream becomes a reality. The brothers, who in hatred sold Joseph into slavery, now stand before the second most powerful man in Egypt hearing him say astonishing words. 'So, now it was not you that sent me hither, but God: and he hath made me a father to Pharaoh, and Lord of all his house, and a ruler throughout all the land of Egypt' (45:8). The word 'father' may be confusing, but it is simply a title of authority in the Egyptian system of rulership.

Joseph's statement has a couple of small things worth noticing. First, it is a subtle hint that his dream of years before was of substance and should not have been taken lightly. Joseph believes it is critical that the brothers recognize that God, not Joseph, did it. The message is clear that one should be alert to what God is teaching. The application on modern Christians should give pause for reflection. When Joseph shared the dream with his brothers, there was no clear and present application except in their envy. They shoved it aside as inapplicable to them, and allowed it to feed their jealousy and anger. Modern people are often prone to hearing the Word of God, but, seeing no clear and present application, shove it aside. Biblical learning is shunned because the immediate relevance is not present. We look to guidance in only that which speaks to the burning, present issues of life. In that fashion, the message of God is missed.

Second, Joseph's rulership was not crafted in Jacob's household, but in Egypt. God has set apart the family of Jacob (from Abraham) to be a great nation. The nation, of which Joseph and his brothers would be part, would bow down to God. All, including Joseph, would acknowledge God's rulership. Joseph's rulership in Egypt, the foreign country, paled in comparison to the great work that God is doing. Better to be a lower person in the nation, which God is making, than to be ruler in Egypt. If the brothers could simply understand their blessing as part of the nation of God, they will have no sense of jealousy of Joseph as ruler in Egypt.

Genesis 45:9-15

9. Haste ye, and go up to my father, and say unto him, Thus saith thy son Joseph, God hath made me lord of all Egypt: come down unto me, tarry not: 10. And thou shalt dwell in the land of Goshen, and thou shalt be near unto me, thou, and thy children, and thy children's children, and thy flocks, and thy herds, and all that thou hast: 11. And there will I nourish thee; for yet there are five years of famine; lest thou, and thy household, and all that thou hast, come to poverty. 12. And, behold, your eyes see, and the eyes of my brother Benjamin, that it is my mouth that speaketh unto you. 13. And ye shall tell my father of all my glory in Egypt, and of all that ye have seen; and ye shall haste and bring down my father hither. 14. And he fell upon his brother Benjamin's neck, and wept; and Benjamin wept upon his neck.

'...thou shalt dwell in Goshen...'

The finale of the tense drama between Joseph and his brothers has come centre stage. He has revealed himself to his brothers, and now applies the coup de' grace. '...Thus saith...Joseph, God hath made me lord of all Egypt: come down unto me, tarry not: And thou shalt dwell in the land of Goshen, and thou shalt be near unto me, thou, and thy children, and thy children's children, and thy flocks, and thy herds, and all that thou hast...for yet there are five years of famine; lest thou, and thy household, and all that thou hast come to poverty...' (45:9-11).

Several things that have been a mystery from the moment we are introduced to Abraham (Genesis 12) are now unfolding. God had said to Abraham, '...I will make of thee a great nation...' (12:2). The reader has wondered when that nation will begin to manifest itself. It is not hard to imagine twelve brothers, their families, and their children's families, isolated in one of the most fertile sections of Egypt could begin to multiply quickly. They will be protected from too much involvement with the Egyptians because of their trade as shepherds, an unclean lifestyle to the Egyptian mind.

The metaphorical picture in the creation of the nation is one of restoration. When God created man he placed him in the Garden of Eden. This was a place designed for man to have regular fellowship with God. After he lost the Garden of Eden by virtue of sin, he lost the sweet fellowship with God. The grand design of the Genesis patriarchal families is the long journey of God working to restore that fellowship. The land of Goshen is a place of fertility where Israel (after the famine ends) can prosper. They can establish the worship of their God in a good place (45:20). Goshen is not the Garden of Eden, but elements of it can be recaptured in a concentrated effort at a 'good' place to worship God. At the point when those people have developed into a nation, they will see the mighty work and glory of God, and become the witness to his glory in the world. Ultimately, through them will come the great redeemer, who shall fulfil the second part of the promise to Abraham '...in thee shall all families of the earth be blessed' (Genesis 12:3). The book of Genesis began with paradise lost, it is coming to conclusion with the hope of paradise regained. This is the hope established in the promise of the seed of the woman, who shall come through the nation spawned by Abraham, and shall culminate in the one person, Jesus Christ.

> With all the debris that the patriarchal families have wrought in their lives, it is wonderful to see the plan of God coming together regardless. The fellowship with God lost in the Garden of Eden can be restored. How do we know? Look at what God has accomplished in the patriarchal families.

'...your eyes see...'

In the story of Joseph's triumph, and the bringing of his father's family into Egypt, the importance of the decision by the family is often overlooked. It is necessary to remember that the brothers had been in a long confrontation with Joseph, and they knew him only as an Egyptian Prince. They had never recognized him. Even when he said, '...I am Joseph...' (45:3), they were not certain. '...his brethren could not answer him; for they were troubled at his presence' (45:3).

Joseph insisted, 'Haste ye...go...to my father and say...God hath made me Lord of all Egypt; come down unto me...thou and thy children and thy children's children, and thy flocks, and thy herds, and all that thou hast: And I will nourish thee; for yet there are five years of famine...' (45:9-11). Jacob and his sons must make a commitment of faith. For Joseph's brothers, it is, 'How can we know you are really Joseph, and are not lying to us about what you will do?' For Jacob, it is, 'How can I know that my hope will not be dashed, and that my sons are not lying to me?' It's interesting to see how the effort was made to have the important steps of faith become a reality.

Joseph handled the problem in an interesting way. 'And, behold, your eyes see, and the eyes of my brother Benjamin, that it is my mouth that speaketh unto you' (45:12). Until this time, Joseph had only spoken to his brothers through an interpreter (Genesis 42:7). He now says, 'Look at my mouth, I am speaking to you in your language with your dialect.' For application purposes one might phrase it like this. 'I understand you and you understand me.' Jesus had something very similar to say about his followers. 'My sheep hear my voice, and I know them, and they follow me' (John 10:27).

For Joseph's brothers, the issue was settled by Joseph's knowledge of them and by his voice. Everyone must make the decision about following God. Jesus asked his disciples to leave all and follow him. Can Jesus be trusted? We must ask 'Does he know us, and do we understand him?' When it becomes clear that his knowledge is superior, that his method of salvation is the only way we can 'live and not die,' then we can act on faith. The question is, do we look and see clearly that it is the voice of Jesus?

The value of forgiveness

The sweet fragrance of forgiveness! It is one of those concepts that is most sublime among humans, and only understood fully within a theological context. When is forgiveness needed? Our first thoughts turn to one who has wronged another. A relationship is badly damaged, and the person who committed the wrong seeks full restoration of the relationship. He, or she, needs forgiveness.

There is a second aspect of forgiveness. That would be in the realm of the one who needs to forgive. It is this need that is hardest to comprehend. When one has been harmed, the tendency is to believe that what he or she needs most is vengeance. The natural drive of humans is to seek some type of revenge. Our favourite stories are the ones that lead us to the good guy getting vengeance on the bad guy.

Unfortunately, real life isn't quite so tidy. Revenge does not get rid of the anger and the hatred. It does not cleanse the heart. It often serves to drive one toward seeking further action on others who were not part of the original hurt. Revenge doesn't satisfy like we thought. The only thing that can cleanse the heart, and provide freedom from the burdens of anger and hatred is forgiveness.

In the saga of Joseph's woes, coming as a result of his brother's actions, the reader has waited to see Joseph get revenge. In the end, there is reconciliation instead. The picture is marvellous to behold. It requires our meditation. The life of Joseph and his brothers could have ended with the brothers in slavery, and Joseph as their master. The reader would have been satisfied with such an ending. The brothers got what they deserved. It would be called a good ending. The actual picture is an even better ending. 'And he (Joseph) fell upon his brother Benjamin's neck, and wept; and Benjamin wept upon his neck. Moreover, he kissed all his brethren, and wept upon them: and after that his brethren talked with him' (45:14-15). The last few words of Genesis 45:15 draw a marked parallel to Genesis 45:3. '…And his brethren could not answer him for they were troubled at his presence.' What made the difference? The ones, who needed to be forgiven, were! The one, who needed to forgive, did! The anger, revenge, hatred are gone. Reconciliation is made possible. That is a truly happy ending.

Genesis 45:16-28

16. And the fame thereof was heard in Pharaoh's house, saying, Joseph's brethren are come: and it pleased Pharaoh well, and his servants. 17. And Pharaoh said unto Joseph, Say unto thy brethren, This do ye; lade your beasts, and go, get you unto the land of Canaan; 18. And take your father and your households, and come unto me: and I will give you the good of the land of Egypt, and ye shall eat the fat of the land. 19. Now thou art commanded, this do ye; take you wagons out of the land of Egypt for your little ones, and for your wives, and bring your father, and come. 20. Also regard not your stuff; for the good of all the land of Egypt is yours. 21. And the children of Israel did so: and Joseph gave them wagons, according to the commandment of Pharaoh, and gave them provision for the way. 22. To all of them he gave each man changes of raiment; but to Benjamin he gave three hundred pieces of silver, and five changes of raiment. 23. And to his father he sent after this manner; ten asses laden with the good things of Egypt, and ten she asses laden with corn and bread and meat for his father by the way. 24. So he sent his brethren away, and they departed: and he said unto them, See that ye fall not out by the way. 25. And they went up out of Egypt, and came into the land of Canaan unto Jacob their father, 26. And told him, saying, Joseph is yet alive, and he is governor over all the land of Egypt. And Jacob's heart fainted, for he believed them not. 27. And they told him all the words of Joseph, which he had said unto them: and when he saw the wagons which Joseph had sent to carry him, the spirit of Jacob their father revived: 28. And Israel said, It is enough; Joseph my son is yet alive: I will go and see him before I die.

A glimpse of God

The Scriptures offer insights into the mind of God that are more than learning experiences for the purifying of our lives. They are little pieces of information that are designed to allow us to have a true relationship with God as father. It is a wonderful thing when our earthly dads open up, and reveal a little of themselves to us, especially when it is shown to unveil wisdom, love, and a sense of integrity. In those kinds of circumstances, love blossoms, and our dads become precious. When God becomes precious to us, our relationship with him goes to a new dimension. Note the wonder of what God has here revealed.

When Pharaoh hears of Joseph's family coming to him, we are told that Pharaoh was pleased (45:16). The reaction of Pharaoh would indicate that he was more than pleased, he was ecstatic. 'And Pharaoh said …go…unto the land of Canaan; And take your father and your households, and come unto me: and I will give you the good of the land of Egypt, and ye shall eat the fat of the land...Also regard not your stuff; for the good of all the land of Egypt is your's' (45:17-20). The Pharaoh was anxious to get Joseph's whole family into Egypt. Why? Consider how Joseph had made the Pharaoh look in the eyes of the world. As the only nation ready for the famine, he was extremely wise, and obviously a great leader. If Joseph, alone, made him look that good, what might his whole family do for him? Pharaoh anxiously extended his goodness to Joseph's family offering them the 'fat of the land' (45:18), and promising to restock any of the stuff they had to leave behind in Canaan (45:20).

The reader knows that God is going to build a great nation out of the family of Jacob. He uses Joseph to build the confidence of a foreign ruler. He brings the family that will be a great nation into that land. Right in the heart of a fertile part of a foreign country, Jacob's family will grow into a great nation. The plan of God is seen to be coming to fruition as the Pharaoh makes this grand gesture. Ultimately, instead of the wisdom of Pharaoh that is remembered, it will be the glory of God, and a prophet named Moses, arising from Jacob's family, which the world remembers. It's fun to watch God at work.

> One of the grandest treats of the Bible is the special moments that we can gaze into the mind and heart of God, and see his nature being manifested. It would be good to meditate on this for a moment and give God thanks for these precious moments when He allows us to see him in fresh ways. God shall give the grandest picture of his nature, and the ultimate revelation of himself in Jesus Christ. 'For God who commanded the light to shine out of darkness, hath shined in our hearts, to give the light of the knowledge of the glory of God in the face of Jesus Christ' (2 Corinthians 4:6).

'...fall not out by the way...'

Joseph had convinced his brothers to bring their families to Egypt. They had returned home and convinced their father Jacob that Joseph was alive and well in Egypt, and that he, and the whole family should move. In the narrative of these two events, other things are worthy of note.

As Joseph sent his brothers back to Canaan to get their families, and to bring their father to Egypt, he offers a gentle reminder. '...See that ye fall not out by the way' (45:24). As the brothers travelled, there would be plenty of time for discussion. They had stood before Joseph when they deemed him a stranger and confessed that God was punishing them for their sins (44:16). The actual sin, for which they deemed themselves facing punishment, was well known to Joseph. The brothers, however, had not stated the sin publicly. As they journeyed, they would know one inevitable fact. Their father, Jacob, would learn why Joseph was in Egypt. Will the brothers be able to stand before their father in confession without arguments among themselves?

This scenario brings the problem of confession of sin to a completely different level. It is a level at which humans often stumble. It is the moment when our sin must be publicly revealed. The Bible teaches that sin is basically against God. 'Against thee, thee only, have I sinned and done this evil...' (Psalms 51:4), was declared by David after committing adultery and murder. Even though sin is against God, there are times when our sin cannot be hidden from our fellowman if things are going to be made right. The brothers had sinned against God, but they had committed a crime against their father, and now must face him with that reality. Joseph had forgiven them. Will their father do the same?

One must see the dilemma. Without having their sin acknowledged before Jacob, he will never see Joseph, and the problem of dealing with the famine remains. The grounds for argument, and dispute about who is most to blame are clearly there when Joseph says, '...see that ye fall not out by the way' (45:24). Sin always leaves us with only difficult options.

'...the words of Joseph...'

The great news that Jacob's sons brought to him did not strike Jacob positively at first. '...And Jacob's heart fainted...' (45:26). In just reading the story one wonders why Jacob would be so downcast when the words are spoken. It is not very difficult to understand when one looks back to Jacob's words at the time he sent his sons to Egypt for the second time. 'And God almighty give you mercy before the man, that he may send away your other brother, and Benjamin. If I be bereaved of my children, I am bereaved' (Genesis 43:14). These were not the words of a confident man who was filled with hope. They are the words of one who has been hurt and expects the worst.

One of the most interesting facets of humanity is the protecting device of expecting bad things, thus we are not disappointed when bad things happen. The other side to that coin is that when good things happen, we don't believe it. The Scripture says, '...for he believed them not' (45:26). It will be of help to consider the nature of the frailty of the human spirit in this area. When Jacob sent his sons into Egypt, the motivation that drove him to that decision was fear. Famine was in the land, but there was food in Egypt. His family would die unless food could be obtained. Note how the fear changed from fear of death to fear of the loss of his sons. (Compare Genesis 43:1-2 with Genesis 43:14). Every fear imaginable engulfed the spirit of Jacob. He had to act because of fear, yet he feared that his action would cause him great hurt. When the sons returned, with Simeon and Benjamin alive and well, Jacob could be satisfied. He had not expected it to occur. A weakened spirit that expects the worst does not know how to grasp hope. '...Jacob's heart fainted...' (45:26). When he heard good news, he must be convinced. There would have been no disbelief at bad news. He was mentally conditioned to hear only that which would discourage.

When one understands this kind of mindset, it is not hard to grasp the reason for Jacob's downcast reaction. He saw the words his sons were telling him only as a means of getting his hopes up to see them dashed on the ground. It is better to have no hope than to see it dashed. The answer for reviving his heart was to focus on the words of Joseph. 'And they told him all the words of Joseph...' (45:27).

> How do we revive hope when all hope is dashed? All of us face moments when hope seems to be lost. It is imperative that we learn to have a larger view of life than the temporariness of this world. In that light, we have access into the mind of Christ. It would be appropriate to ask the Lord to help us learn how to focus on his words to revive our spirit when hope is hard to discern.

'...he saw the wagons...'

The importance of moving the family of Jacob to Egypt is established. Even the Pharaoh got into the act. 'And Pharaoh said unto Joseph, Say unto thy brethren, This do ye; lade your beasts, and go, get you into the land of Canaan; and take your father and your households, and come unto me: and I will give you the good of the land of Egypt, and ye shall eat the fat of the land' (45:17-18). The problem remains to convince Jacob.

The sons of Jacob had been convinced when Joseph spoke to him in their native tongue and dialect (45:12). However, Joseph could not be with them when the message is delivered to Jacob. The first reaction of Jacob is predictable. '...And Jacob's heart fainted, for he believed them not' (45:26). How is Jacob to be convinced?

There are two actions that bring Jacob around. The first is the telling of the words of Joseph. Obviously, the announcement that Joseph is alive would catch Jacob's attention, and create at least an interest in listening. In the words spoken, Jacob must have recognized language revealing his son. Though he did not have Joseph present and saying them, the words carried a power with which Jacob could identify. One is reminded of the reaction of a group of officers sent to arrest Jesus. 'Then came the officers to the chief priests and Pharisees; and they said unto them, Why have ye not brought him? The officers answered, Never man spake like this man' (John 7:45-46). Even today, the words of Jesus, spoken by others, are recognizable in the human soul as words like no one else ever spoke.

The second action to inspire the faith of Jacob is that Joseph sent wagons to carry him to Egypt (45:27). Subtly, the reality for Jacob is, I do not have to take myself to Egypt. Joseph is going to bring me there. He has provided the transportation. The greatest reality for the follower of God is the realization that God issues the call to come to him in obedience, but then, he provides the way. Paul asked '…Who shall deliver me from the body of this death' (Romans 7:24)? He answers, 'I thank God through Jesus Christ, our Lord…' (Romans 7:25). God calls and the believers' trust in Christ is the transportation. Note, '…the spirit of Jacob…revived… (45:27). Through Jesus, The believer is revived. That is the power of the words of one who is called the 'Word' (John 1:1).

'…I will see him…'

The sound of '…the spirit of Jacob their father revived' (45:27), is an extremely pleasant sound. Though the scheming and cunning of Jacob had left us often angry at him, it is good to see some of the old take charge Jacob returning. '…Joseph, my son is yet alive; I will go and see him before I die' (45:28). The writer suddenly turns from the old name Jacob, to the new name, Israel. Remembering the name means 'power with men and power with God,' one can see that the sight of a revived Jacob revives the whole family. Jacob is on his way to see his son who is alive. For the first time in twenty-two years, they are all truly alive.

Certainly, no story ever penned is more sublime than this story. It has everything one could ask: drama, tragedy, and comedy (seen in the brothers' vain actions before Joseph). There are features that reveal it to be much more than a story. In the end, evil is condemned, yet the brothers are reconciled. An old man is restored to his beloved son without insisting on dire consequences for the sons who cost him the last twenty-two years without Joseph. Repentance and forgiveness are the rule. This story is not just a literary masterpiece; it is the actual history of a family in which God worked a miracle. The elements of this family's life bear the marks of a divine source.

Many would examine their own life, and wistfully say, 'such happy endings only occur in stories, or in the Bible. It doesn't happen to me.' There is another way to see it, and it is the proper way. The life of Jacob's family was not exactly a happy one. There were trials, and heartaches, and dastardly deeds. One event of triumph at the end does not repay all the years lost, and all the time spent in ambivalent and hateful relationships. Instead, it is a description of the journey of life. The issue, at the end, is not that things ended happily, but that things ended well. Jacob and his family were in submission to God. He would not get back the years with Joseph that he lost. '...I will go and see him before I die' (45:28). It is enough that Joseph is alive.

It doesn't matter how you and I come to evaluate the whole of our lives. They have been what they have been. Can we finish them without bitterness and anger? Jacob must forgive the sons who took Joseph from him? He must recognize the work that God was doing and rejoice in it. Our lives may not be filled with all the happiness we desire, we may have had more than our share of heartache and misery, but, if we can look and see that God was at work in us, and say, 'that is enough,' then life can at least end well.

Genesis 46:1-34

I. The Family Journeys to Egypt (46:1-27)
1. '...Israel...came to Beersheeba'
2. Setting the stage for the next story
3. Seventy

II. They Came to Goshen (46:28-34)
1. '..he sent Judah...'
2. The primacy of Judah'
3. '...let me die...'
4. Understanding the Nomadic Lifestyle

Genesis 46:1-27

1. And Israel took his journey with all that he had, and came to Beersheba, and offered sacrifices unto the God of his father Isaac. 2. And God spake unto Israel in the visions of the night, and said, Jacob, Jacob. And he said, Here am I. 3. And he said, I am God, the God of thy father: fear not to go down into Egypt; for I will there make of thee a great nation: 4. I will go down with thee into Egypt; and I will also surely bring thee up again: and Joseph shall put his hand upon thine eyes. 5. And Jacob rose up from Beersheba: and the sons of Israel carried Jacob their father, and their little ones, and their wives, in the wagons which Pharaoh had sent to carry him. 6. And they took their cattle, and their goods, which they had gotten in the land of Canaan, and came into Egypt, Jacob, and all his seed with him: 7. His sons, and his sons' sons with him, his daughters, and his sons' daughters, and all his seed brought he with him into Egypt. 8. And these are the names of the children of Israel, which came into

Egypt, Jacob and his sons: Reuben, Jacob's firstborn. 9. And the sons of Reuben; Hanoch, and Phallu, and Hezron, and Carmi. 10. And the sons of Simeon; Jemuel, and Jamin, and Ohad, and Jachin, and Zohar, and Shaul the son of a Canaanitish woman. 11. And the sons of Levi; Gershon, Kohath, and Merari. 12. And the sons of Judah; Er, and Onan, and Shelah, and Pharez, and Zerah: but Er and Onan died in the land of Canaan. And the sons of Pharez were Hezron and Hamul. 13. And the sons of Issachar; Tola, and Phuvah, and Job, and Shimron. 14. And the sons of Zebulun; Sered, and Elon, and Jahleel. 15. These be the sons of Leah, which she bare unto Jacob in Padanaram, with his daughter Dinah: all the souls of his sons and his daughters were thirty and three. 16. And the sons of Gad; Ziphion, and Haggi, Shuni, and Ezbon, Eri, and Arodi, and Areli. 17. And the sons of Asher; Jimnah, and Ishuah, and Isui, and Beriah, and Serah their sister: and the sons of Beriah; Heber, and Malchiel. 18. These are the sons of Zilpah, whom Laban gave to Leah his daughter, and these she bare unto Jacob, even sixteen souls. 19. The sons of Rachel Jacob's wife; Joseph, and Benjamin. 20. And unto Joseph in the land of Egypt were born Manasseh and Ephraim, which Asenath the daughter of Potipherah priest of on bare unto him. 21. And the sons of Benjamin were Belah, and Becher, and Ashbel, Gera, and Naaman, Ehi, and Rosh, Muppim, and Huppim, and Ard. 22. These are the sons of Rachel, which were born to Jacob: all the souls were fourteen. 23. And the sons of Dan; Hushim. 24. And the sons of Naphtali; Jahzeel, and Guni, and Jezer, and Shillem. 25. These are the sons of Bilhah, which Laban gave unto Rachel his daughter, and she bare these unto Jacob: all the souls were seven. 26. All the souls that came with Jacob into Egypt, which came out of his loins, besides Jacob's sons' wives, all the souls were threescore and six; 27. And the sons of Joseph, which were born him in Egypt, were two souls: all the souls of the house of Jacob, which came into Egypt, were threescore and ten.

'...Israel...came to Beersheba'

This passage of Scripture is extremely significant in the narrative of the patriarchal families. Jacob has learned that his son is alive in Egypt. He has started the journey to go and see him before he dies. The reader has noted that Jacob's new name 'Israel' is used as the author talks about the revived Jacob (Genesis 45:28). It is an exciting moment for the whole family as they begin their journey.

Jacob (Israel) stopped at Beersheba, which had been a central place in the journeys of Jacob's father, Isaac (Genesis 26:23, 33). The purpose of Jacob's halting is to offer sacrifices to God. It is notable that the author records Jacob as thinking in terms of the God of his father, Isaac. The result of the sacrifice made is that Jacob received a message from God. Clearly Jacob stopped to offer sacrifices because of a concern. In the message of God, we see his concern. '...fear not to go down into Egypt; for I will there make of thee a great nation: I will go down with thee into Egypt; and I will also surely bring thee up again' (46:3-4).

This little passage infers conversations between Jacob and his father, Isaac. Abraham may have been involved in some of these conversations. The reader of Genesis will recall that Abraham had experienced famine when he first entered the land of Canaan. Abraham responded to that crisis. '...and Abram went down into Egypt to sojourn there; for the famine was grievous in the land' (12:10). Abraham's journey into Egypt led him to sin, and he was severely rebuked. Jacob's sacrifice to God is clearly a remembrance of lessons taught to him at his father's feet. Should he go to Egypt? Isaac, as well, was instructed, '...Go not down into Egypt...' (26:2). Could Jacob be sinning by doing the very thing condemned in his father and grandfather.

Jacob certainly knew from the teaching of his father about this admonition. Even though he probably has a reasonable amount of assurance that he is doing the right thing, he seeks further assurance from God. Jacob is to be commended. In a time such as our present day when the tendency is for sons and daughters to abandon the lessons of the fathers simply because it is the lessons of the fathers, Jacob's example is noteworthy. It is true that God changed the correct action for Jacob, but Jacob made sure he had clear direction from God before abandoning the lesson of his father. The key is that both Isaac and Jacob were in desire of doing the will of God. When humans desire daily a 'Beersheba' where

God's will is sought, we have the promise that he will direct our paths (Proverbs 3:6).

Setting the stage for the next story

The reader of Scripture has been stirred by the intensely emotional story of Joseph and his dealings with his brothers. That story has come to completion, and we begin to read the record detailing the names of Jacob's children. Following Joseph's story, this may, at first, impact the reader as rather dull. However, in the telling of a greater story, this record commands attention.

If the reader is significantly involved, there is a quality of suspense that is being developed. From the beginning of the patriarchal story, there has been the knowledge that a nation would be spawned from Abraham, which would occupy the Promised Land of Canaan. Abraham and Isaac were forbidden to leave the Promised Land. Now, Jacob and his entire family are travelling to Egypt. Further, they have God's blessing! It was shown to Abraham (by vision) that the promised nation would be in a foreign land for four hundred years (15:12-14). The reader now knows that the foreign land will be Egypt and he knows how the nation arrived there. The suspense lies in the knowledge that the family goes to Egypt in the graces of the Pharaoh, but will ultimately be afflicted by Egypt. As we encounter the names of Jacob's family, we must wonder about what is in store for Abraham's children.

Also, it is clear that a new story is being placed before us. The writer is very skilfully drawing us into the next great adventure, and letting us know that the work of God is not finished, even though the exciting story of Joseph has come to conclusion. One might note that the total family of Jacob which begins the new nation, totals seventy (46:27). This connects the creation of the nation of Israel with the original creation of the nations of the world also numbered at seventy. 'When the Most High divided to the nations their inheritance, when he separated the sons of Adam, he set the bounds of the people according to the number of the children of

Israel' (Deuteronomy 32:8). The command that God has on the destiny of the world is clearly in view. The number, seventy, for the nations, and for the new nation reminds us of the Abrahamic promise '...in thee shall all families of the earth be blessed' (12:3). We are also reminded that God's work is always dynamic and exciting. It never ends! It only begins anew!

> The command of God in the history of the nations is a wonder to view. One might pause to reflect on the necessity for God's sovereign control. It is seen in his great love. It does not take a great deal of insight to see how humans were fighting against God. They would have prevented the redemptive work of God, if possible. God always saw to it that humans would fail and his plan would succeed.

Seventy

The story of Genesis brings the reader through many tragic and ironic situations. Ultimately, it becomes clear that it is a story of the failure of humanity to live up to the standards of God. Three great judgements of God upon humanity are presented in the first eleven chapters. Adam and Eve are thrust out of the Garden of Eden (Genesis 3). The world is destroyed by flood (Genesis 6-8). Man is scattered on the earth and given many languages (Genesis 11). With man's sin established, and his inability to live according to God's plan clearly manifested, God acts to begin his redemptive history.

Out of those scattered nations, he chooses one individual (Abram) from whom he will develop a brand new nation. To that nation, he will teach his ways, instruct about himself, and send one who will ultimately bring redemptive blessing to all the nations of the earth (Genesis 12:3). One should consider the awesome nature of such an announcement within the reality of so many different languages now spoken in the earth. How will God accomplish such a task?

The Genesis narrative unfolds as the patriarchal heroes (Abraham, Isaac, Jacob and Joseph) struggle with their relationship to God, and the sin in their life. The reader wonders how the promised nation will appear. The judgement of God upon man has been swift and destructive in the first eleven chapters. As the weaknesses of the patriarchs unfold, will the judgement of God fall upon them?

In each instance, God works to bring about his own purpose, and draw the patriarchs to himself. Humans have not fared well, nor looked very promising throughout the Genesis narrative, but thankfully, God never gives up on them. By his own power, he will make a way of redemption for that which appears unredeemable. The story now brings us to a dramatic moment. '...all the souls of the house of Jacob, which came into Egypt, were threescore and ten' (46:27). Seventy people who are direct blood relatives of Jacob along with in-laws make their way to Egypt. From very small beginnings shall come a great nation. Take a moment and consider the majesty and wonder of that which God was doing in Genesis. What must he be doing in our day as he moves the world to the end of the age?

It is wise here to reflect upon the work of God. Consider his great wisdom and power. Consider the reality that humans had such freedom, yet never took God by surprise. Consider how he continually moved the lives of each person to accomplish his plan. Now, it would be appropriate to ask God to teach us how to always bask in the wonder and majesty of his great work in the affairs of the world and in the affairs of our individual lives.

Genesis 46:28-34

28. And he sent Judah before him unto Joseph, to direct his face unto Goshen; and they came into the land of Goshen. 29. And Joseph made ready his chariot, and went up to meet Israel his father, to Goshen, and presented himself unto him; and he fell on his neck, and wept on his neck a good while. 30. And Israel said unto Joseph, Now let me die, since I have seen thy face, because thou art yet alive. 31. And Joseph said unto his brethren, and unto his father's house, I will go up, and shew Pharaoh, and say unto him, My brethren, and my father's house, which were in the land of Canaan, are come unto me; 32. And the men are shepherds, for their trade hath been to feed cattle; and they have brought their flocks, and their herds, and all that they have. 33. And it shall come to pass, when Pharaoh shall call you, and shall say, What is your occupation? 34. That ye shall say, Thy servants' trade hath been about cattle from our youth even until now, both we, and also our fathers: that ye may dwell in the land of Goshen; for every shepherd is an abomination unto the Egyptians.

'...he sent Judah...'

Often, the Bible gives us subtle hints that we are examining a truly supernatural work. Writing from the standpoint of developing history, God inspires the narrator of that history to open certain windows to the future. Genesis 46:28, which might go unnoticed by the casual reader, brings food for thought for larger biblical reflection. 'And he (Jacob) sent Judah before him unto Joseph, to direct his face unto Goshen; and they came into the land of Goshen.' The words are curious in the King James English. Specifically, they refer to the reality that it is Judah that shall lead Israel to Goshen after receiving directions from Joseph.

The placing of Judah's name at the centre of this event re-emphasises the primacy of Judah and his heritage in Israel's history. Judah has not been the most admirable of characters, but it was he who showed the leadership among his brothers. He came up with the plan to spare Joseph from death (37:25-27). It was Judah who had the appropriate self-sacrificial attitude to convince Jacob to allow Benjamin to return to Egypt resulting in sparing the life of Simeon (Genesis 43:8-9). It was Judah who spoke up and offered himself as a substitute for Benjamin to the Egyptian prince (44:18-34). As such, Judah, not Benjamin, would pay the price for Benjamin's supposed theft of the prized cup (44:12, 33). In today's text it is Judah who is once again the leader who shows the way to Goshen. It is Joseph's plan, but Judah leads the way.

The larger plan of God's redemptive purpose is seen in microscope. Judah, the brother who sacrificed himself is the brother who shows the way. It is out of Judah's tribe that the redeemer will come who shows humanity the way back into God's blessings. If we are astute and take into account the great story beginning with the promise made to Abraham (Genesis 12), the sense of anticipation rises. Who will be this great son of Judah? What shall he do? How can this obscure nation that is filled with characters like Joseph's brothers be headed to such a great destiny? We have seen what God did with Joseph. The story just keeps getting more wonderful and the glory of our God keeps expanding to larger and larger horizons.

> We are often very casual about the grandeur of the Word of God. These little glimpses into the mind of God show us repeatedly that we are dealing with a supernatural book. Perhaps, there should be a time of repentance for moments we may have had a casual attitude about the Word of God.

The primacy of Judah

The story of the Patriarchs has brought us through the development of the family of Jacob. Judah is clearly established as the son of Jacob whose heritage shall rise to primacy in the nation of Israel. It is the family of Jacob that shall be the first in which all sons comprise the special nation God is building from Abraham. Out of one son, Judah, there shall be born the one who shall be leader in the nation. He will be the ultimate fulfilment of the promise made to Abraham. '..in thee shall all families of the earth be blessed' (Genesis 12:3). The author of Genesis gives us another glorious hint of God's plan when Judah's name emerges as the one who leads the family of Jacob to Goshen.

It is a little clue about the plan of God that shall help us later in reading the story of the nation. The primacy of Judah will be a background to the story of Israel's first king. The reader will know that Saul's heritage will not be the kingly line. Saul, of the tribe of Benjamin, does not carry the proper lineage. When David succeeded Saul, the nation could have easily seen the will of God at work in David's ascendance had they understood their own history.

The lesson for us lies in acknowledgement of the way God works in our life. The little lesson that he teaches us today may seem insignificant, but it prepares us for the larger decisions of tomorrow. It may be the means of discerning the will of God when critical decisions must be made. It is easy to read events of our lives as mere circumstance, or to dismiss things as of little or no meaning. Our tendency to do this may cause us to lose the essential lesson that God provided that would aid decision-making at a later moment in our lives.

Many things are mere coincidence. Often, dismissal is a sound approach to analysis of life's events. How can I be sure of knowing when there is a learning event before me? The key is to be found in our focus on God. When one reads the stories of the patriarchs as the story of God's work, it is natural to pick up on God's clues. The person that looks at his personal life in the light of God's work, and places great emphasis on knowing God will be more likely to see when God provides those special teaching moments. The primacy of Judah can be a great guidepost for Israel. We should be alert to the guideposts that God provides for us.

The aids to decision-making can be a great help to us. The problem is to be alert to aids that may be presented to us long before the decision-making moment arrives.

'...let me die...'

There is an interesting exchange between Joseph and his father Jacob that occurs in this passage. It is the first time that Joseph will have seen his father in twenty-five years. The Scripture speaks of the weeping of Joseph at their meeting. Great weeping was characteristic of Joseph (Genesis 45:1-2). There is nothing mentioned of any tears of Jacob. The words of Jacob are provided. 'And Israel said unto Joseph, Now let me die, since I have seen thy face, because thou art yet alive' (46:30).

From the moment that Joseph was sold into Egypt, every word spoken by Jacob is in relation to his death. As age and sadness continue to dominate Jacob's mind, the talk of death becomes more prominent. Even with the glorious reunion with Joseph. Jacob's words are almost a plea for death. '...Now let me die...' (46:30).

There are a couple of lessons that one might take from this. First, it should be noted that Jacob has focused on his death for twenty-five years. There are several more years of life remaining for him. It is sometimes typical of the elderly to want to focus on their death. As with Jacob, a life of pain (either emotional or physical), may produce this kind of obsession. The tendency is to think that age or circumstances predict that death is very near when, in reality, there may be much life, and many years still left. It is sad to think that one views the continuing of life as the less desirable of alternatives. Many aged people have much to offer family and loved ones if they would find the mental focus to consider life. None of us can know for certain the moment of death. Even when old, there are reasons to consider productivity in our life. When God is our focus, he can help us recreate our productivity in ways that our declining bodies can handle.

A second view would rest in the peace of Jacob that the great hurt of his life has been healed. He will not die in anger and sadness, but in the sense of having been redeemed from a sad existence. In this sense, Jacob is saying, 'Life has given me what I required of it, and thus, there is quietness, not despair, at the thought of death.' In either view, there is a statement to be made. There is reason to live, and a comfort in dying. That is what redemption brings to our life.

Joseph was much in need of his father's fellowship when Jacob says, '...Now let me die...' (46:30). That highlights the second lesson. It was an extremely selfish point of view for Jacob. He had been robbed of his son's company for the last twenty-five years. But Joseph had been robbed of the love of a father. Jacob should have given some thought to that and prayed, 'Now let me live.'

Understanding the Nomadic lifestyle

With the family of Jacob arriving in Egypt, Joseph must secure the place that the family will stay. There are several calculations that must be made. There is the simple geography of such a need. The family of Jacob must dwell somewhere. The over-arching theological problem is also a consideration. The family of Jacob will develop into the nation of Israel. The place in which they dwell must allow for some degree of isolation where this family will not become assimilated into Egypt. God will separate them as a people unto himself, and will ultimately establish his mastery over the Egyptian deities.

Joseph's plan is to place Israel in Goshen, a very fertile area very suitable for the keeping of sheep, and somewhat remote to the permanent dwelling places of Egypt. This solves both the geographical and the theological problems. In order to get Jacob's family to Goshen, the brothers are rehearsed by Joseph in the proper way to reply to Pharaoh. This is an acceptable alternative that should work because of the Egyptian's dislike of shepherds (46:34).

This distaste for shepherds is probably related to lifestyle more than to occupation. Shepherds are a nomadic bunch living in tents whereas the Egyptians dwell in permanent quarters. The prejudice will be used by God to accomplish his purpose for Jacob's family.

The event should bring some things to remembrance, and allow understanding of God's long-term plan. Lot's choosing of the plains of Sodom, leaving the hillsides to Abraham, insured that Abraham's family would have the shepherd's mentality. One will recall that Lot ended up being a permanent resident of Sodom (Genesis 19:1-2). Isaac, heir to Abraham, was forced to move continually, and to dig new wells, guaranteeing his nomadic state (26:17). Jacob was made to be on the move as well. The sins of his sons forced his leaving one area for another (see Genesis 34). Ultimately, the famine has brought this family of shepherds to Egypt where the family will become a nation. God's sovereignty manifested itself in many ways. Even the sins of the patriarchal family could not prevent God from fashioning his own divine plan. Ultimately, Abraham's descendants must come to Egypt as shepherds. As shepherds, the move into Egypt could be done without conflict. God knew exactly what he was doing. Do you ever look at the world is out of control? Consider the story of Genesis.

The moment of real peace in our lives is rare and precious. It is that moment when there is calm and assurance. The sense that things are under control allows life to be restored from crisis. The realization of God's control can provide that sense of peace each time we reflect on him and give ourselves to him in worship.

Genesis 47:1-26

I. Negotiating for Goshen (47:1-12)
1. Straight Talk and Hard Work
2. '...Jacob Blessed Pharaoh...'
3. '...few and evil...'

III. Joseph's Wisdom and Jacob's Plea (47:12-26)
1. '...Pharaoh's servants...'
2. '...bury me not in Egypt...'
3. A proper burial site
4. Dichotomy of Jacob and Israel

Genesis 47:1-12

1. Then Joseph came and told Pharaoh, and said, My father and my brethren, and their flocks, and their herds, and all that they have, are come out of the land of Canaan; and, behold, they are in the land of Goshen. 2. And he took some of his brethren, even five men, and presented them unto Pharaoh. 3. And Pharaoh said unto his brethren, What is your occupation? And they said unto Pharaoh, Thy servants are shepherds, both we, and also our fathers. 4. They said moreover unto Pharaoh, For to sojourn in the land are we come; for thy servants have no pasture for their flocks; for the famine is sore in the land of Canaan: now therefore, we pray thee, let thy servants dwell in the land of Goshen. 5. And Pharaoh spake unto Joseph, saying, Thy father and thy brethren are come unto thee: 6. The land of Egypt is before thee; in the best of the land make thy father and brethren to dwell; in the land of Goshen let them dwell: and if thou knowest any men of activity among them, then make them rulers over my cattle. 7. And Joseph brought in Jacob his father, and set him before Pharaoh: and Jacob blessed Pharaoh. 8. And Pharaoh said unto Jacob, How old art thou? 9. And Jacob said unto Pharaoh, The days of the years of my pilgrimage are an hundred and thirty years: few and evil have the days of the years of my life been, and have not attained unto the days of the years of the life of my fathers in the days of their pilgrimage. 10. And Jacob blessed Pharaoh, and went out from before Pharaoh. 11. And Joseph placed his father and his brethren, and gave them a possession in the land of Egypt, in the best of the land, in the land of Rameses, as Pharaoh had commanded. 12. And Joseph nourished his father, and his brethren, and all his father's household, with bread, according to their families.

Straight talk and hard work

There are two lessons worthy of our meditation in this passage. The reader will note the doublet as the same words are repeated from Joseph's instructions in 46:31-34. The reason for repeating is to emphasize the control of God, and his protection for the obedient. Joseph's wisdom is validated as the Pharaoh accepts Joseph's suggestion concerning the land of Goshen (46:31-34). This provides the first lesson. It is amazing to some that Joseph would advise his brothers in this action. Tell the Pharaoh exactly what you need and tell him why. There was no ambiguity at all in their request. It was simple and it made sense.

Christians are often prone to utilizing communication skills that defy logic. We will sometimes insist on some venture arguing that, in some mystical way, God has revealed that it should be done. This methodology is used by Christians through statements, indicating a private conversation with God, the content of which is known only to themselves. The phrasing is usually, 'God spoke to me last night and he told me what we should do!' Immediately, such language defines anyone who disagrees with the venture as disagreeing with God, and allows the person making the statement the position of infallibility as God's spokesperson. How can someone else know that such a word is a word from God?

Another methodology is to create unreal scenarios, such as turn small problems into major crises with inflammatory words to give the impression that desperate action is needed. Sometimes one simply hides the true motivation, which is often self-serving, under the guise of a special, unique message from God. Unless one can fully demonstrate that he has some mystical connection with God that makes his word equal to the Bible, a good rule of thumb is to be able to state in clear language (which makes sense) what you want and why you want it. Many foolish decisions are validated by those claiming some kind of extra-biblical revelation. If you can't do that, maybe the venture should not be attempted.

The second lesson is in the instruction about blessing. When we speak of blessing, it is mostly in terms of what God has done to make life easier, or better. The impact of the event in this passage is clearly that God made life better for the family of Jacob. This was accomplished through the generosity of the Pharaoh. 'And Pharaoh spake unto Joseph saying, Thy father and thy brethren are come unto thee: The land of Egypt is before thee; in the best of the land make thy father and brethren to dwell; in the land of Goshen let them dwell: and if thou knowest any men of activity among them, then make them rulers over my cattle' (47:5-6).

The blessing, added to the family of Jacob, is to increase their work load. In the light of modern culture, which sees work as a curse, this message is quite profound. It is good that the sons of Jacob can work in the caring of their own cattle. It is better that they can work tending to their cattle and to the Pharaoh's cattle. It is quite common to hear Christians pray for the blessing of God to fall upon them. How often do they consider themselves to be asking God to increase their work load as demonstration of his blessing? It might be interesting to see what would happen to a body of believers who prayed 'Lord, give us more work to do.'

The lesson here is remindful of the words of the Incarnate Christ, 'Take my yoke upon you, and learn of me...' (Matthew 11:29). The yoke of Christ involves work. In an age that is prone to think of blessing as a decrease in work, it would be fitting to ask the Lord to teach us anew the blessing to be found in an increased work load.

'...Jacob blessed Pharaoh...'

All biblical stories carry the nature of the sombre and serious in Christian minds. This is because the encounter with these stories is usually in church Bible classes or through preaching. Thus, Bible stories are brought to us in the holy situations of our lives. Because we know Bible stories in the atmosphere of worship, we may occasionally miss the humorous scene. Our text has one such scene.

The setting is the royal court of the Pharaoh. Jacob's family has arrived from Canaan because of the devastating results of famine. They are there to make request of Pharaoh and obtain a place whereby they may sustain themselves during the famine. Literally, Pharaoh holds their life in his hands.

The Pharaoh was not introduced to Jacob until the moment after he grants the request of Joseph's brothers to dwell in Goshen. This is curious, but we immediately learn why. 'And Joseph brought in Jacob his father, and set him before Pharaoh: and Jacob blessed Pharaoh (47:7). Picture this: an old man desperately in need of Pharaoh's favour acts as if he is Pharaoh's superior. The words, '...and Jacob blessed Pharaoh...' (47:7) carry a punch. Jacob was not the least bit intimidated or impressed by Pharaoh's position. The old man who is waiting to die (46:30), in an amazing show of arrogance, blesses the King of Egypt. The portrait conjures up some marvellous pictures in the human mind.

To appropriate its meaning, we are called back to the promise made to Abraham when God said, '...I will bless them that bless thee...' (12:3). The blessing that Jacob gives to Pharaoh may reflect some of that spiritual understanding. It is better to be part of God's kingdom than to be the King of any other kingdom. When Jacob blesses Pharaoh, it is clear that he felt he had something to give to the most powerful man in the world. That insight only comes through a mind that considers with intensity matters spiritual.

The outward picture of Jacob is humorous and arrogant. Inwardly, there may be a spiritual insight to be emulated. That which Jacob has via inheritance in the Abrahamic promise is more valuable than the throne of Egypt. Jacob has the insight to know it.

> The lesson here is remindful of the words of the Incarnate Christ, 'Take my yoke upon you, and learn of me...' (Matthew 11:29). The yoke of Christ involves work. In an age that is prone to think of blessing as a decrease in work, it would be fitting to ask the Lord to teach us anew the blessing to be found in an increased work load.

'...few and evil...'

In Jacob's old age, he is found uttering words which reflect a great deal of insight which experience has taught him. The young Jacob who was so eager for possessions and power, deceived his father, and stole the family blessing from his brother (Genesis 27), is now the aged Jacob unimpressed with the riches of the Pharaoh (47:7). He has learned the deceitfulness of riches, and the greater value of God's blessing. He goes further in his understanding. After the rather arrogant blessing of Pharaoh, he manifests the following note of humility: '...The days of the years of my pilgrimage are an hundred and thirty years: few and evil have the days of the years of my life been, and have not attained unto the days of the years of the life of my fathers in the days of their pilgrimage' (47:9).

Jacob's words are a striking confession, and a portent of a future command of God. The evil of which Jacob has reference is in the reality that he had not honoured God as had his fathers Abraham and Isaac. Also, he had not honoured his fathers in the many times of failure to place God at the forefront of his life. For his sins, Jacob will die outside the Promised Land. The portent in

Jacob's confession is the later promise of God to Israel. 'Honour thy father and thy mother: that thy days may be long upon the land which the Lord thy God giveth thee' (Exodus 20:12). Unlike his father Isaac, who honoured the God of Abraham, and lived out his life in the land of promise, Jacob must finish his life in Egypt.

Jacob's words reflect the inherent sadness of his heart. He knows that his sins have found him out. He willingly acknowledges that he is paying for those sins. As is always true in the Word of God, the confession of sin is a double-edged proposition. It is a moment of sadness and humility, but it is also a moment of triumph. The flesh must pay for its sins, but the soul is restored in a relationship to God. This story ends on a positive note reflecting the triumph that is found in Jacob's confession. '...and gave them a possession in the land of Egypt, in the best of the land...' (47:11). God applies his grace in the light of Jacob's confession. It is not the land of promise, but it is a good place. Confession is good for the soul.

> There is a note of melancholy in Jacob's confession, but we are comforted by God's grace to Jacob. He is in Egypt with his family fully restored. He is exactly where God wanted him to be. There is payment for sins, but it is good to know that God punishes, and in the framework of that punishment works out his will to perfection. It is both bad and good for Jacob. God's grace is applied in wonderful and mysterious ways.

'...Pharaoh's servants...'

The narrative of the Patriarchs, after a great deal of attention given to Joseph and his brothers, returns to the problem of the great famine. A simple, straight-forward reading of these verses may leave one feeling that there is no great spiritual lesson here. Yet, there are some key themes that God has led the author to record. The reader will recall the consistent wording of Jacob and his sons in reflecting on their journey to Egypt to buy bread. '...there is corn in Egypt: get you down...and buy...that we may live, and not die' (Genesis 42:2). '...We will arise and go; that we may live, and not die...' (Genesis 43:8). The same theme is now presented as coming from the mouths of the Egyptian people. '...Give us bread: for why should we die in thy presence...' (47:15)? '...and give us seed, that we may live, and not die...' (47:19).

There are several things already presented in the book but reiterated here. God had used the desire of Joseph's brothers to kill him to put him in a position to save many lives. Joseph had emphasized this to his brothers. '...be not grieved...that ye sold me hither: for God did send me before you to preserve life' (45:5). In chapter 47, we see that Joseph was used to save the lives of the Egyptian people. The value of life is vividly portrayed, as the people are willing to sacrifice everything in order to preserve life. Land, possessions, and their freedom are ultimately given to Pharaoh. (47:25). Modern readers would be somewhat shocked by this turn of events because of the importance of freedom to our culture. It is worth noting that a love of, and appreciation of, freedom springs from one's religion, specifically, the love of God. The author subtly draws this parallel when he analyses the condition of Israel during the same period. '...And Israel dwelt in the land of...Goshen; and they had possessions therein, and grew, and multiplied exceedingly' (47:27). The fact that the Egyptian people were selling themselves to Pharaoh as slaves was a concept that had already been accepted implicitly by the acknowledgement in Egyptian life of the divinity of Pharaoh. Joseph did not radically alter the nature of Egyptian life, but ingeniously kept the economy going through very difficult times while allowing the family of Jacob to prosper.

It is interesting to see the intricate wisdom of God woven into the lives of the patriarchs. Love of God is not just an emotional event. It pays practical benefits, and will keep us from the foolish guidance of the world, which can enslave us.

'...bury me not...in Egypt...'

It is very difficult for us in the modern world to understand the mindset out of which the ancient world spoke. As Jacob nears death, he sends for Joseph and makes a specific request of him. The request was to be established by means of an oath symbolized by a strange method. '...put, I pray thee, thy hand under my thigh, and deal kindly and truly with me; bury me not, I pray thee, in Egypt' (47:29). This strange method has been seen before. 'And Abraham said unto his eldest servant of his house, that ruled over all that he had, Put, I pray thee, thy hand under my thigh: And I will make thee swear by the Lord, the God of heaven, and the God of the earth, that thou shalt not take a wife unto my son of the daughters of the Canaanites...' (24:2-3).

This particular kind of oath accompanied by the hand under the thigh is seen at times when one speaks of that which is of greatest concern. Though the two incidents seem unrelated (Abraham's concern about a wife for his son; Jacob's concern that his body be buried in the land), there is a connecting link. It is their claim on the promise of God. In both instances, the primary concern is the promise of the land. For Abraham, it is crucial that there be no connection with the inhabitants of the land (Canaanites) that would spoil the later claim to the land for the children of Abraham. For Jacob, he must be buried in the land as a symbolic statement that he died claiming the promise as his possession. Jacob did not believe the burial placed him in the land as he would be with his fathers at death (47:30). The burial was instead, a clear statement of that which held priority for Jacob to the people of God that would come after Jacob of that which held priority for Jacob.

For the modern Christian, there is a great deal of comfort and consolation here. Jacob had earlier said '...few and evil have the days...of my life been...' (47:9), Yet, as he approached death, his thoughts were for the future, and he was to go to his grave with great hope. That hope was for self, but it was also for the people of

God who are yet to come. It is nice to know that the people of God have 'hope,' even at death.

A proper burial site

Jacob's desire to be buried in the Promised Land instead of in Egypt became an important symbol for the people of Israel. The 'dry bones' of the ancestors buried in the land was seen as evidence of God's faithfulness to his people. This is illustrated in the vision of Ezekiel as God brought to life the 'valley of dry bones.' God's words to the prophet express the great hope of Israel. '... Behold, O my people, I will open your graves, and cause you to come up out of your graves, and bring you into the land of Israel. And you shall know that I am the Lord, when I have opened your graves, O my people, and brought you up out of your graves' (Ezekiel 37:12-13).

As the reader meditates upon this passage of Scripture, there are two clear lessons that appear. First, there is confrontation with the great wonder of the inspiration of Scripture. Jacob certainly did not peer into the future and know how a later prophet of God would utilize the hope to be found in the bones of the ancestors. God did! It was God who led Jacob to this great concern. The concern did not stop with Jacob. Joseph was to say to the people of the nation '...God will surely visit you, and ye shall carry up my bones from hence...' (50:25). When one considers the images of Jacob's and Joseph's request, greater meaning is added to God's question for Ezekiel. '...Son of man, can these bones live...' (Ezekiel 37:3)? Jacob and Joseph died believing those bones could live. God uses the faith of Jacob and Joseph, connecting the centuries between them and Ezekiel, and uses the same image for the building of Ezekiel's faith. It accomplishes the same thing for us in the wonder of God's inspired Word.

The second great lesson is found in the importance of faith expressions. Though the bones were only symbolic statements, both Jacob and Joseph wanted those who came after them to recognize their heritage of faith. We spend much time trying to leave our children an inheritance. Far more important is the heritage of faith. Do we think seriously enough about the way we communicate the importance of our faith in the inheritance that we desire to pass on to our children?

> One should never underestimate the importance of passing on proper faith to their children. Some have said, 'I want my children to choose for themselves, so I will not emphasize my faith to them.' Such a statement misses the mark entirely. Your children will certainly decide for themselves. You cannot make that decision for them. Someone will teach them of the faith upon which they will decide. Will it be the faith of the redemption of God in Christ that they are taught?

Dichotomy of Jacob and Israel

The Scriptures are a veritable gold mine of great riches. As with any mine, getting to the ore requires some careful digging. This passage carries some big nuggets, but it takes an eye and heart willing to pause and consider some of the unique things that are presented. When Jacob was given a new name by the angel of the Lord (Genesis 32:28), it was a moment of great trauma. It occurred after he had wrestled with the angel for a whole night. The new name was 'Israel' which would be the name the nation of Abraham's children would carry. After being given the new name, the Scripture continues using both names in the narrative of Jacob. Sometimes, he is Jacob; sometimes, he is Israel.

This passage continues the pattern: 'And Israel...' (v. 27), 'And Jacob...' (v. 28), '...the whole age of Jacob was...' (v. 28) '...the time drew nigh that Israel must die...' (v. 29), '...And Israel bowed himself...' (v. 31). Jacob represents the deceiver, the supplanter, reflected in Jacob's own confession, '...few and evil have the days of...my life been...' (47:9). Israel represents the man of faith who struggled with God and found power with him (Genesis 32:28). Why are the names used interchangeably?

The question provides pause for reflection. The various names represent the struggle of human existence. Sometimes we, as Jacob, live by faith in God, sometimes we resort to our own ingenuity and forget God. The nation, which would carry the name, Israel, was to have the same kind of up and down existence. Sometimes they would faithfully serve their God. Often they would forget him and turn to their own way.

In the two names that are carried by the grandson of Abraham, there is the sacred and the profane, the lowly and the sublime. Jacob is a reflection of the human character. It reveals how far God must come to reach us. Israel is a reflection of the power of God to reach and change even the lowest of characters. The great comforting factor for us as we think about Jacob is that God never ceased calling him Israel even though he often acted like Jacob. From the lowliness of Jacob to the wonder of Israel! God can do it, and thankfully, he didn't give up on Jacob and he does not give up on us.

Genesis 48:1-22

I. Joseph's Sons Brought to Jacob (48:1-13)
1. Jacob's statement of faith
2. Jacob's spiritual growth
3. A touch of wonder
4. Ephraim and Manasseh are mine
5. '…I buried her…in…Bethlehem'

II. The Spiritual Musings of Jacob (48:14-19)
1. 'God…before whom my fathers…'
2. The shepherd and the redeemer

III. The Blessing of Ephraim and Manasseh (48:20-22)
1. '…I know it my son…'
2. '…One above thy brethren…'

Genesis 48:1-13

1. And it came to pass after these things, that one told Joseph, behold, thy father is sick: and he took with him his two sons, Manasseh and Ephraim. 2. And one told Jacob, and said, Behold, thy son Joseph cometh unto thee: and Israel strengthened himself, and sat upon the bed. 3. And Jacob said unto Joseph, God Almighty appeared unto me at Luz in the land of Canaan, and blessed me, 4. And said unto me, Behold, I will make thee fruitful, and multiply thee, and I will make of thee a multitude of people; and will give this land to thy seed after thee for an everlasting possession. 5. And now thy two sons, Ephraim and Manasseh, which were born unto thee in the land of Egypt before I came unto thee into Egypt, are mine;

as Reuben and Simeon, they shall be mine. 6. And thy issue, which thou begettest after them, shall be thine, and shall be called after the name of their brethren in their inheritance. 7. And as for me, when I came from Padan, Rachel died by me in the land of Canaan in the way, when yet there was but a little way to come unto Ephrath: and I buried her there in the way of Ephrath; the same is Bethlehem. 8. And Israel beheld Joseph's sons, and said, Who are these? 9. And Joseph said unto his father, They are my sons, whom God hath given me in this place. And he said, Bring them, I pray thee, unto me, and I will bless them. 10. Now the eyes of Israel were dim for age, so that he could not see. And he brought them near unto him; and he kissed them, and embraced them. 11. And Israel said unto Joseph, I had not thought to see thy face: and, lo, God hath shewed me also thy seed. 12. And Joseph brought them out from between his knees, and he bowed himself with his face to the earth. 13. And Joseph took them both, Ephraim in his right hand toward Israel's left hand, and Manasseh in his left hand toward Israel's right hand, and brought them near unto him.

Jacob's statement of faith

The blessing of Joseph's two sons is mentioned in another biblical passage. It is this event which, curiously, the writer of Hebrews chose as the crowning moment of Jacob's life. In the chapter often dubbed the biblical hall of fame for faith we read, 'By faith Jacob, when he was a dying, blessed both the sons of Joseph; and worshipped, leaning upon the top of his staff' (Hebrews 11:21). What are the things that make this event so notable? Consider the following.

There is a very clear statement of Jacob's faith. It is a grand passage, such as we have not seen from Jacob previously. 'God almighty appeared unto me...and blessed me... I will make of thee a multitude of people; and will give this land to thy seed...for an everlasting possession' (48:3-4). Jacob repeats the promise that God made him, but with a couple of minor alterations. First, the words of God were, '...I am God Almighty: be fruitful and multiply; a nation...shall be of thee...' (35:11). Jacob quoted, 'I will make thee...' (48:4). The stress in Jacob's words were based on what God would do as compared to that which appears to be a command or a simple note of encouragement about the future in Genesis 35:11. Genesis 28:13 carries the same promise to Jacob with the further confirmation of God's own 'I will.' The reader will note its connection with God's promise to Abraham and Isaac. Jacob defines the promise in a way that connects it with past and present.

Also, Jacob quotes God as saying that he would '...give this land to thy seed after thee for an everlasting possession' (48:4). Actually, there is no mention in Genesis 35:11 of the land being an everlasting possession. From what source was Jacob's understanding derived? At this point, the wonder of Jacob's words unfold. It is not the words that God spoke to Jacob that are the key, but the words that God spoke to Abraham.

Jacob was claiming the faith of his father, Abraham. It was words spoken to another that were his words. The words 'an everlasting possession' were spoken to Abraham, not to Jacob. '...all the land of Canaan, for an everlasting possession...' (17:8). This is an ultimate statement of faith. No wonder it is that which is included in the faith hall of fame! Is that not the key for us? The Bible is the record of words spoken to another.

> Faith is such a difficult and delicate thing. This passage reveals another of its marvellous nuances. The patriarchs can help us in not experiencing the same painful lessons of turning from the faith.

Jacob's spiritual growth

When word reaches Joseph that his father is extremely ill and is approaching death, he brings his two sons, Ephraim and Manasseh, for a visit to their grandfather. Jacob is energized by their presence.

'...and Israel strengthened himself and sat upon the bed...' (48:2). The reader is then treated to a rather detailed account of the blessing that Jacob gave to the two grandsons.

Instantly, the reader is inclined to recall the vivid scene when Jacob was the young man, receiving blessing from his father, Isaac. As in the earlier case, the older man has poor eyesight and cannot visually distinguish the difference in the two sons (Genesis 27). This passage is noteworthy because the writer of Hebrews records it as the most profound moment of faith in Jacob's life. 'By faith Jacob, when he was a dying, blessed both the sons of Joseph; and worshipped, leaning upon the top of his staff' (Hebrews 11:21). As we compare this event of blessing with the earlier one, the position of Jacob's faith emerges for us.

In the earlier instance, the father and the son acted in disobedience and in foolishness. The blessing was given to the younger Jacob by means of deceiving the father. Isaac had wrongly sought to give the blessing to Esau, the older brother. In the case of Jacob and Esau, the blessing was a private matter with the other brother absent. Here, the matter is settled openly and honestly in the full presence of both brothers. The picture is one of humble acceptance instead of human guilt that produces anger and division. Clearly, Jacob had learned from the earlier situation.

A further note about this event is striking. Why does the blessing go to Ephraim and Manasseh instead of to Joseph. This takes into account the birthright. It is in reality a blessing to Joseph. Through his sons, he shall have two tribes in the nation. The birthright meant that the elder brother received two parts in the inheritance to everyone else's one part. Jacob acted to give Joseph this part of the birthright. Yet, he held back one part from the son of his beloved Rachel. The headship of the nation would go to another brother, Judah (49:8). For Jacob, his heart may have desired to give that part of the blessing to Joseph. But, he bowed to the wisdom and will of God. Faith is shown in Jacob's gentle acquiescence.

The end of Jacob's life is clearly contrasted to the beginning of his life. He has progressed from trying to run things his own way to simple acquiescence to the Will of God. It is a relief to the reader, and brings a smile to the face. It is nice to see this Jacob. The question then comes, 'Can we reach that same point of gentle surrender?'

A touch of wonder

The story of Jacob's blessing of Ephraim and Manasseh has many allusions to other scriptural truth. As it is contemplated, one feels a tingle in the heart that derives from the wonder of such biblical unity from many diversified situations. Jacob's words to Joseph, recite the story of God's promise of blessing to Jacob, and are a marvellous portrait of the way God connects events set apart by centuries. Jacob's recitation of God's words to him (48:4) includes words that were actually spoken to Abraham (Genesis 17). By this, Jacob lays claim to the promises given to his grandfather years earlier. The request of Jacob to be buried in the promised land coupled with Joseph's request that his bones be carried to Israel (50:25) are connected to the vision of Ezekiel in the valley of dry bones, providing an Old Testament allusion to the resurrection.

It is striking when one considers what Jacob added to the words that God spoke to him. It is just as striking to see what part of God's promise to Jacob that he did not relate to Joseph. 'And God said unto him, I am God almighty: be fruitful and multiply; a nation and a company of nations shall be of thee, and kings shall come out of thy loins' (35:11). Jacob did not pass to Joseph's sons the blessing of kings. That belonged to another. 'Judah, thou art he whom thy brethren shall praise: thy hand shall be in the neck of thine enemies; thy father's children shall bow down before thee' (49:8).

The other Scriptures to which Jacob's prophecies allude show us the glory of God's knowledge. Ephraim will not have the blessing of kings, but he will have ascendancy over his brothers. The northern kingdom which shall remove ten tribes from the rule of David's sons shall be referred to as Ephraim. 'Ephraim is joined to idols: let him alone' (Hosea 4:17). Many different families shall lay claim to rulership of the Northern Kingdom, while David, and his progeny as sons of Judah, shall rule forever in the Southern Kingdom.

As one tries to connect the dots between all this writing of blessing, prediction, and historical events, it may seem like a meaningless mass of confusion until you see the whole picture. The intricate threads of a historical needlework are pieced together by God. Such divine handiwork should give us some confidence when we go to God with our needs.

> As one views the words of Jacob, and looks across the aeons of history at the tapestry of God's grand design, the only reaction is amazement. There is a complicated tangle of historical threads that become a beautiful picture of redemption. 'But ye are a chosen generation...Which in time past were not a people, but are now the people of God...' (1 Peter 2:9-10).

'...Ephraim and Manasseh...are mine...'

There is a part of Jacob's blessing that carries great relevance to the historical narrative of the patriarchal lives of Abraham, Isaac, and Jacob. Specifically, it brings to final conclusion the suspense about the nation that shall spring from Abraham. In God's rejection of the elder son, Ishmael, born to Abraham, and his rejection of the elder son, Esau, born to Isaac, the reader is led to wonder how this will ultimately work itself out. Will there be certain children accepted and rejected out of every generation? If so, how can this kind of activity ever be developed into one nation? The words of Jacob end that speculation. '...bless the lads, and let my name be named on them, and the name of my father Abraham and Isaac; and let them grow into a multitude in the midst of the earth' (48:16).

As Jacob reached out to his grandchildren, the only two sons of Joseph and named them both as part of the nation, there is a final stamp placed on the family. All the sons of Jacob, and their heritage, shall be the nation. Reaching past Joseph to bless the grandsons symbolically brings to an end the era of the Patriarchs. It is not the father, who blesses Ephraim and Manasseh, it is the grandfather. The founding fathers of the nation are now forever established.

Jacob continues by saying '...let them grow into a multitude....' (48 16). Chapter 49 of Genesis is the continuation of Jacob's blessing on his other sons. Chapter 50 concludes Joseph's life. We will next encounter the nation Israel more than 400 years later, and we are introduced to them like this. 'And the children of Israel were fruitful, and increased abundantly, and multiplied, and waxed exceeding mighty; and the land was filled with them' (Exodus 1:7). There is no mention of anything in the lives of the nation until they have fulfilled the words of the blessing '...let them grow...' (48:16). Since we have not the great and wonderful stories in the ensuing four hundred years, such as we see in the Patriarchs, can it be said that God was active? He certainly was! The nation was doing exactly as he commanded, and had plenty to study, to acknowledge, and to apply to themselves in the amazing lives of the Patriarchs. They would encounter nothing in which there could not be found a counterpart in the patriarchs' lives. God left them many clues to understand his direction in their lives.

There is the tendency to believe that our lives have not the many adventures and misadventures of the patriarchs; therefore, God is not at work in us. A closer look reveals that there is much in their lives, which correspond to us, and will, if we allow it, provide direction in our lives.

'...I buried her...in...Bethlehem'

As Jacob's conversation with Joseph and his two sons is recounted, the reader may sense some degree of disjointedness. Jacob goes from one thought to another, and it is difficult to see the connection. The important thing to remember is that three distinct things are occurring. First, there is a blessing for Joseph that is delivered by virtue of his two sons being included as part of the nation, thus Joseph has two parts in the heritage of Jacob. Joseph receives the birthright. Second, the blessings are a prophecy, denoting what shall be the construct of the nation in years to come. Third, this is the spiritual delineation of a salvation history that is placed in microscopic view.

The 'salvation history' is to be discovered in phrases like '...the God which fed me all my life long...The Angel which redeemed me from all evil...' (48:15-16). There is another verse that provides an even greater clue. Yet, one wonders how it is connected. 'And as for me, when I come from Padan, Rachel died by me in the land of Canaan in the way, when yet there was but a little way to come unto Ephrath: and I buried her there in the way of Ephrath; the same is Bethlehem' (48:7).

It is interesting that a burial is mentioned in the context of births. Jacob had just spoken of the sons born unto Joseph (48:5), and he refers to the sons that shall be born to them (48:6). Their sons shall be Joseph's inheritance. Strangely, he then speaks of the burial of Rachel at Bethlehem. Can we make a connection to this disconnect?

It becomes apparent when one sees the issue as one of the offspring, not of Rachel. Birth is the issue, not burial. In God's providence, Jacob is inspired to think of his beloved Rachel's burial place. This will instruct the nation about the most profound place of birth in the nation. A later prophet shall explain fully. 'But thou, Bethlehem Ephratah, though thou be little among the thousands of Judah, yet out of thee shall he come forth unto me that is to be ruler in Israel; whose goings forth have been from of old, from everlasting' (Micah 5:2). Jacob was lamenting the loss of his beloved Rachel, but in God's providence a lament is a prophecy of the place where the greatest birth in history shall occur. Thus, the lament fits perfectly in this setting. It, too, is the pronouncement of blessing. There will be a birth, but for the whole nation.

Genesis 48:14-19

14. And Israel stretched out his right hand, and laid it upon Ephraim's head, who was the younger, and his left hand upon Manasseh's head, guiding his hands wittingly; for Manasseh was the firstborn. 15. And he blessed Joseph, and said, God, before whom my fathers Abraham and Isaac did walk, the God which fed me all my life long unto this day, 16. The Angel which redeemed me from all evil, bless the lads; and let my name be named on them, and the name of my fathers Abraham and Isaac; and let them grow into a multitude in the midst of the earth. 17. And when Joseph saw that his father laid his right hand upon the head of Ephraim, it displeased him: and he held up his father's hand, to remove it from Ephraim's head unto Manasseh's head. 18. And Joseph said unto his father, Not so, my father: for this is the firstborn; put thy right hand upon his head. 19. And his father refused, and said, I know it, my son, I know it: he also shall become a people, and he also shall be great: but truly his younger brother shall be greater than he, and his seed shall become a multitude of nations.

'...God, before whom my fathers...'

Jacob's blessing on Joseph's two sons carries significant theological overtones that can be very meaningful to the student of Scripture. It begins with a statement to Joseph, '...God, before whom my fathers Abraham and Isaac did walk, the God which fed me all my life long unto this day, The Angel which redeemed me from all evil, bless the lads...' (48:15-16). As Jacob is dying, he makes a pronouncement about God. He begins with saying, '...God, before whom my fathers Abraham and Isaac did walk...' (48:15).

When one thinks of what Jacob said in the wisdom of the present cultural setting, it would be viewed with scepticism. When attitudes of previous generations are summarily dismissed as antiquated and out of date, and one must somehow dismiss himself from previous generations to be given any credibility, Jacob's approach is soundly criticized. He did not dismiss himself from his fathers, but proudly proclaimed and owned them. It was an urgent statement to Joseph to do the same. Our connection with the saints of the ages is critical to our stability and to our identity. When any generation seeks to reinvent itself as springing only from itself, the result is confusion and the loss of identity.

Jacob, through claiming the faith of his fathers is eliminating the need to ask the philosophical modern day question 'Who am I?' Whenever Christians try to recreate biblical truth to accommodate modern fascination and fancy we lose our identity.

There is a second aspect to this statement that requires some consideration. Jacob was dying. As his life was coming to an end, there was great comfort in knowing that he was following the path of his grandfather and his father who died with confidence in their God. He was following in the path that had been walked before. By a re-creation of biblical truth, a person must walk paths never walked before. The sense of comfort and reassurance that Jacob found is lost. The family connection with the saints who died before may not be so strongly felt when life is vibrant and death is a distant concept, but when the end is near, that family connection becomes very vital. It was great for Jacob to be able to face death knowing that he had the company of Abraham and Isaac. Come to think of it, it's great for us, too!

It is good to prepare for the moment we all face, the end of life on this earth. It is not generally thought about, but the connection with previous generations provides much comfort in that moment. Let us pray for great understanding of these great heroes and for a genuine connection with our heritage in Christ so that the heroes of the past will not be strangers to us as we are draw close to meeting them.

The shepherd and the redeemer

The expression '...God which fed me all my life long...' (48:15) is part of a shepherd's terminology. As one who tended to flocks all his life, it is not surprising that Jacob would use this expression to understand his God. He is stating that God had, in effect, been his shepherd. For Jacob, the words are very much a dynamic confessional in the form of praise. To be one's shepherd is to be with him even in the midst of great peril. Jacob expressed his understanding of the life of one who is a shepherd to his uncle Laban many years earlier. 'Thus I was; in the day the drought consumed me, and the frost by night; and my sleep departed from mine eyes' (Genesis 31:40). A shepherd's life is not an easy one. The confession by Jacob is that it had not been easy for God to shepherd him. He had required God to go with him in many difficult places, but God was always there. That is insight love produced.

The Angel that Jacob has in mind (48:16) is, without doubt, the Angel who visited him at Peniel with whom Jacob wrestled (32:24-30). The antecedent to the word, Angel, is God. It was God in human form (many biblical scholars acknowledge that this is a Christophany, an Old Testament appearance of Jesus Christ), who wrestled with Jacob, gave him a new name, and marked his body by giving him a crippled thigh (32:25). Jacob refers to the crippling as a great blessing in his life. Why? Because of the crippling he learned of the evil of his life. Note '...redeemed me from all evil...' (48:16). As Jacob lies on his death-bed, he praises God for a bodily affliction that established a monument to his acknowledgement of the evil in his life and in his need for dependence on God.

The word 'redeemer' is a great Old Testament word. It reflects the idea of a 'next of kin.' It is one who carries responsibility to protect you in times of trouble. The story of Ruth provides an illustration that expands on the idea of kinsman redeemer. Ruth's life had been shattered by the death of her husband. Her life is reclaimed for her by the action of a kinsman redeemer, Boaz. Jacob's statement of God as redeemer carries the wonder of the reclamation of life. The Angel (God), crippled Jacob at Peniel, but in the process gave Jacob spiritual life. In Jacob's mind, that was an excellent trade. It was made especially wonderful in the time of his dying. The spiritual life would reunite him with his father and grandfather at death.

The great theological truth that rests in the kinsman redeemer is in the Incarnation. Christ took on the form of flesh (becoming our near kinsman) and was in all points tempted like as we are. He pays the price of our sin through his vicarious death, thus claiming us as his bride (Ephesians 5:31-32), and reclaiming us for the family of God.

Genesis 48:20-22

20. And he blessed them that day, saying, In thee shall Israel bless, saying, God make thee as Ephraim and as Manasseh: and he set Ephraim before Manasseh. 21. And Israel said unto Joseph, Behold, I die: but God shall be with you, and bring you again unto the land of your fathers. 22. Moreover I have given to thee one portion above thy brethren, which I took out of the hand of the Amorite with my sword and with my bow.

'...I know it my son...'

The reader of Genesis must acknowledge that the life of Jacob has been filled with all the colour and wonder that make for great stories. His was a life of adventure, daring, audacity, romance, struggle, triumph, tragedy, and we can even throw in a little comedy. Among all the events of his life, it is the moment in which he rises to pronounce blessing upon Ephraim and Manasseh, the sons of Joseph, that the writer of Hebrews denotes as his greatest moment. 'By faith Jacob, when he was a dying, blessed both the sons of Joseph; and worshipped, leaning upon the top of his staff' (Hebrews 11:21).

It is Jacob's greatest moment because it is here that he makes the great statement of his faith. He does that in several ways. The first is his recounting of God's words to him. The second comes in a strange scenario. 'And Joseph took them both, Ephraim in his right hand toward Israel's left hand, and Manasseh in his left hand toward Israel's right hand...And Israel stretched out his right hand, and laid it upon Ephraim's head, who was the younger... And Joseph said unto his father, Not so my father: for this is the first born; put thy right hand upon his head. And his father refused, and said, I know it, my son, I know it...' (48:13-14, 18-19).

One may ask how this event is a statement of faith. Why is there so much stress laid on the pre-eminence of the younger over the older. This theme has appeared before in Genesis with Isaac's preference over Ishmael, and Jacob's preference over Esau. The underlying thought is 'who is most deserving of God's blessing?' It is difficult for humans to think in any other capacity than 'one gets what he deserves.' In Jacob's world, the blessing was the rightful possession of the elder brother, yet the younger received it, the one who should not have had it.

The lesson here is a lesson of grace. God's grace is never given on the basis of deserving, or on the basis of position, but on the basis of God's choice. There is no such thing as being deserving of God's grace, there is only the acceptance and receiving of God's grace. When Jacob stole the blessing from his father, he sought status. When he said to Joseph; '...I know it my son, I know it...' (48:19) he was stating. I know it is not about status, it's about grace. Jacob has finally understood. This is faith.

The emphasis here is on the aspect of grace seen once before. It is totally at God's discretion. We love grace when it is applied to us in forgiveness. We don't like it when we see it applied to someone else who appears favoured over us. Yet, the only way to have the benefits of grace in forgiveness is to have grace manifested as totally in the purview of God.

'...one portion above thy brethren...'

Jacob concludes the blessing of Ephraim and Manasseh with a statement that is somewhat mystifying. 'Moreover I have given to thee one portion above thy brethren, which I took out of the hand of the Amorite with my sword and with my bow' (48:22). It is a difficult passage on two fronts. First, the picture that Jacob gives to himself is not the picture of the Jacob we see in the narratives. He was never one who looked for physical battle, but sought to gain the edge on others by outwitting them. Second, the Bible gives no account of any battle that Jacob had with the Amorites.

To analyse it, and to come to application on it means dependency on the biblical information that we have. There is an encounter that happened with the people of the land. It was, however, Jacob's sons who were involved. The anger of Simeon and Levi over the treatment of their sister, Diana, led to a treachery in which Simeon and Levi slaughtered the people of Shechem (34:25). The word 'portion' (48:22) is the same word as the proper name, Shechem, in the Hebrew, so there is an allusion to the massacre of Chapter 34: Jacob severely chastised his sons for their actions (Genesis 34:30). His chastising them did not mean he did not accept whatever spoils may have come from the encounter. This included the right of ownership to the city which the sons, Simeon and Levi, had ravaged.

Since we only have the scriptural accounting, this seems to be the most natural understanding of the passage. If so, what is the application?

First, in giving ownership to the spoils of the battle to Joseph's sons, Jacob is making sure that neither Simeon, Levi, nor their sons, collect the spoils of their treachery. For us, there is a lesson to be applied. Gain that comes through treachery, or deceit, is never really ours. The nation of Israel was to take possession of the land at God's appointed time, and he would give it to them in such fashion that would demand their thanksgiving and acknowledgement of him. Anything that leads us to fail to acknowledge God, even though it appears profitable to us shall not be retained by us.

The child of God is obligated to learn the lessons of Scripture. To do so will save much heartache and solve many dilemmas before they create pain. The lesson here is that the child of God cannot truly prosper through treachery and deceit. Whatever is gained will ultimately be taken from him.

Genesis 49:1-27

I. The More Notable Sons' Blessings (49:1-12)
1. '...that which shall befall you...'
2. Blessing of Reuben
3. Blessing of Simeon and Levi
4. 'Judah...thy brethren shall praise...'
5. '...lions' whelp...'
6. '...until Shiloh come...'
7. '...shall the gathering of the people be...'
8. '...eyes shall be red with wine...'

II. The Less Notable Sons' Blessing (49:13-21)
1. Blessing of Zebulun and Issachar
2. Blessing of Dan
3. 'Gad...Asher...Naphtali

II. Further Blessings (49:22-27)
1. Blessing of Joseph
2. Blessing of Benjamin

Genesis 49:1-12

1. And Jacob called unto his sons, and said, Gather yourselves together, that I may tell you that which shall befall you in the last days. 2. Gather yourselves together, and hear, ye sons of Jacob; and hearken unto Israel your father. 3. Reuben, thou art my firstborn, my might, and the beginning of my strength, the excellency of dignity, and the excellency of power: 4. Unstable as water, thou shalt not excel; because thou wentest

*up to thy father's bed; then defiledst thou it: he went up to my couch. 5.
Simeon and Levi are brethren; instruments of cruelty are in their habitations. 6. O my soul, come not thou into their secret; unto their assembly,
mine honour, be not thou united: for in their anger they slew a man, and
in their selfwill they digged down a wall. 7. Cursed be their anger, for it
was fierce; and their wrath, for it was cruel: I will divide them in Jacob,
and scatter them in Israel. 8. Judah, thou art he whom thy brethren shall
praise: thy hand shall be in the neck of thine enemies; thy father's children
shall bow down before thee. 9. Judah is a lion's whelp: from the prey, my
son, thou art gone up: he stooped down, he couched as a lion, and as an
old lion; who shall rouse him up? 10. The sceptre shall not depart from
Judah, nor a lawgiver from between his feet, until Shiloh come; and unto
him shall the gathering of the people be. 11. Binding his foal unto the
vine, and his ass's colt unto the choice vine; he washed his garments in
wine, and his clothes in the blood of grapes: 12. His eyes shall be red with
wine, and his teeth white with milk.*

'...that which shall befall you...'

The reading of Genesis 49 is fraught with difficulty in that there is
much poetic language with meanings very obscure. The chapter
is generally labelled the 'blessing of Jacob.' As one reads the pronouncements of Jacob, 'blessing' doesn't always seem accurate.
'Curse' would appear a better description in several instances. The
Hebrew word translated 'blessed' in v. 28 can sometimes mean
curse, so the so-called words of blessing would not have been so
confusing in a Hebrew mindset.

    As one tries to understand what is happening, it is good to bear
in mind that this is not what we moderns would think of in terms of
a reading of the will. This is a prediction of the development of the
nation that shall be spawned by the sons of Jacob. The reality for
the sons is that their lives as individuals are not affected in any way.
After Jacob finishes his blessing and cursing, the sons can walk
away with a 'who cares' mentality. Such an attitude was reflected
when King Hezekiah was told of the trouble that shall come to the
nation of Judah after his lifetime is complete. Hezekiah responds,

'...Good is the word of the Lord...Is it not good, if peace and truth be in my days' (2 Kings 20:19)? The full impact of Jacob's words shall come in future generations, so what is the purpose to the sons?

It's best if we look at the last message of Jacob in terms of prediction, and in terms of a sermon. Just as Jacob had learned by his experiences, and expanded his understanding of God until the time of his death, he expects his sons to continue learning.

From Jacob's message to his sons, we can posit the following learning experiences for them and for us. First, God sees and records the deeds of our lives. The most important deeds of our lives are those which reflect and define our attitude toward the will of God. As the descendants of the twelve sons read the prediction, they will be called upon to submit to God's will. The sons of Jacob must make confession for their actions and seek to live out the rest of their lives in submission.

Second, God can and will use our life for the ultimate teaching of others. You will be an example one way or another. As God works out his blessing and cursing upon future generations, each individual will still have the option of learning and knowing God. That is an option still open to Jacob's sons. In this manner, the words are indeed a blessing.

Blessing of Reuben

Jacob gathers his twelve sons around him. He explains his reason as defining '...that which shall befall you in the last days' (49:1). One is quickly made aware that some of his sons will also be reminded of the past. The expression '...in the last days' (49:1) is better understood as 'in the days to come.' In very poetic language, the sons of Jacob are described, and told that God will mould the nation in accordance with their attributes. Thus, the lives of Jacob's sons, prefigured the history of the nation. Jacob saw the plan of God being demonstrated before him. It is not a prophetic methodology to be initiated, but a demonstration of God's control of the future.

We are to be in submission to God's will, and Jacob is foretelling that which is God's will for the nation.

The prophecy begins with the eldest son, Reuben. '...thou art my firstborn, my might, and the beginning of my strength, the excellency of dignity, and the excellency of power' (49:3). As the first born, Reuben bore the potential for excellence, and the opportunity for leadership. Reuben did not have the inward discipline and character to manifest that opportunity. Instead he is called, 'unstable as water' (49:4). The proof of his instability is seen in one sin reported in Genesis 35:22. '...Reuben went and lay with... his father's concubine....' At the time it occurred, Jacob appeared to ignore the action. We are only told that '...Israel heard it...' (Genesis 35:22). Reuben may be discovering for the first time that Jacob knew about that sin.

Reuben's inability to hang in there and do the right thing was also demonstrated in his lack of leadership with his brothers when they desired to kill Joseph. It was also displayed by a lack of initiative when Benjamin's life was at stake (Genesis 44:11-34). He is 'unstable as water' (49:3). The picture is one of great passion which can unleash itself as flood waters for great destruction, but can never be disciplined enough to produce benefit as a great dam which controls the torrent, and produces great power for a city.

As a historical reflection, the same instability and lack of discipline was displayed in Judges when the tribe of Reuben could not unite to fight against the Canaanites. 'And the princes of Issachar were with Deborah...For the division of Reuben, there were great thoughts of heart....' (Judges 5:15).

The failure to keep passions under control and to do the right thing, is a weakness, which can radically alter the heritage of one's life. Reuben is a sad case of unmet potential. It was his lack of discipline that shall characterize those who are his progeny in the nation. Little did Reuben know that his life was defining his progeny.

'Blessing of Simeon and Levi'

The pronouncements of Jacob upon his twelve sons are a large overview of the history of the nation of Israel. Jacob's words are there to partially explain the work of God to later generations, and to remind them of God's control. The blessings and cursings of Jacob are a reminder of God's watchful eye upon the attitudes by which people live their lives. Reuben lost the ownership of the birthright because of unstable character. Simeon and Levi would have been next in line, but they also acted in a way that cost them. Their violent activity in Chapter 34 had been chastised by Jacob because their actions could prove costly (34:30). Here, the two brothers learn what God thinks of their action.

One must be careful when action is based only in revenge. Simeon and Levi had perceived themselves as defending their sister's honour (34:31). God saw them as acting out of passion, and anger, rather than a clearly defined moral vision. Several of Jacob's words portray it for us: '...instruments of cruelty are in their habitations...in their anger they slew a man...cursed be their anger for it was fierce....' (49:5-7). The attitude and conclusions of Simeon and Levi were not attitudes that contribute to ending a problem, but attitudes that would only enlarge a problem. We humans are often prone to this kind of solution. It is only as we are submitted to God that we can clearly discern solutions instead of enlarging conflicts.

From a historical perspective, the two tribes of the nation, which would come from Simeon and Levi, would be dispersed. As it developed, neither of the tribes would ever obtain any of the land as a clear entitlement or portion. Levi would be designated the tribe of priests whose portion is the temple worship, and Simeon would be dispersed among the inheritance of Judah (Joshua 19:1), and among the northern tribes that split from Judah (2 Chronicles 34:5-6).

The separation has a symbolic message. As a teacher must separate two volatile personalities to maintain order, so Simeon and Levi were separated in the land to demonstrate the danger of passion not placed in submission to the will of God.

One can often rationalize passion by giving it high sounding motivation. It is important to recognize the passion that is uncontrollable and to discern its tendency to lead to rebellion against God.

'Judah...thy brethren shall praise...'

Jacob proceeds with his pronouncements of blessing and cursing on the twelve sons. The blessing on Judah is significantly different. He is set apart, and clearly out-distances the others in terms of praise, and prophecy of greatness. The tribe that shall come from Judah will carry the note of grandeur forever. 'Judah, thou art he whom thy brethren shall praise...' (49:8).

This is significant in two ways. First, Judah is not the recipient of the birthright which was given to Joseph (48:22). The fact that Judah shall be praised above his brethren is a clear note of God's choice. It was Joseph who had saved their lives but it is Judah that shall carry the praise as the stronger of the tribes. 'Moreover he refused the tabernacle of Joseph, and chose not the tribe of Ephraim: But chose the tribe of Judah, the mount Zion which he loved' (Psalms 78:67-68).

Second, the brothers had been known to act jealously as in their rage toward Joseph. Sons born from different mothers, but with the same father, are even more vulnerable to vibrant competition and rivalry than that which is normally seen among siblings. The statement '...whom thy brethren shall praise...' (49:8), indicates a very special coming together of the brothers through the nation. It is almost a miracle. All the tribes shall be united in praise to Judah, and be glad in it. The joy of Israel in praise to Judah is extremely significant.

The united twelve tribes occurred as a historical narrative in the early days of the monarchy, but saw its peak in the reign of David. Solomon (David's son) had a long and successful tenure, but his heavy taxes on the people (2 Chronicles 10:4) allowed some of that unity of praise to crumble. It totally fell apart with Solomon's son, Rehoboam, and disappeared with the development of a divided kingdom.

The uniting of the nation in the years that follow is to be seen symbolically through the hope of Messiah, the one who will renew Israel's glory, and re-establish the throne of David. He shall unify the nation forever and again bring Israel to praise the tribe of Judah. 'In his days Judah shall be saved, and Israel shall dwell safely: and this is his name whereby he shall be called, The Lord our Righteousness' (Jeremiah 23:6). Not only shall Israel unite in praise to the great son of Judah, the whole earth shall praise him.

> Through the Incarnate One, here revealed as coming from the tribe of Judah, the whole world benefits from the blessing on Judah. A moment of praise and thanksgiving is worthwhile for God's mastery in making a nation of Abraham's seed, choosing one obscure individual from the great grandchildren of Abraham, and setting up his line as a kingly line for the nation. To make it more phenomenal, he uses that as means to bless all the families of the earth (12:3). What a great salvation!

'...lion's whelp...'

In the words of Jacob to his twelve sons, we have images placed before us that stir the imagination. They represent that which is to become a historical reality, and as such, are fascinating. The vivid images are meant to pack an emotional wallop. As one contemplates them, there is a certain kind of excitement, and a certain kind of anxiety. That which gives the appearance of being just an ancient story about a man and his sons strangely starts impacting us. A new nation, Israel, is the historical development, but more is in view than the one nation. The reader senses that he or she is somehow involved.

The blessing pronounced on Judah is poetic and sublime. He is described as a young lion. 'Judah is a lion's whelp: from the prey, my son, thou art gone up: he stooped down, he couched as a lion, and as an old lion; who shall rouse him up' (49:9)? One will note the majesty and authority in the picture. The lion catches his prey, and eats it. He lies down to sleep, and who would dare rouse him? He has no fear, as he is in total control, even when he sleeps. It is the character of grand rulership.

In biblical and historical perspective, Israel is told that their king shall come from the tribe of Judah, and this is fulfilled in the anointing of David (I Samuel 16:13). If the tribe of Judah is the lion of Israel, then the greatest son born of Judah is the greatest in the nation. The Bible refers to the greatest son as the Lion of the tribe of Judah. '...behold, the Lion of the tribe of Judah, the Root of David, hath prevailed to open the book, and to loose the seven seals thereof' (Revelation 5:5). In Revelation 5:5, the Lion is roused, and the book is opened that shall seal the fate of the earth.

The amazing picture, which unfolds, is that the lion of the tribe of Judah is also portrayed as another kind of animal. '...Worthy is the Lamb that was slain to receive power, and riches, and wisdom, and strength, and honour, and glory, and blessing' (Revelation 5:12). When the full picture unfolds as to the meaning of the 'lion's whelp' (49:9) image of Judah, the heart is stirred. It is no wonder that a bit of excitement and anxiety fills the reader as the words of Jacob are contemplated. This lion shall one day be full grown, and roused up to judge the whole world, but we shall first see him as the lamb.

God has given to the world the opportunity to respond to the lion of the tribe of Judah as the lamb of God (John 1:29). A note of thanks is appropriate, for in knowing him as the lamb, there shall be no fear when he dons the mantle of the lion.

'...until Shiloh come...'

The more one contemplates the blessing of Judah in the light of historical development, the more one becomes aware that the blessing of Judah is a vicarious blessing on the whole nation of Israel, as well as to the whole earth. When fully comprehended, the other eleven sons of Jacob needed no blessing for they are all included here. Israel is to undergo a long and frightful history. Their rebellion shall bring the judgement of God upon them, but there is a way to know that Israel is not fully abandoned by God as a nation. For the rest of the world, God's action with Judah is a way to know that God is not finished with the world.

'The sceptre shall not depart from Judah, nor a lawgiver from between his feet, until Shiloh come; and unto him shall the gathering of the people be' (49:10).

There are a couple of things, which help the understanding of this part of the blessing of Judah. The sceptre is a sign for royalty, but could also be used to mean other authority, so this does not imply a throne or necessitating a king 'until Shiloh come' (49:10). Also, it is not to be understood as necessitating a particular individual as authority 'until Shiloh come' (49:10). The reference is to Judah, and to his status, or more specifically to the status of the tribe of Judah. In addition, the word Shiloh, is a Hebrew idiom that expresses the idea of ownership. The idea is explained in the words of the prophet Ezekiel '...and it shall be no more, until he come whose right it is...' (Ezekiel 21:27). The expression 'Shiloh' should be understood as the 'one to come who has the right of possession.'

The historical perspective plays out in God's maintenance of the Jewish people. Though scattered through all nations of the earth after 70 A.D. they were able to identify themselves as the Jewish people and reclaim their homeland nearly 2000 years later. Though ten of their tribes (the northern kingdom), have been lost, Jacob's blessing to Judah remains. Through Judah, the people of Israel may know that their nation is still a part of God's plan. Judah returned from captivity in Babylon. The one who is the true owner of the kingship has not yet manifest himself as the lion of the tribe of Judah. Until he does, Israel, and the world, will know through Judah's existence that God is not finished with his earth.

The beauty of this passage is the way that God provides keys to helping us maintain our faith. The primacy of Judah denotes the future kingship of the nation, but additionally provides a comfort to all believers, validating, by its continued existence, that God will not abandon his promise 'til Shiloh come' (49:10).

'...Shall the gathering of the people be'

The continuing unfolding of the blessing that Jacob pronounces on Judah leaves the mind staggering. There is so much said in so few words. Trying to absorb it all leaves one feeling out of breath, and motivated toward praise to God. The survival of the Jewish people for centuries, though scattered among the nations is a wonder in itself. As a scattered people, they have been often persecuted, and many attempts have been made to destroy them. The twentieth century was extremely horrific for the Jewish people. There is a part of the blessing to Judah that should create concern for the nations who would seek to destroy them.

'The sceptre shall not depart form Judah, nor a lawgiver from between his feet, until Shiloh come; and unto him shall the gathering of the people be' (49:10). The phrase translated '...gathering of the people...' (49:10) is better understood in terms of nations. It refers to the concept that the lion of the tribe of Judah (49:9) shall command allegiance from all the nations of the world. Unfortunately, the nation of Israel came to understand this as having reference to Israel's rulership over the nations instead of the rulership of the 'lion'. The nations would not bow at Israel's feet, they would join with Israel in bowing to the lion of the tribe of Judah.

The Psalmist had such a view in mind when he wrote, 'All the ends of the world shall remember and turn unto the Lord: and all the kindreds of the nations shall worship before thee' (Psalms 22:27). That moment is vividly described in the prophetic eye of the future. '...behold, the Lion of the tribe of Judah...Thou art worthy to take the book...for thou wast slain, and hast redeemed us to God by thy blood out of every kindred, and tongue, and people, and nation...And every creature which is in heaven, and on the earth, and under the earth, and such as are in the sea, and all that are in them, heard I saying, Blessing, and honour, and glory, and power, be unto him that sitteth upon the throne....' (Revelation 5:5,9,13).

The promise made to Abraham in Genesis 12:3 '...in thee shall all families of the earth be blessed' is taking on an expanded, and heart-pounding reality through the blessing now placed on Judah. As the reader allows the majesty of this blessing to invade the soul, the command to '...love the Lord thy God with all thy heart, with all thy soul, and with all thy mind' (Matthew 22:37), seems much easier to obey.

> In the daily cares of life, we lose sight of the wonder of God. Such passages of Scripture as this help us to recapture that wonder. We should spend a moment in meditating on the grandeur of God. Consider the creation narrative. Consider the power and majesty as he filled out the heavens, and populated the earth with the animals. Consider his movement among men and his work with the patriarchs of the nation of Israel.

'...eyes shall be red with wine...'

The 'lion of the tribe of Judah' (49:9) shall be a great king. All the nations of the earth shall bow before him. '...unto him shall the gathering of the people be' (49:10). The question arises, 'What shall his kingdom be like? ' Jacob adds words to his blessing on Judah that shall be picked up by many of Israel's prophets who explain the nature of the reign of the great king.

'Binding his foal unto the vine, and his ass's colt unto the choice vine; he washed his garments in wine, and his clothes in the blood of grapes: his eyes shall be red with wine, and his teeth white with milk' (49:11-12). This is a picture of grand prosperity and blessing. The harvest shall be so great that one may tie his animal to the best vine, and allow him to eat. There shall be so much wine that it is as disposable as wash water. '...he washed his garments in wine...' (49:11). The reign of the lion of the tribe of Judah will be a festive and joyful event for all.

The statement concerning the king in (49:12) may be a little surprising in the light of other Scripture texts. He is described as having '...eyes...red with wine...' (49:12). The book of Proverbs writes, 'Who hath woe? Who hath sorrow?...Who hath redness of eyes? They that tarry long at the wine...' (Proverbs 23:29-30). The two passages of Scripture are not contradictory when one understands the nature of the language. The blessing on Judah is poetic language. It is spoken in the extreme, and uses a metaphor to portray abundance and celebration. The Apostle Paul uses the same kind of metaphorical expression when he says 'be not drunk with wine...but be filled with the Spirit' (Ephesians 5:18). One is to have a different kind of intoxication. The blessing on Judah speaks of the intoxication that comes out of the wonder of the reign of the 'lion' (v. 9). Redness of eyes, and whiteness of teeth are expressions of strength. It is the language of trying to describe the indescribable. One goes to the extreme to provide understanding of that which is hard to understand by contrasting it with the easy to understand.

Christians are often prone to mourning the woeful conditions on the earth, and seeing only hopelessness and despair. Take a moment and reflect on God's great plan, and know that there is a lion of the tribe of Judah whose kingdom shall prosper by his great strength.

In a time when humans are often in despair with the evil conditions of the world, and are left without explanation for the inhumanity that exists, the desire for hope is universal.

Where can we go to find it? We might consider a little contemplation on the coming kingdom of the Lion of the tribe
of Judah, also revealed as the '...seed of the woman...'
(Genesis 3:15).

Genesis 49:13-21

*13. Zebulun shall dwell at the haven of the sea; and he shall be for an
haven of ships; and his border shall be unto Zidon. 14. Issachar is a strong
ass couching down between two burdens: 15. And he saw that rest was
good, and the land that it was pleasant; and bowed his shoulder to bear,
and became a servant unto tribute. 16. Dan shall judge his people, as one
of the tribes of Israel. 17. Dan shall be a serpent by the way, an adder in
the path, that biteth the horse heels, so that his rider shall fall backward.
18. I have waited for thy salvation, O Lord. 19. Gad, a troop shall overcome him: but he shall overcome at the last. 20. Out of Asher his bread
shall be fat, and he shall yield royal dainties. 21. Naphtali is a hind let
loose: he giveth goodly words.*

Blessing of Zebulun and Issachar

Except for his words to Joseph, Jacob says least to the younger
brothers of Judah. There are short, terse pronouncements. Very
little is revealed of long-term history for the nation of Israel. This
can be reflected in the fact that ten of the tribes were lost to historical perspective following the fall of the Northern Kingdom, and in
Benjamin's absorption into Judah of the Southern Kingdom.

Zebulun and Issachar are often mentioned together in the
Old Testament. In Jacob's statement, Zebulun is seen as one who
sets his eyes to the sea, and pushes the borders of his inheritance
toward Zidon (49:13). Issachar is a strong donkey whose strength
gets used only as beast of burden (49:14). There is an underlying
theme in Jacob's words that can give application. To understand
it clearly, one needs to see a later word that shall be spoken by

Moses of the tribes of Zebulun and Issachar. 'And of Zebulun he said, rejoice, Zebulun, in thy going out; and, Issachar, in thy tents. They shall call the people into the mountain; there they shall offer sacrifices of righteousness: for they shall suck of the abundance of the seas, and of treasures hid in the sand' (Deuteronomy 33:18-19). When the words of Jacob and Moses are placed together, it makes for a rather unflattering portrayal of the two brothers' descendants. The people of the tribes of Zebulun and Issachar were turned to material wealth. They enjoyed the abundance of the land and the treasures that derived from sea trade. To 'offer sacrifices' (Deuteronomy 33:19) is to worship at the altar of material gain.

The portrait of Zebulun and Issachar speaks volumes to a culture like ours. Issachar is a donkey, a beast of burden. He values his possessions and his ease so much that it cost him his liberty. He will give away the control of his life in order that he may suck up the treasures of the land. This is the picture of a group of people who lost understanding of priority. Being so in love with material gain and ease, and thinking they knew about value, they lost sense of that which is truly valuable. Issachar is later shown as an extremely powerful race of men (I Chronicles 7:5), but without someone to lead them, they would give up liberty to preserve material gain.

> Humans are always vulnerable to valuing a life of materialism and ease above a spiritual relationship with God.

Blessing of Dan

Dan was one of the sons of Jacob born to a concubine. The reader may sense a note of great tragedy in this pronouncement. Clearly, there is anxiety. Jacob cries out at the end of his statement about Dan 'I have waited for thy salvation, O Lord' (49:18). In addition, the tribe noted to be the one that '...shall judge his people...' (49:16) is connected with the image of a serpent. Evidently there is a progression in the tribe from one who brings justice to his people to one who acts as the serpent. One of the most famous of the

Judges (Samson) was a Danite. The serpent imagery recalls the animal who first tempted Eve to sin by telling her she could be as God (Genesis 3:5). Here is the first indication of the corruption of the nation's worship. Dan shall be at the heart of the corruption of the worship of the nation.

In Judges 18, there is an intriguing story about the children of Dan accepting an idol as a part of worship. A centre of worship was established in direct opposition to the worship centre at Shiloh, where the ark of the covenant was located. Later, in the history of the nation, Jeroboam, first king of the Northern Kingdom institutionalized idolatrous worship by setting up a calf of gold to be worshipped at Dan, and at Bethel. Thus, Dan is central to the pollution of the entire worship life of the nation.

Clearly, the worship of the people is central to God's concern. Jacob's cry for the salvation of God may be a prophetic view of the horror of corrupted worship in the nation. In the book of Revelation, there is a listing of the tribes of Israel, stating the number from each tribe that shall be protected in the last days. Dan is not included among them (Revelation 7:4-8). The prophet, Amos, validates the fact that Dan's elimination is connected to his corruption of the nation's worship. 'They that swear by the sin of Samaria, and say, Thy God, O Dan, liveth; and, The manner of Beersheba liveth; even they shall fall, and never rise up again' (Amos 8:14).

The statement of Jacob about Dan is a sermon to the nation of later times. It speaks to us about the seriousness of God concerning the worship of his people. It should give every Christian reason to ponder the seriousness of worship in his life. In an age which tends to trivialize worship, and look upon it as merely a means of self-gratification, or a way to feel good, instead of a holy moment in which to approach God, a look at the tribe of Dan may be very enlightening.

This may be a good time to consider the way that we approach worship. In what way do we value it? Is it more a focus on ourselves trying to get God to pay attention to us, or is it a moment when our hearts are hungry to have him teach us about him? Let us pray that we would not make the mistake of Dan and pervert worship to be a primary focus on us.

'...Gad...Asher...Napthali...'

Of the twelve sons of Jacob, four were born to concubines. All were part of the Northern Kingdom, which split with Judah following Solomon's death in rebellion against Solomon's heir, Rehoboam. The tribe of Dan distinguished itself in infamy as a tribe that contributed heavily to the corruption of worship in the land. The other three tribes spawned from Jacob's concubines have no such notoriety. In effect, Jacob lays out that which shall be their role in the land.

Gad shall be regularly besieged. Choosing to dwell in the land on the east of Jordan, Gad shall be regularly attacked, and will constantly be fending off enemies. They shall become effective warriors (1 Chronicles 12:14-15). There is a promise that they shall overcome in the land.

Asher shall dwell in a part of the land that produces great abundance. Their inheritance in the promised land was the lowlands of Carmel, one of the best parts for producing great harvests. This part of the land provided much of the food for King Solomon (1 Kings 5:11).

Naphtali shall dwell in the highlands, and shall be an uninhibited tribe exhibiting the characteristics of a free-spirited animal. Naphtali is predicted to be a tribe that '...giveth goodly words' (49:21). This is better understood as 'beareth comely fawns,' in keeping with the image of a hind (a gazelle, or free-spirited animal). As people of the highlands, the people of Naphtali will remain a pure blood. Their children shall be strong.

To understand the blessing of Jacob to these sons of the concubines, it is best that these three should be considered one. All three tribes disappeared after the fall of the Northern Kingdom and there is little upon which to gain any historical perspective. The prophetic word to Dan, the other son of a concubine, had been a warning of treachery and carried a sombre note. Dan is referred to as a serpent. Jacob follows that pronouncement with great hope for the other three.

With that understanding, their hope is in service to the tribe of Judah, more specifically to the lion of the tribe of Judah. Engagement in the battle (Gad), servitude in providing the needs of the King (Asher), or maintaining purity in service to God (Naphtali) is the route to blessing. All three are metaphors to the kind of living that Christians are called upon to do.

Genesis 49:22-27

22. Joseph is a fruitful bough, even a fruitful bough by a well; whose branches run over the wall: 23. The archers have sorely grieved him, and shot at him, and hated him: 24. But his bow abode in strength, and the arms of his hands were made strong by the hands of the mighty God of Jacob; (from thence is the shepherd, the stone of Israel:) 25. Even by the God of thy father, who shall help thee; and by the Almighty, who shall bless thee with blessings of heaven above, blessings of the deep that lieth under, blessings of the breasts, and of the womb: 26. The blessings of thy father have prevailed above the blessings of my progenitors unto the utmost bound of the everlasting hills: they shall be on the head of Joseph, and on the crown of the head of him that was separate from his brethren. 27. Benjamin shall ravin as a wolf: in the morning he shall devour the prey, and at night he shall divide the spoil.

Blessing of Joseph

Jacob's blessing on Joseph provides some confusion for biblical readers. There are twelve tribes in Israel, corresponding with twelve sons born to Jacob. There are two grandsons, Ephraim and Manasseh included in the equation of the twelve tribes. This works itself out via the elimination of Joseph as a tribe with his blessing being doubled through his grandsons. This still leaves thirteen. However, with Levi, as the priestly tribe, there are only twelve tribes who receive parcels of the land. One must understand Ephraim and Manasseh as under the sonship of Joseph to get at the number twelve.

In the final days, the twelve tribes are understood by the elimination of the names of Dan and Ephraim. Joseph's name replaces Ephraim, and Dan is eliminated, arguably because of Dan's corruption of the worship life of the nation (Judges 18:30-31). As the blessing of Ephraim was under Joseph, his tribe is not eliminated but assumed under the name of Joseph in Revelation. It is a confusing picture, but shows us how the number gets from fourteen to twelve.

Joseph's tribe from the perspective of Jacob must be seen in a varied context. He speaks of the combination of the two tribes of Ephraim and Manasseh in terms of Joseph. In addition, Jacob has in mind a much larger view of the whole nation. Indeed, as the whole nation is to benefit from the blessing of Judah, the words to Joseph encapsulate the history of all of Israel. The blessing is both specific and national in implication.

As the national implication is present, the historical perspective emerges. Joseph is fruitful. He grew into a large nation (49:22). Specifically, Ephraim and Manasseh had the greater numbers in the population of the nation, '...blessings of the breasts, and of the womb' (49:25). As a nation, they faced war and the hatred of the other nations (49:23-24). God has preserved them through the ages (49:25-26). Joseph was separate from his brothers, being sold into slavery in Egypt. Israel shall also be a separate nation unique unto God (49:26). Even in the present age of the church, Israel, wherever it lives, remains a separate entity, the people known as Jews.

All this is a rather remarkable portrait of history. When one ponders the somewhat confusing nature of Jacob's words of blessing, we can only marvel at their accuracy in the more confusing history of the Jewish people.

One will sometimes be greatly bewildered at the words of the Bible, and find it extremely difficult to fathom all the riches present. It is impossible to grasp all the wondrous works of God, yet the history of the nation he created out of the descendants of Shem, can only lead us to come to his feet, and worship at his great wisdom. The church, the bride of Christ, has the responsibility to lead in proper worship. Let us never fail to understand the awesome responsibility, and pray to avoid the temptation to turn worship into an entity to feed our desire to glorify ourselves.

Blessing of Benjamin

The final son born to Jacob is Benjamin. His mother (Rachel) had died when giving him birth (35:17-19). The blessing that he receives from his father is a prediction of action that shall be seen in the life of the tribe of Benjamin. He is described as a wolf. The words '...shall ravin as a wolf' (49:27) reflect fierceness and spirit as in 'ravenous wolf.' The Chronicles has this comment on the tribe of Benjamin: 'And the sons of Ulam were mighty men of valour, archers, and had many sons, and sons' sons, an hundred and fifty. All these are of the sons of Benjamin' (I Chronicles 8:40). The battlefield tenacity and ability of the tribe is documented in Scripture (Judges 20:21-22; 1 Chronicles 12:2). It was the war-like tribe that was the heritage of Saul, first king of Israel.

Though the portrait the blessing provides is shown to be accurate in the historical perspective of the nation, it is difficult to see the lesson for Israel in such a short statement. The brief description that Jacob provides probably carries an implicit warning. Benjamin will have battlefield ability, but will they always battle on the right side?

The book of Deuteronomy provides an additional note about the tribe of Benjamin. 'And of Benjamin he said, The beloved of the Lord shall dwell in safety by him; and the Lord shall cover him all the day long, and he shall dwell between his shoulders' (Deuteronomy 33:12). The ravenous wolf is spoken of as '...The beloved of the Lord...' When the two blessings are placed together (49:27 and Deuteronomy 33:12), a positive picture emerges. Benjamin makes the right choice, and shall 'dwell in safety' (Deuteronomy 33:12). The historical perspective is reflected in the division of the nation after Solomon's death. Ten tribes secede and begin the Northern Kingdom rebelling against the rule of the son of David, a king from the line of Judah. Benjamin does not secede, but remains with Judah. In the New Testament, the great apostle who is called to take the gospel to the Gentiles identifies himself as '...of the tribe of Benjamin, an Hebrew of the Hebrews...' (Philippians 3:5).

The characteristic of Benjamin that Jacob noted was both good and bad depending on the choice that Benjamin makes. The lesson for us is to make sure that we do not glory in any particular attribute, but to stay alert to the importance of making right choices.

It would be a good moment if we reflect on the way we make choices in our lives. Do we focus on the nature of God, and what would honour him? Do we focus on ourselves and what would honour us? Do we refuse to glory in any ability or talent that we have, understanding that it came from God, and that he can take it away from us?

Genesis 50:1-26

I. Jacob's Death and Elaborate Funeral (50:1-13)
1. '…mourned threescore and ten days'
2. '…all the elders of Egypt'

II. The Brothers after Jacob's Death (50:15-21)
1. The brothers worry
2. '…Forgive I pray thee…'
3. '…we be thy servants…'
4. '…fear ye not…'

III. The Last Days of Joseph (50:22-26)
1. '…brought up upon Joseph's knees
2. 'So Joseph died…'

Genesis 50:1-13

1. And Joseph fell upon his father's face, and wept upon him, and kissed him. 2. And Joseph commanded his servants the physicians to embalm his father: and the physicians embalmed Israel. 3. And forty days were fulfilled for him; for so are fulfilled the days of those which are embalmed: and the Egyptians mourned for him threescore and ten days. 4. And when the days of his mourning were past, Joseph spake unto the house of Pharaoh, saying, If now I have found grace in your eyes, speak, I pray you, in the ears of Pharaoh, saying, 5. My father made me swear, saying, Lo, I die: in my grave which I have digged for me in the land of Canaan, there shalt thou bury me. Now therefore let me go up, I pray thee, and bury my father, and I will come again. 6. And Pharaoh said, Go up, and bury thy father, according as he made thee swear. 7. And Joseph went up to bury his father: and with him went up all the servants of Pharaoh, the elders of his house, and all the elders of the land of Egypt, 8. And all the house of Joseph, and his brethren, and his father's house: only their little ones, and their flocks, and their herds, they left in the land of Goshen. 9. And there went up with him both chariots and horsemen: and it was a very great company. 10. And they came to the threshingfloor of Atad, which is beyond Jordan, and there they mourned with a great and very sore lamentation: and he made a mourning for his father seven days. 11. And when the inhabitants of the land, the Canaanites, saw the mourning in the floor of Atad, they said, This is a grievous mourning to the Egyptians: wherefore the name of it was called Abelmizraim, which is beyond Jordan. 12. And his sons did unto him according as he commanded them: 13. For his sons carried him into the land of Canaan, and buried him in the cave of the field of Machpelah, which Abraham bought with the field for a possession of a buryingplace of Ephron the Hittite, before Mamre.

'...mourned...threescore and ten days'

The death of Jacob is placed before the reader of Scripture in an unusual fashion. For Abraham and Isaac, the earlier patriarchs, we have a simple statement without any colourful details. 'Then Abraham gave up the ghost, and died...' (Genesis 25:8). 'And Isaac gave up the ghost, and died...' (Genesis 35:29).

The scene of Jacob lying back on his bed offers a last scene of peace in a life that had seen little peace. The era of the patriarchs is brought to a close. In spite of weaknesses and conflicts, the nation that God had promised (Genesis 12:3) is now blossoming in Egypt. It will bear Jacob's new name, Israel. The one who gives the nation its name has just finished a series of blessings on his twelve sons, which spell out the coming history of the nation. Much trouble and travail is still to fall on the nation, but there is peace for Jacob. He has filled his role.

Then, there is an elaborate reporting of his funeral. His body is embalmed (50:2). A long period of mourning is carried out (50:3). Joseph seeks permission to take Jacob's body to Canaan for burial, and a description is provided of an elaborate caravan that accompanies this trip (50:4-13). By virtue of Joseph's closeness to the Pharaoh's court, Jacob's death is significant to the nation of Egypt. He is treated as part of the royal family. In the light of God's great plan, the setting is quite ironic. It is almost humorous.

Though promised the land of Canaan, and promised that they would become a great nation, all three patriarchs die without seeing ownership of the land. Yet, as the patriarchal age closes, the last of them, is given a royal funeral. It has the appearance that God is subtly bringing another nation to honour the sovereignty of the patriarchs in the land. The Canaanites, who would ultimately be displaced in the land, notice the caravan, and are reported to call the place of mourning 'Abel-mizraim' (50:11). The expression is a play on a word meaning 'the mourning of the Egyptians.' All Egypt according to the Canaanites is viewed as mourning over Jacob's body. God gives the last patriarch a royal funeral, and has the people, who will be dispossessed of the land, as witnesses to this grand statement of a future reality. The king of the land shall come from Israel.

The spectacle has a touch of grandeur with spiritual overtones. One can sense that there is something going on that is far more than meets the eye. It is an event that will cause one's spine to tingle wondering what the true meaning is. When one realizes that God was delivering a message, the tingle becomes a chill, or a thrill. As one seeks to know God, and to find the capacity of increasing love for him, these little glimpses into his work can stir our hearts with emotion.

'...all the elders of Egypt'

The pomp and grandeur of a funeral is an event the reader of Genesis does not see until the final chapter. The last of the patriarchs is transported by caravan from Egypt to his final resting-place in the land of Canaan. The Canaanites are noted as observing the mourning of the Egyptians. The patriarch, Jacob, is only related to the Egyptians as father of Joseph, who is close to the Pharaoh. The reader is left to wonder why the writer of Genesis makes so much of Jacob's funeral. Why do the Egyptians' activities in the procession seem so important, especially in light of the fact that there was no such treatment for Abraham and Isaac?

It is clear that God is closing the story of the patriarchs with this grand gesture, which acknowledges their role in human history. Egypt is the most powerful nation in the world and God has them mourning the passing of his patriarch. This is a clear statement that should have been remembered by the nation of Israel in later years. God is in control of the nations. At Jacob's death, God has Egypt in mourning. When the page of Scripture is turned, the same nation shall refuse to hear the Word of God when spoken by Moses. Their majestic power shall be broken when the army of Egypt is drowned in the Red Sea.

To Israel, God is stating a message through Jacob's grand funeral. He says, 'I brought Egypt to mourn for your father, Jacob, and to royally honour him. I will bring all nations to royally honour you as long as you are obedient to me.' This is a concept that is stated as a matter-of-fact in another time. 'Behold, I have taught you statutes and judgements, even as the Lord my God commanded me, that ye should do so in the land whither ye go to possess it. Keep therefore and do them; for this is your wisdom and your understanding in the sight of the nations, which shall hear all these statutes, and say, Surely, this great nation is a wise and understanding people' (Deuteronomy 4:5-6). The promise of Deuteronomy 4:5-6, left unfulfilled in the nation, will be fulfilled in the person of Jesus Christ at whose feet all nations shall bow.

It is true that this text is only the story of a funeral (though a grand one). Yet, it says volumes about God's majestic control of history and the nations.

There are so many biblical wonders of the control of God in history. This is a good time to ask ourselves if these reminders have the needed effect on us. Do we find the comfort that such truth should provide? Do we rush to that thought with each worldly crisis, or do we panic with the rest of the world? Do we look at the world and ask for God's insight on how to communicate our trust in him, or do we look at the world, and grow fearful?

Genesis 50:14-21

14. And Joseph returned into Egypt, he, and his brethren, and all that went up with him to bury his father, after he had buried his father. 15. And when Joseph's brethren saw that their father was dead, they said, Joseph will peradventure hate us, and will certainly requite us all the evil which we did unto him. 16. And they sent a messenger unto Joseph, saying, Thy father did command before he died, saying, 17. So shall ye say unto Joseph, Forgive, I pray thee now, the trespass of thy brethren, and their sin; for they did unto thee evil: and now, we pray thee, forgive the trespass of the servants of the God of thy father. And Joseph wept when they spake unto him. 18. And his brethren also went and fell down before his face; and they said, Behold, we be thy servants. 19. And Joseph said unto them, Fear not: for am I in the place of God? 20. But as for you, ye thought evil against me; but God meant it unto good, to bring to pass, as it is this day, to save much people alive. 21. Now therefore fear ye not: I will nourish you, and your little ones. And he comforted them, and spake kindly unto them.

The brothers worry

At the time of Jacob's death, he and his sons (Joseph's brothers) had lived in Egypt for seventeen years (Genesis 47:28). For seventy days, Jacob's family had been in the state of mourning over his death. When the funeral has ended and the brothers return to Egypt, their sins from the past begin to haunt them. 'And when Joseph's brethren saw that their father was dead, they said, Joseph will peradventure hate us, and will certainly requite us all the evil which we did unto him' (Genesis 50:15).

As one reads the story, the reaction of the brothers is quite remarkable. That issue, for the reader, was settled long ago. Joseph had clearly stated his forgiveness, and the brothers should have felt quite secure. '...Joseph said unto to his brethren...be not grieved, nor angry with yourselves, that ye sold me hither: for God did send me before you to preserve life...to preserve you a posterity in the earth, and to save your lives by a great deliverance' (Genesis 45:4-7).

Why do the brothers now fear Joseph? The answer is reason for meditation on the part of the reader. Sin has the ability to soil the mind in a way that destroys sound reasoning. Instead of returning to the memory of Joseph's forgiveness, and his explanation, they thought only of their sin, and reasoned according to the way they understood human nature. The thought that Joseph might actually forgive them was foreign to their thinking. They could suspect only the worst.

The ability to accept forgiveness requires a spiritual touch. When one cannot accept forgiveness, the results can be devastating. One of those results is constant fear. Now that Jacob would not be a factor in Joseph's decisions, Joseph's brethren were afraid for their lives. There are many Christians whose lives are filled with fear based in sins of the past. Every slight disappointment, *every* setback, is seen as the retribution of God. There is never a time when any given setback is perceived as sufficient retribution.

Such fear ultimately translates into a kind of Christian paranoia. It causes a loss of joy, a loss of decision making ability fearing God will punish us by making the choice turn out bad, and a loss of power in our spiritual life. The life becomes paralysed. Joseph's brothers were led to the fabrication of a lie (50:16-17). Instead of going back to normal living, their fears created unnecessary scheming. Accepting Joseph's forgiveness would have made life much easier.

It is tough to forgive, but Joseph's brothers show that it is sometimes tougher to accept forgiveness. How does one know that he is forgiven? Are words enough to prove that forgiveness has occurred? It would be proper to ask God to teach us how to know that we are forgiven.

'...Forgive, I pray thee...'

The body of Jacob has been carried to Canaan and buried in the tomb of his fathers as per his request (49:29-30). Joseph's brothers, fearing that Jacob's death will now incite Joseph to seek revenge for the evil they had caused him, make up a story. 'And they sent a messenger unto Joseph, saying, Thy father did command before he died, saying, So shall ye say unto Joseph, Forgive, I pray thee now, the trespass of thy brethren, and their sin; for they did unto thee evil: and now, we pray thee, forgive the trespass of the servants of the God of thy father...' (50:16-17).

The request of the brothers speaks much about human nature and the shackles that guilt puts on people's lives. The brothers are afraid of Joseph when there was no need. He had forgiven them (45:5-7). They could not think about the necessary things of lives life because fear and guilt pushed their minds in another direction. A close look at the brothers' request reveals the very sinister nature of this kind of fear. To begin with, their story was fictional. Jacob had no need to make such a request, he trusted Joseph. The brothers lie, and proceed to make God part of the lie. '...forgive the trespass of the servants of the God of thy father...' (50:17). The subtle shaping of these words means the brothers are saying to Joseph that God would not be pleased if he acts to avenge himself and to punish them. They presume to be stating the will of God in the same breath in which they are telling a lie. How foolish can we humans be? They were putting words in their father's mouth desecrating his memory, and they were taking the name of God in vain and desecrating his Name. The sin keeps compounding itself.

When fear and guilt rule the life, sin will be king. The subtle lesson here is that the answer to fear and guilt is the acceptance of forgiveness. Most people understand the difficulty of accepting forgiveness. It is derived from our own inability to forgive. He who cannot forgive does not have the means to rationalize the possibility of forgiveness. When one cannot perceive the possibility of forgiveness, the only thing left is fear of retribution, which creates foolish action.

It is by God's power that we come to know and accept the possibility of forgiveness. Jesus taught us to pray '...forgive us our debts, as we forgive our debtors' (Matthew 6:12). It is not a law, it is a reality that knowing the blessing of forgiveness is only possible when we know the giving of forgiveness.

> The learning of forgiveness is critical to our spiritual health in so many ways. An essential part of understanding forgiveness is to know its possibility through our own forgiving attitude.

'...we be thy servants...'

The setting is one of pathos and absurdity. One cannot help but feel pity for Joseph's brothers. They have been reduced to snivelling and infantile scheming. One gazes upon them and wonders why someone doesn't stand up and be a man. '...they sent a messenger unto Joseph saying...Forgive, I pray thee now, the trespass of thy brethren, and their sin...forgive the trespass of the servants of the God of thy father...And his brethren also went and fell down before his face; and they said, Behold, we be thy servants' (50:16-18).

The brothers' cowardice is noted when they sent a messenger instead of confronting Joseph themselves. Also, they prostrated themselves as servants instead of asking for what they really wanted which was the desire to continue their lives as usual. Further, the reader has seen all this before. It had occurred when Joseph established the nature of the relationship (45:5-7). If they fear that the relationship has changed, why not just ask him openly instead of going through this silly scheming?

Joseph's reaction is interesting. '...And Joseph wept when they spake unto him' (50:17). The story of Joseph has documented the strong emotional nature that is his characteristic (45:1-2). The emotion expressed here would appear to have two basic ingredients. First, the appearance of his older brothers acting in such pitiable fashion stirred his sense of compassion. He said, '...fear ye not: I will nourish you, and your little ones. And he comforted them...' (50:21) The brothers were probably relieved, but their actions probably cost them in terms of Joseph's respect. The fear and guilt that had led them to act in such pathos is probably replaced by a bit of embarrassment and self-contempt that they exposed themselves this way. Both of these things can be healthy if the brothers learn their lesson.

The second ingredient of Joseph's emotion is his discernment of his brothers' lack of perception. He rebukes them with the question '...am I in the place of God' (50:19)? When Joseph had tried to teach them of the much bigger picture of God's plan, they were only able to see out of their very small self-involved world. It was that small way of viewing life that led them to sell Joseph into slavery. Joseph must be somewhat frustrated that they still had not learned. '...ye thought evil against me; but God meant it unto good, to bring to pass, as it is this day, to save much people alive' (50:20). If they could have seen the larger view, the forgiveness of Joseph would not have been so hard to accept.

'...fear ye not...'

Joseph's life had been a series of ups and downs. As a young lad, his life was the best of all worlds. Clearly the favoured son of his father, Jacob, he grew up with a view of life as positive. He expected things to always go well for him. He had dreams that spoke of future greatness for himself (Genesis 37). The brothers of Joseph, however, brought his rosy outlook of life to a shocking halt when they sold him into slavery. Fate brings the brothers back into his life. They were suffering from the famine that engulfed the earth, and Joseph, as one of great position in Egypt had power to help them or to destroy them. Joseph, ingeniously helps his brothers, and brings them and his father to Egypt. When Jacob dies, Joseph's brothers fear that Joseph will now seek vengeance on them.

Joseph reacts: 'But as for you, ye thought evil against me; but God meant it unto good...' (50:20). The theology gives the human mind much to think about. Joseph's brothers had clearly done him evil, but Joseph says '...God meant it unto good...' (50:20). Good and evil stand in paradox. Both things are present in one event. What should be our focus?

As this is meditated upon, it should become clear to us that God's ways are above our ways. Many times humans think they can do an evil thing for a good reason, and make an evil thing good. This always fails! The issue in the story of Joseph and his brothers is not that humans can make good happen from an evil event, but that God can. As Joseph examined the events of his life, he gloried in God's ability, and saw vengeance on his part as a means of invalidating the glorious wisdom of God. Joseph's comforting words to his brothers would mean. 'Relax, what you did was overruled by God. Glorify him because he turned your evil to good, and magnify him, because he is deserving.'

The strained relationship that had always been part of the life of Jacob's sons comes to its ultimate climax in these verses. It provides a supreme example of how a Christian should react when wronged by another. It is to be found in the power the victim has over the perpetrator. The power is not of physical strength, or of positional authority, but in an emotional hold on the life of the perpetrator. When one is desperately in need of forgiveness, but forgiveness is withheld, the victim and the perpetrator exchange positions. Though wronged, the victim, by withholding forgiveness persecutes the perpetrator.

Understanding the nature of that exchange explains another reason why forgiveness is often difficult. There is a sense of power and control that one has over the person seeking forgiveness. It is hard to turn loose of that control. Joseph establishes the great example for us in his continuing statement. 'Now therefore fear ye not: I will nourish you, and your little ones. And he comforted them, and spake kindly to them' (50:21).

Joseph's response is a clear methodology for forgiveness. It is to speak and act in a positive expression of good will. '...fear ye not: I will nourish you, and your little ones...' (50:21). The scriptural principle is to repay evil with good (Luke 6:27). It is in the doing of kindness that the words 'I forgive' can make their way from the tongue to actually formulate a forgiving heart.

> Hopefully, one's study of the writing of Genesis can lead to continual focus on God. We must know that evil cannot defeat him because he has the power to turn evil into good. However, we need to pray that we always remember that it is only God, and never us, that can make good happen from an evil event.

Genesis 50:22-26

22. And Joseph dwelt in Egypt, he, and his father's house: and Joseph lived an hundred and ten years. 23. And Joseph saw Ephraim's children of the third generation: the children also of Machir the son of Manasseh were brought up upon Joseph's knees. 24. And Joseph said unto his brethren, I die: and God will surely visit you, and bring you out of this land unto the land which he sware to Abraham, to Isaac, and to Jacob. 25. And Joseph took an oath of the children of Israel, saying, God will surely visit you, and ye shall carry up my bones from hence. 26. So Joseph died, being an hundred and ten years old: and they embalmed him, and he was put in a coffin in Egypt.

'...brought up upon Joseph's knees'

One of the most remarkable lives in biblical history comes to a close. The life that had seen so much travail, and so much frenetic activity finishes with a description of total normalcy. The reader, often wading through tense and exciting events is brought to an ending that is somewhat dull. Yet, reflection on the scene offers some comforting insights. Before us is a man enjoying the simple pleasures of life. '...Joseph lived an hundred and ten years. And Joseph saw Ephraim's children of the third generation: the children also of Machir the son of Manasseh were brought up upon Joseph's knees' (50:22-23).

For many years, Joseph had served God well. In extreme travail, he never backed away from obedience to God. He trusted God in the darkest of days. There was great wisdom given to him in the interpretation of dreams. He had accomplished many wonderful deeds. What is his reward? It is seen in the fact that he doesn't have to accomplish wonderful deeds any more. He can be normal, enjoy his children, and his children's children. It is the ideal way to live.

There were times in Joseph's life when the spectacular was required of him such as the interpretation of dreams. It is the nature of human beings to long for and desire the spectacular as the ideal life. The Bible would tell us the opposite. It is the normal (we would call it dull) that is the ideal. One might satirically say that Joseph was rewarded for his heroism with dullness, and no excitement for the rest of his life.

Again, we are reminded of how much God's way of thinking differs from the thinking of fallen man. There is no greater reward than being able to live our life in simple accord with God's stated purpose for us. 'So God created man...male and female...and God said unto them, 'Be fruitful, and multiply, and replenish the earth, and subdue it...' (1:27-28). As the story of the patriarchal families ends, Joseph epitomizes God's perfection for men, as he enjoys his own contribution to God's command. It may seem dull in the light of all of Joseph's great adventures. My guess is that Joseph would say it was the greatest part of his life.

When humans pause and ponder life in their own pursuit of the spectacular, we usually come to the conclusion that the greatest part of life was the wonderful, simple times when the best relationships of our lives were established and developed. If our story is told, they would be the dullest moments. It is only in the individual's understanding that they are called the best. Our lesson is to better appreciate those dull moments.

In coming to the end of Genesis, it would be good to take a moment of reflection and thank God for the moments of our lives when rest occurs, and we are not longing for the spectacular, but are simply enjoying the wonderful fruit of our knowledge of him.

'So Joseph died...'

The story of Joseph has brought us through one of the most unusual lives in all of history. Many fairy tales tell of the poor unfortunate person who has great luck and discovers the pot of gold, or the Cinderella who finds her handsome prince. Joseph's story of the beloved son, who is sold into slavery to become the man second only to Pharaoh in the land of Egypt, is unique. It is unique because it is clearly established as part of a grand master plan. It is not a feel-good story. It is unique because it is planted squarely in history, and presents the glory of God not of human luck or ingenuity. It is unique because it isn't just a nice story to tell our children to help them have sweet dreams, it teaches much to help them learn about the nature of God. It is unique because of the way it ends. 'And Joseph took an oath of the children of Israel, saying, God will surely visit you, and ye shall carry up my bones from hence. So Joseph died, being an hundred and ten years old: and they embalmed him, and he was put in a coffin in Egypt' (50:25-26).

We are used to our fairy tales ending 'And they lived happily ever after.' Joseph saw things a little differently. His 'happily ever after' would have been in Egypt in human thinking. He was second to Pharaoh. He had great command and power. He had access to much wealth. Yet, there was something better waiting. He promised his children that God would visit them and bring them out of Egypt. They will return to the land promised to Abraham, Isaac, and Jacob (50:24). Our question is, 'How is that better when they were (at the time Joseph spoke) so prosperous in Egypt?' The answer: It is better because it is what God had promised. As Joseph died, he, unlike the fairy tales, saw beyond the present life to a better land. He laid claim to that better land, and left a strong legacy to his children. He desired that they live by the same hope, and lay claim to the better thing. He evoked a promise, '...ye shall carry up my bones from hence' (50: 25). That wish was fulfilled more then four hundred years later. 'And Moses took the bones of Joseph with him....' (Exodus 13:19).

Joseph's bones being taken to the Promised Land seems a strange and unimportant ritual to the modern reader. To Israel, it is a connector of the past to the present. The promised land is more than this life. It is bound in the promise of God. It is an eternal promise in which the past, present, and future will be brought together. The life of Joseph is not over. From this earth, it is temporarily suspended, while he enjoys heaven with his Saviour.

The end of Genesis encapsulates the hope of every Christian. The end of life on this earth only magnifies the wonder of our hope. There is a better land waiting. The Apostle Paul defines the hope. 'Looking for that blessed hope, and the glorious appearing of the great God and our Saviour Jesus Christ' (Titus 2:13). That which began with the hope of the seed of the woman ends with that same hope. For us, we have an advantage on the patriarchs, we know the name of the seed of the woman. He is Jesus, the Incarnate Christ! Let us close with a meditation on the great salvation wrought in Christ, and express our love for the great Saviour.